To Bob
with my best regards
&
thanks what he is doing for
Analysis of Algorithms

Thank you!

Wojtek

W. Lafayette,   09/30/2015

ANALYTIC PATTERN MATCHING

How do you distinguish a cat from a dog by their DNA? Did Shakespeare really write all his plays? Pattern matching techniques can offer answers to these questions and to many others, in contexts from molecular biology to telecommunications to the classification of Twitter content.

This book, intended for researchers and graduate students, demonstrates the probabilistic approach to pattern matching, which predicts the performance of pattern matching algorithms with very high precision using analytic combinatorics and analytic information theory. Part I compiles results for pattern matching problems that can be obtained via analytic methods. Part II focuses on applications to various data structures on words, such as digital trees, suffix trees, string complexity, and string-based data compression. The authors use results and techniques from Part I and also introduce new methodology such as the Mellin transform and analytic depoissonization.

More than 100 end-of-chapter problems will help the reader to make the link between theory and practice.

ANALYTIC PATTERN MATCHING

From DNA to Twitter

PHILIPPE JACQUET

*Institut National de Recherche en Informatique
et en Automatique (INRIA), Rocquencourt*

WOJCIECH SZPANKOWSKI

Purdue University, Indiana

CAMBRIDGE
UNIVERSITY PRESS

CAMBRIDGE
UNIVERSITY PRESS

University Printing House, Cambridge CB2 8BS, United Kingdom

Cambridge University Press is part of the University of Cambridge.

It furthers the University's mission by disseminating knowledge in the pursuit of education, learning and research at the highest international levels of excellence.

www.cambridge.org
Information on this title: www.cambridge.org/9780521876087

© Philippe Jacquet and Wojciech Szpankowski 2015

First published 2015

Printed in the United States of America by Sheridan Books, Inc.

A catalog record for this publication is available from the British Library

Library of Congress Cataloging in Publication data

Jacquet, Philippe, 1958–
Analytic pattern matching from DNA to Twitter / Philippe Jacquet, Institut National de Recherche en Informatique et en Automatique (INRIA), Rocquencourt Wojciech Szpankowski, Purdue University, Indiana.
pages cm
Includes bibliographical references and index.
ISBN 978-0-521-87608-7 (Hardback)
1. Pattern recognition systems. I. Szpankowski, Wojciech, 1952– II. Title.
TK7882.P3J33 2015
519.2–dc23
2014017256

ISBN 978-0-521-87608-7 Hardback

Dedicated to PHILIPPE FLAJOLET,
our mentor and friend.

Contents

Foreword

Early computers replaced calculators and typewriters, and programmers focused on scientific computing (calculations involving numbers) and string processing (manipulating sequences of alphanumeric characters, or strings). Ironically, in modern applications, string processing is an integral part of scientific computing, as strings are an appropriate model of the natural world in a wide range of applications, notably computational biology and chemistry. Beyond scientific applications, strings are the *lingua franca* of modern computing, with billions of computers having immediate access to an almost unimaginable number of strings.

Decades of research have met the challenge of developing fundamental algorithms for string processing and mathematical models for strings and string processing that are suitable for scientific studies. Until now, much of this knowledge has been the province of specialists, requiring intimate familiarity with the research literature. The appearance of this new book is therefore a welcome development. It is a unique resource that provides a thorough coverage of the field and serves as a guide to the research literature. It is worthy of serious study by any scientist facing the daunting prospect of making sense of huge numbers of strings.

The development of an understanding of strings and string processing algorithms has paralleled the emergence of the field of analytic combinatorics, under the leadership of the late Philippe Flajolet, to whom this book is dedicated. Analytic combinatorics provides powerful tools that can synthesize and simplify classical derivations and new results in the analysis of strings and string processing algorithms. As disciples of Flajolet and leaders in the field nearly since its inception, Philippe Jacquet and Wojciech Szpankowski are well positioned to provide a cohesive modern treatment, and they have done a masterful job in this volume.

ROBERT SEDGEWICK
Princeton University

Preface

Repeated patterns and related phenomena in words are known to play a central role in many facets of computer science, telecommunications, coding, data compression, data mining, and molecular biology. One of the most fundamental questions arising in such studies is the frequency of pattern occurrences in a given string known as the text. Applications of these results include gene finding in biology, executing and analyzing tree-like protocols for multiaccess systems, discovering repeated strings in Lempel–Ziv schemes and other data compression algorithms, evaluating string complexity and its randomness, synchronization codes, user searching in wireless communications, and detecting the signatures of an attacker in intrusion detection.

The basic *pattern matching* problem is to find for a given (or random) pattern w or set of patterns W and a text X how many times W occurs in the text X and how long it takes for W to occur in X for the first time. There are many variations of this basic pattern matching setting which is known as *exact string matching*. In approximate string matching, better known as *generalized string matching*, certain words from W are expected to occur in the text while other words are *forbidden* and cannot appear in the text. In some applications, especially in constrained coding and neural data spikes, one puts restrictions on the text (e.g., only text without the patterns 000 and 0000 is permissible), leading to *constrained string matching*. Finally, in the most general case, patterns from the set W do not need to occur as strings (i.e., consecutively) but rather as subsequences; that leads to *subsequence pattern matching*, also known as *hidden pattern matching*.

These various pattern matching problems find a myriad of applications. Molecular biology provides an important source of applications of pattern matching, be it exact or approximate or subsequence pattern matching. There are examples in abundance: finding signals in DNA; finding split genes where exons are interrupted by introns; searching for starting and stopping signals in genes; finding tandem repeats in DNA. In general, for gene searching, hidden pattern matching (perhaps with an exotic constraint set) is the right approach for finding meaningful information. The hidden pattern problem can also be viewed as a close relative of the longest common subsequence (LCS) problem, itself of immediate relevance to computational biology but whose probabilistic aspects are still surrounded by mystery.

Exact and approximate pattern matching have been used over the last 30 years in source coding (better known as data compression), notably in the Lempel–Ziv schemes. The idea behind these schemes is quite simple: when an encoder finds two (longest) copies of a substring in a text to be compressed, the second copy is not stored but, rather, one retains a pointer to the copy (and possibly the length of the substring). The holy grail of universal source coding is to show that, without knowing the statistics of the text, such schemes are asymptotically optimal.

There are many other applications of pattern matching. Prediction is one of them and is closely related to the Lempel–Ziv schemes (see Jacquet, Szpankowski, and Apostol (2002) and Vitter and Krishnan (1996)). Knowledge discovery can be achieved by detecting repeated patterns (e.g., in weather prediction, stock market, social sciences). In data mining, pattern matching algorithms are probably the algorithms most often used. A text editor equipped with a pattern matching predictor can guess in advance the words that one wants to type. Messages in phones also use this feature.

In this book we study pattern matching problems in a probabilistic framework in which the text is generated by a probabilistic source while the pattern is given. In Chapter 1 various probabilistic sources are discussed and our assumptions are summarized. In Chapter 6 we briefly discuss the algorithmic aspects of pattern matching and various efficient algorithms for finding patterns, while in the rest of this book we focus on *analysis*. We apply analytic tools of combinatorics and the analysis of algorithms to discover general laws of pattern occurrences. Tools of analytic combinatorics and analysis of algorithms are well covered in recent books by Flajolet and Sedgewick (2009) and Szpankowski (2001).

The approach advocated in this book is the analysis of pattern matching problems through a formal description by means of regular languages. Basically, such a description of the *contexts* of one, two, or more occurrences of a pattern gives access to the expectation, the variance, and higher moments, respectively. A systematic translation into the *generating functions* of a complex variable is available by methods of analytic combinatorics deriving from the original Chomsky–Schützenberger theorem. The structure of the implied generating functions at a pole or algebraic singularity provides the necessary asymptotic information. In fact, there is an important phenomenon, that of *asymptotic simplification*, in which the essentials of combinatorial-probabilistic features are reflected by the singular forms of generating functions. For instance, variance coefficients come out naturally from this approach, together with a suitable notion of correlation. Perhaps the originality of the present approach lies in this joint use of combinatorial-enumerative techniques and analytic-probabilistic methods.

We should point out that pattern matching, hidden words, and hidden meaning were studied by many people in different contexts for a long time before computer algorithms were designed. Rabbi Akiva in the first century A.D. wrote a collection of documents called *Maaseh Merkava* on secret mysticism and meditations. In the eleventh century the Spaniard Solomon Ibn Gabirol called these secret teachings *Kabbalah*. Kabbalists organized themselves as a secret society dedicated to the study of the ancient wisdom of Torah, looking for mysterious connections and hidden truths, meaning, and words in Kabbalah and elsewhere. Recent versions of this activity are *knowledge discovery and data mining, bibliographic search, lexicographic research, textual data processing*, and even *web site indexing*. Public domain utilities such as `agrep`, `grappe`, and `webglimpse` (developed for example by Wu and Manber (1995), Kucherov and Rusinowitch (1997), and others) depend crucially on approximate pattern matching algorithms for subsequence detection. Many interesting algorithms based on regular expressions and automata, dynamic programming, directed acyclic word graphs, and digital tries or suffix trees have been developed. In all the contexts mentioned above it is of obvious interest to distinguish pattern occurrences from the statistically unavoidable phenomenon of noise. The results and techniques of this book may provide some answers to precisely these questions.

Contents of the book

This book has two parts. In Part I we compile all the results known to us about the various pattern matching problems that have been tackled by analytic methods. Part II is dedicated to the application of pattern matching to various data structures on words, such as digital trees (e.g., tries and digital search trees), suffix trees, string complexity, and string-based data compression and includes the popular schemes of Lempel and Ziv, namely the Lempel–Ziv'77 and the Lempel–Ziv'78 algorithms. When analyzing these data structures and algorithms we use results and techniques from Part I, but we also bring to the table new methodologies such as the Mellin transform and analytic depoissonization.

As already discussed, there are various pattern matching problems. In its simplest form, a pattern $\mathcal{W} = w$ is a single string w and one searches for some or all occurrences of w as a block of consecutive symbols in the text. This problem is known as *exact string matching* and its analysis is presented in Chapter 2 where we adopt a symbolic approach. We first describe a language that contains all occurrences of w. Then we translate this language into a generating function that will lead to precise evaluation of the mean and variance of the number of occurrences of the pattern. Finally, we establish the central and local limit laws, and large deviation results.

In Chapter 2 we assume that the text is generated by a random source without any constraints. However, in several important applications in coding and molecular biology, often the text itself must satisfy some restrictions. For example, codes for magnetic recording cannot have too many consecutive zeros. This leads to consideration of the so-called (d, k) sequences, in which runs of zeros are of length at least d and at most k. In Chapter 3 we consider the exact string matching problem when the text satisfies extra constraints, and we coin the term *constrained pattern matching*. We derive moments for the number of occurrences as well as the central limit laws and large deviation results.

In the *generalized string matching* problem discussed in Chapter 4 the pattern $\mathcal{W}$ is a set of patterns rather than a single pattern. In its most general formulation, the pattern is a pair $(\mathcal{W}_0, \mathcal{W})$ where $\mathcal{W}_0$ is the so-called *forbidden set*. If $\mathcal{W}_0 = \emptyset$ then $\mathcal{W}$ is said to appear in the text X whenever a word from $\mathcal{W}$ occurs as a string, with overlapping allowed. When $\mathcal{W}_0 \neq \emptyset$ one studies the number of occurrences of strings from $\mathcal{W}$ under the condition that there is no occurrence of a string from $\mathcal{W}_0$ in the text. This is *constrained* string matching, since one restricts the text to those strings that do not contain strings from $\mathcal{W}_0$. Setting $\mathcal{W} = \emptyset$ (with $\mathcal{W}_0 \neq \emptyset$), we search for the number of text strings that do not contain any pattern from $\mathcal{W}_0$. In this chapter we present a complete analysis of the generalized string matching problem. We first consider the so-called *reduced set of patterns* in which one string in $\mathcal{W}$ cannot be a substring of another string in $\mathcal{W}$. We generalize our combinatorial language approach from Chapter 2 to derive the mean, variance, central and local limit laws, and large deviation results. Then we analyze the generalized string pattern matching. In our first approach we construct an automaton to recognize a pattern $\mathcal{W}$, which turns out to be a de Bruijn graph. The generating function of the number of occurrences has a matrix form; the main matrix represents the transition matrix of the associated de Bruijn graph. Our second approach is a direct generalization of the language approach from Chapter 2. This approach was recently proposed by Bassino, Clement, and Nicodeme (2012).

In the last chapter of Part I, Chapter 5, we discuss another pattern matching problem called subsequence pattern matching or hidden pattern matching. In this case the pattern $\mathcal{W} = w_1 a_2 \cdots w_m$, where w_i is a symbol of the underlying alphabet, occurs as a subsequence rather than a string of consecutive symbols in a text. We say that $\mathcal{W}$ is hidden in the text. For example, date occurs as a subsequence in the text hid<u>d</u>en p<u>at</u>tern, four times in fact but not even once as a string. The gaps between the occurrences of $\mathcal{W}$ may be bounded or unrestricted. The extreme cases are: the *fully unconstrained* problem, in which all gaps are unbounded, and the *fully constrained* problem, in which all gaps are bounded. We analyze these and mixed cases. Also, in Chapter 5 we present a general model that contains all the previously discussed pattern matchings. In short, we analyze the so-called *generalized subsequence problem*. In this case the pattern is $\mathcal{W} = (\mathcal{W}_1, \ldots, \mathcal{W}_d)$, where $\mathcal{W}_i$ is a collection of strings (a language). We say that the generalized pattern $\mathcal{W}$ occurs in the text X if X contains $\mathcal{W}$ as a *subsequence* $(w_1, w_2, \ldots, w_d)$, where $w_i \in \mathcal{W}_i$. Clearly, the generalized subsequence problem includes all the problems discussed so far. We analyze this generalized pattern matching for general probabilistic dynamic sources, which include Markov sources and mixing sources as recently proposed by Vallée (2001). The novelty of the analysis lies in the translation of probabilities into compositions of operators. Under a mild decomposability assumption, these operators possess spectral representations that allow us to derive precise asymptotic behavior for the quantities of interest.

Part II of the book starts with Chapter 6, in which we describe some data structures on words. In particular, we discuss digital trees, suffix trees, and the two most popular data compression schemes, namely Lempel–Ziv'77 (LZ'77) and Lempel–Ziv'78 (LZ'78).

In Chapter 7 we analyze tries and digital search trees built from *independent* strings. These basic digital trees owing to their simplicity and efficiency, find widespread use in diverse applications ranging from document taxonomy to IP address lookup, from data compression to dynamic hashing, from partial-match queries to speech recognition, from leader election algorithms to distributed hashing tables. We study analytically several tries and digital search tree parameters such as depth, path length, size, and average profile. The motivation for studying these parameters is multifold. First, they are efficient shape measures characterizing these trees. Second, they are asymptotically close to the parameters of suffix trees discussed in Chapter 8. Third, not only are the analytical problems mathematically challenging, but the diverse new phenomena they exhibit are highly interesting and unusual.

In Chapter 8 we continue analyzing digital trees but now those built from correlated strings. Namely we study suffix trees, which are tries constructed from the suffixes of a string. In particular we focus on characterizing mathematically the length of the longest substring of the text occurring at a given position that has another copy in the text. This length, when averaged over all possible positions of the text, is actually the typical *depth* in a suffix trie built over (randomly generated) text. We analyze it using analytic techniques such as generating functions and the Mellin transform. More importantly, we reduce its analysis to the exact pattern matching discussed in depth in Chapter 2. In fact, we prove that the probability generating function of the depth in a suffix trie is asymptotically close to the probability generating function of the depth in a trie that is built over n *independently* generated texts analyzed in Chapter 7, so we have a pretty good understanding of its probabilistic behavior. This allows us to conclude that the depth in a suffix trie is asymptotically normal. Finally, we turn our attention to an application of suffix trees to the analysis of the Lempel–Ziv'77 scheme. We ask the question how many LZ'77 phrases there are in a randomly generated string. This number is known as the multiplicity parameter and we establish its asymptotic distribution.

In Chapter 9 we study a data structure that is the most popular and the hardest to analyze, namely the Lempel–Ziv'78 scheme. Our goal is to characterize probabilistically the number of LZ'78 phrases and its redundancy. Both these tasks drew a lot of attention as being open and difficult until Aldous and Shields (1988) and Jacquet and Szpankowski (1995) solved them for memoryless sources. We present here a simplified proof for extended results: the central limit theorem for the number of phrases and the redundancy as well as the moderate and large deviation findings. We study this problem by reducing it to an analysis of the associated digital search tree, already discussed in part in Chapter 7. In particular, we establish the central limit theorem and large deviations for the total path length in the digital search tree.

Finally, in Chapter 10 we study the string complexity and also the joint string complexity, which is defined as the cardinality of distinct subwords of a string or strings. The string complexity captures the "richness of the language" used in a sequence, and it has been studied quite extensively from the worst case point of view. It has also turned out that the joint string complexity can be used quite successfully for `twitter` classification (see Jacquet, Milioris, and Szpankowski (2013)). In this chapter we focus on an average case analysis. The joint string complexity is particularly interesting and challenging from the analysis point of view. It requires novel analytic tools such as the two-dimensional Mellin transform, depoissonization, and the saddle point method.

Nearly every chapter is accompanied by a set of problems and related bibliography. In the problem sections we ask the reader to complete a sketchy proof, to solve a similar problem, or to actually work on an open problem. In the bibliographical sections we briefly describe some related literature.

Finally, to ease the reading of this book, we illustrate each chapter with an original comic sketch. Each sketch is somewhat related to the topic of the corresponding chapter, as discussed below.

Acknowledgments

This book is dedicated to **Philippe Flajolet**, the father of analytic combinatorics, our friend and mentor who passed away suddenly on March 22, 2011. An obituary – from which we freely borrow here – was recently published by Salvy, Sedgewick, Soria, Szpankowski, and Vallee (2011).

We believe that this book was possible thanks to the tireless efforts of Philippe Flajolet, his extensive and far-reaching body of work, and his scientific approach to the study of algorithms, including the development of the requisite mathematical and computational tools. Philippe is best known for his fundamental advances in mathematical methods for the analysis of algorithms; his research also opened new avenues in various areas of applied computer science, including streaming algorithms, communication protocols, database access methods, data mining, symbolic manipulation, text-processing algorithms, and random generation. He exulted in sharing his passion: his papers had more than a hundred different co-authors (including the present authors) and he was a regular presence at scientific meetings all over the world.

Philippe Flajolet's research laid the foundation of a subfield of mathematics now known as analytic combinatorics. His lifework *Analytic Combinatorics* (Cambridge University Press, 2009, co-authored with R. Sedgewick) is a prodigious achievement, which now defines the field and is already recognized as an authoritative reference. Analytic combinatorics is a modern basis for the quantitative study of combinatorial structures (such as words, trees, mappings, and graphs), with applications to probabilistic study of algorithms based on these structures. It also strongly influences other scientific areas, such as statistical physics, computational biology, and information theory. With deep historic roots in classical analysis, the basis of the field lies in the work of Knuth, who put the study of algorithms onto a firm scientific basis, starting in the late 1960s with his classic series of books. Philippe Flajolet's work took the field forward by introducing original approaches into combinatorics based on two types of methods: symbolic and analytic. The symbolic side is based on the automation of decision procedures in combinatorial enumeration to derive characterizations of generating functions. The analytic side treats those generating functions as functions in the complex plane and leads to a precise characterization of limit distributions.

Finally, Philippe Flajolet was the leading figure in the development of a large international community (which again includes the present authors) devoted to research on probabilistic, combinatorial, and asymptotic methods in the analysis of algorithms. His legacy is alive through this community. We are still trying to cope with the loss of our friend and mentor.

While putting the final touches to this book, the tragic shooting occurred in Paris of the famous French cartoonists at Charlie Hebdo. We are sure that this event would shock Philippe Flajolet, who had an inimitable sense of humour. He mocked himself and his friends. We were often on the receiving end of his humour. We took it, as most did, as a proof of affection. Cartoonists and scientists have something in common: offending the apparent truth is a necessary step toward better knowledge.

There is a long list of other colleagues and friends from whom we benefited through their encouragement and constructive comments. They have helped us in various ways during our work on the analysis of algorithms and information theory. We mention here only a few: Alberto Apostolico, Yongwook Choi, Luc Devroye, Michael Drmota, Ananth Grama, H-K. Hwang, Svante Janson, John Kieffer, Chuck Knessl, Yiannis Kontoyiannis, Mehmet Koyuturk, Guy Louchard, Stefano Lonardi, Pierre Nicodeme, Ralph Neininger, Gahyuan Park, Mireille Régnier, Yuriy Reznik, Bob Sedgewick, Gadiel Seroussi, Brigitte Vallée, Sergio Verdu, Mark Ward, Marcelo Weinberger. We thank Bob Sedgewick for writing the foreword.

Finally, no big project like this can be completed without help from our families. We thank Véronique, Manou, Lili, Mariola, Lukasz and Paulina from the bottom of our hearts.

This book has been written over the last five years, while we have been traveling around the world carrying (electronically) numerous copies of various drafts. We have received invaluable help from the staff and faculty of INRIA, France and the Department of Computer Sciences at Purdue University. The second author is grateful to the National Science Foundation, which has supported his work over the last 30 years. We have also received support from institutions around the world that have hosted us and our book: INRIA, Rocquencourt; Alcatel-Lucent, Paris; LINCS, Paris; the Gdańsk University of Technology, Gdańsk; the University of Hawaii; and ETH, Zurich. We thank them very much.

PHILIPPE JACQUET
WOJTEK SZPANKOWSKI

About the sketches

In order to ease the reading of this book, full of dry equations, Philippe drew a comic sketch for each chapter. In these sketches we introduced two recurrent comic characters. They are undefined animals like rats, worms, or lizards, sometimes more like fish or butterflies. We, Wojtek and Philippe, appear in some sketches: Wojtek with his famous moustache appears as the butterfly hunter and Philippe appears as a fisherman.

For us patterns are like small animals running over a text, and we see a text like a forest or a garden full of words, as illustrated below. We have given names

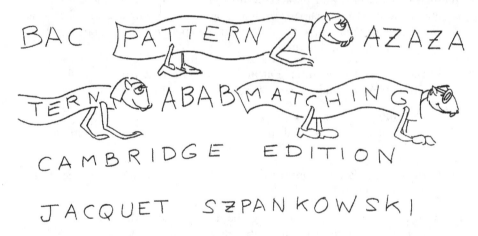

to these two animals: Pat for Patricia Tern, and Mat for Mathew Tching. They are mostly inspired by Philippe's twin cats, Calys and Gypsie who often play and hide wherever they can.

Let us give you some hints on how to read these sketches:

1. The probabilistic model chapter shows Pat and Mat in a chess game, because probability and games are deeply entangled concepts. Here is the

question: who will win the game (chess mat) and who will lose (pat)? Colours in the checker board are omitted in order to complicate the puzzle.

2. In exact string matching, Pat and Mat are in their most dramatic situation: escaping the pattern matching hunters.

3. In the constrained pattern matching chapter, Pat and Mat must escape a stubborn pattern matching hunter who is ready to chase them in the hostile (constrained) submarine context.

4. In general string matching, the issue is how to catch a group of patterns. This is symbolised by a fisherman holding several hooks. Whether the fisherman looks like Philippe is still an open question, but he tried his best.

5. In the subsequence pattern matching chapter, Pat and Mat are butterflies facing a terrible hunter. Yes, he looks like Wojtek, but without his glasses, so that the butterflies have a chance.

6. In the algorithms and data structures chapter, Pat and Mat are resting under the most famous pattern matching data structure: the tree. In this case, the tree is an apple tree, and Mat is experiencing the gravity law as Isaac Newton did in his time.

7. In the digital trees chapter, Pat and Mat find themselves in the situation of Eve and Adam and are collecting the fruits of knowledge from the tree.

8. In the suffix tree and Lempel–Ziv'77 chapter, Mat tries to compress his pal. Yes, it is really painful, but they are just cartoon characters, aren't they?

9. In the Lempel–Ziv'78 compression chapter, Pat is having her revenge from the previous chapter.

10. At least in the string complexity chapter, Pat and Mat are achieving a concerted objective: to enumerate their common factors, the small kid animals of "AT", "A", and "T". Congratulations to the parents.

11. In the bibliography section, Pat and Mat find some usefulness in their existence by striving to keep straight the impressive pile of books cited in this work.

Part I

ANALYSIS

CHAPTER 1

Probabilistic Models

In this book we study pattern matching problems in a probabilistic framework. We first introduce some general probabilistic models of generating sequences. The reader is also referred to Alon and Spencer (1992), Reinert, Schbath, and Waterman (2000), Szpankowski (2001) and Waterman (1995a) for a brief introduction to probabilistic models. For the convenience of the reader, we recall here some definitions.

We also briefly discuss some analytic tools such as generating functions, the residue theorem, and the Cauchy coefficient formula. For in-depth discussions the reader is referred to Flajolet and Sedgewick (2009) and Szpankowski (2001).

1.1.   Probabilistic models on words

Throughout we shall deal with sequences of discrete random variables. We write $(X_k)_{k=1}^{\infty}$ for a one-sided infinite sequence of random variables; however, we will often abbreviate it as X provided that it is clear from the context that we are talking about a sequence, not a single variable. We assume that the sequence $(X_k)_{k=1}^{\infty}$ is defined over a finite alphabet $\mathcal{A} = \{a_1, \ldots, a_V\}$ of size V. A partial sequence is denoted as $X_m^n = (X_m, \ldots, X_n)$ for $m < n$. Finally, we shall always assume that a probability measure exists, and we will write $P(x_1^n) = P(X_k = x_k, \, 1 \leq k \leq n, \, x_k \in \mathcal{A})$ for the probability mass, where we use lower-case letters for a realization of a stochastic process.

Sequences are generated by information sources, usually satisfying some constraints. We also refer to such sources as *probabilistic models*. Throughout, we assume the existence of a stationary probability distribution; that is, for any string w we assume that the probability that the text X contains an occurrence of w at position k is equal to $P(w)$ independently of the position k. For $P(w) > 0$, we denote by $P(u|w)$ the conditional probability, which equals $P(wu)/P(w)$.

The most elementary information source is a *memoryless source*; also known as a *Bernoulli source*:

(B) MEMORYLESS OR BERNOULLI SOURCE. The symbols from the alphabet $\mathcal{A} = \{a_1, \ldots, a_V\}$ occur independently of one another; thus the string $X = X_1 X_2 X_3 \cdots$ can be described as the outcome of an infinite sequence of Bernoulli trials in which $P(X_j = a_i) = p_i$ and $\sum_{i=1}^{V} p_i = 1$. Throughout, we assume that at least for one i we have $0 < p_i < 1$.

In many cases, assumption (B) is not very realistic. When this is the case, assumption (B) may be replaced by:

(M) MARKOV SOURCE. There is a Markov dependency between the consecutive symbols in a string; that is, the probability $p_{ij} = P(X_{k+1} = a_j | X_k = a_i)$ describes the conditional probability of sampling symbol a_j immediately after symbol a_i. We denote by $\mathrm{P} = \{p_{ij}\}_{i,j=1}^{V}$ transition matrix and by $\boldsymbol{\pi} = (\pi_1, \ldots, \pi_V)$ the stationary row vector satisfying $\boldsymbol{\pi}\mathrm{P} = \boldsymbol{\pi}$. (Throughout, we assume that the Markov chain is irreducible and aperiodic.) A general Markov source of order r is characterized by the $V^r \times V$ the transition matrix with coefficients $P(j \in \mathcal{A} \mid u)$ for $u \in \mathcal{A}^r$.

In some situations more general sources must be considered (for which one still can obtain a reasonably precise analysis). Recently, Vallée (2001) introduced *dynamic sources*, which we briefly describe here and will use in the analysis of the generalized subsequence problem in Section 5.6. To introduce such sources we start with a description of a *dynamic system* defined by:

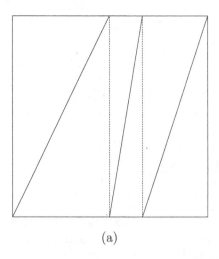 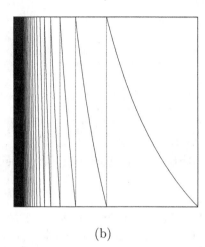

(a)   (b)

Figure 1.1. Plots of $\mathcal{I}_m$ versus x for the dynamic sources discussed in Example 1.1.1: (a) a memoryless source with shift mapping $T_m(x) = (x - q_m)/p_{m+1}$ for $p_1 = 1/2$, $p_2 = 1/6$, and $p_3 = 1/3$; (b) a continued fraction source with $T_m(x) = 1/x - m = \langle 1/x \rangle$.

- a topological partition of the unit interval $\mathcal{I} = (0, 1)$ into a disjoint set of open intervals $\mathcal{I}_a, a \in \mathcal{A}$;

- an encoding mapping e which is constant and equal to $a \in \mathcal{A}$ on each $\mathcal{I}_a$;

- a shift mapping $T : \mathcal{I} \to \mathcal{I}$ whose restriction to $\mathcal{I}_a$ is a bijection of class $\mathcal{C}^2$ from $\mathcal{I}_a$ to $\mathcal{I}$; the local inverse of T restricted to $\mathcal{I}_a$ is denoted by h_a.

Observe that such a dynamic system produces infinite words of $\mathcal{A}^\infty$ through the encoding e. For an initial $x \in \mathcal{I}$ the source outputs a word, say $w(x) = (e(x), (e(T(x)), \ldots)$.

(DS) PROBABILISTIC DYNAMIC SOURCE. A source is called a *probabilistic dynamic source* if the unit interval of a dynamic system is endowed with a probability density f.

Example 1.1.1. A memoryless source associated with the probability distribution $\{p_i\}_{i=1}^V$, where V can be finite or infinite, is modeled by a dynamic source in which the components $w_k(x)$ are independent and the corresponding topological partition of $\mathcal{I}$ is defined as follows:

$$\mathcal{I}_m := (q_m, q_{m+1}], \qquad q_m = \sum_{j<m} p_j.$$

In this case the shift mapping restricted to $\mathcal{I}_m$, $m \in \mathcal{A}$, is defined as

$$T_m = \frac{x - q_m}{p_{m+1}}, \qquad q_m < x \leq q_{m+1}.$$

In particular, a symmetric V-ary memoryless source can be described by

$$T(x) = \langle Vx \rangle, \qquad e(x) = \lfloor Vx \rfloor,$$

where $\lfloor x \rfloor$ is the integer part of x and $\langle x \rangle = x - \lfloor x \rfloor$ is the fractional part of x. In Figure 1.1(a) we assume $\mathcal{A} = \{1, 2, 3\}$ and $p_1 = 1/2$, $p_2 = 1/6$, and $p_3 = 1/3$, so that $q_1 = 0$, $q_1 = 1/2$, $q_2 = 2/3$, and $q_4 = 1$. Then

$$T_1 = 2x, \qquad T_2 = 6(x - 1/2), \qquad T_3 = 3(x - 2/3).$$

For example, if $x = 5/6$ then

$$w(x) = (e(x), e(T_3(x)), e(T_2(T_3(x))), \ldots) = (3, 2, 1, \ldots).$$

Here is another example of a source with a memory related to continued fractions. The alphabet $\mathcal{A}$ is the set of all natural numbers and the partition of $\mathcal{I}$ is defined as $\mathcal{I}_m = (1/(m+1), 1/m)$. The restriction of T to $\mathcal{I}_m$ is the decreasing linear fractional transformation $T(x) = 1/x - m$, that is,

$$T(x) = \langle 1/x \rangle, \qquad e(x) = \lfloor 1/x \rfloor.$$

Observe that the inverse branches h_m of the mapping $T(x)$ are defined as $h_m(x) = 1/(x + m)$ (see Figure 1.1(b)).   ∎

Let us observe that a word of length k, say $w = w_1 w_2 \ldots w_k$, is associated with the mapping $h_w := h_{w_1} \circ h_{w_2} \circ \cdots \circ h_{w_k}$, which is an inverse branch of T^k. In fact all words that begin with the same prefix w belong to the same *fundamental interval*, defined as $\mathcal{I}_w = (h_w(0), h_w(1))$. Furthermore, for probabilistic dynamic sources with density f one easily computes the probability of w as the measure of the interval $\mathcal{I}_w$.

The probability $P(w)$ of a word w can be explicitly computed through a special *generating operator* $\mathbf{G}_w$, defined as follows

$$\mathbf{G}_w[f](t) := |h'_w(t)| f \circ h_w(t). \tag{1.1}$$

One recognizes in $\mathbf{G}_w[f](t)$ a density mapping, that is, $\mathbf{G}_w[f](t)$ is the density of f mapped over $h_w(t)$. The probability of w can then be computed as

$$P(w) = \left| \int_{h_w(0)}^{h_w(1)} f(t)dt \right| = \int_0^1 |h_w'(t)|f \circ h_w(t)dt = \int_0^1 \mathbf{G}_w[f](t)dt. \quad (1.2)$$

Let us now consider a concatenation of two words w and u. For memoryless sources $P(wu) = P(w)P(u)$. For Markov sources one still obtains the product of the *conditional* probabilities. For dynamic sources the product of probabilities is replaced by the product (composition) of the generating operators. To see this, we observe that

$$\mathbf{G}_{wu} = \mathbf{G}_u \circ \mathbf{G}_w, \quad (1.3)$$

where we write $\mathbf{G}_w := \mathbf{G}_w[f](t)$. Indeed, $h_{wu} = h_w \circ h_u$ and

$$\mathbf{G}_{wu} = h_w' \circ h_u h_u' f \circ h_w \circ h_u$$

while $\mathbf{G}_w = h_w' f \circ h_w$ and so

$$\mathbf{G}_u \circ \mathbf{G}_w = h_u' h_w' \circ h_u f \circ h_w \circ h_u,$$

as desired.

Another generalization of Markov sources, namely the *mixing source*, is very useful in practice, especially for dealing with problems of data compression or molecular biology when one expects long(er) dependency between the symbols of a string.

(MX) (STRONGLY) ψ-MIXING SOURCE. Let $\mathcal{F}_m^n$ be a σ-field generated by the sequence $(X_k)_{k=m}^n$ for $m \leq n$. The source is called *mixing* if there exists a bounded function $\psi(g)$ such that, for all $m, g \geq 1$ and any two elements of the σ-field (events) $A \in \mathcal{F}_1^m$ and $B \in \mathcal{F}_{m+g}^\infty$, the following holds:

$$(1 - \psi(g))P(A)P(B) \leq P(AB) \leq (1 + \psi(g))P(A)P(B). \quad (1.4)$$

If, in addition, $\lim_{g \to \infty} \psi(g) = 0$ then the source is called *strongly* mixing.

In words, the model (MX) postulates that the dependency between $(X_k)_{k=1}^m$ and $(X_k)_{k=m+g}^\infty$ gets weaker and weaker as g becomes larger (note that when the sequence (X_k) is independent and identically distributed (i.i.d.) we have $P(AB) = P(A)P(B)$). The degree of dependency is characterized by $\psi(g)$. A weaker mixing condition, namely ϕ-*mixing*, is defined as follows:

$$-\phi(g) \leq P(B|A) - P(B) \leq \phi(g), \qquad P(A) > 0, \quad (1.5)$$

provided that $\phi(g) \to 0$ as $g \to \infty$. In general, strong ψ-mixing implies the ϕ-mixing condition but not vice versa.

1.2.   Probabilistic tools

In this section, we briefly review some probabilistic tools used throughout the book. We will concentrate on the different types of *stochastic convergence*.

The first type of convergence of a sequence of random variables is known as *convergence in probability*. The sequence X_n converges to a random variable X in probability, denoted $X_n \to X$ (pr.) or $X_n \overset{pr}{\to} X$, if, for any $\varepsilon > 0$,

$$\lim_{n \to \infty} P\left(|X_n - X| < \varepsilon\right) = 1.$$

It is known that *if $X_n \overset{pr}{\to} X$ then $f(X_n) \overset{pr}{\to} f(X)$ provided that f is a continuous function* (see Billingsley (1968)).

Note that convergence in probability does not say that the difference between X_n and X becomes very small. What converges here is the *probability* that the difference between X_n and X becomes very small. It is, therefore, possible, although unlikely, for X_n and X to differ by a significant amount and for such differences to occur infinitely often. A stronger kind of convergence that does not allow such behavior is *almost sure convergence* or *strong convergence*. This convergence ensures that *the set of sample points for which X_n does not converge to X has probability zero*. In other words, a sequence of random variables X_n converges to a random variable X almost surely, denoted $X_n \to X$ a.s. or $X_n \overset{(a.s.)}{\to} X$, if, for any $\varepsilon > 0$,

$$\lim_{N \to \infty} P(\sup_{n \geq N} |X_n - X| < \varepsilon) = 1.$$

From this formulation of almost sure convergence, it is clear that if $X_n \to X$ (a.s.), the probability of infinitely many large differences between X_n and X is zero. As the term "strong" implies, almost sure convergence implies convergence in probability.

A simple sufficient condition for almost sure convergence can be inferred from the *Borel–Cantelli lemma*, presented below.

Lemma 1.2.1 (Borel–Cantelli). *If $\sum_{n=0}^{\infty} P(|X_n - X| > \varepsilon) < \infty$ for every $\varepsilon > 0$ then $X_n \overset{a.s.}{\to} X$.*

Proof. This follows directly from the following chain of relationships:

$$P\left(\sup_{n \geq N} |X_n - X| \geq \varepsilon\right) = P\left(\bigcup_{n \geq N} |X_n - X| \geq \varepsilon\right) \leq \sum_{n \geq N} P(|X_n - X| \geq \varepsilon) \to 0.$$

The inequality above is a consequence of the fact that the probability of a union of events is smaller than the sum of the probability of the events (see Boole's or the union inequality below). The last convergence is a consequence of our assumption that $\sum_{n=0}^{\infty} P(|X_n - X| > \varepsilon) < \infty$. ∎

A third type of convergence is defined on distribution functions $F_n(x)$. The sequence of random variables X_n *converges in distribution* or *converges in law* to the random variable X, this convergence being denoted as $X_n \xrightarrow{d} X$, if

$$\lim_{n \to \infty} F_n(x) = F(x) \tag{1.6}$$

for each point of continuity of $F(x)$. In Billingsley (1968) it was proved that the above definition is equivalent to the following: $X_n \xrightarrow{d} X$ *if*

$$\lim_{n \to \infty} \mathbf{E}[f(X_n)] = \mathbf{E}[f(X)] \tag{1.7}$$

for all bounded continuous functions f.

The next type of convergence is *convergence in mean of order p* or *convergence in L^p*, which postulates that $\mathbf{E}[|X_n - X|^p] \to 0$ as $n \to \infty$. We write this type of convergence as $X_n \xrightarrow{L^p} X$. Finally, we introduce *convergence in moments* for which $\lim_{n \to \infty} \mathbf{E}[X_n^p] = \mathbf{E}[X^p]$ for any $p \geq 1$.

We now describe the relationships (implications) between the various types of convergence. The reader is referred to Billingsley (1968) for a proof.

Theorem 1.2.2. *We have the following implications:*

$$X_n \xrightarrow{a.s.} X \quad \Rightarrow \quad X_n \xrightarrow{pr} X, \tag{1.8}$$

$$X_n \xrightarrow{L^p} X \quad \Rightarrow \quad X_n \xrightarrow{pr} X, \tag{1.9}$$

$$X_n \xrightarrow{pr} X \quad \Rightarrow \quad X_n \xrightarrow{d} X, \tag{1.10}$$

$$X_n \xrightarrow{L^p} X \quad \Rightarrow \quad \mathbf{E}[X_n^p] \to \mathbf{E}[X^p]. \tag{1.11}$$

No other implications hold in general.

It is easy to devise an example showing that convergence in probability does not imply convergence in mean (e.g., take $X_n = n$ with probability $1/n$ and $X_n = 0$ with probability $1 - 1/n$). To obtain convergence in mean from convergence in probability one needs somewhat stronger conditions. For example, if $|X_n| \leq Y$ and $\mathbf{E}[Y] < \infty$ then, by the *dominated convergence theorem*, we know that convergence in probability implies convergence in mean. To generalize, one introduces so-called uniform integrability. *It is said that a sequence* $\{X_n,\ n \geq 1\}$ *is uniformly integrable if*

$$\sup_{n \geq 1} \mathbf{E}\left[|X_n| I(|X_n| > a)\right] \to 0 \qquad (1.12)$$

when $a \to \infty$; here $I(B)$ is the indicator function, equal to 1 if A holds and 0 otherwise. The above is equivalent to

$$\lim_{a \to \infty} \sup_{n \geq 1} \int_{|x| > a} x\, dF_n(x) = 0.$$

Then the following is true, as shown in Billingsley (1968): *if* X_n *is uniformly integrable then* $X_n \overset{pr}{\to} X$ *implies that* $X_n \overset{L^1}{\to} X$.

In the probabilistic analysis of algorithms, inequalities are very useful for establishing these stochastic convergences. We review now some inequalities used in the book.

Boole's or the union inequality. For any set of events $A_1, \ldots, A_n$ the following is true:

$$P(A_1 \cup A_2 \cup \cdots \cup A_n) \leq P(A_1) + P(A_2) + \cdots + P(A_n). \qquad (1.13)$$

The proof follows from iterative applications of $P(A_n \cup A_2) \leq P(A_1) + P(A_2)$, which is obvious.

Markov's inequality. For a nonnegative function $g(\cdot)$ and a random variable X,

$$P(g(X) \geq t) \leq \frac{\mathbf{E}[g(X)]}{t} \qquad (1.14)$$

holds for any $t > 0$. Indeed, we have the following chain of obvious inequalities:

$$\mathbf{E}[g(X)] \geq \mathbf{E}\left[g(X)I(g(X) \geq t)\right] \geq t\mathbf{E}[I(g(X) \geq t)] = tP(g(X) \geq t),$$

where we recall that $I(A)$ is the indicator function of event A.

Chebyshev's inequality. If one replaces $g(X)$ by $|X - \mathbf{E}[X]|^2$ and t by t^2 in Markov's inequality then we have

$$P(|X - \mathbf{E}[X]| \geq t) \leq \frac{\mathrm{Var}[X]}{t^2}, \qquad (1.15)$$

which is known as Chebyshev's inequality.

Schwarz's inequality (also called the **Cauchy–Schwarz** inequality). Let X and Y be such that $\mathbf{E}[X^2] < \infty$ and $\mathbf{E}[Y^2] < \infty$. Then

$$\mathbf{E}[|XY|]^2 \leq \mathbf{E}[X^2]\mathbf{E}[Y^2], \qquad (1.16)$$

where throughout the book we shall write $\mathbf{E}[X]^2 = (\mathbf{E}[X])^2$.

Jensen's inequality. Let $f(\cdot)$ be a downward convex function, that is, for $\lambda \in (0,1)$

$$\lambda f(x) + (1 - \lambda)f(y) \geq f(\lambda x + (1 - \lambda)y).$$

Then

$$f(\mathbf{E}[X]) \leq \mathbf{E}[f(X)]; \tag{1.17}$$

equality holds when $f(\cdot)$ is a linear function.

Minkowski's inequality. *If* $\mathbf{E}[|X|^p] < \infty$, *and* $\mathbf{E}[|Y|^p] < \infty$ *then* $\mathbf{E}[|X + Y||^p < \infty$ *and*

$$\mathbf{E}[|X + Y|^p]^{1/p} \leq \mathbf{E}[|X|^p]^{1/p} + \mathbf{E}[|Y|^p]^{1/p} \tag{1.18}$$

for $1 \leq p < \infty$.

Inequality on means. Let $(p_1, p_2, \ldots, p_n)$ be a probability vector such that $\sum_{i=1}^n p_i = 1$ and $(a_1, a_2, \ldots, a_n)$ any vector of positive numbers. The *mean of order* $b \neq 0$ $(-\infty \leq b \leq \infty)$ is defined as

$$M_n(b) := \left(\sum_{i=1}^n p_i a_i^b \right)^{1/b}.$$

The inequality on means asserts that $M_n(b)$ is a nondecreasing function of b

$$r < s \quad \Rightarrow \quad M_n(r) \leq M_n(s); \tag{1.19}$$

equality holds if and only if $a_1 = a_2 = \cdots = a_n$. Furthermore, we have **Hilbert's inequality on means** which states that

$$\lim_{b \to -\infty} M_n(b) = \min\{a_1, \ldots, a_n\}, \tag{1.20}$$

$$\lim_{b \to \infty} M_n(b) = \max\{a_1, \ldots, a_n\}. \tag{1.21}$$

First and second moment methods. In establishing convergence in probability, the following two inequalities are of particular interest:
(i) *First moment method.* For a nonnegative integer random variable X, the following holds:

$$P(X > 0) \leq \mathbf{E}[X]; \tag{1.22}$$

this is obvious by the definition of the expectation and the discreteness of X.
(ii) *Second moment method.* For a nonnegative discrete random variable X, the following holds:

$$P(X > 0) \geq \frac{(\mathbf{E}[X])^2}{\mathbf{E}[X^2]}. \tag{1.23}$$

To see this we apply Schwarz's inequality (1.16), to obtain

$$\mathbf{E}[X]^2 = \mathbf{E}[I(X \neq 0)X]^2 \leq \mathbf{E}[I(X \neq 0)]\mathbf{E}[X^2] = P(X \neq 0)\mathbf{E}[X^2],$$

from which the inequality (1.23) follows.

Chernov's bound. Let $S_n = X_1 + \cdots + X_n$. Then

$$P(S_n \geq x) \leq \min_{\lambda > 0} \left\{ e^{-\lambda x} \mathbf{E}[e^{\lambda S_n}] \right\} \qquad (1.24)$$

provided that the right-hand side exists for some $\lambda > 0$.

Hoeffding and Azuma inequality. Let $S_n = X_1 + \cdots + X_n$ for independent X_i such that $a_i \leq X_i \leq b_i$ for some constants a_i, b_i for $1 \leq i \leq n$. Then

$$P(|S_n| > x) \leq 2 \exp \left(-\frac{2x^2}{(b_1 - a_1)^2 + \cdots + (b_n - a_n)^2} \right). \qquad (1.25)$$

A more in depth discussion of large deviation inequalities can be found in Bucklew (1990), Dembo and Zeitouni (1993), Durrett (1991), Janson (2004) and Szpankowski (2001).

Berry–Esseen inequality. When deriving the generating functions of discrete structures, we often obtain an error term. To translate such an analytic error term into a distribution error term, we often use the Cauchy estimate. In some situations, however, the following estimate of Berry and Esseen is very useful. The proof can be found in Durrett (1991) or Feller (1971). We write $|||f|||_\infty := \sup_x |f(x)|$.

Lemma 1.2.3 (Berry–Esseen inequality). *Let F and G be distribution functions with characteristic functions $\phi_F(t)$ and $\phi_G(t)$. Assume that G has a bounded derivative. Then*

$$|||F - G|||_\infty \leq \frac{1}{\pi} \int_{-T}^{T} \left| \frac{\phi_F(t) - \phi_G(t)}{t} \right| dt + \frac{24}{\pi} \frac{|||G'|||_\infty}{T} \qquad (1.26)$$

for any $T > 0$.

This inequality is used to derive Hwang's power law Hwang (1994, 1996) which we quote below.

Theorem 1.2.4 (Hwang, 1994). *Assume that the moment generating functions $M_n(s) = \mathbf{E}[e^{sX_n}]$ of a sequence of random variables X_n are analytic in the disk $|s| < \rho$ for some $\rho > 0$ and satisfy there the expansion*

$$M_n(s) = e^{\beta_n U(s) + V(s)} \left(1 + O\left(\frac{1}{\kappa_n} \right) \right) \qquad (1.27)$$

for $\beta_n, \kappa_n \to \infty$ as $n \to \infty$, where $U(s), V(s)$ are analytic in $|s| < \rho$. Assume also that $U''(0) \neq 0$. Then

$$\mathbf{E}[X_n] = \beta_n U'(0) + V'(0) + O(\kappa_n^{-1}), \tag{1.28}$$

$$\mathrm{Var}[X_n] = \beta_n U''(0) + V''(0) + O(\kappa_n^{-1}) \tag{1.29}$$

and, for any fixed x,

$$P\left(\frac{X_n - \beta_n U'(0)}{\sqrt{\beta_n U''(0)}} \leq x\right) = \Phi(x) + O\left(\frac{1}{\kappa_n} + \frac{1}{\sqrt{\beta_n}}\right), \tag{1.30}$$

where $\Phi(x)$ is the distribution function of the standard normal distribution.

1.3. Generating functions and analytic tools

In this book we systematically view generating functions as analytic complex functions. Here, we briefly review some often used facts. The reader is referred to Flajolet and Sedgewick (2009) and Szpankowski (2001) for a detailed discussion; the book by Henrici (1997) is a good source of knowledge about complex analysis.

The *generating function* of a sequence $\{a_n\}_{n\geq 0}$ (e.g., representing the size of the objects belonging to a certain class) is defined as

$$A(z) = \sum_{n\geq 0} a_n z^n,$$

where the meaning of z is explained below. In this *formal power series* we are assuming that $A(z)$ is an algebraic object, more precisely, that the set of such formal power series forms a *ring*. In this case z does not take any particular value, but one can identify the coefficient at z^n. Moreover, we can manipulate formal power series to discover new identities and establish recurrences and exact formulas for the coefficients. The convergence of $A(z)$ is not an issue.

In the *analytic theory* of generating functions, we assume that z is a complex number, and the issue of convergence is now pivotal. In fact, the singularity points of $A(z)$ (i.e., points where $A(z)$ is not defined) determine the asymptotics of the coefficients.

Convergence issues are addressed by the Hadamard theorem.

Theorem 1.3.1 (Hadamard). *There exists a number $0 \leq R \leq \infty$ such that the series $A(z)$ converges for $|z| < R$ and diverges for $|z| > R$. The radius of convergence R can be expressed as*

$$R = \frac{1}{\limsup_{n\to\infty} |a_n|^{\frac{1}{n}}}, \tag{1.31}$$

where by convention $1/0 = \infty$ *and* $1/\infty = 0$. *The function* $A(z)$ *is analytic for* $|z| < R$.

For our purposes it is more important to find the coefficient of $A(z)$ at z^n, which we write as

$$a_n = [z^n]A(z).$$

Cauchy's theorem allows us to compute the coefficient at z^n as a complex integral. If $A(z)$ is analytic in the vicinity of $z = 0$ then

$$a_n = [z^n]A(z) = \frac{1}{2\pi i} \oint \frac{A(z)}{z^{n+1}} dz \qquad (1.32)$$

where the integral is around any simple curve (contour) encircling $z = 0$. Indeed, since $A(z)$ is analytic at $z = 0$ it has a convergent series representation

$$A(z) = \sum_{k \geq 0} a_k z^k.$$

Thus

$$\oint \frac{A(z)}{z^{n+1}} dz = \sum_{k \geq 0} a_k \oint z^{-(n+1-k)} dz = 2\pi i a_n,$$

where the last equality follows from

$$\oint z^{-n} dz = \int_0^1 e^{-2\pi i(n-1)} dt = \begin{cases} 2\pi i & \text{for } n = 1 \\ 0 & \text{otherwise.} \end{cases}$$

The interchange of the integral and sum above is justified since the series converges uniformly.

Finally, we should mention that Cauchy's formula is often used to establish a bound on the coefficients a_n. Let

$$M(R) = \max_{|z| \leq R} |A(z)|.$$

Then for all $n \geq 0$

$$|a_n| \leq \frac{M(R)}{R^n}, \qquad (1.33)$$

which follows immediately from (1.32) and a trivial majorization under the integral.

In most cases, the Cauchy integral (1.32) is computed through the *Cauchy residue theorem*, which we discuss next. The residue of $f(z)$ at a point a is the coefficient at $(z - a)^{-1}$ in the Laurent expansion of $f(z)$ around a, and it is written as

$$\text{Res}\,[f(z);\ z = a] := f_{-1} = \lim_{z \to a} (z - a)f(z).$$

There are many rules to evaluate the residues of simple poles and the reader can find them in any standard book on complex analysis (e.g., Henrici (1997)). For example, if $f(z)$ and $g(z)$ are analytic around $z = a$, then

$$\text{Res}\left[\frac{f(z)}{g(z)};\ z = a\right] = \frac{f(a)}{g'(a)}, \qquad g(a) = 0, \quad g'(a) \neq 0; \qquad (1.34)$$

if $g(z)$ is not analytic at $z = a$ then

$$\text{Res}[f(z)g(z);\ z = a] = f(a)\,\text{Res}[g(z);\ z = a]. \qquad (1.35)$$

Evaluating the residues of multiple poles is much more computationally involved. Actually, the easiest way is to use the `series` command in MAPLE, which produces a series development of a function. The residue is simply the coefficient at $(z - a)^{-1}$.

Residues are very important in evaluating contour integrals such as the Cauchy integral (1.32).

Theorem 1.3.2 (Cauchy residue theorem). *If $f(z)$ is analytic within and on the boundary of a simple closed curve C except at a finite number of poles $a_1, a_2, \ldots, a_N$ within C having residues $\text{Res}[f(z);\ z = a_1], \ldots, \text{Res}[f(z);\ z = a_N]$, respectively, then*

$$\frac{1}{2\pi i} \int_C f(z)dz = \sum_{j=1}^{N} \text{Res}[f(z);\ z = a_j],$$

where the curve C is traversed counterclockwise. Also, the following holds

$$f^{(k)}(z) = \frac{k!}{2\pi i} \oint \frac{f(w)dw}{(w - z)^{k+1}} \qquad (1.36)$$

where $f^{(k)}(z)$ is the kth derivative of $f(z)$.

Sketch of proof.   Let us assume there is only one pole at $z = a$. Since $f(z)$ is meromorphic, it has a Laurent expansion, which after integration over C leads to

$$\int_C f(z)dz = \sum_{n \geq 0} f_n \int_C (z - a)^n dz + f_{-1} \int_C \frac{dz}{z - a} = 2\pi i\,\text{Res}[f(z), z = a],$$

since the first integral is zero.   ∎

1.4. Special functions

Throughout this book we will often make use of special functions such as the Euler gamma function $\Gamma(z)$ and the Riemann zeta function $\zeta(z)$. We briefly review some properties of these functions.

1.4.1. Euler's gamma function

A desire to generalize $n!$ to the complex plane led Euler to introduce one of the most useful special functions, namely, the *gamma function*. It is defined as follows:

$$\Gamma(z) = \int_0^\infty t^{z-1} e^{-t} dt, \qquad \Re(z) > 0. \tag{1.37}$$

To see that the above integral generalizes $n!$, let us integrate it by parts. We obtain

$$\Gamma(z+1) = -\int_0^\infty t^z d\left(e^{-t}\right) = z\Gamma(z). \tag{1.38}$$

Observe now that $\Gamma(1) = 1$, and so $\Gamma(n+1) = n!$ for natural n, as desired.

To analytically extend $\Gamma(z)$ to the whole complex plane, we first extend the definition to $-1 < \Re(z) < 0$ by considering (1.38) and writing

$$\Gamma(z) = \frac{\Gamma(z+1)}{z}, \qquad -1 < \Re(z) < 0.$$

Since $\Gamma(z+1)$ is well defined for $-1 < \Re(z) < 0$ (indeed, $\Re(z+1) > 0$), we can enlarge the region of definition to the strip $-1 < \Re(z) < 0$. However, at $z = 0$ there is a pole whose residue is easy to evaluate; that is,

$$\mathrm{Res}[\Gamma(z); z = 0] = \lim_{z \to 0} z\Gamma(z) = 1.$$

In general, let us assume that we have already defined $\Gamma(z)$ up to the strip $-n < \Re(z) < -n+1$. Then, extension to $-n-1 < \Re(z) < -n$ is obtained as

$$\Gamma(z) = \frac{\Gamma(z+n+1)}{z(z+1)\cdots(z+n)}.$$

The residue at $z = -n$ becomes

$$\mathrm{Res}[\Gamma(z); z = -n] = \lim_{z \to -n} (z+n)\Gamma(z) = \frac{(-1)^n}{n!} \tag{1.39}$$

for all $n = 0, 1, \ldots$

Closely related to the gamma function is the *beta function*, defined as

$$B(w, z) = \int_0^1 t^{w-1}(1 - t)^{z-1}dt, \qquad \Re(w) > 0 \text{ and } \Re(z) > 0. \qquad (1.40)$$

It is easy to see that

$$B(w, z) = \frac{\Gamma(w)\Gamma(z)}{\Gamma(w + z)}. \qquad (1.41)$$

In many applications Stirling's asymptotic formula for $n!$ proves to be extremely useful. Not surprisingly, then, the same is true for the asymptotic expansion of the gamma function. It can be proved that

$$\Gamma(z) = \sqrt{2\pi}z^{z-1/2}e^{-z}\left(1 + \frac{1}{12z} + \frac{1}{288z^2} + \cdots\right)$$

for $z \to \infty$ when $|\arg(z)| < \pi$.

Finally, when bounding the gamma function along the imaginary axis it is useful to know the following estimate:

$$|\Gamma(x + iy)| \sim \sqrt{2\pi}|y|^{x-1/2}e^{-\pi|y|/2} \qquad \text{as} \qquad |y| \to \pm\infty \qquad (1.42)$$

for any real x and y.

Psi function. The derivative of the logarithm of the gamma function plays an important role in the theory and applications of special functions. It is known as the *psi function* and is thus defined as

$$\psi(z) = \frac{d}{dz}\ln\Gamma(z) = \frac{\Gamma'(z)}{\Gamma(z)}.$$

The following can be proved:

$$\psi(z) = -\gamma + \sum_{n=0}^{\infty}\left(\frac{1}{n + 1} - \frac{1}{z + n}\right), \qquad z \neq 0, -1, -2, \ldots \qquad (1.43)$$

From the above, we conclude that the psi function possesses simple poles at all nonpositive integers and that

$$\mathrm{Res}[\psi(z); z = -n] = \lim_{z \to -n}(z + n)\psi(z) = -1, \qquad n \in \mathbb{N}. \qquad (1.44)$$

Laurent's expansions. As we observed above, the gamma function and the psi function have simple poles at all nonpositive integers. Thus one can expand these functions around $z = -n$ using a Laurent series. The following is known (cf. Temme (1996)):

$$\Gamma(z) = \frac{(-1)^n}{n!} \frac{1}{(z+n)} + \psi(n+1) \tag{1.45}$$

$$+ \frac{1}{2}(z+n)\left(\pi^2/3 + \psi^2(n+1) - \psi'(n+1)\right) + O((z+n)^2),$$

$$\psi(z) = \frac{-1}{z+n} + \psi(m+1) + \sum_{k=2}^{\infty}\left((-1)^n\zeta(n) + \sum_{i=1}^{k} i^{-k}\right)(z+n)^{k-1}, \tag{1.46}$$

where $\zeta(z)$ is the Riemann zeta function defined in (1.49) below. In particular,

$$\Gamma(z) = \frac{1}{z} - \gamma + O(z), \tag{1.47}$$

$$\Gamma(z) = \frac{-1}{z+1} + \gamma - 1 + O(z+1). \tag{1.48}$$

We shall use these expansions quite often in this book.

1.4.2. Riemann's zeta function

The Riemann zeta function $\zeta(z)$ is a fascinating special function, which still hides from us some beautiful properties (e.g., the Riemann conjecture concerning the zeros of $\zeta(z)$). We will uncover merely the tip of the iceberg. The reader is referred to Titchmarsh and Heath-Brown (1988) for a more in-depth discussion. The Riemann zeta function is defined as

$$\zeta(z) = \sum_{n=1}^{\infty} \frac{1}{n^z}, \qquad \Re(z) > 1. \tag{1.49}$$

The *generalized* zeta function $\zeta(z, a)$ (also known as the Hurwitz zeta function) is defined as

$$\zeta(z, a) = \sum_{n=0}^{\infty} \frac{1}{(n+a)^z}, \qquad \Re(z) > 1,$$

where $a \neq 0, -1, -2, \ldots$ is a constant. It is evident that $\zeta(z, 1) = \zeta(z)$.

We know that $\zeta(z)$ has only one pole at $z = 1$. It can be proved that its Laurent series around $z = 1$ is

$$\zeta(z) = \frac{1}{z-1} + \sum_{k=0}^{\infty} \frac{(-1)^k \gamma_k}{k!}(z-1)^k, \tag{1.50}$$

where the γ_k are the so-called Stieltjes constants for $k \geq 0$:

$$\gamma_k = \lim_{m \to \infty} \left(\sum_{i=1}^{m} \frac{\ln^k i}{i} - \frac{\ln^{k+1} m}{k+1} \right).$$

In particular, $\gamma_0 = \gamma = 0.577215\ldots$ is the Euler constant, and $\gamma_1 = -0.072815\ldots$ From the above we conclude that

$$\mathrm{Res}[\zeta(z); z = 1] = 1.$$

We shall use the ζ function often in this book.

1.5. Exercises

1.1   Prove that the $(k+1)$th moment of a discrete nonnegative random variable X is given by

$$\mathbf{E}[X^{k+1}] = \sum_{m \geq 0} P(X > m) \sum_{i=0}^{k} (m+1)^{k-i} m^i,$$

and, in particular, that

$$\mathbf{E}[X] = \sum_{m \geq 0} P(X > m).$$

1.2   Prove the following result: *if X_n is a sequence of nonnegative random variables such that $X_n \overset{a.s.}{\to} X$ and $\mathbf{E}[X_n] \to \mathbf{E}[X]$ then $X_n \overset{L^1}{\to} X$.*

1.3   Prove that if $X_n \overset{pr}{\to} X$ then $f(X_n) \overset{pr}{\to} f(X)$ provided that f is a continuous function.

1.4   Let $X = X_1 + \cdots + X_m$ where the X_j are binary random variables. Prove that

$$P(X > 0) \geq \sum_{j=1}^{m} \frac{\mathbf{E}[X_j]}{\mathbf{E}[X | X_j = 1]}.$$

1.5   Prove the following inequality, known as the *fourth moment method*:

$$\mathbf{E}[|X|] \geq \frac{\mathbf{E}[X^2]^{3/2}}{\mathbf{E}[X^4]^{1/2}},$$

provided that it possesses the first four moments.

1.6   Extend Liouville's theorem to polynomial functions, that is, prove that
       if $f(z)$ is of at most polynomial growth, that is, $|f(z)| \le B|z|^r$ for some
       $r > 0$, then it is a polynomial.

1.7   Estimate the growth of the coefficients $f_n = [z^n]f(z)$ of

$$f(z) = \frac{1}{(1-z)(1-2^z)}.$$

1.8   Using the Weierstrass product formula for the gamma function, that is,

$$\frac{1}{\Gamma(z)} = ze^{\gamma z} \prod_{n=1}^{\infty} \left[\left(1 + \frac{z}{n} \right) e^{-z/n} \right],$$

       prove the expansion (1.43) of the psi function

$$\psi(z) = -\gamma + \sum_{n=0}^{\infty} \left(\frac{1}{n+1} - \frac{1}{z+n} \right), \qquad z \ne 0, -1, -2, \dots$$

1.9   Prove the following asymptotic expansion for $\Re(b-a) > 0$ (see Temme
       (1996)):

$$\frac{\Gamma(z+a)}{\Gamma(z+b)} \sim z^{a-b} \sum_{n=0}^{\infty} c_n \frac{\Gamma(b-a+n)}{\Gamma(b-a)} \frac{1}{z^n} \qquad \text{as } z \to \infty \qquad (1.51)$$

       where

$$c_n = (-1)^n \frac{B_n^{a-b+1}(a)}{n!},$$

       and $B_n^{(w)}(x)$ are the so-called *generalized Bernoulli polynomials* defined
       as

$$e^{xz} \left(\frac{z}{e^z - 1} \right)^w = \sum_{n=0}^{\infty} \frac{B_n^{(w)}(x)}{n!} z^n \qquad |z| < 2\pi.$$

       Hint. Express the ratio $\Gamma(z+a)/\Gamma(z+b)$ in terms of the beta function,
       that is, write

$$\frac{\Gamma(z+a)}{\Gamma(z+b)} = \frac{B(z+a, b-a)}{\Gamma(b-a)}.$$

       Then use the integral representation of the beta function to show that

$$\frac{\Gamma(z+a)}{\Gamma(z+b)} = \frac{1}{\Gamma(b-a)} \int_0^\infty u^{b-a-1} e^{-zu} f(u) du,$$

       where

$$f(u) = e^{-au} \left(\frac{1-e^{-u}}{u} \right)^{b-a-1}.$$

Bibliographical notes

Probabilistic models for words are discussed in many standard books. Markov models are presented in Billingsley (1961) and Rabiner (1989); however, our presentation follows Karlin and Ost (1987). Dynamic sources were introduced by Vallée (2001), and expanded in Clément, Flajolet, and Vallée (2001) and in Bourdon and Vallée (2002). Bradley (1986) gave a brief and rigorous description of mixing sources. General stationary ergodic sources are discussed in Shields (1969).

In this book the emphasis is on the analysis of pattern matching problems by analytic methods in a probabilistic framework. Probabilistic tools are discussed in depth in Alon and Spencer (1992), Szpankowski (2001) and Waterman (1995b) (see also Arratia and Waterman (1989, 1994)). Analytic techniques are thoroughly explained in Flajolet and Sedgewick (2009) and Szpankowski (2001). The reader may also consult Bender (1973), Hwang (1996), Jacquet and Szpankowski (1994, 1998) and Sedgewick and Flajolet (1995). Power law for generating functions was proposed by Hwang (1994, 1996).

Special functions are discussed in depth in many classical books, such as Olver (1974) and Temme (1996), however, Abramowitz and Stegun (1964) is still the best source of formulas for special functions. The Riemann function is well explained in Titchmarsh and Heath-Brown (1988).

CHAPTER 2

Exact String Matching

In the *exact string matching* problem we are searching for a given pattern $w = w_1 w_2 \cdots w_m$ of length m in a text X over an alphabet $\mathcal{A}$. In the *probabilistic* version of the problem, which is the subject of this book, the text $X = X_1^n = X_1 \cdots X_n$ of length n is generated by a random source. We will deal mostly with pattern matching problems with fixed length patterns, that is, we shall assume throughout that $m = O(1)$. However, in Section 2.5.4 we analyze a version of the problem in which the pattern length m grows with the text length n.

2.1. Formulation of the problem

There are several parameters of interest in string matching, but two stand out. The first is the number of times that the pattern w occurs in the text X which we denote as $O_n = O_n(w)$ and define formally by

$$O_n(w) = \left| \{ i : \ X_{i-m+1}^i = w, \ m \le i \le n \} \right|.$$

We can write $O_n(w)$ in an equivalent form as follows:

$$O_n(w) = I_m + I_{m+1} + \cdots + I_n \tag{2.1}$$

where $I_i = 1$ if w occurs at position i and $I_i = 0$ otherwise.

The second parameter is the *waiting time* T_w, defined as the first time that w occurs in the text X; that is,

$$T_w := \min\{n : X_{n-m+1}^n = w\}.$$

One can also define T_j as the minimum length of text in which the pattern w occurs j times. Clearly, $T_w = T_1$. Observe the following relation between O_n and T_w:

$$\{T_w > n\} = \{O_n(w) = 0\}. \tag{2.2}$$

More generally,

$$\{T_j \leq n\} = \{O_n(w) \geq j\}. \tag{2.3}$$

Relation (2.3) is called the *duality principle*. In fact, exact pattern matching can be analyzed through the discrete random variable O_n or the continuous random variable T_w. In this book we mostly concentrate on the frequency of pattern occurrences O_n. The reader is referred to Chapter 6 of Lothaire (2005) for an alternative approach based on T_j.

Our goal is to estimate the frequency of pattern occurrences O_n in a text generated by memoryless or Markov sources. We allow a pattern w to overlap when counting occurrences (e.g., if $w = abab$ then it occurs twice in $X = abababb$ when overlapping is allowed, but only once if overlapping is not allowed). We study the probabilistic behavior of O_n through two generating functions, namely

$$N_r(z) = \sum_{n \geq 0} P(O_n(w) = r)z^n,$$

$$N(z, x) = \sum_{r=1}^{\infty} N_r(z)x^r = \sum_{r=1}^{\infty} \sum_{n=0}^{\infty} P(O_n(w) = r)z^n x^r$$

which are defined for $|z| \leq 1$ and $|x| \leq 1$. We note that $P(O_n(w) = r)$ is the probability that in a text X the pattern w occurs r times.

Throughout this book we adopt a combinatorial approach to string matching, that is, we use combinatorial calculus to find combinatorial relationships between sets of words satisfying certain properties (i.e., languages).

2.2. Language representation

We start our combinatorial analysis with some definitions. For any language $\mathcal{L}$ we define its *generating function* $L(z)$ as

$$L(z) = \sum_{u \in \mathcal{L}} P(u) z^{|u|},$$

where $P(u)$ is the stationary probability of occurrence of the word u and $|u|$ is the length of u.[1] We also assume that $P(\varepsilon) = 1$, where ε is the empty word. Notice that $L(z)$ is defined for all complex z such that $|z| < 1$. In addition, we define the *w-conditional generating function* of $\mathcal{L}$ as

$$L_w(z) = \sum_{u \in \mathcal{L}} P(u|w) z^{|u|} = \sum_{u \in \mathcal{L}} \frac{P(wu)}{P(w)} z^{|u|}.$$

Since we are allowing overlaps, the structure of the pattern w has a profound impact on the number of occurrences. To capture this, we introduce the autocorrelation language and the autocorrelation polynomial.

Given a string w, we define the *autocorrelation set*

$$S = \{w_{k+1}^m : \; w_1^k = w_{m-k+1}^m\}, \tag{2.4}$$

where m is the length of the pattern w. By $\mathcal{P}(w)$ we denote the set of position numbers $k \geq 1$ satisfying $w_1^k = w_{m-k+1}^m$. Thus if $w = vu$ or $w = ux$ for some words v, x, and u then x belongs to S and $|u| \in \mathcal{P}(w)$. Notice that $\varepsilon \in S$. The generating function of the language S is denoted as $S(z)$ and we call it the *autocorrelation polynomial*. Its w-conditional generating function is denoted $S_w(z)$. In particular, for Markov sources of order 1,

$$S_w(z) = \sum_{k \in \mathcal{P}(w)} P(w_{k+1}^m | w_k^k) z^{m-k}. \tag{2.5}$$

Before we proceed, let us present a simple example illustrating the definitions introduced so far.

Example 2.2.1. Let us assume that $w = aba$ over a binary alphabet $\mathcal{A} = \{a, b\}$. Observe that $\mathcal{P}(w) = \{1, 3\}$ and $S = \{\varepsilon, ba\}$. Thus, for an unbiased memoryless source we have $S(z) = 1 + z^2/4$, while for the Markov model of order 1 we obtain $S_{aba}(z) = 1 + P(w_2^3 = ba|w_1 = a)z^2 = 1 + p_{ab}p_{ba}z^2$. ∎

---

[1]We use $|\cdot|$ for both the cardinality of a set and the length of a pattern, but this should not lead to any confusion.

Our goal is to estimate the number of pattern occurrences in a text. Alternatively, we can seek the generating function of a language that consists of all words containing certain occurrences of a pattern w. Given the pattern w, we introduce the following languages:

(i) $\mathcal{T}_r$, a set of words each containing exactly r occurrences of w;

(ii) the "right" language $\mathcal{R}$, a set of words containing only one occurrence of w, located at the right-hand end of the word;

(iii) the "ultimate" language $\mathcal{U}$, defined as

$$\mathcal{U} = \{u : \ wu \in \mathcal{T}_1\}, \tag{2.6}$$

that is, a word u belongs to $\mathcal{U}$ if wu has exactly one occurrence of w, at the left-hand end of wu;

(iv) the "minimal" language $\mathcal{M}$, defined as

$$\mathcal{M} = \{v : \ wv \in \mathcal{T}_2, \text{ i.e., } w \text{ occurs at the right-hand end of } wv\},$$

that is, $\mathcal{M}$ is a language such that any word in $w\mathcal{M}$ has exactly two occurrences of w, at the left-hand and right-hand ends. Here $w \cdot \mathcal{M}$ means that the pattern w is concatenated with all possible words of the language $\mathcal{M}$.[2]

Example 2.2.2. Let $\mathcal{A} = \{a, b\}$ and $w = abab$. Then $v = aaabab \in \mathcal{R}$ (see (ii) above) since there is only one occurrence of w, at the right-hand end of v. Also, $u = bbbb \in \mathcal{U}$ (see (iii) above) since wu has only one occurrence of w at the left-hand end; but $v = abbbb \notin \mathcal{U}$ since $wv = ababbbb$ has two occurrences of w. Furthermore, $ab \in \mathcal{M}$ (see (iv) above) since $wab = ababab \in \mathcal{T}_2$ has two occurrences of w, at the left-hand and the right-hand ends. Finally, $t = bbababababbbababbb \in \mathcal{T}_3$, and one observes that $t = vm_1m_2u$ where $v = bbabab \in \mathcal{R}$, $m_1 = ab \in \mathcal{M}$, $m_2 = bbabab \in \mathcal{M}$, and $u = bb \in \mathcal{U}$.   ∎

We now describe the languages $\mathcal{T}_r$ and $\mathcal{T}_{\geq 1} = \bigcup_{r \geq 1} \mathcal{T}_r$ (the sets of words containing exactly r and at least one occurrence of w) in terms of $\mathcal{R}$, $\mathcal{M}$, and $\mathcal{U}$. Recall that $\mathcal{M}^r$ denotes the concatenation of r languages $\mathcal{M}$ and $\mathcal{M}^0 = \{\varepsilon\}$. Also, we have that $\mathcal{M}^+ = \cup_{r \geq 1} \mathcal{M}^r$ and $\mathcal{M}^* = \cup_{r \geq 0} \mathcal{M}^r$.

---

[2]We mostly write wu when concatenating two words w and u but we will use $\cdot$ to represent the concatenation between a word and a language or languages (e.g., $w \cdot \mathcal{M}$).

Theorem 2.2.3. *The languages $\mathcal{T}_r$ for $r \geq 1$ and $\mathcal{T}_{\geq 1}$ satisfy the relation*

$$\mathcal{T}_r = \mathcal{R} \cdot \mathcal{M}^{r-1} \cdot \mathcal{U}, \tag{2.7}$$

and therefore

$$\mathcal{T}_{\geq 1} = \mathcal{R} \cdot \mathcal{M}^* \cdot \mathcal{U}. \tag{2.8}$$

In addition, we have

$$\mathcal{T}_0 \cdot w = \mathcal{R} \cdot \mathcal{S}. \tag{2.9}$$

Proof. To prove (2.7), we obtain the decomposition of $\mathcal{T}_r$ as follows. The first occurrence of the pattern w in a word belonging to $\mathcal{T}_r$ determines a prefix $p \in \mathcal{T}_r$ that is in $\mathcal{R}$. After concatenating a nonempty word v we create the second occurrence of w provided that $v \in \mathcal{M}$. This process is repeated $r - 1$ times. Finally, after the last w occurrence we add a suffix u that does not create a new occurrence of w, that is, wu is such that $u \in \mathcal{U}$. Clearly, a word belongs to $\mathcal{T}_{\geq 1}$ if for some $1 \leq r < \infty$ it is in $\mathcal{T}_r$. The derivation of (2.9) is left to the reader as Exercise 2.3 at the end of the chapter. ∎

Example 2.2.4. Let $w = TAT$. The following word belongs to the language $\mathcal{T}_3$:

$$\overbrace{CCTAT}^{\mathcal{R}} \underbrace{AT}_{\mathcal{M}} \underbrace{GATAT}_{\mathcal{M}} \overbrace{GGA}^{\mathcal{U}}$$

as is easy to check. ∎

We now prove the following result, which summarizes the relationships between the languages $\mathcal{R}$, $\mathcal{M}$, and $\mathcal{U}$.

Theorem 2.2.5. *The languages $\mathcal{M}$, $\mathcal{R}$, and $\mathcal{U}$ satisfy*

$$\mathcal{M}^* = \mathcal{A}^* \cdot w + \mathcal{S}, \tag{2.10}$$

$$\mathcal{U} \cdot \mathcal{A} = \mathcal{M} + \mathcal{U} - \{\varepsilon\}, \tag{2.11}$$

$$w \cdot (\mathcal{M} - \varepsilon) = \mathcal{A} \cdot \mathcal{R} - \mathcal{R}. \tag{2.12}$$

Proof. We first deal with (2.10). Clearly, $\mathcal{A}^* w$ contains at least one occurrence of w on the right, hence $\mathcal{A}^* \cdot w \subset \mathcal{M}^*$. Furthermore, a word v in $\mathcal{M}^*$ is not in $\mathcal{A}^* \cdot w$ if and only if its size $|v|$ is smaller than $|w|$ (e.g., consider $v = ab \in \mathcal{M}$ for $w = abab$). Then the second w occurrence in wv overlaps with w, which means that v is in $\mathcal{S}$.

Let us turn now to (2.11). When one adds a character $a \in \mathcal{A}$ directly after a word u from $\mathcal{U}$, two cases may occur. Either wua still does not contain a second occurrence of w (which means that ua is a nonempty word of $\mathcal{U}$) or a new w appears, clearly at the right-hand end. Hence $\mathcal{U} \cdot \mathcal{A} \subseteq \mathcal{M} + \mathcal{U} - \varepsilon$. Now let $v \in \mathcal{M} - \varepsilon$; then by definition $wv \in \mathcal{T}_2 \subseteq \mathcal{U}\mathcal{A} - \mathcal{U}$, which proves (2.11).

We now prove (2.12). Let $x = av$, where $a \in \mathcal{A}$, be a word in $w \cdot (\mathcal{M} - \varepsilon)$. As x contains exactly two occurrences of w, located at its left-hand and right-hand ends, v is in $\mathcal{R}$ and x is in $\mathcal{A} \cdot \mathcal{R} - \mathcal{R}$; hence $w \cdot (\mathcal{M} - \varepsilon) \subseteq \mathcal{A} \cdot \mathcal{R} - \mathcal{R}$. To prove that $\mathcal{A} \cdot \mathcal{R} - \mathcal{R} \subseteq w \cdot (\mathcal{M} - \varepsilon)$, we take a word avw from $\mathcal{A} \cdot \mathcal{R}$ that is not in $\mathcal{R}$. Then avw contains a second w-occurrence starting in av. As vw is in $\mathcal{R}$, its only possible position is at the left-hand end, and so x must be in $w \cdot (\mathcal{M} - \varepsilon)$. This proves (2.12).   ■

2.3. Generating functions

The next step is to translate the relationships between languages into the associated generating functions. Therefore, we must now select the probabilistic model according to which the text is generated. We will derive results for a Markov model of order 1. We adopt the following notation. To extract a particular element, say with index (i, j), from a matrix P, we shall write $[\mathrm{P}]_{i,j} = p_{i,j}$. We recall that we have $(\mathrm{I} - \mathrm{P})^{-1} = \sum_{k \geq 0} \mathrm{P}^k$, where I is the identity matrix, provided that $\| \mathrm{P} \| < 1$, for a matrix norm $\| \cdot \|$. We also write Π for the stationary matrix that consists of $|\mathcal{A}|$ identical rows given by $\boldsymbol{\pi}$. By Z we denote the *fundamental matrix* $\mathrm{Z} = (\mathrm{I} - (\mathrm{P} - \Pi))^{-1}$. Finally, for Markov sources of order 1, we often use the following obvious identity:

$$P(u) = P(u_1 u_2 \cdots u_m) = P(u_1)P(u_2 \cdots u_m | u_1) = \boldsymbol{\pi}_{u_1} P(u_2 \cdots u_m | u_1) \quad (2.13)$$

for any $u \in \mathcal{A}^m$.

The next lemma translates the language relationships (2.10)–(2.12) into the generating functions $M_w(z)$, $U_w(z)$, and $R(z)$ of the languages $\mathcal{M}$, $\mathcal{U}$, and $\mathcal{R}$ (we recall that the first two generating function are *conditioned* on w appearing just before any word from $\mathcal{M}$ and $\mathcal{U}$). We define a function

$$F(z) = \frac{1}{\boldsymbol{\pi}_{w_1}} \left[\sum_{n \geq 0} (\mathrm{P} - \Pi)^{n+1} z^n \right]_{w_m, w_1} = \frac{1}{\boldsymbol{\pi}_{w_1}} [(\mathrm{P} - \Pi)(\mathrm{I} - (\mathrm{P} - \Pi)z)^{-1}]_{w_m, w_1}$$

$$(2.14)$$

for $|z| < \| \mathrm{P} - \Pi \|^{-1}$, where $\boldsymbol{\pi}_{w_1}$ is the stationary probability of the first symbol w_1 of w. For memoryless sources $F(z) = 0$.

Lemma 2.3.1. *For stationary Markov sources (of order 1), the generating functions associated with the languages $\mathcal{M}, \mathcal{U}$, and $\mathcal{R}$ satisfy*

$$\frac{1}{1 - M_w(z)} = S_w(z) + P(w)z^m \left(\frac{1}{1 - z} + F(z) \right), \tag{2.15}$$

$$U_w(z) = \frac{M_w(z) - 1}{z - 1}, \tag{2.16}$$

$$R(z) = P(w)z^m \cdot U_w(z), \tag{2.17}$$

provided that the underlying Markov chain is aperiodic and ergodic. If the source is memoryless then $F(z) = 0$.

Proof. We first prove (2.16). Let us consider the language relationship (2.11), which we rewrite as $\mathcal{U} \cdot \mathcal{A} - \mathcal{U} = \mathcal{M} - \varepsilon$. Observe that $\sum_{b \in \mathcal{A}} p_{ab} z = z$. Hence, the set $\mathcal{U} \cdot \mathcal{A}$ yields (conditioning on the left-hand end occurrence of w)

$$\sum_{u \in \mathcal{U}} \sum_{b \in \mathcal{A}} P(ub|w)z^{|ub|} = \sum_{a \in \mathcal{A}} \sum_{u \in \mathcal{U}, \ell(u) = a} P(u|w)z^{|u|} \sum_{b \in \mathcal{A}} p_{ab} z = U_w(z)z,$$

where $\ell(u)$ denotes the last symbol of the word u. Of course, $\mathcal{M} - \varepsilon$ and $\mathcal{U}$ translate into $M_w(z) - 1$ and $U_w(z)$, and (2.16) is proved.

We now turn our attention to (2.17) and use the relationship (2.12), $w \cdot \mathcal{M} - w = \mathcal{A} \cdot \mathcal{R} - \mathcal{R}$. In order to compute the *conditional* generating function of $\mathcal{A} \cdot \mathcal{R}$ we proceed as follows:

$$\sum_{ab \in \mathcal{A}^2} \sum_{bv \in \mathcal{R}} P(abv)z^{|abv|} = z^2 \sum_{a \in \mathcal{A}} \sum_{b \in \mathcal{A}} \pi_a p_{ab} \sum_{bv \in \mathcal{R}} P(v|v_{-1} = b)z^{|v|}.$$

Owing to the stationarity of the underlying Markov chain, $\sum_a \pi_a p_{ab} = \pi_b$. As $\pi_b P(v|v_{-1} = b) = P(bv)$, we get $zR(z)$. Furthermore, $w \cdot \mathcal{M} - w$ translates into $P(w)z^m(M_w(z) - 1)$. Then by (2.16), proved above, we have

$$P(w)z^m U_w(z)(z - 1) = P(w)z^m(M_w(z) - 1),$$

which after simplification leads to (2.17).

Finally, we deal with (2.15) and prove it using (2.10). The left-hand side of (2.10) involves the language $\mathcal{M}$, hence we must condition on the left-hand end occurrence of w. In particular, $\bigcup_{r \geq 1} \mathcal{M}^r + \varepsilon$ of (2.10) translates into $1/(1 - M_w(z))$. Now we deal with the term $\mathcal{A}^* \cdot w$ on the right-hand side of (2.10), which we use in the form

$$w \cdot \mathcal{M}^* = w \cdot \mathcal{A}^* \cdot w + w \cdot \mathcal{S}.$$

Thus, conditioning on the left-hand end occurrence of w, the generating function $A_w(z)$ of $\mathcal{A}^* \cdot w$ is given by

$$A_w(z) = \sum_{n \geq 0} \sum_{|u|=n} z^{n+m} P(uw | u_{-1} = w_m)$$

$$= \sum_{n \geq 0} \sum_{|u|=n} z^n P(uw_1 | u_{-1} = w_m) P(w_2 \cdots w_m | w_1) z^m.$$

We have $P(w_2 \cdots w_m | w_1) = P(w) / \pi_{w_1}$ and, for $n \geq 0$:

$$\sum_{|u|=n} P(uw_1 | u_{-1} = w_m) = [\mathrm{P}^{n+1}]_{w_m, w_1}$$

where, we recall, w_m is the last character of w. In summary, the language $\mathcal{A}^* \cdot w$ contributes $P(w) z^m \left[\frac{1}{\pi_{w_1}} \sum_{n \geq 0} \mathrm{P}^{n+1} z^n \right]_{w_m, w_1}$ while the language $\mathcal{S} - \{\varepsilon\}$ contributes $S_w(z) - 1$. Using the equality $\mathrm{P}^{n+1} - \Pi = (\mathrm{P} - \Pi)^{n+1}$ (which follows from consecutive applications of the identity $\Pi \mathrm{P} = \mathrm{P} \Pi = \Pi$) and observing, that for any symbols a and b,

$$\left[\frac{1}{\pi_b} \sum_{n \geq 0} \Pi z^n \right]_{ab} = \sum_{n \geq 0} z^n = \frac{1}{1 - z},$$

we obtain the sum in (2.15) and complete the proof of the lemma.   ∎

Lemma 2.3.1, together with Theorem 2.2.3, suffices to derive the generating functions $N_r(z)$ and $N(z, x)$ from Section 2.1 in an explicit form.

Theorem 2.3.2.   *Let w be a given pattern of size m and X be a random text of length n generated according to a stationary Markov chain with transition probability matrix* P. *Define*

$$D_w(z) = (1 - z) S_w(z) + z^m P(w)(1 + (1 - z) F(z)). \qquad (2.18)$$

Then

$$N_0(z) = \frac{1 - R(z)}{1 - z} = \frac{S_w(z)}{D_w(z)}, \qquad (2.19)$$

$$N_r(z) = R(z) M_w^{r-1}(z) U_w(z), \qquad r \geq 1, \qquad (2.20)$$

$$N(z, x) = R(z) \frac{x}{1 - x M_w(z)} U_w(z), \qquad (2.21)$$

where

$$M_w(z) = 1 + \frac{z-1}{D_w(z)}, \tag{2.22}$$

$$U_w(z) = \frac{1}{D_w(z)}, \tag{2.23}$$

$$R(z) = z^m P(w) \frac{1}{D_w(z)}. \tag{2.24}$$

We recall that for memoryless sources $F(z) = 0$, and hence

$$D(z) = (1-z)S(z) + z^m P(w). \tag{2.25}$$

Proof. We only need to comment on the derivation of $N_0(z)$ since the rest follows directly from our previous results. Observe that

$$N_0(z) = \sum_{n \geq 0} P(O_n = 0)z^n = \sum_{n \geq 0}(1 - P(O_n > 0))z^n = \frac{1}{1-z} - \sum_{r=1}^{\infty} N_r(z);$$

from thus the first expression follows (2.20). The second expression is a direct translation of $\mathcal{T}_0 \cdot w = \mathcal{R} \cdot \mathcal{A}$ (see (2.9)), which reads $N_0(z)P(w)z^m = R(z)S_w(z)$ in terms of the corresponding generating functions.   ∎

Memoryless source. For a memoryless source $F(z) = 0$, and therefore $D(z) = (1-z)S(z) + z^m P(w)$. Note that conditioning on w is not necessary. Thus, from Section 2.1,

$$N(z, x) = \frac{z^m P(w)x}{D(z)\left[D(z) - x(D(z) + z - 1)\right]}.$$

In $N(z, x)$ we have summed from $r = 1$. If we set $\overline{N}(z, x) = N(z, x) + N_0(z)$ then

$$\overline{N}(z, x) = \frac{x + (1-x)S(z)}{(1-z)((1-x)S(z) + x) + z^m P(w)(1-x)}. \tag{2.26}$$

2.4.   Moments

In the previous section we derived explicit formulas for the generating functions $N(z, x) = \sum_{n \geq 0} \mathbf{E}[x^{O_n}]z^n$ and $N_r(z)$. These formulas can be used to obtain explicit and asymptotic expressions for the moments of O_n, the central limit theorem, large deviation results, and the Poisson law. We start with derivations of the mean and the variance of O_n.

Theorem 2.4.1. *Under the assumptions of Theorem 2.3.2 one has, for $n \geq m$,*

$$\mathbf{E}[O_n(w)] = P(w)(n - m + 1) \tag{2.27}$$

and

$$\mathrm{Var}[O_n(w)] = nc_1 + c_2 + O(R^{-n}), \qquad \text{for } R > 1, \tag{2.28}$$

where

$$c_1 = P(w)(2S_w(1) - 1 - (2m - 1)P(w) + 2P(w)E_1)), \tag{2.29}$$

$$\begin{aligned} c_2 = P(w)((m-1)(3m-1)P(w) - (m-1)(2S_w(1) - 1) - 2S'_w(1)) \\ -2(2m-1)P(w)^2 E_1 + 2E_2 P(w)^2 \end{aligned} \tag{2.30}$$

and the constants E_1, E_2 are given by

$$E_1 = \frac{1}{\pi_{w_1}}[(\mathrm{P} - \Pi)\mathrm{Z}]_{w_m, w_1}, \qquad E_2 = \frac{1}{\pi_{w_1}}[(\mathrm{P}^2 - \Pi)\mathrm{Z}^2]_{w_m, w_1}$$

with, as we recall, $\mathrm{Z} = (\mathrm{I} - (\mathrm{P} - \Pi))^{-1}$.

Proof. Notice that first moment estimate can be derived directly from the definition of the stationary probability of w. In order to obtain the higher moments we will use analytic tools applied to generating functions. We can compute the first two moments of O_n from $N(z, x)$ since $\mathbf{E}[O_n] = [z^n]N_x(z, 1)$ and $\mathbf{E}[O_n(N_n - 1)] = [z^n]N_{xx}(z, 1)$ where $N_x(z, 1)$ and $N_{xx}(z, 1)$ are the first and second derivatives of $N(z, x)$ with respect to the variable x at $(z, 1)$. By Theorem 2.3.2 we find that

$$N_x(z, 1) = \frac{z^m P(w)}{(1 - z)^2},$$

$$N_{xx}(z, 1) = \frac{2z^m P(w)M_w(z)D_w(z)}{(1 - z)^3}.$$

Now we observe that both expressions admit as a numerator a function that is analytic beyond the unit circle. Furthermore, for a positive integer $k > 0$,

$$[z^n](1 - z)^{-k} = \binom{n + k - 1}{k - 1} = \frac{\Gamma(n + k)}{\Gamma(k)\Gamma(n + 1)}, \tag{2.31}$$

where $\Gamma(x)$ is the Euler gamma function. We find that for $n \geq m$,

$$\mathbf{E}[O_n] = [z^n]N_u(z, 1) = P(w)[z^{n-m}](1 - z)^{-2} = (n - m + 1)P(w).$$

In order to estimate the variance we introduce

$$\Phi(z) = 2z^m P(w)M_w(z)D_w(z),$$

and observe that

$$\Phi(z) = \Phi(1) + (z-1)\Phi'(1) + \frac{(z-1)^2}{2}\Phi''(1) + (z-1)^3 f(z), \qquad (2.32)$$

where $f(z)$ is the remainder of the Taylor expansion of $\Phi(z)$ up to order 3 at $z = 1$. Hence, by (2.31) we arrive at

$$\mathbf{E}[O_n(O_n - 1)] = [z^n]N_{xx}(z,1) = \Phi(1)\frac{(n+2)(n+1)}{2} - \Phi'(1)(n+1) + \frac{1}{2}\Phi''(1).$$

However, $\mathcal{M}_w(z)D_w(z) = D_w(z) + (1-z)$, which is easy to evaluate except for the term

$$[z^n]\frac{2z^{2m}P(w)^2 F(z)}{(1-z)^2},$$

where $F(z)$, defined in (2.14), is analytic beyond the unit circle for $|z| \leq R$, with $R > 1$. Then the first two terms in the Taylor expansion of $F(z)$ are $E_1 + (1-z)E_2$, and applying (2.31) yields the result. ∎

Memoryless source. For memoryless sources $P = \Pi$, so $E_1 = E_2 = 0$ and (2.28) vanishes for $n \geq 2m-1$, since $\Phi(z)$ and thus $f(z)$ in (2.32) are polynomials of degree $2m-2$ and $[z^n](z-1)f(z)$ is 0 for $n \geq 2m-1$. Thus

$$\mathrm{Var}[O_n(w)] = nc_1 + c_2 \qquad (2.33)$$

with

$$c_1 = P(w)(2S(1) - 1 - (2m-1)P(w)),$$
$$c_2 = P(w)((m-1)(3m-1)P(w) - (m-1)(2S(1) - 1) - 2S'(1)).$$

In passing we mention again that from the generating function $N(z,x)$ we can compute all moments of O_n.

2.5. Limit laws

In this section we estimate asymptotically $P(O_n(w) = r)$ for various ranges of r, including small $r = O(1)$, the central law regime $r = \mathbf{E}[O_n] + \xi\mathrm{Var}[O_n]$ for fixed ξ, and large deviation regime $r = (1+\delta)\mathbf{E}[O_n)]$ for some $\delta > 0$ (see Theorems 2.5.1, 2.5.3, and 2.5.4). These laws are derived under the assumption that the given pattern w is of fixed length m, that is, $\mathbf{E}[O_n] = nP(w) \to \infty$ if $n \to \infty$. In fact, we assume $m = O(1)$. When $\mathbf{E}[O_n] = nP(w) = O(1)$ the Gaussian law cannot hold, and one enters the rare events regime, which we discuss in the next section.

2.5.1. Pattern count probability for small values of r

In this subsection we estimate the asymptotic probability $P(O_n = r)$ when the number of times that the pattern of interest occurs in a text, r, is fixed and small.

Theorem 2.5.1. *Assume that $m = O(1)$. For a Markov source, let ρ_w be the root of $D_w(z) = 0$ having the smallest modulus and multiplicity 1 (see Lemma 2.5.2 below). Then ρ_w is real and such that $\rho_w > 1$, and there exists $\rho > \rho_w$ such that, for fixed $r > 1$,*

$$P(O_n(w) = r) = \sum_{j=1}^{r+1} (-1)^j a_j \binom{n}{j-1} \rho_w^{-(n+j)} + O(\rho^{-n}), \qquad (2.34)$$

where

$$a_{r+1} = \frac{\rho_w^m P(w)\,(\rho_w - 1)^{r-1}}{(D_w'(\rho_w))^{r+1}} \qquad (2.35)$$

and the remaining coefficients can be computed according to

$$a_j = \frac{1}{(r+1-j)!} \lim_{z \to \rho_w} \frac{d^{r+1-j}}{dz^{r+1-j}} \left(N_r(z)(z - \rho_w)^{r+1} \right) \qquad (2.36)$$

with $j = 1, 2, \ldots, r$. For $r = 0$ we have

$$P(O_n(w) = 0) = -\frac{S(\rho_w)}{D'(\rho_w)} \rho_w^{-(n+1)} + O(\rho^n) \qquad (2.37)$$

where $\rho > \rho_w$; $N_r(z)$ and $S_w(z)$ are given by (2.20) and (2.5).

In order to prove Theorem 2.5.1, we need the following simple result.

Lemma 2.5.2. *The equation $D_w(z) = 0$ has at least one root, and all its roots are of modulus greater than 1.*

Proof. The singularities of $D_w(z) = (1 - z)/(1 - M_w(z))$ are clearly poles of $1/(1 - M_w(z))$. As $1/(1 - M_w(z))$ is the generating function of the language $\mathcal{M}^*$, it converges for $|z| < 1$ and has no pole of modulus smaller than 1. Since $D_w(1) \neq 0$, $z = 1$ is a simple pole of $1/(1 - M_w(z))$. As all its coefficients are real and non negative, there is no other pole of modulus $|z| = 1$. It follows that the roots of $D_w(z)$ are all of modulus greater than 1. The existence of a root is guaranteed since $D_w(z)$ is either a polynomial (in the Bernoulli model) or a ratio of polynomials (in the Markov model). ∎

Proof of Theorem 2.5.1. We first rewrite the formula (2.20) for $N_r(z)$ as follows, for $r \geq 1$:

$$N_r(z) = \frac{z^m P(w)(D_w(z) + z - 1)^{r-1}}{D_w^{r+1}(z)} . \tag{2.38}$$

Observe that $P(O_n(w) = r)$ is the coefficient at z^n of $N_r(z)$. By Hadamard's theorem 1.3.1, the asymptotics of the coefficients of a generating function depend on the singularities of the generating function itself. In our case the generating function $N_r(z)$ is a rational function, thus we can only expect poles (for which the denominator $D_w(z)$ vanishes). Lemma 2.5.2 above establishes the existence and properties of such a pole. Therefore the generating function $N_r(z)$ can be expanded around the root of $D_w(z)$ of smallest modulus. Say this root is ρ_w. Then the Laurent series becomes

$$N_r(z) = \sum_{j=1}^{r+1} \frac{a_j}{(z - \rho_w)^j} + \widetilde{N}_r(z) \tag{2.39}$$

where $\widetilde{N}_r(z)$ is analytic in $|z| < \rho'$ and ρ' is defined as $\rho' = \inf\{|\rho| : \rho > \rho_w \text{ and } D_w(\rho) = 0\}$. The a_j satisfy (2.36). The formula (2.38) simplifies into (2.35) for the leading coefficient a_{r+1}. As a consequence of the analyticity we have, for $1 < \rho_w < \rho < \rho'$,

$$[z^n]\widetilde{N}^{(r)}(z) = O(\rho^{-n}).$$

Hence the term $\widetilde{N}_r(z)$ contributes only to the lower terms in the asymptotic expansion of $N_r(z)$. After some algebra, and noting as in (2.31) that

$$[z^n]1(1-z)^{-k-1} = \binom{n+k}{n},$$

Theorem 2.5.1 is proved. For $r = 0$ we use the explicit expression (2.19) for $N_0(z)$ and the Cauchy residue theorem 1.3.2 to find the probability $P(O_n = 0)$.
∎

2.5.2. Central limit laws

In the next theorem we establish the central limit theorem in its strong form (i.e., the local limit theorem). In this subsection we merely sketch the proof. Detailed proofs for a more general case of the generalized pattern matching are presented in Chapter 4. Throughout this section we assume that $nP(w) \to \infty$.

Theorem 2.5.3. *For an aperiodic and ergodic Markov source, let $nP(w) \to \infty$. Then*

$$P(O_n(w) \le \mathbf{E}[O_n] + \xi\sqrt{\mathrm{Var}[O_n]}) = \left(1 + O\left(\frac{1}{\sqrt{n}}\right)\right) \frac{1}{\sqrt{2\pi}} \int_{-\infty}^{\xi} e^{-t^2/2} dt.$$
(2.40)

If, in addition, $p_{ij} > 0$ for all $i, j \in \mathcal{A}$ then, for any bounded real interval B,

$$\sup_{\xi \in B} \left| P(O_n(w) = \lfloor \mathbf{E}[O_n] + \xi\sqrt{\mathrm{Var}[O_n]} \rfloor) - \frac{1}{\sqrt{2\pi\mathrm{Var}(O_n)}} e^{-\frac{1}{2}\xi^2} \right| = o\left(\frac{1}{\sqrt{n}}\right)$$
(2.41)

as $n \to \infty$.

Proof. Let $r = \lfloor \mathbf{E}[O_n] + \xi\sqrt{\mathrm{Var}[O_n]} \rfloor$ with $\xi = O(1)$. We will compute $P(O_n(w) \le r)$ (in the case of the central limit theorem) and $P(O_n(w) = r)$ (in the case of the local limit theorem) for $r = \mathbf{E}(O_n) + \xi\sqrt{\mathrm{Var}(O_n)}$ when $\xi = O(1)$. Let $\nu_n = \mathbf{E}[O_n(w)] = (n - m + 1)P(w)$ and $\sigma_n^2 = \mathrm{Var}[O_n(w)] = c_1 n + O(1)$. To establish the normality of $(O_n(w) - \nu_n)/\sigma_n$ it suffices, according to Lévy's continuity theorem, to prove the following:

$$\lim_{n \to \infty} e^{-\tau \nu_n / \sigma_n} N_n(e^{\tau/\sigma_n}) = e^{\tau^2/2}$$
(2.42)

for complex τ (actually, $\tau = iv$ suffices). Again by Cauchy's coefficient formula (1.32),

$$\mathbf{E}[x^{O_n}] =: N_n(x) = \frac{1}{2\pi i} \oint \frac{N(z, x)}{z^{n+1}} dz = \frac{1}{2\pi i} \oint \frac{x P(w)}{D_w^2(z)(1 - x M_w(z)) z^{n+1-m}} dz,$$

where the integration is along a circle around the origin. The evaluation of this integral is standard and appeals to the Cauchy residue theorem 1.3.2. Namely, we enlarge the circle of integration to a larger circle, with, say radius $R > 1$, such that the larger circle contains the dominant pole of the integrand function. Since $D_w(1) \ne 1$, observe that the Cauchy integral over the larger circle is $O(R^{-n})$. Let us now substitute $x = e^t$ and $z = e^\rho$. Then the poles of the integrand are the roots of the equation

$$1 - e^t M_w(e^\rho) = 0.$$
(2.43)

This equation implicitly defines in some neighborhood of $t = 0$ a unique C^∞ function $\rho(t)$, satisfying $\rho(0) = 0$. Notably, all other roots ρ satisfy $\inf |\rho| = \rho' > 0$. The residue theorem with $e^{\rho'} > R > e^\rho > 1$ now leads to

$$N_n(e^t) = C(t) e^{-(n+1-m)\rho(t)} + O(R^{-n})$$
(2.44)

where
$$C(t) = \frac{P(w)}{D_w^2(\rho(t)) M_w'(\rho(t))}.$$

To study the properties of $\rho(t)$, we observe that $\mathbf{E}[O_n(w)] = [t] \log N_n(e^t)$ and $\sigma_n^2 = [t^2] \log N_n(e^t)$, where we recall again that $[t^r] f(t)$ denotes the coefficient of $f(t)$ at t^r. In our case $\nu_n = -n\rho'(0) + O(1)$ and $\sigma_n^2 = -n\rho''(0) + O(1)$. Now, in (2.44) set $t = \tau/\sigma_n \to 0$ for some complex τ. Since uniformly in t we have $\rho(t) = t\rho'(0) + \rho''(0)t^2/2 + O(t^3)$ for $t \to 0$, our estimate (2.44) leads to

$$e^{-\tau\nu_n/\sigma_n} N_n(e^{\tau/\sigma_n}) = \exp\left(\frac{\tau^2}{2} + O(n\tau^3/\sigma_n^3)\right)$$
$$= e^{\tau^2/2}\left(1 + O(1/\sqrt{n})\right),$$

which proves (2.40) without the error term. After applying the Berry–Esseen inequality, one can derive the error term $O(1/\sqrt{n})$. The reader is encouraged to fill in the missing details. We will prove a more general version in Theorem 4.2.6 of Chapter 4.

To establish the local limit theorem we observe that if $p_{ij} > 0$ for all $i, j \in \mathcal{A}$ then $\rho(t) > 0$ for $t \neq 0$ (see Exercise 2.8). In fact, we can obtain a much more refined local limit result. Indeed, we find for $x = o(n^{1/6})$,

$$P(O_n = \mathbf{E}[O_n] + \xi\sqrt{nc_1}) = \frac{1}{\sqrt{2\pi nc_1}} e^{-\frac{1}{2}\xi^2}\left(1 - \frac{\kappa_3}{2c_1^{3/2}\sqrt{n}}\left(\xi - \frac{\xi^3}{3}\right)\right)$$
$$+ O(n^{-3/2}), \tag{2.45}$$

where κ_3 is a constant. This completes the proof of Theorem 2.5.3. ∎

In the central law regime, we conclude that the normalized random variable $(O_n - \mathbf{E}[O_n])/\sqrt{\mathrm{Var}[O_n]}$ converges also in moments to the moments of the standard normal distribution. This follows from the fact just proved, that the normalized generating function converges to an analytic function, namely $e^{\tau^2/2}$ for τ complex in the vicinity of zero. Since an analytic function has well-defined derivatives, convergence in moments follows. We shall leave a formal proof to the reader (see Exercise 2.7).

2.5.3. Large deviations

Finally, we establish precise large deviations for O_n, still under the assumption that $nP(w) \to \infty$. Large deviation results play a central role in many applications, most notably in data mining and molecular biology, since they allow one to establish thresholds for determining over-represented and under-represented patterns.

Theorem 2.5.4.   *Assume that $m = O(1)$. Let $r = a\mathbf{E}[O_n]$ with $a = (1+\delta)P(w)$ for $\delta \neq 0$. For complex t, define $\rho(t)$ to be the root of*

$$1 - e^t M_w(e^\rho) = 0 \qquad (2.46)$$

and define ω_a and σ_a by

$$-\rho'(\omega_a) = a, \qquad -\rho''(\omega_a) = \sigma_a^2.$$

Then

$$P(O_n(w) = (1+\delta)\mathbf{E}[O_n]) \sim \frac{1}{\sigma_a\sqrt{2\pi(n-m+1)}} e^{-(n-m+1)I(a)+\theta_a}, \qquad (2.47)$$

where $I(a) = a\omega_a + \rho(\omega_a)$ and

$$\theta_a = \log \frac{P(w)e^{m\rho(\omega_a)}}{D_w(e^{\rho(\omega_a)}) + (1 - e^{\rho(\omega_a)})D_w'(e^{\rho(\omega_a)})}, \qquad (2.48)$$

and $D_w(z)$ was defined in (2.18).

Proof. From (2.44) we conclude that

$$\lim_{n\to\infty} \frac{\log N_n(e^t)}{n} = -\rho(t).$$

By the Gärtner–Ellis theorem we find that

$$\lim_{n\to\infty} \frac{\log P(O_n > na)}{n} = -I(a)$$

where

$$I(a) = a\omega_a + \rho(\omega_a)$$

with ω_a a solution of $-\rho'(t) = a$. A stronger version of the above result is possible and we will derive it in Chapter 4. In fact, we will use (2.45) to do this and the "shift of mean" technique to be discussed next.

As in the local limit regime, we could use Cauchy's formula to compute the probability $P(O_n = r)$ for $r = \mathbf{E}[O_n] + \xi O(\sqrt{n})$, but formula (2.45) is only good for $\xi = O(1)$; we need $\xi = O(\sqrt{n})$ for large deviations. To expand its validity we shift the mean of the generating function $N_n(x)$ to a new value, say $m = an = (1+\delta)P(w)(n-m+1)$, so that we can again apply the local limit theorem (2.45) around the new mean. To accomplish this, let us rewrite (2.44) as

$$N_n(e^t) = C(t)[g(t)]^{n-m+1} + O(R^{-n})$$

for any $R > 0$, where $g(t) = e^{-\rho(t)}$. (In the derivation below, for simplicity we will drop the $O(R^{-n})$ term.) The above suggests that $N_n(e^t)$ is the moment generating function of a sum S_n of $n - m + 1$ "almost" independent random variables $X_1, \ldots, X_{n-m+1}$ having moment generating function $g(t)$ and an independent random variable Y whose moment generating function is $C(t)$. Observe that $\mathbf{E}(S_n) = (n - m + 1)P(w)$, while we need to estimate the tail of S_n around $(1 + \delta)(n - m + 1)P(w)$. To achieve this, we introduce a new random variable, $\widetilde{X}_i$, whose moment generating function $\widetilde{g}(t)$ is given by

$$\widetilde{g}(t) = \frac{g(t + \omega)}{g(\omega)},$$

where ω will be chosen later. Then the mean and variance of the new variable $\widetilde{X}$ are

$$\mathbf{E}[\widetilde{X}] = \frac{g'(\omega)}{g(\omega)} = -\rho'(\omega),$$

$$\mathrm{Var}[\widetilde{X}] = \frac{g''(\omega)}{g(\omega)} - \left(\frac{g'(\omega)}{g(\omega)}\right)^2 = -\rho''(\omega).$$

Let us now choose ω_a such that

$$-\rho'(\omega_a) = \frac{g'(\omega_a)}{g(\omega_a)} = a = P(w)(1 + \delta)$$

(we will prove the uniqueness of this expression in the next chapter). Then the new sum $\widetilde{S}_n - Y = \widetilde{X}_1 + \cdots + \widetilde{X}_{n-m+1}$ has a new mean $(1 + \delta)P(w)(n - m + 1) = a(n - m + 1)$, and hence we can apply to $\widetilde{S}_n - Y$ the local limit result (2.45). To translate from $\widetilde{S}_n - Y$ to S_n we use the following simple formula (see Exercise 2.9):

$$[e^{tM}]\,(g^n(t)) = \frac{g^n(\omega)}{e^{\omega M}}[e^{tM}]\left(\frac{g^n(t + \omega)}{g^n(\omega)}\right), \qquad (2.49)$$

where $M = a(n - m + 1)$ and, as before, $[e^{tn}]g(t)$ denotes the coefficient of $g(t)$ at $z^n = e^{tn}$ (where $z = e^t$). Now we can apply (2.45) to the right-hand side of the above equation, to arrive at

$$[e^{tM}]\left(\frac{g^M(t + \omega)}{g^M(\omega)}\right) \sim \frac{1}{\sigma_a\sqrt{2\pi(n - m + 1)}}.$$

To obtain the final result we must take into account the effect of Y whose moment generating function is $C(t)$. This leads to the replacement of $a = 1 + \delta$ by $a =$

$1 + \delta + C'(0)/n$, resulting in the correction term $e^{\theta_a} = e^{C'(0)\omega_a}$. Theorem 2.5.4 is proved.   ∎

We now illustrate the above results with an example taken from molecular biology.

Example 2.5.5. Biologists apply the so-called Z-score and p-value to determine whether biological sequences such as DNA or protein contain a biological signal, that is, an under-represented or over-represented pattern. A fundamental question is how one classifies an occurrence of a pattern as significant. Here, the term "significant" is used for observed data that are interesting, surprising, suspicious, or perhaps most importantly, meaningful; we classify a pattern as significant if it is unlikely to occur fortuitously, that is, in a randomly generated instance of the problem. Thus, we compare the experimental data with a reference model, which in our case is the probabilistic model developed in this book.

In particular, the Z-score and p-value are defined as

$$Z(w) = \frac{\mathbf{E}[O_n] - O_n(w)}{\sqrt{\mathrm{Var}[O_n(w)]}},$$
$$pval(r) = P(O_n(w) > r).$$

The Z-score indicates by how many standard deviations the observed value $O_n(w)$ is away from the mean. Clearly, this score makes sense only if one can prove, as in Theorem 2.5.3, that Z satisfies (at least asymptotically) the central limit theorem (CLT). However, the p-value is used for rare occurrences, far from the mean, where one needs to apply large deviation results as in Theorem 2.5.4.

The ranges of validity of the Z-score and p-value are important, as illustrated in Table 2.1 where results for 2008 nucleotide long fragments of *A.thaliana* (a plant genome) are presented. In the table for each 9-mer the number of observations is presented in the first column followed by the large deviations probability computed from Theorem 2.5.4 and the Z-score. We observe that for $AATTGGCGG$ and $AAGACGGTT$ the Z-scores are about 48 (which indicates that these two strings have the same statistical significance) while the p-values differ by two orders of magnitude. In fact the occurrences of these 9-mers are very rare and therefore the Z-score is not an adequate measure.   ∎

2.5.4.   Poisson laws

In this section we will assume that $\mathbf{E}[O_n] = nP(w)$ is small and does not grow with n. We concentrate on the case when $\lim_{m\to\infty} nP(w) = \lambda > 0$, which

Oligomer	Obs.	p-val (large dev.)	Z-sc.
AATTGGCGG	2	8.059×10^{-4}	48.71
TTTGTACCA	3	4.350×10^{-5}	22.96
ACGGTTCAC	3	2.265×10^{-6}	55.49
AAGACGGTT	3	2.186×10^{-6}	48.95
ACGACGCTT	4	1.604×10^{-9}	74.01
ACGCTTGG	4	5.374×10^{-10}	84.93
GAGAAGACG	5	0.687×10^{-14}	151.10

Table 2.1. The Z score and the p-values of tandem repeats in *A.thaliana*.

leads to the compound Poisson distribution. We also analyze the case when $\lim_{m \to \infty} nP(w) = 0$.

Let us first review the situation. When $\mathbf{E}[O_n] = nP(w)$ is very small, the number of pattern occurrences tends to zero, too. Clearly, the Gaussian law cannot hold; rather we should expect a Poisson distribution of rare events. However, periodic patterns may overlap, introducing dependency, as we have already observed. This results in a *compound Poisson* limit law. More precisely, we will establish in this section that the limit law is the Polýa–Aeppli distribution with parameters $\tilde{\lambda} = nP(w)/S_w(1)$ and $\theta = (S_w(1) - 1)/S_w(1)$. The Polýa–Aeppli distribution is a convolution of the Poisson distribution $\mathrm{Po}(\tilde{\lambda})$ and the shifted geometric distribution $\mathrm{Geom}(\theta)$ that starts at 1. The Polýa–Aeppli limiting distribution for the pattern counts has an easy interpretation. Occurrences come in clumps of intensity $\tilde{\lambda}$ and size governed by a geometric distribution with parameter θ. We now make this more precise. The next result gives our main findings of this section.

Theorem 2.5.6. *For a Markov source (of order 1), let $nP(w) \to \lambda > 0$ while $mP(w) \to 0$. Then the probability generating function $N_n(x)$ for the pattern counts becomes, for any x in a compact set,*

$$N_n(x) = \exp\left(\frac{nP(w)}{S_w(1)} \frac{x - 1}{1 - x\frac{S_w(1)-1}{S_w(1)}} \right) \left(1 + O(mP(w) + O(nP^2(w)))\right) \quad (2.50)$$

as $n \to \infty$. In other words, the limiting distribution of the pattern counts is the convolution of a Poisson and a geometric distribution, that is, $\mathrm{Po}(\tilde{\lambda}) \star \mathrm{Geom}(\theta)$,

where

$$\tilde{\lambda} = \frac{nP(w)}{S_w(1)} \qquad \text{and} \qquad \theta = \frac{S_w(1) - 1}{S_w(1)};$$

this constitutes the Polýa–Aeppli distribution.

Proof. We present here only the proof for a memoryless source. This extension to Markov sources is left as Exercise 2.11.

The starting point is the bivariate generating function $\bar{N}(z, x) = N(z, x) + N_0(z) = \sum_{r \geq 0} \sum_{n \geq 0} P(O_n(w_=r)x^r z^n$, which is given by (2.26):

$$\bar{N}(z, x) = \frac{x + (1 - x)S(z)}{(1 - z)((1 - x)S(z) + x) + z^m P(w)(1 - x)}.$$

To find the probability generating function $N_n(x) = \mathbf{E}[x^{O_n(w)}] = [z^n]\bar{N}(z, x)$, we apply the Cauchy coefficient formula to yield

$$N_n(x) = \frac{1}{2\pi i} \oint \frac{x + (1 - x)S(z)}{(1 - z)((1 - x)S(z) + x) + z^m P(w)(1 - x)} \frac{dz}{z^{n+1}}.$$

The evaluation of this integral is standard. We apply the residue theorem, to find that

$$N_n(x) = -\text{Res}(\bar{N}(z, x)z^{-(n+1)}, \ z = z_0(x)) + O(R^{-n})$$

where $R > 1$ and $z_0(x)$ is the smallest root of the denominator of $N_n(x)$, i.e., the smallest root of

$$(1 - z)((1 - x)S(z) + x) + z^m P(w)(1 - x) = 0.$$

For $mP(w) \to 0$, we realize that this root must be close to unity; thus we define $z_0(x) = 1 + \varepsilon(x)$. Simple but tedious algebra reveals that

$$\varepsilon(x) = \frac{P(w)(1 - x)}{x + (1 - x)S(1)} \left(1 + O(mP(w))\right).$$

This leads to

$$N_n(x) = \exp\left(\frac{nP(w)}{S(1)} \cdot \frac{x - 1}{1 - x\frac{S(1)-1}{S(1)}}\right)\left(1 + O(mP(w) + O(nP^2(w))\right)$$

which further translates into the Polýa–Aeppli distribution.   ∎

The condition $nP(w) = O(1)$ of the above theorem holds when $m = O(\log n)$, but we can infer the limiting distribution even for $nP(w) \to 0$, that is, when

m grows faster than logarithmically. In this case we additionally assume that $mP(w) = o(nP(w))$, hence that m grows more slowly than n. Then our estimate (2.50) still holds. In view of this we conclude that

$$N_n(x) = 1 + \frac{nP(w)}{S(1)} \frac{x-1}{1 - x\frac{S(1)-1}{S(1)}} + o(nP(w)).$$

We can translate this into the following limiting distribution:

$$P(O_n(w) = k) = \frac{nP(w)}{S^2(1)} \left(\frac{S(1)-1}{S(1)} \right)^k \tag{2.51}$$

for $k \geq 1$. In Exercise 2.12 the reader is asked to extend (2.51) when $m = \Theta(n)$.

2.6. Waiting times

We shall now discuss the waiting times T_w and T_j, where $T_w = T_1$ is the first time that the pattern w occurs in the text while T_j is the minimum length of text in which w occurs j times. Fortunately, we do not need to rederive the generating function of T_j since, as we have already indicated in (2.3), the following *duality principle* holds:

$$\{O_n \geq j\} = \{T_j \leq n\}$$

and, in particular, $\{T_w > n\} = \{O_n = 0\}$. Therefore, if

$$T(x, z) = \sum_{n \geq 0} \sum_{j \geq 0} P(T_j = n) z^n x^j$$

then by the duality principle we have

$$(1 - x)T(x, z) + x(1 - z)N(z, x) = 1,$$

and we can obtain $T(x, z)$ using $N(z, x)$ from Theorem 2.3.2.

Finally, observe that the above duality principle implies that

$$\mathbf{E}[T_w] = \sum_{n \geq 0} P(O_n = 0) = N_0(1).$$

In particular, for *memoryless sources*, from Theorem 2.3.2 we conclude that

$$N_0(z) = \frac{z^m S(z)}{(1 - z)S(z) + z^m P(w)}.$$

Hence

$$\mathbf{E}[T_w] = \sum_{n \geq 0} P(O_n(w) = 0) = N_0(1) = \frac{S(1)}{P(w)}$$

$$= \sum_{k \in \mathcal{P}(w)} \frac{1}{P(w_1^k)} = \frac{1}{P(w)} + \sum_{k \in \mathcal{P}(w) - \{m\}} \frac{1}{P(w_1^k)}. \tag{2.52}$$

We have just recovered an old result of Feller (1970).

2.7.　Exercises

2.1　　Find the autocorrelation set for $w = ababbbaababbbaa$. Assuming that the text was generated by a memoryless source with $p_a = 0.3$, find the autocorrelation polynomial.

2.2　　Let $\mathcal{A} = \{a, b, c\}$. Find the generating function of the language $\mathcal{A}^* - \{\varepsilon\} - \{a\} - \{b\} - \{c\}$.

2.3　　Prove (2.9), that is, that $\mathcal{T}_0 \cdot w = \mathcal{R} \cdot \mathcal{S}$.

2.4　　For an alphabet $\mathcal{A} = \{\alpha, \beta\}$ define the following language

$$\mathcal{U}_w^{(\alpha)} = \{v \; : \; v \text{ starts with } \alpha \text{ and } wv \text{ has exactly one occurrence of } w\alpha$$
$$\text{and no occurrences of } w\beta\},$$

where v is a word of the language and w is the pattern of interest. Compute its generating function (see Section 8.3 of Chapter 8).

2.5　　For the alphabet $\mathcal{A} = \{\alpha, \beta\}$ define the language

$$\mathcal{H}_w^{(\alpha)} = \mathcal{M}_w \cap (\alpha \mathcal{A}^*)$$

that is, the words of the language $\mathcal{M}_w$ that begin with α. Compute the generating function of $\mathcal{H}_w$ (see (8.49) of Chapter 8).

2.6　　In Theorem 2.4.1 we proved that for an irreducible aperiodic Markov chain $\text{Var}[O_n] = nc_1 + c_2$ (see (2.28)). Prove that $c_1 > 0$.

2.7　　Prove that $(O_n - \mathbf{E}[O_n])/\sqrt{\text{Var}[O_n]}$ converges in moments to the appropriate moments of the standard normal distribution.

2.8　　Let $\rho(t)$ be a root of $1 - e^t M_{\mathcal{W}}(e^\rho) = 0$. Observe that $\rho(0) = 0$. Prove that $\rho(t) > 0$ for $t \neq 0$ for $p_{ij} > 0$ for all $i, j \in \mathcal{A}$.

2.9　　For any nonnegative integers n and m and some α, prove the following change of variables:

$$[z^m] G^n(z) = \frac{G^n(\alpha)}{\alpha^m} [z^m] \left(\frac{G(\alpha z)}{G(\alpha)} \right)^n$$

where $G(z)$ is a generating function.

2.10   Prove the expression (2.48) for θ_a of Theorem 2.5.4 (see Denise and Régnier (2004)).

2.11   Prove Theorem 2.5.6 for Markov sources.

2.12   Assume that $m = \alpha n$ for some $\alpha < 1$. Prove that the limiting distribution (2.51) still holds provided that n is replaced by $(1 - \alpha)n$.

Bibliographical notes

In this chapter we analyzed exact pattern matching in a probabilistic framework that goes back to Feller (1970) who computed the probability of a pattern occurrence when overlapping is allowed. Our approach is founded on the work of Guibas and Odlyzko (1981a) and Guibas and Odlyzko (1981b), who derived the moment generating function for the number of strings that do not contain a given pattern. Extensions of the Guibas and Odlyzko approach to biased memoryless sources were discussed in Breen, Waterman, and Zhang (1985) and Fudos, Pitoura, and Szpankowski (1996). The Markov model was tackled by Li (1980) and Chryssaphinou and Papastavridis (1988a, 1988b), who estimated the number of word occurrences. The variance of the word count was discussed in Kleffe and Borodovsky (1992). The presentation in this chapter follows very closely the work of Régnier and Szpankowski (1998a) and Régnier (2000). A more probabilistic approach was adopted in Prum, Rodolphe, and Turckheim (1995). Example 2.5.5 was taken from Denise, Régnier, and Vandenbogaert (2001). We finally mention some other work on exact string matching such as Cowan (1991), Robin and Daudin (1999) and Robin and Daudin (2001).

The Gaussian law for memoryless sources can be found in Waterman (1995a). The extension to Markov sources is due to Prum et al. (1995) who used a probabilistic method and Régnier and Szpankowski (1998a) who used an analytic approach. See also Reinert et al. (2000). The large deviation results presented here are from Régnier and Szpankowski (1998a) and Denise and Régnier (2004); see also Schbath (1995). Finally, the compound Poisson process law is due to Chryssaphinou, Papastavridis, and Vaggelatou (2001), Arratia, Goldstein, and Gordon (1990), Godbole (1991), Godbole and Schaffner (1993) and Robin (2002) for memoryless sources; for Markov sources it was discussed in Geske, Godbole, Schaffner, Skolnick, and Wallstrom (1995) and Reinert and Schbath (1998). The derivation presented here using an analytic approach is somewhat new. In passing we mention that the exact distribution of the number of clumps (clusters of overlapping words) was provided by Stefanov (2003).

CHAPTER 3

Constrained Exact String Matching

The main idea of constrained pattern matching is to search for pattern strings in a text satisfying certain additional structural restrictions (e.g., that some patterns are forbidden); such a text is known also as a constrained sequence. In digital communication systems such as magnetic and optical recording, the main purpose of constrained pattern matching is to improve performance by matching the system characteristics to those of the channel. In biology, constrained sequences are in abundance (e.g., the spike trains of neuronal data). In this chapter our goal is to study and understand some aspects of pattern matching in constrained sequences.

To simplify our presentation we restrict our analysis further, to so-called (d, k) sequences, in which runs of zeros cannot be smaller than d nor larger than k, where $0 \leq d < k$. Such sequences have proved to be useful in digital recording and biology. In digital recording they have been widely used in hard disk drives and digital optical disks such as CDs, DVDs, and Blu-ray. In biology, the spike trains of neuronal data recorded from different neurons in the brain of an animal seem to satisfy structural constraints that exactly match the framework of (d, k) binary sequences. This follows from the fact that a neuron cannot fire two spikes in too short a time; this translates into the constraint that the induced binary spike train needs to contain at least a certain number of 0s, corresponding to no activity, between any two consecutive 1s, corresponding to spikes.

In these applications one often requires that the word w constituting the pattern of interest does not occur or occurs only a few times in a (d, k) sequence. Therefore, we study here the following problem: given such a word w, how many times does it occur in a (d, k) sequence? For such a problem we coin the term *constrained pattern matching*, which is a natural extension of the exact pattern matching discussed in the previous chapter. As throughout this book, we study this problem in a probabilistic framework. However, to simplify our presentation we restrict our discussion to memoryless sources, leaving the analysis of Markov sources to the exercises.

3.1. Enumeration of (d, k) sequences

As a warm-up for this chapter, we consider the enumeration of (d, k) sequences, that is, we will count the number of (d, k) sequences of length n. This count is needed to compute the Shannon capacity of a noiseless constrained channel.

Let $\mathcal{W}_{d,k}$ denote the collection of all (d, k) sequences. We also define the set

$$\mathcal{A}_{d,k} = \{\underbrace{0\ldots0}_{d}, \ldots, \underbrace{0\ldots0}_{k}\},$$

that is, a set of runs of zeros of length between d and k. Its generating function is

$$A(z) = z^d + z^{d+1} + \cdots + z^k = \frac{z^d - z^{k+1}}{1 - z}. \tag{3.1}$$

We now observe that $\mathcal{W}_{d,k}$ for $d > 0$ can be symbolically written as

$$\mathcal{W}_{d,k} = \mathcal{A}_{d,k} \cdot \left(\varepsilon + \{1\} \cdot \mathcal{A}_{d,k} + (\{1\} \cdot \mathcal{A}_{d,k})^2 + \cdots (\{1\} \cdot \mathcal{A}_{d,k})^k + \cdots\right)(\varepsilon + \{1\})$$
$$+ \{1\} \cdot \left(\varepsilon + (\mathcal{A}_{d,k} \cdot \{1\}) + \cdots (\mathcal{A}_{d,k} \cdot \{1\})^k + \cdots\right)(\varepsilon + \mathcal{A}_{d,k}), \tag{3.2}$$

where $\cdot$ denotes a Cartesian product of sets (that is, the concatenation of words). Equation (3.2) basically says that the members of the collection $\mathcal{W}_{d,k}$ of (k, d) sequences

- either start with an allowed run of 0s followed by repeated 1s and allowed runs of 0s, followed by a 1 or an empty symbol;

- or start with a 1 followed by repeated 1s and allowed runs of 0s, followed by an allowed run of 0s or an empty symbol.

The language construction (3.2) can be written in a simpler way using a *sequence construction*. For a language $\mathcal{B}$ we write

$$SEQ(\mathcal{B}) = \varepsilon + \mathcal{B} + \mathcal{B} \times \mathcal{B} + \mathcal{B} \times \mathcal{B} \times \mathcal{B} + \cdots . \tag{3.3}$$

Thus (3.2) can be written as

$$\mathcal{W}_{d,k} = \mathcal{A}_{d,k} \cdot SEQ(\{1\} \cdot \mathcal{A}_{d,k}) + \{1\} \cdot SEQ(\{1\} \cdot \mathcal{A}_{d,k}) \left(\varepsilon + \mathcal{A}_{d,k}\right).$$

The generating function of the language $\mathcal{W}_{d,k}$ is given by

$$W_{d,k}(z) = \sum_{u \in \mathcal{W}_{d,k}} z^{|u|} = \sum_{n=0}^{\infty} z^n W_n,$$

where $W_n := [z^n]W_{d,k}(z)$ is the number of (d, k) sequences of length n. Since language concatenation translates into products of generating functions, (3.2) directly implies that

$$W_{d,k}(z) = \frac{A(z) + z(1 + A(z))}{1 - zA(z)}, \tag{3.4}$$

where $A(z)$ is given by (3.1). Extracting the coefficient at z^n (e.g., using MAPLE), one finds exactly the number of (d, k) sequences of length n. For example, there are $W_{20} = 3151$ constraint sequences with $d = 1$ and $k = 3$.

In order to obtain the asymptotics of $W_n := [z^n]W_{d,k}(z)$ we apply Cauchy's formula. Let $B(z) = zA(z)$ and let the roots of

$$1 - zA(z) = 0$$

be $\rho_0 < |\rho_1| \le \ldots < |\rho_k|$. The smallest root ρ_0 is *real* and less than 1. Indeed, $B(0) = 0A(0) = 0$, $B(1) = k + d - 1 > 0$, and $B(z)$ is an increasing function in the interval $(0, 1)$. Let us also define

$$\lambda_0 = \frac{1}{\rho_0}.$$

Then, from Cauchy's formula,

$$W_n = \frac{1}{2\pi i} \oint \frac{W_{d,k}(z)}{z^{n+1}} dz = \frac{1 + \rho_0 + \rho_0^2}{1 + A'(\rho_0)\rho_0^2} \left(\frac{1}{\rho_0}\right)^{n+1} + O(r^n), \qquad (3.5)$$

where $r < 1/\rho_0$. Then Shannon's capacity, defined as

$$C_{d,k} = \lim_{n\to\infty} \frac{1}{n} \log W_n,$$

then becomes

$$C_{d,k} = \log \lambda_0 + O(1/n). \qquad (3.6)$$

For $d = 0$ we need to modify slightly our derivation since now the symbol 1 does not separate runs of 0s. In this case we have to replace (3.2) by a simpler expression, namely

$$\mathcal{W}_{0,k} = \mathcal{A}_{0,k} \cdot \left(\varepsilon + (\{1\} \cdot \mathcal{A}_{0,k}) + (\{1\} \cdot \mathcal{A}_{0,k})^2 + \cdots + (\{1\} \cdot \mathcal{A}_{0,k})^k + \cdots\right),$$

which leads to

$$W_{0,k}(z) = \frac{A(z)}{1 - zA(z)}.$$

In particular, there must be 1024 $(0, 10)$ sequences and, indeed, $[z^{10}]W_{0,10}(z) = 1024$.

Later in this chapter we will need the number of (d, k) sequences that start with 0 and end with 1; we call them *restricted* (d, k) *sequences*. We denote such a set by $\mathcal{W}_{d,k}^r$. Clearly

$$\mathcal{W}_{d,k}^r = \varepsilon + \mathcal{B}_{d,k} + \mathcal{B}_{d,k} + \cdots + \mathcal{B}_{d,k}^k + \cdots = SEQ(\mathcal{B}), \qquad (3.7)$$

where $\mathcal{B}_{d,k} = \mathcal{A}_{d,k} \cdot \{1\}$. The above translates into the generating function $W_{d,k}^r(z)$ as follows:

$$W_{d,k}^r(z) = \frac{1}{1 - zA(z)} = \frac{1}{1 - B(z)}. \qquad (3.8)$$

Then $W_n^r = [z^n]W_{d,k}^r(z)$ and, by Cauchy's formula,

$$W_n^r = \frac{1}{B(1/\lambda_0)} \lambda_0^{n+1} + O(r^n) \qquad (3.9)$$

where, as before, $\rho_0 = 1/\lambda_0$ is the smallest real root of $B(z) = 1$.

3.1.1. Languages and generating functions

We now focus on the main topic of this chapter, namely pattern matching in constrained sequences. In this chapter, by constrained sequences we mean (d,k) sequences. In fact, for ease of presentation we first derive all results for *restricted* (d,k) sequences, which start with 0 and end with 1. We will relax this assumption in Section 3.6. We are aiming to find the probability distribution of the number of occurrences of a given pattern w in a (d,k) sequence generated by a binary memoryless source. Here w is a pattern that is itself a (d,k) sequence, and pattern overlapping is allowed.

We recall two languages defined in the previous section, namely

$$\mathcal{A}_{d,k} = \{\underbrace{0\ldots0}_{d}, \cdots, \underbrace{0\ldots0}_{k}\}$$

the *extended alphabet* (see the text after (3.7))

$$\mathcal{B}_{d,k} = \mathcal{A}_{d,k} \cdot \{1\} = \{\underbrace{0\cdots0}_{d}1, \ldots, \underbrace{0\cdots0}_{k}1\}.$$

The elements of $\mathcal{B}_{d,k}$ are known as super-symbols. Restricted (d,k) sequences are built over $\mathcal{B}_{d,k}$. More importantly, we also count pattern occurrences over the super-symbols of $\mathcal{B}_{d,k}$, not over $\mathcal{A}$, as illustrated in the next example.

Example 3.1.1. Let the pattern $w = 01$. This super-symbol does *not* occur in the restricted $(d,k) = (1,4)$ sequence 0010001. But the sequence does contain two other super-symbols, 001 and 0001, from $\mathcal{B}_{d,k}$. ∎

As in the previous chapter, we now introduce some languages that play a major role in our analysis. We start by considering the autocorrelation set over the extended alphabet $\mathcal{B}_{d,k}$. Let $w = w_1 \cdots w_m \in \{0,1\}^m$ with $w_m = 1$ so that w is itself a restricted (d,k) sequence. In $\mathcal{B}_{d,k}$ we have the decomposition $w = \beta_1 \cdots \beta_{m'}$, where $\beta_i \in \mathcal{B}_{d,k}$ and $\sum_{i=1}^{m'} |\beta_i| = m$. Let $\mathcal{S}$ denote the *autocorrelation set* of w over $\mathcal{B}_{d,k}$, that is,

$$\mathcal{S} = \{\beta_{\ell+1}^{m'} : \beta_1^{\ell} = \beta_{m'-\ell+1}^{m'}\}, \qquad 1 \le \ell \le m',$$

where $\beta_i^j = \beta_i \cdots \beta_j$ and $\beta_i^j = \varepsilon$ if $i > j$. Notice that, by definition, the autocorrelation set always contains the empty word ε.

As in the previous chapter we introduce four languages, $\mathcal{T}_r^{(d,k)}$, $\mathcal{R}^{(d,k)}$, $\mathcal{U}^{(d,k)}$, and $\mathcal{M}^{(d,k)}$ as follows, given a restricted (d,k) pattern w defined over $\mathcal{B}_{d,k}$:

(i) $\mathcal{T}_r^{(d,k)}$, the set of all (d,k) sequences containing exactly r occurrences of w;

(ii) the "right" language $\mathcal{R}^{(d,k)}$, the set of all (d,k) sequences containing only one occurrence of w, located at the right-hand end;

(iii) the "ultimate" language $\mathcal{U}^{(d,k)}$, defined by

$$\mathcal{U}^{(d,k)} = \{u :\ wu \in \mathcal{T}_1^{(d,k)}\},$$

that is, a word u belongs to $\mathcal{U}^{(d,k)}$ if u is a (d,k) sequence and wu has exactly one occurrence of w, at the left-hand end of wu;

(iv) the "universal" language $\mathcal{M}^{(d,k)}$, defined by

$$\mathcal{M}^{(d,k)} = \{v :\ wv \in \mathcal{T}_2^{(d,k)} \text{ and } w \text{ occurs at the right-hand end of } wv\},$$

that is, any word in $\{w\} \cdot \mathcal{M}^{(d,k)}$ has exactly two occurrences of w, one at the left-hand end and the other at the right-hand end.

To simplify our notation we drop the upper index (d,k). It is easy to see that, for $r \geq 1$,

$$\mathcal{T}_r = \mathcal{R} \cdot \mathcal{M}^{r-1} \cdot \mathcal{U}, \tag{3.10}$$
$$\mathcal{T}_0 \cdot \{w\} = \mathcal{R} \cdot \mathcal{S}. \tag{3.11}$$

In order to find relationships between the languages $\mathcal{R}$, $\mathcal{M}$, and $\mathcal{U}$, we extend the approach discussed in the previous chapter, to yield

$$\mathcal{M}^* = \mathcal{B}^* \cdot \{w\} + \mathcal{S}, \tag{3.12}$$
$$\mathcal{U} \cdot \mathcal{B} = \mathcal{M} + \mathcal{U} - \{\varepsilon\}, \tag{3.13}$$
$$\{w\} \cdot \mathcal{M} = \mathcal{B} \cdot \mathcal{R} - (\mathcal{R} - \{w\}), \tag{3.14}$$

where $\mathcal{B}^*$ is the set of all restricted (d,k) sequences, that is,

$$\mathcal{B}^* = SEQ(\mathcal{B}) = \{\varepsilon\} + \mathcal{B} + \mathcal{B}^2 + \mathcal{B}^3 + \cdots .$$

Similarly, $\mathcal{M}^* = \sum_{i=0}^{\infty} \mathcal{M}^i$, where $\mathcal{M}^0 = \{\varepsilon\}$. For example, (3.12) indicates that any word in the language $\mathcal{M}^*$ is either in $\mathcal{S}$ (if the length of the word from $\mathcal{M}^*$ is smaller than that of w) or it must end with w.

At this point we need to set up a probabilistic framework. Throughout, we assume that a binary sequence is generated by a binary memoryless source with p the probability of emitting a zero and $q = 1 - p$. We will find the conditional probability distribution of the number of occurrences of w in a (d, k) sequence. We also compute the probability that a randomly generated sequence is a (d, k) sequence.

The language relationships (3.12)–(3.14) are translated into probability generating functions:

$$\frac{1}{1 - M(z)} = \frac{1}{1 - B(z)} z^m P(w) + S(z), \tag{3.15}$$

$$U(z) = \frac{M(z) - 1}{B(z) - 1}, \tag{3.16}$$

$$R(z) = z^m P(w) U(z), \tag{3.17}$$

where

$$B(z) = p^d q z^{d+1} + p^{d+1} q z^{d+2} + \cdots + p^k q z^{k+1}$$

$$= z q \frac{(zp)^d - (zp)^{k+1}}{1 - zp}. \tag{3.18}$$

In particular, from (3.10), (3.11), and above one finds that

$$T_0(z) = \frac{S(z)}{D(z)}, \tag{3.19}$$

$$T_r(z) = \frac{z^m P(w)(D(z) + B(z) - 1)^{r-1}}{D(z)^{r+1}}, \tag{3.20}$$

where

$$D(z) = S(z)(1 - B(z)) + z^m P(w). \tag{3.21}$$

Let O_n be a random variable representing the number of occurrences of w in a (regular) binary sequence of length n. Then the generating function $T_r(z)$ for (d, k) sequences is defined as follows:

$$T_r(z) = \sum_{n \geq 0} P(O_n = r, \mathcal{D}_n) z^n,$$

where $\mathcal{D}_n$ is the event that a randomly generated binary sequence of length n is a (d, k) sequence. Let us also define the bivariate generating function $T(z, x)$ as

$$T(z, x) = \sum_{r \geq 0} T_r(z) x^r = \sum_{r \geq 0} \sum_{n \geq 0} P(O_n = r, \mathcal{D}_n) z^n x^r.$$

From (3.10) and (3.11) we find that

$$T(z, x) = R(z) \frac{x}{1 - x M(z)} U(z) + T_0(z). \tag{3.22}$$

Observe that $T(z,x)$ is not a bivariate probability generating function since $[z^n]T(z,1) \neq 1$, but we can easily make it into a *conditional* probability generating function. First, define

$$P(\mathcal{D}_n) = [z^n]T(z,1)$$

as the probability that a randomly generated sequence of length n is a (d,k) sequence. We also introduce the short-hand notation $O_n(\mathcal{D}_n)$ for the conditional number of occurrences of w in a (d,k) sequence. More formally,

$$P(O_n(\mathcal{D}_n) = r) = P(O_n = r \mid \mathcal{D}_n).$$

Therefore, the probability generating function for $O_n(\mathcal{D}_n)$ is

$$\mathbf{E}[x^{O_n(\mathcal{D}_n)}] = \frac{[z^n]T(z,x)}{[z^n]T(z,1)}.$$

Next, we derive moments and establish several limit laws for $P(O_n(\mathcal{D}) = r)$ for various ranges of r. Throughout this chapter we assume that m is fixed, that is, $nP(w) \to \infty$. In Exercise 3.4 we ask the reader to extend our analysis to the case when $nP(w) = O(1)$ and so establish the Poisson limit law.

3.2.   Moments

We start with the first two moments of the word count. The expected value of $O_n(\mathcal{D}_n)$ is

$$\mathbf{E}[O_n(\mathcal{D}_n)] = \frac{[z^n]T_x(z,1)}{[z^n]T(z,1)}, \tag{3.23}$$

where $T_x(z,1)$ is the derivative of $T(z,x)$ at $x = 1$, and

$$\mathbf{E}[O_n(\mathcal{D}_n)(O_n(\mathcal{D}_n) - 1)] = \frac{[z^n]T_{xx}(z,1)}{[z^n]T(z,1)},$$

is the second factorial moment, where $T_{xx}(z,1)$ is the second derivative with respect to x at $x = 1$.

Our first main result is presented next.

Theorem 3.2.1. *Let $\rho := \rho(p)$ be the unique positive real root of $B(z) = 1$ where $B(z)$ is defined in (3.18), and let $\lambda = 1/\rho$. Then the probability of generating a (d,k) sequence is equal to*

$$P(\mathcal{D}_n) = \frac{1}{B'(\rho)}\lambda^{n+1} + O(\omega^n), \tag{3.24}$$

for some $\omega < \lambda$. Furthermore,

$$\mathbf{E}[O_n(\mathcal{D}_n)] = \frac{(n - m + 1)P(w)}{B'(\rho)}\lambda^{-m+1} + O(1),$$

and the variance is given by

$$\mathrm{Var}[O_n(\mathcal{D}_n)] = (n - m + 1)P(w)\left[\frac{(1 - 2m)P(w)}{B'(\rho)^2}\lambda^{-2m+2}\right. \tag{3.25}$$

$$\left. + \frac{P(w)B''(\rho)}{B'(\rho)^3}\lambda^{-2m+1} + \frac{2S(\rho) - 1}{B'(\rho)}\lambda^{-m+1}\right] + O(1), \tag{3.26}$$

for large n.

We will prove Theorem 3.2.1 in several steps. We first obtain asymptotic formulas for the mean and the variance of $O_n(\mathcal{D}_n)$. From (3.15)–(3.22), we find

$$T(z, 1) = \frac{1}{1 - B(z)}, \quad quad T_x(z, 1) = \frac{z^m P(w)}{(1 - B(z))^2},$$

and

$$T_{xx}(z, 1) = \frac{2z^m P(w)M(z)}{U(z)(1 - B(z))^3} = \frac{2z^m P(w)D(z)}{(1 - B(z))^3} - \frac{2z^m P(w)}{(1 - B(z))^2}.$$

By Cauchy's coefficient formula and the residue theorem (see Chapter 1) we find that

$$P(\mathcal{D}_n) = [z^n]T(z, 1) = [z^n]\frac{1}{1 - B(z)} = \frac{1}{B'(\rho)}\lambda^{n+1} + O(\omega^n),$$

where ρ is the unique positive real root of $B(z) = 1$, $\lambda = 1/\rho$, and $\omega < \lambda$. In the lemma below we prove that there always exists a unique positive real root of $B(z) = 1$, which is greater than 1 and whose modulus is the smallest complex root.

Lemma 3.2.2. *The equation $B(z) = 1$ has one positive real root ρ that is greater than 1. All other roots ρ' satisfy $|\rho'| > \rho$.*

Proof. By definition, $B(z) := p^d q z^{d+1} + p^{d+1} q z^{d+2} + \cdots + p^k q z^{k+1}$. Let $f(z) = 1 - B(z)$. Then we observe that $f(1) = 1 - B(1) > 0$ and $\lim_{z \to \infty} f(z) = -\infty$. We also see that $f'(z) = -B'(z) < 0$ for $z > 0$, that is, $f(z)$ is a decreasing function. Therefore, $f(z) = 0$ has one real root on $(1, \infty)$.

To prove the second part of the theorem, we appeal to Rouché's theorem. Let ρ be the real root, and let $h(z) = 1$ and $g(z) = -B(z)$. We consider a closed contour $C = \{z : |z| = \rho - \varepsilon\}$ where ε is an arbitrarily small positive constant. Rouché's theorem (see Henrici (1997)) states that if $f(z) = g(z) + h(z) = 1 - B(z)$ and $h(z) = 1$ are analytic inside and on C and if $|g(z)| < |h(z)| = 1$ then $h(z)$ and $f(z) = g(z) + h(z) = 1 - B(z)$ have the same number of zeros inside C. At points on C we have

$$|g(z)| \le p^d q |z|^{d+1} + p^{d+1} q |z|^{d+2} + \cdots + p^k q |z|^{k+1}$$
$$= p^d q (\rho - \varepsilon)^{d+1} + p^{d+1} q (\rho - \varepsilon)^{d+2} + \cdots + p^k q (\rho - \varepsilon)^{k+1}$$
$$< p^d q \rho^{d+1} + p^{d+1} q \rho^{d+2} + \cdots + p^k q \rho^{k+1} = 1 = |h(z)|.$$

Thus, by Rouché's theorem $f(z)$ and $h(z) = 1$ have the same number of zeros inside C, that is, $f(z)$ has no root inside C. Therefore, all other complex roots ρ' satisfy $|\rho'| \ge \rho$.

Suppose that another complex root ρ' satisfies $|\rho'| = \rho$, that is, $\rho' = \rho e^{i\theta}$ for some θ. Then

$$|1| = |B(\rho')| = |p^d q \rho^{d+1} e^{i(d+1)\theta} + p^{d+1} q \rho^{d+2} e^{i(d+2)\theta} + \cdots + p^k q \rho^{k+1} e^{i(k+1)\theta}|$$
$$\le p^d q \rho^{d+1} |e^{i(d+1)\theta}| + p^{d+1} q \rho^{d+2} |e^{i(d+2)\theta}| + \cdots + p^k q \rho^{k+1} |e^{i(k+1)\theta}|$$
$$= p^d q \rho^{d+1} + p^{d+1} q \rho^{d+2} + \cdots + p^k q \rho^{k+1} = 1.$$

In the second line, equality holds only when $\theta = 2\pi j$ for some integer j. Thus, ρ' must be a real root, which is ρ; all other roots ρ' satisfy $|\rho'| > \rho$. ∎

To find moments, we proceed as follows. Consider

$$[z^n] T_x(z, 1) = [z^n] \frac{z^m P(w)}{(1 - B(z))^2} = \frac{P(w)}{B'(\rho)^2} \left((n - m + 1)\lambda + \frac{B''(\rho)}{B'(\rho)} \right) \lambda^{n-m+1}$$
$$+ O(\omega^n).$$

Thus

$$\mathbf{E}[O_n(\mathcal{D}_n)] = \frac{[z^n] T_x(z, 1)}{[z^n] T(z, 1)} = \frac{(n - m + 1) P(w)}{B'(\rho)} \lambda^{-m+1} + O(1).$$

Similarly,

$$\mathrm{Var}[O_n(\mathcal{D}_n)] = \frac{[z^n] T_{xx}(z, 1)}{[z^n] T(z, 1)} + \mathbf{E}[O_n(\mathcal{D}_n)] - \mathbf{E}[O_n(\mathcal{D}_n)]^2.$$

After some algebra, we can establish the formula for the variance in (3.26).

3.3. The probability count

We will now estimate the probability $P(O_n(\mathcal{D}) = r)$ for various values of r. We start with fixed r.

Theorem 3.3.1. *Let* $\tau := \tau(p, w)$ *be the smallest positive real root of* $D(z) = 0$ *where* $D(z)$ *is defined in (3.21), and let* $\rho := \rho(p) < \tau$ *be the unique positive real root of* $B(z) = 1$. *Then, for* $r = O(1)$ *with* $r \geq 1$,

$$P(O_n(\mathcal{D}_n) = r) \sim \frac{P(w)B'(\rho)(1 - B(\tau))^{r-1}}{D'(\tau)^{r+1}\tau^{r-m}} \binom{n - m + r}{r} \left(\frac{\rho}{\tau}\right)^{n+1}.$$

for large n.

Proof. By Cauchy's coefficient formula and the residue theorem,

$$P(O_n = r, \mathcal{D}_n) = [z^n]T_r(z) = [z^{n-m}]\frac{P(w)(D(z) + B(z) - 1)^{r-1}}{D(z)^{r+1}}$$

$$= \sum_{j=1}^{r+1}(-1)^j a_j \binom{n - m + j - 1}{j - 1}\left(\frac{1}{\tau}\right)^{n-m+j} + O(t^n),$$

where $\tau < t^{-1}$ is the smallest positive real root of $D(z) = 0$, and

$$a_{r+1} = \frac{P(w)(B(\tau) - 1)^{r-1}}{D'(\tau)^{r+1}}.$$

In Lemma 3.3.2 below we prove that there exists at least one positive real root of $D(z) = 0$, which is greater than ρ. Finally, we find that

$$P(O_n(\mathcal{D}_n) = r) := P(O_n = r | \mathcal{D}_n) = \frac{P(O_n = r, \mathcal{D}_n)}{P(\mathcal{D}_n)}$$

$$\sim \frac{P(w)B'(\rho)(1 - B(\tau))^{r-1}}{D'(\tau)^{r+1}} \binom{n - m + r}{r} \frac{\rho^{n+1}}{\tau^{n-m+r+1}},$$

as desired. $\blacksquare$

Thus to complete the proof, we need to show the existence of a positive root of $D(z)$, and we present this next. We should point out that in Lemma 2.5.2 we established this existence in the case of exact pattern matching.

Lemma 3.3.2. *The equation* $D(z) = 0$ *has at least one positive real root* τ, *and this root is greater than* ρ.

Proof. For $0 \leq z \leq \rho$, we observe that $D(z) := S(z)(1 - B(z)) + z^m P(w) > 0$. This follows from the fact that $S(z) > 0$ and $1 - B(z) > 0$ (for $0 < z < \rho$). Note also that $D(0) = 1$ and $D(\rho) = \rho^m P(w)$.

Now let us consider $z > \rho$. Let m' be the length of the pattern over the extended alphabet $\mathcal{B}_{d,k}$. Notice that $d + 1 \leq m/m' \leq k + 1$. First, let us assume that $m' = 1$, that is, $d + 1 \leq m \leq k + 1$. Then, since $S(z) = 1$ and $P(w) = p^{m-1}q$,

$$D(z) = 1 - B(z) + p^{m-1}qz^m.$$

Thus $D(z) \to -\infty$ as $z \to \infty$ because $B(z)$ has at least two terms, one of which cancels out $p^{m-1}qz^m$. Therefore, there exists at least one real root on (ρ, ∞).

Now we can assume that $m' \geq 2$, and first consider when m/m' is either $d+1$ or $k+1$, that is, the pattern is periodic. If $m/m' = d+1$ then $P(w) = (p^d q)^{m'}$, so

$$S(z) = 1 + p^d qz^{d+1} + \left(p^d qz^{d+1}\right)^2 + \cdots + \left(p^d qz^{d+1}\right)^{m'-1},$$

and this leads to

$$D(z) = 1 - S(z)(B(z) - p^d qz^{d+1}).$$

Thus, again $D(z) \to -\infty$ as $z \to \infty$. The same is true when $m/m' = k+1$. Therefore, there exists at least one real root.

Next, we consider the case $d+1 < m/m' < k+1$; we will show that $D(z_0) \leq 0$ for some positive z_0. Let us define two integers, ℓ and u, as the largest integer smaller than m/m' and the smallest integer larger than m/m', respectively. Then

$$D(z) \leq 1 - B(z) + z^m P(w)$$
$$= (1 - p^{\ell-1}qz^\ell)(1 - p^{u-1}qz^u) - (B(z) - p^{\ell-1}qz^\ell - p^{u-1}qz^u)$$
$$- p^{\ell+u-2}q^2 z^{\ell+u} + p^{m-m'}q^{m'}z^m.$$

If $m = \ell + u$ then m' must be 2. Thus,

$$D(z) \leq (1 - p^{\ell-1}qz^\ell)(1 - p^{u-1}qz^u) - (B(z) - p^{\ell-1}qz^\ell - p^{u-1}qz^u),$$

and either $z_0 = \left(p^{\ell-1}q\right)^{-1/\ell}$ or $z_0 = \left(p^{u-1}q\right)^{-1/u}$ makes $D(z_0) \leq 0$.

If $m \neq \ell + u$, then we choose z_0 as the root of the equation $p^{m-m'}q^{m'}z^m = p^{\ell+u-2}q^2 z^{\ell+u}$, that is,

$$z_0 = \left(p^{\ell+u-2-m+m'}q^{2-m'}\right)^{1/(m-\ell-u)}.$$

After some algebra we arrive at

$$D(z_0) \leq (1 - p^{\ell-1}qz_0^\ell)(1 - p^{u-1}qz_0^u) = (1 - (q/p)^x)(1 - (p/q)^y),$$

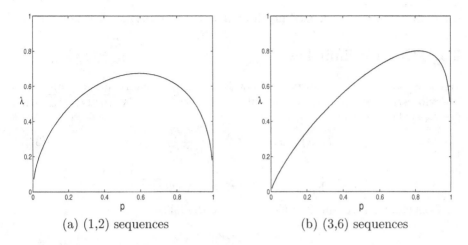

(a) (1,2) sequences   (b) (3,6) sequences

Figure 3.1. Plots of λ versus p for (a) $(1,2)$ sequences; and (b) $(3,6)$ sequences.

where
$$x = \frac{m - \ell m' - (u - \ell)}{m - \ell - u}$$

and
$$y = \frac{u m' - m - (u - \ell)}{m - \ell - u}.$$

Here we can observe that x and y have the same sign and from this observation we can easily see that $D(z_0) \leq 0$. Hence, there always exists a positive z_0 such that $D(z_0) \leq 0$, and consequently there always exists at least one positive real root on $(\rho, z_0]$.   ∎

Finally, we offer some remarks. In Figure 3.1, we plot $\lambda = 1/\rho$ versus p for various (d, k) sequences. Observe that the probability $P(\mathcal{D}_n) \asymp \lambda^n$ is asymptotically maximized for some $p \neq 0.5$ (corresponding to a biased source), and this may be used to design better run-length coding.

Observe also that when the binary source is unbiased ($p = q = 1/2$), we can count the number $N_n(r)$ of (d, k) sequences of length n that contain w exactly r times, by computing $[z^n] T_r(2z)$ (with r fixed with respect to n.) In fact, $N_n(r) = 2^n P(O_n = r, \mathcal{D}_n)$ and so one can find the asymptotics of $N_n(r)$ from part (i) of Theorem 3.3.1. In particular, the Shannon entropy is

$$C(r) = \lim_{n \to \infty} \frac{\log_2 N_n(r)}{n} = \log_2 \left(\frac{2}{\tau} \right),$$

where $\tau = \tau(1/2, w)$ is defined in Theorem 3.3.1 for $p = 1/2$.

3.4.   Central limit law

We now establish the central limit law for fixed m, that is, for $nP(w) \to \infty$. We will estimate $P(O_n(\mathcal{D}_n) = r)$ for $r = \mathbf{E}[O_n(\mathcal{D}_n)] + \xi\sqrt{\mathrm{Var}[O_n(\mathcal{D}_n)]}$ with $\xi = O(1)$. Define

$$T_n(x) = \mathbf{E}[u^{O_n(D_n)}] = \frac{[z^n]T(z,x)}{[z^n]T(z,1)} \tag{3.27}$$

and

$$\mu_n = \mathbf{E}[O_n(\mathcal{D}_n)], \qquad \sigma_n = \sqrt{\mathrm{Var}[O_n(\mathcal{D}_n)]}.$$

By Goncharov's theorem, it suffices to prove the following:

$$\lim_{n\to\infty} e^{-\nu\mu_n/\sigma_n}T_n(e^{\nu/\sigma_n}) = e^{\nu^2/2},$$

for all $\nu = it'$ where $-\infty < t' < \infty$. However, we shall now establish that the above holds for complex ν.

Theorem 3.4.1.   *For $r = \mathbf{E}[O_n(\mathcal{D}_n)] + \xi\sqrt{\mathrm{Var}[O_n(\mathcal{D}_n)]}$ with $\xi = O(1)$,*

$$\frac{O_n(\mathcal{D}_n) - \mathbf{E}[O_n(\mathcal{D}_n)]}{\sqrt{\mathrm{Var}[O_n(\mathcal{D}_n)]}} \xrightarrow{d} N(0,1),$$

as $n \to \infty$.

Proof. Let $\rho(x)$ be the smallest real root of $1 - xM(z) = 0$. We easily find that the pole of $T_0(z)$ is always greater than $\rho(x)$. Then, by Cauchy's coefficient formula and the residue theorem, from (3.22) we obtain

$$[z^n]T(z,x) = c(x)\lambda^{n+1}(x) + O(\omega^n(x)), \tag{3.28}$$

$$c(x) = \frac{R(\rho(x))U(\rho(x))}{M'(\rho(x))},$$

and $\lambda(x) = 1/\rho(x)$ where $|\omega(x)| < \lambda(x)$. Thus, by (3.27),

$$P(\mathcal{D}_n)T_n(x) = c(x)\lambda^{n+1}(x) + O(\omega^n(x)), \tag{3.29}$$

since $P(\mathcal{D}_n) = [z^n]T(z,1)$.

Let $x = e^t$ and $t = \nu/\sigma_n$. Since $t \to 0$ and $x \to 1$ as $n \to \infty$, expanding in a Taylor series around $t = 0$ we arrive at

$$\lambda(e^t) = \lambda(1) + \lambda'(1)t + \frac{\lambda''(1) + \lambda'(1)}{2}t^2 + O(t^3). \tag{3.30}$$

Now let us find $\lambda'(1)$ and $\lambda''(1)$. From (3.28) we observe that

$$[z^n]T_x(z,1) = (n+1)c(1)\lambda^n(1)\lambda'(1) + c'(1)\lambda^{n+1}(1) + O(n\omega^n(1)). \quad (3.31)$$

By (3.23), (3.28), and (3.31) we obtain

$$\lambda'(1) = \frac{\mu_n}{n+1}\lambda(1) - \frac{c'(1)}{(n+1)c(1)}\lambda(1) + O\left(n\theta^n(1)\right), \quad (3.32)$$

where $\theta(x) = \omega(x)/\lambda(x)$. We note that $|\theta(x)| < 1$. Similarly, after some algebra, we arrive at

$$\lambda''(1) = \left(\frac{\sigma_n^2 - \mu_n}{n+1} + \frac{\mu_n^2}{(n+1)^2}\right)\lambda(1) + O\left(\frac{1}{n}\right). \quad (3.33)$$

Using (3.29), (3.30), (3.32), (3.33), and the fact that $t = O\left(1/\sqrt{n}\right)$, we find that

$$P(\mathcal{D}_n)T_n(e^t) = c(x)\lambda^{n+1}(x) \cdot (1 + O(\theta^n(x)))$$
$$= c(x)\lambda^{n+1}(1)\left[1 + \frac{\mu_n}{n+1}t + \frac{1}{2}\left(\frac{\sigma_n^2}{n+1} + \frac{\mu_n^2}{(n+1)^2}\right)t^2 + O(t^3)\right]^{n+1}$$
$$\times (1 + O(\theta^n(x))).$$

Therefore

$$e^{-\nu\mu_n/\sigma_n}P(\mathcal{D}_n)T_n(e^{\nu/\sigma_n}) = c(x)\lambda^{n+1}(1)\left(1 + \frac{\sigma_n^2}{2(n+1)}t^2 + O(t^3)\right)^{n+1}$$
$$(1 + O(\theta^n(x)))$$

and

$$\lim_{n\to\infty} e^{-\nu\mu_n/\sigma_n}T_n(e^{\nu/\sigma_n}) = \lim_{n\to\infty}\left(1 + \frac{\nu^2}{2(n+1)} + O(t^3)\right)^{n+1} = \exp\left(\frac{\nu^2}{2}\right).$$

This completes the proof. ∎

3.5. Large deviations

Finally we establish the large deviation results, that is, we compute $P(O_n(\mathcal{D}_n) = r)$ for $r = (1 + \delta)\mathbf{E}[O_n(\mathcal{D}_n)]$ for some $\delta > 0$. Let a be a real constant such that $na = (1 + \delta)\mathbf{E}[O_n(\mathcal{D}_n)]$. We will compute $P(O_n(\mathcal{D}_n) = na)$ asymptotically for the case when na is an integer (when na is not an integer, we need to replace na by the closest integer). Clearly,

$$P(O_n(D_n) = na) = [x^{na}]T_n(x) = \frac{[z^n][x^{na}]T(z, x)}{[z^n]T(z, 1)}. \qquad (3.34)$$

By (3.22),

$$[x^{na}]T(z, x) = [x^{na}]\left(T_0(z) + xR(z)U(z)\sum_{i=0}^{\infty}(xM(z))^i \right)$$

$$= R(z)U(z)M(z)^{na-1} = \frac{P(w)z^m}{[D(z)]^2}M(z)^{na-1}.$$

Hence, Cauchy's coefficient formula leads to

$$[z^n][x^{na}]T(z, x) = \frac{1}{2\pi i}\oint \frac{P(w)z^m}{[D(z)]^2}M(z)^{na-1}\frac{1}{z^{n+1}}dz,$$

where integration is along any contour around zero in the convergence circle.

In order to derive the large deviation results, we need to apply the *saddle point method*. We now review this method. It is summarized in Table 3.1. The reader is referred to Flajolet and Sedgewick (2009) and Szpankowski (2001) for an in-depth discussion.

Following Table 3.1, we define the function $h_a(z)$ of a complex variable z as

$$h_a(z) = a\log M(z) - \log z,$$

such that

$$[z^n][x^{na}]T(z, x) = \frac{1}{2\pi i}\oint e^{nh_a(z)}g(z)dz,$$

where

$$g(z) = \frac{P(w)z^{m-1}}{D(z)^2 M(z)}.$$

In the lemma below, we characterize some properties of $h_a(z)$ that are needed to estimate the integral.

Lemma 3.5.1. *The following holds.*

(i) *There exists a unique real root z_a of the equation $h_a'(z) = 0$ that satisfies $0 < z_a < \rho$ for some constant a.*

(ii) *$h_a''(z_a) > 0$.*

Table 3.1. Summary of the saddle point approximation.

Input. Let $g(z)$ be analytic in $|z| < R$ ($0 < R < +\infty$) with nonnegative Taylor coefficients and "fast growth" as $z \to R^-$. Let $h(z) := \log g(z) - (n+1)\log z$.
Output. The asymptotic formula (3.39) for $g_n := [z^n]g(z)$:

$$g_n = \frac{1}{2i\pi} \int_{\mathcal{C}} g(z) \frac{dz}{z^{n+1}} = \frac{1}{2i\pi} \int_{\mathcal{C}} e^{h(z)} \, dz, \qquad (3.35)$$

where $\mathcal{C} = \{z \mid |z| = r\}$ is a loop around $z = 0$.

(SP1) **Saddle point contour.** Assume that $g'(z)/g(z) \to +\infty$ as $z \to R^-$. Let $r = r(n)$ be the unique positive root of the saddle point equation, when $r \to R$ as $n \to \infty$

$$h'(r) = 0 \qquad \text{or} \qquad \frac{rg'(r)}{g(r)} = n + 1. \qquad (3.36)$$

(SP2) **Basic split.** Assume that $h'''(r)^{1/3}h''(r)^{-1/2} \to 0$. Define $\delta = \delta(n)$, the *range* of the saddle point, by $\delta = \left| h'''(r)^{-1/6}h''(r)^{-1/4} \right|$, so that $\delta \to 0$, $h''(r)\delta^2 \to \infty$, and $h'''(r)\delta^3 \to 0$. Split $\mathcal{C}$ into $\mathcal{C}_0 \cup \mathcal{C}_1$, where $\mathcal{C}_0 = \{z \in \mathcal{C} \mid |\arg(z)| \leq \delta\}$, and $\mathcal{C}_1 = \{z \in \mathcal{C} \mid |\arg(z)| \geq \delta\}$.

(SP3) **Elimination of tails.** Assume that $|g(re^{i\theta})| \leq |g(re^{i\delta})|$ on $\mathcal{C}_1$. Then

$$\left| \int_{\mathcal{C}_1} e^{h(z)} \, dz \right| = O\left(|e^{-h(re^{i\delta})}| \right). \qquad (3.37)$$

(SP4) **Local approximation.** Assume that $h(re^{i\theta}) - h(r) - \frac{1}{2}r^2\theta^2 h''(r) = O(|h'''(r)\delta^3|)$ on $\mathcal{C}_0$. Then the central integral is asymptotic to a complete Gaussian integral, and

$$\frac{1}{2i\pi} \int_{\mathcal{C}_0} e^{h(z)} \, dz = \frac{g(r)r^{-n}}{\sqrt{2\pi h''(r)}} \left(1 + O(|h'''(r)\delta^3|) \right). \qquad (3.38)$$

(SP5) **Collection.** Assumptions (SP1), (SP2), (SP3), and (SP4) imply the estimate

$$[z^n]g(z) = \frac{g(r)r^{-n}}{\sqrt{2\pi h''(r)}} \left(1 + O(|h'''(r)\delta^3|) \right) \sim \frac{g(r)r^{-n}}{\sqrt{2\pi h''(r)}}. \qquad (3.39)$$

(iii) $h_a(z_a) < -\log \rho$.

Proof. By the definition of $h_a(z)$,

$$h'_a(z) = \frac{aM'(z)}{M(z)} - \frac{1}{z} =$$

$$\frac{-D(z)^2 + (azB'(z) + 1 - B(z))D(z) + az(1 - B(z))D'(z)}{zD(z)(D(z) - 1 + B(z))}.$$

We notice that the denominator is always positive for $0 < z < \rho$.

Let us define $f_a(z)$, a function of a real variable z, as the numerator of $h'_a(z)$. That is, by the definition of $D(z)$ in (3.21),

$$f_a(z) = [(1 - S(z))S(z) + azS'(z)](1 - B(z))^2$$
$$+ z^m P(w)[azB'(z) + (1 - 2S(z) + am)(1 - B(z)) - z^m P(w)].$$

We find that

$$f_a(\rho) = \rho^m P(w)(a\rho B'(\rho) - \rho^m P(w)) > 0 \qquad (3.40)$$

since, for large n,

$$a = (1 + \delta)\frac{\mathbf{E}[O_n(D_n)]}{n} = (1 + \delta)\frac{\rho^{m-1}}{B'(\rho)}P(w)\left(1 - O\left(\frac{1}{n}\right)\right) > \frac{\rho^{m-1}}{B'(\rho)}P(w).$$

First, we consider the case when the pattern is not self-overlapping, that is, $S(z) \equiv 1$. Then

$$f_a(z) = z^m P(w)[azB'(z) + (am - 1)(1 - B(z)) - z^m P(w)].$$

The term of smallest degree in $f_a(z)$ is $(am - 1)P(w)z^m$, and its coefficient is negative since $a < 1/m$. Thus, there exists a sufficiently small $\varepsilon > 0$ such that $f_a(\varepsilon) < 0$. By this and (3.40), there exists a real root z_a of $h'_a(z) = 0$.

Second, we consider the case when the pattern is self-overlapping, that is,

$$S(z) = 1 + c_r z^r + \text{higher order terms} \qquad (0 < r < m),$$

where r is the smallest degree of the nonconstant terms and c_r is a positive constant. Then the term of smallest degree in $f_a(z)$ becomes $(ar - 1)c_r z^r$, and its coefficient is negative since $a < 1/m < 1/r$. As in the first case, $f_a(\varepsilon) < 0$ for sufficiently small $\varepsilon > 0$, and we get the same result. The uniqueness comes from this result and part (ii) of the lemma because $h'_a(z)$ is continuous on $z \in [0, \rho]$.

Next, we prove part (ii). By definition,

$$h'_a(z_a) = \frac{aM'(z_a)}{M(z_a)} - \frac{1}{z_a} = 0. \qquad (3.41)$$

However, we can write $M(z) = \sum_{i \geq 0} p_i z^i$ with $p_i \geq 0$ since $M(z)$ is the probability generating function of the language $\mathcal{M}$. Then

$$\frac{M'(z_a)}{M(z_a)} = \frac{\sum_{i \geq 0} i p_i z_a^{i-1}}{\sum_{i \geq 0} p_i z_a^i} = \frac{1}{z_a} \sum_{i \geq 0} i \frac{p_i z_a^i}{\sum_{j \geq 0} p_j z_a^j} = \frac{1}{z_a} \mathbf{E}[X], \qquad (3.42)$$

where X is a random variable such that

$$P(X = i) = \frac{p_i z_a^i}{\sum_{j \geq 0} p_j z_a^j} \qquad \text{for } i \geq 0.$$

From (3.41) and (3.42), we see that $\mathbf{E}[X] = 1/a$. Now let us compute $h_a''(z_a)$. We have

$$h_a''(z_a) = \frac{a M''(z)}{M(z)} - a \left(\frac{M'(z)}{M(z)} \right)^2 + \frac{1}{z_a^2}$$

$$= \frac{a}{z_a^2} \mathbf{E}[X(X-1)] - a \left(\frac{\mathbf{E}[X]}{z_a} \right)^2 + \frac{1}{z_a^2} = \frac{a}{z_a^2} \mathrm{Var}[X].$$

Therefore $h_a''(z_a) > 0$ because the distribution is definitely not concentrated at one value. This proves part (ii) of the lemma.

Finally, to prove part (iii) we observe that $h_a(\rho) = -\log \rho$ and $h_a'(z) > 0$ for $z_a < z \leq \rho$. Therefore $h_a(z_a) < h_a(\rho) = -\log \rho$. This completes the proof of the lemma. ∎

Now we are in a position to formulate our main result of this section. As always in this chapter we assume that m is fixed, or more generally that $nP(w) \to \infty$.

Theorem 3.5.2. *For $r = (1+\delta)\mathbf{E}[O_n(\mathcal{D}_n)]$ with $\delta > 0$, let a be a real constant such that $na = (1+\delta)\mathbf{E}[O_n(\mathcal{D}_n)]$ is an integer and let*

$$h_a(z) = a \log M(z) - \log z.$$

We denote by z_a the unique real root of the equation $h_a'(z) = 0$ such that $z_a \in (0, \rho)$. Then

$$P(O_n(\mathcal{D}_n) = na) = \frac{c_1 e^{-nI(a)}}{\sqrt{2\pi n}} \left[1 + \frac{c_2}{n} + O\left(\frac{1}{n^2} \right) \right]$$

and

$$P(O_n(\mathcal{D}_n) \geq na) = \frac{c_1 e^{-nI(a)}}{\sqrt{2\pi n}(1 - M(z_a))} \left[1 + O\left(\frac{1}{n} \right) \right],$$

where

$$I(a) = -\log \rho - h_a(z_a) > 0 \qquad (3.43)$$

and

$$c_1 = \frac{\rho B'(\rho) g(z_a)}{\tau_a}, \quad g(z) = \frac{P(w) z^{m-1}}{D(z)^2 M(z)}, \quad \tau_a^2 = h_a''(z_a).$$

The constant c_2 is explicitly computed below in (3.5).

Proof. We follow now the steps outlined in Table 3.1. This can be viewed as an illustration of an application of the saddle point method.

Let z_a be the unique positive real root of the equation $h_a'(z) = 0$. To evaluate the integral on $\mathcal{C} = \{z : |z| = z_a\}$ we first split $\mathcal{C}$ into $\mathcal{C}_0$ and $\mathcal{C}_1$ where $\mathcal{C}_0 = \{z \in \mathcal{C} : |\arg(z)| \le \theta_0\}$ and $\mathcal{C}_1 = \{z \in \mathcal{C} : |\arg(z)| \ge \theta_0\}$ for some θ_0. That is,

$$[z^n][x^{na}] T(z, x) = I_0 + I_1,$$

where

$$I_0 = \frac{1}{2\pi i} \int_{\mathcal{C}_0} e^{n h_a(z)} g(z) dz, \quad \text{and} \quad I_1 = \frac{1}{2\pi i} \int_{\mathcal{C}_1} e^{n h_a(z)} g(z) dz.$$

We compute I_0 first and show that $|I_1|$ is exponentially smaller than I_0.

Now set $\theta_0 = n^{-2/5}$ and compute I_0 with the change of variable $z = z_a e^{i\theta}$:

$$I_0 = \frac{z_a}{2\pi} \int_{-\theta_0}^{+\theta_0} \exp(n h_a(z_a e^{i\theta}) + i\theta) g(z_a e^{i\theta}) d\theta.$$

To simplify the notation, let us define some variables as follows:

$$\tau_a^2 = h_a''(z_a) \text{ (cf. part (ii) of Lemma 3.5.1)}, \quad \beta_a = \frac{h_a^{(3)}(z_a)}{3! \tau_a^3}, \quad \text{and} \quad \gamma_a = \frac{h_a^{(4)}(z_a)}{4! \tau_a^4}.$$

Using a Taylor series around $\theta = 0$, we arrive at

$$h_a(z_a e^{i\theta}) = h_a(z_a) - \frac{\tau_a^2 z_a^2}{2} \theta^2 - \left(\beta_a \tau_a^3 z_a^3 + \frac{\tau_a^2 z_a^2}{2} \right) i\theta^3$$

$$+ \left(\gamma_a \tau_a^4 z_a^4 + \frac{3}{2} \beta_a \tau_a^3 z_a^3 + \frac{7}{24} \tau_a^2 z_a^2 \right) \theta^4 + O(\theta^5)$$

since $h_a'(z_a) = 0$. When $|\theta| \le \theta_0$, $n\theta^k \to 0$ $(k \ge 3)$ as $n \to \infty$. Thus, using the Taylor series, we get

$$e^{n h_a(z_a e^{i\theta}) + i\theta} = \exp\left(n h_a(z_a) - \frac{\tau_a^2 z_a^2}{2} n\theta^2 \right) \left(1 + \alpha(\theta) + \frac{\alpha(\theta)^2}{2!} + \frac{\alpha(\theta)^3}{3!} + \cdots \right),$$

where

$$\alpha(\theta) = i\theta - \left(\beta_a \tau_a^3 z_a^3 + \frac{\tau_a^2 z_a^2}{2}\right) in\theta^3 + \left(\gamma_a \tau_a^4 z_a^4 + \frac{3}{2}\beta_a \tau_a^3 z_a^3 + \frac{7}{24}\tau_a^2 z_a^2\right) n\theta^4$$
$$+ O(n\theta^5).$$

For $\omega_0 = \tau_a z_a n^{1/10}$ we then have

$$I_0 = \frac{e^{nh_a(z_a)}}{2\pi\tau_a\sqrt{n}} \int_{-\omega_0}^{+\omega_0} \exp\left(-\frac{\omega^2}{2}\right) \left(1 + \alpha(\omega) + \frac{\alpha(\omega)^2}{2!} + \cdots\right)$$
$$\times g\left(z_a e^{i\omega/(\tau_a z_a \sqrt{n})}\right) d\omega.$$

We observe that each term of odd degree of ω in

$$\left(1 + \eta(\omega) + \frac{\eta(\omega)^2}{2!} + \frac{\eta(\omega)^3}{3!} + \cdots\right) g\left(z_a e^{i\omega/(\tau_a z_a \sqrt{n})}\right),$$

contributes nothing to the integral. Thus, using the Taylor series of the function $g\left(z_a e^{i\omega/(\tau_a z_a \sqrt{n})}\right)$ around $\omega = 0$, we arrive at

$$I_0 = \frac{e^{nh_a(z_a)}}{2\pi\tau_a\sqrt{n}} \int_{-\omega_0}^{+\omega_0} \exp\left(-\frac{\omega^2}{2}\right) \left(A + B\omega^2 + C\omega^4 + D\omega^6 + O\left(\frac{1}{n^2}\right)\right) d\omega$$

where

$$A = g(z_a), \quad B = -\frac{1}{n}\left(\frac{g''(z_a)}{2\tau_a^2} + \frac{3g'(z_a)}{2\tau_a^2 z_a} + \frac{g(z_a)}{2\tau_a^2 z_a^2}\right),$$

$$C = \frac{1}{n}\left(g'(z_a)\left(\frac{\beta_a}{\tau_a} + \frac{1}{2\tau_a^2 z_a}\right) + g(z_a)\left(\gamma_a + \frac{5\beta_a}{2\tau_a z_a} + \frac{19}{24\tau_a^2 z_a^2}\right)\right),$$

and

$$D = -\frac{g(z_a)}{2n}\left(\beta_a + \frac{1}{2\tau_a z_a}\right)^2.$$

Using the fact that, as $\omega_0 \to \infty$,

$$\int_{\omega_0}^{+\infty} x^k e^{-\frac{x^2}{2}} dx = O\left(e^{-\frac{1}{2}\omega_0^2}\right), \quad \text{and} \quad \int_{-\infty}^{+\infty} x^{2k} e^{-\frac{x^2}{2}} dx = \frac{\Gamma(2k)}{2^{k-1}\Gamma(k)}\sqrt{2\pi},$$

we finally obtain

$$I_0 = \frac{g(z_a)e^{nh_a(z_a)}}{\tau_a\sqrt{2\pi n}}\left[1 + \frac{1}{n}\left(\frac{3\beta_a g'(z_a)}{\tau_a g(z_a)} - \frac{g''(z_a)}{2\tau_a^2 g(z_a)} + 3\gamma_a - \frac{15\beta_a^2}{2}\right) + O\left(\frac{1}{n^2}\right)\right].$$
$$\tag{3.44}$$

It is easy to see that the main contribution to the large deviations comes from I_0. Thus, we only need to show that I_1 is small.

We will compute a bound on $|I_1|$ and show that it is exponentially smaller than I_0. We can write $I_1 = I_1^+ + I_1^-$, where

$$I_1^+ = \frac{z_a}{2\pi} \int_{\theta_0}^{\pi} e^{nh_a(z_a e^{i\theta})} g(z_a e^{i\theta}) e^{i\theta} d\theta, \quad I_1^- = \frac{z_a}{2\pi} \int_{\theta_0}^{\pi} e^{nh_a(z_a e^{i\theta})} g(z_a e^{i\theta}) e^{i\theta} d\theta.$$

First we need to consider $M(z)$, the probability generating function for the nonempty language $\mathcal{M}$. Clearly, the coefficients of $M(z)$ are all nonnegative; also $M(z)$ is aperiodic, which is the subject of Lemma 3.5.3 below. Granted the aperiodicity of $M(z)$, by the nonnegativity of the coefficients the function $|M(z_a e^{i\theta})|$ has a unique maximum at $\theta = 0$. It is also infinitely differentiable at $\theta = 0$. Consequently there exists an angle $\theta_1 \in (0, \pi)$ such that

$$\left| M(z_a e^{i\theta}) \right| \leq \left| M(z_a e^{i\theta_1}) \right| \quad \text{for } \theta \in [\theta_1, \pi],$$

and $|M(z_a e^{i\theta})|$ is decreasing for $\theta \in [0, \theta_1]$. Thus, for large n,

$$\left| M(z_a e^{i\theta}) \right| \leq \left| M(z_a e^{i\theta_0}) \right| \quad \text{for } \theta \in [\theta_0, \pi],$$

since $\theta_0 = n^{-2/5} < \theta_1$. Therefore, for $\theta \in [\theta_0, \pi]$,

$$\left| e^{nh_a(z_a e^{i\theta})} \right| = \frac{\left| M(z_a e^{i\theta}) \right|^{na}}{z_a^n} \leq \frac{\left| M(z_a e^{i\theta_0}) \right|^{na}}{z_a^n} = \left| e^{nh_a(z_a e^{i\theta_0})} \right|,$$

and this leads to

$$|I_1^+| \leq \frac{z_a \max(g)}{2\pi} \int_{\theta_0}^{\pi} \left| e^{nh_a(z_a e^{i\theta})} \right| d\theta \leq \frac{z_a \max(g)}{2\pi} \int_{\theta_0}^{\pi} \left| e^{nh_a(z_a e^{i\theta_0})} \right| d\theta$$

$$= \frac{z_a(\pi - \theta_0) \max(g)}{2\pi} \exp\left(nh_a(z_a) - \frac{\tau_a^2 z_a^2}{2} n^{\frac{1}{5}} + O(n^{-\frac{1}{5}}) \right) = O\left(I_0 e^{-cn^{\frac{1}{5}}} \right),$$

where $\max(g)$ is the maximum of $|g(z_a e^{i\theta})|$ for $\theta \in [\theta_0, \pi]$ and c is a positive constant. Similarly, $|I_1^-|$ is bounded. Thus $[z^n][x^{na}]T(z, x) = I_0 + I_1 = I_0\left(1 + O\left(e^{-cn^{1/5}} \right) \right)$.

Finally, by (3.24), (3.34), (3.44) and the above we have

$$P(O_n(D_n) = na) = \frac{\rho B'(\rho) g(z_a) e^{-nI(a)}}{\tau_a \sqrt{2\pi n}}$$

$$\times \left[1 + \frac{1}{n}\left(\frac{3\beta_a g'(z_a)}{\tau_a g(z_a)} - \frac{g''(z_a)}{2\tau_a^2 g(z_a)} + 3\gamma_a - \frac{15\beta_a^2}{2} \right) + O\left(\frac{1}{n^2} \right) \right],$$

where $I(a) = -\log \rho - h_a(z_a)$, which is positive. This establishes our result; the constant c_2 can be extracted from (3.5). ∎

To complete the proof we need to prove the following lemma.

Lemma 3.5.3. *The probability generating function $M(z)$ is aperiodic if the length of a pattern w defined over the extended alphabet $\mathcal{B}_{d,k}$ is greater than 1.*

Proof. To prove the aperiodicity of $M(z)$, we will show that there always exist two words, u_1 and u_2, in $\mathcal{M}$ whose lengths differ by 1. Let $\mathcal{B}_{d,k} = \{\beta_d, \beta_{d+1}, \ldots, \beta_k\}$ and ℓ be the length of the pattern w defined over $\mathcal{B}_{d,k}$ ($\ell \geq 2$). We consider the following two cases: (a) some super-symbols of $\mathcal{B}_{d,k}$ do not appear in w; (b) all such super-symbols appear in w.

To prove the first case, let β_i be super-symbol that does not appear in w. Then, clearly both $\beta_i \beta_d \beta_i w$ and $\beta_i \beta_{d+1} \beta_i w$ are in $\mathcal{M}$ and their difference in length is 1.

Now we prove the second case. For this, we consider three subcases, and for each subcase we find two words in $\mathcal{M}$ which differ by 1 in length for each subcase:

Subcase (i), $|\mathcal{B}_{d,k}| \geq 3$: Let

$$u_1 = \underbrace{\beta_d \cdots \beta_d}_{\ell} \beta_d \underbrace{\beta_d \cdots \beta_d}_{\ell} w \quad \text{and} \quad u_2 = \underbrace{\beta_d \cdots \beta_d}_{\ell} \beta_{d+1} \underbrace{\beta_d \cdots \beta_d}_{\ell} w.$$

Then w can occur in wu_1 only at the left-hand and the right-hand ends because the occurrence of w elsewhere would imply that

$$w = \underbrace{\beta_d \cdots \beta_d}_{\ell},$$

which would contradict the assumption that all super-symbols appear in w. Similarly, w occurs in wu_2 only at the two ends. Otherwise, w would have only one or two kinds of super-symbol, which contradicts the assumption. Thus both u_1 and u_2 are in $\mathcal{M}$.

Subcase (ii), $|\mathcal{B}_{d,k}| = 2$ and $\ell \geq 3$. Let β_i be a super-symbol that appears more than once in w. Then, by a similar argument to that for the first case,

$$\underbrace{\beta_j \cdots \beta_j}_{\ell} \beta_i u_1 = \underbrace{\beta_j \cdots \beta_j}_{\ell} w \quad \text{and} \quad u_2 = \underbrace{\beta_j \cdots \beta_j}_{\ell} \beta_j \underbrace{\beta_j \cdots \beta_j}_{\ell} w$$

are in $\mathcal{M}$, and their lengths differ by 1 because $|i - j| = 1$.

Subcase (iii), $|\mathcal{B}_{d,k}| = 2$ and $\ell = 2$. In this case, w must be either $\beta_d \beta_k$ or $\beta_k \beta_d$. Thus $\beta_d w$ and $\beta_k w$ are in $\mathcal{M}$. Therefore $M(z)$ is aperiodic. ∎

3.6. Some extensions

First, we relax our assumption that the (d, k) sequences are restricted. A small modification can extend our previous analysis to *all* (d, k) sequences. Let $\mathcal{T}_r^{all}$ be the set of all (d, k) sequences containing exactly r occurrences of w. Then, for $d \geq 1$,

$$\mathcal{T}_r^{all} = \{\varepsilon, 1\} \cdot \mathcal{T}_r \cdot (\{\varepsilon\} + \mathcal{A}_{d,k}); \qquad (3.45)$$

the generating functions and asymptotic expressions can be derived from this expression.

Next, we consider pattern occurrences in a *binary* alphabet rather than extended alphabet $\mathcal{B}_{d,k}$ (e.g., $w = 01$ occurs twice in the $(1, 4)$ sequence 0010001 over $\mathcal{A}\{0, 1\}$ and not at all over $\mathcal{B}_{d,k}$). Again, let $w = w_1 \cdots w_m \in \{0, 1\}^m$ with $w_m = 1$, and let w be represented over $\mathcal{B}_{d,k}$, that is, $w = \beta_1 \cdots \beta_{m'}$ where $\beta_i \in \mathcal{B}_{d,k}$. Then the autocorrelation set $\mathcal{S}_2$ over the *binary* alphabet is defined as

$$\mathcal{S}_2 = \{w_{\ell+1}^m : w_1^\ell = w_{m-\ell+1}^m\}, \qquad 1 \leq \ell \leq m.$$

Using the languages $\mathcal{T}_r$, $\mathcal{R}$, $\mathcal{M}$, and $\mathcal{U}$ defined after Example 3.1.1, we find

$$\mathcal{T}_r = \mathcal{R} \cdot \mathcal{M}^{r-1} \cdot \mathcal{U}, \qquad (3.46)$$

$$\mathcal{T}_0 \cdot \mathcal{Z} \cdot \{w\} = \mathcal{R} \cdot \mathcal{S}_2, \qquad (3.47)$$

$$\mathcal{M}^* = \mathcal{B}^* \cdot \mathcal{Z} \cdot \{w\} + \mathcal{S}_2, \qquad (3.48)$$

$$\mathcal{U} \cdot \mathcal{B} = \mathcal{M} + \mathcal{U} - \{\varepsilon\}, \qquad (3.49)$$

$$\mathcal{Z} \cdot \{w\} \cdot \mathcal{M} = \mathcal{B} \cdot \mathcal{R} - (\mathcal{R} - \mathcal{Z} \cdot \{w\}), \qquad (3.50)$$

where $\mathcal{Z} = \{\varepsilon, 0, 00, \ldots, 0^{k+1-|\beta_1|}\}$, and 0^k denotes a run of zeros of length k. We now replace $\mathcal{S}$ by $\mathcal{S}_2$ and $\{w\}$ by $\mathcal{Z} \cdot \{w\}$ in (3.10)–(3.14). The key idea is that any word in $\mathcal{Z} \cdot \{w\}$ is now considered to contain an occurrence of w. Applying the same techniques as above we can derive the generating functions and asymptotic results (see Exercise 3.8).

3.7. Application: significant signals in neural data

In this section we illustrate how our theoretical results can be used to obtain some accurate statistical inferences from biological data. We apply Theorem 3.5.2 to detect under- and over-represented structures in neuronal data (spike trains). We shall first argue that neuronal data are best represented by constrained sequences. Indeed, current technology allows for the simultaneous recording of the spike trains from 100 (or more) different neurons in the brain of a live animal. Such experiments have produced enormous amounts of extremely

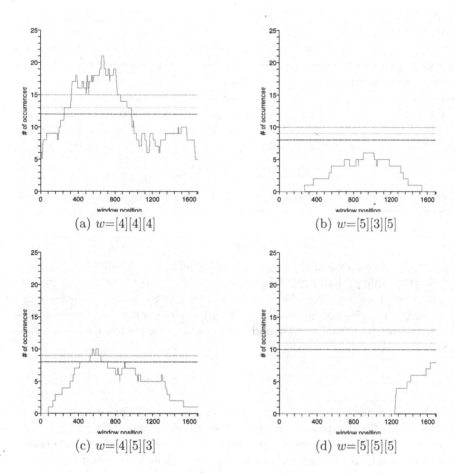

Figure 3.2. The number of occurrences of w within a window of size 500, where $[i]$ stands for the pattern $0\cdots01$ with $i-1$ zeros, for three thresholds corresponding to $\alpha_{th} = 10^{-6}, 10^{-7}, 10^{-8}$.

valuable data, and a core research area in neuroscience is devoted to developing accurate and precise statistical tools to quantify and describe the information that is contained in this data (see Paninski (2003)). Because of the nature of the biological mechanisms that produce them, spike train data satisfy structural constraints that match the framework of (d, k) binary sequences, as discussed in the introduction to this chapter.

We will consider the single-electrode experimental data from cortical neurons under random current injection. The details can be found in Jolivet, Rauch, Luscher, and Gerstner (2006). This spike timing data can be transformed into a (d, k) sequence by setting the time resolution and dividing the time into *bins* of the same size. Each time bin is represented by a bit 0 or 1. If there is a spike in a certain time bin, the bin is represented by 1; otherwise it is represented by 0. Having this in mind, and using our large deviation results, we can derive a threshold, O_{th}, above which pattern occurrences will be classified as statistically significant. The threshold is defined as the minimum value of O_{th} such that

$$P(O_n(\mathcal{D}_n) \geq O_{th}) \leq \alpha_{th},$$

where α_{th} is a given probability threshold. From Theorem 3.5.2 we easily conclude that, for α_{th} in the range of the large deviation domain, the threshold is $O_{th} = na_{th}$, where

$$a_{th} \approx I^{-1}(\log(1/\alpha_{th})/n),$$

and $I^{-1}(\cdot)$ is the inverse of the function $I(a)$ defined in (3.43) of Theorem 3.5.2.

To set up our probabilistic reference model, we need to fix the parameters d, k, and p. First, we find d and k by inspecting the binary sequence (e.g., by finding the minimum and maximum lengths of runs of zeros between spikes in the sequence). Then we can find p by solving the following simultaneous equations in the variables ρ and p:

$$B(\rho) = 1 \quad \text{and} \quad 1 - p = \frac{1}{\rho B'(\rho)}.$$

Note that the coefficients of $B(z)$ depend on p. The second equation follows from the fact that $\rho B'(\rho)$ captures the average length of symbols of $\mathcal{B}_{d,k}$ in a (d, k) sequence, and thus its reciprocal represents $1 - p$. In other words, we estimate p indirectly through the estimation of d and k. One might be tempted to estimate p by just counting the total number of 0s and dividing it by the length of the sequence. But this could lead to a poor estimate since a large portion of the (d, k) sequence set may not be typical.

In our experiment we set the size of the time bin to 3 ms and obtained a $(d, k) = (1, 6)$ sequence of length 2193 with $p = 0.752686$. Figure 3.2 shows the number of occurrences for various patterns w within a (sliding) window of size 1.5 s over a long neural sequence; here we use the short-hand notation $[i]$ for the pattern

$$\underbrace{0 \cdots 0}_{i-1} 1.$$

The three horizontal lines represent the thresholds for $\alpha_{th} = 10^{-6}$, 10^{-7}, and 10^{-8}, respectively. As expected, the thresholds vary with the structure of w.

If the number of occurrences exceeds the threshold at some position, we claim that the pattern occurrence is statistically significant in that window. This observation can be used as a starting point for the interpretation of neural signals, although there is still a huge interpretive gap between the patterns of spike trains and their meaning in a real nervous system. In passing we observe that one would obtain quite different threshold values if the constraints were ignored.

3.8. Exercises

3.1   Enumerate the (d, k) sequences that start with 00 and end with 11.

3.2   Enumerate the $(1, 4)$ sequences that do not contain the pattern $w = 001$.

3.3   Enumerate the $(1, 4)$ sequences with at least one occurrence of $w = 01$ and no occurrences of $w = 001$.

3.4   Establish the limit laws for $P(O_n(\mathcal{D}) = r)$ when $nP(w) = O(1)$ and for $nP(w) \to 0$. Follow the derivations in Section 2.5.4 of Chapter 2.

3.5   In this chapter we studied pattern matching only in (d, k) sequences. Observe that a (d, k) sequence can be obtained as an output of an automaton. In fact, a large class of constrained sequences can be generated by automation (see Marcus, Roth, and Siegel (1988)). Extend our analysis to such a larger class of constrained sequences.

3.6   Estimate the average numbers of occurrences of $w_1 = 001$ and $w_2 = 0001$ in a $(1, 6)$ sequence.

3.7   Establish the central limit theorem and the large deviations for non-restricted (d, k) sequences as described in (3.45).

3.8   Using (3.46)–(3.50) establish the central limit theorem and the large deviations for pattern occurrences over a binary alphabet.

3.9   Extend our analysis to Markov sources.

3.10   Consider the following constrained pattern matching problem. Let $W = 010011$. Analyze the number of occurrences of $w = 0101$ in binary sequences of length n that do not contain W.

Bibliographical notes

Constrained pattern matching, under the name *constrained coding*, is usually discussed in the context of information theory; see for example Marcus et al. (1988). Constrained pattern matching has been discussed in only a few publications; see Moision, Orlitsky, and Siegel (2001). Our presentation in this chapter is based on the paper by Choi and Szpankowski (2011).

In fact, (d, k) sequences have been analyzed in information theory since Shannon, with some recent contributions: Dembo and Kontoyiannis (2002), Kolesnik and Krachkovsky (1991), Marcus et al. (1988), Zehavi and Wolf (1988). It should be added that pattern matching in constrained sequences can in principle be analyzed by various versions of generalized pattern matching, as will be discussed in Chapter 4. See also Bender and Kochman (1993), Flajolet, Szpankowski, and Vallée (2006) and Nicodème, Salvy, and Flajolet (1999).

It should be pointed out that the number of pattern occurrences may differ significantly from the normal distribution, if the text is generated by some rational languages, as shown in Banderier, Bodini, Ponty, and Bouzid (2012).

The saddle point method is discussed in many books, e.g., Flajolet and Sedgewick (2009), Olver (1974) and Szpankowski (2001).

CHAPTER 4

Generalized String Matching

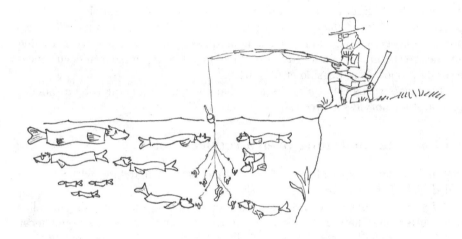

In this chapter we consider generalized pattern matching, in which a set of patterns (rather than a single pattern) is given. We assume here that the pattern is a pair of sets of words $(\mathcal{W}_0, \mathcal{W})$, where $\mathcal{W} = \bigcup_{i=1}^{d} \mathcal{W}_i$ consists of the sets $\mathcal{W}_i \subset \mathcal{A}^{m_i}$ (i.e., all words in $\mathcal{W}_i$ have a fixed length m_i). The set $\mathcal{W}_0$ is called the *forbidden set*. For $\mathcal{W}_0 = \emptyset$ one is interested in the number of pattern occurrences $O_n(\mathcal{W})$, defined as the *number of patterns* from $\mathcal{W}$ occurring in a text X_1^n generated by a (random) source. Another parameter of interest is the *number of positions* in X_1^n where a pattern from $\mathcal{W}$ appears (clearly, several patterns may occur at the same positions but words from $\mathcal{W}_i$ must occur in different locations); this quantity we denote as Π_n. If we define $\Pi_n^{(i)}$ as the number of positions where a word from $\mathcal{W}_i$ occurs, then

$$O_n(\mathcal{W}) = \Pi_n^{(1)} + \cdots + \Pi_n^{(d)}.$$

Notice that at any given position of the text and for a given i only one word from $\mathcal{W}_i$ can occur.

For $\mathcal{W}_0 \neq \emptyset$ one studies the number of occurrences $O_n(\mathcal{W})$ under the condition that $O_n(\mathcal{W}_0) := \Pi_n^{(0)} = 0$, that is, there is no occurrence of a pattern from $\mathcal{W}_0$ in the text X_1^n. This could be called *constrained* pattern matching since one restricts the text to those strings that do not contain strings from $\mathcal{W}_0$. A simple version of constrained pattern matching was discussed in Chapter 3 (see also Exercises 3.3, 3.6, and 3.10).

In this chapter we first present an analysis of generalized pattern matching with $\mathcal{W}_0 = \emptyset$ and $d = 1$, which we call the *reduced pattern set* (i.e., no pattern is a substring of another pattern). This is followed by a detailed analysis of (nonreduced) generalized pattern matching. We describe two methods of analysis. First, for general pattern matching (i.e., with a nonreduced set), we apply the de Bruijn's automaton and spectral analysis of matrices to obtain the central and local limit laws as well as the large deviation results. Then, we present a novel language approach to nonreduced generalized pattern matching and derive the multivariate generating functions describing pattern occurrences recently proposed by Bassino et al. (2012).

Throughout this chapter we assume that the text is generated by a (nondegenerate) memoryless source (B), as defined in Chapter 1.

4.1. String matching over a reduced set

We analyze here a special case of generalized pattern matching with $\mathcal{W}_0 = \emptyset$ and $d = 1$. For this case we shall write $\mathcal{W}_1 := \mathcal{W} = \{w_1, \ldots, w_K\}$, where w_i ($1 \leq i \leq K$) are given patterns with fixed length $|w_i| = m$. We shall generalize the results from Chapter 2 for exact pattern matching, but here we omit most proofs since we will present more general results with proofs in the next section.

As before, let $\mathcal{T}_{\geq 1}$ be a language of words containing at least one occurrence from the set $\mathcal{W}$ and, for any nonnegative integer r, let $\mathcal{T}_r$ be the language of words containing exactly r occurrences from $\mathcal{W}$. In order to characterize $\mathcal{T}_r$ we introduce some additional languages for any $1 \leq i, j \leq K$:

- $\mathcal{M}_{ij} = \{v : w_i v \in \mathcal{T}_2 \text{ and } w_j \text{ occurs at the right-hand end of } v\}$;

- $\mathcal{R}_i$, the set of words containing only one occurrence of w_i, located at the right-hand end;

- $\mathcal{U}_i = \{u : w_i u \in \mathcal{T}_1\}$, a set of words u such that the only occurrence of $w_i \in \mathcal{W}$ $w_i u$ is at the left-hand end.

We also need to generalize the autocorrelation set and the autocorrelation polynomial to the case where there is a set of patterns. For any given two strings w and u, let

$$S_{w,u} = \{u_{k+1}^m : w_{m-k+1}^m = u_1^k\}$$

be the *correlation set*. Notice that $S_{w,u} \neq S_{u,w}$. The set of positions k satisfying $u_1^k = w_{m-k+1}^m$ is denoted as $\mathcal{P}(w,u)$. If $w = xv$ and $u = vy$ for some words x, y v, then $y \in S_{w,u}$ and $|v| \in \mathcal{P}(w,u)$. The correlation polynomial $S_{w,u}(z)$ of w and u is the associated generating function of $S_{w,u}$, that is,

$$S_{w,u}(z) = \sum_{k \in \mathcal{P}(w,u)} P(u_{k+1}^m) z^{m-k}.$$

In particular, for $w_i, w_j \in \mathcal{W}$ we define $S_{i,j} := S_{w_i,w_j}$. The *correlation matrix* is then denoted as $\mathbf{S}(z) = \{S_{w_i w_j}(z)\}_{i,j=1,K}$.

Example 4.1.1. Consider a DNA sequence over the alphabet $\mathcal{A} = \{A, C, G, T\}$ generated by a memoryless source with $P(A) = 1/5$, $P(C) = 3/10$, $P(G) = 3/10$ and $P(T) = 1/5$. Let $w_1 = ATT$ and $w_2 = TAT$. Then the correlation matrix $\mathbf{S}(z)$ is

$$\mathbf{S}(z) = \begin{pmatrix} 1 & \frac{z^2}{25} \\ \frac{z}{5} & 1 + \frac{z^2}{25} \end{pmatrix}$$

as is easy to see. ∎

In order to analyze the number of occurrences $O_n(\mathcal{W})$ and its generating functions we first generalize the language relationships presented in Theorem 2.2.3 of Chapter 2. Observe that

$$\mathcal{T}_r = \sum_{1 \leq i,j \leq K} \mathcal{R}_i \mathcal{M}_{ij}^{r-1} \mathcal{U}_j,$$

$$\mathcal{T}_{\geq 1} = \sum_{r \geq 1} \sum_{1 \leq i,j \leq K} \mathcal{R}_i \mathcal{M}_{ij}^{r-1} \mathcal{U}_j;$$

here $\sum$ denotes the disjoint union of sets. As in Theorem 2.2.5 of Chapter 2, one finds the following relationships between the languages just introduced

$$\bigcup_{k \geq 1} \mathcal{M}_{i,j}^k = \mathcal{A}^* \cdot w_j + \mathcal{S}_{ij} - \delta_{ij}\varepsilon, \qquad 1 \leq i, j \leq K, \qquad (4.1)$$

$$\mathcal{U}_i \cdot \mathcal{A} = \bigcup_j \mathcal{M}_{ij} + \mathcal{U}_i - \varepsilon, \qquad 1 \leq i \leq K, \qquad (4.2)$$

$$\mathcal{A} \cdot \mathcal{R}_j - (\mathcal{R}_j - w_j) = \bigcup_i w_i \mathcal{M}_{ij}, \qquad 1 \leq j \leq K, \qquad (4.3)$$

$$\mathcal{T}_0 \cdot w_j = \mathcal{R}_j + \bigcup_i \mathcal{R}_i(\mathcal{S}_{ij} - \varepsilon), \qquad 1 \leq i, j \leq K \qquad (4.4)$$

where δ_{ij} is 1 when $i = j$ and zero otherwise.

Let us now analyze $O_n(\mathcal{W})$ in a probabilistic framework when the text is generated by a memoryless source. Then the above language relationships translate directly into generating functions. However, before we proceed, we will adopt the following notation. Lower-case letters are reserved for vectors, and these are assumed to be column vectors (e.g., $\mathbf{x}^t = (x_1, \ldots, x_K)$) except for vectors of generating functions, which we denote by upper-case letters (e.g., $\mathrm{U}^t(z) = (U_1(z), \ldots, U_K(z))$, where $U_i(z)$ is the generating function of the language $\mathcal{U}_{w_i}$). In the above, the upper index t denotes the transpose. We shall use upper-case letters for matrices (e.g., $\mathrm{S}(z) = \{S_{w_i w_j}(z)\}_{i,j=1,K}$). In particular, we write I for the identity matrix, and $\mathbf{1}^t = (1, \ldots, 1)$ for a vector of 1s.

Now we are ready to present exact formulas for the generating functions $N_r(z) = \sum_{n \geq 0} P(O_n(\mathcal{W}) = r) z^n$ and $N(z, x) = \sum_{k \geq 0} N_r(z) x^r$. The following theorem is a direct consequence of our definitions and language relationships.

Theorem 4.1.2. *Let $\mathcal{W} = \{w_1, \ldots, w_K\}$ be a given set of reduced patterns each of fixed length m (thus no pattern in $\mathcal{W}$ is a subpattern of another pattern in $\mathcal{W}$) and let X be a random text of length n produced by a memoryless source. The generating functions $N_r(z)$ and $N(z, x)$ can be computed as follows:*

$$N_r(z) = \mathrm{R}^t(z) \mathrm{M}^{r-1}(z) \mathrm{U}(z), \qquad (4.5)$$

$$N(z, x) = \mathrm{R}^t(z) x (\mathrm{I} - x\mathrm{M}(z))^{-1}, \mathrm{U}(z) \qquad (4.6)$$

where, writing $\mathrm{w}^t = (P(w_1), \ldots, P(w_K))$ and $\mathbf{1}^t = (1, 1, \ldots, 1)$, we have

$$\mathrm{M}(z) = (\mathrm{D}(z) + (z - 1)\mathrm{I}) \mathrm{D}(z)^{-1}, \qquad (4.7)$$

$$(\mathrm{I} - \mathrm{M}(z))^{-1} = \mathrm{S}(z) + \frac{z^m}{1 - z} \mathbf{1} \cdot \mathrm{w}^t, \qquad (4.8)$$

$$\mathrm{U}(z) = \frac{1}{1 - z}(\mathrm{I} - \mathrm{M}(z)) \cdot \mathbf{1}, \qquad (4.9)$$

$$\mathrm{R}^t(z) = \frac{z^m}{1 - z} \mathrm{w}^t \cdot (\mathrm{I} - \mathrm{M}(z)), \qquad (4.10)$$

and

$$D(z) = (1 - z)S(z) + z^m \mathbf{1} \cdot \mathbf{w}^t.$$

Using these results and following in the footsteps of our analysis in Chapter 2 of exact pattern matching, we arrive at the following.

Theorem 4.1.3. *Let a text X be generated by a memoryless source with $P(w_i) > 0$ for $i = 1, \ldots, K$ and $P(\mathcal{W}) = \sum_{w_i \in \mathcal{W}} P(w_i) = \mathbf{w}^t \cdot \mathbf{1}$.*

(i) *The following hold:*

$$\mathbf{E}[O_n(\mathcal{W})] = (n - m + 1)P(\mathcal{W}),$$
$$\mathrm{Var}([_n(\mathcal{W})]) = (n - m + 1)\left(P(\mathcal{W}) + P^2(\mathcal{W}) - 2mP^2(\mathcal{W}) + 2\mathbf{w}^t(S(1) - \mathsf{I})\mathbf{1}\right)$$
$$+ m(m - 1)P^2(\mathcal{W}) - 2\mathbf{w}^t S'(1) \cdot \mathbf{1},$$

where $S'(1)$ denotes the derivative of the matrix $S(z)$ at $z = 1$.

(ii) *Let $\rho_\mathcal{W}$ be the smallest root of multiplicity 1 of $\det D(z) = 0$ outside the unit circle $|z| \leq 1$. There exists $\rho > \rho_\mathcal{W}$ such that, for $r = O(1)$,*

$$P(O_n(\mathcal{W}) = r) = (-1)^{r+1}\frac{a_{r+1}}{r!}(n)_r \rho_\mathcal{W}^{-(n-m+r+1)}$$
$$+ \sum_{j=1}^{r}(-1)^j a_j \binom{n}{j-1}\rho_\mathcal{W}^{-(n+j)} + O(\rho^{-n}),$$

where the a_r are computable constants.

(iii) *Define $r = \lfloor \mathbf{E}[O_n] + \xi\sqrt{\mathrm{Var}[O_n]} \rfloor$ for a fixed ξ. Then*

$$\lim_{n \to \infty} P(O_n(w) \leq \mathbf{E}[O_n] + \xi\sqrt{\mathrm{Var}[O_n]}) = \frac{1}{\sqrt{2\pi}}\int_{-\infty}^{\xi} e^{-t^2/2}dt. \qquad (4.11)$$

(iv) *Let $r = (1 + \delta)\mathbf{E}[O_n]$ with $\delta \neq 0$, and let $a = (1 + \delta)P(\mathcal{W})$. Define $\tau(t)$ to be the root of*

$$\det(\mathsf{I} - e^t M(e^\tau)) = 0$$

and define ω_a and σ_a to be given by

$$-\tau'(\omega_a) = -a, \qquad -\tau''(\omega_a) = \sigma_a^2.$$

Then, for integer r,

$$P(O_n(\mathcal{W}) = r) \sim \frac{1}{\sigma_a\sqrt{2\pi(n - m + 1)}}e^{-(n-m+1)I(a)+\theta_a},$$

where $I(a) = a\omega_a + \tau(\omega_a)$ and θ_a is a computable constant (see Exercise 4.3).

We sketch here only the derivation for part (iii) since in the next section we provide more general results with rigorous proofs. Our starting point is

$$N(z,x) = \mathsf{R}^t(z)x(\mathsf{I} - x\mathsf{M}(z))^{-1}\mathsf{U}(z),$$

shown in Theorem 4.1.2 to hold for complex $|z| < 1$ and $|x| < 1$. We may proceed in two different ways.

Method A: Determinant approach. Observe that

$$(\mathsf{I} - x\mathsf{M}(z))^{-1} = \frac{\mathsf{B}(z,x)}{\det(\mathsf{I} - x\mathsf{M}(z))}$$

where $\mathsf{B}(z,x)$ is a complex matrix. Set

$$Q(z,x) := \det(\mathsf{I} - x\mathsf{M}(z)),$$

and let $z_0 := \rho(x)$ be the smallest root of

$$Q(z,x) = \det(\mathsf{I} - x\mathsf{M}(z)) = 0.$$

Observe that $\rho(1) = 1$ by (4.8).

For our central limit result, we restrict our interest to $\rho(x)$ in the vicinity of $x = 1$. Such a root exists and is unique since for real z the matrix $\mathsf{M}(z)$ has all positive coefficients. The Perron–Frobenius theorem implies that all other roots $\rho_i(x)$ are of smaller modulus. Finally, one can analytically continue $\rho(x)$ to a complex neighborhood of x. Thus Cauchy's formula yields, for some $A < 1$,

$$\begin{aligned}
N_n(x) := [z^n]N(z,x) &= \frac{1}{2\pi i}\oint \frac{\mathsf{R}^t(z)\mathsf{B}(z,x)\mathsf{U}(z)}{Q(z,x)}\frac{dz}{z^{n+1}}\\
&= C(x)\rho^{-n}(x)(1 + O(A^n)),
\end{aligned}$$

where $C(x) = -\mathsf{R}^t(\rho(x))\mathsf{B}(\rho(x),x)\mathsf{U}(\rho(x))\rho^{-1}(x)/Q'(\rho(x),x)$. As in the proof of Theorem 2.5.3, we recognize a quasi-power form for $N_n(x)$, and this leads directly (e.g., by an application of the Levy continuity theorem or Goncharev's theorem) to the central limit result presented in (4.11).

Method B: Eigenvalue approach. We apply now the Perron–Frobenius theorem for positive matrices together with a matrix spectral representation to obtain even more precise asymptotics. Our starting point is the following formula

$$[\mathsf{I} - x\mathsf{M}(z)]^{-1} = \sum_{k=0}^{\infty} x^k\mathsf{M}^k(z). \tag{4.12}$$

Now observe that $M(z)$ for real z, say t, is a positive matrix since each element $M_{ij}(t)$ is the generating function of the language $\mathcal{M}_{ij}$ and, for any $v \in \mathcal{M}_{ij}$ we have $P(v) > 0$ for memoryless sources. Let $\lambda_1(t), \lambda_2(t), \ldots, \lambda_K(t)$ be the eigenvalues of $M(t)$. By the Perron–Frobenius result we know that $\lambda_1(t)$ is simple real, and that $\lambda_1(t) > |\lambda_i(t)|$ for $i \geq 2$. (To facilitate further derivations we will also assume that the $\lambda_i(x)$ are simple, but this assumption will not have any significant impact on our asymptotics as we shall see below.) Let $\mathbf{l}_i$ and $\mathbf{r}_i$, $i = 1, \ldots, K$ be the left and right eigenvectors corresponding to eigenvalues $\lambda_1(t), \lambda_2(t), \ldots, \lambda_K(t)$, respectively. We set $\langle \mathbf{l}_1, \mathbf{r}_1 \rangle = 1$, where $\langle \mathbf{x}, \mathbf{y} \rangle$ is the scalar product of the vectors $\mathbf{x}$ and $\mathbf{y}$. Since $\mathbf{r}_i$ is orthogonal to the left eigenvector $\mathbf{r}_j$ for $j \neq i$, we can write, for any vector $\mathbf{x}$,

$$\mathbf{x} = \langle \mathbf{l}_1, \mathbf{x} \rangle \mathbf{r}_1 + \sum_{i=2}^{K} \langle \mathbf{l}_i, \mathbf{x} \rangle \mathbf{r}_i.$$

This yields

$$M(t)\mathbf{x} = \langle \mathbf{l}_1, \mathbf{x} \rangle \lambda_1(t) \mathbf{r}_1 + \sum_{i=2}^{K} \langle \mathbf{l}_i, \mathbf{x} \rangle \lambda_i(t) \mathbf{r}_i$$

since $M(t)\mathbf{r}_i = \lambda_i(t)\mathbf{r}_i$. But $M^k(t)$ has eigenvalues $\lambda_1^k(t), \lambda_2^k(t), \ldots, \lambda_K^k(t)$; thus, dropping even our assumption that the eigenvalues $\lambda_2, \ldots, \lambda_K$ are simple, we arrive at

$$M^k(t)\mathbf{x} = \langle \mathbf{l}_1, \mathbf{x} \rangle \lambda_1^k(t) \mathbf{r}_1 + \sum_{i=2}^{K'} q_i(k) \langle \mathbf{l}_i, \mathbf{x} \rangle \lambda_i^k(t) \mathbf{r}_i, \qquad (4.13)$$

where the $q_i(k)$ are polynomials in k ($q_i(k) \equiv 1$ when the eigenvalues $\lambda_2, \ldots, \lambda_K$ are simple). Finally, we observe that we can analytically continue $\lambda_1(t)$ to the complex plane owing to the separation of $\lambda_1(t)$ from the other eigenvalues leading to $\lambda_1(z)$.

Now applying (4.13) to (4.12) and using it in the formula for $N(z, x)$ derived in Theorem 4.1.2 we obtain (for simple $\lambda_i(t)$)

$$N(z, x) = \mathbf{R}^t(z) x[\mathbf{I} - x M(z)]^{-1} \mathbf{U}(z)$$

$$= x \mathbf{R}^t(z) \left(\sum_{k=0}^{\infty} x^k \lambda_1^k(z) \langle \mathbf{l}_1(z), \mathbf{U}(z) \rangle \mathbf{r}_1(z) \right.$$

$$\left. + \sum_{i=2}^{K'} x^k \lambda_i^k(z) \langle \mathbf{l}_i(z), \mathbf{U}(z) \rangle \mathbf{r}_i(z) \right)$$

$$= \frac{x C_1(z)}{1 - x \lambda_1(z)} + \sum_{i=2}^{K'} \frac{x C_i(z)}{1 - x \lambda_i(z)}$$

for some polynomials $C_i(z)$. This representation enables us to apply the Cauchy formula, yielding, as before, for $A < 1$ and a polynomial $B(x)$,

$$N_n(x) := [z^n]N(z,x) = B(x)\rho^{-n}(x)(1 + O(A^n)),$$

where $\rho(x)$ is the smallest root of $1 - x\lambda(z) = 0$, which coincides with the smallest root of $\det(I - xM(x)) = 0$. In the above $A < 1$ since $\lambda_1(z)$ dominates all the other eigenvalues. In the next section we return to this method and discuss it in more depth.

4.2. Generalized string matching via automata

In this section we deal with a general pattern matching problem where the words in $\mathcal{W}$ are of all different lengths, that is, $\mathcal{W} = \bigcup_{i=1}^{d} \mathcal{W}_i$ such that $\mathcal{W}_i$ is a subset of $\mathcal{A}^{m_i}$ with all m_i different. For the present we keep $\mathcal{W}_0 = \emptyset$ (i.e., there are no forbidden words) but we will consider the case $\mathcal{W}_0 \neq \emptyset$ at the end of the section. We present here a powerful method based on finite automata, i.e., the de Bruijn graph. This approach is very versatile but unfortunately is not as insightful as the combinatorial approach discussed so far.

Our goal is to derive the probability generating function $N_n(x) = \mathbf{E}[x^{O_n(\mathcal{W})}]$ for the number of occurrences in the text of patterns from the set $\mathcal{W}$. We start by building an automaton that scans the text $X_1 X_2 \cdots X_n$ and recognizes occurrences of patterns from $\mathcal{W}$. As a matter of fact, our automaton corresponds to the de Bruijn graph, which we describe in what follows. Let $M = \max\{m_1, \ldots, m_d\} - 1$ and $\mathcal{B} = \mathcal{A}^M$. The de Bruijn automaton is built over the state space $\mathcal{B}$. Let $b \in \mathcal{B}$ and $a \in \mathcal{A}$. Then the transition from state b resulting from the scanning of symbol a of the text is to $\hat{b} \in \mathcal{B}$ such that

$$\hat{b} = b_2 b_3 \cdots b_M a;$$

that is, the leftmost symbol of b is erased and symbol a is appended at the right. We shall denote such a transition as $ba \mapsto \hat{b}$ or $ba \in \mathcal{A}\hat{b}$, since the first symbol of b has been deleted owing to the scanning of symbol a. When scanning a text of length $n - M$ one constructs an associated path of length $n - M$ in the de Bruijn automaton that begins at a state formed by the first M symbols of the text, that is, $b = X_1 X_2 \cdots X_M$. In addition, we denote the edges of the graph by the transition symbol a.

Example 4.2.1. Let $\mathcal{W} = \{ab, aab, aba\}$. Then $M = 2$; the corresponding de Bruijn graph is presented in Figure 4.1.

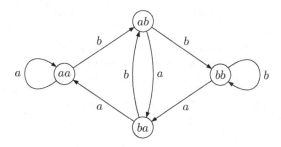

Figure 4.1. The de Bruijn graph for $\mathcal{W} = \{ab, aab, aba\}$.

To record the *number* of pattern occurrences we equip the automaton with a counter $\Delta(b, a)$. When a transition occurs, we increment $\Delta(b, a)$ by the number of occurrences of patterns from $\mathcal{W}$ in the text ba. Since all occurrences of patterns from $\mathcal{W}$ ending with a are contained in text of the form ba, we realize that

$$\Delta(b, a) = O_{M+1}(\mathcal{W}, ba) - O_M(\mathcal{W}, b),$$

where $O_k(\mathcal{W}, u)$ is the number of pattern occurrences in a text u of length k. Having built such an automaton, we construct an $|\mathcal{A}|^M \times |\mathcal{A}|^M$ transition matrix $T(x)$ as a function of a complex variable x such that

$$
\begin{aligned}
[T(x)]_{b,\hat{b}} &:= P(a)x^{\Delta(b,a)} [\![\, ba \in \mathcal{A}\hat{b} \,]\!] \\
&= P(a)x^{O_{M+1}(\mathcal{W},ba)-O_M(\mathcal{W},b)} [\![\, \hat{b} = b_2 b_3 \cdots b_M a \,]\!],
\end{aligned}
\tag{4.14}
$$

where Iverson's bracket convention is used:

$$
[\![B]\!] = \begin{cases} 1 & \text{if the property } B \text{ holds,} \\ 0 & \text{otherwise.} \end{cases}
$$

Example 4.2.2. Let us consider the same set of words as in Example 4.2.1, that is, $\mathcal{W} = \{ab, aab, aba\}$. The transition matrix $T(x)$ is shown below:

$$
T(x) = \begin{array}{c} \\ aa \\ ab \\ ba \\ bb \end{array} \begin{array}{cccc} aa & ab & ba & bb \end{array} \\
\begin{pmatrix}
P(a) & P(b)\,x & 0 & 0 \\
0 & 0 & P(a)\,x^2 & P(b) \\
P(a) & P(b) & 0 & 0 \\
0 & 0 & P(a) & P(b)
\end{pmatrix}
$$

Next, we extend the above construction to scan a text of length $k \geq M$. By the combinatorial properties of matrix products, the entry of index $b, \hat{b}$ of the matrix product $\mathrm{T}^k(x)$ accumulates all terms corresponding to starting in state b and ending in state $\hat{b}$ and records the total number of occurrences of patterns $\mathcal{W}$ found upon scanning the last k letters of the text. Therefore,

$$\left[\mathrm{T}^k(x)\right]_{b,\hat{b}} = \sum_{v \in \mathcal{A}^k} P(v)\, x^{O_{M+k}(\mathcal{W},bv) - O_M(\mathcal{W},b)}. \tag{4.15}$$

Now define a vector $\mathbf{x}(x)$ indexed by b as

$$[\mathbf{x}(x)]_b = P(b)\, x^{O_M(\mathcal{W},b)}.$$

Then, the summation of all the entries of the row vector $\mathbf{x}(x)^t \mathrm{T}^k(x)$ is achieved by means of the vector $\mathbf{1} = (1, \ldots, 1)$, so that the quantity $\mathbf{x}(x)^t \mathrm{T}^k(x)\mathbf{1}$ represents the probability generating function of $O_{k+M}(\mathcal{W})$ taken over all texts of length $M + k$; this is seen that in fact

$$\mathbf{E}[x^{O_n(\mathcal{W})}] = \sum_v P(v) x^{O_n(\mathcal{W},v)}.$$

Now setting $n = M + k$ we can prove the following theorem.

Theorem 4.2.3. *Consider a general pattern $\mathcal{W} = (\mathcal{W}_1, \ldots, \mathcal{W}_d)$ with $M = \max\{m_1, \ldots, m_d\} - 1$. Let $\mathrm{T}(x)$ be the transition matrix defined as*

$$[\mathrm{T}(x)]_{b,\hat{b}} := P(a) x^{O_{M+1}(\mathcal{W},ba) - O_M(\mathcal{W},b)} [\![\, \hat{b} = b_2 b_3 \cdots b_M a \,]\!],$$

where $b, \hat{b} \in \mathcal{A}^M$ and $a \in \mathcal{A}$. Then

$$N_n(x) = \mathbf{E}[x^{O_n(\mathcal{W})}] = \mathbf{b}^t(x)\mathrm{T}^n(x)\mathbf{1} \tag{4.16}$$

where $\mathbf{b}^t(x) = \mathbf{x}^t(x)\mathrm{T}^{-M}(x)$. Also,

$$N(z,x) = \sum_{n \geq 0} N_n(x) z^n = \mathbf{b}^t(x)(\mathsf{I} - x\mathrm{T}(x))^{-1}\mathbf{1} \tag{4.17}$$

for $|z| < 1$.

Let us now return for a moment to the reduced pattern case discussed in the previous section and compare the expression (4.17) given here with expression (4.6) of Theorem 4.1.2, which we repeat below:

$$N(z,x) = \mathrm{R}^t(z)x(\mathsf{I} - x\mathsf{M}(z))^{-1}\mathsf{U}(z).$$

Although there is a striking resemblance of these formulas they are actually quite different. In (4.6) $M(z)$ is a matrix representing generating functions of languages $\mathcal{M}_{ij}$, while $T(x)$ is a function of x and is the transition matrix of the associated de Bruijn graph. Nevertheless, the eigenvalue method discussed in the first section of this chapter can be directly applied to derive the limit laws of $O_n(\mathcal{W})$ for a general set of patterns $\mathcal{W}$. We shall discuss it next.

To study the asymptotics of $O_n(\mathcal{W})$ we need to estimate the growth of $T^n(x)$, which is governed by the growth of the largest eigenvalue as we have already seen in the previous sections. Here, however, the situation is a little more complicated since the matrix $T(x)$ is irreducible but not necessary primitive. To be more precise, $T(x)$ is *irreducible* if its associated de Bruijn graph is strongly connected, while for the *primitivity* of $T(x)$ we require that the greatest common divisor of the cycle weights of the de Bruijn graph is equal to 1.

Let us first verify irreducibility of $T(x)$. As is easy to check, the matrix is irreducible since for any $g \geq M$ and $b, \hat{b} \in \mathcal{A}^M$ there are two words $w, v \in \mathcal{A}^g$ such that $bw = v\hat{b}$ (e.g., for $g = M$ one can take $w = \hat{b}$ and $v = b$). Thus $T^g(x) > 0$ for $x > 0$ which is sufficient for irreducibility.

Let us now have a closer look at the primitivity of $T(x)$. We start with a precise definition. Let $\psi(b, \hat{b}) := \Delta(ba)$ where $ba \mapsto \hat{b}$ is the counter value for a transition b to $\hat{b}$. Let $\mathcal{C}$ be a cycle in the associated de Bruijn graph. Define the total weight of the cycle $\mathcal{C}$ as

$$\psi(\mathcal{C}) = \sum_{b, \hat{b} \in \mathcal{C}} \psi(b, \hat{b}).$$

Finally, we set $\psi_\mathcal{W} = \gcd(\psi(\mathcal{C}) : \mathcal{C} \text{ is a cycle})$. If $\psi_\mathcal{W} = 1$ then we say the $T(x)$ is primitive.

Example 4.2.1 (*continued*). Consider again the matrix $T(x)$ and its associated graph shown in Figure 4.1. There are six cycles with respective weights $0, 3, 2, 0, 0, 1$; therefore $\psi_\mathcal{W} = 1$ and $T(x)$ is primitive. Consider now another matrix

$$T(x) = \begin{pmatrix} P(a) & P(b)\,x^4 \\ P(a)\,x^2 & P(b)\,x^3 \end{pmatrix}.$$

This time there are three cycles with weights $0, 6$, and 3, and $\psi_\mathcal{W} = 3$. The matrix is not primitive. Observe that the characteristic polynomial $\lambda(x)$ of this matrix is a polynomial in x^3. ∎

Observe that the diagonal elements of $T^k(x)$ (i.e., its trace) are polynomials in x^ℓ if and only if ℓ divides $\psi_\mathcal{W}$; therefore, the characteristic polynomial $\det(z\mathbf{I} - T(x))$ of $T(x)$ is a polynomial in $u^{\psi_\mathcal{W}}$. Indeed, it is known that for any matrix

A

$$\det(I - A) = \exp\left(\sum_{k \geq 0} -\frac{\mathrm{Tr}[A^k]}{k}\right)$$

where $\mathrm{Tr}[A]$ is the trace of A.

The asymptotic behavior of the generating function $N_n(x) = \mathbf{E}[x^{O_n(\mathcal{W})}]$, and hence $O_n(\mathcal{W})$, depends on the growth of $\mathrm{T}^n(x)$. The next lemma summarizes some useful properties of $\mathrm{T}(x)$ and its eigenvalues. For a matrix $\mathrm{T}(x)$ of dimension $|\mathcal{A}|^M \times |\mathcal{A}|^M$ we denote by $\lambda_j(x)$, for $j = 1, \ldots, R = |\mathcal{A}^M|$, its eigenvalues and we assume that $|\lambda_1(x)| \geq |\lambda_2(x)| \geq \cdots \geq |\lambda_R(x)|$. To simplify the notation, we often drop the index of the largest eigenvalue, writing $\lambda(x) := \lambda_1(x)$. Observe that $\varrho(x) = |\lambda(x)|$ is known as the *spectral radius* and is given by

$$\varrho(x) = \lim_{n \to \infty} \| \mathrm{T}^n(x) \|^{1/n}$$

where $\| \cdot \|$ is any matrix norm.

Lemma 4.2.4.   *Let $\mathcal{G}_M(\mathcal{W})$ and $\mathrm{T}(x)$ denote, respectively, the de Bruijn graph and its associated matrix defined in (4.14), for a general pattern $\mathcal{W}$. Assume $P(\mathcal{W}) > 0$.*

(i) *For $x > 0$ the matrix $\mathrm{T}(x)$ has a unique dominant eigenvalue $\lambda(x)$ ($> \lambda_j(x)$ for $j = 2, \ldots, |\mathcal{A}^M|$) that is strictly positive and a dominant eigenvector $\mathbf{r}(x)$ whose entries are all strictly positive. Furthermore, there exists a complex neighborhood of the real positive axis on which the mappings $u \to \lambda(x)$ and $u \to \mathbf{r}(x)$ are well defined and analytic.*

(ii) *Define $\Lambda(s) := \log \lambda(e^s)$ for complex s. For real s the function $s \to \Lambda(s)$ is strictly increasing and strictly convex. In addition,*

$$\Lambda(0) = 1, \qquad \Lambda'(0) = P(\mathcal{W}) > 0, \qquad \Lambda''(0) := \sigma^2(\mathcal{W}) > 0.$$

(iii) *For any $\theta \in (0, 2\pi)$ and t real $\varrho(te^{i\theta}) \leq \varrho(t)$.*

(iv) *For any $\theta \in (0, 2\pi)$, if $\psi_{\mathcal{W}} = 1$ then for t real $\varrho(te^{i\theta}) < \varrho(t)$; otherwise $\psi_{\mathcal{W}} = d > 1$ and $\varrho(te^{i\theta}) = \varrho(t)$ if and only if $\theta = 2k\pi/d$.*

Proof. We first prove (i). Take $x > 0$ real and positive. Then the matrix $\mathrm{T}(x)$ has positive entries, and for any exponent $g \geq M$ the gth power of $\mathrm{T}(x)$ has strictly positive entries, as shown above (see the irreducibility of $\mathrm{T}(x)$). Therefore, by the Perron–Frobenius theorem there exists an eigenvalue $\lambda(x)$ that dominates strictly all the others. Moreover, it is simple and strictly positive. In other words, one has

$$\lambda(x) := \lambda_1(x) > |\lambda_2(x)| \geq |\lambda_3(x)| \geq \cdots .$$

Furthermore, the corresponding eigenvector $\mathbf{r}(x)$ has all its components strictly positive. Since the dominant eigenvalue is separate from the other eigenvalues, by perturbation theory there exists a complex neighborhood of the positive real axis where the functions $x \to \lambda(x)$ and $x \to \mathbf{r}(x)$ are well-defined and analytic. Moreover, $\lambda(x)$ is an algebraic function since it satisfies the characteristic equation $\det(\lambda\mathsf{I} - \mathsf{T}(x)) = 0$.

We now prove part (ii). The increasing property for $\lambda(x)$ (and thus for $\Lambda(s)$) is a consequence of the fact that if A and B are nonnegative irreducible matrices such that $A_{i,j} \geq B_{i,j}$ for all (i,j), then the spectral radius of A is larger than the spectral radius of B.

For the convexity of $\Lambda(s)$ it is sufficient to prove that, for $u, v > 0$,

$$\lambda(\sqrt{uv}) \leq \sqrt{\lambda(u)}\sqrt{\lambda(v)}.$$

Since eigenvectors are defined up to a constant, one can always choose eigenvectors $\mathbf{r}(\sqrt{uv})$, $\mathbf{r}(u)$, and $\mathbf{r}(v)$ such that

$$\max_i \frac{r_i(\sqrt{uv})}{\sqrt{r_i(u)\,r_i(v)}} = 1.$$

Suppose that this maximum is attained at some index i. We denote by P_{ij} the coefficient at u in $\mathsf{T}(u)$, that is, $P_{ij} = [u^\psi][\mathsf{T}(u)]_{ij}$. By the Cauchy-Schwarz inequality we have

$$\lambda(\sqrt{uv})r_i(\sqrt{uv}) = \sum_j P_{ij}\left(\sqrt{uv}\right)^{\psi(i,j)} r_j(\sqrt{uv})$$

$$\leq \sum_j P_{ij}(\sqrt{uv})^{\psi(i,j)}\sqrt{r_j(u)\,r_j(v)}$$

$$\leq \left(\sum_j P_{ij}\,u^{\psi(i,j)}\,r_j(u)\right)^{1/2}\left(\sum_j P_{ij}\,v^{\psi(i,j)}\,r_j(v)\right)^{1/2}$$

$$= \sqrt{\lambda(u)}\sqrt{\lambda(v)}\,\sqrt{r_i(u)\,r_i(v)},$$

which implies the convexity of $\Lambda(s)$. To show that $\Lambda(s)$ is strictly convex, we argue as follows: Observe that for $u = 1$ the matrix $\mathsf{T}(u)$ is stochastic, hence $\lambda(1) = 1$ and $\Lambda(0) = 0$. As we shall see below, the mean and the variance of $O_n(\mathcal{W})$ are asymptotically equal to $n\Lambda'(0)$ and $n\Lambda''(0)$, respectively. From the formulation of the lemma, we conclude that $\Lambda'(0) = P(\mathcal{W}) > 0$ and $\Lambda''(0) = \sigma^2(\mathcal{W}) > 0$. Therefore, $\Lambda'(s)$ and $\Lambda''(s)$ cannot be always zero and (since they are analytic) they cannot be zero on any interval. This implies that $\Lambda(s)$ is strictly increasing and strictly convex.

We now establish part (iii). For $|x| = 1$, and t real and positive, consider two matrices $T(t)$ and $T(xt)$. From (i) we know that for $T(t)$ there exists a dominant strictly positive eigenvalue $\lambda := \lambda(t)$ and a dominant eigenvector $\mathbf{r} := \mathbf{r}(t)$ whose entries r_j are all strictly positive. Consider an eigenvalue ν of $T(xt)$ and its corresponding eigenvector $s := s(x)$. Denote by v_j the ratio s_j/r_j. One can always choose $\mathbf{r}$ and s such that $\max_{1 \le j \le R} |v_j| = 1$. Suppose that this maximum is attained for some index i. Then

$$|\nu s_i| = \left| \sum_j P_{ij} (xt)^{\psi(i,j)} s_j \right| \le \sum_j P_{ij} t^{\psi(i,j)} r_j = \lambda r_i. \tag{4.18}$$

We conclude that $|\nu| \le \lambda$, and part (iii) is proven.

Now we deal with part (iv). Suppose now that the equality $|\nu| = \lambda$ holds. Then, the inequalities in (4.18) become equalities. First, for all indices ℓ such that $P_{i,\ell} \ne 0$, we deduce that $|s_\ell| = r_\ell$ and v_ℓ has modulus 1. For these indices ℓ, we have the same equalities in (4.18) as for the index i. Finally, the transitivity of the de Bruijn graph entails that each complex v_j is of modulus 1. The converse of the triangular inequality shows that for every edge $(i, j) \in \mathcal{G}_M(\mathcal{W})$ we have

$$u^{\psi(i,j)} v_j = \frac{\nu}{\lambda} v_i,$$

and for any cycle $\mathcal{C}$ of length L we conclude that

$$\left(\frac{\nu}{\lambda} \right)^L = u^{\psi(\mathcal{C})}.$$

However, for any pattern $\mathcal{W}$ there exists a cycle $\mathcal{C}$ of length 1 with weight $\psi(\mathcal{C}) = 0$, as is easy to see. This proves that $\nu = \lambda$ and that $u^{\psi(\mathcal{C})} = 1$ for any cycle $\mathcal{C}$. If $\psi_\mathcal{W} = \gcd(\psi(\mathcal{C}), \mathcal{C} \text{ cycle}) = 1$, then $u = 1$ and $\varrho(te^{i\theta}) < \varrho(t)$ for $\theta \in (0, 2\pi)$.

Suppose now that $\psi_\mathcal{W} = d > 1$. Then the characteristic polynomial and the dominant eigenvalue $\lambda(v)$ are functions of v^d. The lemma is proved. ∎

Lemma 4.2.4 provides the main technical support to prove the forthcoming results in particular, to establish the asymptotic behavior of $T^n(x)$ for large n. Indeed, our starting point is (4.17), to which we apply the spectral decomposition in (4.13) to conclude that

$$N(z, x) = \frac{c(x)}{1 - z\lambda(x)} + \sum_{i \ge 2} \frac{c_i(x)}{(1 - z\lambda_i(x))^{\alpha_i}},$$

where $\alpha_i \geq 1$ are integers. In the above, $\lambda(x)$ is the dominant eigenvalue while $|\lambda_i(x)| < \lambda(x)$ are the other eigenvalues and $c_i(x)$ are polynomials. The numerator of the first term is the expression $c(x) = \mathbf{b}^t(x)\langle \mathbf{l}(x), \mathbf{1}\rangle\mathbf{r}(x)$, where $\mathbf{l}(x)$ and $\mathbf{r}(x)$ are the left and the right dominant eigenvectors and $\mathbf{b}^t(x)$ was defined after (4.16). Then Cauchy's coefficient formula implies that

$$N_n(x) = c(u)\lambda^n(x)(1 + O(A^n)) \tag{4.19}$$

for some $A < 1$. Equivalently, the moment generating function $\mathbf{E}[e^{sO_n(\mathcal{W})}]$ of $O_n(\mathcal{W})$ is given by the following uniform approximation in a neighborhood of $s = 0$:

$$\mathbf{E}[e^{sO_n(\mathcal{W})}] = d(s)\lambda^n(e^s)(1 + O(A^n)) = d(s)\exp\left(n\Lambda(s)\right)(1 + O(A^n)) \tag{4.20}$$

where $d(s) = c(e^s)$ and $\Lambda(s) = \log\lambda(e^s)$.

There is another, more general, derivation of (4.19). Observe that the spectral decomposition of $\mathrm{T}(x)$ when x lies in a sufficiently small complex neighborhood of any compact subinterval of $(0, +\infty)$ is of the form

$$\mathrm{T}(x) = \lambda(x)\mathrm{Q}(x) + \mathrm{R}(x) \tag{4.21}$$

where $\mathrm{Q}(x)$ is the projection onto the dominant eigensubspace and $\mathrm{R}(x)$ is a matrix whose spectral radius equals $|\lambda_2(x)|$. Therefore,

$$\mathrm{T}^n(x) = \lambda^n(x)\mathrm{Q}(x) + \mathrm{R}^n(x)$$

leads to the estimate (4.19). The next result follows immediately from (4.20).

Theorem 4.2.5. *Let* $\mathcal{W} = (\mathcal{W}_0, \mathcal{W}_1, \ldots, \mathcal{W}_d)$ *be a generalized pattern, with* $\mathcal{W}_0 = \emptyset$, *generated by a memoryless source. For large* n

$$\mathbf{E}[O_n(\mathcal{W})] = n\Lambda'(0) + O(1) = nP(\mathcal{W}) + O(1), \tag{4.22}$$
$$\mathrm{Var}[O_n(\mathcal{W})] = n\Lambda''(0) + O(1) = n\sigma^2(\mathcal{W}) + O(1), \tag{4.23}$$

where $\Lambda(s) = \log\lambda(e^s)$ *and* $\lambda(u)$ *is the largest eigenvalue of* $\mathrm{T}(u)$. *Furthermore,*

$$P(O_n(\mathcal{W}) = 0) = C\lambda^n(0)(1 + O(A^n)),$$

where $C > 0$ *is a constant and* $A < 1$.

Now we establish limit laws, starting with the central limit law and the corresponding local limit law.

Theorem 4.2.6. *Under the same assumption as for Theorem 4.2.5, the following holds:*

$$\sup_{\xi \in B} \left| P\left(\frac{O_n(\mathcal{W}) - nP(\mathcal{W})}{\sigma(\mathcal{W})\sqrt{n}} \leq \xi \right) - \frac{1}{\sqrt{2\pi}} \int_{-\infty}^{\xi} e^{-t^2/2} \, dt \right| = O\left(\frac{1}{\sqrt{n}} \right), \quad (4.24)$$

where B is a bounded real interval.

Proof. The uniform asymptotic expansion (4.20) of a sequence of moment generating functions is known as a quasi-powers approximation. Then an application of the classical Levy continuity theorem leads to the Gaussian limit law. An application of the Berry–Esseen inequality (see Lemma 1.2.3 of Chapter 1) or Hwang's power law (see Theorem 1.2.4 of Chapter 1) provides the speed of convergence, which is $O(1/\sqrt{n})$. This proves the theorem.   ∎

Finally, we deal with large deviations.

Theorem 4.2.7. *Under the same assumption as for Theorem 4.2.5, let ω_a be a solution of*

$$\omega\lambda'(\omega) = a\lambda(\omega) \qquad\qquad (4.25)$$

for some $a \neq P(\mathcal{W})$, where $\lambda(x)$ is the largest eigenvalue of $\mathrm{T}(x)$. Define the large deviation rate

$$I(a) = a \log \omega_a - \log \lambda(\omega_a). \qquad\qquad (4.26)$$

Then there exists a constant $C > 0$ such that $I(a) > 0$ for $a \neq P(\mathcal{W})$ and

$$\lim_{n\to\infty} \frac{1}{n} \log P\left(O_n(\mathcal{W}) \leq an \right) = -I(x) \qquad \text{if } 0 < x < P(\mathcal{W}) \qquad (4.27)$$

$$\lim_{n\to\infty} \frac{1}{n} \log P\left(O_n(\mathcal{W}) \geq an \right) = -I(x) \qquad \text{if } P(\mathcal{W}) < x < C. \qquad (4.28)$$

Proof. We now establish (4.27). The variable $O_n(\mathcal{W})$ by definition has at most linear growth, and so there exists a constant C such that $O_n(\mathcal{W}) \leq Cn + O(1)$. Let $0 < x < P(\mathcal{W})$. Cauchy's coefficient formula provides the probability

$$P\left(O_n(\mathcal{W}) \leq k = na \right) = \frac{1}{2i\pi} \int_{|x|=r} \frac{N_n(x)}{x^k} \frac{dx}{x(1-x)}.$$

For ease of exposition, we first discuss the case of a primitive pattern. We recall that a pattern is primitive if $\psi_{\mathcal{W}} = \gcd(\psi(\mathcal{C}),\ \mathcal{C}$ is a cycle$) = 1$. The strict domination property expressed in Lemma 4.2.4(iv) for primitive patterns implies that the above integrand is strictly maximal at the intersection of the circle $|x| = r$ and the positive real axis. Near this axis, where the contribution of the integrand is concentrated, the following uniform approximation holds, with $k = na$:

$$\frac{N_n(x)}{x^{na}} = \exp\left(n\left(\log \lambda(x) - a \log x\right)\right)\left(1 + o(1)\right). \tag{4.29}$$

The saddle point equation is then obtained by canceling the first derivative, yielding

$$F(\omega) := \frac{\omega \lambda'(\omega)}{\lambda(\omega)} = a, \tag{4.30}$$

and this equation coincides with (4.25). Note that the function F is exactly the derivative of $\Lambda(s)$ at the point $s := \log \omega$. Since $\Lambda(s)$ is strictly convex, the left-hand side is an increasing function of its argument, as stated in Lemma 4.2.4(ii). Also, we know from this lemma that $F(0) = 0$, $F(1) = P(\mathcal{W})$, while we set $F(\infty) = C$. Thus, for any real a in $(0, C)$, equation (4.30) always admits a unique positive solution, which we denote by $\omega \equiv \omega_a$. Moreover, for $a \neq P(\mathcal{W})$, one has $\omega_a \neq 1$. Since the function

$$f(x) = -\log \frac{\lambda(x)}{x^a} \tag{4.31}$$

(see (4.25)) admits a strict maximum at $x = \omega_a$, this maximum $I(a)$ is strictly positive. Finally, the usual saddle point approximation, as given in Table 3.1, applies and one finds that

$$P\left(\frac{O_n(\mathcal{W})}{n} \leq a\right) = \left(\frac{\lambda(\omega_a)}{\omega_a^a}\right)^n \Theta(n), \tag{4.32}$$

where $\Theta(n)$ is of order $n^{-1/2}$. To see the latter, define $f(x)$ as in (4.31). Then (4.29) becomes

$$\frac{N_n(x)}{x^{na}} = \exp\left(-nf(x)\right)\left(1 + o(1)\right).$$

By a Taylor expansion around the saddle point ω_a we have

$$f(x) = f(\omega_a) + \frac{1}{2}(x - \omega_a)^2 f''(\omega_a) + O((x - \omega_a)^3 f'''(x')),$$

where $f''(\omega_a) > 0$ and

$$\exp(-nf(\omega_a)) = \left(\frac{\lambda(\omega_a)}{\omega_a^a}\right)^n$$

is the first factor in (4.32). Furthermore

$$\Theta(n) := \int \exp\left(-\frac{1}{2}(x - \omega_a)^2 f''(\omega_a)\right) dx = \sqrt{\frac{2\pi}{nf''(\omega_a)}},$$

as expected.

In summary, the large deviation rate is

$$I(a) = -\log \frac{\lambda(\omega_a)}{\omega_a^a} \qquad \text{with} \qquad \frac{\omega_a \lambda'(\omega_a)}{\lambda(\omega_a)} = a$$

as given in the theorem.

In the general case, when the pattern is not primitive, the strict inequality of Lemma 4.2.4(iv) is not satisfied, and several saddle points may be present on the circle $|x| = r$, which would lead to some oscillation. We must, in this case, use the weaker inequality of Lemma 4.2.4(iii), namely, $\varrho(te^{i\theta}) \leq \varrho(t)$, which replaces the strict inequality. However, the factor $(1 - x)^{-1}$ present in the integrand of (4.29) attains its maximum modulus for $|t| = r$ solely at $t = r$. Thus, the contribution of possible saddle points can affect only a fraction of the contribution from $t = r$. Consequently, (4.27) and (4.26) continue to be valid. A similar reasoning provides the right-hand tail estimate, with $I(a)$ still given by (4.26). This completes the proof of (4.27).   ∎

We complete this analysis with a local limit law.

Theorem 4.2.8.   *If* $\mathrm{T}(u)$ *is primitive then*

$$\sup_{\xi \in B} \left| P\left(O_n = nP(\mathcal{W}) + \xi\sigma(\mathcal{W})\sqrt{n}\right) - \frac{1}{\sigma(\mathcal{W})\sqrt{n}} \frac{e^{\xi^2/2}}{\sqrt{2\pi}} \right| = o\left(\frac{1}{\sqrt{n}}\right) \qquad (4.33)$$

where B *is a bounded real interval. Furthermore, under the above additional assumption, one can find constants* σ_a *and* θ_a *such that*

$$P(O_n(\mathcal{W}) = a\mathbf{E}[O_n]) \sim \frac{1}{\sigma_a\sqrt{2\pi n}}, e^{-nI(a)+\theta_a} \qquad (4.34)$$

where $I(a)$ *is defined in (4.26) above.*

Proof Stronger "regularity conditions" are needed in order to obtain local limit estimates. Roughly, one wants to exclude the possibility that the discrete distribution is of a lattice type, supported by a nontrivial sublattice of integers. (For instance, we need to exclude the possibility that $O_n(\mathcal{W})$ is always odd or of the parity of n, and so on.) Observe first that the positivity and irreducibility of the matrix $\mathrm{T}(u)$ is not enough, as shown in Example 4.2.1.

By Lemma 4.2.4 one can estimate the probability distribution of $O_n(\mathcal{W})$ by the saddle point method in the case when $\mathcal{W}$ is primitive. Again, one starts from Cauchy's coefficient integral,

$$P(O_n(\mathcal{W}) = k) = \frac{1}{2i\pi} \int_{|x|=1} N_n(x) \frac{dx}{x^{k+1}}, \qquad (4.35)$$

where k is of the form $k = nP(\mathcal{W}) + \xi\sigma(\mathcal{W})\sqrt{n}$. Property (iv) of Lemma 4.2.4 grants us precisely the fact that any closed arc of the unit circle not containing $x = 1$ brings an exponentially negligible contribution. A standard application of the saddle point technique, given in Table 3.1, then completes the proof of the local limit law of Theorem 4.2.8. The precise large deviation results follow from the local limit result and an application of the method of shift discussed in the proof of Theorem 2.5.4.   ∎

Finally, consider a general pattern drawn from the set $\mathcal{W} = (\mathcal{W}_0, \mathcal{W}_1, \ldots, \mathcal{W}_d)$ with nonempty forbidden set $\mathcal{W}_0$. In this case we study the number of occurrences $O_n(\mathcal{W}|\mathcal{W}_0 = 0)$ of patterns $\mathcal{W}_1, \ldots, \mathcal{W}_d$ under the condition that there is no occurrence in the text of any pattern from $\mathcal{W}_0$.

Fortunately, we can recover almost all the results from our previous analysis after redefining the matrix $\mathbf{T}(x)$ and its de Bruijn graph. We now change (4.14) to

$$[\mathbf{T}(x)]_{b,\hat{b}} := P(a)x^{\Delta(b,a)}[\![\, ba \in \mathcal{A}\hat{b} \text{ and } ba \not\subset \mathcal{W}_0 \,]\!], \qquad (4.36)$$

where $ba \subset \mathcal{W}_0$ means that any *subword* of ba (i.e., part of the word ba) belongs to $\mathcal{W}_0$. In other words we are forcing the matrix $\mathbf{T}(x)$ to be zero at any position that leads to a word containing patterns from $\mathcal{W}_0$, that is, we are eliminating from the de Bruijn graph any transition that contains a forbidden word. Having constructed the matrix $\mathbf{T}(x)$, we can repeat all the previous results; however, it is much harder to find explicit formulas even for the mean and the variance (see Exercise 4.5).

4.3.   Generalized string matching via a language approach

In this section we again study the nonreduced set of patterns $\mathcal{W} = \bigcup_{i=1}^{d} \mathcal{W}_i$ with $\mathcal{W}_0 = \emptyset$; however, here we will often write explicitly $\mathcal{W} = \{w_1, \ldots, w_s\}$ for $s = \sum_{i=1}^{d} m_i$ patterns in $\mathcal{W}$. Our goal is to find the generating function for the number of occurrences, but now focusing more on the multivariate generating function of the vector $\mathbf{O}(\mathcal{W}, v) = (O(w_1, v), \ldots, O(w_s, v))$, where v is a word representing the text and $O(v, w_i)$ counts the number of pattern w_i occurrences in v. We have already used this notation in the last section. More precisely, we introduce the multivariate generating function

$$F(z, \mathbf{x}) = \sum_{v \in \mathcal{A}^*} \pi(v)z^{|v|} \prod_{i=1}^{s} x_i^{O(w_i, v)}, \qquad (4.37)$$

where $\pi(v)$ is a weight function for v. This generalizes our approach from the previous sections. Indeed, if we set $\pi(v) = P(v)$ then the multivariate generating function $F(z, \mathbf{x})$ becomes the probability generating function

$$N(z, \mathbf{x}) = \sum_{v \in \mathcal{A}^*} z^{|v|} \mathbf{E}[\mathbf{x}^{\mathbf{O}(\mathcal{W}, v)}],$$

where we use the short-hand notation $\mathbf{x}^{\mathbf{j}} = \prod_{i=1}^{s} x_i^{j_r}$. Furthermore, if we set $\pi(v) = 1$ then $F(z, \mathbf{x})$ becomes the enumerative generating function.

In this section we follow Bassino et al. (2012) who proposed a novel approach via languages that directly extends our analyses from previous chapters.

4.3.1. Symbolic inclusion–exclusion principle

We first explain a way of counting pattern occurrences based on the inclusion–exclusion principle. In Chapter 2 we constructed the language $\mathcal{T}_r$, whose words each contain exactly r copies of words from $\mathcal{W}$. When $\mathcal{W}$ is nonreduced such a construction is quite complicated, as seen in the last section. Here we present a new approach that directly generalizes the language approach of Chapter 2 and Section 4.1. We shall construct a language $\mathcal{Q}$ that contains *some* occurrences from $\mathcal{W}$ and we shall allow the over-counting of some patterns. We then use the *symbolic inclusion–exclusion principle* to remedy this situation.

We illustrate our ideas with a few examples.

Example 4.3.1. Let us first consider a single pattern $w = aaa$ and let the text be represented by a single word $v = aaaa$. Observe that w may occur in the following three situations: $[aaa]a$, $a[aaa]$ and $[aa[a]aa]$, where we indicate the pattern occurrence by $[aaa]$. Observe that in the third case, two occurrences of $w = aaa$ overlap. Well, clearly this last case captures all we need but it is much easier to describe the three cases together. For this we introduce informally a language, called a *cluster* $\mathcal{C}$, that describes the situation in which several pattern occurrences overlap, one after another, without any gap between patterns (e.g., $[aa[a]aa]$ is a cluster). Then the three situations can be described by the following language:

$$\mathcal{Q} = \{\mathcal{C}\mathcal{A}, \mathcal{A}\mathcal{C}, \mathcal{C}\}$$

where $\mathcal{A}$ is the alphabet. The generating function of $\mathcal{Q}$ with $\pi(v) = 1$ is

$$Q(z, x) = z^4(1 + x + x + x^2),$$

where x counts the occurrences and z measures the length of the text. Clearly, this is not the enumerative generating function, which in this case is $F(z, x) = z^4 x^2$. But we observe that $F(z, x) = Q(z, x - 1)$. Here we have taken advantage of the symbolic inclusion–exclusion principle, which we explain next. ∎

As mentioned above, the main technical tool behind this new idea is the symbolic inclusion–exclusion principle. Let $\mathcal{Q}$ be a language in which some patterns may occur (we call them *marked*) while others are unmarked. The point to observe is that this language $\mathcal{Q}$ is easy to construct. The language $\mathcal{T}$ that leads to the generating function $F(z,x)$ is much harder to construct, and for a general pattern $\mathcal{W}$ too complex; in that language we count pattern occurrences *only once*, while in $\mathcal{Q}$ we may use a "marked" pattern or not. The latter is reflected in the generating function by the replacement of x by $1 + x$ (i.e., we set it to 1 if a pattern is unmarked and to x if it is marked). In other words, the symbolic inclusion–exclusion principle reads (see Flajolet and Sedgewick (2009))

$$Q(z,x) = F(z, x + 1), \tag{4.38}$$

or $F(z,x) = Q(z, x - 1)$.

Example 4.3.2. Let us apply the inclusion–exclusion principle that we have just learned to rediscover the probability generating function (2.26) from Chapter 2, which counts the number of occurrences of the only pattern w in the set $\mathcal{W} = \{w\}$ for a memoryless source. In that case we have

$$\mathcal{Q} = \text{SEQ}(\mathcal{A}) \cdot \text{SEQ}\left(w \cdot \text{SEQ}(\mathcal{S} \setminus \varepsilon) \cdot \text{SEQ}(\mathcal{A})\right),$$

where we recall that $\mathcal{S}$ is the autocorrelation set. The expression $w \cdot \text{SEQ}(\mathcal{S} \setminus \varepsilon)$ describes the structure of a cluster of overlapping occurrences. This specification can be translated to the present context using general principles ($\text{SEQ}(\mathcal{L}) \mapsto (1 - L(z,v))^{-1}$ for instance), and yields the bivariate generating function

$$Q(z,x) = \sum_{v \in \mathcal{A}^*} \sum_{\text{marked } w \text{ in } v} \pi(v) z^{|v|} x^{\# \text{ marked occurrences}}$$

$$= \frac{1}{1 - z\pi(\mathcal{A})} \frac{1}{1 - \pi(w) x z^{|w|} \frac{1}{1 - x(S(z) - 1)} \frac{1}{1 - z\pi(\mathcal{A})}}$$

$$= \frac{1}{1 - z\pi(\mathcal{A}) - \frac{x\pi(w) z^{|w|}}{1 - x(S(z) - 1)}}.$$

Then, by the symbolic inclusion–exclusion principle, we find directly that

$$F(z,x) = \sum_{v \in \mathcal{A}^*} \pi(v) z^{|v|} x^{O(v,w)} = Q(z, x - 1).$$

Setting $\pi(w) = P(w)$ we recover (2.26). ∎

4.3.2.   Multivariate generating function

In this section derive the multivariate generating function for a non-reduced set of patterns $\mathcal{W} = \{w_1, \ldots, w_s\}$:

$$F(z, \mathbf{x}) = \sum_{v \in \mathcal{A}^*} \pi(v) z^{|v|} \mathbf{x}^{\mathbf{O}(\mathcal{W}, v)}$$

from which we recover $F(\mathbf{x}) = [z^n] F(z, \mathbf{x})$. In particular, if the weight $\pi(v)$ is equal to the probability $P(v)$ then $F(\mathbf{x})$ becomes the probability generating function

$$N_n(\mathbf{x}) = \mathbf{E} \left[\mathbf{x}^{\mathbf{O}(\mathcal{W}, v)} \right] = [z^n] F(z, \mathbf{x}).$$

We first construct a set $\mathcal{Q}$ containing marked pattern occurrences from $\mathcal{W}$ and then apply the symbolic inclusion–exclusion principle to recover the set $\mathcal{T}_r$ of r pattern occurrences. We illustrate our approach on a simple example.

Example 4.3.3. Let $\mathcal{W} = \{aaa, aba\}$ and let the text be $v = aaaaba$. We recall that a cluster $\mathcal{C}$ is a consecutive text that is "covered" by patterns from $\mathcal{W}$; that is, any two consecutive symbols in a cluster belong to $\mathcal{W}$. For example, $v = [a[aa][a]ba]$ is a cluster. Clearly, there are only two occurrences of $w_1 = aaa$ and one occurrence of $w_2 = aba$. We will see that $N(z, x_1, x_2) = z^6 x_1^2 x_2$ and we can construct it through the inclusion–exclusion principle.

Therefore, we first build a set $\mathcal{Q}$ with some (marked) occurrences of $\mathcal{W}$. This is rather easy, if we know how to construct a cluster $\mathcal{C}$. Granted this and, in symbolic calculus, writing $\mathcal{A}$ for a symbol from the alphabet and $\mathcal{C}$ for a cluster, we have

$$\mathcal{Q} = \{\mathcal{AAAAAA}, \ \mathcal{CAAA}, \ \mathcal{ACAA}, \ \mathcal{AAAC}, \ \mathcal{CC}, \ \mathcal{AC}, \ \mathcal{CCAA}, \ \mathcal{C}\},$$

which translates into the generating function

$$Q(z, x_1, x_2) = z^6 (1 + x_1 + x_1 + x_2 + x_1 x_2 + x_1 x_2 + x_1^2 + x_1^2 x_2).$$

Then the inclusion–exclusion "miracle" produces

$$F(z, x_1, x_2) = Q(z, x_1 - 1, x_2 - 1) = z^6 x_1^2 x_2$$

as required.   ∎

We will follow the above approach to construct the multivariate generating function $F(z, \mathbf{x})$ from the generating function $Q(z, \mathbf{x})$ of a simpler language $\mathcal{Q}$ in which (by over-counting) we mark certain pattern occurrences and ignore others. We need to define more formally a cluster and its generating function.

We call a word v a *clustering word* if any two consecutive positions in v are covered by a word from $W = \{w_1, \ldots, w_s\}$. Position i in the word v is *covered* by a word w if $w = v_{j-|v|+1}^{j}$ for some $j \in \{|w|, \ldots, |v|\}$ and $j - |w| + 1 \leq i \leq j$. The language of all clustering words for a given set W is denoted $\mathcal{K}_W$. Then a cluster $\mathcal{C}$ formed from a clustering word $v \in \mathcal{K}_W$ is a set

$$\mathcal{C} = \{\, \mathcal{P}_w : \ w \in W \,\}$$

containing sets $\mathcal{P}_w$ of occurrence positions covering v, each set corresponding to a particular word w from W. Thus, a cluster is a subset of the occurrence positions in the clustering words. Moreover, every two consecutive positions i and $i + 1$ in v are covered by at least one occurrence of some $w \in W$. More formally,

$$\forall i \in \{1, \ldots, |v|-1\} \quad \exists w \in W, \exists p \in \mathcal{P}_w \quad \text{such that} \quad p - |w| + 1 \leq i < i+1 \leq p.$$

The set of clusters with respect to the clustering words built over W is denoted $\mathcal{L}_W$. Furthermore, $\mathcal{L}_W(v)$ is the subset of $\mathcal{L}_W$ corresponding to the clustering-word $v \in \mathcal{K}_W$. For a cluster $\mathcal{C} = \{\mathcal{P}_w : \ w \in W\}$ we also define $v(\mathcal{C})$, the corresponding (unique) clustering word, and $|\mathcal{C}|_w$, the number of marked occurrences of the word w in the cluster; thus

$$|\mathcal{C}|_w = |\mathcal{P}_w|.$$

Example 4.3.4. Let $W = \{baba, ab\}$ and suppose that we have a clustering word $v = abababa$, so that $v \in \mathcal{K}_W$. Then

$$\mathcal{L}_W(v) = \{\{\mathcal{P}_{ab} = \{2,4,6\}, \mathcal{P}_{baba} = \{5,7\}\}, \{\mathcal{P}_{ab} = \{2,6\}, \mathcal{P}_{baba} = \{5,7\}\},$$
$$\{\mathcal{P}_{ab} = \{2,4\}, \mathcal{P}_{baba} = \{5,7\}\}, \{\mathcal{P}_{ab} = \{2\}, \mathcal{P}_{baba} = \{5,7\}\}\}$$

as is easy to verify.   ∎

With this notation, we can define the generating function of clusters $\xi(z, \mathbf{t})$ as follows:

$$\xi(z, \mathbf{t}) = \sum_{v \in \mathcal{K}_W} \sum_{\mathcal{C} \in \mathcal{L}_W(v)} z^{|v|} \pi(v) t_1^{|\mathcal{C}|_{w_1}} \ldots t_s^{|\mathcal{C}|_{w_s}}, \qquad (4.39)$$

where we recall that $|\mathcal{C}|_w$ is the number of pattern w occurrences in the cluster $\mathcal{C}$.

Now we can describe a language $\mathcal{Q}$ consisting of all text words v with *some* (marked) patterns W. Clearly

$$\mathcal{Q} = SEQ(\mathcal{A} + \mathcal{C})$$

since $v\mathcal{Q}$ can be decomposed into symbols from $\mathcal{A}$ or from the cluster $\mathcal{C}$, as shown in Example 4.3.3. The generating function of this language is

$$Q(z, \mathbf{x}) = \frac{1}{1 - A(z) - \xi(z, \mathbf{x})}.$$

Then, by the symbolic inclusion–exclusion principle we finally arrive at our main result of this subsection, namely the generating function for the word counts,

$$F(z, \mathbf{x}) = \frac{1}{1 - A(z) - \xi(z, \mathbf{x} - \mathbf{1})} \tag{4.40}$$

where $\mathbf{1} = (1, \ldots, 1)$.

This is the starting point for the extraction of the moments and limiting distributions of $O_n(\mathcal{W})$ provided that we can find an expression for the cluster generating function $\xi(z, \mathbf{x})$, which we will do next.

4.3.3. Generating function of a cluster

Thus, in order to complete our analysis we need to derive the generating function of a cluster for $\mathcal{W}$. For a single word $\mathcal{W} = \{w\}$, the generating function of a cluster was presented in Jacquet and Szpankowski (1994), but for a nonreduced set $\mathcal{W}$ we need a major extension. We shall again follow the derivation from Bassino et al. (2012).

In the nonreduced case a word w_i may occur within another word from $\mathcal{W}$. In order to generate the clusters properly we introduce the notion of the *right extension* of a pair of words (h_1, h_2). This notion is similar to the correlation set of two words h_1 and h_2 defined in Section 4.1 but differs in two important aspects: (i) overlapping is not allowed to occur at the beginning of h_1; and (ii) the extension cannot be an empty word, that is, some symbols must be added to the right of h_1. More formally we define it as follows.

Definition 4.3.5 (Right extension set). The right extension set of a pair of words (h_1, h_2) is given by

$$\mathcal{E}_{h_1, h_2} = \{e : \text{ there exists } e' \in \mathcal{A}^+ \text{ such that } h_1 e = e' h_2 \quad \text{with } 0 < |e| < |h_2|\}.$$

For a set of words $\mathcal{W} = \{w_1, \ldots, w_s\}$ we define the right extension matrix as

$$\mathcal{E} = \left(\mathcal{E}_{w_i, w_j}\right)_{1 \leq i, j \leq s}.$$

Note that when h_1 and h_2 have no factor relation (i.e., one word is not a substring of another word) the right extension set $\mathcal{E}_{h_1, h_2}$ is the correlation set of

h_1 to h_2. Furthermore, when $h_1 = h_2$ the set $\mathcal{E}_{h_1,h_2}$ is the autocorrelation set $\mathcal{S} - \varepsilon$ of h_1 (the empty word does not belong to $\mathcal{E}_{h_1,h_2}$).

We now illustrate the right extension set and matrices with a few examples.

Example 4.3.6. (i) For $\mathcal{W} = (ab, aba)$, we have $\mathcal{E} = \begin{pmatrix} \emptyset & \emptyset \\ b & ba \end{pmatrix}$.

(ii) For $\mathcal{W} = (a^3 = aaa, a^7 = aaaaaaa)$, we have

$$\mathcal{E} = \begin{pmatrix} a + aa & a^5 + a^6 \\ a + aa & a + a^2 + a^3 + a^4 + a^5 + a^6 \end{pmatrix}.$$

(iii) For $\mathcal{W} = (aa, ab, ba, baaab)$, we have $\mathcal{E} = \begin{pmatrix} a & b & \emptyset & \emptyset \\ \emptyset & \emptyset & a & aaab \\ a & b & \emptyset & \emptyset \\ \emptyset & \emptyset & a & aaab \end{pmatrix}$.

Having this in mind, we now introduce the right extension graph (see Figure 4.2), in analogy to the de Bruijn graph of the previous section.

Definition 4.3.7 (Right extension graph). Let $\mathcal{W} = \{w_1, \ldots, w_s\}$; the right extension graph $\mathcal{G}_{\mathcal{W}} = (V, E)$ of the set of words $\mathcal{W}$ is the directed labeled graph such that:

(i) the set of vertices is $V = \{\varepsilon\} \cup \mathcal{W}$;

(ii) the set of edges is

$$E = \{\varepsilon \xrightarrow{w} w, \ w \in \mathcal{W}\} \cup \{w \xrightarrow{y} w', \ w, w' \in \mathcal{W} \text{ and } y \in \mathcal{E}(w, w')\}.$$

In order to translate this combinatorial description of clusters into generating functions, we need to introduce two quantities, namely a vector $\mathbf{w}^{\circ}$ and a matrix C. Basically, when a word w_m is a factor of a word w_i it may be marked or remain unmarked during the marking process; the latter induces a term $(1 + t_m)$, where t_m is indeterminate, in the associated multivariate generating function.

Definition 4.3.8 (Inclusion–exclusion formal marking). Let $\mathbf{w} = (w_1, \ldots, w_s)$ be a vector of s words. Then the formal marking of $\mathbf{w}$, denoted by $\mathbf{w}^{\circ}$, is a vector with its ith coordinate element equal to

$$\mathbf{w}_i^{\circ} = \pi(w_i) z^{|w_i|} \prod_{m \neq i} (1 + t_m)^{|w_i|_m},$$

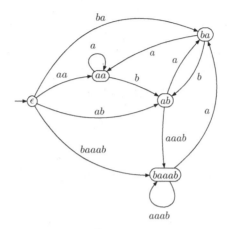

Figure 4.2. Graph $\mathcal{G}_\mathcal{W}$ for $\mathcal{W} = \{aa, ab, ba, baaab\}$. We remark that several paths may correspond to the same labeling. For instance the word $baaab$ corresponds to different paths $\varepsilon \overset{baaab}{\to} baaab$, and $\varepsilon \overset{ba}{\to} ba \overset{a}{\to} aa \overset{a}{\to} aa \overset{b}{\to} ab$.

where $|w_i|_m$ is the number of occurrences of the word w_m in the word w_i. The formal marking of the matrix of right extension sets $\mathcal{E}$ is the matrix $C = \{C_{ij}\}_{i,j=1}^s$, where

$$C_{i,j} = \sum_{e \in \mathcal{E}_{i,j}} \pi(e) z^{|e|} \prod_{m \neq j} (1 + t_m)^{\min(|w_i e|_m - |w_i|_m, |w_j|_m)}. \qquad (4.41)$$

Example 4.3.9. The above definitions are illustrated in Figure 4.2 for $\mathcal{W} = \{aa, ab, ba, baaab\}$. Here

$$\mathcal{E} = \begin{pmatrix} a & b & \emptyset & \emptyset \\ \emptyset & \emptyset & a & aaab \\ a & b & \emptyset & \emptyset \\ \emptyset & \emptyset & a & aaab \end{pmatrix},$$

and

$$C = \begin{pmatrix} z\pi(a) & z\pi(b) & 0 & 0 \\ 0 & 0 & z\pi(a) & z^4\pi(aaab)(1 + t_{ba})(1 + t_{aa})^2(1 + t_{ab}) \\ z\pi(a) & z\pi(b) & 0 & 0 \\ 0 & 0 & z\pi(a) & z^4\pi(aaab)(1 + t_{ba})(1 + t_{aa})^2(1 + t_{ab}) \end{pmatrix}.$$

In the above definition, there is a need for the min operator since when considering the right extension matrix we are only counting factor occurrences that begin and finish within the last occurrence considered (w_j in the definition) and also finish inside the extension; on the contrary, when analyzing a single word w we consider *all* factor occurrences, and we note this particular case by the symbol $\circ$ in superscript.

Example 4.3.6 (*continued*). We now develop Example 4.3.6 further by taking $\pi(a) = \pi(b) = 1$.

(i) For $\mathcal{W} = (ab, aba)$, we have $C = \begin{pmatrix} 0 & 0 \\ z & z^2(1 + t_1) \end{pmatrix}$.

(ii) For $\mathcal{W} = (a^3 = aaa, a^7 = aaaaaaa)$, the matrix C is given by

$$\begin{pmatrix} z + z^2 & (1 + t_1)^5(z^5 + z^6) \\ z + z^2 & (1 + t_1)z + (1 + t_1)^2 z^2 + (1 + t_1)^3 z^3 + (1 + t_1)^4 z^4 + (1 + t_1)^5(z^5 + z^6) \end{pmatrix}$$

as is easy to see. Here the crucial point is to determine which factor occurrences lie within the last occurrence (hence the min operator in (4.41)) and finish within the extension.

(iii) For $\mathcal{W} = (aa, ab, ba, baaab)$ (see Figure 4.2) we have

$$C = \begin{pmatrix} z & z & 0 & 0 \\ 0 & 0 & z & z^4(1 + t_1)^2(1 + t_2)(1 + t_3) \\ z & z & 0 & 0 \\ 0 & 0 & z & z^4(1 + t_1)^2(1 + t_2)(1 + t_3) \end{pmatrix}.$$

With the notation as above we are ready to present our main result of this section, that is, the generating function for clusters.

Theorem 4.3.10. *The generating function $\xi(z, \mathbf{t})$ for the clusters built over $\mathcal{W} = \{w_1, \ldots, w_s\}$ is given by*

$$\xi(z, \mathbf{t}) = \mathbf{w}^\circ \Delta(\mathbf{t}) \cdot (\mathsf{I} - C\Delta(\mathbf{t}))^{-1} \cdot \mathbf{1}, \tag{4.42}$$

where $\mathbf{w} = (w_1, \ldots, w_s)$, $\mathbf{t} = (t_1, \ldots, t_s)$, and $\Delta(\mathbf{t})$ is an $s \times s$ diagonal matrix with entries $t_1, \ldots, t_s$.

Proof. The matrix C is a formal expression of the transition matrix of the graph $\mathcal{G}_\mathcal{W}$ where the vertex ε and its corresponding edges have been removed. Some occurrences of the word w_i (for each $i \in \{1, \ldots, n\}$) are marked with the formal variables t_i in the labels of $\mathcal{G}_\mathcal{W}$. More precisely, a word occurrence w_i obtained when visiting a vertex w_i is marked by the formal variable t_i, and appears in the calculus through the diagonal matrix $\Delta(\mathbf{t})$ in (4.42); in contrast, a factor occurrence can be marked or not (this does not change the path in the graph), hence providing a term of the form $\prod_{m \neq i}(t_m + 1)^k$ where k is the number of possible new occurrences. The first transition from ε to any $w \in \mathcal{W}$ is handled similarly. So the paths with $k+1$ transitions in $\mathcal{G}_{\mathcal{W}}$ starting from ε have generating function

$$\mathbf{w}^\circ \Delta(\mathbf{t}) \cdot (C\Delta(\mathbf{t}))^k \cdot \mathbf{1}.$$

Finally we use the quasi-inverse notation $\sum_{j=0}^{\infty} (C\Delta(\mathbf{t}))^j = (\mathsf{I} - C\Delta(\mathbf{t}))^{-1}$ to complete the proof. ∎

We consider two examples.

Example 4.3.11.   For $\mathcal{W} = \{w\}$, we have

$$\xi(z, t) = \frac{tw^\circ}{1 - tC(z)} = \frac{t\pi(w)z^{|w|}}{1 - t(S(z) - 1)}, \tag{4.43}$$

where $S(z)$ is the autocorrelation polynomial.

Now let $\mathcal{W} = \{w_1, w_2\}$. We can compute explicitly $\xi(z, t_1, t_2)$ by Cramer's rule:

$$\xi(z, t_1, t_2) = \frac{t_1 w_1^\circ + t_2 w_2^\circ - t_1 t_2 \left(w_2^\circ [C_{2,2} - C_{1,2}] + w_2^\circ [C_{1,1} - C_{2,1}]\right)}{1 - t_2 C_{2,2} - t_1 C_{1,1} + t_1 t_2 (C_{1,1} C_{2,2} - C_{2,1} C_{1,2})}, \tag{4.44}$$

and this expression is computable from the right extension matrix of $\{w_1, w_2\}$. ∎

Example 4.3.12.   Let $\mathcal{W} = (a^3, a^7)$. Recall that the right extension matrix $\mathcal{E}$ (see Example 4.3.6(ii)) is:

$$\mathcal{E} = \begin{pmatrix} a + a^2 & a^5 + a^6 \\ a + a^2 & a + a^2 + a^3 + a^4 + a^5 + a^6 \end{pmatrix}.$$

If we take $\pi(w) = 1$ for all words w (the unweighted "enumerative" model where each word has weight 1), we have $\mathbf{w}^\circ = (z^3, (1 + t_1)^5 z^7)$, and

$$C_{1,1} = z + z^2, \quad C_{1,2} = (1 + t_1)^5 (z^5 + z^6), \quad C_{2,1} = z + z^2,$$

$$C_{2,2} = (1 + t_1)z + (1 + t_1)^2 z^2 + (1 + t_1)^3 z^3 + (1 + t_1)^4 z^4 + (1 + t_1)^5 (z^5 + z^6).$$

By substituting these values in (4.44), the generating function $\xi(z, t_1, t_2)$ can be easily computed. ∎

Finally, we observe that when the set $\mathcal{W}$ is reduced, that is, when no word of $\mathcal{W}$ is a factor of another, the clusters are uniquely defined by a path in the graph $\mathcal{G}_\mathcal{W}$. So $\mathbf{w}^\circ$ and C do not depend on any of the variables t_i. Hence, in (4.42), the variables t_i appear only inside $\Delta(\mathbf{t})$. This constitutes another formulation of the result of Goulden and Jackson (1983).

4.3.4. Moments and covariance

In this section we return to the word count $O_n(\mathcal{W})$ and again compute the moments as well as the covariance matrix for a memoryless source. Thus we define

$$\pi(\mathcal{W}) = \sum_{w \in \mathcal{W}} P(w).$$

When considering the *total* number of occurrences from $\mathcal{W}$ we simply set all $x_i = x$ in the cluster generating function. We shall write

$$\Xi(z, x) := \xi(z, x, \ldots, x).$$

Then (4.40) becomes

$$N(z, x) = \frac{1}{1 - z - \Xi(z, x - 1)}$$

with $\Xi(z, 0) = 0$ since $N(z, 1) = 1/(1 - z)$. Setting $\Xi_x(z) = \frac{\partial}{\partial x}\Xi(z, x)\big|_{x=0}$ and $\Xi_{xx}(z) = \frac{\partial^2}{\partial x^2}\Xi(z, x)\big|_{x=0}$ and using basic algebra, we have

$$\sum_{n \geq 0} \mathbf{E}[O_n] z^n = \frac{\partial}{\partial x} N(z, x)\bigg|_{x=1} = \frac{\Xi_x(z)}{(1 - z)^2}$$

$$\sum_{n \geq 0} \mathbf{E}[O_n^2] z^n = \frac{\partial^2}{\partial x^2} N(z, x)\bigg|_{x=1} + \frac{\partial}{\partial x} N(z, x)\big|_{x=1}$$

$$= \frac{2\Xi_x(z)^2}{(1 - z)^3} + \frac{\Xi_{xx}(z) + \Xi_x(z)}{(1 - z)^2}.$$

It is easy to see that $\Xi_x(z) = \sum_{w \in \mathcal{W}} P(w) z^{|w|}$ (for the case of clusters with one and only one marked occurrence). The expression for $\Xi_{xx}(z)$ takes into account that some words of $\mathcal{W}$ are factors of others:

$$\Xi_{xx}(z) = \sum_{u,v \in \mathcal{W}} \left(2P(u)|u|_v z^{|u|} + \sum_{e \in \mathcal{E}_{u,v}} 2P(ue) z^{|ue|} \right),$$

with the convention that $|u|_u = 1$.

In summary, using the above and the Cauchy residue theorem we arrive at

$$\mathbf{E}[O_n] = \sum_{w \in \mathcal{W}} P(w)(n - |w| + 1)$$

$$\frac{1}{n}\text{Var}[O_n] = \sum_{w \in \mathcal{W}} P(w) - \sum_{u,v \in \mathcal{W}} P(u)P(v)(|u| + |v| - 1)$$

$$+ \sum_{u,v \in \mathcal{W}} 2P(u)P(\mathcal{E}_{u,v}) + \sum_{u,v \in \mathcal{W}} 2P(u)|u|_v + o(1).$$

If $\mathcal{W} = \{w\}$ then

$$\lim_{n \to \infty} \frac{1}{n}\text{Var}[O_n] = P(w) + 2P(w)P(\mathcal{E}_{w,w}) - (2|w| - 1)P(w)^2,$$

as already given in Theorem 2.4.1.

Finally, we will compute the covariance matrix for words co-occurrence. We prove the following result.

Theorem 4.3.13. *The normalized asymptotic correlation coefficient of occurrences for two patterns $\mathcal{W}_i$ and $\mathcal{W}_j$ satisfies*

$$\mathbf{Cov}(\mathcal{W}_1, \mathcal{W}_2) = \sum_{\substack{u \in \mathcal{W}_i \\ v \in \mathcal{W}_j}} (P(u)P(\mathcal{E}_{u,v}) + P(v)P(\mathcal{E}_{v,u}) - (|u| + |v| - 1)P(u)P(v))$$

$$(4.45)$$

$$+ P(\mathcal{W}_i \cap \mathcal{W}_j) + \sum_{\substack{u \in \mathcal{W}_i \\ v \in \mathcal{W}_j}} (|u|_v P(u) + |v|_u P(v)) + o(1),$$

with the convention that $|u|_u = 1$.

Proof. Let $\mathcal{U}$ and $\mathcal{V}$ be two sets of words. We first decompose the set $\mathcal{U} \cup \mathcal{V}$ as a direct sum:

$$\mathcal{U} \cup \mathcal{V} = (\mathcal{U} \setminus \mathcal{V}) \cup (\mathcal{V} \setminus \mathcal{U}) \cup (\mathcal{U} \cap \mathcal{V}).$$

In order to ease the notation, we will index the variables in the generating function $\xi(z, \mathbf{x})$ by words, i.e., the variable x_u corresponds to the word u. Then we consider the generating function of clusters for the three disjoint sets $\mathcal{U}' = \mathcal{U} \setminus \mathcal{V}$, $\mathcal{V}' = \mathcal{V} \setminus \mathcal{U}$, and $\mathcal{W} = \mathcal{U} \cap \mathcal{V}$, where $\mathbf{x} = (x_u)_{u \in \mathcal{U} \cup \mathcal{V}}$ with respective variables x_1, x_2, and x_3:

$$\Xi(z, x_1, x_2, x_3) = \xi(z, \mathbf{x})|_{\substack{x_u = x_1 \text{ for } u \in \mathcal{U} \setminus \mathcal{V} \\ x_u = x_2 \text{ for } u \in \mathcal{V} \setminus \mathcal{U} \\ x_u = x_3 \text{ for } u \in \mathcal{U} \cap \mathcal{V}}}, \qquad (4.46)$$

that is, we simply substitute the variables x_1, x_2 and x_3 for the words appearing in each of the three sets.

Let $N(z, x, y)$ be the corresponding generating function counting occurrences. We have, by (4.40), since occurrences in $\mathcal{U} \cap \mathcal{V}$ are marked twice

$$N(z, x, y) = \frac{1}{1 - z - \Xi(z, x - 1, y - 1, xy - 1)}. \tag{4.47}$$

By construction, since $N(z, 1, 1) = 1/1 - z$, we have

$$\Xi(z, 0, 0, 0) = 0.$$

To simplify the notation, we set

$$\Xi_i(z) = \left. \frac{\partial}{\partial t_i} \Xi(z, x_1, x_2, x_3) \right|_{(x_1, x_2, x_3) = (0,0,0)} \qquad \text{for } i = 1, 2, 3,$$

$$\Xi_{ij}(z) = \left. \frac{\partial^2}{\partial x_i \partial x_j} \Xi(z, x_1, x_2, x_3) \right|_{(x_1, x_2, x_3) = (0,0,0)} \qquad \text{for } i, j \in \{1, 2, 3\}.$$

Denoting X_n and Y_n, respectively, as the number of occurrences in $\mathcal{U}$ and $\mathcal{V}$, we obtain by (4.47)

$$\sum_{n \geq 0} \mathbf{E}[X_n] z^n = \left. \left(\frac{\partial}{\partial x} N(z, x, y) \right) \right|_{x=y=1} = \frac{1}{(1 - z)^2} \left(\Xi_1(z) + \Xi_3(z) \right)$$

$$\sum_{n \geq 0} \mathbf{E}[Y_n] z^n = \left. \left(\frac{\partial}{\partial y} N(z, x, y) \right) \right|_{x=y=1} = \frac{1}{(1 - z)^2} \left(\Xi_2(z) + \Xi_3(z) \right),$$

which yields

$$\mathbf{E}[X_n] = \sum_{u \in \mathcal{U}} (n - |u| + 1) P(u), \qquad \mathbf{E}[Y_n] = \sum_{u \in \mathcal{V}} (n - |u| + 1) P(u).$$

Thus we also have

$$\sum_{n \geq 0} \mathbf{E}[X_n Y_n] z^n = \left. \frac{\partial^2}{\partial x \partial y} N(z, x, y) \right|_{x=y=1}$$

$$= 2 \frac{(\Xi_1(z) + \Xi_3(z))(\Xi_2(z) + \Xi_3(z))}{(1 - z)^3}$$

$$+ \frac{\Xi_{12}(z) + \Xi_{13}(z) + \Xi_{23}(z) + \Xi_{33}(z) + \Xi_3(z)}{(1 - z)^2}$$

$$= 2 \frac{\Xi_1(z) \Xi_2(z)}{(1 - z)^3} + \frac{\Xi_{12}(z)}{(1 - z)^2} + 2 \frac{\Xi_3(z)^2}{(1 - z)^3} + \frac{\Xi_{33}(z) + \Xi_3(z)}{(1 - z)^2}$$

$$+ 2 \frac{\Xi_3(z)(\Xi_1(z) + \Xi_2(z))}{(1 - z)^3} + \frac{\Xi_{13}(z) + \Xi_{23}(z)}{(1 - z)^2}.$$

A Taylor expansion at $z = 1$ gives for $i = 1, 2, 3$

$$\Xi_i(z) = \Xi_i(1) - (1 - z)\Xi_i'(1) + o(1 - z)$$

which leads to

$$
\begin{aligned}
\mathbf{E}[X_n Y_n] = &(n + 1)(n + 2)\left(\Xi_1(1) + \Xi_3(1)\right)\left(\Xi_2(1) + \Xi_3(1)\right) \\
&+ (n + 1)\left[\left(\Xi_1'(1) + \Xi_3'(1)\right)\left(\Xi_2(1) + \Xi_3(1)\right)\right. \\
&+ \left(\Xi_1(1) + \Xi_3(1)\right)\left(\Xi_2'(1) + \Xi_3'(1)\right) \\
&\left.+ \Xi_{12}(1) + \Xi_{13}(1) + \Xi_{23}(1) + \Xi_{33}(1) + \Xi_3(1)\right] + o(n).
\end{aligned}
$$

Observe that

$$\Xi_1(1) + \Xi_3(1) = \sum_{u \in \mathcal{U}} P(u),$$

$$\Xi_{13}(1) = \sum_{u \in \mathcal{U} \setminus \mathcal{V}} \sum_{v \in \mathcal{V} \cap \mathcal{U}} \left(P(u)|u|_v + P(u)P(\mathcal{E}_{u,v}) + P(v)|v|_u + P(v)\pi(\mathcal{E}_{v,u})\right).$$

In summary, after some computations we find that

$$
\begin{aligned}
\frac{1}{n}\mathbf{Cov}[X_n, Y_n] = &\sum_{u \in \mathcal{U}} \sum_{v \in \mathcal{V}} \left(P(u)P(\mathcal{E}_{u,v}) + P(v)P(\mathcal{E}_{v,u})\right) \\
&- (|u| + |v| - 1)P(u)\pi(v)) \\
&+ P(\mathcal{U} \cap \mathcal{V}) + \sum_{u \in \mathcal{U}} \sum_{v \in \mathcal{V}} (|u|_v P(u) + |v|_u P(v)) + o(1).
\end{aligned}
$$

Substituting $\mathcal{U}$ and $\mathcal{V}$ respectively by $\mathcal{W}_i$ and $\mathcal{W}_j$ leads to (4.45).   ∎

The limiting distribution of $O_n(\mathcal{W})$ could be derived using the Perron–Frobenius characterization. Extension to the multivariate case, that is, the multivariate central limit theorem for $\mathbf{O}_n(\mathcal{W}) = (O_n(w_1), \ldots, O_n(w_s))$ is possible; however, the computation is quite troublesome because of the need to avoid degenerate cases. Details can be found in Bender and Kochman (1993) and Bassino et al. (2012).

4.4.   Exercises

4.1   Extend the analysis of Chapter 4 to multisets $\mathcal{W}$, that is, to the case where a word w_i may occur several times in $\mathcal{W}$.

4.2   Prove the language relationships (4.1)–(4.4).

4.3   Derive an explicit formula for the constant θ_a in Theorem 4.1.3(iv).

4.4 With the notation of Section 4.2 build the de Bruijn graph for $\mathcal{W} = \{aba, bb, abab, bab, bba\}$ and then construct the matrix $\mathbf{T}(x)$. Finally, derive the mean and the variance of $O_n(\mathcal{W})$ in this case; see Theorem 4.2.5.

4.5 Find explicit formulas for the values of the mean $\mathbf{E}[O_n(\mathcal{W})]$ and the variance $\mathrm{Var}[O_n(\mathcal{W})]$ for the generalized pattern matching discussed in Section 4.2 in the cases where $\mathcal{W}_0 = \emptyset$ and $\mathcal{W}_0 \neq \emptyset$.

4.6 Using the Berry–Esseen inequality, verify the error term $O(1/\sqrt{n})$ in Theorem 4.2.6.

4.7 Derive explicit formulas for the constants σ_a and θ_a in (4.34) to be found in Theorem 4.2.8.

4.8 Using the Berry–Esseen inequality carry out detailed derivations to establish the error term in Theorem 4.2.6.

4.9 Enumerate the (d, k) sequences over a non binary alphabet (i.e., generalize the analysis of Section 3.1).

4.10 With the notation of Section 4.3.4 verify the following two identities:

$$\Xi_x(z) = \sum_{w \in \mathcal{W}} P(w) z^{|w|},$$

$$\Xi_{xx}(z) = \sum_{u,v \in \mathcal{W}} \left(2P(u)|u|_v z^{|u|} + \sum_{e \in \mathcal{E}_{u,v}} 2P(ue) z^{|ue|} \right).$$

Bibliographical notes

The generalized string matching problem discussed here was introduced and analyzed in Bender and Kochman (1993). However, our presentation follows a different path simplifying previous analyses. Among others, Bender and Kochman (1993) established a general (conditional) central limit law and local limit laws. Unfortunately, the explanations in Bender and Kochman (1993) lacked details and were expressed, without any references to de Bruijn graphs or correlation sets. Thus, in this chapter we have aimed to simplify and modernize the findings of Bender and Kochman (1993).

An analysis of string matching over a reduced set of patterns appears in Régnier and Szpankowski (1998b) (see also Guibas and Odlyzko (1981b)). An automaton approach to motif finding was proposed in Nicodème, Salvy, and Flajolet (2002). Section 4.2 is based on Flajolet et al. (2006). Section 4.3 is based on the novel approach proposed in Bassino et al. (2012) (see also Bassino, Clement, Fayolle, and Nicodeme (2007)). The language approach to two general patterns was also discussed in Denise and Régnier (2004) with an application to statistical significance of over-represented oligonucleotides presented in Denise et al. (2001). The cluster approach for a single pattern was first analyzed in Jacquet and Szpankowski (1994).

The Perron–Frobenius theory and the spectral decomposition of matrices can be found in Gantmacher (1959), Karlin and Taylor (1975) and Kato (1980); see also Flajolet and Sedgewick (2009) and Szpankowski (2001). Operator theory is discussed in Kato (1980).

The symbolic inclusion–exclusion principle presented here is taken from Flajolet and Sedgewick (2009), which follows the encyclopedic treatise of Goulden and Jackson (1983).

CHAPTER 5

Subsequence String Matching

As explained at the start of Chapter 4, in the generalized string matching problem, given a pattern $\mathcal{W}$ one searches for some or all occurrences of $\mathcal{W}$ as a block of consecutive symbols in a text. Here we concentrate on *subsequence string matching*. In this case, we are searching for a given pattern $\mathcal{W} = w_1 w_2 \cdots w_m$ in the text $X = x_1 x_2 \cdots x_n$ as a *subsequence*, that is, we are looking for indices $1 \le i_1 < i_2 < \cdots < i_m \le n$ such that $x_{i_1} = w_1$, $x_{i_2} = w_2$, ..., $x_{i_m} = w_m$. We also say that the word $\mathcal{W}$ is "hidden" in the text; thus we call this the *hidden pattern* problem. For example, date occurs as a subsequence in the text hidden pattern, in fact four times but not even once as a string of consecutive symbols.

More specifically, we allow the possibility of imposing an additional set of constraints $\mathcal{D}$ on the indices $i_1, i_2, \ldots, i_m$ to record a valid subsequence occurrence. For a given set of integers d_j ($d_j \geq 1$, possibly $d_j = \infty$), one should have $(i_{j+1} - i_j) \leq d_j$. More formally, the hidden pattern specification is determined by a pair $(\mathcal{W}, \mathcal{D})$ where $\mathcal{W} = w_1 \cdots w_m$ is a word of length m and the *constraint* $\mathcal{D} = (d_1, \ldots, d_{m-1})$ satisfies $1 \leq d_i \leq \infty$ for all $1 \leq i \leq m$.

The case when all d_j are infinite is called the (fully) *unconstrained problem*. When all d_j are finite, we speak of the (fully) *constrained* problem. In particular, the case where all d_j equal 1 reduces to the exact string matching problem. Furthermore, observe that when all $d_j < \infty$ (the case of a fully constrained problem), the problem can be treated as generalized string matching, discussed in Chapter 4. In this case the general pattern $\mathcal{W}$ is a set consisting of all words satisfying a constraint $\mathcal{D}$. However, when even one d_j is infinite the techniques discussed so far are not well suited to handle the situation. Therefore, in this chapter we develop new methods that facilitate such analysis.

5.1. Problem formulation

If an m-tuple $I = (i_1, i_2, \ldots, i_m)$, $1 \leq i_1 < i_2 < \cdots < i_m$, satisfies the constraint $\mathcal{D}$ with $i_{j+1} - i_j \leq d_j$ then it is called a *position tuple*. Let $\mathcal{P}_n(\mathcal{D})$ be the set of all positions subject to the separation constraint $\mathcal{D}$, and furthermore satisfying $i_m \leq n$. Also let $\mathcal{P}(\mathcal{D}) = \bigcup_n \mathcal{P}_n(\mathcal{D})$. An *occurrence* of the pattern $\mathcal{W}$ subject to the constraint $\mathcal{D}$ is a pair (I, X) formed by a position $I = (i_1, i_2, \ldots, i_m)$ of $\mathcal{P}_n(\mathcal{D})$ and a text $X = x_1 x_2 \cdots x_n$ for which $x_{i_1} = w_1, x_{i_2} = w_2, \ldots, x_{i_m} = w_m$.

Example 5.1.1. If $\#$ represents a don't-care symbol and its subscript denotes a strict upper bound on the length of the associated gap, a typical pattern may look like this

$$ab\#_2 r\# ac\# a\# d\#_4 a\# br\# a \tag{5.1}$$

where $\#$ equals $\#_\infty$ and $\#_1$ is omitted; that is, ab should occur first contiguously, followed by r with a gap of less than two symbols, followed anywhere later in the text by ac, etc.   ∎

Observe that an occurrence of a pattern can be viewed as a text in which the positions at which the pattern occurs have been distinguished in some way. The number Ω of occurrences of a pattern $\mathcal{W}$ in the text X as a subsequence subject to the constraint $\mathcal{D}$ is then a sum of characteristic variables:

$$\Omega(X) = \sum_{I \in \mathcal{P}_{|X|}(\mathcal{D})} Z_I(X), \tag{5.2}$$

where
$$Z_I(X) := [\![\mathcal{W} \text{ occurs at position } I \text{ in } X]\!].$$
When the text X is of length n, we often write $\Omega_n := \Omega(X)$.

In order to proceed we need to introduce the important notion of blocks and aggregates. In the general case we assume that the subset $\mathcal{F}$ of indices j for which d_j is finite $(d_j < \infty)$ has cardinality $m - b$ with $1 \leq b \leq m$. The two extreme values of b, namely, $b = m$ and $b = 1$, describe the (fully) unconstrained and the (fully) constrained problem, respectively. Thus, the subset $\mathcal{U}$ of indices j for which d_j is unbounded $(d_j = \infty)$ has cardinality $b - 1$. It then separates the pattern $\mathcal{W}$ into b independent subpatterns called blocks and denoted by $\mathcal{W}_1, \mathcal{W}_2, \ldots, \mathcal{W}_b$. All the possible d_j "inside" any $\mathcal{W}_r$ are finite and form a subconstraint $\mathcal{D}_r$, so that a general hidden pattern specification $(\mathcal{W}, \mathcal{D})$ is equivalently described as a b-tuple of fully constrained hidden patterns $((\mathcal{W}_1, \mathcal{D}_1), (\mathcal{W}_2, \mathcal{D}_2), \ldots, (\mathcal{W}_b, \mathcal{D}_b))$.

Example 5.1.1 (*continued*). Consider again
$$ab\#_2 r\#ac\#a\#d\#_4 a\#br\#a,$$
in which one has $b = 6$, the six blocks being
$$\mathcal{W}_1 = a\#_1 b\#_2 r, \quad \mathcal{W}_2 = a\#_1 c, \quad \mathcal{W}_3 = a, \quad \mathcal{W}_4 = d\#_4 a, \quad \mathcal{W}_5 = b\#_1 r, \quad \mathcal{W}_6 = a.$$

In the same way, an occurrence position $I = (i_1, i_2, \ldots, i_m)$ of $\mathcal{W}$ subject to the constraint $\mathcal{D}$ gives rise to b suboccurrences, $I^{[1]}, I^{[2]}, \ldots, I^{[b]}$, the rth term $I^{[r]}$ representing an occurrence of $\mathcal{W}_r$ subject to constraint $\mathcal{D}_r$. The rth block $B^{[r]}$ is the closed segment whose end points are the extremal elements of $I^{[r]}$ and the *aggregate* of position I, denoted by $\alpha(I)$, is the collection of these b blocks.

Example 5.1.2. Consider the pattern from Example 5.1.1, and assume the occurrence position tuple is
$$I = (6, 7, 9, 18, 19, 22, 30, 33, 50, 51, 60).$$
This satisfies the constraint $\mathcal{D}$ and gives rise to six subpositions,

$$\overbrace{(6,7,9)}^{I^{[1]}}, \quad \overbrace{(18,19)}^{I^{[2]}}, \quad \overbrace{(22)}^{I^{[3]}}, \quad \overbrace{(30,33)}^{I^{[4]}}, \quad \overbrace{(50,51)}^{I^{[5]}}, \quad \overbrace{(60)}^{I^{[6]}};$$

accordingly, the resulting aggregate $\alpha(I)$,

$$\overbrace{[6,9]}^{B^{[1]}}, \quad \overbrace{[18,19]}^{B^{[2]}}, \quad \overbrace{[22]}^{B^{[3]}}, \quad \overbrace{[30,33]}^{B^{[4]}}, \quad \overbrace{[50,51]}^{B^{[5]}}, \quad \overbrace{[60]}^{B^{[6]}},$$

has six blocks. ∎

5.2.   Mean and variance analysis

Hereafter, we will assume that the word $\mathcal{W}$ is given and that the text X is generated by a (nondegenerate) *memoryless* source. The first moment of the number of pattern occurrences $\Omega(X)$ is easily obtained by describing the collection of such occurrences in terms of formal languages, as discussed in Chapter 4. We adopt this approach here, and build languages satisfying certain properties. When analyzing occurrences we weight these languages by text probabilities, and this leads to the corresponding generating functions.

Let us start by building a language that allows us to compute the expected number of subsequence occurrence and its variance. We consider the collection of position–text pairs

$$\mathcal{O} := \{(I, X);\ \ I \in \mathcal{P}_{|X|}(\mathcal{D})\},$$

the size of an element (I, X) being by definition the length n of the text X. The weight of an element (I, X) of $\mathcal{O}$ is taken to be equal to $Z_I(X)P(X)$, where $P(X)$ is the probability of generation of the text. In this way $\mathcal{O}$ can also be regarded as the collection of all pattern occurrences weighted by the probability of the text. The corresponding generating function of $\mathcal{O}$ equipped with this weight is

$$O(z) = \sum_{(I,X)\in\mathcal{O}} Z_I(X)P(X)\, z^{|X|} = \sum_{X} \left(\sum_{I\in\mathcal{P}_{|X|}(\mathcal{D})} Z_I(X) \right) P(X)z^{|X|},$$

where the inner sum is exactly $\Omega(X)$ as defined in (5.2). Thus

$$O(z) = \sum_{X} \Omega(X)P(X)\, z^{|X|} \ = \sum_{n} \mathbf{E}[\Omega_n]z^n. \tag{5.3}$$

As a consequence, one has $[z^n]O(z) = \mathbf{E}[\Omega_n]$, so that $O(z)$ serves as the generating function of the sequence of expectations $\mathbf{E}(\Omega_n)$.

However, each pattern occurrence can be viewed as a "context", with an initial string, then the first letter of the pattern, then a separating string, then the second letter, etc. The collection $\mathcal{O}$ is therefore described combinatorially by

$$\mathcal{O} = \mathcal{A}^\star \times \{w_1\} \times \mathcal{A}^{<d_1} \times \{w_2\} \times \mathcal{A}^{<d_2} \times \ldots \times \{w_{m-1}\} \times \mathcal{A}^{<d_{m-1}} \times \{w_m\} \times \mathcal{A}^\star. \tag{5.4}$$

Here, for $d < \infty$, $\mathcal{A}^{<d}$ denotes the collection of all words of length strictly less than d, i.e., $\mathcal{A}^{<d} := \bigcup_{i<d} \mathcal{A}^i$, whereas for $d = \infty$ we write $\mathcal{A}^{<\infty} := \mathcal{A}^\star =$

$\bigcup_{i<\infty} \mathcal{A}^i$. The generating functions associated with $\mathcal{A}^{<d}$ and $\mathcal{A}^{<\infty}$ are

$$A^{<d}(z) = 1+z+z^2+\cdots+z^{d-1} = \frac{1-z^d}{1-z}, \qquad A^{<\infty}(z) = 1+z+z^2+\cdots = \frac{1}{1-z}.$$

Thus, the description (5.4) of occurrences automatically translates, for memoryless sources, into

$$O(z) \equiv \sum_{n\geq 0} \mathbf{E}[\Omega_n]\, z^n = \left(\frac{1}{1-z}\right)^{b+1} \left(\prod_{i=1}^{m} p_{w_i} z\right) \left(\prod_{i\in\mathcal{F}} \frac{1-z^{d_i}}{1-z}\right), \qquad (5.5)$$

where $\mathcal{F}$ is the set of indices i for which $d_i < \infty$. One finally obtains

$$\mathbf{E}[\Omega_n] = [z^n]O(z) = \frac{n^b}{b!} \left(\prod_{i\in\mathcal{F}} d_i\right) P(\mathcal{W}) \left(1 + O\left(\frac{1}{n}\right)\right), \qquad (5.6)$$

and a complete asymptotic expansion could easily be obtained.

For the analysis of the variance and especially of the higher moments, it is essential to work with a centered random variable Ξ defined, for each n, as

$$\Xi_n = \Omega_n - \mathbf{E}[\Omega_n] = \sum_{I\in\mathcal{P}_n(\mathcal{D})} Y_I, \qquad (5.7)$$

where $Y_I = Z_I - \mathbf{E}[Z_I] = Z_I - P(\mathcal{W})$. The second moment of the centered variable Ξ equals the variance of Ω_n and, with the centered variables defined by (5.7), one has

$$\mathbf{E}[\Xi_n^2] = \sum_{I,J\in\mathcal{P}_n(\mathcal{D})} \mathbf{E}[Y_I Y_J]. \qquad (5.8)$$

From this last equation, we can see that we need to analyze *pairs of positions* $(I,X), (J,X) = (I,J,X)$ relative to a common text X. We denote by $\mathcal{O}_2$ this set, that is,

$$\mathcal{O}_2 = \{(I,J,X);\ \ I,J \in \mathcal{P}_{|X|}(\mathcal{D})\},$$

and we weight each element (I,J,X) by $Y_I(X)Y_J(X)P(X)$. The corresponding generating function, which enumerates pairs of occurrences, is

$$O_2(z) = \sum_{(I,J,X)\in\mathcal{O}_2} Y_I(X)Y_J(X)P(X)\, z^{|X|}$$

$$= \sum_{X} \left(\sum_{I,J\in\mathcal{P}_{|X|}(\mathcal{D})} Y_I(X)Y_J(X)\right) P(X) z^{|X|}$$

and, with (5.8), we obtain

$$O_2(z) = \sum_{n \geq 0} \sum_{I,J \in \mathcal{P}_n(\mathcal{D})} \mathbf{E}[Y_I Y_J] \, z^n = \sum_{n \geq 0} \mathbf{E}[\Xi_n^2] \, z^n.$$

The process entirely parallels the derivation of (5.3) and one has $[z^n]O_2(z) = \mathbf{E}[\Xi_n^2]$, so that $O_2(z)$ serves as the generating function (in the usual sense) of the sequence of moments $\mathbf{E}[\Xi_n^2]$.

In order to characterize the language $\mathcal{O}_2$ we need a better understanding of the properties of the pair (I, J). There are two kinds of pair (I, J), depending on whether I and J intersect or not. When I and J do not intersect, the corresponding random variables Y_I and Y_J are independent (for a memoryless source), and the corresponding covariance $\mathbf{Cov}[Y_I Y_J]$ reduces to 0. As a consequence, one may restrict attention to pairs of occurrences (I, J) that intersect at one place at least. Suppose that there exist two occurrences of a pattern $\mathcal{W}$ at positions I and J which intersect at ℓ distinct places. We then denote by $\mathcal{W}_{I \cap J}$ the subpattern of $\mathcal{W}$ that occurs at the position $I \cap J$ and by $P(\mathcal{W}_{I \cap J})$ the probability of this subpattern. Observe that

$$\mathbf{E}[Z_I Z_J] = \frac{P^2(\mathcal{W})}{P(\mathcal{W}_{I \cap J})} [\![\mathcal{W} \text{ agrees on } I \cap J]\!]$$

where $[\![\mathcal{W} \text{ agree on } I \cap J]\!]$ is 1 if the pattern $\mathcal{W}$ at positions I is the same as at positions J and is 0 if this is not the case. Thus

$$\mathbf{E}[Y_I Y_J] = \mathbf{E}[Z_I Z_J] - \mathbf{E}[Z_I]\mathbf{E}[Z_J] = P^2(\mathcal{W}) \left(\frac{[\![\mathcal{W} \text{ agrees on } I \cap J]\!]}{P(\mathcal{W}_{I \cap J})} - 1 \right)$$

$$= P^2(\mathcal{W}) e(I, J) \tag{5.9}$$

where the *correlation number* $e(I, J)$ is defined as

$$e(I, J) = \frac{[\![\mathcal{W} \text{ agrees on } I \cap J]\!]}{P(\mathcal{W}_{I \cap J})} - 1. \tag{5.10}$$

One may remark that this relation remains true even if the pair (I, J) does not intersect, since, in this case, one has $P(\mathcal{W}_{I \cap J}) = P(\varepsilon) = 1$.

The asymptotic behavior of the variance is driven by the amount of overlap of the blocks involved in I and J rather than simply by the cardinality of $I \cap J$. In order to formalize this, define first the (joint) *aggregate* $\alpha(I, J)$ to be the system of blocks obtained by merging together all intersecting blocks of the two aggregates $\alpha(I)$ and $\alpha(J)$. The number of blocks $\beta(I, J)$ of $\alpha(I, J)$ plays a fundamental rôle here, since it measures the *degree of freedom* of the pairs; we also call $\beta(I, J)$ the degree of pair (I, J). Figure 5.1 illustrates this notion graphically.

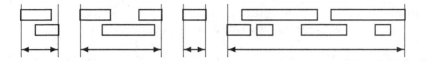

Figure 5.1. A pair of position tuples I, J with $b = 6$ blocks each and their joint aggregates; the number of degrees of freedom is here $\beta(I, J) = 4$.

Example 5.2.1. Consider a pattern $\mathcal{W} = \boxed{a\#_3 b\#_4 r}\,\#\,\boxed{a\#_4 c}$ composed of two blocks, indicated by the boxes. The text *aarbarbccaracc* contains several valid occurrences of $\mathcal{W}$ including two at positions $I = (2, 4, 6, 10, 13)$ and $J = (5, 7, 11, 12, 13)$. The individual aggregates are $\alpha(I) = \{[2, 6], [10, 13]\}, \alpha(J) = \{[5, 11], [12, 13]\}$ so that the joint aggregates are $\alpha(I, J) = [2, 13]$ and $\beta(I, J) = 1$. The pair (I, J) has exactly degree 1. ∎

When I and J intersect there exists at least one block of $\alpha(I)$ that intersects a block of $\alpha(J)$, so that the degree $\beta(I, J)$ is at most equal to $2b - 1$. Next, we partition $\mathcal{O}_2$ according to the value of $\beta(I, J)$

$$\mathcal{O}_2^{[p]} := \{(I, J, X) \in \mathcal{O}_2 : \quad \beta(I, J) = 2b - p\}$$

for the collection of groups (I, J, X) of occurrences for which the degree of freedom equals $2b - p$. From the preceding discussion, only $p \geq 1$ needs to be considered and so

$$O_2(z) = O_2^{[1]}(z) + O_2^{[2]}(z) + O_2^{[3]}(z) + \cdots + O_2^{[2b]}(z).$$

As we will see next, asymptotically it is only the first term of this sum that matters.

In order to conclude the discussion, we need the notion of full pairs: a pair (I, J) of $\mathcal{P}_q(\mathcal{D}) \times \mathcal{P}_q(\mathcal{D})$ is *full* if the joint aggregate $\alpha(I, J)$ completely covers the interval $[1, q]$; see Figure 5.2. (Clearly, the possible values of length q are finite since q is at most equal to 2ℓ, where ℓ is the length of the constraint $\mathcal{D}$.)

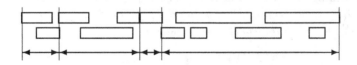

Figure 5.2. A full pair of position tuples (I, J) with $b = 6$ blocks each.

Example 5.2.2. Consider again the pattern $\mathcal{W} = a\#_3 b\#_4 r\#a\#_4 c$. The text *aarbarbccaracc* also contains two other occurrences of $\mathcal{W}$, at positions $I' = (1, 4, 6, 12, 13)$ and $J' = (5, 7, 11, 12, 14)$. Now, I' and J' intersect, and the aggregates are $\alpha(I') = \{[1, 6], [12, 13]\}, \alpha(J') = \{[5, 11], [12, 14]\}$, so that $\alpha(I', J') = \{[1, 11], [12, 14]\}$. We have here an example of a full pair of occurrences, with the number of blocks $\beta(I', J')$ equal to 2. ∎

There is a fundamental translation invariance due to the independence of symbols in the memoryless model that entails a combinatorial isomorphism (represented by $\cong$)

$$\mathcal{O}_2^{[p]} \cong (\mathcal{A}^\star)^{2b-p+1} \times \mathcal{B}_2^{[p]},$$

where $\mathcal{B}_2^{[p]}$ is the subset of $\mathcal{O}_2$ formed with full pairs (I, J) such that $\beta(I, J)$ equals $2b - p$. In essence, the gaps can be all grouped together (in number they are $2b-p+1$, which is translated by $(\mathcal{A}^\star)^{2b-p+1}$), while what remains constitutes a full occurrence. The generating function of $\mathcal{O}_2^{[p]}$ is accordingly

$$O_2^{[p]}(z) = \left(\frac{1}{1-z}\right)^{2b-p+1} B_2^{[p]}(z)$$

where $B_2^{[p]}(z)$ is the generating function of the collection $\mathcal{B}_2^{[p]}$. From our earlier discussion, it must be a *polynomial*. Now, an easy dominant pole analysis entails that $[z^n]O_2^{[p]} = O(n^{2b-p})$. This proves that the dominant contribution to the variance is given by $[z^n]O_2^{[1]}$, which is of order $O(n^{2b-1})$.

The variance $\mathbf{E}[\Xi_n^2]$ involves the constant $B_2^{[1]}(1)$ that is the total weight of the collection $\mathcal{B}_2^{[1]}$. Recall that this collection is formed of intersecting full pairs of occurrences of degree $2b - 1$. The polynomial $B_2^{[1]}(z)$ is itself the generating function of the collection $\mathcal{B}_2^{[1]}$, and it is conceptually an extension of the autocorrelation polynomial introduced in Chapter 2. We shall return to both polynomials in the next section.

We summarize our findings in the following theorem.

Theorem 5.2.3. *Consider a general constraint $\mathcal{D}$ with a number of blocks b and $m = O(1)$. The mean and the variance of the number of occurrences Ω_n of a pattern $\mathcal{W}$ subject to the constraint $\mathcal{D}$ satisfy*

$$\mathbf{E}[\Omega_n] = \frac{P(\mathcal{W})}{b!}\left(\prod_{j\,:\,d_j<\infty} d_j\right) n^b \left(1 + O(n^{-1})\right),$$

$$\mathrm{Var}[\Omega_n] = \sigma^2(\mathcal{W})n^{2b-1}\left(1 + O(n^{-1})\right),$$

where the variance coefficient $\sigma^2(\mathcal{W})$ involves an autocorrelation coefficient $\kappa(\mathcal{W})$:

$$\sigma^2(\mathcal{W}) = \frac{P^2(\mathcal{W})}{(2b-1)!} \, \kappa^2(\mathcal{W}) \qquad with \qquad \kappa^2(\mathcal{W}) := \sum_{(I,J)\in\mathcal{B}_2^{[1]}} e(I,J). \qquad (5.11)$$

The set $\mathcal{B}_2^{[1]}$ is the collection of all pairs of position tuples (I, J) that satisfy three conditions: (i) they are full; (ii) they are intersecting; (iii) there is a single pair (r, s) with $1 \leq r, s \leq b$ for which the rth block $B^{[r]}$ of $\alpha(I)$ and the sth block $C^{[s]}$ of $\alpha(J)$ intersect.

The computation of the autocorrelation coefficient $\kappa(\mathcal{W})$ reduces to b^2 computations of correlations $\kappa(\mathcal{W}_r, \mathcal{W}_s)$ relative to pairs $(\mathcal{W}_r, \mathcal{W}_s)$ of blocks. Note that each correlation of the form $\kappa(\mathcal{W}_r, \mathcal{W}_s)$ involves a totally constrained problem and is discussed below. Let $D(\mathcal{D}) := \prod_{i:\ d_i<\infty} d_i$. Then one has

$$\kappa^2(\mathcal{W}) = D^2(\mathcal{D}) \sum_{1\leq r,s\leq b} \frac{1}{D(\mathcal{D}_r)D(\mathcal{D}_s)} \binom{r+s-2}{r-1}\binom{2b-r-s}{b-r} \kappa(\mathcal{W}_r, \mathcal{W}_s),$$

$$(5.12)$$

where $\kappa(\mathcal{W}_r, \mathcal{W}_s)$ is the sum of the $e(I, J)$ in (5.11) taken over all full intersecting pairs (I, J) formed with a position tuple I of block $\mathcal{W}_r$ and subject to constraint $\mathcal{D}_r$, and a position tuple J of block $\mathcal{W}_s$, subject to constraint $\mathcal{D}_s$. Let us explain formula (5.12) in words: for a pair (I, J) of the set $\mathcal{B}_2^{[1]}$, there is a single pair (r, s) of indices with $1 \leq r, s \leq b$ for which the rth block $B^{[r]}$ of $\alpha(I)$ and the sth block $C^{[s]}$ of $\alpha(J)$ intersect. So, there exist $r + s - 2$ blocks before the block $\alpha(B^{[r]}, C^{[s]})$ and $2b - r - s$ blocks after it. We thus have three different degrees of freedom: (i) the relative order of the blocks $B^{[i]}(i < r)$ and the blocks $C^{[j]}(j < s)$, and similarly the relative order of the blocks $B^{[i]}(i > r)$ and the blocks $C^{[j]}(j > s)$; (ii) the lengths of the blocks (there are D_j possible lengths for the jth block); (iii) finally, the relative positions of the blocks $B^{[r]}$ and $C^{[s]}$.

In particular, in the unconstrained case, the parameter b equals m and each block $\mathcal{W}_r$ is reduced to a symbol, w_r. Then the correlation coefficient $\kappa^2(\mathcal{W})$ is given by

$$\kappa^2(\mathcal{W}) := \sum_{1\leq r,s\leq m} \binom{r+s-2}{r-1}\binom{2m-r-s}{m-r} [\![w_r = w_s]\!] \left(\frac{1}{P(w_r)} - 1\right). \quad (5.13)$$

In words, once one fixes the position of the intersection, called the pivot, then amongst the $r + s - 2$ symbols smaller than the pivot one assigns freely $r - 1$ symbols to the first occurrence and the remaining $s - 1$ symbols to the second occurrence. One proceeds similarly for the $2m - r - s$ symbols larger than the pivot.

5.3. Autocorrelation polynomial revisited

Finally, we compare the autocorrelation coefficient $\kappa(\mathcal{W})$ with the autocorrelation polynomial $S_w(z)$ introduced in Chapter 2 in the context of exact string matching. Let $w = w_1 w_2 \cdots w_m$ be a string of length m; all the symbols of w must occur at consecutive places, so that a valid position I is an interval of length m. We recall that the autocorrelation set $\mathcal{P}(w) \subset [1, m]$ involves all indices k such that the prefix w_1^k coincides with the suffix w_{m-k+1}^m. Here, an index $k \in \mathcal{P}(w)$ relates to a intersecting pair of positions (I, J) and one has $w_1^k = w_{I \cap J}$.

Recall that the autocorrelation polynomial $S_w(z)$ is defined in (2.5) of Chapter 2 by

$$S_w(z) = \sum_{k \in \mathcal{P}_w} P(w_{k+1}^m) z^{m-k} = P(w) \sum_{k \in \mathcal{P}(w)} \frac{1}{P(w_1^k)} z^{m-k}.$$

Let us also define

$$C_w(z) = \sum_{k \in \mathcal{P}(w)} z^{m-k}.$$

Since the polynomial $B_2^{[1]}(z)$ of the language $\mathcal{B}_2^{[1]}$ involves the coefficients $e(I, J)$ defined in (5.10), it can be written as a function of the two autocorrelation polynomials A_w and C_w, as follows:

$$B_2^{[1]}(z) = P(w) z^m \left(A_w(z) - P(w) C_w(z) \right). \tag{5.14}$$

Put simply, the variance coefficient of the hidden pattern problem extends the classical autocorrelation quantities associated with strings.

5.4. Central limit laws

Our goal now is to prove that a sequence Ω_n appropriately centered and scaled tends to the normal distribution. We consider the following standardized random variable $\widetilde{\Xi}_n$ which is defined for each n by

$$\widetilde{\Xi}_n := \frac{\Xi_n}{n^{b-1/2}} = \frac{\Omega_n - \mathbf{E}[\Omega_n]}{n^{b-1/2}}, \tag{5.15}$$

where b is the number of blocks of the constraint $\mathcal{D}$. We shall show that $\widetilde{\Xi}_n$ behaves asymptotically as a normal variable with mean 0 and standard deviation σ. By the classical *moment convergence theorem*, this is established once all moments of $\widetilde{\Xi}_n$ are known to converge to the appropriate moments of the standard normal distribution.

We remind the reader that if G is a standard normal variable (i.e., a Gaussian distributed variable with mean 0 and standard deviation 1) then, for any integral $s \geq 0$,

$$\mathbf{E}[G^{2s}] = 1 \cdot 3 \cdots (2s - 1), \qquad \mathbf{E}[G^{2s+1}] = 0. \tag{5.16}$$

We shall accordingly distinguish two cases based on the parity of r, $r = 2s$ and $r = 2s + 1$, and prove that

$$\mathbf{E}[\Xi_n^{2s+1}] = o(n^{(2s+1)(b-1/2)}), \qquad \mathbf{E}[\Xi_n^{2s}] \sim \sigma^{2s} \left(1 \cdot 3 \cdots (2s - 1)\right) n^{2sb-s}, \tag{5.17}$$

which implies the Gaussian convergence of $\widetilde{\Xi}_n$.

Theorem 5.4.1. *The random variable Ω_n over a random text of length n generated by a memoryless source asymptotically obeys a* central limit law *in the sense that its distribution is asymptotically normal. That is, for all $x = O(1)$, one has*

$$\lim_{n \to \infty} P\left(\frac{\Omega_n - \mathbf{E}[\Omega_n]}{\sqrt{\mathrm{Var}[\Omega_n]}} \leq x\right) = \frac{1}{\sqrt{2\pi}} \int_{-\infty}^{x} e^{-t^2/2} \, dt. \tag{5.18}$$

Proof. The proof below is combinatorial; it basically reduces to grouping and enumerating adequately the various combinations of indices in the sum that expresses $\mathbf{E}[\Xi_n^r]$. Recall that $\mathcal{P}_n(\mathcal{D})$ is formed from all the sets of positions in $[1, n]$ subject to the constraint $\mathcal{D}$ and set $\mathcal{P}(\mathcal{D}) := \bigcup_n \mathcal{P}_n(\mathcal{D})$. Then, distributing the terms in Ξ^r yields

$$\mathbf{E}[\Xi_n^r] = \sum_{(I_1,\ldots,I_r) \in \mathcal{P}_n^r(\mathcal{D})} \mathbf{E}[Y_{I_1} \cdots Y_{I_r}]; \tag{5.19}$$

Y_I was defined after (5.7). An r-tuple of sets $(I_1, \ldots, I_r)$ in $\mathcal{P}^r(\mathcal{D})$ is said to be *friendly* if each I_k intersects at least one other I_ℓ, with $\ell \neq k$ and we let $\mathcal{Q}^{(r)}(\mathcal{D})$ be the set of all friendly collections in $\mathcal{P}^r(\mathcal{D})$. For $\mathcal{P}^r$, $\mathcal{Q}^{(r)}$, and their derivatives below, we add the subscript n each time the situation is particularized to texts of length n. If $(I_1, \ldots, I_r)$ does not lie in $\mathcal{Q}^{(r)}(\mathcal{D})$ then

$$\mathbf{E}[Y_{I_1} \cdots Y_{I_r}] = 0,$$

since at least one Y_I is independent of the other factors in the product and the Y_I are centered: $\mathbf{E}[Y_I]0$. One can thus restrict attention to friendly families and obtain the basic formula

$$\mathbf{E}[\Xi_n^r] = \sum_{(I_1,\ldots,I_r) \in \mathcal{Q}_n^{(r)}(\mathcal{D})} \mathbf{E}[Y_{I_1} \cdots Y_{I_r}], \tag{5.20}$$

where the sum involves fewer terms than in (5.19). From here we proceed in two stages, dealing separately with the odd and even moments. First, we restrict attention to friendly families that give rise to the dominant contribution and introduce a suitable subfamily $\mathcal{Q}_*^{(r)} \subset \mathcal{Q}^{(r)}$ that neglects the moments of odd order, which are small. Next, the family $\mathcal{Q}_*^{(r)}$ for even order r involves a symmetry and it suffices to consider another smaller subfamily $\mathcal{Q}_{**}^{(r)} \subset \mathcal{Q}_*^{(r)}$, that corresponds to a "standard" form of position tuple intersection; this last reduction gives rise to precisely the even Gaussian moments.

Odd moments. Given $(I_1, \ldots, I_r) \in \mathcal{Q}^{(r)}$, the aggregate $\alpha(I_1, I_2, \ldots, I_r)$ is defined as the aggregation of $\alpha(I_1) \cup \cdots \cup \alpha(I_r)$. Next, the *number of blocks* of $(I_1, \ldots, I_r)$ is the number of blocks of the aggregate $\alpha(I_1, \ldots, I_r)$; if p is the total number of intersecting blocks of the aggregate $\alpha(I_1, \ldots, I_r)$, the aggregate $\alpha(I_1, I_2, \ldots I_r)$ has $rb - p$ blocks. As previously, we say that the family $(I_1, \ldots, I_r)$ of $\mathcal{Q}_q^{(r)}$ is *full* if the aggregate $\alpha(I_1, I_2, \ldots I_r)$ completely covers the interval $[1, q]$. In this case, the length of the aggregate is at most $rd(m-1)+1$, and the generating function of full families is a polynomial $P_r(z)$ of degree at most $rd(m-1)+1$ with $d = \max_{j \in \mathcal{F}} d_j$, where we recall that the set of indices j for which $d_j < \infty$ is denoted by $\mathcal{F}$. Then, the generating function of those families of $\mathcal{Q}^{(r)}$ whose block number equals k is of the form

$$\left(\frac{1}{1-z}\right)^{k+1} P_r(z),$$

whose block number equals k is $O(n^k)$. This observation proves that the dominant contribution to (5.20) arises from friendly families with a maximal block number. It is clear that the minimum number of intersecting blocks of any element of $\mathcal{Q}^{(r)}$ equals $\lceil r/2 \rceil$, since it coincides exactly with the minimum number of edges of a graph with r vertices which contains no isolated vertex. Thus the maximum block number of a friendly family equals $rb - \lceil r/2 \rceil$. In view of this fact and the remarks above regarding cardinalities, we immediately have

$$\mathbf{E}\left[\Xi_n^{2s+1}\right] = O\left(n^{(2s+1)b-s-1}\right) = o\left(n^{(2s+1)(b-1/2)}\right)$$

which establishes the limit form of odd moments in (5.17).

Even Moments. We are thus left with estimating the even moments. The dominant term relates to friendly families of $\mathcal{Q}^{(2s)}$ with an intersecting block number equal to s, whose set we denote by $\mathcal{Q}_*^{(2s)}$. In such a family, each subset I_k intersects one and only one other subset I_ℓ. Furthermore, if the blocks of $\alpha(I_h)$ are denoted by $B_h^{[u]}, 1 \leq u \leq b$, there exists only one block $B_k^{[u_k]}$ of $\alpha(I_k)$ and only one block $B_\ell^{[u_\ell]}$ of $\alpha(I_\ell)$ that contain the points of $I_k \cap I_\ell$. This defines an involution τ such that $\tau(k) = \ell$ and $\tau(\ell) = k$ for all pairs of indices (ℓ, k) for which I_k and I_ℓ intersect. Furthermore, given the symmetry relation

$$\mathbf{E}[Y_{I_1} \cdots Y_{I_{2s}}] = \mathbf{E}[Y_{I_{\rho(1)}} \cdots Y_{I_{\rho(2s)}}]$$

it suffices to restrict attention to the friendly families of $\mathcal{Q}_\star^{(2s)}$ for which the involution τ is the standard one with cycles $(1, 2)$, $(3, 4)$, etc.; for such "standard" families whose set is denoted by $\mathcal{Q}_{\star\star}^{(2s)}$, the pairs that intersect are thus (I_1, I_2), $\ldots$, (I_{2s-1}, I_{2s}). Since the set $\mathcal{K}_{2s}$ of involutions of $2s$ elements has cardinality $K_{2s} = 1 \cdot 3 \cdot 5 \cdots (2s - 1)$, the equality

$$\sum_{\mathcal{Q}_{\star n}^{(2s)}} \mathbf{E}[Y_{I_1} \cdots Y_{I_{2s}}] = K_{2s} \sum_{\mathcal{Q}_{\star\star n}^{(2s)}} \mathbf{E}[Y_{I_1} \cdots Y_{I_{2s}}], \qquad (5.21)$$

entails that we can work now solely with standard families.

The class of position tuples relative to standard families is $\mathcal{A}^\star \times (\mathcal{A}^\star)^{2sb-s-1} \times \mathcal{B}_{2s}^{[s]} \times \mathcal{A}^\star$; this class involves the collection $\mathcal{B}_{2s}^{[s]}$ of all full friendly $2s$-tuples of position tuples with their numbers of blocks equal to s. Since $\mathcal{B}_{2s}^{[s]}$ is exactly a shuffle of s copies of $\mathcal{B}_2^{[1]}$ (as introduced in the study of the variance), the associated generating function is

$$\left(\frac{1}{1-z} \right)^{2sb-s+1} (2sb - s)! \left(\frac{B_2^{[1]}(z)}{(2b-1)!} \right)^s,$$

where $B_2^{[1]}(z)$ is the autocorrelation polynomial already introduced (see (5.14)). Upon taking coefficients, we obtain the estimate

$$\sum_{\mathcal{Q}_{\star\star n}^{(2s)}} \mathbf{E}[Y_{I_1} \cdots Y_{I_{2s}}] \sim n^{(2b-1)s} \sigma^{2s}. \qquad (5.22)$$

In view of the formulas (5.19)–(5.22) above, this yields the estimate of the even moments and leads to the second relation in (5.17). This completes the proof of Theorem 5.4.1. ∎

The even Gaussian moments eventually come out as the number of involutions, which corresponds to a fundamental asymptotic symmetry present in the problem. In this perspective the specialization of the proof to the fully unconstrained case is reminiscent of the derivation of the usual central limit theorem (dealing with sums of independent variables) by moment methods.

5.5. Limit laws for fully constrained pattern

In this section, we strengthen our results for a *fully constrained pattern*, in which all gaps d_j are finite. We set $D = \prod_j d_j$. Observe that in this case we can reduce the subsequence problem to a generalized string matching problem in which the generalized pattern $\mathcal{W}$ consists of all words that satisfy $(\mathcal{W}, \mathcal{D})$. Thus our results of Chapter 4 apply, in particular Theorems 4.2.6 and 4.2.8. This leads to the following result.

Theorem 5.5.1. *Consider a fully constrained pattern with the mean and variance found in Theorem 5.2.3 for the case $b = 1$ and $m = O(1)$.*

(i) *The random variable Ω_n satisfies a* central limit law *with speed of convergence $1/\sqrt{n}$:*

$$\sup_x \left| P\left(\frac{\Omega_n - DP(\mathcal{W})n}{\sigma(\mathcal{W})\sqrt{n}} \leq x \right) - \frac{1}{\sqrt{2\pi}} \int_{-\infty}^x e^{-t^2/2}\, dt \right| = O\left(\frac{1}{\sqrt{n}} \right). \quad (5.23)$$

(ii) Large deviations *from the mean value have an exponentially small probability: there exist a constant $\eta > 0$ and a nonnegative function $I(x)$ defined throughout $(0, \eta)$ such that $I(x) > 0$ for $x \neq DP(\mathcal{W})$ and*

$$\left\{ \begin{aligned} \lim_{n\to\infty} \frac{1}{n} \log P\left(\frac{\Omega_n}{n} \leq x \right) &= -I(x) \quad \text{if } 0 < x < DP(\mathcal{W}), \\ \lim_{n\to\infty} \frac{1}{n} \log P\left(\frac{\Omega_n}{n} \geq x \right) &= -I(x) \quad \text{if } DP(\mathcal{W}) < x < \eta \end{aligned} \right\}, \quad (5.24)$$

except for at most a finite number of exceptional values of x. More precisely,

$$I(x) = -\log \frac{\lambda(\zeta)}{\zeta^x} \quad \text{with } \zeta \equiv \zeta(x) \text{ defined by} \quad \frac{\zeta\lambda'(\zeta)}{\lambda(\zeta)} = x \quad (5.25)$$

where $\lambda(x)$ is the largest eigenvalue of the matrix $\mathrm{T}(x)$ of the associated de Bruijn graph constructed for $\mathcal{W} = \{v : v = w_1 u_1 w_2 \cdots w_{m-1} u_{m-1} w_m$, where $u_i \in \mathcal{A}^{d_i - 1}$, $1 \leq i \leq m - 1\}$ (see Section 4.2).

(iii) *For primitive patterns a* local limit law *holds:*

$$\sup_k \left| P\left(\Omega_n = k \right) - \frac{1}{\sigma(\mathcal{W})\sqrt{n}} \frac{e^{x(k)^2/2}}{\sqrt{2\pi}} \right| = o\left(\frac{1}{\sqrt{n}} \right), \quad (5.26)$$

where

$$x(k) = \frac{k - DP(\mathcal{W})n}{\sigma(\mathcal{W})\sqrt{n}}$$

for $n \to \infty$.

Example 5.5.2. Subsequence pattern matching finds a myriad of applications, including in biology and computer security. In intrusion detection within the context of computer security, if one wants to detect "suspicious" activities (e.g., signatures viewed as subsequences in an audit file), it is important to set up a threshold in order to avoid false alarms. This problem can be rephrased as one of finding a threshold $\alpha_0 = \alpha_0(\mathcal{W}; n, \beta)$ such that

$$P(\Omega_n > \alpha_0) \leq \beta,$$

for small given β (say $\beta = 10^{-5}$). Based on the frequencies of letters and the assumption that a memoryless model is (at least roughly) relevant, one can estimate the mean value and variance. The Gaussian limits given by Theorems 5.4.1 and 4.2.6 then reduce the problem to solving an approximate system, which in the (fully) constrained case reads

$$\alpha_0 = nP(\mathcal{W}) + x_0 \sigma(\mathcal{W}) \sqrt{n}, \qquad \beta = \frac{1}{\sqrt{2\pi}} \int_{x_0}^{\infty} e^{-t^2/2} \, dt.$$

This system admits the approximate solution

$$\alpha_0 \approx nP(\mathcal{W}) + \sigma(\mathcal{W}) \sqrt{2n \log(1/\beta)}, \tag{5.27}$$

for small β. If intrusions are rare events then one needs to apply a large deviations approach. We do not discuss this here, and the reader is referred to Janson (2004). ∎

5.6. Generalized subsequence problem

In the *generalized subsequence problem* the pattern is a sequence $\mathcal{W} = (\mathcal{W}_1, \ldots, \mathcal{W}_d)$, where each $\mathcal{W}_i$ is a set of strings (i.e., a language). We say that the generalized pattern $\mathcal{W}$ occurs in a text X if X contains $\mathcal{W}$ as a *subsequence* $(w_1, \ldots, w_d)$, where $w_i \in \mathcal{W}_i$. An occurrence of the pattern in X is a sequence

$$(u_0, w_1, u_1, \ldots, w_d, u_d)$$

such that $X = u_0 w_1 u_1 \cdots w_d u_d$, where $u_i \in \mathcal{A}^*$. We shall study the associated language $\mathcal{L}$, which can be described as

$$\mathcal{L} = \mathcal{A}^* \times \mathcal{W}_1 \times \mathcal{A}^* \times \mathcal{W}_d \times \mathcal{A}^*. \tag{5.28}$$

More precisely, an occurrence of $\mathcal{W}$ is a sequence of d disjoint intervals $I = (I_1, I_2, \ldots, I_d)$ such that $I_j := [i_j^1, i_j^2]$, where $1 \leq i_j^1 \leq i_j^2 \leq n$ is a portion of text X_1^n where $w_j \in \mathcal{W}_j$ occurs. We denote by $\mathcal{P}_n := \mathcal{P}_n(\mathcal{W})$ the set of all valid occurrences I. The number of occurrences Ω_n of $\mathcal{W}$ in the text X of size n is then

$$\Omega_n = \sum_{I \in \mathcal{P}_n(\mathcal{L})} Z_I, \qquad (5.29)$$

where $Z_I(X) := [\![\mathcal{W} \text{ occurs at position } I \text{ in } X]\!]$.

In passing, we observe that the generalized subsequence problem is the most general pattern matching considered so far. It contains exact string matching (see Chapter 2), generalized string matching (see Chapter 4), and subsequence pattern matching as discussed in this chapter. In this section we present an analysis of the first two moments of Ω_n for the generalized subsequence pattern matching problem in the case of the dynamic sources discussed in Chapter 1.

We start with a brief description of the methodology of the generating operators used in the analysis of dynamic sources. We recall from Chapter 1 that the *generating operator* $\mathbf{G}_w$ is defined by $\mathbf{G}_w[f](t) := |h'_w(t)| f \circ h_w(t)$ for a density function f and a word w. In particular, (1.2) states that $P(w) \int_0^1 f(t)dt = \int_0^1 \mathbf{G}_w[f](t)dt$ for any function $f(t)$, which implies that $P(w)$ is an eigenvalue of the operator $\mathbf{G}_w$. Furthermore, the generating operator for wu is $\mathbf{G}_{wu} = \mathbf{G}_u \circ \mathbf{G}_w$, where w and u are words (see (1.3)) and $\circ$ is the composition of operators.

Consider now a language $\mathcal{B} \subset \mathcal{A}^*$. Its *generating operator* $\mathbf{B}(z)$ is then defined as

$$\mathbf{B}(z) := \sum_{w \in \mathcal{B}} z^{|w|} \, \mathbf{G}_w.$$

We observe that the ordinary generating function $B(z)$ of the language $\mathcal{B}$ is related to the generating operators. Indeed,

$$B(z) := \sum_{w \in \mathcal{B}} z^{|w|} P(w) = \sum_{w \in \mathcal{B}} z^{|w|} \int_0^1 \mathbf{G}_w[f](t)dt = \int_0^1 \mathbf{B}(z)[f](t)dt. \qquad (5.30)$$

If $\mathbf{B}(z)$ is well defined at $z = 1$ then $\mathbf{B}(1)$ is called the *normalized operator* of $\mathcal{B}$. In particular, using (1.1) we obtain

$$P(\mathcal{B}) = \sum_{w \in \mathcal{B}} P(w) = \int_0^1 \mathbf{B}(1)dt.$$

Furthermore, the operator

$$\mathbf{G} := \sum_{a \in \mathcal{A}} \mathbf{G}_a, \qquad (5.31)$$

is the normalized operator of the alphabet $\mathcal{A}$ and plays a fundamental role in the analysis.

From the product formula (1.3) for generating operators $\mathbf{G}_w$ we conclude that unions and Cartesian products of languages translate into sums and compositions of the associated operators. For instance, the operator associated with $\mathcal{A}^\star$ is

$$(I - z\mathbf{G})^{-1} := \sum_{i \geq 0} z^i \mathbf{G}^i,$$

where $\mathbf{G}^i = \mathbf{G} \circ \mathbf{G}^{i-1}$.

In order to proceed, we must restrict our attention to a class of dynamic sources, called *decomposable*, that satisfy two properties: (i) there exist a unique positive dominant eigenvalue λ and a dominant eigenvector denoted as φ (which is unique under the normalization $\int \varphi(t)dt = 1$); (ii) there is a spectral gap between the dominant eigenvalue and other eigenvalues. These properties entail the separation of the operator $\mathbf{G}$ into two parts (see also (4.21)):

$$\mathbf{G} = \lambda \mathbf{P} + \mathbf{N} \tag{5.32}$$

such that the operator $\mathbf{P}$ is the projection relating to the dominant eigenvalue λ while $\mathbf{N}$ is the operator relating to the remainder of the spectrum (see Chapter 4). Furthermore, it is easy to see that (see Exercise 5.12)

$$\mathbf{P} \circ \mathbf{P} = \mathbf{P}, \tag{5.33}$$
$$\mathbf{P} \circ \mathbf{N} = \mathbf{N} \circ \mathbf{P} = 0. \tag{5.34}$$

The last property implies that for any $i \geq 1$ (see also (4.13)),

$$\mathbf{G}^i = \lambda^i \mathbf{P} + \mathbf{N}^i. \tag{5.35}$$

In particular, for the *density* operator $\mathbf{G}$ the dominant eigenvalue $\lambda = P(\mathcal{A}) = 1$ and φ is the unique stationary distribution. The function 1 is the left eigenvector. Then, using (5.35), we arrive at

$$(I - z\mathbf{G})^{-1} = \frac{1}{1-z}\mathbf{P} + \mathbf{R}(z), \tag{5.36}$$

where

$$\mathbf{R}(z) := (I - z\mathbf{N})^{-1} - \mathbf{P} = \sum_{k \geq 0} z^k (\mathbf{G}^k - \mathbf{P}). \tag{5.37}$$

Observe that the first term in (5.36) has a pole at $z = 1$ and, owing to the spectral gap, the operator $\mathbf{N}$ has spectral radius $\nu < \lambda = 1$. Furthermore, the operator $\mathbf{R}(z)$ is analytic in $|z| < 1/\nu$ and, again thanks to the existence of the spectral gap, the series $\mathbf{R}(1)$ is of geometric type. We shall point out below that the speed of convergence of $\mathbf{R}(z)$ is closely related to the decay of the correlation between two consecutive symbols. Finally, we list some additional properties of the operators just introduced (see Exercise 5.12) that are true for any function $g(t)$ defined between 0 and 1:

$$\mathbf{N}[\varphi] = 0, \qquad\qquad \mathbf{P}[g](t) = \varphi(t) \int_0^1 g(t')dt' \qquad (5.38)$$

$$\int_0^1 \mathbf{P}[g](t)dt = \int_0^1 g(t)dt, \quad \int_0^1 \mathbf{N}[g](t)dt = 0, \qquad (5.39)$$

where φ is the stationary density.

The theory built so far allows us, among other things, to define precisely the correlation between languages in terms of generating operators. From now on we restrict our analysis to so-called *nondense* languages $\mathcal{B}$ for which the associated generating operator $\mathbf{B}(z)$ is analytic in a disk $|z| > 1$. First, observe that for a nondense language $\mathcal{B}$ the normalized generating operator $\mathbf{B}$ satisfies

$$\int_0^1 \mathbf{P} \circ \mathbf{B} \circ \mathbf{P}[g](t) = P(\mathcal{B}) \left(\int_0^1 g(t)dt \right). \qquad (5.40)$$

Let us now define the correlation coefficient between two languages, say $\mathcal{B}$ with generating operator $\mathbf{B}$ and $\mathcal{C}$ with generating operator $\mathbf{C}$. Two types of correlations may occur between such languages. If $\mathcal{B}$ and $\mathcal{C}$ do not overlap then $\mathcal{B}$ may precede $\mathcal{C}$ or follow $\mathcal{C}$. We define the *correlation coefficient* $c(\mathcal{B}, \mathcal{C})$ (and in an analogous way $c(\mathcal{C}, \mathcal{B})$) by

$$P(\mathcal{B})P(\mathcal{C})c(\mathcal{B},\mathcal{C}) := \sum_{k \geq 0} \left[P(\mathcal{B} \times \mathcal{A}^k \times \mathcal{C}) - P(\mathcal{B})P(\mathcal{C}) \right]$$

$$= \int_0^1 \mathbf{C} \circ \mathbf{R}(1) \circ \mathbf{B}[\varphi](t). \qquad (5.41)$$

To see that (5.41) holds we observe, using (5.32)–(5.40), that

$$\int_0^1 \mathbf{C} \circ \mathbf{R}(1) \circ \mathbf{B}[\varphi](t)dt = \int_0^1 \mathbf{C} \circ \left(\sum_{k \geq 0} (\mathbf{G}^k - \mathbf{P}) \right) \circ \mathbf{B}[\varphi](t)dt$$

$$= \sum_{k \geq 0} \left(\int_0^1 \mathbf{C} \circ \mathbf{G}^k \circ \mathbf{B}[\varphi](t)dt - \int_0^1 \mathbf{C} \circ \mathbf{P} \circ \mathbf{B}[\varphi](t) \right)$$

$$= \sum_{k \geq 0} \left(P(\mathcal{B} \times \mathcal{A}^k \times \mathcal{B}) - P(\mathcal{B})P(\mathcal{C}) \right).$$

We say that $\mathcal{B}$ and $\mathcal{C}$ overlap if there exist words b, u, and c such that $u \neq \varepsilon$ and $(bu, uc) \in (\mathcal{B} \times \mathcal{C}) \cup (\mathcal{C} \times \mathcal{B})$. We denote by $\mathcal{B} \uparrow \mathcal{C}$ the set of words overlapping the words from $\mathcal{B}$ and $\mathcal{C}$. The correlation coefficient of the overlapping languages $\mathcal{B}$ and $\mathcal{C}$ is defined as

$$d(\mathcal{B}, \mathcal{C}) := \frac{P(\mathcal{B} \uparrow \mathcal{C})}{P(\mathcal{B}) P(\mathcal{C})}. \tag{5.42}$$

Finally, the total correlation coefficient $\gamma(\mathcal{B}, \mathcal{C})$ between $\mathcal{B}$ and $\mathcal{C}$ is defined as

$$\gamma(\mathcal{B}, \mathcal{C}) = c(\mathcal{B}, \mathcal{C}) + c(\mathcal{C}, \mathcal{B}) + d(\mathcal{B}, \mathcal{C}). \tag{5.43}$$

Thus

$$P(\mathcal{B})P(\mathcal{C})\gamma(\mathcal{B}, \mathcal{C}) = P(\mathcal{B} \uparrow \mathcal{C})$$
$$+ \sum_{k \geq 0} \left[P(\mathcal{B} \times \mathcal{A}^k \times \mathcal{C}) + P(\mathcal{C} \times \mathcal{A}^k \times \mathcal{B}) - 2P(\mathcal{B})P(\mathcal{C}) \right].$$

We shall need the coefficients γ, c, and d in the analysis of the generalized subsequence problem for dynamic sources.

We will now derive the mean and variance of the number of occurrences $\Omega_n(\mathcal{W})$ of a generalized pattern as a subsequence, for a dynamic source. Here is a sketch of the forthcoming proof.

- We first describe the generating operators of the language $\mathcal{L}$ defined in (5.28), that is,

$$\mathcal{L} = \mathcal{A}^* \times \mathcal{W}_1 \times \mathcal{A}^* \cdots \mathcal{W}_d \times \mathcal{A}^*.$$

  It will turn out that the quasi-inverse operator $(I - z\mathbf{G})^{-1}$ is involved in such a generating operator.
- We then decompose the operator with the help of (5.36). We obtain a term related to $(1-z)^{-1}\mathbf{P}$ that gives the main contribution to the asymptotics, and another term coming from the operator $\mathbf{R}(z)$.
- We then compute the generating function of $\mathcal{L}$ using (5.30).
- Finally, we extract the asymptotic behavior from the generating function.

The main finding of this section is summarized in the next theorem.

Theorem 5.6.1. *Consider a decomposable dynamical source endowed with the stationary density φ and let $\mathcal{W} = (\mathcal{W}_1, \mathcal{W}_2, \ldots, \mathcal{W}_d)$ be a generalized nondense pattern.*
(i) The expectation $\mathbf{E}(\Omega_n)$ of the number of occurrences of the generalized pattern $\mathcal{W}$ in a text of length n satisfies asymptotically

$$\mathbf{E}(\Omega_n(\mathcal{W})) = \binom{n+d}{d} P(\mathcal{W}) + \binom{n+d-1}{d-1} P(\mathcal{W}) \left[C(\mathcal{W}) - T(\mathcal{W}) \right] + O(n^{d-2}),$$

where

$$T(\mathcal{W}) = \sum_{i=1}^{d} \sum_{w \in \mathcal{W}_i} \frac{|w| P(w)}{P(\mathcal{W}_i)} \tag{5.44}$$

is the average text length, and the correlation coefficient $C(\mathcal{W})$ is the sum of the correlations $c(\mathcal{W}_{i-1}, \mathcal{W}_i)$ between the languages $\mathcal{W}_i$ and $\mathcal{W}_{i+1}$, as defined by (5.41).

(ii) *The variance of Ω_n is asymptotically equal to*

$$\mathrm{Var}[\Omega_n(\mathcal{W})] = \sigma^2(\mathcal{W}) \, n^{2d-1} \left(1 + O(n^{-1})\right), \tag{5.45}$$

where

$$\sigma^2(\mathcal{W}) = P^2(\mathcal{W}) \left[\frac{d - 2T(\mathcal{W})}{d!(d-1)!} + \frac{\gamma(\mathcal{W})}{(2d-1)!} \right]$$

and the total correlation coefficient $\gamma(\mathcal{W})$ can be computed from

$$\gamma(\mathcal{W}) := \sum_{1 \le i, j \le d} \binom{i+j-2}{i-1} \binom{2d-i-j}{d-i} \gamma(\mathcal{W}_i, \mathcal{W}_j),$$

where $\gamma(\mathcal{W}_i, \mathcal{W}_{i+1})$ is defined in (5.43).

Proof. We prove only part (i), leaving the proof of part (ii) as Exercise 5.13. We shall start with the language $\mathcal{L}$ defined in (5.28). Its generating operator is

$$\mathbf{L}(z) = (I - z\mathbf{G})^{-1} \circ \mathbf{L}_d(z) \circ (I - z\mathbf{G})^{-1} \circ \cdots \circ \mathbf{L}_1(z) \circ (I - z\mathbf{G})^{-1}. \tag{5.46}$$

After applying the transformation (5.35) and using (5.36), we obtain an operator

$$\mathbf{M}_1(z) = \left(\frac{1}{1-z} \right)^{d+1} \mathbf{P} \circ \mathbf{L}_d(z) \circ \mathbf{P} \circ \cdots \circ \mathbf{P} \circ \mathbf{L}_1(z) \circ \mathbf{P}$$

that has a pole of order $d+1$ at $z = 1$. Near $z = 1$, each operator $\mathbf{L}_i(z)$ is analytic and admits an expansion

$$\mathbf{L}_i(z) = \mathbf{L}_i + (z-1)\mathbf{L}_i'(1) + O(z-1)^2.$$

Therefore, the leading term of the expansion is

$$\left(\frac{1}{1-z} \right)^{d+1} \mathbf{P} \circ \mathbf{L}_r \circ \mathbf{P} \circ \cdots \circ \mathbf{P} \circ \mathbf{L}_1 \circ \mathbf{P}. \tag{5.47}$$

The term second in importance is actually a sum of d terms, each obtained by replacing the operator $\mathbf{L}_i(z)$ by its derivative $\mathbf{L}_i'(1)$ at $z = 1$. The corresponding generating function $M_1(z)$ satisfies, near $z = 1$,

$$M_1(z) = \left(\frac{1}{1-z} \right)^{d+1} P(\mathcal{W}) - \left(\frac{1}{1-z} \right)^{d} P(\mathcal{W}) T(\mathcal{W}) + O\left(\frac{1}{1-z} \right)^{d-1}, \tag{5.48}$$

where the average text length $T(\mathcal{W})$ was defined in (5.44).

After applying (5.35) to $\mathbf{L}(z)$, we obtain an operator $\mathbf{M}_2(z)$ that has a pole of order d at $z = 1$. This operator is a sum of $d+1$ terms, each term containing an occurrence of the operator $\mathbf{R}(z)$ between two generating operators, those of the languages $\mathcal{W}_{i-1}$ and $\mathcal{W}_i$. The corresponding generating function $M_2(z)$ has also a pole of order d at $z = 1$ and satisfies, near $z = 1$,

$$M_2(z) = \left(\frac{1}{1-z}\right)^d P(\mathcal{W}) \sum_{i=2}^{d} c(\mathcal{W}_{i-1}, \mathcal{W}_i) + O\left(\frac{1}{1-z}\right)^{d-1}.$$

The correlation coefficient $c(\mathcal{B}, \mathcal{C})$ of $\mathcal{B}$ and $\mathcal{C}$ was defined in (5.41). To complete the proof we need only to extract the coefficients of $P(z)/(1-z)^d$, as discussed in previous sections. ∎

5.7. Exercises

5.1   Find an explicit formula for the generating function $B_2^{[p]}(z)$ of the collection $\mathcal{B}_2^{[p]}$.

5.2   Design a dynamic programming algorithm to compute the correlation algorithm $\kappa^2(\mathcal{W})$ presented in (5.12).

5.3   Establish the rate of convergence for the Gaussian law from Theorem 5.4.1.

5.4   For the fully unconstrained subsequence problem, establish the large deviation results (see Janson (2004)).

5.5   Prove (5.14).

5.6   Show that
$$\mathbf{E}[\Omega_n \log \Omega_n] - \mathbf{E}[\Omega_n] \log \mathbf{E}[\Omega] = O(n^{b-1})$$
for large n and $m = O(1)$.

5.7   Provide a detailed proof of Theorem 5.5.1.

5.8   A pattern $\mathcal{W} = \{w_1, \ldots, w_d\}$ consists of a set of patterns w_i. The pattern $\mathcal{W}$ is said to occur as a subsequence in a text if any of the w_i occurs as a subsequence. Analyze for a memoryless source this generalization of subsequence pattern matching.

5.9   Let w be a pattern. Set a window size W with $|w| \leq W \leq n$. Consider *windowed subsequence pattern matching*, in which w must appear as a subsequence within the window W. Analyze the number of windows that have at least one occurrence of w as a subsequence within a window (see Gwadera, Atallah, and Szpankowski (2003)).

5.10   In this exercise we find a different representation for Ω_n, namely as a product of random matrices. The reader is asked to prove the following result.

> **Proposition 5.7.1.**   *Consider a binary alphabet $\mathcal{A} = \{0, 1\}$. Let matrices $T(a)$ be defined for $a \in \mathcal{A}$ by*
>
> $$T(a): \quad T_{i,i}(a) = 1, T_{i+1,i}(a) = [\![w_i = a]\!], T_{i,j}(a) = 0 \quad (i \notin \{j - 1, j\}).$$
>
> *The random variable Ω_n is then*
>
> $$\Omega_n = (0, \ldots, 0, 1)\, B_n\, (1, 0, \ldots, 0)^t$$
>
> *where B_n is a random product of n matrices, each factor in the product being chosen as $T(0)$ or $T(1)$ with probabilities p or $1 - p$, respectively.*

5.11   Establish the following formula for the multivariate generating function $F_n(\mathbf{z}) = \mathbf{E}[\mathbf{z}^{\Omega_n}]$ of Ω_n. Let $\mathcal{A} = \{0, 1\}$ and the R_0, R_1 be two polynomial substitutions on $\mathbf{z} = (z_0, z_1, \ldots, z_m)$, defined by

$$R_a: \quad u_0 \mapsto z_0, \quad z_j \mapsto z_{j-1} z_j^{[\![w_j = a]\!]}$$

for $a \in \mathcal{A}$. The probability generating function $F_n(\mathbf{z}) = \mathbf{E}[\mathbf{z}^{\Omega_n}]$ satisfies the recursion

$$F_{n+1}(\mathbf{z}) = p R_0 [F_n(\mathbf{z})] + (1 - p) R_1 [F_n(\mathbf{z})], \qquad F_0(\mathbf{z}) = u_0.$$

5.12   Prove the generating operator identities (5.32)–(5.35) and (5.38)–(5.40).

5.13   Prove the second part of Theorem 5.6.1, that is, derive the formula (5.45) for the variance of $\Omega_n(\mathcal{W})$.

5.14   Does the central limit theorem hold for the generalized subsequence problem discussed in Section 5.6? What about large deviations?

5.15   We now consider the unconstrained subsequence problem (i.e., the gaps d_j between symbols are infinite); however, now we will assume that the pattern length m grows linearly with n. More precisely, we assume that $m = \theta n$ for $0 < \theta < 1$. Clearly, we still have

$$\mathbf{E}[\Omega_n(w)] = \binom{n}{m} P(w).$$

For typical patterns w, that is, when $P(w) \sim 2^{-mH(p)}$ where $H(p) = -p \log p - (1 - p) \log(1 - p)$ is the entropy, prove that

$$\mathbf{E}[\Omega_n(w)] \sim 2^{n(H(\theta) - \theta H(p))}.$$

5.16   For the problem discussed in Exercise 5.15, establish that

$$\text{Var}[\Omega_n(w)] = \sum_{k=1}^{m} \binom{n}{2m-k} P^2(w)\kappa^2(w) \qquad (5.49)$$

where $k = |I \cap J|$ and

$$\kappa^2(w) = \sum_{\substack{1 \le r_1 < \cdots r_k \le m \\ 1 \le s_1 < \cdots s_k \le m}} \binom{r_1 + s_1 - 2}{r_1 - 1}\binom{r_2 - r_1 + s_2 - s_1 - 2}{r_2 - r_1 - 1}$$

$$\times \binom{2m - r_k - s_k}{m - r_k} \cdots \prod_{i=1}^{k} [\![w_{r_i} = w_{s_i}]\!]\left(\frac{1}{P(w_{r_1} \cdots w_{r_k})} - 1\right)$$

and where positions r_i and s_i are "common", i.e., in I and J they overlap.

5.17   We are again in the same setting as in Exercise 5.15, that is, $m = \theta n$. In Exercise 5.16 we computed the variance. However, it is very difficult to obtain its asymptotics. To build up our intuition, assume now that the pattern $w = 0^m$ consists of m zeros. Clearly when X^n is composed of k 1s and $n - k$ 0s, then obviously $\Omega_n(0^m) = \binom{n-k}{m}$ and therefore

$$P\left(\Omega_n(0^m) = \binom{n-k}{m}\right) = \binom{n}{k} p^k (1-p)^{n-k}.$$

Prove that

$$\frac{1}{n}\log \mathbf{E}[\Omega_n^2(0^m)] \sim 2(q + \theta p - \delta)H(\theta/(q + \theta p - \delta)) + H((1-\theta)p + \delta)$$
$$+ ((1-\theta)p + \delta)\log p + (q + \theta p - \delta)\log q,$$

where $q = 1 - p$ and

$$\delta = \frac{q - \sqrt{q^2 + 4\theta(1-\theta)pq}}{2}.$$

Note that

$$\text{Var}[\Omega_n(0^m)] \sim \mathbf{E}[\Omega_n^2(0^m)] \sim 2^{n\beta(\theta,p)}$$

for large n.

Bibliographical notes

The subsequence problem has not been addressed in its generality previously, except in Flajolet, Guivarc'h, Szpankowski, and Vallée (2001) and Flajolet et al. (2006). Some specific instances of the subsequence problem were discussed in Gentleman (1994) and Gentleman and Mullin (1989). However, various approximate and "don't care" pattern matching problems have been presented in many publications, e.g., Adebiyi, Jiang, and Kaufmann (2001), Cobbs (1995), Landau and Schmidt (1993), Luczak and Szpankowski (1997), Régnier and Szpankowski (1998b) and Sagot (1998).

   This chapter was based almost entirely on Flajolet et al. (2006) (see also Flajolet et al. (2001) and Dembo and Kontoyiannis (2002)). Applications to intrusion detection are discussed in Gwadera et al. (2003). Large deviation results for the subsequence problem were proposed by Janson (2004). The generalized subsequence pattern matching discussed in Section 5.6 was taken from Bourdon and Vallée (2002). The operator generating function approach for dynamic sources was developed by Vallée (2001) and Clément et al. (2001).

Part II

APPLICATIONS

CHAPTER 6

Algorithms and Data Structures

The second part of the book, which begins with this chapter, is tuned towards the applications of pattern matching to data structures and algorithms on strings. In particular, we study digital trees such as tries and digital search trees, suffix trees, the Lempel–Ziv'77 and Lempel–Ziv'78 data compression algorithms, and string complexity (i.e., how many distinct words there are in a string).

In the present chapter we take a break from analysis and describe some popular data structures on strings. We will present simple constructions of digital

trees known as *tries* and *digital search trees* and will analyze these structures in
the chapters to come.

6.1.   Tries

A *trie* or prefix tree, is an ordered tree data structure. Its purpose is to store
keys, usually represented by strings, known in this context as records. Tries
were proposed by de la Briandais (1959) and Fredkin (1960), who introduced
the name; it is derived from re*trie*val. Tries belong to a large class of *digital
trees* that store strings in one form or another. In this chapter, besides tries we
also consider two other digital trees, namely suffix trees and digital search trees.

A trie – like every recursive data structure – consists of a root and $|\mathcal{A}|$
subtrees, where $\mathcal{A}$ is an alphabet; each of the subtrees is also a trie. Tries store
strings or records in leaves while their internal nodes act as routing nodes to the
leaves. The edges to the subtrees are usually labeled by the symbols from $\mathcal{A}$.
To insert a new string into an existing trie, one follows a path dictated by the
symbols of the new string until an empty terminal node is found (i.e., no other
string shares the same prefix), in which the string is stored. Observe that we
either store the whole string or just the suffix that is left after the path to the
leaf. When drawing a trie, we sometimes will represent leaves as square nodes
to distinguish them from branching nodes.

We now present some pseudo-codes that build tries over a set

$$\mathcal{W} = \{w^1, \cdots, w^n\}$$

of strings $w^i = w_1^i w_2^i \ldots$ written over the alphabet $\mathcal{A}$. Some comments are in
order. A tree, denoted as $\mathcal{T}$, should be understood as the pointer to the root
of a trie. In fact, for any $x \in \mathcal{A}$, we denote by $\mathcal{T}.x$ a pointer to the subtree of
$\mathcal{T}$ corresponding to the symbol $x \in \mathcal{A}$. Furthermore, we denote by $record(\mathcal{T})$ a
string stored in a node pointed by $\mathcal{T}$. Observe that for internal (routing) nodes
$record(\mathcal{T}) = \mathbf{nil}$ while for terminal nodes $record(\mathcal{T})$ is nonempty.

We will use the constructor method to build a tree containing a string w in
the root and having all its $|\mathcal{A}|$ subtrees empty. The pseudo-code achieving it is
presented below.

procedure TRIE(w)
  $\mathcal{T} \leftarrow$ TRIE()
  $record(\mathcal{T}) \leftarrow w$
  for each $a \in \mathcal{A}$
    do $\mathcal{T}.a \leftarrow \mathbf{nil}$
  return ($\mathcal{T}$)

Now we construct a trie by first inserting a word $w \in \mathcal{W}$. Below we give a code containing the procedure $\text{READ}(w)$, which extracts and returns the first symbol of w when $w \neq \textbf{nil}$ or returns $\textbf{nil}$ when $w = \textbf{nil}$.

procedure $\text{INSERTTRIE}(w, \mathcal{T})$
  if $\mathcal{T} = \textbf{nil}$ **then return** $(\text{TRIE}(w))$
  if $record(\mathcal{T}) = \textbf{nil}$
    then $\begin{cases} x \leftarrow \text{READ}(w) \\ \mathcal{T}.x = \text{INSERT}(w, \mathcal{T}.x) \end{cases}$

    else $\begin{cases} w2 \leftarrow record(\mathcal{T}) \\ y \leftarrow \text{READ}(w2) \\ record(\mathcal{T}) \leftarrow \textbf{nil} \\ \mathcal{T}.y \leftarrow \text{TRIE}(w2) \\ x \leftarrow \text{READ}(w) \\ \mathcal{T}.x \leftarrow \text{INSERTTRIE}(w, \mathcal{T}.x) \end{cases}$
  return $(\mathcal{T})$

Finally, we complete the trie construction in the pseudo-code below.

procedure $\text{BUILDTRIE}(\mathcal{W})$
  $\mathcal{T} \leftarrow \textbf{nil}$
  if $\mathcal{W} = \emptyset$ **then return** $(\mathcal{T})$
  for each $w \in \mathcal{W}$
    do $\mathcal{T} \leftarrow \text{INSERTTRIE}(\mathcal{W}, \mathcal{T})$
  return $(\mathcal{T})$

To retrieve all strings stored in a trie $\mathcal{T}$ we follow the paths to all leaves and read the strings, as presented below.

procedure $\text{EXTRACTTRIE}(\mathcal{T})$
  if $\mathcal{T} = \textbf{nil}$ **then return** $(\emptyset)$
  if $record(\mathcal{T}) \neq \textbf{nil}$ **then return** $(\{record(\mathcal{T})\})$
  $rw \leftarrow \emptyset$
  for each $x \in \mathcal{A}$
    do $\begin{cases} \mathcal{W} \leftarrow \text{EXTRACTTRIE}(\mathcal{T}.x) \\ \textbf{for each } w \in \mathcal{W} \\ \quad \textbf{do } rw \leftarrow rw + \{xw\} \end{cases}$
  return (rw)

We notice that the path to a string in a trie is the shortest prefix of the original string that is *not* a prefix of another string stored in the trie. We also notice that the trie does not depend on the order of insertion of the strings.

Example 6.1.1.   Let $\mathcal{W} = \{abaa, abba, babb, aabb, abbb\}$. Figure 6.1 shows the corresponding trie.

■

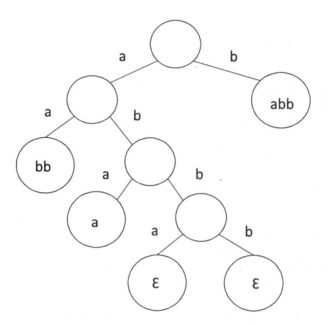

Figure 6.1. A trie built over $\mathcal{W} = \{abaa, abba, babb, aabb, abbb\}$.

There is a variation of tries, called b-tries, where the leaves may contain up to b strings. The basic trie corresponds to $b = 1$. In the general case the field record of a node is a set of no more than b records. This leads to a variation of the pseudo-code, as shown below.

procedure INSERTTRIE($w, \mathcal{T}$)

if $\mathcal{T} = $ **nil** **then return** $(\text{TRIE}(w))$
if $record(\mathcal{T}) = $ **nil**
   then $\begin{cases} x \leftarrow \text{READ}(w) \\ \mathcal{T}.x = \text{INSERTTRIE}(w, \mathcal{T}.x) \end{cases}$

   else $\begin{cases} aw2 \leftarrow record(\mathcal{T}) \\ aw2 \leftarrow aw2 + \{w\} \\ \textbf{if } |aw2| \leq b \textbf{ then } \mathcal{T} \leftarrow \text{TRIE}(aw2) \\ \\ \textbf{else} \begin{cases} record(\mathcal{T}) \leftarrow \textbf{nil} \\ \textbf{for each } w2 \in aw2 \\ \textbf{do} \begin{cases} y \leftarrow \text{READ}(w2) \\ \mathcal{T}.y \leftarrow \text{INSERTTRIE}(w2, \mathcal{T}.y) \end{cases} \end{cases} \end{cases}$

return $(\mathcal{T})$

Example 6.1.2. In Figure 6.2 we present an example of a 2-trie constructed
from the strings: *abaa, abba, babb, aabb, abbb.*   ∎

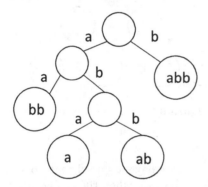

Figure 6.2. A 2-trie built from $\mathcal{W} = \{abaa, abba, babb, aabb, abbb\}$.

The case $b = 0$ is special since for it all records are **nil**. In other words,
strings are stored as paths to the leaves. We shall call such a trie a noncompact
trie or a prefix tree. However, we will not deal with such tries in this book. The
pseudo-code for insertion in a 0-trie is presented below.

procedure INSERTTRIE($w, \mathcal{T}$)
  if $\mathcal{T} =$ **nil** **then** $\mathcal{T} \leftarrow$ TRIE(**nil**)
  $x \leftarrow$ READ(w)**while** $x \neq \$$
    do $\mathcal{T}.x \leftarrow$ INSERTTRIE($w, \mathcal{T}.x$)
  $\mathcal{T}.\$ \leftarrow$ TRIE(**nil**)
  return ($\mathcal{T}$)

Example 6.1.3. Let $\mathcal{W} = \{abaa, abba, babb, aabb, abbb\}$. Figure 6.3 shows the 0-trie built from $\mathcal{W}$. ■

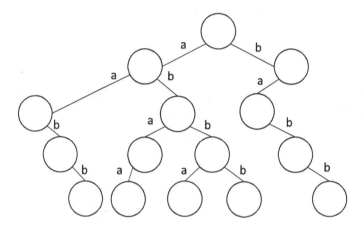

Figure 6.3. A 0-trie or spaghetti trie.

    In the discussion so far, we have assumed that no string in a trie is a prefix of another string. This is the case when the strings are potentially infinite. In order to consider *finite* strings we introduce an extra symbol, say $\$$, at the end of all strings. This new symbol is different from any symbol of $\mathcal{A}$ and indicates that the string terminates. In this case the trie is a $(|\mathcal{A}| + 1)$-tree. The subtree that corresponds to the symbol $\$$ always has its record equal to **nil**.

6.2.   Suffix trees

The *suffix tree* of a word w is simply a trie built over successive suffixes of w, where w can be unbounded in length. In other words, the (infinite) suffix tree

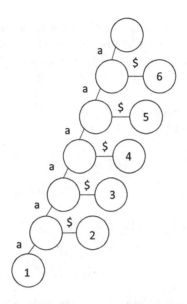

Figure 6.4. Suffix tree for $w = a^6$.

built over n suffixes is a trie over the set $\mathcal{W} = \{w_1 w_2 \cdots, w_2 w_3 \cdots, \ldots, w_n \cdots\}$.
A finite suffix tree is built over successive finite suffixes of $w\$$, that is, over the
set $\mathcal{W}\$ = \{w_1 \cdots w_n\$, \ldots, w_n\$\}$, where we use the special terminal character $\$$
to create finite length suffixes. We will work mostly with infinite suffix trees and
for brevity will refer to them just as suffix trees.

The pseudo-codes to construct suffix trees resemble those for tries. In particular, we have:

procedure BUILDSUFFIXTREE(w)
  $\mathcal{T} \leftarrow$ **nil**
  if $w =$ **nil** **then return** ($\mathcal{T}$)
  while $w \neq$ **nil**
    do $\begin{cases} x \leftarrow \text{READ}(w) \\ \mathcal{T} \leftarrow \text{INSERTTRIE}(w, \mathcal{T}) \end{cases}$
  return ($\mathcal{T}$)

The original string is easy to recover from such a trie, since it is the longest
string it contains. However, one can construct a more economical version of
the suffix tree by storing in the leaves the rank of the suffix in the original

string instead of the whole sequence of the suffix (or its remaining part). By the "rank" we mean the position of the first symbol of the suffix in w. Therefore in a suffix tree the field record is replaced by the field rank (which is set at -1 in the internal nodes). The conversion code is as follows, where n is the length of original text:

procedure CONVERTSUFFIXTREE$(n, \mathcal{T})$
  if $\mathcal{T} = $ **nil** **then return** (**nil**)
  if $record(\mathcal{T}) \neq$ **nil**
    then $\begin{cases} rank(\mathcal{T}) \leftarrow n - |record(\mathcal{T})| \\ \textbf{return } (\mathcal{T}) \end{cases}$
  $rank(\mathcal{T}) \leftarrow -1$
  for each $a \in \mathcal{A}$
    do $\{\mathcal{T}.a \leftarrow$ CONVERTSUFFIXTREE$(n - 1, \mathcal{T}.a)$
  return $(\mathcal{T})$

Example 6.2.1. Figure 6.4 shows the suffix tree built over the string $w = aaaaaa = a^6\$$ while Figure 6.5 shows the suffix tree for $w = abaabb\$$. ∎

The reconstruction of the original text is easy. For this it suffices to extract for each suffix its rank and its path to its leaf. The following procedure returns an array S, where $S[i]$ is the path to the leaf of the ith suffix.

procedure EXTRACTARRAYSUFFIX$(\mathcal{T})$
  $R \leftarrow$ EXTRACTSETSUFFIX$(\mathcal{T})$
  for each $(w, i) \in R$
    do $S[i] \leftarrow w$
  return (S)

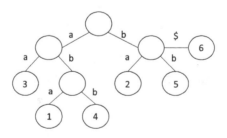

Figure 6.5. Suffix tree for $w = abaabb$.

procedure ExtractSetSuffix($\mathcal{T}$)
  if $\mathcal{T} = $ **nil** **then return** ($\emptyset$)
  if $rank(\mathcal{T}) \neq -1$ **then return** (**nil**, $rank(\mathcal{T})$)
  $S \leftarrow \emptyset$
  for each $a \in \mathcal{A} + \{\$\}$
  do $\begin{cases} Sa \leftarrow \text{ExtractSetSuffix}(\mathcal{T}.a) \\ \textbf{for each } (w, i) \in Sa \\ \quad \textbf{do } S \leftarrow S + \{(aw, i)\} \end{cases}$
  return (S)

In the next section we present one of many possible applications of suffix trees, namely an application to code words for the Lempel–Ziv'77 data compression algorithm.

We will return to suffix trees in Chapter 8, where we present an analysis of their depth and show to what extent they resemble tries.

6.3. Lempel–Ziv'77 scheme

We now briefly discuss one of the most popular data compression algorithms designed in 1977 by Ziv and Lempel and known as the Lempel–Ziv'77 algorithm or LZ'77. The Lempel–Ziv algorithm partitions or parses a sequence into *phrases* that are similar in some sense. Depending on how such a parsing is encoded we have different versions of the algorithm. However, the basic idea is to find the longest prefix of a yet uncompressed sequence that occurs in an already compressed sequence. For this task, the *associated suffix tree* is very useful, as we shall see below.

More specifically, let us assume that the first n symbols of the sequence $X_1^n = X_1, \ldots, X_n$ is given to the encoder and the decoder. This initial string is sometimes called the *database string* or *training sequence*. Then we search for the longest prefix $X_{n+1}^{n+\ell}$ of X_{n+1}^∞ which has a copy in X_1^n, that is, the largest integer ℓ such that $X_{n+1}^{n+\ell} = X_m^{m+\ell-1}$ for some prescribed range of m and ℓ. We denote this largest integer ℓ as D_n. Depending on the ranges for m and ℓ, we can have different versions of the LZ'77 scheme.

The code built for LZ'77 consists of a sequence of triple (m, ℓ, char), where char is the symbol $X_{m+\ell}$, m is a pointer to a position in the string, and ℓ is the length of the repeated substring occurring at position m. Since the pointer to m needs $\log_2 n$ bits, the length ℓ can be coded in $O(\log D_n)$ bits and char requires $\log |\mathcal{A}|$ bits, we conclude that the code length is equal to $\log_2 n + O(\log D_n) + \log_2 |\mathcal{A}|$ bits.

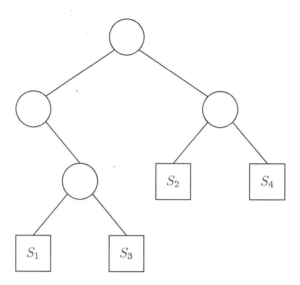

Figure 6.6. Suffix tree built from the first four suffixes of $X = 1010010001\cdots$; thus $S_1 = X_1^{10} = 1010010001$, $S_2 = X_2^{10} = 010010001$, $S_3 = X_3^{10} == 10010001$ and $S_4 = X_4^{10} == 010001$.

The heart of all versions of the Lempel–Ziv scheme is the algorithm that finds the longest prefix of length D_n that occurs in a database string of length n. It turns out that the suffix tree discussed in the previous section can be used efficiently to find such a prefix. Indeed, let us consider a sequence $X = 1010010001\cdots$, and assume that X_1^4 is the database string. The suffix tree built over X_1^4 is shown in Figure 6.6. Let us now look for D_4, that is, the longest prefix of X_5^∞ that occurs in the database X_1^4. In the growing database implementation it is X_5^8 since this is equal to X_2^5. We can see this by inserting the fifth suffix of X into the suffix tree from Figure 6.6, which leads to the suffix tree shown in Figure 6.7. In these two figures we denote the leaves by squares to distinguish them from the internal nodes.

6.4.   Digital search tree

The digital search tree (DST) is another digital tree structure. Unlike in a trie, the records in a DST are stored in all the nodes. The root contains either the first record or an empty record, depending on the application. As with tries, to

$$S_1 = 1010010001 \qquad S_4 = 0010001$$
$$S_2 = 010010001 \qquad S_5 = 010001$$
$$S_3 = 10010001$$

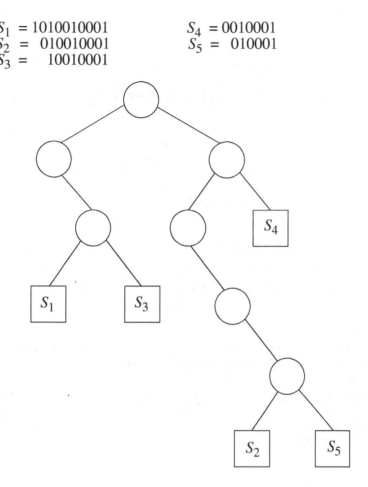

Figure 6.7. Suffix tree built from the first five suffixes $S_1, \dots, S_5$ of $X = 1010010001 \dots$ where $S_5 = 010001$.

recover stored records we read the DST from the root to all nodes, concatenating the sequence of symbols along paths and the records stored in nodes.

Let us assume that we insert into a digital tree n records $w^1, \dots, w^n$, where each record is a string (perhaps infinite) over the alphabet $\mathcal{A}$. More precisely, the root usually contains the first string although in some applications the root may contain an empty string. The next string occupies the ath child of the root if its first symbol is $a \in \mathcal{A}$. The remaining strings are stored in available nodes which are directly attached to already existing nodes in the tree. The search for an existing node in the tree follows the prefix structure of a string, as for tries. That is, if the next symbol in a string is $a \in \mathcal{A}$ then we move to the subtree corresponding to a. This is illustrated in the next example.

Example 6.4.1.   Let $\mathcal{W} = \{abb, babb, aabb, abbb\}$. Figure 6.8 shows the DST built over $\mathcal{W}$. ∎

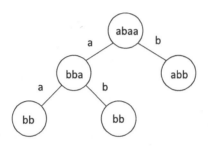

Figure 6.8. A digital search tree over $\mathcal{W} = \{abb, babb, aabb, abbb\}$.

The pseudo-code that builds a digital tree is very similar to that for tries, so we list below just the three procedures: DST(w), INSERTDST($w, \mathcal{T}$), and BUILDDST($\mathcal{W}$).

procedure DST(w)
   $\mathcal{T} \leftarrow$ DST()
   $record(\mathcal{T}) \leftarrow w$
   for each $a \in \mathcal{A}$
      do $\mathcal{T}.a \leftarrow$ **nil**
   return ($\mathcal{T}$)

procedure INSERTDST($w, \mathcal{T}$)
   if $\mathcal{T} =$ **nil**   **then return** (DST(w))
   $x \leftarrow$ READ(w)
   $\mathcal{T}.x \leftarrow$ INSERTDST($w, \mathcal{T}.x$)
   return ($\mathcal{T}$)

procedure BUILDDST($\mathcal{W}$)

$\mathcal{T} \leftarrow \textbf{nil}$
if $\mathcal{W} = \emptyset$ **then return** $(\mathcal{T})$
for each $w \in \mathcal{W}$
   do $\mathcal{T} \leftarrow \text{INSERTDST}(\mathcal{W}, \mathcal{T})$
return $(\mathcal{T})$

A few comments are in order. Notice that the shape, or structure, of a DST depends on the order of string insertion. However, a particular DST shape can be obtained via several insertion orders. For this it suffices that the partial order of strings starting with the same symbol is not modified. The enumeration of such trees is an interesting problem. In particular, for the enumeration of DST trees with a given total path, the reader is referred to Seroussi (2006a) (see also Knessl and Szpankowski (2005) and Seroussi (2006b)).

The recovery of a set of strings is very similar to the extraction from a trie, with the addition that one must also extract the records in the internal nodes:

procedure $\text{EXTRACTDST}(\mathcal{T})$
  if $\mathcal{T} = \textbf{nil}$ **then return** $(\emptyset)$
  $S \leftarrow record(\mathcal{T})$
  for each $a \in \mathcal{A}$
    do $\begin{cases} Sa \leftarrow \text{EXTRACTDST}(\mathcal{T}.a) \\ \textbf{for each } w \in Sa \\ \quad \textbf{do } S \leftarrow S + \{aw\} \end{cases}$
  return (S)

6.5. Parsing trees and Lempel–Ziv'78 algorithm

A digital search tree has an equivalent suffix tree image, which is sometimes called the parsing tree and is used in variable-to-fixed compression algorithms. However, unlike suffix trees, parsing trees do not necessarily contain all suffixes of the original text. To understand this better, we need to say a few words about variable-to-fixed codes.

A variable-to-fixed-length encoder partitions the source string over the alphabet $\mathcal{A}$ into a sequence of variable-length phrases. Each phrase belongs to a given dictionary of source strings. A uniquely parsable dictionary is represented by a *complete parsing tree*, i.e., a tree in which every internal node has exactly $|\mathcal{A}|$ children nodes. The dictionary entries correspond to the *leaves* of the associated parsing tree. The encoder maps each parsed string into the fixed-length binary code word corresponding to its dictionary entry. There are several well-known variable-to-fixed algorithms. Here we concentrate on the Lempel–Ziv'78 scheme, which we describe next.

Let us first consider the parsing process. The idea is to partition a sequence, say w, into variable phrases, each of which is a path from the root to a leaf in the associated parsing tree. This parsing tree is a digital search tree. At the beginning the associated DST contains the **nil** string in the root. The first suffix is then inserted into the tree. The path to its leaf is the prefix of w and forms the first phrase. The next suffix of w to be inserted is the suffix that starts just after the phrase created in the insertion of the first suffix. This process is repeated until the text is exhausted or the tree contains the required number of suffixes or leaves, corresponding to the code words or entries in the code dictionary.

Let us first present the pseudo-codes constructing a parsing tree.

procedure BUILDPARSINGTREE(m, w)
$\mathcal{T} \leftarrow \text{DST}(\textbf{nil})$
$k \leftarrow 0$
while $k < m$
$\quad$**do** $\begin{cases} k \leftarrow k + 1 \\ (w, \mathcal{T}) \leftarrow \text{INSERTPHRASE}(w, \mathcal{T}) \end{cases}$
return $(\mathcal{T})$

procedure INSERTPHRASE$(w, \mathcal{T})$
$\quad$**if** $\mathcal{T} = \textbf{nil}$ **then return** $(w, \text{DST}(w))$
$x \leftarrow \text{READ}(w)$
$(w, \mathcal{T}.x) \leftarrow \text{INSERTPHRASE}(w, \mathcal{T}.x)$
return $(w, \mathcal{T})$

As with a suffix tree, it is more convenient to replace the strings that are stored in the nodes by their rank. The corresponding change in the above code is rather trivial, since it consists of carrying the integer k into the argument of INSERTPHRASE(). Below we give a version of the code which is not recursive.

procedure BUILDPHRASETREE(w, m)
$\mathcal{T}_m \leftarrow \text{DST}(0)$
$k \leftarrow 1$
while $k \leq m$
$\quad$**do** $\begin{cases} x \leftarrow \text{READ}(w) \\ \mathcal{T}' \leftarrow \mathcal{T}_m \\ \textbf{while } \mathcal{T}'.x \neq \textbf{nil} \\ \quad \textbf{do } \begin{cases} \mathcal{T}' \leftarrow \mathcal{T}'.x \\ x \leftarrow \text{READ}(w) \end{cases} \\ \mathcal{T}'.x \leftarrow \text{DST}(k) \\ k \leftarrow k + 1 \end{cases}$
return $(\mathcal{T}_m)$

where we use the following constructor

procedure DST(k)
  $\mathcal{T} \leftarrow$ DST()
  $rank(\mathcal{T}) \leftarrow k$
  for each $a \in \mathcal{A}$
    do $\mathcal{T}.a \leftarrow$ **nil**
  return ($\mathcal{T}$)

Example 6.5.1. The infinite sequence $w = a^\infty = aaaaa \cdots$ is parsed into increasing sequences $()(a)(a^2)(a^3) \cdots$, etc. The tree given by BUILDDST($w, 3$) is shown in Figure 6.9. ∎

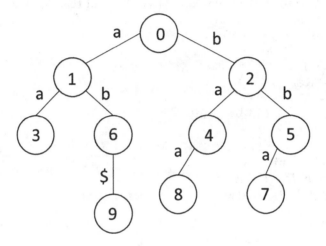

Figure 6.9. Digital search tree for an infinite sequence limited to the first three phrases ($m = 3$).

Now we are ready to describe the Lempel–Ziv'78 compression algorithm. In general, it is a *dictionary-based* scheme, which partitions a sequence into phrases (sometimes called blocks) of variable size such that a new phrase is the shortest substring that has not appeared previously as a phrase. Every such phrase is encoded by a tuple made of a pointer and a symbol from $\mathcal{A}$. The pointer is the index of the longest prefix which appeared before as a phrase, and the symbol one must append to this prefix in order to make the new phrase. Thus the LZ'78 code consists of a sequence of (`pointer, symbol`) tuples. To be more specific, let us continue with Example 6.5.1. We now replace each phrase by the pair (`pointer`,`symbol`), where the pointer is the rank number of the parent phrase in the associated tree and the symbol is the extra symbol added to the parent phrase to create the current phrase. In our example, we obtain

$$(0a)(1a)(2a)\cdots.$$

This is in fact the Lempel–Ziv'78 partition of a^∞. Observe that knowledge of this last sequence is equivalent to knowledge of the tree and is therefore sufficient to reconstruct the original text.

The previous code can be adapted to a finite sequence w as shown below. To make this rigorous we have to assume that the text w ends with an extra symbol $\$$ never occurring before in the text. To each node in $\mathcal{T}(w)$ there corresponds a phrase in the parsing algorithm. Let $L(w)$ be the path length of $\mathcal{T}(w)$, that is, the sum of paths to all the nodes in the tree. We find that $L(w) = |w|$.

procedure BUILDDST(w)

$\mathcal{T} \leftarrow$ TREE(0)

$k \leftarrow 1$

while $w \neq$ **nil**

    do $\begin{cases} x \leftarrow \text{READ}(w) \\ \mathcal{T}' \leftarrow \mathcal{T} \\ \textbf{while } \mathcal{T}'.x \neq \textbf{nil}\&w \neq \textbf{nil} \\ \quad \textbf{do } \begin{cases} \mathcal{T}' \leftarrow \mathcal{T}'.x \\ x \leftarrow \text{READ}(w) \end{cases} \\ \textbf{if } \mathcal{T}'.x = \textbf{nil} \\ \quad \textbf{then } \mathcal{T}'.x \leftarrow \text{TREE}(k) \\ \quad \textbf{else } \mathcal{T}'.\$ \leftarrow \text{TREE}(k) \\ k \leftarrow k + 1 \end{cases}$

return $(\mathcal{T})$

Example 6.5.2. Let $w = abaababbabbbabaaab\$$. The corresponding parsing tree in the Lempel–Ziv'78 scheme is presented in Figure 6.10. The phrase sequence is the following:

$$()(a)(b)(aa)(ba)(bb)(ab)(bba)(baa)(ab).$$

Replacing each phrase by the pointer and the extra symbol leads to

$$(0a)(0b)(1a)(2a)(2b)(1b)(5a)(4a)(6\$)$$

which is the Lempel–Ziv'78 code for w. ■

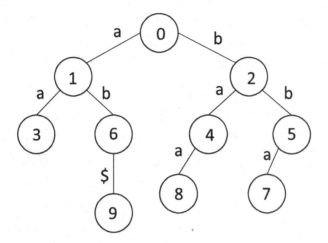

Figure 6.10. Digital search tree for the finite sequence $w = abaababbabbbabaaab$.

Observe that knowledge of the tree $\mathcal{T}(w)$ without the node sequence order is not sufficient to recover the original text w. But knowledge of $\mathcal{T}(w)$ together with the rank number will reconstruct the original text w, as shown below:

procedure REBUILD($\mathcal{T}$)
  for $i \leftarrow 1$ **to** $|\mathcal{T}|$
    do $wt[i] \leftarrow$ **nil**
  $wt \leftarrow$ RETRIEVE($\mathcal{T}, wt, $**nil**$)$
  return (wt)

procedure RETRIEVE($\mathcal{T}, wt, w$)
  $wt[rank(\mathcal{T})] \leftarrow w$
  for each $a \in \mathcal{A}$
    do $\{$**if** $\mathcal{T}.a \neq$ **nil then** $wt \leftarrow$ RETRIEVE($\mathcal{T}.a, wt, wa$)
  if $\mathcal{T}.\$ \neq$ **nil then** $wt[rank(\mathcal{T}.\$)] \leftarrow w$
  return (wt)

To summarize, we present one more example that will help us to understand universal types.

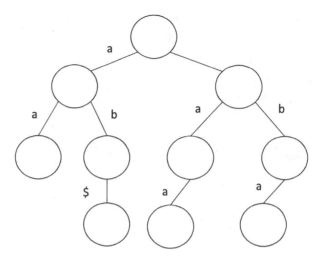

Figure 6.11. The digital search tree for *abaababbabbaabbaab* which is the same as in Figure 6.10 for *abaababbabbbabaaab*.

Example 6.5.3. Consider the sequence *abaababbabbbabaab*, which partitions into

$$(a)(b)(aa)(ba)(bb)(ab)(bba)(baa).$$

The associated digital tree is presented in Figure 6.10. Now consider another string *abaababbabbaabba* that is parsed into

$$(a)(b)(aa)(ba)(bb)(baa)(bba)$$

and the associated digital tree is presented in Figure 6.11. But both figures are the same! In fact, both sequences parse into the same *set* of phrases, even if these parsings are different. Notice that phrase number 7 and phrase number 8 are inverted. We say that both strings belong to the same universal types, as discussed in the example below.   ∎

In this last example we show that different sequences may lead to the same digital search tree. We say that such sequences belong to the same universal type, as discussed in depth in Seroussi (2006a).

Example 6.5.4. Figure 6.12 shows two different Lempel–Ziv'78 trees, (a) and (b), each corresponding to the same *set* of phrases. In Figure 6.12(a) sequences

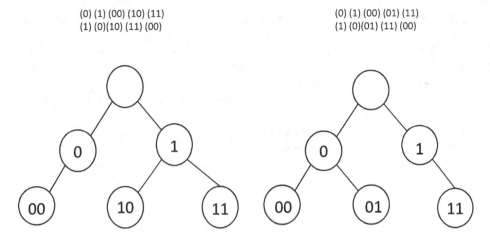

Figure 6.12. Two universal types and the corresponding trees

01001011 and 10101100 lead to the following set of phrases $\{0, 1, 00, 10, 11\}$. In Figure 6.12(b) the set of phrases is $\{0, 1, 00, 01, 11\}$. ∎

Bibliographical notes

The algorithmic aspects of pattern matching have been presented in numerous books. We mention here Crochemore and Rytter (1994) and Gusfield (1997) (see also Apostolico (1985)). Public domain utilities such as `agrep`, `grappe`, and `webglimpse` for finding general patterns were developed by Wu and Manber (1995), Kucherov and Rusinowitch (1997), and others. Various data compression schemes are presented in Burrows and Wheeler (1994), Crochemore, Mignosi, Restivo, and Salemi (2000), Dembo and Kontoyiannis (2002), Wyner and Ziv (1989), Wyner (1997), Yang and Kieffer (1998), Ziv and Lempel (1978) and Ziv and Merhav (1993). In particular, the Lempel–Ziv'77 algorithm was first presented in Ziv and Lempel (1977), while the Lempel-Ziv'78 scheme was described in Ziv and Lempel (1978). We present an analysis of the LZ'77 algorithm in Chapter 8. The LZ'78 algorithm is discussed in some depth in Chapter 9.

The "brute force" construction of a suffix tree (by insertion of the suffixes one at a time) requires, in the worst case, quadratic time while the average time complexity is $O(n \log n)$; see Alon and Spencer (1992). There are, however, several $O(n \log |\mathcal{A}|)$ constructions. The algorithm by McCreight (1976) and the one by Blumer et al. (1985) are variations on Weiner (1973). Note that these algorithms take only a linear time for finite alphabets. All these constructions are *offline* because they process the text in the reverse order from right to left. An online algorithm by Ukkonen (1995) also achieves linear time. Farach (1997) proposed an optimal construction for large alphabets.

There are several other well known variable-to-fixed algorithms such as Khodak (1969) and Tunstall (1967). The reader is referred to Drmota, Reznik, and Szpankowski (2010) and Savari and Gallager (1997) for in-depth analyses of the Tunstall and Khodak algorithms.

CHAPTER 7

Digital Trees

Digital trees are fundamental data structures on words. Among them *tries* and *digital search trees* stand out because they have a myriad of applications. Owing to their simplicity and efficiency, tries have found widespread use in diverse applications ranging from document taxonomy to IP address lookup, from data compression to dynamic hashing, from partial-match queries to speech recognition, from leader election algorithms to distributed hashing tables.

Tries are prototype data structures useful for many indexing and retrieval purposes. We described their construction in detail in Chapter 6, so here we only briefly review some facts. Tries were first proposed by de la Briandais (1959) for information processing. Fredkin (1960) suggested the current name, part of the word re*trie*val. Tries are trees whose nodes are vectors of characters or digits; they are a natural choice of data structure when the input records involve the notion of alphabets or digits. Given a sequence of n words over the alphabet $\mathcal{A} = \{a_1, \ldots, a_{|\mathcal{A}|}\}$, $|\mathcal{A}| \geq 2$, we construct a trie as follows. If $n = 0$ then the trie is empty. If $n = 1$ then a single external node holding the word is allocated. If $n \geq 1$ then the trie consists of a root (i.e., internal) node directing words to $|\mathcal{A}|$ subtrees according to the first symbol of each word, and words directed to the same subtree are themselves tries. The *internal nodes* in tries are branching nodes, used merely to direct records to each subtrie; the record strings are all stored in *external nodes*, which are leaves of such tries. In Figure 6.1 a binary trie built over five records is shown.

Digital search trees were discussed in Section 6.4. In a *digital search tree* (DST) record strings are directly stored in nodes. For a binary alphabet $\mathcal{A} = \{0, 1\}$, the root contains the first string (or an empty string) and the next string occupies the right or the left child of the root depending on whether its first symbol is 0 or 1. The remaining strings are stored in nodes which are directly attached to already existing nodes in the tree. The search for an available node follows the prefix structure of a new string. Sometimes external nodes are added to such constructed trees, as was shown in Figure 6.8. These external nodes are positions where the next inserted string may end up.

In this chapter, we analyze various digital tree shape parameters (e.g., depth, path length, profile) in a probabilistic framework. As throughout this book, we assume that the n words that are stored (strings, sequences, records) are generated by memoryless or Markov sources. We mostly study digital trees built over a binary alphabet $\mathcal{A} = \{0, 1\}$ and denote by $p = P(0)$ the probability of generating a zero; we also write $q = 1 - p$. However, all results presented in this chapter can be quite easily generalized to a general alphabet $\mathcal{A}$.

7.1. Digital tree shape parameters

We now define some shape parameters of a digital tree. Throughout we assume that n strings (records) are inserted into a tree. To simplify our presentation we will focus on tries, but our definitions work also for digital search trees.

For a trie built from n strings (see Figure 7.1) we define:

- the *depth* $D_n(i)$ to the ith (external) node as the path length from the root to the ith node or, equivalently, the level of the ith node;

- the *typical depth* D_n as the path length to a randomly selected node, that

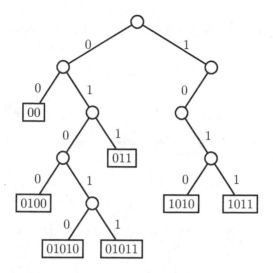

Figure 7.1. A trie built over $n = 7$ record strings, $00\cdots$, $011\cdots$, $0100\cdots$, $01010\cdots$, $01011\cdots$, $1010\cdots$, and $1011\cdots$.

is,

$$P(D_n = k) = \frac{1}{n}\sum_{i=1}^{n} P(D_n(i) = k);$$

- the *depth of insertion* $D_n(n+1)$ as the depth of the new, $(n+1)$th, string inserted into a trie built from n strings;

- the *path length* L_n as the sum of the depths to all (external) nodes, that is,

$$L_n = \sum_{i=1}^{n} D_n(i);$$

- the *height* H_n as the longest path, that is,

$$H_n = \max_{1 \le i \le n}\{D_n(i)\};$$

- the *fillup level* F_n as the last level containing all internal nodes, that is,

$$F_n = \max_{\ell \ge 0}\{\#\text{ internal nodes at level k} = |\mathcal{A}|^{\ell}\};$$

- the *shortest path* R_n as the length of the shortest path from the root to an *external node*, that is,

$$R_n = \min_{1 \leq i \leq n} \{D_n(i)\};$$

- the *size* S_n as the number of (internal) nodes in the tree;

- the *internal profile* $I_{n,k}$ as the number of internal nodes at level k (see Figure 7.2);

- the *external profile* $B_{n,k}$ as the number of external nodes at level k (see Figure 7.2).

There are relationships between these parameters. For example, all parameters can be expressed in terms of the external and internal profiles. Indeed,

$$L_n = \sum_j j I_{n,j},$$
$$H_n = \max\{j : B_{n,j} > 0\},$$
$$R_n = \min\{j : B_{n,j} > 0\},$$
$$F_n = \max\{j : I_{n,j} = 2^j\},$$
$$S_n = \sum_j I_{n,j}.$$

We also have the following relationship between the typical depth D_n and the average external profile $\mathbf{E}[B_{n,k}]$:

$$P(D_n = k) = \frac{\mathbf{E}[B_{n,k}]}{n}. \tag{7.1}$$

The reader is asked in Exercise 7.1 to provide a simple argument to prove equation (7.1).

Another parameter, the *multiplicity parameter* M_n, is of interest, especially for the suffix trees to be discussed in Chapter 8. To define M_n, let us first introduce a useful notion, that of the *alignment* C_{ij}, the length of the longest common prefix of the ith and jth strings. Observe that we have the following relationships:

$$D_n(i) = \max_{1 \leq j \leq n} \{C_{ij}, \; j \neq i\} + 1, \tag{7.2}$$
$$H_n = \max_{i \neq j} \{C_{ij}\} + 1. \tag{7.3}$$

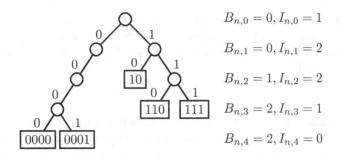

Figure 7.2. A trie of $n = 5$ record strings; the rectangles holding the
records are external nodes and the circles represent internal nodes.

Then the multiplicity parameter M_n is defined as

$$M_n = \#\{j : \ C_{j,n+1} + 1 = D_n(n+1), \ 1 \leq j \leq n\} \qquad (7.4)$$

where we recall that $D_n(n+1) = \max_j C_{j,n+1} + 1$ is the depth of insertion. In
other words, M_n is the number of strings that have the longest common prefix
with the $(n+1)$th (inserted) string. In terms of the underlying trie, built from
the first n strings, the multiplicity parameter M_n is the size of the subtree rooted
at the branching point of the (new) insertion of the $(n+1)$th string.

7.2. Moments

In this section we focus on evaluating the moments (mostly the mean and variance) of some shape parameters of tries and digital trees. We do our analysis for
binary alphabets but all results can be extended easily to an arbitrary alphabet.

7.2.1. Average path length in a trie by Rice's method

Let us consider a trie built over n strings generated by a binary memoryless
source with p the probability of generating a zero and $q = 1 - p$. We first
deal with the average depth $\mathbf{E}[D_n]$ and the average path length $\mathbf{E}[L_n]$. Clearly,
$\mathbf{E}[L_n] = n\mathbf{E}[D_n]$, thus we need to evaluate only one of these parameters. It
turns out that the average path length is easier to derive.

Let $l_n = \mathbf{E}[L_n]$ in a binary trie. It should be easy to see that l_n satisfies the
following recurrence for $n \geq 2$:

$$l_n = n + \sum_{k=0}^{n} \binom{n}{k} p^k q^{n-k} (l_k + l_{n-k}) \qquad (7.5)$$

with $l_0 = l_1 = 0$. Indeed, n strings at the root are split into left and right subtrees according to whether the first symbol of these strings is 0 or 1. The probability that k out of n strings starts with 0 is binomially distributed, i.e., it is equal to

$$\binom{n}{k} p^k q^{n-k}.$$

Finally, the subtrees are tries of sizes k and $n - k$, respectively.

The above recurrence falls into a general recurrence of the following form

$$x_n = a_n + \sum_{k=0}^n \binom{n}{k} p^k q^{n-k}(x_k + x_{n-k}), \quad n \ge 2 \tag{7.6}$$

with $x_0 = x_1 = 0$ and a_n a given sequence (in our case $a_n = n$). We can solve (7.6) using an exponential generating function, defined as

$$X(z) = \sum_{n \ge 0} x_n \frac{z^n}{n!}.$$

We also define the *Poisson transform* as $\widetilde{X}(z) = X(z)e^{-z}$. Then, after multiplying by $z^n/n!$ and using the convolution formula, we arrive at the following functional equation for $\widetilde{X}(z)$:

$$\widetilde{X}(z) = \widetilde{A}(z) + \widetilde{X}(zp) + \widetilde{X}(zq) - a_0 e^{-z} - a_1 z e^{-z} \tag{7.7}$$

where $\widetilde{A}(z) = A(z)e^{-z} = e^{-z} \sum_{n=0}^{\infty} a_n z^n/n!$. Since $\widetilde{x}_n = n![z^n]\widetilde{X}(z)$,[1] the quantities $\widetilde{x}_n$ and x_n are related by

$$x_n = \sum_{k=0}^n \binom{n}{k} \widetilde{x}_k. \tag{7.8}$$

To solve (7.5) we need to introduce the *binomial inverse relations*, defined as

$$\hat{a}_n = \sum_{k=0}^n \binom{n}{k} (-1)^k a_k, \qquad a_n = \sum_{k=0}^n \binom{n}{k} (-1)^k \hat{a}_k \tag{7.9}$$

which follow immediately from the exponential functional relations

$$\hat{A}(z) = A(-z)e^z, \qquad A(z) = \hat{A}(-z)e^z$$

---

[1] See (1.32) for the meaning of the notation $[z^n]\widetilde{X}(z)$.

or the simple combinatorial relation[2]

$$\llbracket n = k \rrbracket = \sum_{j=0}^{n} (-1)^{j+k} \binom{n}{j} \binom{j}{k}.$$

For example, in Exercise 7.2 we ask the reader to prove, for nonnegative r, that

$$a_n = \binom{n}{r}, \qquad \hat{a}_n = (-1)^r \delta_{n,r}$$

where $\delta_{n,r} = 1$ if $n = r$ and zero otherwise.

After comparing the coefficients of $\widetilde{X}(z)$ at z^n in (7.7) we can solve the recurrence (7.5). We give the solution in the following simple lemma.

Lemma 7.2.1. *The recurrence (7.6) has the following solution*

$$x_n = \sum_{k=2}^{n} (-1)^k \binom{n}{k} \frac{\hat{a}_k + ka_1 - a_0}{1 - p^k - q^k}, \tag{7.10}$$

where $n![z^n]\widetilde{A}(z) = \widetilde{a}_n := (-1)^n \hat{a}_n$. Furthermore,

$$\hat{x}_n = \frac{\hat{a}_k + ka_1 - a_0}{1 - p^k - q^k} \tag{7.11}$$

for all n.

Proof. Comparing the coefficients at z^k of (7.7) we find

$$\widetilde{x}_k = \frac{\widetilde{a}_k - (-1)^k a_0 - a_1(-1)^{k-1}k}{1 - p^k - q^k}.$$

Noting that $\widetilde{a}_k = (-1)^k \hat{a}_k$ and using (7.8) completes the proof. ∎

In view of this, we can also derive an exact expression for the average path length, namely

$$l_n = \sum_{k=2}^{n} (-1)^k \binom{n}{k} \frac{k}{1 - p^k - q^k} \tag{7.12}$$

for $n \geq 2$. We should point out that (7.12) has the form of an alternating sum. This suggests that the asymptotics of l_n may require sophisticated analytic tools. This turns out to be the case, as we shall see next.

---

[2]Recall that $\llbracket a = b \rrbracket = 1$ if and only if $a = b$.

In order to find an asymptotic expansion of l_n, we appeal to the so-called Rice method. Let us consider a general alternating sum of the form

$$S_n[f] := \sum_{k=m}^{n} (-1)^k \binom{n}{k} f_k$$

for some fixed m and any function f that enjoys a valid analytic continuation to a complex plane.

Theorem 7.2.2 (Rice's formula). *Let $f(s)$ be an analytic continuation of $f(k) = f_k$ that contains the half line $[m, \infty)$. Then*

$$S_n[f] := \sum_{k=m}^{n} (-1)^k \binom{n}{k} f_k = \frac{(-1)^n}{2\pi i} \int_{\mathcal{C}_{[m,n]}} f(z) \frac{n!}{z(z-1)\cdots(z-n)} dz$$

$$= -\frac{1}{2\pi i} \int_{\mathcal{C}_{[m,n]}} B(n+1,-z) f(z) dz, \qquad (7.13)$$

where $\mathcal{C}_{[m,n]}$ is a positively oriented curve that encircles $[m,n]$ and does not include any of the integers $0, 1, \ldots, m-1$ and where $B(x,y) = \Gamma(x)\Gamma(y)/\Gamma(x+y)$ is the beta function.

Proof. This requires a direct application of the residue calculus after noting that the poles within $\mathcal{C}$ of the integrand are at $k = m, m+1, \ldots, n$ and that

$$\text{Res}\left[\frac{n!}{z(z-1)\cdots(z-n)} f(z); \; z=k \right] = (-1)^{n-k} \binom{n}{k} f(k).$$

This completes the proof.   ∎

Another representation of $S_n[f]$ is sometimes easier to handle computationally. (It was called by Knuth (1998) the gamma method.) In this case, however, we need to restrict f to *polynomial growth*, that is, $f(s) = O(|s|^k)$ for some k as $s \to \infty$. In fact, when evaluating the integral in the Rice method, we must usually impose some growth condition on f over large circles. The proof uses a simple residue theorem argument, as above, and is left to the reader to perform in Exercise 7.4.

Theorem 7.2.3 (Szpankowski, 1988). *Let $f(z)$ be of polynomial growth at infinity and let it be analytic to the left of the vertical line $(\frac{1}{2} - m - i\infty, \frac{1}{2} - m + i\infty)$.*

Then

$$S_n[f] = \frac{1}{2\pi i} \int_{\frac{1}{2}-m-i\infty}^{\frac{1}{2}-m+i\infty} f(-s)B(n+1,s)dz \qquad (7.14)$$

$$= \frac{1}{2\pi i} \int_{\frac{1}{2}-m-i\infty}^{\frac{1}{2}-m+i\infty} f(-s)n^{-s}\Gamma(s)\left(1 - \frac{s(s+1)}{2n}\right. \qquad (7.15)$$

$$+ \frac{s(1+s)}{24n^2}(3(1+s)^2 + s - 1) + O(n^{-3})\Big) ds, \qquad \Re(s) > 0,$$

where as before $B(x,y) = \Gamma(x)\Gamma(y)/\Gamma(x+y)$ is the beta function.

We now note that (7.12) falls into the Rice method paradigm. If we apply Theorem 7.2.3 to (7.12), that translates into

$$l_n = \frac{1}{2\pi i} \int_{-\frac{3}{2}-i\infty}^{-\frac{3}{2}+i\infty} \frac{-sB(n+1,s)}{1-p^{-s}-q^{-s}} n^{-s}ds$$

$$= -\frac{1+O(1/n)}{2\pi i} \int_{-\frac{3}{2}-i\infty}^{-\frac{3}{2}+i\infty} \frac{\Gamma(s+1)}{1-p^{-s}-q^{-s}} n^{-s}ds, \qquad (7.16)$$

where the integration is along the vertical line $(-\frac{3}{2}-i\infty, -\frac{3}{2}+i\infty)$ in the complex plane. In what follows, we ignore the error term, which is of order $O(1/n)$.

We can apply a standard approach, sometimes called the "closing-the-box method", to estimate the integral (7.16). We consider the rectangle $\mathcal{R}$ shown in Figure 7.3. To simplify our notation, set

$$X^*(s) = \frac{\Gamma(s+1)}{1-p^{-s}-q^{-s}}.$$

Then the integral of $X^*(s)n^{-s}$ along $\mathcal{R}$ can be divided into four parts as follows:

$$\lim_{A\to\infty} \int_{\mathcal{R}} = \lim_{A\to\infty} \left(\int_{c-iA}^{c+iA} + \int_{c+iA}^{M+iA} + \int_{M+iA}^{M-iA} + \int_{M-iA}^{c-iA} \right)$$

where $c = 3/2$. We are interested in the first integral since the second and the fourth integrals contribute $O(e^{-\alpha A})$ for some $\alpha > 0$, owing to the smallness property of the gamma function presented in (1.42) of Chapter 1. The contribution of the third integral is computed as follows. For any $M > 0$,

$$\left| \int_{M+i\infty}^{M-i\infty} X^*(s)n^{-s}ds \right| = \left| \int_{+\infty}^{-\infty} X^*(M+it)n^{-M-it}dt \right|$$

$$\leq |n^{-M}| \int_{+\infty}^{-\infty} |X^*(M+it)|dt = O(n^{-M}),$$

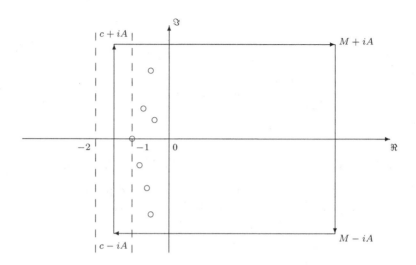

Figure 7.3. The integration contour (the circles represent the zeroes of $p^{-s} + q^{-s} = 1$.

since the integral in the last line exists owing to the properties of the gamma function. Now, by the Cauchy residue theorem, we find for any $M > 0$

$$\frac{1}{2\pi i} \int_{c-i\infty}^{c+i\infty} X^*(s) n^{-s} ds = - \sum_{s_k \in \mathcal{Z}} \mathrm{Res}[X^*(s) n^{-s}, s = s_k] + O(n^{-M}), \quad (7.17)$$

where the s_k are singularities of the function $X^*(s) n^{-s}$. The minus sign is a consequence of the clockwise orientation of the contour $\mathcal{R}$.

In order to evaluate the residues of (7.17) we must examine the locations of the zeros of the characteristic equation $1 - p^{-s} - q^{-s} = 0$, that is, we need to study the properties of the set $\mathcal{Z} = \{s \in \mathbb{C} : p^{-s} + q^{-s} = 1\}$. We can prove the following lemma:

Lemma 7.2.4 (Jacquet, 1989; Schachinger, 1993). *Suppose that $0 < p < q < 1$ with $p + q = 1$, and let*

$$\mathcal{Z} = \{s \in \mathbb{C} : p^{-s} + q^{-s} = 1\}.$$

Then
(i) All $s \in \mathcal{Z}$ satisfy

$$-1 \le \Re(s) \le \sigma_0,$$

where σ_0 is a real positive solution of $1 + q^{-s} = p^{-s}$. Furthermore, for every integer k there uniquely exists $s_k \in \mathcal{Z}$ with

$$\frac{(2k-1)\pi}{\log(1/p)} < \Im(s_k) < \frac{(2k+1)\pi}{\log(1/p)}$$

and consequently $\mathcal{Z} = \{s_k : k \in \mathbb{Z}\}$.

(ii) *If $\log q / \log p$ is irrational then $s_0 = -1$ and $\Re(s_k) > -1$ for all $k \neq 0$.*

(iii) *If $\log q / \log p = r/d$ is rational, where $\gcd(r, d) = 1$ for integers $r, d > 0$, then $\Re(s_k) = -1$ if and only if $k \equiv 0 \bmod d$. In particular $\Re(s_1), \dots, \Re(s_{d-1}) > -1$ and*

$$s_k = s_{k \bmod d} + \frac{2(k - k \bmod d)\pi i}{\log p}, \qquad (7.18)$$

that is, all $s \in \mathcal{Z}$ are uniquely determined by $s_0 = -1$ and by $s_1, s_2, \dots, s_{d-1}$, and their imaginary parts constitute an arithmetic progression. Furthermore, there exists $\delta > 0$ such that all remaining solutions s_k satisfy $\Re(s_k) \leq s_0 - \delta$ for $k \neq 0$.

Proof. We first prove part (i). If $p < q$ and $\sigma = \Re(s) < -1$, then we have $|p^{-s} + q^{-s}| \leq p^{-\sigma} + q^{-\sigma} < p + q = 1$. Next, there uniquely exists $\sigma_0 > 0$ with $1 + q^{-\sigma_0} = p^{-\sigma_0}$, and we have $1 + q^{-\sigma} > p^{-\sigma}$ if and only if $\sigma < \sigma_0$. Now if $p^{-s} + q^{-s} = 1$, then $1 + q^{-\Re(s)} \geq |1 - q^{-s}| = |p^{-s}| = p^{-\Re(s)}$. Consequently $\Re(s) \leq \sigma_0$.

Let B_k denote the set

$$B_k = \{s \in \mathbb{C} : -2 \leq \Re(s) \leq \sigma_0 + 1, \ (2k-1)\pi/\log p \leq \Im(s) \leq (2k+1)\pi/\log p\}.$$

We will show that B_k contains exactly one point of $\mathcal{Z}$ for each k. First, the function $f(s) = p^{-s} - 1$ has exactly one zero, at $\tilde{s}_k = (2k\pi i)/\log p \in B_k$. We shall show that $|q^{-s}| < |p^{-s} - 1|$ on the boundary of B_k. Thus, by Rouche's theorem[3] (cf. Henrici (1997)) the function $g(s) = p^{-s} - 1 + q^{-s}$ also has exactly one zero in B_k as required. We now prove that $|q^{-s}| < |p^{-s} - 1|$ to complete the proof of part (i). If $\Im(s) = (2k \pm 1)\pi/\log p$, then $p^{-s} - 1 = -p^{-\Re(s)} - 1$. Next, observe that $p < q$ implies that for all real σ we have $q^{-\sigma} < 1 + p^{-\sigma}$. Consequently, $|q^{-s}| = q^{-\Re(s)} < 1 + p^{-\Re(s)} = |1 - p^{-s}|$. If $\Re(s) = -2$, then it follows from $p^2 + q^2 < 1$ that $|q^{-s}| = q^2 < 1 - p^2 \leq |1 - p^{-s}|$. Finally, if $\Re(s) = \sigma_0 + 1$ then we have $q^{-\sigma_0-1} + 1 < p^{-\sigma_0-1}$ and, thus, $|q^{-s}| = q^{-\sigma_0-1} <$

---

[3]Recall that Rouche's theorem states that if $f(z) = g(z) + h(z)$ and $h(z)$ are analytic inside and on a contour C and are such that $|g(z)| < |h(z)|$ then $h(z)$ and $f(z) = g(z) + h(z)$ have the same number of zeros inside C.

$p^{-\sigma_0-1} - 1 = |1 - p^{-s}|$. This completes the proof that $|q^{-s}| < |p^{-s} - 1|$ on the boundary of B_k.

For part (ii), suppose that $s = -1 + it$ for some $t \neq 0$ and $p^{-s} + q^{-s} = pe^{-it\log p} + qe^{-it\log q} = 1$. Of course, this is only possible if there exist (non-zero) integers $\tilde{d}, \tilde{r}$ with $t\log p = 2\pi\tilde{d}$ and $t\log q = 2\pi\tilde{r}$. This implies that $\log p/\log q = \tilde{d}/\tilde{r}$ is rational. Conversely, if $\log p/\log q$ is irrational, then it follows that all $s \in \mathcal{Z}$ with $s \neq -1$ satisfy $\Re(s) > -1$.

Finally, for part (iii), suppose that $\log p/\log q = d/r$ is rational, where we assume that d and r are coprime positive integers. It is immediately clear that all s of the form $s = -1 + 2\ell\pi id/\log p$, where ℓ is an arbitrary integer, are contained in $\mathcal{Z}$. This means that

$$s_{\ell d} = -1 + 2\ell\pi id/\log p = s_0 + 2\ell\pi id/\log p.$$

Similarly we get

$$s_{\ell d+j} = s_j + 2\pi i\ell d/\log p$$

for $j = 1, 2, \ldots, d-1$. It remains to show that $\Re(s_j) > -1$ for $j = 1, 2, \ldots, d-1$. From the proof of (ii) it follows that every $s \in \mathcal{Z}$ with $\Re(s) = -1$ has imaginary part $\Im(s) = 2\pi\tilde{d}/\log p$, where $\tilde{d}$ is an integer with $\log p/\log q = \tilde{d}/\tilde{r}$. Thus, $\tilde{d}$ is an integer multiple of d, that is, $\tilde{d} = \ell d$ and consequently $s = s_{\ell d}$. ∎

Remark 7.2.5. The above lemma plays a role in many places in this book. Therefore, we will generalize it to any alphabet $\mathcal{A}$. For this we must first define rationally related numbers.

Definition 7.2.6. We say that the members of the set $\{\log p_a\}_{a\in\mathcal{A}}$ are *rationally related* if there exists a positive real number L such that the $\log p_a$ are integer multiples of L, that is, $\log p_a = -n_a L$, $n_a \in \mathbb{Z}_{>0}$, $(a \in \mathcal{A})$. Equivalently this means that all the ratios $(\log p_a)/(\log p_b)$ are rational. Without loss of generality we can assume that L is as large as possible which implies that $\gcd(n_a, a \in \mathcal{A}) = 1$. Similarly, we say that the members of $\{\log p_a\}_{a\in\mathcal{A}}$ are *irrationally related* if they are not rationally related.

In this general case, the *characteristic equation* is

$$\sum_{a\in\mathcal{A}} p_a^{-s} = 1. \tag{7.19}$$

Its roots s_k satisfy the above lemma with some alteration, mostly for the rationally related case. To be more precise, let $\log p_a = Ln_a$ for some real L and integers n_a for $a \in \mathcal{A}$. Then (7.19) can be written as

$$\sum_{a\in\mathcal{A}} z^{n_a} = 1, \quad z = e^{-Ls}. \tag{7.20}$$

Let $K = \max_a\{n_a\}$. Hence, we can say that (7.20) is a polynomial of degree K, and by the fundamental theorem of algebra we know that it has K roots, which we denote as $z_0, z_1, \ldots, z_{K-1}$. Notice that the corresponding roots s_j are given by

$$s_j = \frac{-1}{L}\log z_j \tag{7.21}$$

for $j = 0, 1, \ldots, K - 1$. In particular, $s_0 = -1$ corresponds to $z_0 = e^L$. In fact, all the roots s_k of the characteristic equation (7.19) can be written as (somewhat abusing the notation)

$$s_k = s_j + \frac{2\pi i k}{L}, \qquad k \in \mathbb{Z},$$

for any integer k and $j = 0, \ldots, K - 1$ with s_j given by (7.21).   ∎

Now, we are in a position to complete our asymptotic expansion of the average path length $l_n = \mathbf{E}[L_n]$. In order to compute the residues we shall use the following expansions for $w = s - s_0$ (in our case $s_0 = -1$):

$$\Gamma(s+1) = \frac{1}{s+1} - \gamma + O(s+1), \tag{7.22}$$

$$n^{-s} = n - n\log n(s+1) + O((s+1)^2), \tag{7.23}$$

$$\frac{1}{1 - p^{-s} - q^{-s}} = -\frac{1}{h}\frac{1}{s+1} + \frac{h_2}{2h^2} + O(s+1), \tag{7.24}$$

where $h = -p\ln p - q\ln q$, $h_2 = p\ln^2 p + q\ln^2 q$, and $\gamma = 0.577215\ldots$ is the Euler constant.

Theorem 7.2.7. *Consider a binary trie built over n strings generated by a memoryless source.*
(i) *If $\log p/\log q$ is irrational then*

$$\mathbf{E}[L_n] = \frac{n}{h}\log_2 n + \frac{n}{h}\left(\gamma + \frac{h_2}{2h}\right) + o(n),$$

where we recall that $h = -p\log_2 p - q\log_2 q$ is the source entropy rate, $h_2 = p\log_2^2 p + q\log_2^2 q$, and $\gamma = 0.577\ldots$ is Euler's constant.
(ii) *If $\log p/\log q = d/r$ is rational with $\gcd(r, d) = 1$, where $r, d \in \mathbb{Z}$, then*

$$\mathbf{E}[L_n] = \frac{n}{h}\log_2 n + \frac{n}{h}\left(\gamma + \frac{h_2}{2h} - \Phi_0(\log n)\right) + \sum_{j=1}^{d} n^{-s_i}\frac{1}{h(s_i)}\Phi_i(\log n)$$

$$+ O(\log n) \tag{7.25}$$

$$= \frac{n}{h}\log_2 n + \frac{n}{h}\left(\gamma + \frac{h_2}{2h} - \Phi_0(\log n)\right) + O(n^{1-\varepsilon}), \tag{7.26}$$

with $\Re(s_i) > -1$ for $i = 1, \ldots d - 1$ as in Lemma 7.2.4(iii);

$$h(s_i) = -p^{-s_i} \log p - q^{-s_i} \log q$$

and

$$\Phi_0(x) = \sum_{k \neq 0} \Gamma\left(\frac{2k\pi k}{L}\right) \exp\left(-\frac{2k\pi k}{L}x\right), \qquad (7.27)$$

$$\Phi_i(x) = \sum_{k \neq 0} \Gamma\left(1 + s_i + \frac{2k\pi k}{L}\right) \exp\left(-\frac{2k\pi k}{L}x\right) \qquad (7.28)$$

are continuous periodic functions with period 1, mean zero, a small amplitude, and $L = \log p/d$.

Proof. The proof follows directly from (7.17), computing the residues at s_k. Notice that $s_0 = -1$ is a double pole, leading to the main term of $\mathbf{E}[L_n]$, while s_k for $k \neq 0$ contributes to the periodic functions $\Phi_i(x)$ for each s_i, $i = 0, \ldots, d$. The main periodic function $\Phi_0(x)$ is the residue at $s_k = s_0 + 2\pi i k/L$ and contributes $n\Phi_0(\log n)$ while the other zeros $s_k = s_i + 2\pi i k/L$, $i \neq 0$, lead to $n^{-s_i}\Phi_i(\log n)$ and contribute $O(n^{1-\varepsilon})$ for some $\varepsilon > 0$. ∎

Remark 7.2.8. Theorem 7.2.7 extends, as stated, to a general alphabet $\mathcal{A}$ with

$$h = -\sum_{a \in \mathcal{A}} p_a \log p_a, \qquad h_2 = \sum_{a \in \mathcal{A}} p_a \log^2 p_a, \qquad h(s_i) = -\sum_{a \in \mathcal{A}} p_a^{-s_i} \log p_a.$$

In this case, we need to use a general L as in Definition 7.2.6. ∎

7.2.2. Average size of a trie

In this subsection we apply the methodology just learned to estimate the average size of a trie, that is, the average number of internal nodes in a trie generated by a memoryless model.

Let S_n be the size and define $s_n = \mathbf{E}[S_n]$. Then s_n satisfies the following recurrence for $n \geq 2$

$$s_n = 1 + \sum_{k=0}^{n} \binom{n}{k} p^k q^{n-k} (s_k + s_n),$$

with $s_0 = s_1 = 0$. This falls under the general recurrence (7.6) and can be solved using Lemma 7.2.1. We find that

$$s_n = \sum_{k=2}^{n} (-1)^k \binom{n}{k} \frac{k-1}{1 - p^k - q^k}.$$

Applying Theorem 7.2.3 we arrive at

$$s_n = -(1 + O(1/n)) \int_{-\frac{3}{2}-i\infty}^{-\frac{3}{2}+i\infty} \frac{\Gamma(s)(s+1)}{1 - p^{-s} - q^{-s}} n^{-s} ds.$$

We next follow in the footsteps of our analysis from the last subsection. Since the characteristic equation $1 - p^{-s} - q^{-s}$ is the same as in the analysis of the path length, the roots s_k satisfy Lemma 7.2.4. In particular, $s_0 = -1$. However, unlike in the path length case, s_0 is a single pole owing to the factor $s+1$. Also, we need the expansion

$$\Gamma(s) = -\frac{1}{s+1} + 1 - \gamma + O(s+1)$$

together with (7.23) and (7.24).

We have the following result.

Theorem 7.2.9. *Consider a trie built over n strings generated by a memoryless source over a finite alphabet $\mathcal{A}$.*
(i) If $\log p_1, \ldots, \log p_{|\mathcal{A}|}$ are irrationally related, then

$$\mathbf{E}[S_n] = \frac{n}{h} + o(n),$$

where h is the entropy rate defined in (7.29).
(ii) If $\log p_1, \ldots, \log p_{|\mathcal{A}|}$ are rationally related then

$$\mathbf{E}[S_n] = \frac{n}{h} (1 + \Phi_0(\log n)) + O(n^{1-\varepsilon}) \tag{7.29}$$

for any $\varepsilon > 0$, where $\Phi_0(x)$ is defined in (7.27) of Theorem 7.2.7.

7.2.3. Average depth in a DST by Rice's method

We now consider a digital search tree, as defined in Chapter 6. An example of a binary digital tree is shown in Figure 6.8. In this section we use the Rice method to estimate the mean and variance of the typical depth, that is, the path length from the root to a randomly selected node. The reader is referred to Section 9.3.1 of Chapter 9 for an extension of this analysis to moments of the path length.

Let $I_{n,k}$ denote the number of internal nodes at level k in a digital tree built over n binary strings generated by a memoryless source. To derive a recurrence on the typical depth D_n we observe as in Section 7.1 that

$$P(D_n = k) = \frac{\mathbf{E}[I_{n,k}]}{n}. \tag{7.30}$$

We shall work initially with the average profile and so we define the generating function $B_n(u) = \sum_{k=0}^{\infty} \mathbf{E}[I_{n,k}]u^k$, which satisfies for a binary DST the recurrence

$$B_{n+1}(u) = 1 + u \sum_{j=0}^{n} \binom{n}{j} p^j q^{n-j} (B_j(u) + B_{n-j}(u)) \tag{7.31}$$

with $B_0(u) = 0$. This recurrence arises naturally in our setting when we consider the left and the right subtrees of the root, and note that j strings will go to the left subtree with probability

$$\binom{m}{j} p^j q^{m-j}.$$

To solve (7.31), let us multiply both sides by $z^n/n!$ to arrive at

$$B'_z(z, u) = e^z + uB(pz, u)e^{qz} + uB(qz, u)e^{pz},$$

where

$$B(z, u) = \sum_{n=0}^{\infty} B_n(u) \frac{z^n}{n!}$$

and $B'_z(z, u)$ is the derivative of $B(z, u)$ with respect to z. We now multiply this functional equation by e^{-z} and introduce the Poisson transform $\widetilde{B}(z, u) = B(z, u)e^{-z}$. This leads to a new functional equation, namely

$$\widetilde{B}'(z, u) + \widetilde{B}(z, u) = 1 + u(\widetilde{B}(zp, u) + \widetilde{B}(zq, u)).$$

Now comparing the coefficients at z^n one finds that

$$\widetilde{B}_{n+1}(u) = \delta_{m,0} - \widetilde{B}_n(u)(1 - up^n - uq^n),$$

where $\delta_{0,m}$ is the Kronecker symbol. It now suffices to note that

$$B_n(u) = \sum_{k=0}^{m} \binom{n}{k} \widetilde{B}_k(u)$$

to finally obtain

$$B_n(u) = n - (1-u) \sum_{k=2}^{n} (-1)^k \binom{n}{k} Q_{k-2}(u) \qquad (7.32)$$

where

$$Q_k(u) = \prod_{j=2}^{k+1} (1 - up^j - uq^j), \quad Q_0(u) = 1. \qquad (7.33)$$

Using our analysis from subsection 7.2.1, we present in Theorem 7.2.10 below our findings for the mean and the variance of the depth in a DST. In Remark 7.2.11 we re-prove the theorem using the Rice method.

Theorem 7.2.10 (Kirschenhofer & Prodinger, 1988; Szpankowski, 1991). *The average depth* $\mathbf{E}[D_n]$ *in a binary digital search tree attains the following asymptotics as* $n \to \infty$;

$$\mathbf{E}[D_n] = \frac{1}{h} \left(\log n + \gamma - 1 + \frac{h_2}{2h} - \eta + \Delta_1(\log n) \right) + O\left(\frac{\log n}{n} \right), \qquad (7.34)$$

where, as we recall, h *is the entropy,* $h_2 = p \log^2 p + q \log^2 q$, $\gamma = 0.577\ldots$ *is the Euler constant, and*

$$\eta = \sum_{k=1}^{\infty} \frac{p^{k+1} \log p + q^{k+1} \log q}{1 - p^{k+1} - q^{k+1}} . \qquad (7.35)$$

When $\log p / \log q$ *is irrational we have*

$$\lim_{x \to \infty} \Delta_1(x) = 0,$$

while if $\log p / \log q = d/r$ *for some integers* d, r, *then* $\Delta_1(x) = \Delta_0(x) + \tilde{\Delta}(x)$ *is a periodic function with a small amplitude such that* $\lim_{x \to \infty} \tilde{\Delta}(x) = 0$ *and*

$$\Delta_0(x) = \sum_{k \neq 0}^{\infty} \Gamma\left(-1 + \frac{2\pi i k d}{\log p} \right) \exp\left(-\frac{2\pi i k d}{\log p} \log x \right). \qquad (7.36)$$

The variance of D_n *satisfies*

$$\mathrm{Var}[D_n] = \frac{h_2 - h^2}{h^3} \log n + A + \Delta_2(\log n) + O\left(\frac{\log^2 n}{n} \right), \qquad (7.37)$$

where A is a constant (see Exercise 7.5) and $\Delta_2(x)$ is a fluctuating function with a small amplitude. In the symmetric case $(p = q)$, the coefficient at $\log n$ becomes zero and

$$\mathrm{Var}[D_n] = \frac{1}{12} + \frac{1}{\log^2 2} \cdot \frac{\pi^2}{6} - \eta - \beta + \Delta(\log_2 n) - [\Delta^2]_0 + O\left(\frac{\log^2 n}{n}\right) \quad (7.38)$$

where

$$\eta = \sum_{j=1}^{\infty} \frac{1}{2^j - 1}, \qquad \beta = \sum_{j=1}^{\infty} \frac{1}{(2^j - 1)^2},$$

the function $\Delta_2(x)$ is continuous with period 1 and mean zero, and the term $[\Delta^2]_0 < 10^{-10}$ is the mean of $\Delta^2(x)$.

Proof. We present only a sketch of the proof using the approach of Theorem 7.2.3. It suffices to derive the asymptotics of the average path length $l_n := n\mathbf{E}[D_n]$ and the second factorial moment of the path length,

$$l_n^2 := n\mathbf{E}[D_n(D_n - 1)].$$

But $l_n = B_n'(1)$ and $l_n^2 = B_n''(1)$ where $B_n'(1)$ and $B_n''(1)$ are the first and the second derivatives of $B_n(u)$ at $u = 1$. Note that

$$\mathrm{Var}[D_n] = \frac{l_n^2}{n} + \frac{l_n}{n} - \left(\frac{l_n}{n}\right)^2.$$

We should point out here that the variance of the path length $\mathrm{Var}[L_n]$ requires a quite different analysis, which is summarized in Theorem 9.3.1 of Chapter 9.

Using (7.32), after some algebra we arrive at the following two recurrences for all $n \geq 0$

$$l_{n+1} = n + \sum_{k=0}^{n} \binom{n}{k} p^k q^{n-k} (l_k + l_{n-k}), \quad (7.39)$$

$$l_{n+1}^2 = 2(l_{n+1} - n) + \binom{n}{k} p^k q^{n-k} (l_k^2 + l_{n-k}^2) \quad (7.40)$$

with $l_0 = l_0^2 = 0$. The recurrence (7.39) resembles (7.31). Therefore, its solution is

$$l_n = \sum_{k=2}^{n} (-1)^k \binom{n}{k} Q_{k-2}, \quad (7.41)$$

where

$$Q_k = Q_k(1) = \prod_{j=2}^{k+1} (1 - p^j - q^j).$$

This is an alternating sum with a kernel Q_k of polynomial growth, so either Rice's method in Theorem 7.2.2 or Theorem 7.2.3 can be used. We use the latter method first, and then in Remark 7.2.11 following this proof we outline Rice's approach. We need the analytic continuation of Q_k, but this is easy. Define

$$Q(s) = \frac{P(0)}{P(s)},$$

where $P(s) = \prod_{j=2}^{\infty}(1 - p^{s+j} - q^{s+j})$. Then $Q_k = Q(s)|_{s=k}$ and, by Theorem 7.2.3, we have

$$l_n = \frac{1 + O(1/n)}{2\pi i} \int_{-\frac{3}{2}-i\infty}^{-\frac{3}{2}+i\infty} \Gamma(s)n^{-s}Q(-s-2)ds \tag{7.42}$$
$$= -\sum_{s_{k,j}} \mathrm{Res}(\Gamma(s)n^{-s}Q(-s-2), \; s = s_{k,j}),$$

where the $s_{k,j}$ are roots of

$$p^{j-2-s} + q^{j-2-s} = 1 \tag{7.43}$$

for integers k. To consider all singularities we must also take into account the singularities of the gamma function at $s = 0$ and $s = -1$ together with the roots of (7.43). In particular, $s_{0,2} = -1$ and $s_{0,3} = 0$. An easy extension of Lemma 7.2.4 applies to (7.43). The main contribution comes from $s_{0,2} = -1$. We use the expansions (7.22)–(7.24) together with

$$Q(-s-2) = \frac{P(0)}{P(-s-2)} = \frac{1}{1 - p^{-s} - q^{-s}} \frac{P(0)}{P(-s-1)}.$$

To find an expansion for $P(0)/P(-s-1)$ we use a simple result for the products of functions. Namely, if

$$F(z) = \prod_j \frac{1}{1 - f_j(z)}$$

for differentiable functions $f_j(z)$ then Taylor's expansion at $z = z_0$ is

$$F(z) = F(z_0)\left(1 + \sum_j \frac{f_j'(z_0)}{1 - f_j(z_0)}(z - z_0) + O((z - z_0)^2)\right). \tag{7.44}$$

Thus $Q(-s-2)$ has the following Laurent expansion:

$$Q(-s-2) = -\frac{1}{h}\frac{1}{s+1} + \frac{\eta}{h} + \frac{h_2}{2h^2} + (s+1)\frac{\eta h_2}{2h^2} + O((s+1)^2). \tag{7.45}$$

Finally, extracting the coefficient at $(s+1)^{-1}$, we establish the leading term of the asymptotics without $\Delta_1(x)$ as in the analysis of the path length of a trie. To obtain $\Delta_1(x)$ and, in particular, $\Delta_0(x)$ we must consider the roots at $s_{k,2}$ for $k \neq 0$. Using Lemma 7.2.4 we finally prove (7.34). The double pole at $s = 0$ contributes an $O(\log n)$ term.

The asymptotics of l_n^2 can be obtained in a similar manner but algebra is more involved. We need to find the binomial inverse to l_n. Solution (7.41) implies that $\hat{l}_n = Q_{n-2}$. With this in mind we obtain directly

$$l_n^2 = -2 \sum_{k=2}^{n} \binom{n}{k} (-1)^k Q_{k-2} T_{k-2},$$

where

$$T_n = \sum_{i=2}^{n+1} \frac{p^i + q^i}{1 - p^i - q^i}.$$

We need an analytic continuation of T_n. A "mechanical" derivation works here upon observing that

$$T_{n+1} = T_n + \frac{p^{n+2} + q^{n+2}}{1 - p^{n+2} - q^{n+2}}.$$

Replacing n by z we obtain

$$T(s) = T(s+1) - \frac{p^{s+2} + q^{s+2}}{1 - p^{+2} - q^{s+2}},$$

for which after some iterations we find

$$T(s) = T(\infty) - \sum_{i=2}^{\infty} \frac{p^{s+i} + q^{s+i}}{1 - p^{s+i} - q^{s+i}}.$$

Setting $s = 0$ in the above, knowing that $T(0) = 0$ we finally arrive at

$$T(s) = \eta - \sum_{i=2}^{\infty} \frac{p^{s+i} + q^{s+i}}{1 - p^{s+i} - q^{s+i}},$$

where η was defined in (7.35). The above derivation can easily be made rigorous by observing that all series involved do converge for $\Re(z) > -2$.   ∎

Remark 7.2.11. Now we re-prove Theorem 7.2.10 using Rice's method from Theorem 7.2.2. We have

$$l_n = -\frac{1}{2\pi i} \int_{\mathcal{C}_{[2,n]}} B(n+1,-z)Q(z-2)dz$$

with the same notation as before. Now we expand the contour of integration to a larger curve $\mathcal{C}$ that includes all singularities of the integral and excludes $[2,n]$. Then

$$l_n = \sum_{z_{k,j}} \mathrm{Res}[B(n+1,-z)Q(z-2); z = z_{k,j}],$$

where the $z_{k,j}$ are the roots of

$$p^{z+j} + q^{z+j} = 1.$$

Notice that for $\log p/\log q = d/r$, where d and r are integers in the rational case, $z_{k,j} = 3 - j + 2\pi i d/\log p$ for $j \geq 2$. The main contribution to the sum comes from the roots $z_{0,2} = 1$ and $z_{0,3} = 0$. In particular, we need the following Laurent expansions:

$$B(n+1,-z) = \frac{n}{z-1} + n(\bar{H}_{n+1} - 1) + O(z),$$

$$Q(z-2) = \frac{1}{1-p^z-q^z} \frac{P(0)}{P(z-1)},$$

where $\bar{H}_n = \sum_{i=1}^{n} 1/i$ is the harmonic sum. For the last term we then use (7.44). This leads to findings in Theorem 7.2.10.

Remark 7.2.12. It is easy to extend our result to any finite alphabet. In particular, a more detailed asymptotic analysis leads to

$$\mathbf{E}[L_n] = n\mathbf{E}[D_n] = \frac{n}{h}\left(\log n + \frac{h_2}{2h} + \gamma - 1 - \eta + \Delta_1(\log m)\right) \qquad (7.46)$$

$$+ \frac{1}{h}\left(\log m + \frac{h_2}{2h} + \gamma - \eta - \sum_{a\in\mathcal{A}} \log p_a - \frac{1}{2}\right),$$

where

$$\eta = -\sum_{k\geq 2} \frac{\sum_{a\in\mathcal{A}} p_a^k \log p_a}{1 - \sum_{a\in\mathcal{A}} p_a^k}$$

and h and h_2 are defined in (7.29). ∎

In passing we point out that $\mathrm{Var}[L_n]$ is much harder to analyze. We will discuss it in Section 9.3.1 of Chapter 9 where, in Theorem 9.3.1, we present detailed results concerning the mean and the variance of L_n and in Theorem 9.3.3 we establish the central limit theorem for the path length L_n of a digital search tree. These results for DST presented in Section 9.3 are proved using refined analytic depoissonization and Mellin transform.

7.2.4. Multiplicity parameter by Mellin transform

In this section we continue analyzing the moments of shape parameters; however, we now use new techniques such as analytic depoissonization and the Mellin transform to establish our results. Both techniques are carefully explained in the recent books by Szpankowski (2001) and Flajolet and Sedgewick (2009) but, for the reader's convenience, we summarize the basic properties of depoissonization and the Mellin transform in Tables 7.1 and 7.2.

We also deal here with a new parameter, namely the multiplicity parameter M_n defined in Section 7.1. Actually, we can interpret M_n in a different way. Consider a randomized selection algorithm that has n initial participants and a moderator. At the outset, n participants and one moderator are present. Each has a biased coin with a probability p of showing a head when flipped; as always $q = 1 - p$. At each stage of the selection process the moderator flips its coin once; the participants remain for subsequent rounds if and only if their result agrees with the moderator's result. Note that all participants are eliminated in finitely many rounds with probability 1. We let M_n denote the number of participants remaining in the last nontrivial round (i.e., the final round in which some participants still remain). This, as it turns out, is the same as the multiplicity parameter defined in Section 7.1 since the game can be viewed in terms of a trie. Indeed, consider a trie built from strings of 0s and 1s drawn from an i.i.d. source. We restrict attention to the situation where n such strings have already been inserted into a trie. When the $(n+1)$th string is inserted into the trie, M_n denotes the size of the subtree that starts at the branching point of this new insertion.

Our goal is to evaluate the mean and the variance of M_n. However, instead we will compute all the factorial moments of M_n, that is,

$$\mathbf{E}[M_n^{\underline{j}}] = \mathbf{E}[M_n(M_n - 1) \cdots (M_n - j + 1)].$$

We define the exponential generating function

$$W_j(z) = \sum_{n \geq 0} \mathbf{E}[(M_n)^{\underline{j}}] \frac{z^n}{n!}$$

and its Poisson transform as $\widetilde{W}_j(z) = W_j(z)e^{-z}$. To find a functional equation for $W_j(z)$ observe that for any function f on tries we have

$$\mathbf{E}[f(M_n)] = p^n(qf(n) + p\mathbf{E}[f(M_n)]) + q^n(pf(n) + q\mathbf{E}[f(M_n)])$$
$$+ \sum_{k=1}^{n-1} \binom{n}{k} p^k q^{n-k} \left(p\mathbf{E}[f(M_k)] + q\mathbf{E}[f(M_{n-k})]\right). \quad (7.47)$$

Thus, in particular,

$$\mathbf{E}[(M_n)^{\underline{j}}] = p^n(qn^{\underline{j}} + p\mathbf{E}[(M_n)^{\underline{j}}]) + q^n(pn^{\underline{j}} + q\mathbf{E}[(M_n)^{\underline{j}}])$$
$$+ \sum_{k=1}^{n-1} \binom{n}{k} p^k q^{n-k} (p\mathbf{E}[(M_k)^{\underline{j}}] + q\mathbf{E}[(M_{n-k})^{\underline{j}}]). \quad (7.48)$$

We derive an asymptotic solution as $n \to \infty$ for these recurrence relations using poissonization, the Mellin transform, and depoissonization. The idea is to replace a fixed-size population model (i.e., a model in which the number n of initial participants or string is fixed) by a poissonized model, in which the number of strings/participants is a Poisson random variable with mean n. This is affectionately referred to as "poissonizing" the problem. So, we let the number of strings be N, a random variable that has a Poisson distribution and mean n (i.e., $P(N = j) = e^{-n}n^j/j!$ $\forall j \geq 0$). We apply a Poisson transform to the exponential generating function $W_j(z)$, which yields

$$\widetilde{W}_j(z) = \sum_{n \geq 0} \mathbf{E}[(M_n)^{\underline{j}}] \frac{z^n}{n!} e^{-z}$$

where in general z is complex. From (7.48) we conclude that

$$\widetilde{W}_j(z) = q(pz)^j e^{-qz} + p(qz)^j e^{-pz} + p\widetilde{W}_j(pz) + q\widetilde{W}_j(qz). \quad (7.49)$$

In order to solve (7.49) we apply a Mellin transform, defined for a real function on $(0, \infty)$ by

$$\mathcal{M}[f(x); s] = f^*(s) = \int_0^\infty f(x) x^{s-1} \, dx.$$

We give the properties of the Mellin transform in Table 7.1.

We next determine the fundamental strip of $\widetilde{W}_j(x)$ as defined in property (M2) of Table 7.1, that is, we determine where the Mellin transform $\widetilde{W}_j^*(s)$ of $\widetilde{W}_j(x)$ exists. We therefore need to understand the behavior of $\widetilde{W}_j(x)$ for $x \to 0$ and $x \to \infty$. Observe that

$$\widetilde{W}_j(x) = q(px)^j e^{-qx} + p(qx)^j e^{-px} + p\widetilde{W}_j(px) + q\widetilde{W}_j(qx)$$

$$= q(px)^j \sum_{k \geq 0} \frac{(-qx)^k}{k!} + p(qx)^j \sum_{k \geq 0} \frac{(-px)^k}{k!}$$

$$+ p \sum_{n \geq 0} \mathbf{E}[(M_n)^{\underline{j}}] \frac{(px)^n}{n!} \sum_{k \geq 0} \frac{(-px)^k}{k!}$$

$$+ q \sum_{n \geq 0} \mathbf{E}[(M_n)^{\underline{j}}] \frac{(qx)^n}{n!} \sum_{k \geq 0} \frac{(-qx)^k}{k!}$$

$$\rightarrow q(px)^j + p(qx)^j + p\mathbf{E}[(M_j)^{\underline{j}}] \frac{(px)^j}{j!} + q\mathbf{E}[(M_j)^{\underline{j}}] \frac{(qx)^j}{j!}$$

$$= O(x^j) \qquad \text{as} \quad x \rightarrow 0.$$

We expect that $\widetilde{W}_j(x) = O(1) = O(x^0)$ as $x \rightarrow \infty$. So, by property (M2) of Table 7.1, the Mellin transform $\widetilde{W}_j^*(s)$ of $\widetilde{W}_j(x)$ exists for $\Re(s) \in (-j, 0)$, which is the fundamental strip. Furthermore,

$$\mathcal{M}(e^{-x}; s) = \int_0^\infty e^{-x} x^{-s} \, dx = \Gamma(s).$$

Using property (M3) of Table 7.1, we can solve (7.49) in terms of the Mellin transform, arriving at

$$\widetilde{W}_j^*(s) = \frac{\Gamma(s + j) \left(p^j q^{-s-j+1} + q^j p^{-s-j+1} \right)}{(1 - p^{-s+1} - q^{-s+1})}. \tag{7.54}$$

From Table 7.1 we note that the Mellin transform is a special case of the Fourier transform. So, there is an inverse Mellin transform, given in property (M4). Since $\widetilde{W}_j$ is continuous on $(0, \infty)$,

$$\widetilde{W}_j(x) = \frac{1}{2\pi i} \int_{-\frac{1}{2} - i\infty}^{-\frac{1}{2} + i\infty} \widetilde{W}_j^*(s) x^{-s} \, ds \tag{7.55}$$

since $c = -1/2$ is in the fundamental strip of $\widetilde{W}_j(x) \; \forall j \geq 1$. This is true for real x; however, we can analytically continue it to complex z around the positive real axis.

We now restrict attention to the case where $\log p / \log q$ is rational. Thus we can write $\log p / \log q = d/r$ for some relatively prime $r, d \in \mathbb{Z}$. Then, by Lemma 7.2.4 we know that the set of dominating poles of $\widetilde{W}_j^*(s) x^{-s}$ is exactly

$$s_k = \frac{2kd\pi i}{\ln p} \quad k \in \mathbb{Z}.$$

Table 7.1. Main properties of the Mellin transform.

(M1) **Direct and inverse Mellin transforms.** Let c belong to the *fundamental strip* defined below. Then, for a real function $f(x)$ defined on $(0, \infty)$,

$$f^*(s) := \mathcal{M}(f(x); s) = \int_0^\infty f(x) x^{s-1} dx \iff f(x) = \frac{1}{2\pi i} \int_{c-i\infty}^{c+i\infty} f^*(s) x^{-s} ds.$$

$$(7.50)$$

(M2) **Fundamental strip.** The Mellin transform of $f(x)$ exists in the *fundamental strip* $\Re(s) \in (-\alpha, -\beta)$, where

$$f(x) = O(x^\alpha), \qquad x \to 0 \qquad f(x) = O(x^\beta) \qquad x \to \infty$$

for $\beta < \alpha$.

(M3) **Harmonic sum property.** By linearity and the scale rule $\mathcal{M}(f(ax); s) = a^{-s} \mathcal{M}(f(x); s)$, we have

$$f(x) = \sum_{k \geq 0} \lambda_k g(\mu_k x) \qquad \iff \qquad f^*(s) = g^*(s) \sum_{k \geq 0} \lambda_k \mu_k^{-s}. \qquad (7.51)$$

(M4a) **Asymptotics of $f(x)$ and singularities of $f^*(s)$ for $x \to 0$.**

$$f(x) = \sum_k c_k x^\xi (\log x)^k + O(x^M) \qquad \iff \qquad f^*(s) \asymp \sum_k c_k \frac{(-1)^k k!}{(s+\xi)^{k+1}}. \quad (7.52)$$

(i) *Direct mapping.* Assume that as $x \to 0^+$ function $f(x)$ admits the asymptotic expansion (7.52) for some $-M < -\alpha$ and $k > 0$. Then, for $\Re(s) \in (-M, -\beta)$, the transform $f^*(s)$ satisfies the singular expansion (7.52).

(ii) *Converse mapping.* Assume that $f^*(s) = O(|s|^{-r})$ with $r > 1$, as $|s| \to \infty$ and that $f^*(s)$ admits the singular expansion (7.52) for $\Re(s) \in (-M, -\beta)$. Then $f(x)$ satisfies the asymptotic expansion (7.52) at $x \to 0^+$.

(M4b) **Asymptotics of $f(x)$ and singularities of $f^*(s)$ for $x \to \infty$.** Corresponding to (M4a) we have an asymptotic property for $x \to \infty$, namely

$$f(x) = -\sum_k (-1)^k \frac{d_k}{k!} x^\xi (\log x)^k + O(x^{-M}) \qquad \iff \qquad f^*(s) \asymp \sum_k \frac{d_k}{(s+\xi)^{k+1}},$$

$$(7.53)$$

for $\beta \leq \Re(s) < M$.

In addition we will have nondominating poles $s_{k,j} = s_j + 2\pi kid/\log p$ with $\Re(s_j) > 0$ $(j = 1, \ldots, d-1)$ that contribute $O(x^{-\varepsilon})$, hence we ignore these singularities from now on.

We observe that $\widetilde{W}_j^*(s)x^{-s}$ has simple poles at each s_k. The integral (7.55) can be evaluated in exactly the same manner as in Section 7.2.1 by the closing-the-box method. This leads to

$$\widetilde{W}_j(x) = -\sum_{k\in\mathbb{Z}} \operatorname{Res}[\widetilde{W}_j^*(s)x^{-s};\ s_k] + O(x^{-\varepsilon}) \tag{7.56}$$

where the term $O(x^{-\varepsilon})$ comes from the nondominating poles. We are now left with evaluating the residues.

We claim that

$$\widetilde{W}_j(x) = \Gamma(j)\frac{q(p/q)^j + p(q/p)^j}{h} + \frac{1}{h}\delta_j(\log_{1/p} x) + O(x^{-\varepsilon}), \tag{7.57}$$

where

$$\delta_j(t) = \sum_{k\neq 0} e^{2kr\pi it}\Gamma(s_k + j)\left(p^j q^{-s_k-j+1} + q^j p^{-s_k-j+1}\right).$$

To prove the claim, we first observe that, if $k \in \mathbb{Z}$, then

$$\operatorname{Res}[\widetilde{W}_j^*(s)x^{-s};\ s_k] = x^{-s_k}\operatorname{Res}[\widetilde{W}_j^*(s);\ s_k]$$
$$= -\frac{e^{2kd\pi i\log x/\log p}\Gamma(s_k+j)\left(p^j q^{-s_k-j+1} + q^j p^{-s_k-j+1}\right)}{h}$$

Then (7.57) follows immediately from (7.56).

Finally, we need to depoissonize our results. Recall that, in the original problem statement, n is a large fixed integer. Most of our analysis has utilized a model where n is a Poisson random variable. Therefore, to obtain results about the problem as originally stated, it is necessary to depoissonize our results. Observe that (7.57) is a solution to the poissonized version of the problem. We utilize the depoissonization techniques shown in Table 7.2; in particular, Theorem 7.2.13. By (7.57) it follows that

$$|\widetilde{W}_j(z)| = \left|\Gamma(j)\frac{q(p/q)^j + p(q/p)^j}{h} + \frac{1}{h}\delta_j(\log_{1/p} z) + O(z^{-M})\right|$$
$$\leq \left|\Gamma(j)\frac{q(p/q)^j + p(q/p)^j}{h}\right| + \frac{1}{h}\left|\delta_j(\log_{1/p} z)\right| + O(|z|^{-M})$$
$$= O(1), \qquad \text{since } |\delta_j| \text{ is uniformly bounded on } \mathbb{C}.$$

Therefore, there exist real-valued constants $c_M, c_{j,M}, z_M, z_{j,M}$ such that

$$|\widetilde{W}_j(z)| \leq c_{j,M}|z|^0 \ \forall z \in S_{\pi/4} = \{z\ :\ |\arg(z)| \leq \pi/4\} \text{ with } |z| \geq z_{j,M}.$$

Table 7.2. Main properties of analytic depoissonization.

Let g_n be a sequence of n. Define the Poisson transform as $\widetilde{G}(z) = \sum_{n \geq 0} g_n \frac{z^n}{n!} e^{-z}$.

Theorem 7.2.13. *Assume that in a linear cone $\mathcal{S}_\theta = \{z : |\arg(z)| \leq \theta\}$ ($\theta < \pi/2$) the following two conditions hold simultaneously.*
(I) *For $z \in \mathcal{S}_\theta$ and some real $B, R > 0, \beta$*

$$|z| > R \quad \Rightarrow \quad |\widetilde{G}(z)| \leq B|z|^\beta. \tag{7.58}$$

(O) *For $z \notin \mathcal{S}_\theta$ and $A, \alpha < 1$:* $|z| > R \quad \Rightarrow \quad |\widetilde{G}(z)e^z| \leq A\exp(\alpha|z|)$. *Then, for large n,*

$$g_n = \widetilde{G}(n) + O(n^{\beta-1}). \tag{7.59}$$

To extend to distributions we investigate double-index sequences $g_{n,k}$ (e.g, $g_{n,k} = P\{X_n = k\}$). Define $\widetilde{G}(z, u) = \sum_{n=0}^\infty \frac{z^n}{n!} e^{-z} \sum_{k=0}^\infty g_{n,k} u^k$; $\widetilde{G}_k(z) = \sum_{n=1}^\infty g_{n,k} \frac{z^n}{n!} e^{-z}$.

Theorem 7.2.14 (Jacquet and Szpankowski, 1998). *Let $\widetilde{G}_k(z)$ be a sequence of Poisson transforms of $g_{n,k}$. Let the following two conditions hold:*
(I) *For $z \in \mathcal{S}_\theta$ and a slowly varying function $\Psi(x)$,*

$$|z| > R \quad \Rightarrow \quad |\widetilde{G}_n(z)| \leq Bn^\beta |\Psi(n)|. \tag{7.60}$$

(O) *For z outside the linear cone $\mathcal{S}_\theta$,* $|z| = n \quad \Rightarrow \quad |\widetilde{G}_n(z)e^z| \leq n^\gamma \exp(n - An^\alpha)$. *Then for large n*

$$g_{n,n} = \widetilde{G}_n(n) + O(n^{\beta-1}\Psi(n)). \tag{7.61}$$

Define the Poisson mean $\widetilde{X}(z) = \widetilde{G}'_u(z, 1)$ and $\widetilde{V}(z) = \widetilde{G}''_u(z, 1) + \widetilde{X}(z) - \left(\widetilde{X}(z)\right)^2$.

Theorem 7.2.15. *Let $\widetilde{X}(z) = O(z^\beta \Psi(z))$ and $\widetilde{V}(z) = O(z^\beta \Psi(z))$ in a linear cone $\mathcal{S}_\theta$ and appropriate conditions (O) outside the cone be satisfied. Then*

$$\mathbf{E}[X_n] = \widetilde{X}(n) - \frac{1}{2}n\widetilde{X}^{\langle 2 \rangle}(n) + O(n^{\beta-2}\Psi(n)), \tag{7.62}$$

$$\mathrm{Var}[X_n] = \widetilde{V}(n) - n[\widetilde{X}'(n)]^2 + O(n^{\beta-1}\Psi(n)). \tag{7.63}$$

So condition (I) of Theorem 7.2.13 in Table 7.2 is satisfied. In Section 7.2.5 below we verify condition (O) of the same theorem using a technique known as *increasing domains* that will find further applications in this book.

In summary, we prove the following final result.

Theorem 7.2.16. *Let $s_k = \frac{2kd\pi i}{\ln p}$ $\forall k \in \mathbb{Z}$, where $\frac{\ln p}{\ln q} = \frac{d}{r}$ for some relatively prime $r, d \in \mathbb{Z}$ (recall that we are interested in the situation where $\frac{\ln p}{\ln q}$ is rational). Then*

$$\mathbf{E}[(M_n)^{\underline{j}}] = \Gamma(j)\frac{q(p/q)^j + p(q/p)^j}{h} + \frac{1}{h}\delta_j(\log_{1/p} n) + O(n^{-1})$$

where

$$\delta_j(t) = \sum_{k \neq 0} e^{2kd\pi it}\Gamma(s_k + j)\left(p^j q^{-s_k - j + 1} + q^j p^{-s_k - j + 1}\right)$$

and Γ is the Euler gamma function.

Note that δ_j is a periodic function that has small magnitude and exhibits fluctuations. For instance, when $p = 1/2$ then

$$1/\ln 2 |\delta_j(t)| \leq \frac{1}{\ln 2}\sum_{k \neq 0}\left|\Gamma\left(j - \frac{2ki\pi}{\ln 2}\right)\right|.$$

The approximate values of

$$\frac{1}{\ln 2}\sum_{k \neq 0}\left|\Gamma\left(j - \frac{2ki\pi}{\ln 2}\right)\right|$$

are given in Table 7.3 for the first 10 values of j.

We note that if $\ln p/\ln q$ is irrational then $\delta_j(x) \to 0$ as $x \to \infty$. So δ_j does not exhibit fluctuations when $\ln p/\ln q$ is irrational.

Remark 7.2.17. Recently Gaither and Ward (2013) extended the above results to an arbitrary alphabet. In particular, it is easy to establish that for any finite alphabet $\mathcal{A}$ we have

$$\mathbf{E}[(M_n)^{\underline{j}}] = \Gamma(j)\frac{\sum_{a \in \mathcal{A}} p_a((1 - p_a)/p_a)^j}{h} + \frac{1}{h}\delta_j(\log_{1/p} n) + o(1). \qquad (7.64)$$

If the members of $\{\log p_a\}_{a \in \mathcal{A}}$ are rationally related then the error term $o(1)$ can be improved to $O(n^{-\varepsilon})$, and we have

$$\delta_j(t) = \sum_{k \in \in \mathbb{Z} \setminus \{0\}} e^{2kt\pi i/L}\Gamma(s_k + j)\sum_{a \in \mathcal{A}}(1 - p_i)^j p_i^{-s_k - j + 1}$$

with L as defined in Remark 7.2.5.   ∎

j	$\frac{1}{\ln(2)} \sum_{k \neq 0} \left| \Gamma\left(j - \frac{2ki\pi}{\ln(2)}\right) \right|$
1	1.4260×10^{-5}
2	1.3005×10^{-4}
3	1.2072×10^{-3}
4	1.1527×10^{-2}
5	1.1421×10^{-1}
6	1.1823×10^{0}
7	1.2853×10^{1}
8	1.4721×10^{2}
9	1.7798×10^{3}
10	2.2737×10^{4}

Table 7.3. The oscillating function $\delta_j(x)$ for $p = 1/2$.

7.2.5. Increasing domains

In order to verify conditions (I) and (O) of the depoissonization given in Table 7.2 we often need to prove some inequalities for a function, say $\widetilde{W}_j(z)$, defined over the whole complex plane by a functional equation, such as (7.49). We accomplish this by using induction over so-called *increasing domains*, which we discuss next.

Let us define, for integers $m = 0, 1, \ldots$ and a constant λ such that $0 < \max\{p, q\} \leq \lambda^{-1} < 1$, $\mathcal{D}_m$ a sequence of increasing domains (see Figure 7.4), where

$$\mathcal{D}_m = \{z : \xi\delta \leq |z| \leq \xi\lambda^{m+1}\}$$

for some constant $\xi > 0$ and $\delta \leq \min\{p, q\}$. Observe that

$$z \in \mathcal{D}_{m+1} - \mathcal{D}_m \quad \Rightarrow \quad pz, qz \in \mathcal{D}_m . \tag{7.65}$$

The property (7.65) is crucial for applying mathematical induction over m in order to establish appropriate bounds on $\widetilde{G}(z)$ over the whole complex plane.

Let us illustrate how to use this property for $\widetilde{W}_j(z)$ satisfying (7.49). In fact, we will check condition (O), that is, prove that outside the cone $\mathcal{S}_\theta$ there exists $\alpha < 1$ such that $|\widetilde{W}_j(z)| < e^{\alpha|z|}$.

Now assume that $z \notin \mathcal{S}_\theta$. We first observe that $|e^z| = e^{\Re(z)} \leq e^{\alpha|z|}$, where $\alpha \geq \cos\theta \geq \cos(\arg(z))$. Induction over the increasing domains can be applied as before, however, this time we consider $\overline{\mathcal{D}}_m = \mathcal{D}_m \cap \overline{\mathcal{S}}_\theta$, where $\overline{\mathcal{S}}_\theta$ is the

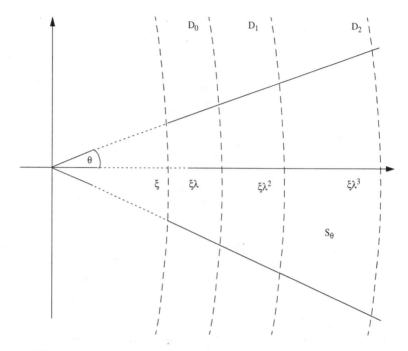

Figure 7.4. The linear cone $\mathcal{S}_\theta$ and the increasing domains $\mathcal{D}_m$.

complementary set to $\mathcal{S}_\theta$. Noting that

$$\Re(z) = |z|\cos(\arg(z)) \le |z|\cos\theta \le \alpha|z|$$

we always can find $\alpha > \cos(\theta)$ such that the following inequalities are simultaneously satisfied

$$|(pz)^j e^{pz}| \le \frac{1}{2}e^{\alpha|z|}, \quad |(qz)^j e^{qz}| \le \frac{1}{2}e^{\alpha|z|}$$
$$|e^{pz}| \le \frac{1}{2}e^{p\alpha|z|}, \quad |e^{qz}| \le \frac{1}{2}e^{q\alpha|z|}.$$

Then by (7.49)

$$|\widetilde{W}_j(z)e^z| \le q|(pz)^j e^{-pz}| + p|(qz)^j e^{-qz}| + p|\widetilde{W}_j(pz)e^{pz}e^{qz}| + q|\widetilde{W}_j(qz)e^{qz}e^{pz}|$$
$$\le \frac{1}{2}qe^{\alpha|z|} + \frac{1}{2}pe^{\alpha|z|} + pe^{\alpha|zp|}|e^{zq}| + qe^{\alpha|qz|}|e^{zp}| \le e^{\alpha|z|},$$

which proves our claim.

7.3. Limiting distributions

In this section we use analytic tools to establish the limiting distributions of the depth in tries and digital search trees as well as the asymptotic distribution of the multiplicity parameter.

7.3.1. Depth in a trie

We derive here the limiting distribution of the depth D_n^T in a trie. We use the index T to distinguish it from the depth in a suffix tree, which we shall discuss in the next chapter. We recall that D_n^T represents the typical depth in a trie built from n independently generated strings. We consider a general finite size alphabet $\mathcal{A}$. We define the probability generating function as

$$D_n^T(u) = \mathbf{E}[u^{D_n^T}]$$

for u complex. We first prove the following asymptotic expression for $D_n^T(u)$. To derive it we use the pattern matching approach from Chapter 2 (see also Section 8.1). Let w be a given word. Then

$$P(D_n < k) = \sum_{w \in \mathcal{A}^k} P(w)(1 - P(w))^{n-1}, \quad n \geq 1. \tag{7.66}$$

Indeed, for a given i consider the depth $D^T(i)$ to the ith external node. The condition $D_n^T(i) < k$ holds if there is a word $w \in \mathcal{A}^k$ such that the prefix of the ith string is equal to w and no other prefixes of $n - 1$ strings are equal to w. Clearly, the typical depth D^T and the depth of the ith node $D^T(i)$ are equally distributed. Thus we have

$$D_n^T(u) = \frac{1-u}{u} \sum_{w \in \mathcal{A}^*} u^{|w|} P(w)(1 - P(w))^{n-1}, \quad n \geq 1 \tag{7.67}$$

by noticing that

$$\sum_{k \geq 1} P(D_n^T < k)u^k = \frac{u\mathbf{E}[u^{D_n^T}]}{1 - u}.$$

This allows us to prove the following useful lemma.

Lemma 7.3.1. *Assume that a trie is built from n strings over a finite alphabet $\mathcal{A}$ generated by a memoryless source that is biased (i.e., not all symbol probabilities are equal). Then, there exists $\varepsilon > 0$ such that*

$$D_n^T(u) = \frac{(1-u)}{h(u)} n^{-s_0(u)}(\Gamma(s_0(u)) + P(\log n, u)) + O(n^\varepsilon),$$

where $h(u) = -\sum_{a \in \mathcal{A}} p_a^{1-s_0(u)} \log p_a$, $s_0(u)$ is the unique real solution of

$$u \sum_{a \in \mathcal{A}} p_a^{1-s_0(u)} = 1, \tag{7.68}$$

and $P(\log n, u)$ is a periodic function, with small amplitude in the case when $\log p_1, \ldots, \log p_{|\mathcal{A}|}$ are rationally related; otherwise, $P(\log n, u)$ converges to zero when $n \to \infty$.

To prove this lemma we need an extension of Lemma 7.2.4 concerning the roots of a characteristic functional equation like (7.68). We formulate it for the binary case.

Lemma 7.3.2. *Suppose that $0 < p_1 < p_2 < 1$ with $p_1 + p_2 = 1$ and that u is a real number with $|u - 1| \leq \delta$ for some $0 < \delta < 1$. Let*

$$\mathcal{Z}(u) = \{s \in \mathbb{C} : p_1^{1-s} + p_2^{1-s} = 1/u\}.$$

Then
(i) All $s \in \mathcal{Z}(u)$ satisfy

$$s_0(u) \leq \Re(s) \leq \sigma_0(u),$$

where $s_0(u) < 1$ is the (unique) real solution of $p_1^{1-s} + p_2^{1-s} = 1/u$ and $\sigma_0(u) > 1$ is the (unique) real solution of $1/u + p_2^{1-s} = p_1^{1-s}$. Furthermore, for every integer k there uniquely exists $s_k(u) \in \mathcal{Z}(u)$ such that

$$(2k-1)\pi/\log(1/p_1) < \Im(s_k(u)) < (2k+1)\pi/\log(1/p_1)$$

and consequently $\mathcal{Z}(u) = \{s_k(u) : k \in \mathbb{Z}(u)\}$.

(ii) If $\log p_2 / \log p_1$ is irrational, then $\Re(s_k(u)) > \Re(s_0(u))$ for all $k \neq 0$.
(iii) If $\log p_2 / \log p_1 = r/d$ is rational, where $\gcd(r, d) = 1$ for integers $r, d > 0$, then we have $\Re(s_k(u)) = \Re(s_0(u))$ if and only if $k \equiv 0 \bmod d$. In particular $\Re(s_1(u)), \ldots, \Re(s_{d-1}(u)) > \Re(s_0(u))$ and

$$s_k(u) = s_{k \bmod d}(u) + \frac{2(k - k \bmod d)\pi i}{\log p_1},$$

that is, all $s \in \mathcal{Z}(u)$ are uniquely determined by $s_0(u)$ and $s_1(u), s_2(u), \ldots, s_{d-1}(u)$, and their imaginary parts constitute an arithmetic progression.

One interesting consequence is that in the irrational case we have

$$\min_{|u-1| \leq \delta} (\Re(s_k(u)) - \Re(s_0(u))) > 0 \tag{7.69}$$

for all $k \neq 0$. This is due to the fact that $s_k(u)$ varies continuously in u.

Proof. Now we are in a position to prove Lemma 7.3.1. As in Section 7.2.4, we apply the Mellin transform. Let

$$T^*(s, u) = \int_0^\infty x^{s-1} \frac{u}{1-u} D_x^T(u) dx$$

be the Mellin transform with respect to n of $D_n^T(u)$, see (7.67). Then

$$T^*(s, u) = \sum_{w \in \mathcal{A}^*} u^{|w|} \frac{P(w)}{1 - P(w)} (-\log(1 - P(w)))^{-s} \Gamma(s)$$

for $\Re(s) > 0$ since

$$\mathcal{M}((1 - P(w))^n; s) = \Gamma(s)(-\log(1 - P(w)))^{-s}.$$

For s bounded, $(-\log(1 - P(w)))^{-s} = P(w)^{-s}(1 + O(sP(w)))$; thus we conclude that

$$T^*(s, u) = \Gamma(s) \left(\frac{u \sum_{a \in A} p_a^{1-s}}{1 - u \sum_{a \in A} p_a^{1-s}} + g(s, u) \right),$$

where

$$g(s, u) = O \left(\frac{|u|s \sum_{a \in A} p_a^{2-\Re(s)}}{1 - |u| \sum_{a \in A} p_a^{2-\Re(s)}} \right).$$

Let $s_0(u)$ be the unique real root of the characteristic equation (7.68). The other roots are denoted as $s_k(u)$ for integer $k \neq 0$, as presented in Lemma 7.3.2. Notice that by (7.69) we have, for all k,

$$\Re(s_k(u)) \geq s_0(u), \tag{7.70}$$

and the inequality is strict for the irrational case. Using the inverse Mellin transform, as given in (M1) and (M4) of Table 7.1, we find that

$$D_n^T = \frac{1 - u}{2i\pi u} \int_{-i\infty}^{+i\infty} T^*(s, u) n^{-s} ds.$$

We now consider $|u| < \delta^{-1}$ for $\delta < 1$. Then there exists ε such that for $\Re(s) \leq \varepsilon$ the function $g(s, u)$ has no singularity. Moving the integration path to the left of $\Re(s) = \varepsilon$ and applying the residue theorem, we find the following estimate

$$D_n^T(u) = (1 - u) \frac{\Gamma(s_0(u))}{h(u)} n^{-s_0(u)} + (1 - u) \sum_k \frac{\Gamma(s_k(u))}{h_k(u)} n^{-s_k(u)} + O(n^{-\varepsilon}), \tag{7.71}$$

with $h(u) = -\sum_{a \in \mathcal{A}} p_a^{1-s_0(u)} \log p_a$ and $h_k(u) = -\sum_{a \in \mathcal{A}} p_a^{1-s_k(u)} \log p_a$. When the $\log p_a$ are rationally related, by Lemma 7.3.2 the roots $s_k(u)$ have the same real part as $s_0(u)$ and are equally spaced on the line $\Re(s) = \Re(s_0(u))$. In this case their contribution to (7.71) is

$$n^{-s_0(u)} \sum_{k \neq 0} \frac{\Gamma(s_k(u))}{h_k(u)} \exp(-(s_k(u) - s_0(u)) \log n).$$

When the $\log p_a$ are irrationally related, this contribution is negligible when compared to $n^{s_0(u)}$; this follows from (7.70) which in this case reads as $\Re(s_k(u)) > s_0(u)$. ∎

In order to establish the central limit theorem (CLT) for the depth, it suffices to observe that, for $t \to 0$,

$$s_0(e^t) = -c_1 t - \frac{c_2}{2} t^2 + O(t^3), \tag{7.72}$$

where $c_1 = 1/h$ and $c_2 = (h_2 - h^2)/h^3$; that is basically the Taylor expansion of $s_0(u)$ around $u = 1$.

We now consider the *asymmetric case*, that is, the case when the p_a are not all equal, corresponding to a biased memoryless source. From the expression for $D_n^T(u)$ we can find immediately the first and the second moments via the first and the second derivatives of $D_n^T(u)$ at $u = 1$ with the appropriate asymptotic expansion in $c_1 \log n$ and in $c_2 \log n$. In fact we obtained this in Theorem 7.2.1 using Rice's method. In order to find the limiting normal distribution we use Lemma 7.3.1 to find that

$$e^{-tc_1 \log n / \sqrt{c_2 \log n}} D_n^T \left(e^{t/\sqrt{c_2 \log n}} \right) \to e^{t^2/2}$$

since

$$n^{-s_0(u)} = \exp\left(c_1 t \sqrt{\log n / c_2} + \frac{t^2}{2} + O(1/\sqrt{\log n}) \right),$$

$$(1 - e^t) \frac{\Gamma(s_0(e^t))}{h(s_0(e^t))} = \frac{-t}{h} \frac{-1}{c_1 t} + O(t^2) = 1 + O(t^2), \quad t \to 0.$$

By Levy's continuity theorem, we conclude the following result.

Theorem 7.3.3. *Under the assumptions of Lemma 7.3.1*

$$\frac{D_n^T - c_1 \log n}{\sqrt{c_2 \log n}} \to N(0, 1)$$

where

$$c_1 = \frac{1}{h}, \qquad c_2 = \frac{h_2 - h^2}{h^3},$$

and $N(0,1)$ is the standard normal distribution. Here, $h = -\sum_{i=1}^{V} p_i \log p_i$ and $h_2 = \sum_{i=1}^{V} p_i \log^2 p_i$.

Remark 7.3.4. For the symmetric case (i.e., all $p_a = 1/|\mathcal{A}|$), there is no normal limiting distribution since $c_2 = 0$ and therefore the variance is $O(1)$. To find the limiting distribution, if it exists, we return to (7.66). For now let $V = |\mathcal{A}|$. Then from (7.66) we find that

$$P(D_n < k) = (1 - V^{-k})^{n-1}.$$

Next, we find an asymptotic distribution around

$$k = \lfloor \log_V n \rfloor + m = \log_V n - \langle \log_V n \rangle + m$$

for some integer m, where $\langle x \rangle = x - \lfloor x \rfloor$ is the fractional part of x. We obtain

$$P(D_n < \lfloor \log_V n \rfloor + m) = (1 + O(1/n)) \exp\left(-V^{-m + \langle \log_V n \rangle}\right).$$

Owing to the factor $\langle \log_V n \rangle$ there is no limiting distribution. However, we can say, replacing V by $|\mathcal{A}|$, that

$$\liminf_{n\to\infty} P(D_n < \lfloor \log_{|\mathcal{A}|} n \rfloor + m) = \exp\left(-|\mathcal{A}|^{-m}\right), \tag{7.73}$$

$$\limsup_{n\to\infty} P(D_n < \lfloor \log_{|\mathcal{A}|} n \rfloor + m) = \exp\left(-|\mathcal{A}|^{-m+1}\right), \tag{7.74}$$

for any integer m. Furthermore, from the above or using the same approach as in Section 7.2.3 we can precisely estimate the variance:

$$\text{Var}[D_n] = \frac{\pi^2}{6\log^2 V} + \frac{1}{12} + P_2(\log n) + O(n^{-\varepsilon}), \tag{7.75}$$

where $P_2(\log n)$ is a periodic function with small amplitude.   ∎

7.3.2. Depth in a digital search tree

In this section we use a different approach, namely the Rice method, to establish the limiting distribution of the depth in a digital search tree (DST). We prove the following result.

Theorem 7.3.5 (Louchard and Szpankowski, 1995). *For a biased binary memoryless source $(p \neq q)$, the limiting distribution of D_n is normal, that is,*

$$\frac{D_n - \mathbf{E}[D_n]}{\sqrt{\text{Var}[D_n]}} \to N(0,1), \tag{7.76}$$

where $\mathbf{E}[D_n]$ and $\text{Var}[D_n]$ are given by (7.34) and (7.37) of Theorem 7.2.10, respectively. Furthermore, the moments of D_n converge to the appropriate moments of the normal distribution. More generally, for any complex ϑ,

$$e^{-\vartheta c_1 \log n} \mathbf{E}[e^{\vartheta D_n / \sqrt{c_2 \log n}}] = e^{\frac{\vartheta^2}{2}} \left(1 + O\left(\frac{1}{\sqrt{\log n}}\right)\right), \tag{7.77}$$

where $c_1 = 1/h$ and $c_2 = (h_2 - h^2)/h^3$.

Proof. We shall work with the probability generating function for the depth, $D_n(u)$, which is equal to $B_n(u)/n$ where $B(u)$ was defined in Section 7.2.3. Then by (7.32) we have

$$D_n(u) = 1 - \frac{1-u}{n} \sum_{k=2}^{n} (-1)^k \binom{n}{k} Q_{k-2}(u), \tag{7.78}$$

where we recall that

$$Q_k(u) = \prod_{j=2}^{k+1} (1 - up^j - uq^j).$$

Let $\mu_n = \mathbf{E}[D_n]$ and $\sigma_n^2 = \text{Var}[D_n]$. Theorem 7.2.10 implies that

$$\mu_n = c_1 \log n + O(1),$$
$$\sigma_n^2 = c_2 \log n + O(1),$$

where $c_1 = 1/h$ and $c_2 = (h_2 - h^2)/h^3$. Again we use Goncharov's theorem to establish the normal distribution of D_n by showing that

$$\lim_{n \to \infty} e^{-\vartheta \mu_n / \sigma_n} D_n(e^{\vartheta / \sigma_n}) = e^{\vartheta^2 / 2}, \tag{7.79}$$

where ϑ is a complex number. By Levy's continuity theorem, this will establish both the limiting distribution and the convergence in moments for D_n.

We now derive the asymptotics for the probability generating function $D_n(u)$ around $u = 1$. We will assume that $u = e^v$ and, since $\sigma_n = O(\sqrt{\log n})$, we define $v = \vartheta / \sigma_n \to 0$. Note that $1 - D_n(u)$, given by (7.78), has the form of an alternating sum. We now apply the Rice method or, more precisely, Theorem 7.2.3.

To do so, however, we need an analytical continuation of $Q_k(u)$ defined in (7.33). Denote this as $Q(u, s)$ and observe that

$$Q(u, s) = \frac{P(u, 0)}{P(u, s)} = \frac{Q_\infty(u)}{P(u, s)}, \tag{7.80}$$

where $P(u, s) = \prod_{j=2}^\infty (1 - up^{s+j} - uq^{s+j})$. Using Theorem 7.2.3 we arrive at

$$1 - D_n(u) = \frac{1 - u}{n2\pi i} \int_{-3/2-i\infty}^{-3/2+i\infty} \Gamma(s)n^{-s}Q(u, -s - 2)ds + e_n, \tag{7.81}$$

where

$$e_n = O(1/n^2) \int_{-3/2-i\infty}^{-3/2+i\infty} \Gamma(s)n^{-s}sQ(u, -s - 2)ds = O(1/n),$$

as we shall soon see. As usual, we evaluate the integral in (7.81) by the residue theorem. We compute the residues to the *right* of the line of integration in (7.81). The gamma function has its singularities at $s_{-1} = -1$ and $s_0 = 0$, and in addition we have an infinite number of zeros $s_{k,j}(v)$ ($j = 2, 3, \ldots$, $k = 0 \pm 1, \pm 2, \ldots$) of $P(e^v, -s - 2)$, the denominator of $Q(e^v, -s - 2)$, where we have substituted $u = e^v$. More precisely, the $s_{k,j}(v)$ are the zeros of

$$p^{-s-2+j} + q^{-s-2+j} = e^{-v}. \tag{7.82}$$

The dominating contribution to the asymptotics comes from $s_{0,j}(v)$ and s_1. Indeed, the contributions of the first two singularities at s_{-1} and s_0 are, respectively, $(1-u)Q(u, -1) = 1$ and $(1-u)Q(u, -2)/n = O(1/n)$. We now concentrate on the contribution from $s_{0,j}(v)$. In this case, one can solve equation (7.82) to derive an asymptotic expansion as follows (see also (7.72)):

$$s_{0,j}(v) = j - 3 - \frac{v}{h} + \frac{1}{2}\left(\frac{1}{h} - \frac{h_2}{h^3}\right)v^2 + O(v^3), \tag{7.83}$$

for integer $j \geq 2$ and $v \to 0$. We also note that $\Im(s_{k,j}(v)) \neq 0$ for $k \neq 0$.

Now let

$$R_k^j(v) = \text{Res}[(1 - e^v p^{-s-2+j} + e^v q^{-s-2+j})^{-1}; \quad s = s_{k,j}(v)],$$
$$g(s) = \Gamma(s)Q(u, -s - 1).$$

In what follows, we use the expansion

$$Q(u, -s - 2) = \frac{1}{1 - u(p^{-s} + q^{-s})} \frac{Q_\infty(u)}{P(u, -s - 1)}$$
$$= -\frac{w^{-1}}{h} - \frac{\theta}{h} + \frac{h_2}{2h^2} + w\frac{\theta h_2}{2h^2} + O(w^2),$$

where $w = s - s_{0,j}(v)$. Then

$$-D_n(e^v) = R_0^2(v)g(s_{0,2}(v))(1 - e^v)n^{-1}n^{-s_{0,2}(v)}$$

$$+ \sum_{j=3}^{\infty} R_0^j(v)g(s_{0,j}(v))(1 - e^v)n^{-1}n^{-s_{0,j}(v)} \qquad (7.84)$$

$$+ \sum_{\substack{k=-\infty \\ k \neq 0}}^{\infty} \sum_{j=2}^{\infty} R_k^j(v)g(s_{k,j}(v))(1 - e^v)n^{-1}n^{-s_{k,j}(v)} + O(1).$$

We consider the above three terms separately:

(a) $j = 2$ and $k = 0$. Set $v = \vartheta/\sigma_n = \vartheta/\sqrt{c_2 \log n}$. Then by (7.83)

$$n^{-s_{0,2}(v)} = n \exp\left(\frac{\vartheta}{h}\sqrt{\frac{\log n}{c_2}} + \frac{\vartheta^2}{2}\right).$$

In addition, the following hold:

$$R_0^2(v) = -1/h + O(v),$$
$$g(s_{0,2}(v)) = -h/v + O(1),$$

and finally $1 - e^{-v} = v + O(1)$. Therefore, we obtain

$$e^{-\vartheta\mu_n/\sigma_n}R_0^2(v)g(s_{0,2}(v))(1 - e^{-v})m^{-s_{0,2}(v)-1} \to -e^{\vartheta^2/2}. \qquad (7.85)$$

(b) $j \geq 3$ and $k = 0$. In this case we can repeat the analysis from case (a) to get

$$e^{-\vartheta\mu_n/\sigma_n}R_0^2(v)g(s_{0,2}(v))(1 - e^{-v})n^{-s_{0,2}(v)-1} \to O(n^{2-j}e^{\vartheta^2/2}), \qquad (7.86)$$

so this term is an order of magnitude smaller than the first term in (7.84).

(c) $k \neq 0$. Fix $j = 2$. Observe that

$$\sum_{\substack{k=-\infty \\ k \neq 0}}^{\infty} R_k^2(v)g(s_{k,2}(v))(1 - e^v)n^{-1}n^{-s_{k,2}(v)} = O(vn^{-1-\Re(s_{k,2}(v))}).$$

By the same argument as in Lemma 7.3.2 we conclude that $\Re(s_{k,j}) \geq j - 3 + O(v)$. If $\Re(s_{k,j}) > j - 3 + O(v)$ then the term $O(vm^{-1-\Re(s_{k,2}(v))})$ is negligible compared with $O(n^{2-j})$. Otherwise, that is, for $s_{k,j}$ such that $\Re(s_{k,j}) = j - 3 + O(v)$, we observe that the error term is $O(vn^{j-2})$.

Actually, we can do better using the following observation (the reader is asked to prove it in Exercise 7.9):

$$\Re(s_{k,2}(v)) \geq s_{0,2}(\Re(v)).$$

Then the sum becomes

$$\sum_{\substack{k=-\infty \\ k \neq 0}}^{\infty} R_k^2(v)g(s_{k,2}(v))(1 - e^v)n^{-1}n^{-s_{k,2}(v)}$$

$$= n^{-1-\Re(s_{0,2}(v))}O(vn^{\Re(s_{0,2}(v))-s_{0,2}(\Re(v))}) = n^{-1-\Re(s_{0,2}(v))}O(vn^{-\beta v^2}),$$

for some β. Finally, consider general $j \geq 3$. As in case (b), we note that $n^{-s_{k,j}(v)}$ contributes $O(n^{2-j})$, so this term is negligible. All other roots (in the rational case) with $\Re(s_{k,j}(v)) > s_{0,j}(v)$ (see Lemma 7.3.2(iii)) contribute negligible terms.

Putting everything together we note that as $v = O(1/\sqrt{n}) \to 0$ for $n \to \infty$,

$$e^{-\vartheta \mu_n/\sigma_n}D_n(e^{\vartheta/\sigma_n}) = e^{\vartheta^2/2}(1 + O(vn^{-\beta v^2}) + O(1/n)) \to e^{\vartheta^2/2}, \qquad (7.87)$$

which proves the theorem. ∎

7.3.3. Asymptotic distribution of the multiplicity parameter

Finally, we analyze the "asymptotic distribution" of the multiplicity parameter M_n using the depoissonization technique. We say asymptotic distribution rather than limiting distribution since, as we shall see, M_n does not in fact have a limiting distribution.

In this section we prove the following main result.

Theorem 7.3.6. Let $s_k = \frac{2kd\pi i}{\ln p}$ $\forall k \in \mathbb{Z}$, where $\frac{\ln p}{\ln q} = \frac{d}{r}$ for some relatively prime $r, s \in \mathbb{Z}$. Then

$$\mathbf{E}[u^{M_n}] = -\frac{q\ln(1 - pu) + p\ln(1 - qu)}{h} + \frac{1}{h}\delta(\log_{1/p} n, u) + O(n^\varepsilon) \qquad (7.88)$$

where

$$\delta(t, u) = \sum_{k \neq 0} e^{2kd\pi it}\Gamma(s_k)\left(q(1 - pu)^{-s_k} + p(1 - qu)^{-s_k} - p^{-s_k+1} - q^{-s_k+1}\right).$$

It follows immediately that

$$\mathbf{E}[u^{M_n}] = \sum_{j=1}^{\infty} \left(\frac{p^j q + q^j p}{jh} + \frac{1}{h} \sum_{k \neq 0} \frac{e^{2kd\pi i \log_{1/p} n} \Gamma(s_k)(p^j q + q^j p)(s_k)^{\overline{j}}}{j!} \right) + O(n^{-\varepsilon})$$

$$(7.89)$$

where we recall that $z^{\overline{j}} = z(z+1)\cdots(z+j-1)$, *and*

$$P(M_n = j) = \frac{p^j q + q^j p}{jh} + + \frac{1}{h} \sum_{k \neq 0} \frac{e^{2kd\pi i \log_{1/p} n} \Gamma(s_k)(p^j q + q^j p)(s_k)^{\overline{j}}}{j!} + O(n^{-\varepsilon}),$$

$$(7.90)$$

that is, the nonfluctuating part of $P(M_n = j)$ *represents the logarithmic series distribution shown in Figure 7.5. When* $\log p / \log q$ *is irrational, the fluctuating part converges to zero as* $t \to \infty$.

Proof. We shall follow our analysis from Section 7.2.4. We define the exponential generating function

$$G(z, u) = \sum_{n \geq 0} \mathbf{E}[u^{M_n}] \frac{z^n}{n!}$$

for complex $u \in \mathbb{C}$, which, by (7.47), satisfies

$$\mathbf{E}[u^{M_n}] = p^n(qu^n + p\mathbf{E}[u^{M_n}]) + q^n(pu^n + q\mathbf{E}[u^{M_n}]) \qquad (7.91)$$

$$+ \sum_{k=1}^{n-1} \binom{n}{k} p^k q^{n-k} (p\mathbf{E}[u^{M_k}] + q\mathbf{E}[u^{M_{n-k}}]).$$

As in Section 7.2.4, the Poisson transform $\widetilde{G}(z, u) = G(z, u)e^{-z}$ of $G(z, u)$ satisfies

$$\widetilde{G}(z, u) = qe^{(pu-1)z} + pe^{(qu-1)z} - pe^{-pz} - qe^{-qz} + p\widetilde{G}(pz, u) + q\widetilde{G}(qz, u). \quad (7.92)$$

Using properties of the Mellin transform, as summarized in Table 7.1, we conclude that the Mellin transform $G^*(s, u)$ of $\widetilde{G}(z, u)$ exists in $\Re(s) \in (-1, 0)$ and that

$$G^*(s, u) = \frac{\Gamma(s) \left(q(1 - pu)^{-s} + p(1 - qu)^{-s} - p^{-s+1} - q^{-s+1} \right)}{(1 - p^{-s+1} - q^{-s+1})}.$$

Now, we are in a position to find the inverse Mellin transform for $z \to \infty$ on a cone around the real axis (see property (M4) in Table 7.1) and then depoissonize, as described in Table 7.2 (see Theorem 7.2.14). We claim, that for any $\varepsilon > 0$,

$$\widetilde{G}(z, u) = -\frac{q \ln (1 - pu) + p \ln (1 - qu)}{h} - 1 + \frac{1}{h} \delta(\log_{1/p} z, u) + O(x^{-\varepsilon}), \quad (7.93)$$

where

$$\delta(t,u) = \sum_{k \neq 0} e^{2kd\pi it} \Gamma(s_k) \left(q(1-pu)^{-s_k} + p(1-qu)^{-s_k} - p^{-s_k+1} - q^{-s_k+1} \right).$$

Formally, we will derive it first for z real and then by analytic continuation extend to a cone around the real axis. Indeed, as before we first conclude that

$$\widetilde{G}(z,u) = \sum_{k \in \mathbb{Z}} -\mathrm{Res}[G^*(s,u)z^{-s};\ s_k] + O(z^{-M}). \tag{7.94}$$

If $k \neq 0$ then

$$\mathrm{Res}[G^*(s,u)z^{-s};\ s_k] = z^{-s_k}\mathrm{Res}[G^*(s,u);\ s_k] = \exp\left(2kd\pi i \log_{1/p} z\right)$$

$$\times \frac{\Gamma(s_k)\left(q(1-pu)^{-s_k} + p(1-qu)^{-s_k} - p^{-s_k+1} - q^{-s_k+1}\right)}{p^{-s_k+1}\ln p + q^{-s_k+1}\ln q}.$$

Now we compute $\mathrm{Res}[G^*(s,u)z^{-s};\ z_0]$. We first observe that

$$\Gamma(s)\left(q(1-pu)^{-s} + p(1-qu)^{-s} - p^{-s+1} - q^{-s+1}\right)$$
$$= (s^{-1} + O(1))\left(-q\ln(1-pu)s - p\ln(1-qu)s + p\ln(p)s\right.$$
$$\left. +q\ln(q)s + O(s^2)\right)$$
$$= -q\ln(1-pu) - p\ln(1-qu) + p\ln p + q\ln q + O(s).$$

It follows that

$$\mathrm{Res}[G^*(s,u)z^{-s};\ s_0] = z^{-s_0}\mathrm{Res}[G^*(s,u);\ s_0] = \frac{q\ln(1-pu) + p\ln(1-qu)}{h} + 1.$$

Combining these results, the claim given in (7.93) now follows from (7.94). Finally, Theorem 7.2.14 allows us to depoissonize (7.94). To see that (7.89) follows from (7.88), consider the following. From (7.88), we have

$$\mathbf{E}[u^{M_n}] = -\frac{q\ln(1-pu) + p\ln(1-qu)}{h} + \frac{1}{h}\delta(\log_{1/p} n, u) + O(n^{-\varepsilon}). \tag{7.95}$$

Observe that

$$-\frac{q\ln(1-pu) + p\ln(1-qu)}{h} = \sum_{j=1}^{\infty}\left(\frac{p^j q + q^j p}{jh}\right)u^j.$$

Also note that

$$\delta(\log_{1/p} n, u) = \sum_{k \neq 0} \frac{e^{2kr\pi i\log_{1/p} n}\Gamma(s_k)\left(q(1-pu)^{-s_k} + p(1-qu)^{-s_k}\right)}{p^{-s_k+1}\ln p + q^{-s_k+1}\ln q}$$

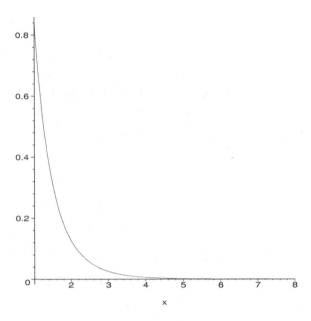

Figure 7.5. The logarithmic series distribution.

$$+\sum_{k\neq0}\frac{e^{2kr\pi i\log_{1/p}n}\Gamma(s_k)\left(-p^{-s_k+1}-q^{-s_k+1}\right)}{p^{-s_k+1}\ln p+q^{-s_k+1}\ln q}$$

$$=\sum_{j=1}^{\infty}\sum_{k\neq0}\frac{e^{2kr\pi i\log_{1/p}n}\Gamma(s_k)(p^jq+q^jp)(s_k)^{\overline{j}}}{j!}$$

since $p^{s_k}=q^{s_k}=1$. Then we apply these observations to (7.95) to conclude that (7.89) holds. Finally, we observe that (7.90) is an immediate corollary of (7.89).   ∎

As mentioned above, the nonfluctuating part of the M_n distribution (7.90) is known as the *logarithmic series distribution* and has mean $1/h$. It is presented in Figure 7.5.

Remark 7.3.7. It is easy to extend this analysis to a finite alphabet $\mathcal{A}$. In particular, for the rational case

$$P(M_n=j)=\sum_{a\in\mathcal{A}}\frac{q_a^jp_a}{jh}+\frac{1}{h}\sum_{k\in\mathbb{Z}\setminus\{0\}}\frac{e^{2k\pi i\log n/L}\Gamma(s_k)(s_j)^{\overline{j}}\sum_{b\in\mathcal{A}}q_b^jp_b}{j!}+O(n^{-\varepsilon}),$$

where $q_a = 1 - p_a$ and with L as defined in Remark 7.2.5. In the irrational case the last two terms are $o(1)$.   ∎

7.4. Average profile of tries

In this section of the chapter, we shall focus on establishing the asymptotic properties of the average profile of a trie. Recall that we introduced two profiles for a trie: the *external profile* $B_{n,k}$ and the *internal profile* $I_{n,k}$, defined respectively as the numbers of external and internal nodes at level k; see Figure 7.2. Hereafter, we mostly discuss the average $\mu_{n,k} = \mathbf{E}[B_{n,k}]$ of the external profile.

Let $B_n^k(u) = \mathbf{E}[u^{B_{n,k}}]$ be the probability generating function for the external profile $B_{n,k}$. It is easy to see that it satisfies the following recurrence for $n \geq 2$:

$$B_n^k(u) = \sum_{i=0}^n \binom{n}{i} p^i q^{n-i} B_i^{k-1}(u) B_{n-i}^{k-1}(u)$$

with $B_n^0 = 1$ for $n \neq 1$ and $B_1^0 = u$. Then the average external profile

$$\mu_{n,k} = \mathbf{E}(B_{n,k}) = \frac{d}{du} B_n^k(u) \mid_{u=1}$$

becomes

$$\mu_{n,k} = \sum_{0 \leq j \leq n} \binom{n}{j} p^j q^{n-j} (\mu_{j,k-1} + \mu_{n-j,k-1}), \qquad (7.96)$$

for $n \geq 2$ and $k \geq 1$ with initial values $\mu_{n,0} = 0$ for all $n \neq 1$ and 1 for $n = 1$. Furthermore, $\mu_{0,k} = 0, k \geq 0$, and

$$\mu_{n,k} = \begin{cases} 0 & \text{if } k \geq 1, \\ 1 & \text{if } k = 0. \end{cases}$$

We use poissonization and depoissonization and the Mellin transform (see Tables 7.1 and 7.2) to find the asymptotics of $\mu_{n,k}$ for a wide range of n and k, mostly for $k = \Theta(\log n)$. Our starting point is an exact formula for the Poisson transform

$$\tilde{M}_k(z) := \sum_{n \geq 0} \mu_{n,k} \frac{z^n}{n!} e^{-z}$$

of $\mu_{n,k}$; we also write $M_k(z) = \tilde{M}_k(z) e^z$ for the exponential generating function of $\mu_{n,k}$.

Lemma 7.4.1. *The Poisson generating function $\tilde{M}_k(z)$ satisfies the following integral representation for $k \geq 1$ and $\Re(z) > 0$*

$$\tilde{M}_k(z) = \frac{1}{2\pi i} \int_{\rho-i\infty}^{\rho+i\infty} z^{-s} \Gamma(s+1) g(s) \left(p^{-s} + q^{-s}\right)^k ds, \qquad (7.97)$$

where $g(s) := 1 - 1/(p^{-s} + q^{-s})$. When $\rho > -2$ the integral is absolutely convergent for $\Re(z) > 0$.

Proof. We consider the recurrence (7.96) with initial conditions $\mu_{n,k} = \delta_{n,1}\delta_{k,0}$ when either $n \leq 1$ and $k \geq 0$ or $k = 0$ and $n \geq 0$. Note that

$$\mu_{n,1} = n \left(pq^{n-1} + qp^{n-1}\right) \qquad (n \geq 2).$$

By (7.96) it follows that

$$M_k(z) = e^{qz} M_{k-1}(pz) + e^{pz} M_{k-1}(qz) \qquad (k \geq 2),$$

with $M_1(z) = z(pe^{qz} + qe^{pz} - 1)$. Thus $\tilde{M}_k(z)$ satisfies

$$\tilde{M}_k(z) = \tilde{M}_{k-1}(pz) + \tilde{M}_{k-1}(qz), \qquad (7.98)$$

and using property (M3) of Table 7.1, the Mellin transform $M_k^*(s)$ of $\tilde{M}_k(z)$, is given by, for $k > 1$,

$$M_k^*(s) = M_{k-1}^*(p^{-s} + q^{-s}).$$

Iterating it and noting that

$$M_1^*(s) = \Gamma(s+1)(p^{-s} + q^{-s} - 1)$$

we prove (7.97).

To justify the absolute convergence of the integral, we apply the Stirling formula for the gamma function (with complex parameter)

$$\Gamma(s+1) = \sqrt{2\pi s} \left(\frac{s}{e}\right)^s \left(1 + O\left(|s|^{-1}\right)\right),$$

uniformly as $|s| \to \infty$ and $|\arg s| \leq \pi - \varepsilon$, which implies that

$$|\Gamma(\rho + it)| = \Theta(|t|^{\rho-1/2} e^{-\pi|t|/2}), \qquad (7.99)$$

uniformly for $|t| \to \infty$ and $\rho = o(|t|^{2/3})$. The integrand in (7.97) is analytic for $\Re(s) > -2$ and bounded above by

$$z^{-\rho-it}\Gamma(\rho+1+it)g(\rho+it)\left(p^{-\rho-it} + q^{-\rho-it}\right)^k$$
$$= O\left(|z|^{-\rho}|t|^{\rho+1/2}e^{-\pi|t|/2+\arg(z)t}(p^{-\rho} + q^{-\rho})^k\right),$$

for large $|t|$. This completes the proof of the lemma. ∎

Observe that we have another integral representation for $\mu_{n,k}$, namely

$$\mu_{n,k} = \frac{1}{2\pi i} \int_{(\rho)} \frac{\Gamma(n+1)\Gamma(s+1)}{\Gamma(n+1+s)} g(s) \left(p^{-s} + q^{-s}\right)^k ds \qquad \rho > -2, \quad (7.100)$$

where (ρ) denotes the vertical line of integration $(\rho - i\infty, \rho + \infty)$. This follows from

$$\mu_{n,k} = \frac{n!}{2\pi i} \int z^{-n-1} e^z \tilde{M}_k(z) dz \qquad (7.101)$$

$$= \frac{n!}{2\pi i} \int z^{-n-1} e^z \left(\frac{1}{2\pi i} \int z^{-s} \Gamma(s+1) g(s) \left(p^{-s} + q^{-s}\right)^k ds \right) dz$$

$$= \frac{n!}{2\pi i} \int \Gamma(s+1) g(s) \left(p^{-s} + q^{-s}\right)^k \left(\frac{1}{2\pi i} \int z^{-n-1-s} e^z dz \right) ds$$

$$= \frac{n!}{2\pi i} \int \frac{\Gamma(s+1)}{\Gamma(n+s+1)} g(s) \left(p^{-s} + q^{-s}\right)^k ds.$$

The depoissonization results given in Table 7.2 allow us to show that $\mu_{n,k} \sim \tilde{M}_k(n)$. So, we will mostly work with $\tilde{M}_k(n)$. Before we present our main result and its proof, we discuss the ideas behind our derivation.

In what follows, we mostly concentrate on analyzing the average profile for $k = \alpha \log n$. For this range, observe that (7.97) gives us

$$\tilde{M}_k(n) = \frac{1}{2\pi i} \int_{\rho - i\infty}^{\rho + i\infty} g(s) \Gamma(s+1) n^{-s} (p^{-s} + q^{-s})^k ds$$

$$= \frac{1}{2\pi i} \int_{c - i\infty}^{c + i\infty} g(s) \Gamma(s+1) \exp(h(s) \log n) ds, \qquad k = \alpha \log n$$

where $g(s) = p^{-s} + q^{-s} - 1$ (note that $g(0) = g(-1) = 0$). In the above,

$$h(s) = \alpha \log(p^{-s} + q^{-s}) - s$$

for $k = \alpha \log n$. Actually, we should write $\alpha_{n,k}$ for α but for now we simplify it to just α. For $k = \Theta(\log n)$, the function under the integral grows with n. Thus the saddle point method, summarized in Table 3.1, can be used. The saddle point ρ occurs where $h'(\rho) = 0$, and it is easy to show that

$$\left(\frac{p}{q} \right)^{-\rho} = \frac{\alpha \log(1/p) - 1}{1 - \alpha \log(1/q)}$$

and notice that for $r = p/q > 1$ we have $r^{it_j} = 1$ for $t_j = 2\pi j/\log r$, $j \in \mathbb{Z}$, which indicates an infinite number of saddle points along the line $\Re(s) = \rho$. Throughout we assume that $p > q$, hence $r > 1$ and thus

$$\rho = \frac{-1}{\log r} \log \left(\frac{\alpha \log q^{-1} - 1}{1 - \alpha \log p^{-1}} \right), \quad \frac{1}{\log q^{-1}} < \alpha < \frac{1}{\log p^{-1}}. \qquad (7.102)$$

Furthermore,

$$\left| p^{-\rho - it} + q^{-\rho - it} \right| = p^{-\rho} + q^{-\rho}.$$

Therefore, there are indeed *infinitely many* saddle points $\rho + it_j$ for $t_j = 2\pi j/\log r$, $j \in \mathbb{Z}$ on the vertical line $\Re(s) = \rho$ that contribute to the leading term of the asymptotic expression.

Let us now make some additional observations. The real saddle point ρ will move along the whole real line from ∞ to $-\infty$ as α varies from $\log(1/q)$ to $\log(1/p)$. More precisely, $\rho \to \infty$ as

$$\alpha \downarrow 1/\log q^{-1} =: \alpha_1,$$

and $\rho \to -\infty$ when

$$\alpha \uparrow 1/\log p^{-1}.$$

When $\rho \to \infty$ we need to consider the gamma function $\Gamma(s)$ in the expression for the saddle point. Also, when ρ moves from ∞ to $-\infty$, that is, when α moves from $\log(1/q)$ to $\log(1/p)$, the saddle point ρ coalesces with the poles of $\Gamma(s+1)$ at $s = -2, -3, \ldots$ The pole at $s = -2$ is dominant and occurs at

$$\alpha_2 := \frac{p^2 + q^2}{p^2 \log(1/p) + q^2 \log(1/q)}.$$

In fact, the average profile undergoes a "phase transition" around $\alpha = \alpha_2$. We describe this precisely in the next theorem.

Theorem 7.4.2. *Consider a trie built over a binary memoryless source with $p > q := 1 - p$. If k satisfies*

$$\alpha_1 \left(\log n - \log \log \log n + \omega_n \right) \leq k \leq \alpha_2 (\log n - \omega_n \sqrt{\log n}), \qquad (7.103)$$

where $\alpha_1 = 1/\log(1/q)$ and ω_n is an arbitrarily slowly growing function, then

$$\mu_{n,k} = G_1 \left(\rho; \log_{p/q} p^k n \right) \frac{n^{-\rho} \left(p^{-\rho} + q^{-\rho} \right)^k}{\sqrt{2\pi \beta_2(\rho) k}} \left(1 + O \left(\frac{1}{k(p/q)^\rho} + \frac{1}{k(\rho + 2)^2} \right) \right),$$
$$(7.104)$$

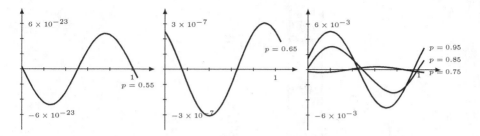

Figure 7.6. The fluctuating part of the periodic function $G_1(x)$ for $p = 0.55, 0.65, \ldots, 0.95$.

where $\rho = \rho(n, k) > -2$ is chosen to satisfy the saddle-point equation

$$
\begin{aligned}
\frac{d}{d\rho}\left(\rho^\rho e^{-\rho} n^{-\rho}(p^{-\rho} + q^{-\rho})^k\right) &= 0 \quad \text{if } \rho \geq 1; \\
\frac{d}{d\rho}\left(n^{-\rho}(p^{-\rho} + q^{-\rho})^k\right) &= 0 \qquad \text{if } \rho \leq 1.
\end{aligned}
\tag{7.105}
$$

For $\rho < 1$ we have

$$
\rho = \frac{1}{\log(p/q)} \log\left(\frac{\log n - k\log(1/p)}{k\log(1/q) - \log n}\right).
\tag{7.106}
$$

Furthermore,

$$
\beta_2(\rho) := \frac{p^{-\rho}q^{-\rho}\log(p/q)^2}{(p^{-\rho} + q^{-\rho})^2},
\tag{7.107}
$$

$$
G_1(\rho; x) = \sum_{j \in \mathbb{Z}} g(\rho + it_j)\Gamma(\rho + 1 + it_j)e^{-2j\pi ix} \qquad (t_j := 2j\pi/\log(p/q))
$$

where $g(s) = 1 - 1/(p^{-s} + q^{-s})$, and $G_1(\rho, x)$ is a 1-periodic function shown in Figure 7.6.

Proof. In order to estimate (7.100) asymptotically we apply the saddle point methods *twice*: first to find the inverse Mellin transform and then to depoissonize. Observe first that by depoissonization

$$
\mu_{n,k} = \frac{n!}{2\pi i} \int_{\substack{|z|=n \\ |\arg(z)| \leq \theta_0}} z^{-n-1}e^z \tilde{M}_k(z)dz + O\left(e^{-cn^{1/5}}\tilde{M}_k(n)\right),
\tag{7.108}
$$

where the O-term is justified by applying the following estimate for $M_k(z)$

$$
|M_k(re^{i\theta})| \leq M_k(r)e^{-cr\theta^2} \qquad r > 0; |\theta| \leq \pi,
\tag{7.109}
$$

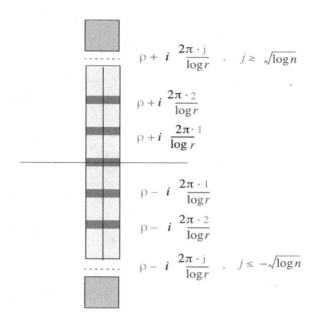

Figure 7.7. Location of the saddle points on the line $\rho + it_j$.

for all $k = k(n) \geq 1$ and some constant $c > 0$. We only need to evaluate $\tilde{M}_k(n)$ and obtain precise local expansions for $\tilde{M}_k(ne^{i\theta})$ when $|\theta| \leq \theta_0$. To estimate the first integral of (7.108), we first focus on estimating $\tilde{M}_k(n)$ and then extend the same approach to derive the asymptotics of $\tilde{M}_k(ne^{i\theta})$. This suffices to prove that $\mu_{n,k} \sim \tilde{M}_k(n)$.

In order to evaluate $\tilde{M}_k(n)$ by the inverse Mellin transform, we first move the line of integration of (7.97) to $\Re(s) = \rho$, so that

$$\tilde{M}_k(n) = \frac{1}{2\pi} \int_{-\infty}^{\infty} J_k(n; \rho + it) dt, \qquad (7.110)$$

where $\rho > -2$ is the saddle point chosen according to (7.105), and we use the abbreviation

$$J_k(n; s) := n^{-s}\Gamma(s+1)g(s)(p^{-s} + q^{-s})^k.$$

We now show that the integral (7.110) is small for $|t| \geq \sqrt{\log n}$, and then assess the main contribution of the saddle points falling in the range $|t| \leq \sqrt{\log n}$. This is illustrated in Figure 7.7.

Assume, from now on, that ρ is chosen as in (7.105). We show that for $|t| \geq \sqrt{\log n}$ the integral in (7.110) is asymptotically negligible. For ease of notation, we write here $L_n = \log n$. Since $\rho > -2$ satisfies (7.106), we have, by (7.99),

$$\frac{1}{2\pi} \int_{|t| \geq \sqrt{L_n}} J_k(n; \rho + it) dt = O\left(n^{-\rho}(p^{-\rho} + q^{-\rho})^k \int_{\sqrt{L_n}}^{\infty} |\Gamma(\rho + 1 + it)| dt\right)$$

$$= O\left(n^{-\rho}(p^{-\rho} + q^{-\rho})^k \int_{\sqrt{L_n}}^{\infty} t^{\rho + 1/2} e^{-\pi t/2} dt\right)$$

$$= O\left(L_n^{\rho/2 + 1/4} e^{-\pi \sqrt{L_n}/2} n^{-\rho}(p^{-\rho} + q^{-\rho})^k\right).$$

However, on the one hand,

$$\rho \leq \frac{1}{\log(p/q)} \left(\log \log n - \log \omega_n + \log \frac{\log(p/q)}{\log(1/q)} + o(1)\right), \qquad (7.111)$$

implying in particular that $\rho = O(\log \log n)$. On the other hand, $\rho \geq -2 + \omega_n L_n^{-1/2}$, so that $n^{-\rho}(p^{-\rho} + q^{-\rho})^k = O(n^2)$, and thus we obtain

$$L_n^{\rho/2 + 1/4} e^{-\pi \sqrt{L_n}/2} = O\left(e^{-\pi \sqrt{L_n}/2 + O(\log \log n^2)}\right) = O\left(\Gamma(\rho + 2) e^{-\sqrt{L_n}}\right),$$

for large enough n. The last O-term holds uniformly for $\rho \geq -2 + \omega_n L_n^{-1/2}$. In summary, the integral for $|t| > \sqrt{\log n}$ is exponentially negligible.

Now, we consider $|t| \leq \sqrt{\log n}$. Let j_0 be the largest integer j for which

$$\frac{2j\pi}{\log(p/q)} \leq \sqrt{L_n}.$$

Then we can split the integral over $\int_{|t| \leq \sqrt{L_n}}$ as follows:

$$\int_{|t| \leq \sqrt{L_n}} J_k(n; \rho + it) dt = \sum_{|j| < j_0} \int_{|t - t_j| \leq \pi/\log(p/q)} J_k(n; \rho + it) dt$$

$$+ \int_{t_{j_0} \leq |t| \leq \sqrt{L_n}} J_k(n; \rho + it) dt.$$

The last integral is bounded above by

$$O\left(\Gamma(\rho + 2) n^{-\rho}(p^{-\rho} + q^{-\rho})^k e^{-\sqrt{L_n}}\right),$$

by the same argument as that used above. It remains to evaluate the integrals

$$T_j := \frac{1}{2\pi} \int_{|t - t_j| \leq \pi/\log(p/q)} J_k(n; \rho + it) dt,$$

for $|j| < j_0$.

We derive first a uniform bound for $|p^{-\rho-it} + q^{-\rho-it}|$. By the elementary inequalities and

$$\sqrt{1-x} \leq 1 - \frac{x}{2} \qquad (x \in [0,1]),$$

we have

$$|p^{-\rho-it} + q^{-\rho-it}| = (p^{-\rho} + q^{-\rho}) \sqrt{1 - \frac{2p^{-\rho}q^{-\rho}}{(p^{-\rho} + q^{-\rho})^2} (1 - \cos(t\log(p/q)))}$$

$$\leq (p^{-\rho} + q^{-\rho}) \left(1 - \frac{p^{-\rho}q^{-\rho}}{(p^{-\rho} + q^{-\rho})^2} (1 - \cos((t - t_j)\log(p/q)))\right)$$

$$\leq (p^{-\rho} + q^{-\rho}) \left(1 - \frac{2p^{-\rho}q^{-\rho}}{\pi^2(p^{-\rho} + q^{-\rho})^2} (t - t_j)^2 \log(p/q)^2\right)$$

$$\leq (p^{-\rho} + q^{-\rho}) e^{-c_0(t-t_j)^2}, \tag{7.112}$$

uniformly for $|t - t_j| \leq \pi/\log(p/q)$, where

$$c_0 = c_0(\rho) := \frac{2p^{-\rho}q^{-\rho}\log(p/q)^2}{\pi^2(p^{-\rho} + q^{-\rho})^2} = \frac{2}{\pi^2}\beta_2(\rho).$$

We now set

$$v_0 := \begin{cases} k^{-2/5} & \text{if } -2 < \rho \leq 1; \\ (c_0 k)^{-2/5} & \text{if } \rho \geq 1, \end{cases}$$

and split the integration range into two parts: $|t - t_j| \leq v_0$ and $v_0 < |t - t_j| \leq \pi/\log(p/q)$, as shown in Figure 7.7. (We assume that k is sufficiently large that $v_0 < \pi/\log(p/q)$.)

Consider first the case $-2 < \rho \leq 1$. From the inequality (7.112), it follows that

$$T_j'' := \frac{1}{2\pi} \int_{v_0 \leq |t-t_j| \leq \pi/\log(p/q)} J_k(n; \rho + it) dt \tag{7.113}$$

$$= O\left(|\Gamma(\rho + 2 + it_j)|n^{-\rho}(p^{-\rho} + q^{-\rho})^k \int_{k^{-2/5}}^\infty e^{-c_0 k v^2} dv\right)$$

$$= O\left(n^{-\rho}(p^{-\rho} + q^{-\rho})^k k^{-3/5} e^{-c_0 k^{1/5}} \times \begin{cases} |\Gamma(\rho + 1 + it_j)| & \text{if } j \neq 0, \\ 1, & \text{if } j = 0, \end{cases}\right),$$

for each $|j| \leq j_0$.

When $\rho \geq 1$ and k satisfies (7.103), we have

$$
T_j'' = O\left(|\Gamma(\rho + 1 + it_j)| n^{-\rho} \left(p^{-\rho} + q^{-\rho}\right)^k \int_{(c_0 k)^{-2/5}}^{\infty} e^{-c_0 k v^2} dv \right)
$$

$$
= O\left(|\Gamma(\rho + 1 + it_j)| n^{-\rho} \left(p^{-\rho} + q^{-\rho}\right)^k (c_0 k)^{-3/5} e^{-(c_0 k)^{1/5}} \right),
$$

for $|j| \leq j_0$.

It remains to evaluate the integrals T_j for t in the range $|t - t_j| \leq v_0$. Note that by our choice of t_j,

$$
p^{-\rho - it_j} + q^{-\rho - it_j} = p^{-it_j} \left(p^{-\rho} + q^{-\rho}\right) = q^{-it_j} \left(p^{-\rho} + q^{-\rho}\right),
$$

so that

$$
\frac{p^{-\rho - it} + q^{-\rho - it}}{p^{-\rho - it_j} + q^{-\rho - it_j}} = 1 + \sum_{\ell \geq 1} \frac{i^\ell (t - t_j)^\ell}{\ell!} \frac{p^{-\rho - it_j} \log(1/p)^\ell + q^{-\rho - it_j} \log(1/q)^\ell}{p^{-\rho - it_j} + q^{-\rho - it_j}}
$$

$$
= 1 + \sum_{\ell \geq 1} \frac{i^\ell (t - t_j)^\ell}{\ell!} \frac{p^{-\rho} \log(1/p)^\ell + q^{-\rho} \log(1/q)^\ell}{p^{-\rho} + q^{-\rho}}.
$$

It follows that

$$
\log\left(p^{-\rho - it} + q^{-\rho - it}\right) = \log\left(p^{-\rho - it_j} + q^{-\rho - it_j}\right) + \sum_{\ell \geq 1} \frac{\beta_\ell(\rho)}{\ell!} i^\ell (t - t_j)^\ell,
$$

where, in particular,

$$
\beta_1(\rho) = \frac{p^{-\rho} \log(1/p) + q^{-\rho} \log(1/q)}{p^{-\rho} + q^{-\rho}}.
$$

The remaining manipulation is then straightforward using the saddle point method. We use the local expansions

$$
\left(\frac{p^{-\rho - it} + q^{-\rho - it}}{p^{-\rho - it_j} + q^{-\rho - it_j}} \right)^k = \exp\left(k \sum_{1 \leq \ell \leq 3} \frac{\beta_\ell(\rho)}{\ell!} i^\ell (t - t_j)^\ell + O(k|\beta_4(\rho)||t - t_j|^4) \right),
$$

and

$$
\Gamma(\rho + 1 + it) g(\rho + it) = \begin{cases} C_0 + C_1 i(t - t_j) + O\left(\dfrac{(t - t_j)^2}{(\rho + 2)^2} \right), & -2 < \rho \leq 1; \\[2ex] \Gamma(\rho + 1 + it_j) e^{(\log \rho) i (t - t_j)} \left(1 + C_2 i(t - t_j) \right. \\ \left. + O(|C_2|^3 |t - t_j|^2) \right) \left(g(\rho + it_j) \right. \\ \left. + g'(\rho + it_j) i(t - t_j) + O\left(|t - t_j|^2\right) \right), & \text{if } \rho \geq 1, \end{cases}
$$

where

$$C_0 := \Gamma(\rho+1+it_j)g(\rho+it_j);$$
$$C_1 := g(\rho+it_j)\Gamma(\rho+1+it_j)\psi(\rho+1+it_j) + g'(\rho+it_j)\Gamma(\rho+1+it_j),$$

with $\psi(s) = \Gamma'(s)/\Gamma(s)$ the logarithmic derivative of the gamma function, and

$$C_2 := \psi(\rho+1+it_j) - \log\rho \qquad (\rho \geq 1).$$

Here C_0 and C_1 are defined to take their limiting values when $\rho = -1$ and $j = 0$, namely,

$$C_0 := p\log(1/p) + q\log(1/q),$$
$$C_1 := -\frac{2p-1}{2}\left(p\log(p)^2 - q\log(q)^2\right) - C_0\gamma - 2pq\log(p)\log(q).$$

Note that $\psi(\rho+1+it_j) - \log\rho = O(\log(1+|t_j|))$. It follows that for $|j| < j_0$

$$T_j = \frac{g(\rho+it_j)}{\sqrt{2\pi\beta_2(\rho)k}}\Gamma(\rho+1+it_j)n^{-\rho-it_j}\left(p^{-\rho}+q^{-\rho}\right)^k p^{-ikt_j}$$
$$\times\left(1 + O\left(\frac{1}{k\beta_2(\rho)} + \frac{1}{k(\rho+2)^2}\right)\right).$$

Summing over together the various $|j| < j_0$ and collecting all estimates, we obtain

$$\tilde{M}_k(n) = \frac{n^{-\rho}\left(p^{-\rho}+q^{-\rho}\right)^k}{\sqrt{2\pi\beta_2(\rho)k}}\sum_{|j|<j_0} g(\rho+it_j)\Gamma(\rho+1+it_j)(p^k n)^{-it_j}$$
$$\times\left(1 + O\left(\frac{1}{k(p/q)^\rho} + \frac{1}{k(\rho+2)^2}\right)\right).$$

Finally, to complete the depoissonization and to estimate the integral in (7.108), we need a more precise expansion for $\tilde{M}_k(ne^{i\theta})$ for small θ. The above proof by the saddle-point method can be easily extended *mutatis mutandis* to $\tilde{M}_k(z)$ for complex values of z lying in the right half-plane since we can write (7.98) as follows:

$$\tilde{M}_k(ne^{i\theta}) = \frac{1}{2\pi i}\int_{(\rho)} n^{-s}e^{-i\theta s}\Gamma(s+1)g(s)\left(p^{-s}+q^{-s}\right)^k ds,$$

where $\rho > -2$ and $|\theta| \leq \pi/2 - \varepsilon$. The result is

$$\tilde{M}_k(ne^{i\theta}) = \frac{(p^{-\sigma}+q^{-\sigma})^k}{\sqrt{2\pi\beta_2(\rho)k}}\sum_{|j|<j_0} g(\sigma+it_j)\Gamma(\sigma+1+it_j)(ne^{i\theta})^{-\rho-it_j}p^{-ikt_j}$$
$$\times\left(1 + O\left(\frac{1}{k(p/q)^\rho} + \frac{1}{k(\rho+2)^2}\right)\right), \qquad\qquad (7.114)$$

uniformly for $|\theta| \leq \pi/2 - \varepsilon$ and k lying in the range (7.103). This completes the proof of (7.104). ∎

Before we continue discussing the asymptotic behavior of the average profile, let us mention here an interesting consequence of Theorem 7.4.2. Theorem 7.3.3 gave the CLT theorem for the depth D_n of a trie. Is there a corresponding local limit theorem (LLT) for this depth? Surprisingly, the answer is no, as the result just proved shows. Indeed, recall that the distribution of the depth D_n is given by $P(D_n = k) = \mu_{n,k}/n$. Observe that for

$$k = \frac{1}{h}(\log n + x\sqrt{h^{-1}\beta_2(-1)\log n}),$$

that is, for $\alpha = 1/h$, where h is the entropy rate, $\rho = 1$ and (7.104) becomes

$$\mu_{n,k} = \frac{\sqrt{h}\, G_1\left(-1; \log_{p/q} p^k n\right)}{\log(p/q)\sqrt{2\pi pq}} \frac{n}{\sqrt{\log n}} e^{-x^2/2}\left(1 + O\left(\frac{1+|x|^3}{\sqrt{\log n}}\right)\right), \quad (7.115)$$

uniformly for $x = o(\log n^{1/6})$. Thus

$$P(D_n = k) = G_1\left(-1; \log_{p/q} p^k n\right) \frac{e^{-x^2/2}}{\sqrt{2\pi \mathrm{Var}[D_n]}}\left(1 + O\left(\frac{1+|x|^3}{\sqrt{\log n}}\right)\right), \quad (7.116)$$

uniformly for $x = o(\log n^{1/6})$, where

$$\mathrm{Var}[D_n] \sim (h_2 - h^2)/h^3 \log n,$$

as in Theorem 7.3.3. The appearance of the unusual periodic function G_1 means that D_n satisfying the central limit theorem but *not* a local limit theorem (of the usual form).

Let us now move to other ranges of $k = \Theta(\log n)$. What happens to $\mu_{n,k}$ when $\alpha > \alpha_2$? The answer is provided in the next theorem.

Theorem 7.4.3. *If*

$$k \geq \alpha_2\left(\log n + \omega_n\sqrt{\alpha_2\beta_2(-2)\log n}\right), \quad (7.117)$$

where β_2 is defined in (7.107), then

$$\mu_{n,k} = 2pqn^2(p^2 + q^2)^{k-1}\left(1 + O\left(\omega_n^{-1}e^{-\omega_n^2/2 + O(\omega_n^3/\sqrt{\log n})}\right)\right), \quad (7.118)$$

uniformly for $1 \ll \omega_n = o(\sqrt{\log n})$.

Proof. To prove (7.118), we move the line of integration of the integral in (7.97) (this is allowable by the absolute convergence of the integral) to $\Re(s) = \rho$, where

$$\rho := -2 - \frac{\omega_n}{\sqrt{\alpha_2 \beta_2(-2) \log n}}.$$

Thus $\tilde{M}_k(ne^{i\theta})$ equals the residue of the integrand at $s = -2$ (the dominant term in (7.118)) plus the value of the integral along $\Re(s) = \rho$:

$$\tilde{M}_k(ne^{i\theta}) = |g(-2)|n^2 e^{2i\theta}(p^2 + q^2)^k + \frac{1}{2\pi}\int_{-\infty}^{\infty} J_k(ne^{i\theta}; \rho + it)dt,$$

where $|g(-1)| = 2pq/(p^2 + q^2)$. We need only estimate the last integral. By the same analysis as that used for T_j'' (see (7.113)) and the inequality (7.112), we have

$$\frac{1}{2\pi}\left(\int_{|t|\leq\pi/\log(p/q)} + \sum_{|j|\geq 1}\int_{|t-t_j|\leq\pi/\log(p/q)}\right) J_k(ne^{i\theta}; \rho + it)dt$$

$$= O\left(|\Gamma(\rho+1)|n^{-\rho}\left(p^{-\rho}+q^{-\rho}\right)^k\int_{|t|\leq\pi/\log(p/q)} e^{-c_0 k t^2}dt\right)$$

$$+ O\left(n^{-\rho}\left(p^{-\rho}+q^{-\rho}\right)^k\sum_{|j|\geq 1}\left|\Gamma\left(\rho+1+\frac{2|j|-1}{\log(p/q)}\pi i\right)\right|\right.$$

$$\left. e^{(2|j|+1)\pi|\theta|/\log(p/q)}\int_{|t-t_j|\leq\pi/\log(p/q)} e^{-c_0 k(t-t_j)^2}dt\right)$$

$$= O\left(\frac{k^{-1/2}}{|\rho+2|}n^{-\rho}\left(p^{-\rho}+q^{-\rho}\right)^k\right) = O\left(\omega_n^{-1}n^{-\rho}\left(p^{-\rho}+q^{-\rho}\right)^k\right),$$

where we have used (7.99) to bound the sum

$$\sum_{|j|\geq 1}\left|\Gamma\left(\rho+1+\frac{2|j|-1}{\log(p/q)}\pi i\right)\right| e^{(2|j|+1)\pi|\theta|/\log(p/q)}$$

$$= O\left(\sum_{|j|\geq 1}(2|j|-1)^{\rho+1/2}\exp\left(-\frac{\pi^2(2|j|-1)}{2\log(p/q)} + \frac{(2|j|+1)\pi|\theta|}{\log(p/q)}\right)\right)$$

$$= O(1),$$

uniformly for $|\theta| \leq \pi/2 - \varepsilon$.

By our choice of ρ and by straightforward expansion, we have

$$\frac{\omega_n^{-1} n^{-\rho} (p^{-\rho} + q^{-\rho})^k}{n^2 (p^2 + q^2)^k} = O\left(\omega_n^{-1} e^{-\log n(\rho+2) + \frac{k}{\alpha_2}(\rho+2) + \frac{k}{2}\beta_2(-2)(\rho+2)^2 + O(k|\rho+2|^3)}\right)$$

$$= O\left(\omega_n^{-1} e^{-\omega_n^2/2 + O(\omega_n^3/\sqrt{\log n})}\right).$$

Thus

$$\tilde{M}_k(ne^{i\theta}) = |g(-2)|(ne^{i\theta})^2 (p^2 + q^2)^k \left(1 + O\left(\omega_n^{-1} e^{-\omega_n^2/2 + O(\omega_n^3/\sqrt{\log n})}\right)\right),$$
(7.119)

uniformly for $|\theta| \leq \pi/2 - \varepsilon$. Substituting this into (7.108), we deduce the desired result (7.118). ∎

Finally, let us say a word about the behavior of $\mu_{n,k}$ for $k < \alpha_1 \log n$ or, more precisely, for $1 \leq k \leq \alpha_1(\log n - \log \log \log n + O(1))$. Because the proof of the following theorem is elementary, in Exercise 7.10 we ask the reader to provide the missing details.

Theorem 7.4.4. *Define*

$$k_m := \alpha_1 \left(\log n - \log \log \log n + \log\left(\frac{p}{q} - 1\right) + m \log \frac{p}{q}\right) \qquad m \geq 0,$$
(7.120)

$$S_{n,k,j} := \binom{k}{j} p^j q^{k-j} n \left(1 - p^j q^{k-j}\right)^{n-1} \qquad 0 \leq j \leq k.$$

For convenience, set $k_{-1} = 0$. Assume that $m \geq 0$. If

$$k_{m-1} + \frac{\alpha_1 \omega_n}{\log \log n} \leq k \leq k_m - \frac{\alpha_1 \omega_n}{\log \log n},$$
(7.121)

then

$$\mu_{n,k} = S_{n,k,m} \left(1 + O((m+1)e^{-\omega_n})\right).$$
(7.122)

If $k = k_m + \alpha_1 x / \log \log n$, where $x = o(\sqrt{\log \log n})$, then

$$\mu_{n,k} = S_{n,k,m} \left(1 + \frac{p\alpha_1 e^x}{q(m+1)}\right) \left(1 + O\left(x^2 \log \log n^{-1} + (m+1) \log n^{-(1-q/p)}\right)\right)$$
(7.123)

for large n.

This completes our discussion of the average profile. The reader may consult Park, Hwang, Nicodeme, and Szpankowski (2009) to find further results such as the variance, limiting distribution, and internal profile for tries (see also the exercises below).

7.5.   Exercises

7.1   Establish (7.1) for tries and digital search trees.

7.2   Prove the following pair of binomial inverse relations:

$$a_n = \binom{n}{r}, \qquad \hat{a}_n = (-1)^r \delta_{n,r}$$

for any nonnegative integer $0 \leq r \leq n$.

7.3   Consider the following system of two-dimensional recurrences:

$$b(n+1,0) = n + \sum_{k=0}^{n} \binom{n}{k} p^k q^{n-k} \left(b(k,0) + b(n-k,k) \right), \quad \text{for } n \geq 2,$$

and

$$b(n,d) = n + \sum_{k=0}^{n} \binom{n}{k} p^k q^{n-k} \left(b(k,d-1) + b(n-k,k+d-1) \right)$$

for $n \geq 2$, $d \geq 1$. Observe that for $d = \infty$ this gives

$$b(n,\infty) = \sum_{\ell=2}^{n} (-1)^\ell \binom{n}{\ell} \frac{\ell}{1 - p^\ell - q^\ell},$$

which is exactly our recurrence (7.5) for the average external path (so that $b(n,\infty) = l_n = \mathbf{E}[L_n]$) for which we gave the solution in Theorem 7.2.7. Therefore, set

$$\widetilde{b}(n,d) = b(n,\infty) - b(n,d)$$

and prove the following result (see Choi, Knessl, and Szpankowski (2012)).

Theorem 7.5.1.   *For $n \to \infty$ and $d = O(1)$ the difference $b(n,\infty) - b(n,d) = \widetilde{b}(n,d)$ is of order $O(\log^2 n)$ for $n \to \infty$. More precisely*

$$\widetilde{b}(n,d) = \frac{1}{2h \log(1/p)} \log^2 n - \frac{d}{h} \log n$$

$$+ \left[\frac{1}{2h} - \frac{1}{h \log p} \left(\gamma + 1 + \frac{h_2}{2h} + \Psi(\log_p n) \right) \right] \log n + O(1),$$

where $\Psi(\cdot)$ is the periodic function

$$\Psi(x) = \sum_{k=-\infty, k \neq 0}^{\infty} \left(1 + \frac{2k\pi id}{\log p} \right) \Gamma\left(-\frac{2k\pi id}{\log p} \right) e^{2k\pi irx}$$

and $\log p / \log q = d/r$ *is rational. If* $\log p / \log q$ *is irrational, the term involving* Ψ *is absent.*

7.4   Prove Theorem 7.2.3 (see Szpankowski (1988a, 2001)).

7.5   Compute the constant A in (7.37) of Theorem 7.2.10.

7.6   Prove (7.75), which holds for a symmetric trie.

7.7   Establish the asymptotics of the variance of the path length, $\mathrm{Var}[L_n]$, for tries and digital search trees (see Kirschenhofer, Prodinger, and Szpankowski (1989b, 1989a, 1994), Jacquet and Szpankowski (1995)).

7.8   Derive asymptotic expression for the variance of the size, $\mathrm{Var}[S_n]$, in tries (see Régnier and Jacquet (1989)).

7.9   Let $s_{j,k}$ $(j = 1, 2, \ldots$ and $k = 0, \pm 1, \ldots)$ be a solution of (7.82). Prove that

$$\Re(s_{k,2}(v)) \geq s_{0,2}(\Re(v))$$

(cf. see Jacquet and Régnier (1986)).

7.10   Prove Theorem 7.4.4 (see Park et al. (2009)).

7.11   Prove the following theorem concerning the variance $\sigma_{n,k}^2 = \mathrm{Var}[B_{n,k}]$ (see Park et al. (2009)). Below we use the same notation as in Section 7.4.

Theorem 7.5.2.   (i) *If* $1 \leq k \leq \alpha_1(1 + o(1)) \log n$, *then*

$$\sigma_{n,k}^2 \sim \mu_{n,k}. \tag{7.124}$$

(ii) *If* $\alpha_1(\log n - \log \log \log n + \omega_n) \leq k \leq \alpha_2(\log n - \omega_n \sqrt{\log n})$, *then*

$$\sigma_{n,k}^2 = G_2\left(\rho; \log_{p/q} p^k n\right) \frac{n^{-\rho} \left(p^{-\rho} + q^{-\rho}\right)^k}{\sqrt{2\pi \beta_2(\rho) k}} \tag{7.125}$$

$$\times \left(1 + O\left(\frac{1}{k(p/q)^\rho} + \frac{1}{k(\rho + 2)^2}\right)\right),$$

where $\rho = \rho(n, k) > -2$ *is given by (7.105) and*

$$G_2(\rho; x) = \sum_{j \in \mathbb{Z}} h(\rho + it_j)\Gamma(\rho + 1 + it_j)e^{-2j\pi i x} \qquad t_j := 2j\pi / \log(p/q).$$

(iii) *If* $k \geq \alpha_2(1 - o(1)) \log n$ *then*

$$\sigma_{n,k}^2 \sim 2\mu_{n,k}. \tag{7.126}$$

7.12   Using Theorem 7.5.2 from the previous exercise, prove, for the following limiting distributions for the external profile.

Theorem 7.5.3.   (i) If $\sigma_{n,k} \to \infty$ then

$$\frac{B_{n,k} - \mu_{n,k}}{\sigma_{n,k}} \xrightarrow{d} \mathcal{N}(0,1), \tag{7.127}$$

where $\mathcal{N}(0,1)$ denotes a standard normal random variable and $\xrightarrow{d}$ stands for convergence in distribution.
(ii) If $\sigma_{n,k} = \Theta(1)$ then

$$P\left(B_{n,k} = 2m\right) = \frac{\lambda_0^m}{m!} e^{-\lambda_0} + o(1), \tag{7.128}$$
$$P\left(B_{n,k} = 2m+1\right) = o(1),$$

uniformly for finite $m \geq 0$, where $\lambda_0 := pqn^2(p^2 + q^2)^{k-1}$.

7.13   In this exercise we ask the reader to extend our results obtained for the external profile $B_{n,k}$ to the internal profile $I_{n,k}$. In particular, define

$$\alpha_0 := \frac{2}{\log(1/p) + \log(1/q)}.$$

We now list asymptotic approximations of $\mathbf{E}[I_{n,k}]$ for various ranges of k, and ask the reader to establish them.
(a) The asymptotics of $\mathbf{E}[I_{n,k}]$ when $1 \leq k \leq \alpha_1(1 + o(1)) \log n$:

$$\mathbf{E}[I_{n,k}] = 2^k - \mathbf{E}[B_{n,k}](1 + o(1)), \tag{7.129}$$

uniformly in k.
(b) The asymptotics of $\mathbf{E}[I_{n,k}]$ when $\alpha_1(\log n - \log \log \log n + w_n) \leq k \leq \alpha_0(\log n - \omega_n \sqrt{\log n})$:

$$\mathbf{E}[I_{n,k}] = 2^k - G_3\left(\rho; \log_{p/q} p^k n\right) \frac{n^{-\rho} (p^{-\rho} + q^{-\rho})^k}{\sqrt{2\pi \beta_2(\rho)k}}$$
$$\times \left(1 + O\left(\frac{1}{k(p/q)^\rho} + \frac{1}{k\rho^2}\right)\right),$$

where $\rho = \rho(n,k) > 0$ satisfies the saddle point equation (7.105), $\beta_2(\rho)$ is the same as in (7.107) and

$$G_3(\rho; x) = \sum_{j \in \mathbb{Z}} (\rho + 1 + it_j)\Gamma(\rho + it_j)e^{-2j\pi i x}$$

where $t_j := 2j\pi/(\log(p/q))$.

(c) The asymptotics of $\mathbf{E}[I_{n,k}]$ when $k = \alpha_0(\log n + o(\log n^{2/3}))$:

$$k = \alpha_0(\log n + \xi\sqrt{\alpha_0\beta_2(0)\log n}),$$

where

$$\alpha_0\beta_2(0) = 2(\log(1/p) + \log(1/q))/\log(p/q)^2$$

and

$$\xi = o(\log n^{1/6}),$$

and then

$$\mathbf{E}[I_{n,k}] = 2^k\Phi(-\xi)\left(1 + O\left(\frac{1 + |\xi|^3}{\sqrt{\log n}}\right)\right),$$

uniformly in ξ, where $\Phi(x)$ denotes the standard normal distribution function.

(d) The asymptotics of $\mathbf{E}[I_{n,k}]$ when $\alpha_0(\log n + \omega_n\sqrt{\log n}) \le k \le \alpha_2(\log n - \omega_n\sqrt{\log n})$:

$$\mathbf{E}[I_{n,k}] = G_3\left(\rho; \log_{p/q} p^k n\right)\frac{n^{-\rho}(p^{-\rho} + q^{-\rho})^k}{\sqrt{2\pi\beta_2(\rho)k}}$$
$$\left(1 + O\left(\frac{1}{k(p/q)^\rho} + \frac{1}{k(\rho+2)^2}\right)\right),$$

with ρ, $\beta_2(\rho)$ and G_3 as defined above.

(e) The asymptotics of $\mathbf{E}[I_{n,k}]$ when $k = \alpha_2(\log n + o(\log n^{2/3}))$: In this case, we write

$$k = \alpha_0(\log n + \xi\sqrt{\alpha_2\beta_2(-2)\log n}),$$

and then we have

$$\mathbf{E}(I_{n,k}) = \frac{1}{2}\Phi(\xi)n^2(p^2 + q^2)^k\left(1 + O\left(\frac{1 + |\xi|^3}{\sqrt{\log n}}\right)\right),$$

uniformly for $\xi = o(\log n^{1/6})$.

(f) The asymptotics of $\mathbf{E}[I_{n,k}]$ when $k \ge \alpha_2(\log n + \omega_n\sqrt{\log n})$:

$$\mathbf{E}[I_{n,k}] = \frac{1}{2}n^2(p^2 + q^2)^k\left(1 + O\left(\omega_n^{-1}e^{-\omega_n^2/2 + O(\omega_n^3 \log n^{-1/2})}\right)\right)$$

as $n \to \infty$.

The reader should consult Park et al. (2009).

7.14   In Section 7.1 we expressed the height H_n, the shortest path R_n, and
        the fillup level F_n in terms of the internal and external profile. Using
        the results of Section 7.4 and the above exercises, prove the following
        corollaries.

Corollary 7.5.4.   *(Height of a trie). Let $H_n := \max\{k : B_{n,k} > 0\}$
be the height of a random trie. Then*

$$\frac{H_n}{\log n} \to \frac{1}{\log(p^2 + q^2)^{-1}}$$

in probability.

Corollary 7.5.5.   *(Shortest path length of tries). Define*

$$\hat{k} := \begin{cases} \alpha_1 \left(\log n - \log\log\log n - \log m_0 + m_0 \log(p/q) - \dfrac{\log\log\log n}{m_0 \log\log n} \right), \\ \alpha_1 (\log n - \log\log n), \end{cases}$$

*depending whether $p \neq q$ or not, respectively, where $m_0 := \lceil 1/(p/q - 1) \rceil$
and*

$$k_S := \begin{cases} \lceil \hat{k} \rceil & \text{if } p \neq q, \\ \lfloor \hat{k} \rfloor & \text{if } p = q. \end{cases}$$

If $p \neq q$ then

$$R_n = \begin{cases} k_S & \text{if } \langle \hat{k} \rangle \log\log n \to \infty, \\ k_S \text{ or } k_S - 1 & \text{if } \langle \hat{k} \rangle \log\log n = O(1), \end{cases}$$

*with high probability; we recall that $\langle x \rangle$ is the fractional part of x. If
$p = q = 1/2$, then*

$$R_n = \begin{cases} k_S + 1, & \text{if } \langle \hat{k} \rangle \log n \to \infty, \\ k_S \text{ or } k_S + 1, & \text{if } \langle \hat{k} \rangle \log n = O(1), \end{cases}$$

with high probability.

Corollary 7.5.6.   *(Fillup level of a trie) If $p \neq q$ then*

$$F_n = \begin{cases} k_S - 1 & \text{if } \langle \hat{k} \rangle \log\log n \to \infty, \\ k_S - 2 \text{ or } k_S - 1 & \text{if } \langle \hat{k} \rangle \log\log n = O(1), \end{cases}$$

with high probability; if $p = q = 1/2$ then

$$F_n = \begin{cases} k_S & \text{if } \langle \hat{k} \rangle \log n \to \infty, \\ k_S \text{ or } k_S - 1 & \text{if } \langle \hat{k} \rangle \log n = O(1). \end{cases}$$

7.15 For $p = q = 1/2$ we have $\alpha_0 = \alpha_1 = \alpha_2 = 1/\log 2$, hence the internal and external profiles become particularly simple. Derive these results.

7.16 Extend the profile results presented in Section 7.4 to a general finite alphabet.

7.17 In a b-trie the external node is allowed to store up to b strings. The regular trie corresponds to $b = 1$. Extend the results of this chapter to b-tries.

7.18 Extend the analyses of this chapter to Markov sources. In particular, prove the CLT for the depths in a trie and in a digital search tree built over n independent strings generated by a Markov source.

More precisely, define $P = \{p_{ij}\}_{i,j=1}^V$ to be a positive transition matrix for the underlying stationary Markov sources with the stationary distribution $\boldsymbol{\pi} = (\pi_1, \ldots, \pi_V)$. Define a new matrix $P(s) = \{p_{ij}^{-s}\}_{i,j=1}^V$ for some complex s with principal left eigenvector $\boldsymbol{\pi}(s)$ and principal right eigenvector $\boldsymbol{\psi}(s)$ associated with the largest eigenvalue $\lambda(s)$, as follows:

$$\boldsymbol{\pi}(s)P(s) = \lambda(s)\boldsymbol{\pi}(s),$$
$$P(s)\boldsymbol{\psi}(s) = \lambda(s)\boldsymbol{\psi}(s),$$

where $\boldsymbol{\pi}(s)\boldsymbol{\psi}(s) = 1$. In particular, observe that

$$\dot{\lambda}(-1) = h = -\sum_{i=1}^V \pi_i \sum_{j=1}^V p_{ij} \log p_{ij},$$

where h is the entropy rate of the underlying Markov process. Prove the following result.

Theorem 7.5.7 (Jacquet, Szpankowski, and Tang, 2001). *Let a digital search tree be built from n strings generated independently by a Markov stationary source with transition probabilities $P = \{p_{ij}\}_{i,j=1}^V$ that are positive. Then*

$$\mathbf{E}[D_m] = \frac{1}{\dot{\lambda}(-1)}\left(\log n + \gamma - 1 + \dot{\lambda}(-1) + \frac{\ddot{\lambda}(-1)}{2\dot{\lambda}^2(-1)}\right.$$
$$\left. -\vartheta - \boldsymbol{\pi}\dot{\boldsymbol{\psi}}(-1) + \delta_1(\log n)\right) + O\left(\frac{\log n}{m}\right),$$

$$\mathrm{Var}[D_n] = \frac{\ddot{\lambda}(-1) - \dot{\lambda}^2(-1)}{\dot{\lambda}^3(-1)}\log n + O(1),$$

where $\dot{\lambda}(-1)$ and $\ddot{\lambda}(-1)$ are the first and second derivatives of $\lambda(s)$ at $s = -1$. Here $\vartheta = \pi\dot{\mathbf{x}}(-2)$ where

$$\dot{\mathbf{x}}(-2) := \sum_{i=1}^{\infty} \left(\mathsf{Q}^{-1}(-2) \cdots \mathsf{Q}^{-1}(-i)(\mathsf{Q}^{-1}(s))'|_{s=-i-1}\mathsf{Q}^{-1}(-i-2) \cdots \right) \mathsf{K},$$

$$\mathsf{K} = \left(\prod_{i=0}^{\infty} Q^{-1}(-2-i) \right)^{-1} \boldsymbol{\psi}.$$

Here $\boldsymbol{\psi} = (1,\ldots,1)$ and $\mathsf{Q}(s) = \mathsf{I} - \mathrm{P}(s)$. The function $\delta_1(x)$ is a fluctuating function with a small amplitude when

$$\frac{\log p_{ij} + \log p_{1i} - \ln p_{1j}}{\ln p_{11}} \in \mathbb{Q}, \qquad i, j = 1, 2, \ldots, V,$$

where $\mathbb{Q}$ is the set of rational numbers. If the above does not hold, then $\lim_{x\to\infty} \delta_1(x) = 0$.

For details see Jacquet, Szpankowski, and Tang (2001).

Bibliographical notes

Digital trees (i.e., tries, PATRICIA tries, and digital search trees, denoted as DSTs) have been intensively studied over the last forty years due to their many applications ranging from data compression (see Lonardi, Szpankowski, and Ward (2007), Ward and Szpankowski (2005)) to bioinformatics (see Gusfield (1997), Waterman (1995a)) to distributed hash tables (see Naor and Wieder (2003), Devroye, Lugosi, Park, and Szpankowski (2009)).

Tries were first proposed by de la Briandais (1959) in the late 1950s for information processing; Fredkin (1960) suggested the current name, part of the term re*trie*val. Digital search trees were introduced by Coffman and Eve (1970) under the name *sequence hash trees*. One of the first analytic approaches to digital trees, which launched the analysis of algorithms, was presented in volume 3 of Knuth (1998), in Chapter 6.3. Knuth applied the so-called *gamma function method*, which later led to Theorem 7.2.3 proved in Szpankowski (1988a). The reader is referred to books Drmota (2009), Mahmoud (1992), Sedgewick (1983), Sedgewick and Flajolet (1995) and Szpankowski (2001) for a systematic treatment of the methodology used to analyze digital trees.

Trie and digital search trees parameters have been analyzed extensively in many contexts:

- for the depth D_n see Devroye (1982, 1992, 1999), Jacquet and Régnier (1986), Jacquet and Szpankowski (1994), Kirschenhofer and Prodinger

(1988), Louchard (1994), Pittel (1986), Schachinger (2001), Szpankowski (1987) and Szpankowski (1988b);

- for the total path length L_n see Clément et al. (2001), Devroye (1984), Kirschenhofer et al. (1989b), Neininger and Rüschendorf (2004), Schachinger (1995, 2001, 2004) and Szpankowski (1987);

- for the size S_n see Clément et al. (2001), Jacquet and Regnier (1998), Jacquet and Szpankowski (1994), Kirschenhofer and Prodinger (1991), Knuth (1998), Neininger and Rüschendorf (2004), Rachev and Ruschendorf (1995), Régnier and Jacquet (1989), Schachinger (1995, 2001) and Schachinger (2004);

- for the height H_n see Clément et al. (2001), Devroye (1984, 1992, 1999, 2002), Flajolet (1983), Flajolet and Steyaert (1982), Jacquet and Régnier (1986), Pittel (1985, 1986) and Szpankowski (1991);

- for the shortest path length R_n see Pittel (1985, 1986);

- for the fill-up (or saturation) level F_n see Knessl and Szpankowski (2004) and Pittel (1985)

- the multiplicity parameter is discussed in Ward and Szpankowski (2005) and Lonardi et al. (2007).

Section 7.2.1 was based on Kirschenhofer and Prodinger (1988) and Szpankowski (1988b) while the variance for unbiased memoryless sources was first derived in Kirschenhofer et al. (1989b). Lemma 7.2.4 was proved in Schachinger (2000). The limiting distribution for the depth in a trie was taken from Jacquet and Régnier (1986); the Markov extension can be found in Jacquet and Szpankowski (1991). The depth of a digital search tree, considered in Sections 7.2.3 and 7.3.2, was taken from Louchard and Szpankowski (1995). The analysis of the multiplicity parameter was first discussed in Ward and Szpankowski (2005) and Lonardi et al. (2007). Finally, the profile of a trie was analyzed in Park (2006) and Park et al. (2009). For the average profile of a DST and Patricia trie see the recent papers by Drmota and Szpankowski (2009), Knessl and Szpankowski (2009) and Magner, Knessl, and Szpankowski (2014), respectively. See also Drmota (2009).

CHAPTER 8

Suffix Trees and Lempel–Ziv'77

In this chapter we discuss a (compact) *suffix tree* (also known as a suffix trie) and the Lempel–Ziv'77 (LZ'77) data compression scheme. Suffix trees are the most popular type of data structure on words while LZ'77 is one of the fundamental data compression schemes. We discussed both the suffix tree and the LZ'77 algorithm in some depth in Chapter 6 so here we only briefly review the basic facts.

A suffix trie is a trie built from the suffixes of a single string. In Figure 8.1 we show the suffix trie (tree) built from the first four suffixes of $X = 0101101110$. More precisely, when building a trie from the first n infinite suffixes $X_1^\infty, X_2^\infty, \ldots,$

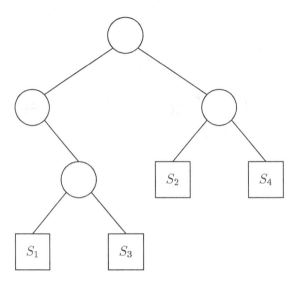

Figure 8.1. Suffix tree built from the first five suffixes of $X = 0101101110$, i.e. 0101101110, 101101110, 01101110, 1101110.

X_n^∞ of X, as shown in Figures 8.1 and 8.2, we call it an infinite suffix tree or simply a suffix tree. We also consider a finite version, called a finite suffix tree, built from the finite suffixes $X_1^n, \ldots X_n^n$ of X; however, in this case we would need to append the suffixes with a special symbol not belonging to the alphabet. In this chapter we mostly deal with infinite suffix trees, which is what we mean here when we say "suffix trees". We will leave the analysis of finite suffix trees to Section 8.1.2, the remarks, and chapter exercises.

Thus, we present here the probabilistic behavior of suffix trees when the input string X is potentially of infinite length and is generated by a probabilistic source. We will concentrate on a memoryless source over a finite alphabet $\mathcal{A}$. Extensions to Markov sources are possible as presented in Fayolle and Ward (2005), but we will not consider them in this chapter.

We will also discuss here, the Lempel–Ziv'77 algorithm presented in Chapter 6. We recall that it partitions a sequence into phrases. The basic idea is to find the longest prefix of an as yet unprocessed (uncompressed) sequence that occurs in the already processed (compressed) sequence. Let us assume that the first n symbols X_1^n are given to the encoder and the decoder. In the standard Lempel–Ziv'77 scheme, the next phrase is the longest prefix as yet uncompressed) $X_{n+1}^{n+\ell}$ of X_{n+1}^∞ that is repeated in X_1^n. If we denote the length of

$S_1 = 0\ 1\ 0\ 1\ 1\ 0\ 1\ 1\ 1\ 0$
$S_2 = 1\ 0\ 1\ 1\ 0\ 1\ 1\ 1\ 0$
$S_3 = 0\ 1\ 1\ 0\ 1\ 1\ 1\ 0$

$S_4 = 1\ 1\ 0\ 1\ 1\ 1\ 0$
$S_5 = 1\ 0\ 1\ 1\ 1\ 0$

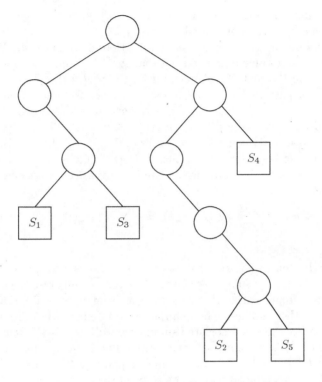

Figure 8.2. Suffix tree built from the first five suffixes of $X = 0101101110$, i.e. 0101101110, 101101110, 01101110, 1101110, 101110.

this next phrase by $D_n(n+1)$, then this length corresponds to the largest ℓ such that $X_{n+1}^{n+\ell} = X_m^{m+\ell-1}$ for some prescribed range of m and ℓ. We have chosen to denote the length of this phrase by $D_n(n+1)$ because it is the depth of insertion in a suffix tree built from the first n suffixes; it is why we are discussing suffix trees and LZ'77 in the same chapter. For example, from Figure 8.2 we can find the fifth phrase of $X = 0101101110$ (i.e. the path to S_5), which is 10111.

8.1.   Random tries resemble suffix trees

In this section we discuss the typical depth D_n in a suffix tree built from the first n suffixes of a string generated by a memoryless source. We first redefine the depth D_n in terms of the number of occurrences of a given pattern and its generating function. This will allow us to take advantage of many results on pattern occurrences presented in Chapter 2.

Let i be an arbitrary integer smaller than or equal to n. We define $D_n(i)$ to be the largest value of $k \leq n$ such that X_i^{i+k-1} occurs in at least two positions before n in the text X. We recall from Chapter 2 that $O_n(w)$ is the number of times that pattern w occurs in a text X_1^n. Therefore, $D_n(i)$ can be characterized as $O_{n+k-1}(X_i^{i+k-1}) \geq 2$, where we explicitly note that any occurrence of X_i^{i+k-1} must occur before the position $n + k - 1$. Clearly $O_{n+k-1}(X_i^{i+k-1}) \geq 1$ since X_i^{i+k-1} is already counted as a factor of X_1^{n+k-1}. Our goal is to determine the probabilistic behavior of a "typical" $D_n(i)$, that is, we define D_n to be equal to $D_n(i)$ when i is randomly and uniformly selected between 1 and n. More precisely,

$$P(D_n = \ell) = \frac{1}{n} \sum_{i=1}^{n} P(D_n(i) = \ell)$$

for any $1 \leq \ell \leq n$.

We hasten to observe that the quantity D_n is also the depth of a randomly selected suffix in a suffix tree. Observe that in a suffix tree the path from the root to node i (representing the ith suffix) is the shortest suffix that distinguishes it from all other suffixes. The quantity $D_n(i)$ defined above represents the depth of the suffix i in the associated suffix trie, while D_n is the *typical depth*, that is, the depth of a randomly selected terminal node in the suffix tree.

Let k be an integer greater than or equal to 1 (the case $k = 0$ is trivial). Let $w \in \mathcal{A}^k$ be an arbitrary word of size k. Observe that

$$P(D_n(i) \geq k \text{ and } X_i^{i+k-1} = w) = P(O_{n+k-1}(w) \geq 2 \text{ and } X_i^{i+k-1} = w).$$

Furthermore, if $O_{n+k-1}(w) = r$ then there are exactly r positions $i \leq n$ such that $X_i^{i+k-1} = w$; hence

$$\sum_{i=1}^{n} P(O_{n+k-1}(w) = r \text{ and } X_i^{i+k-1} = w) = rP(O_{n+k-1}(w) = r).$$

Recall from Chapter 2 that

$$N_n(u) = \mathbf{E}[u^{O_n(w)}] = \sum_{r \geq 0} P(O_n(w) = r)u^r$$

is the probability generating function for $O_n(w)$. We shall sometimes write $N_{n,w}(u)$ to underline the fact that the pattern w is given. From the above considerations we conclude that

$$P(D_n \geq k) = \frac{1}{n} \sum_{i=1}^{n} P(D_n(i) \geq k)$$

$$= \sum_{w \in \mathcal{A}^k} \frac{1}{n} \sum_{i=1}^{n} P(D_n(i) \geq k \text{ and } X_i^{i+k-1} = w)$$

$$= \sum_{w \in \mathcal{A}^k} \frac{1}{n} \sum_{i=1}^{n} \sum_{r \geq 2} P(O_{n+k-1}(w) = r \text{ and } X_i^{i+k-1} = w)$$

$$= \frac{1}{n} \sum_{w \in \mathcal{A}^k} \sum_{r \geq 2} r P(O_{n+k-1}(w) = r).$$

However,

$$\sum_{r \geq 2} r P(O_{n+k-1}(w) = r) = \sum_{r \geq 0} r P(O_{n+k-1}(w) = r) - N'_{n+k-1,w}(0),$$

where $N'_{n,w}(0) = P(O_n(w) = 1)$ denotes the derivative of $N_{n,w}(u) = \mathbf{E}[u^{O_n(w)}]$ at $u = 0$. Since $\sum_{r \geq 0} r P(O_{n+k-1}(w) = r)$ is equal to the average number of occurrences of the word w inside X_1^{n+k-1}, it is also equal to $nP(w)$. Thus

$$P(D_n \geq k) = \sum_{w \in \mathcal{A}^k} \left(P(w) - \frac{1}{n} N'_{n+k-1,w}(0) \right)$$

$$= 1 - \frac{1}{n} \sum_{w \in \mathcal{A}^k} N'_{n+k-1,w}(0). \tag{8.1}$$

Now let $D_n(u) = \mathbf{E}[u^{D_n}] = \sum_k P(D_n = k)u^k$ be the probability generating function for D_n. Then (8.1) implies that, we include the specific but trivial case of $|w| = 0$,

$$D_n(u) = \frac{1}{n} \frac{(1-u)}{u} \sum_{w \in \mathcal{A}^*} u^{|w|} N'_{n+\max\{0,|w|-1\},w}(0),$$

where we have used again the fact that

$$\sum_{k \geq 0} P(D_n \geq k)u^k = \frac{u\mathbf{E}[u^{D_n}] - 1}{u - 1}.$$

Then the bivariate generating function $D(z, u) = \sum_n n D_n(u) z^n$ (notice the unusual definition of $D(z, u)$, containing the factor n) becomes

$$D(z, u) = \frac{1 - u}{u} \sum_{w \in \mathcal{A}^*} \frac{u^{|w|}}{z^{(|w|-1)^+}} \frac{\partial}{\partial u} N_w(z, 0), \tag{8.2}$$

where $a^+ = \max\{0, a\}$, and

$$N_w(z, u) = \sum_{n=0}^{\infty} N_{n,w}(u) z^n = \sum_{n=0}^{\infty} \sum_{r=0}^{\infty} P(O_n(w) = r) z^n u^r.$$

In Chapter 2 we worked with $\sum_{n=0}^{\infty} \sum_{r=1}^{\infty} P(O_n(w) = r) z^n u^r$ (notice that the second sum starts at $r = 1$) and in (2.21) we provided an explicit formula. Adding the term

$$\sum_{n \geq 0} P(O_n(w) = 0) z^n =: N_0(z) = \frac{S_w(z)}{D_w(z)}$$

found in (2.26), we obtain

$$N_w(z, u) = \frac{z^{|w|} P(w)}{D_w^2(z)} \frac{u}{1 - u M_w(z)} + \frac{S_w(z)}{D_w(z)},$$

where $M_w(z)$ is defined in (2.22) and $D_w(z) = (1 - z) S_w(z) + z^{|w|} P(w)$, found in (2.25) with $S_w(z)$ being the autocorrelation polynomial for w presented in Section 2.2. Since

$$\frac{\partial}{\partial u} N_w(z, u) \big|_{u=0} = z^{|w|} \frac{P(w)}{D_w^2(z)}, \tag{8.3}$$

we finally arrive at the following lemma which is the starting point of our subsequent analysis.

Lemma 8.1.1. *The bivariate generating function $D(z, u)$ for $|u| < 1$ and $|z| \leq 1$ is given by*

$$D(z, u) = \frac{1 - u}{u} \sum_{w \in \mathcal{A}^*} u^{|w|} z \frac{P(w)}{D_w^2(z)}, \tag{8.4}$$

with

$$D_w(z) = (1 - z) S_w(z) + z^{|w|} P(w),$$

where $S_w(z)$ is the autocorrelation polynomial for w.

Let D_n^T be the typical depth in a trie built from n independent infinite strings generated by the memoryless source. We studied tries in Chapter 7. We denote by $D_n^T(u) = \mathbf{E}[u^{D_n^T}]$ the probability generating function for D_n^T. We next state a very important fact establishing the asymptotic equivalence of random suffix trees and independent tries. We will prove it in Section 8.1.1.

Theorem 8.1.2. *Consider a suffix tree built from the n suffixes of an infinite string generated by a memoryless source over alphabet $\mathcal{A}$. There exist $\varepsilon > 0$ and $\rho > 1$ such that, for all $|u| \leq \rho$,*

$$D_n(u) - D_n^T(u) = O(n^{-\varepsilon}) \tag{8.5}$$

for sufficiently large n.

Let us stop here and ponder the importance of the above result. It basically says that the distribution of the depth in a suffix tree is asymptotically the same as the distribution of the depth in a trie built from n i.i.d. strings. Thus random suffix trees resemble random tries. In fact, the assumption of a memoryless source is not a restriction since the above statement can be extended to Markov sources, as proved in Fayolle and Ward (2005).

Using this finding and results for tries proved in Chapter 7 we can formulate the following more explicit characterization of suffix trees.

Theorem 8.1.3. *Let $h = -\sum_{a \in \mathcal{A}} p_a \log p_a$ be the entropy rate of a source, and $h_2 = \sum_{a \in \mathcal{A}} p_a \log^2 p_a$. Then we have the following*

(i) For a biased memoryless source (i.e., $p_a \neq p_b$ for some $a \neq b \in \mathcal{A}^2$) there exists for $\varepsilon > 0$

$$\mathbf{E}[D_n] = \frac{1}{h} \log n + \frac{\gamma}{h} + \frac{h_2}{h^2} + \Phi_0(\log n) + O(n^{-\varepsilon}), \tag{8.6}$$

$$\mathrm{Var}[D_n] = \frac{h_2 - h^2}{h^3} \log n + O(1) \tag{8.7}$$

where $\Phi_0(\cdot)$ defined in (7.27) is a periodic function with small amplitude in the case when the $\log p_a$ are rationally related; otherwise it converges to zero.

Furthermore, $(D_n - \mathbf{E}[D_n])/\mathrm{Var}[D_n]$ is asymptotically normal with mean zero and variance 1, for fixed $x \in \mathbb{R}$ we have

$$\lim_{n \to \infty} P\{D_n \leq \mathbf{E}(D_n) + x\sqrt{\mathrm{Var}(D_n)}\} = \frac{1}{\sqrt{2\pi}} \int_{-\infty}^{x} e^{-t^2/2} dt,$$

and, for all integer m,

$$\lim_{n \to \infty} \mathbf{E}\left[\frac{D_n - \mathbf{E}(D_n)}{\sqrt{\mathrm{Var} D_n}}\right]^m = \begin{cases} 0 & \text{when } m \text{ is odd} \\ \frac{m!}{2^{m/2}(m/2)!} & \text{when } m \text{ is even.} \end{cases}$$

(ii) *For an unbiased source (i.e., $\forall a \in \mathcal{A}$ $p_a = 1/|\mathcal{A}|$), we have $h_2 = h^2$, which implies that $\mathrm{Var}[D_n] = O(1)$ or, more precisely, for some $\varepsilon > 0$ (see Remark 7.3.4),*

$$\mathrm{Var}[D_n] = \frac{\pi^2}{6 \log^2 |\mathcal{A}|} + \frac{1}{12} + \Phi_2(\log n) + O(n^{-\varepsilon}),$$

where $\Phi_2(\log n)$ is a periodic function with small amplitude. The limiting distribution of D_n does not exist, but one finds (7.73)–(7.74) or in another form

$$\lim_{n \to \infty} \sup_x \left| P(D_n \leq x) - \exp(-n|\mathcal{A}|^{-x}) \right| = 0,$$

for any real x.

Theorem 8.1.3 tells us that the typical depth is normally distributed, with average depth asymptotically equal to $h^{-1} \log n$ and variance $\Theta(\log n)$ for a biased memoryless source. In the unbiased case, the variance is $O(1)$ and the (asymptotic) distribution is of the extreme distribution type. Interestingly, as said above and proved below, the depth in a suffix tree (built over *one* string sequence generated by a memoryless source) is asymptotically equivalent to the depth in a trie built over n *independently* generated strings. Thus suffix trees resemble tries! Actually, this is not so surprising if one notes that n suffixes of X typically overlap only on $O(\log n)$ positions. Thus considering $O(n/\log n)$ suffixes instead of n suffixes, we are dealing with $O(n/\log n)$ almost independent strings that create a trie resembling probabilistically the original suffix tree.

8.1.1. Proof of Theorem 8.1.2

The proof of Theorem 8.1.2 hinges on establishing the asymptotic equivalence between D_n and the typical depth D_n^T in a trie built from n *independent* sequences. We analyzed the typical depth D_n^T of tries in Section 7.3.1. In particular, we found the following representation.

Lemma 8.1.4. *For all $n \geq 1$,*

$$D_n^T(u) = \frac{1-u}{u} \sum_{w \in \mathcal{A}^*} u^{|w|} P(w)(1 - P(w))^{n-1},$$

$$D^T(z, u) = \frac{1-u}{u} \sum_{w \in \mathcal{A}^*} u^{|w|} \frac{z P(w)}{(1 - z + P(w)z)^2}$$

for all $|u| \leq 1$ and $|z| < 1$.

Proof. From (7.66) we know that

$$P(D_n^T(i) < k) = \sum_{w \in \mathcal{A}^k} P(w)(1 - P(w))^{n-1}, \quad n \geq 1.$$

Indeed, $D_n^T(i) < k$ if there is a word $w \in \mathcal{A}^k$ such the prefix of the ith string is equal to w and no other text prefix is equal to w. The rest is trivial. ∎

Our goal now is to prove that $D_n(u)$ and $D_n^T(u)$ are asymptotically close as $n \to \infty$. This requires several preparatory steps, outlined below, that will lead to

$$D_n^T(u) - D_n(u) = (1 - u)O(n^{-\varepsilon}), \tag{8.8}$$

for some $\varepsilon > 0$ and all $|u| < \beta$ for $\beta > 1$. Consequently,

$$|P(D_n \leq k) - P(D_n^T \leq k)| = O(n^{-\varepsilon}\beta^{-k}) \tag{8.9}$$

for all positive integers k. Indeed, from Cauchy's theorem we have

$$P(D_n \leq k) - P(D_n^T \leq k) = \frac{1}{2\pi i(1-u)} \int_{|u|=\beta} \frac{D_n^T(u) - D_n(u)}{u^{k+1}} du,$$

which immediately leads to (8.9). In conclusion, in Theorem 7.3.3 we proved that D_n^T is asymptotically normal; hence we expect D_n to be normal, as stated in Theorem 8.1.3, provided that we can prove Theorem 8.1.2, which we take up next.

We start with a lemma indicating that for most words w the autocorrelation polynomial $S_w(z)$ is close to 1 for some nonnegative z. This lemma is particularly crucial to our analysis shedding light on the analytical properties of the autocorrelation polynomial.

We need some definitions. We recall that $\mathcal{P}(w)$, for $w \in \mathcal{A}^k$, is the autocorrelation set, that is, the set of positions i such that $w_1^i = w_{k-i+1}^k$. Notice that we always have $k \in \mathcal{P}(w)$. We denote by $\overline{\mathcal{P}(w)}$ the symmetric set: $\overline{\mathcal{P}(w)} = \{j, \ k - j + 1 \in \mathcal{P}(w)\}$. Notice that $1 \in \overline{\mathcal{P}(w)}$. We fix an arbitrary integer m greater than 1, say $m = 2$; and denote by $\mathcal{B}_k$ the subset of $\mathcal{A}^k$ consisting of the words $w \in \mathcal{A}^k$ such that $\min\{\overline{\mathcal{P}(w)} - \{1\}\} > k/m$.

Lemma 8.1.5. *Let $p = \max_{a \in \mathcal{A}}\{p_a\}$ and let $m \geq 1$. There exists $\theta > 1$ such that for all $\rho > 1$, the following hold:*

$$\forall w \in \mathcal{B}_k, \forall \rho > 1: \ S_w(\rho) \leq 1 + (\rho\delta_1)^k \theta \tag{8.10}$$

and

$$\sum_{w \in \mathcal{A}^k - \mathcal{B}_k} P(w) \leq \theta \delta_2^k \tag{8.11}$$

with $\delta_1 = p^{1/m}$ and $\delta_2 = p^{1-1/m}$.

Proof. To simplify the notation, let P_k be the probability measure on $\mathcal{A}^k$ such that for any boolean expression $A(w)$, $P_k(A(w)) = \sum_{w \in \mathcal{A}^k} \llbracket A(w) = \text{true} \rrbracket P(w)$. Thus we need to prove that $P_k(w \notin \mathcal{B}_k) \leq \theta \delta_2^k$.

Let i be an integer greater than 1 such that $1 + i \in \overline{\mathcal{P}(w)}$, that is, such that $w_1^{k-i} = w_{1+i}^k$. It is easy to see that

$$P_k(1 + i \in \overline{\mathcal{P}(w)}) = \left(\sum_{a \in \mathcal{A}} p_a^{\lfloor k/i \rfloor + 1} \right)^r \left(\sum_{a \in \mathcal{A}} p_a^{\lfloor k/i \rfloor} \right)^{i-r}, \qquad (8.12)$$

where $r = k - \lfloor k/i \rfloor i$, the remainder of the division of k by i. The reader is asked in Exercise 8.2 to prove (8.12), but it is easy to understand. Consider $i \leq k/2$ such that the first $k - i$ symbols exactly coincide with the last $k - i$ symbols. This can only happen if the word w is periodic with period of length i. This observation leads to (8.12). Therefore,

$$P_k(1 + i \in \overline{\mathcal{P}(w)}) \leq \left(\sum_{a \in \mathcal{A}} p_a p^{\lfloor k/i \rfloor} \right)^r \left(\sum_{a \in \mathcal{A}} p_a p^{\lfloor k/i) \rfloor - 1} \right)^{i-r}$$

$$\leq p^{r \lfloor k/i \rfloor} p^{(i-r) \lfloor k/i \rfloor + r - i} = p^{k-i}.$$

Thus

$$P_k(w \notin \mathcal{B}_k) = P_k \left(\min(\overline{\mathcal{P}(w)} - \{1\}) < \frac{k}{m} \right)$$

$$\leq \sum_{i \leq k/m} P_k(i + 1 \in \overline{\mathcal{P}(w)}) \leq \frac{p^{k - k/m}}{1 - p}.$$

Now, assume that $w \in \mathcal{B}_k$, that is, $\min(\overline{\mathcal{P}(w)} - \{1\}) > k/m$; then

$$S_w(\rho) - 1 \leq \sum_{i > k - k/m} \rho^{k-i} p^{k-i} \leq \rho^k \frac{p^{k/m}}{1 - p}$$

for all $\rho > 1$. Equations (8.10) and (8.11) will be satisfied if we select $\theta = (1 - p)^{-1}$. ∎

Notice that: (i) by making m large enough we can have δ_2 arbitrarily close to p while δ_1 gets closer to 1; (ii) by choosing ρ such that $\rho \delta_1 < 1$ we can make $S_w(\rho)$ arbitrarily close to 1 for large k.

In the next lemma we show that $D(z, u)$ can be analytically continued above the unit disk, that is, for $|u| > 1$.

Lemma 8.1.6. *Let $|z| < 1$; the generating function $D(z, u)$ is defined for all $|u| < \min\{\delta_1^{-1}, \delta_2^{-1}\}$.*

Proof. From Lemma 8.1.1 we know that

$$D(z, u) = \frac{1 - u}{u} \sum_{w \in \mathcal{A}^*} u^{|w|} \frac{P(w)z}{D_w(z)^2},$$

with $D_w(z) = (1 - z)S_w(z) + z^{|w|}P(w)$. Define

$$D_1(z, u) = \frac{1 - u}{u} \sum_{w \in \mathcal{A}^+} u^{|w|} \frac{P(w)z}{D_w(z)^2},$$

where $\mathcal{A}^+ = \mathcal{A}^* - \{\varepsilon\}$, that is, the set of all nonempty words. For all $w \in \mathcal{A}^+$ and z such that $|z| < 1$,

$$\left| \frac{zP(w)}{D_w(z)^2} \right| = \left| \sum_{n=0}^{\infty} P(O_{n+|w|-1}(w) = 1)z^n \right|$$

$$\leq \sum_{n=0}^{\infty} nP(w)|z|^n = \frac{zP(w)}{(1 - |z|)^2}.$$

Hence

$$\frac{1}{|D_w(z)|^2} \leq \frac{1}{(1 - |z|)^2}.$$

Let $|u| \leq 1$ and $|z| < 1$. Consider the following identity:

$$\sum_{w \in \mathcal{A}^+} u^{|w|} \frac{P(w)z}{(1 - z)^2} = \frac{zu}{(1 - u)(1 - z)^2}.$$

Thus, when $|z| \leq 1$,

$$D_1(z, u) - \frac{z}{(1 - z)^2} = \frac{1 - u}{u} \sum_{w \in \mathcal{A}^+} u^{|w|} P(w)z \left(\frac{1}{D_w^2(z)} - \frac{1}{(1 - z)^2} \right)$$

$$= \frac{(u - 1)}{u} \sum_{w \in \mathcal{A}^+} u^{|w|} P(w) \frac{z \left(D_w(z) - (1 - z) \right) \left(D_w(z) + (1 - z) \right)}{D_w^2(z)(1 - z)^2}.$$

Now we observe that $S_w(z) - 1$ is a polynomial with positive coefficients and that

$$|S_w(z)| \leq \sum_{i \geq 0} p^i |z|^i \leq \frac{1}{1 - |z|p} \leq \frac{1}{1 - p}$$

when $|z| \leq 1$; thus

$$|D_w(z)| \leq (|1 - z|)\frac{1}{1 - p} + p^k \leq B$$

for some $B > 0$. Therefore

$$\left| D_1(z, u) - \frac{z}{(1 - z)^2} \right| \leq \frac{|1 - u|}{|u|(1 - |z|)^4} B \sum_{k=0}^{\infty} u^k \sum_{w \in \mathcal{A}^k} P(w) f(w, z)$$

with

$$f(w, z) = |D_w(z) - (1 - z)|.$$

We already know that $\max_{w \in \mathcal{A}^*}\{f(w, z)\} \leq B + 2$. We now consider

$$\sum_{w \in \mathcal{A}^k} P(w) f(w, z).$$

Let $w \in \mathcal{B}_k$. From Lemma 8.1.5 we know that

$$S_w(1) \leq 1 + \delta_1^k \theta.$$

Since $S_w(z) - 1$ is a polynomial with positive coefficients:

$$S_w(1) - 1 \leq \delta_1^k \theta \quad \Rightarrow \quad \forall |z| \leq 1 : |S_w(z) - 1| \leq \delta_1^k \theta.$$

Therefore, since $P(w) \leq p^k \leq \delta_1^k$ we have

$$f(w, z) \leq |1 - z|\delta_1^k \theta + P(w) = O(\delta_1^k) .$$

Consequently,

$$\sum_{w \in \mathcal{B}_k} P(w) f(w, z) \leq (|1 - z| + B)\delta_1^k \theta.$$

Finally, we consider $w \in \mathcal{A}^k - \mathcal{B}_k$. Since $f(w, z) \leq B + 2$, from Lemma 8.1.5 we find that

$$\sum_{w \in \mathcal{A}^k - \mathcal{B}_k} P(w) f(w, z) \leq (B + 2)\theta \delta_2^k.$$

In summary,

$$\sum_{k=0}^{\infty} u^k \sum_{w \in \mathcal{A}^k} P(w) f(w, z)$$

converges for all $|u| < \min\{\delta_1^{-1}, \delta_2^{-1}\}$, as réquired.   ■

We need two other technical lemmas.

Lemma 8.1.7. *There exists K, a constant $\rho' > 1$ and $\alpha > 0$ such that, for all w with $|w| \geq K$, we have*

$$|S_w(z)| \geq \alpha$$

for $|z| \leq \rho'$ with $p\rho' < 1$.

Proof. Let ℓ be an integer and $\rho' > 1$ be such that $p\rho' + (p\rho')^\ell < 1$. Let $k > \ell$ and let w be such that $|w| = k$. Let $1 + i = \min(\mathcal{P}(w) - \{1\})$. If $i \geq \ell$ then, for all z such that $|z| \leq \rho'$, we have

$$|S_w(z)| \geq 1 - \sum_{j=\ell}^{j=k}(p\rho')^j \geq 1 - \frac{(p\rho')^\ell}{1 - p\rho'}.$$

We now consider the case $i < \ell$. Let $q = \lfloor k/i \rfloor$ and $r = k - iq$ (thus $r < i$). As in the proof of lemma 8.1.5 we have $w = w_i^q w_r$, w_i, and w_r being respectively, the prefixes of lengths i and r of the word w. Notice that w_r is also a prefix of w_i.

Since $1 + i = \min\{\overline{\mathcal{P}(w)} - \{1\}\}$, there are no other elements in $\overline{\mathcal{P}(w)}$ between position 1 and position $1 + i$ and consequently no other positions, other than 1 plus multiples of i, between 1 and $1 + (q - 1)i$. Since the positions between $(q-1)i$ and k correspond to the positions of $\overline{\mathcal{P}(w_i w_r)}$ translated by $(q - 1)i - 1$ we have the identity

$$S_w(z) = \sum_{j=0}^{j=q-1} (P(w_i)z^i)^j + (P(w_i)z^i)^{q-1}(S_{w_i w_r}(z) - 1)$$

$$= \frac{1 - (P(w_i)z^i)^q}{1 - P(w_i)z^i} + (P(w_i)z^i)^{q-1}(S_{w_i w_r}(z) - 1),$$

where $S_{w_i w_r}(z)$ is the autocorrelation polynomial of $w_i w_r$. Since $|S_{w_i w_r}(z) - 1| \leq p\rho'/(1 - p\rho')$, this implies that

$$|S_w(z)| \geq \frac{1 - (p\rho')^{qi}}{1 + (p\rho')^i} - \frac{(p\rho')^{i(q-1)+1}}{1 - p\rho'}.$$

Since $(p\rho')^\ell < 1 - p\rho'$ we have

$$|S_w(z)| \geq \frac{1 - (p\rho')^{qi}}{1 + (p\rho')^i} - \frac{(p\rho')^{(q-1)i+1}}{(p\rho')^\ell}$$

$$\geq \frac{1 - (p\rho')^{qi} - (p\rho')^{(q-1)i+1-\ell}(1 + (p\rho')^i)}{1 + (p\rho')^i}$$

$$\geq \frac{1 - 3(p\rho')^{(q-1)i+1-\ell}}{1 + (p\rho')^i} \geq \frac{1 - 3(p\rho')^{(q-1)i+1-\ell}}{1 + p\rho'}.$$

Let j be an integer such that $3(p\rho')^{j\ell} < 1$ and choose $K = (j+3)\ell$. Since $qi > k - i \geq k - \ell$, thus for $k > K$, we have $(q-1)i + 1 - \ell > k - 3\ell$ and

$$|S_w(z)| \geq \frac{1 - 3(p\rho')^{j\ell}}{1 + p\rho'} > 0;$$

taking $\alpha = (1 - (p\rho') - 3(p\rho')^{j\ell})(1 + p\rho')$ completes the proof.   ∎

Lemma 8.1.8. *There exists an integer K' such that for $|w| \geq K'$ there is only one root of $D_w(z)$ in the disk $|z| \leq \rho'$ for $\rho' > 1$.*

Proof. Let K_1 be such that $(p\rho')^{K_1} < (\rho' - 1)\alpha$ holds for α and ρ' as in Lemma 8.1.7. Write $K' = \max\{K, K_1\}$, where K is defined above. Note also that the above inequality implies that for all w such that $|w| > K'$ we have $P(w)(\rho')^{|w|} < (\rho'-1)\alpha$. Hence, for $|w| > K'$ we have $|P(w)z^{|w|}| < |(z-1)S_w(z)|$ on the circle $|z| = \rho' > 1$. Therefore, by Rouché's theorem the polynomial $D_w(z)$ has the same number of roots as $(1-z)S_w(z)$ in the disk $|z| \leq \rho'$. But the polynomial $(1-z)S_w(z)$ has only a single root in this disk, since by Lemma 8.1.7 we have $|S_w(z)| > 0$ in $|z| \leq \rho'$.   ∎

We have just established that there exists a smallest root of $D_w(z) = 0$, which we denote as A_w. Let C_w and D_w be the first and the second derivatives of $D_w(z)$ at $z = A_w$, respectively. Using bootstrapping, one easily obtains the following expansions:

$$A_w = 1 + \frac{1}{S_w(1)} P(w) + O(P(w)^2), \tag{8.13}$$

$$C_w = -S_w(1) + \left(k - \frac{2S'_w(1)}{S_w(1)} \right) P(w) + O(P(w)^2), \tag{8.14}$$

$$E_w = -2S'_w(1) + \left(k(k-1) - \frac{3S''_w(1)}{S_w(1)} \right) P(w) + O(P(w)^2), \tag{8.15}$$

where $S'_w(1)$ and $S''_w(1)$ respectively denote the first and the second derivatives of $S_w(z)$ at $z = 1$. Note that $A_w \geq 1 + P(w)$ since $S(1) \leq 1$.

Finally, we are ready to compare $D_n(u)$ with $D_n^T(u)$ in order to conclude that they do not differ too much as $n \to \infty$. Let us define two new generating functions $Q_n(u)$ and $Q(z, u)$ that represent the difference between $D_n(u)$ and $D_n^T(u)$:

$$Q_n(u) = \frac{u}{1-u} \left(D_n(u) - D_n^T(u) \right),$$

and

$$Q(z, u) = \sum_{n=0}^{\infty} n\, Q_n(u) z^n = \frac{u}{1-u} \left(D(z, u) - D^T(z, u) \right).$$

Thus

$$Q(z, u) = \sum_{w \in \mathcal{A}^*} u^{|w|} P(w) z \left(\frac{1}{D_w(z)^2} - \frac{1}{(1 - z + P(w)z)^2} \right).$$

It is not difficult to establish the asymptotics of $Q_n(u)$ by appealing to Cauchy's theorem. This is done in the following lemma.

Lemma 8.1.9. *Let* $\delta = \max\{\delta_1, \delta_2\}$. *For all* $1 < \rho \le \rho'$ *and for all* u *such that* $u \le (\delta\rho)^{-1}$, *the following evaluation holds:*

$$Q_n(u) = \frac{1}{n} f_n(u),$$

where

$$f_n(u) = \sum_{w \in \mathcal{A}^*} f_n(w, u)$$

with

$$f_n(w, u) = u^{|w|} P(w) \left(A_w^{-n} \left(\frac{n}{C_w^2 A_w} + \frac{E_w}{C_w^3} \right) - n(1 - P(w))^{n-1} \right)$$
$$+ I_n(w, \rho, u) \tag{8.16}$$

for large n *with* $\sum_{w \in \mathcal{A}^*} |I_n(w, \rho, u)| = O(\rho^{-n})$.

Proof. By Cauchy's formula

$$f_n(u) = \frac{1}{2i\pi} \oint Q(z, u) \frac{dz}{z^{n+1}},$$

where the integration is along a contour contained in the unit disk that encircles the origin. Let w be such that $|w| \ge K'$, where K' was defined in Lemma 8.1.8. From the proof of Lemma 8.1.8 we conclude that $D_w(z)$ and $1 - z + P(w)z$ have only one root in $|z| \le \rho$ for some $\rho > 1$. Now we enlarge the integration contour to a circle of radius ρ that contains the dominant singularities. Then, applying Cauchy's residue theorem we obtain

$$f_n(w, u) = \frac{1}{2i\pi} \oint u^{|w|} P(w) \frac{dz}{z^n} \left(\frac{1}{D_w(z)^2} - \frac{1}{(1 - z + P(w)z)^2} \right)$$
$$= u^{|w|} P(w) \left(\frac{A_w^{-n}}{u} \left(\frac{n + 1 - |w|}{C_w^2 A_w} + \frac{E_w}{C_w^3} \right) - n(1 - P(w))^{n-1} \right)$$
$$+ I_n(w, \rho, u),$$

where

$$I_n(w, \rho, u) = \frac{P(w)}{2i\pi} \int_{|z|=\rho} u^{|w|} \frac{dz}{z^n} \left(\frac{1}{D_w(z)^2} - \frac{1}{(1 - z + P(w)z)^2} \right).$$

To bound $I_n(w, \rho, u)$ contribution we argue in exactly the same manner as in the proof of Lemma 8.1.6. We fix an integer k and consider $\sum_{w \in \mathcal{A}^k} |I_n(w, \rho, u)|$. For $w \in \mathcal{A}^k$ let

$$I_n(w, \rho) = \left| \frac{1}{2i\pi} \int_{|z|=\rho} \frac{dz}{z^n} \left(\frac{1}{D_w(z)^2} - \frac{1}{(1 - z + P(w)z)^2} \right) \right|. \qquad (8.17)$$

We have

$$|I_n(w, \rho, u)| = |u|^k P(w) I_n(w, \rho).$$

Our goal now is to show that

$$\sum_{w \in \mathcal{A}^k} |I_n(w, \rho, u)| = O((\rho \delta |u|)^k \rho^{-n}),$$

so that the sum of the $I_n(w, \rho, u)$ converges for $|u| \le (\rho \delta)^{-1}$ and decays exponentially with integer n. Selecting $\rho \delta < 1$ will terminate the proof.

By Lemma 8.1.7 we know that

$$I_n(w, \rho) \le \rho^{-n} \left(\frac{\rho}{(\rho - 1)^2 \alpha^2} + \frac{\rho}{(\rho - 1)^2} \right),$$

thus by Lemma 8.1.5 we have for all $w \in \mathcal{A}^k - \mathcal{B}_k$

$$\sum_{w \in \mathcal{A}^k - \mathcal{B}_k} P(w) I_n(w, \rho) = O(\delta_2^k \rho^{-n}).$$

Furthermore,

$$I_n(w, \rho) = \left| \frac{1}{2i\pi} \int_{|z|=\rho} \frac{dz}{z^n} \frac{(D_w(z) - (1 - z) + P(w)z)(D_w(z) + 1 - z - P(w)z)}{D_w(z)^2 (1 - z + P(w)z)^2} \right|.$$

Let $w \in \mathcal{B}_k$. We know from Lemma 8.1.6 that

$$|D_w(z) - (1 - z) + P(w)| \le |\rho - 1|\theta(\delta_1 \rho)^k + P(w)\rho^k = O((\delta_1 \rho)^k)$$

and thus, for $w \in \mathcal{B}_k$, we conclude that $I_n(w, \rho) = O((\delta_1 \rho)^k \rho^{-n})$. This leads to

$$\sum_{w \in \mathcal{A}^k} I_n(w, \rho, u) = O((\delta \rho u)^k \rho^{-n})$$

for $\delta = \max\{\delta_1, \delta_2\}$ and consequently, for $|u| < (\delta\rho)^{-1}$,

$$\sum_{w \in \mathcal{A}^*} I_n(w, \rho, u) = O\left(\frac{1}{1 - \rho\delta|u|}\rho^{-n}\right),$$

which concludes the proof. ∎

In the next lemma we show that $Q_n(u) \to 0$ as $n \to \infty$.

Lemma 8.1.10. *Let* $\delta = \max\{\delta_1, \delta_2\}$. *For all* β *such that* $1 < \beta < \delta^{-1}$, *there exists* $\varepsilon > 0$ *such that* $Q_n(u) = (1 - u)O(n^{-\varepsilon})$ *uniformly for* $|u| \leq \beta$.

Proof. Our starting point is the asymptotic expansion (8.16). Using the expansion (8.15) for E_w and Lemma 8.1.5 we can show easily that

$$\sum_{w \in \mathcal{A}^*} u^{|w|} P(w) A_w^{-n} \frac{E_w}{C_w^3} = O(1).$$

Therefore, by Lemma 8.1.9 we arrive at

$$Q_n(u) = \sum_{w \in \mathcal{A}^*} u^{|w|} P(w) \left(\frac{A_w^{-n-1}}{C_w^2} - (1 - P(w))^{n-1}\right) + O(1/n).$$

Now let $f_w(x)$ be a function defined for real x by

$$f_w(x) = \frac{A_w^{-x-1}}{C_w^2} - (1 - P(w))^{x-1}. \tag{8.18}$$

It turns out that

$$\sum_{w \in \mathcal{A}^*} u^{|w|} f_w(x) P(w) < \infty.$$

To be convinced of this it suffices to notice that by (8.13) this function is uniformly bounded on all $x \geq 0$ and $w \in \mathcal{A}^*$ by some $f_{\max}$, and therefore

$$\sum_k \sum_{\mathcal{A}^k - \mathcal{B}_k} u^{|w|} f_w(x) P(w) = \sum_k O(u^k \delta^k) < \infty$$

when $|u| < \beta$. When $w \in \mathcal{B}_k$, since $S_w(1) - 1$ and $S'(w)$ are both $O(P(w))$ we have

$$f_w(x) = (1 + P(w))^{-x} O\left(kP(w) + xP(w)^2\right).$$

Noticing that

$$(1 + P(w))^x x P(w) = \mu x e^{-\mu x} \frac{P(w)}{\log(1 + P(w))} = O(1)$$

with $\mu = \log(1 + P(w))$, we get

$$\sum_k \sum_{w \in \mathcal{B}_k} u^k x P(w)^3 (1 + P(w))^{-x} P(w) = O\left(\frac{1}{1 - p|u|}\right).$$

We also have $\sum_k k P(w)^2 \leq 1/(1 - p|u|)^2$. In view of this, we conclude that

$$\sum_{w \in \mathcal{A}^*} u^{|w|} P(w) f_w(x) < \infty$$

is absolutely convergent for all $x \geq 0$ and u such that $|u| \leq \beta$. The function $f_w(x)$ decreases exponentially for $x \to \infty$, and therefore its Mellin transform

$$f_w^*(s) = \int_0^\infty f_w(x) x^{s-1} dx$$

exists for $\Re(s) > 0$ since $f_w(0) \neq 0$ (see Table 7.1 for the properties of the Mellin transform). However, for our analysis we need a larger strip of convergence. Therefore, we introduce a modified function,

$$\bar{f}_w(x) = f_w(x) - f_w(0)e^{-x},$$

which also decreases exponentially for $x \to +\infty$ but is $O(x)$ for $x \to 0$. For this function the Mellin transform $\bar{f}_w^*(s)$ is well defined for $\Re(s) > -1$. In this region, again using the properties of the Mellin transform from Table 7.1, we obtain

$$\bar{f}_w^*(s) = \Gamma(s)\left(A_w^{-1} \frac{(\log A_w)^{-s} - 1}{C_w^2} - \frac{(-\log(1 - P(w)))^{-s} - 1}{1 - P(w)}\right).$$

Let $g^*(s, u)$ be the Mellin transform of the series $\sum_{w \in \mathcal{A}^*} u^{|w|} P(w) \bar{f}_w(x)$ which exists at least in the strip $(-1, 0)$. Formally, we have

$$g^*(s, u) = \sum_{w \in \mathcal{A}^*} u^{|w|} P(w) \bar{f}_w^*(s).$$

It turns out that this Mellin transform exists in $\Re(s) \in (-1, c)$ for some $c > 0$, as the next lemma – which we prove below – states.

Lemma 8.1.11. *The function $g^*(s, u)$ is analytic in $\Re(s) \in (-1, c)$ for some $c > 0$.*

Assuming that Lemma 8.1.11 is granted, we have

$$Q_n(u) = \frac{1}{2i\pi} \int_{\varepsilon-i\infty}^{\varepsilon+i\infty} g^*(s,u) n^{-s} ds + O(1/n) + \sum_{w\in\mathcal{A}^*} u^{|w|} P(w) f_w(0) e^{-n},$$

for some $\varepsilon \in (0,c)$. Notice that the last term of the above expression contributes $O(e^{-n})$ for $|u| < \beta$ and can be safely ignored. Furthermore, a simple majorization under the integral gives the evaluation $Q_n(u) = O(n^{-\varepsilon})$ since by Lemma 8.1.11 $g^*(s,u)$ is analytic for $\Re(s) \in (0,c)$. This completes the proof provided that we can establish Lemma 8.1.11. ∎

Let us now finalize our analysis by providing a *proof of Lemma 8.1.11*. We will establish the absolute convergence of $g^*(s,u)$ for all s such that $\Re(s) \in (-1,c)$ and $|u| \le \beta$. Let us define

$$h(s,u) = \frac{g^*(s,u)}{\Gamma(s)}.$$

We set $h(s,u) = h_1(s,u) + h_2(s,u)$ where

$$h_1(s,u) = \frac{1}{\Gamma(s)} \sum_{w\in\mathcal{B}_{|w|}} u^{|w|} P(w) \bar{f}_w^*(s),$$

$$h_2(s,u) = \frac{1}{\Gamma(s)} \sum_{w\notin\mathcal{B}_{|w|}} u^{|w|} P(w) \bar{f}_w^*(s).$$

We first prove that $h_2(s,u)$ is well defined for $\Re(s) > -1$ and $|u| < \beta$ for all $w \notin \mathcal{B}_{|w|}$. Then we deal with the harder problem of establishing the existence of $h_1(s,u)$.

Let k be an integer and let $w \notin \mathcal{B}_k$. Notice that

$$\frac{1}{\Gamma(s)} \bar{f}_w^*(s) = A_w^{-1} \frac{(\log A_w)^{-s} - 1}{C_w^2} - \frac{(-\log(1-P(w)))^{-s} - 1}{1 - P(w)}$$

is uniformly bounded for all complex values of s such that $\Re(s) > 0$. However for $w \in \mathcal{B}_k$ we also know that

$$\sum_{w\in\mathcal{A}^k-\mathcal{B}_k} P(w) = O(\delta_2^k),$$

thus

$$h_2(s,u) = O\left(\frac{1}{1-\delta_2|u|}\right).$$

This implies that $h(s, u)$ is defined for all s, such that $\Re(s) \geq 0$, provided that $|u| \leq \beta$. But $f_w^*(0) = 0$, hence the pole at $s = 0$ of $\Gamma(s)$ is canceled by the zero in the numerator and $h_2(s, u)$ is defined for $\Re(s) > -1$.

The case $w \in \mathcal{B}_k$ needs more attention but leads to similar derivations as before. Note that for any fixed s we have the following:

$$(\log A_w)^{-s} = \left(\frac{P(w)}{1 + S_w(1)} \right)^{-s} (1 + O(P(w)))^{-s},$$

$$(- \log(1 - P(w)))^{-s} = P(w)^{-s}(1 + O(P(w)))^{-s}.$$

One must be careful with the manipulation of the "big oh" terms when the exponents are complex numbers. In particular, we have, for any given quantity $\mu > 0$,

$$\left| e^{-\mu s} - 1 \right| = \left| (e^{-\mu \Re(s)} - 1) \cos(\mu \Im(s)) \right|$$
$$+ 1 - \cos(\mu \Im(s)) + |\sin(\mu \Im(s))| e^{-\mu \Re(s)}.$$

Thus $e^{-\mu s} - 1 = 1 + O(|s|\varepsilon)$ as long as $\Re(s)$ and μ are bounded quantities. So for $\Re(s)$ bounded we have (replacing μ by $\log(1 + O(P(w)))$ in both expressions)

$$(1 + O(P(w)))^{-s} = 1 + O(|s|P(w)).$$

From this estimate we derive

$$\frac{(\log A_w)^{-s} - 1}{A_w^{2-|w|} C_w^2} - \frac{(- \log(1 - P(w)))^{-s} - 1}{1 - P(w)}$$
$$= P(w)^{-s} \left((S_w(1))^s (1 + O(|s|P(w))) - (1 + O(|s|P(w))) + O(|w|P(w)) \right).$$

From the assumption that $w \in \mathcal{B}_k$ we know by Lemma 8.1.5 that $S_w(1) = 1 + O(\delta_2^k)$, and therefore

$$(S_w(1))^s = 1 + O(|s|\delta_1^k).$$

Since $P(w) = O(\delta_1^k)$,

$$\frac{(\log A_w)^{-s} - 1}{A_w^{2-|w|} C_w^2} - \frac{(- \log(1 - P(w)))^{-s} - 1}{1 - P(w)} = O(|s|\delta_1^k).$$

We have $|P(w)^{-s}| = P(w)^{-\Re(s)}$, hence

$$h_2(s, u) = \sum_{k=0}^{\infty} |u|^k O(|s|\delta_1^k) \sum_{w \in \mathcal{B}_k} P(w)^{1 - \Re(s)}.$$

Since

$$\sum_{w \in \mathcal{B}_k} P(w)^{1-\Re(s)} \leq \sum_{a \in \mathcal{A}} p_a^{1-\Re(s)},$$

the sum converges for

$$\left(\sum_{a \in \mathcal{A}} p_a^{1-\Re(s)}\right) |u| \delta_1 < 1,$$

which is the case if $|u| \leq \beta < \delta_1$ for c such that

$$\sum_{a \in \mathcal{A}} p_a^{1-c} < \beta \delta_1.$$

(Notice that $\sum_{a \in \mathcal{A}} p_a^{1-\Re(s)} \to 1$ when $\Re(s) \to 0$.) As before, the pole of $\Gamma(s)$ at $s = 0$ cancels out since $f^*(0) = 0$ and therefore $h_2(0, u) = 0$. In summary, $g^*(s, u)$ does not show any singularities in the strip $\Re(s) \in (-1, c)$; it is well defined there. ∎

Since

$$f_n(w, 1) = P(O_n(w) = 1) - nP(w)(1 - P(w))^{n-1}$$

as a consequence of our proof, we conclude with the following corollary regarding the probability $P(O_n(w) = 1)$. We will use it in Chapter 10.

Corollary 8.1.12. *Let k be an integer and let $w \in \mathcal{A}^k$. For all $\varepsilon > 0$*

$$P(O_n(w) = 1) = nP(w)(1 - P(w))^{n-1} + O(n^{1-\varepsilon} P(w)^{1-\varepsilon} \delta_1^k) + f_w(0)e^{-n} \quad (8.19)$$

when $w \in \mathcal{B}_k$, where $f_w(x)$ was defined in (8.18). Furthermore, when $w \notin \mathcal{B}_k$,

$$P(O_n(w) = 1) = nP(w)(1 - P(w))^{n-1} + O(n^{1-\varepsilon} P(w)^{1-\varepsilon}) + f_w(0)e^{-n} \quad (8.20)$$

where $\sum_{w \in \mathcal{A}^*} |f_w(0)| < \infty$.

8.1.2. Suffix trees and finite suffix trees are equivalent

We now investigate the typical depth of a *finite* suffix tree. Recall that by a finite suffix tree we mean a suffix tree built from the first n suffixes of a finite string $X_1^n \$$ where $\$ \notin \mathcal{A}$ is a special symbol. As before, by suffix tree we mean a tree built from the first n suffixes of the infinite string X_1^∞.

We leave as Exercise 8.6 the proof that the probability generating function $D_n^{FS}(u)$ for the typical depth in a finite suffix tree satisfies

$$P(D_n^{FS} \geq k) = \frac{1}{n} \sum_{w \in \mathcal{A}^k} (n + 1 - |w|)^+ P(w) - N'_{n,w}(0), \quad (8.21)$$

where we use the notation $a^+ = \max\{0, a\}$. From (2.27) we observe that

$$\sum_r r P(O_n(w) = r) = (n + 1 - |w|)P(w);$$

thus any occurrence of w must fit into the first $n + 1 - |w|$ positions in X_1^n. Therefore

$$D_n^{FS}(u) = \frac{1}{n}\frac{1 - u}{u}\left(\Delta_n(u) + \sum_{w \in \mathcal{A}^*} u^{|w|} N'_{n,w}(0)\right),$$

with

$$\Delta_n(u) = \sum_{k \geq 0}(n - (n + 1 - k)^+)u^k = \frac{2u - 1 - u^{n+2}}{(1 - u)^2};$$

however, the exact form of $\Delta_n(u)$ is irrelevant. In view of this we have

$$D^{FS}(z, u) = \frac{1 - u}{u}\left(\Delta(z, u) + \sum_{w \in \mathcal{A}^*} \frac{\partial}{\partial u} N_w(z, 0)\right),$$

where

$$\Delta(z, u) = \sum_n \Delta_n(u) z^n$$

and again its exact form is not important. Finally, by borrowing the formula for $N_w(z, u)$ from Chapter 2 or just using (8.3), we have

$$D^{FS}(z, u) = \frac{1 - u}{u}\left(\Delta(z, u) + \sum_{w \in \mathcal{A}^*} (zu)^{|w|}\frac{P(w)}{D_w^2(z)}\right).$$

Our goal is to prove the following theorem which establishes the equivalence of finite suffix trees and tries built from independent strings.

Theorem 8.1.13. *There is an $\varepsilon > 0$ for $|u| \leq \beta$ with $\beta > 1$ such that*

$$D_n^{FS}(u) - D_n^T(u) = O(n^{-\varepsilon})$$

for large n.

We will prove the theorem in two steps. In the first step we prove that a random finite suffix tree resembles a random *finite trie*, defined below. That is, we prove the following:

$$D_n^{FS}(u) - D_n^{FT}(u) = O(n^{-\varepsilon})$$

where $D_n^{FT}(u)$ is the generating function defined by

$$D^{FT}(z, u) = \sum_n n D_n^{FT}(u) = \frac{1-u}{u} \left(\Delta(z, u) + \sum_{w \in \mathcal{A}^*} (zu)^{|w|} \frac{P(w)}{(1 - z + P(w)z)^2} \right).$$

From the above we may also conclude that

$$D_n^{FT}(u) = \frac{1}{n} \frac{1-u}{u} \left(\Delta_n(u) + \sum_{w \in \mathcal{A}} P(w)(n - |w| + 1)^+ (1 - P(w))^{n-|w|} \right).$$

The quantity $D_n^{FT}(u)$ is the probability generating function for the typical depth in a tree structure that we tentatively call a *thinning* trie. In a thinning trie we delete one string at each level of the tree. In other words, one string is stored at the root (level 0) and the remaining $n - 1$ strings are dispatched into the subtrees. At level 1 we again delete one string at random while the remaining $n - 2$ strings are dispatched into the subsubtrees, and so forth. Thus at level n (if attained) no more strings remain. This mimics a finite suffix tree quite well since the nth suffix remains at the root, thanks to the special final symbol $. The $(n - 1)$th suffix is stored at level 1, and so forth. A finite suffix tree cannot reach level n though this is still possible for suffix trees with infinite suffixes.

Unfortunately, the thinning trie does not have a recursive definition. (Recently Choi et al. (2012) analyzed a similar trie, called (d, n)-trie.) Thus we cannot use the nice recurrences that we used in Chapter 7. However, we still can prove that a thinning trie resembles a regular trie.

Lemma 8.1.14. *There exists $\varepsilon > 0$ such that, for $|u| \leq \beta$,*

$$D_n^{FT}(u) - D_n^T(u) = O(n^{-\varepsilon})$$

for large n.

Proof. Let

$$D_n^{FT}(u) - D_n^T(u) = \frac{1}{n} \frac{1-u}{u} Q_n^T(u).$$

We basically need to prove that the quantity

$$Q_n^T(u) = - \sum_{w \in \mathcal{A}^k} u^{|w|} P(w) \left[n \left((1 - P(w))^{n-1} - 1 \right) \right.$$
$$\left. - (n - |w| + 1)^+ \left((1 - P(w))^{n-|w|} - 1 \right) \right]$$

is $O(n^{1-\varepsilon})$ for $|u| \leq \beta$. We have the upper bound

$$|Q_n^T(u)| \leq |f_n(u)| + |g_n(u)|$$

where

$$f_n(u) = \sum_{w \in \mathcal{A}^k} u^{|w|} P(w) n \left((1 - P(w))^{n-1} - 1\right) = n \sum_{w \in \mathcal{A}^k} u^{|w|} f_w(n-1)$$

with $f_w(x) = P(w)(((1 - P(w))^x - 1)$, and

$$g_n(u) = \sum_{|w| \leq n} u^{|w|} P(w)(n+1-|w|)^+ \left((1 - P(w))^{n-|w|} - 1\right).$$

We already know, via the use of the Mellin transform, that $f_n(u) = O(n^{1-\varepsilon})$ for ε and β such that $\beta \sum_{a \in \mathcal{A}} p_a^{1+\varepsilon} < 1$.

We can rewrite $g_n(u)$ as follows:

$$g_n(u) = \sum_{|w| \leq n} u^{|w|} P(w) n \left((1 - P(w))^{n-1} - 1\right) (1 - P(w))^{1-|w|}$$

$$+ \sum_{|w| \leq n} n \left((1 - P(w))^{n-1} - 1\right)$$

$$- \sum_{|w| \leq n} (|w| - 1) u^{|w|} P(w) \left((1 - P(w))^{n-1} - 1\right) (1 - P(w))^{1-|w|}$$

$$- \sum_{|w| \leq n} (|w| - 1) \left((1 - P(w))^{n-1} - 1\right). \tag{8.22}$$

Since $(1 - P(w))^{1-|w|} = O(1)$ it turns out that all the right-hand side terms are of order $O(f_n(|u|))$ (see Exercise 8.7)) which in turn is of order $O(n^{1-\varepsilon})$, as required. ∎

Now we are in a position to prove Theorem 8.1.13. we need to show that $D_n^{FS}(u) - D_n^{FT}(u) = O(n^{-\varepsilon})$, which we do in what follows. Let

$$D_n^{FS}(u) - D_n^{FT}(u) = \frac{1}{n} \frac{1-u}{u} Q_n^F(u).$$

By the Cauchy formula,

$$Q_n^F(u) = \frac{1}{2i\pi} \oint Q^F(z, u) \frac{dz}{z^{n+1}},$$

where

$$Q^F(z, u) = \sum_{w \in \mathcal{A}^*} (uz)^{|w|} P(w) \left(\frac{1}{D_w^2(z)} - \frac{1}{(1 - z + P(w)z)^2}\right).$$

This quantity is similar to $Q(z, u)$ from the previous section. However, in $Q^F(z, u)$ the factor $u^{|w|}z$ is now replaced by $(zu)^{|w|}$. The proof proceeds in the same way as for $Q(z, u)$. The function $Q^F(z, u)$ has the same poles as $Q(z, u)$ at $z = A_w$ and $z = (1 - P(w))$ for $w \in \mathcal{A}^*$. Define

$$f_n^F(w, \rho, u) = \left| \frac{1}{2i\pi} \int_{|z|=\rho} \frac{dz}{z^{n-|w|}} \left(\frac{1}{D_w(z)^2} - \frac{1}{(1 - z + P(w)z)^2} \right) \right|.$$

It is easy to show that

$$f_n^F(w, \rho, u) \leq \rho^{|w|} f_n(w, \rho, u),$$

where $f_n(w, \rho, u)$ is defined in (8.17) in the previous section. Thus (as the reader is asked to prove in Exercise 8.8)

$$\sum_{w \in \mathcal{A}^*} P(w) f_n^F(w, \rho, u) = O\left(\frac{\rho^{-n}}{1 - \rho^2 \delta |u|} \right). \tag{8.23}$$

Finally, we estimate the residues over the poles of $Q^F(z, u)$. We need to deal with the following sum over $w \in \mathcal{A}^*$:

$$u^{|w|} P(w) \left[\frac{A_w^{|w|-n}}{u} \left(\frac{n+1-|w|}{C_w^2 A_w} + \frac{E_w}{C_w^3} \right) - n(1 - P(w))^{n-1+|w|} \right].$$

However,

$$A_w^{|w|-n} = A_w^{-n}(1 + O(|w|P(w)))$$
$$(1 - P(w))^{n-1+|w|} = (1 - P(w))^{n-1}(1 + O(|w|P(w))).$$

Thus the above sum is fundamentally equivalent to

$$u^{|w|} P(w) \left(\frac{A_w^{-n}}{u} \left[\frac{n+1-|w|}{C_w^2 A_w} + \frac{E_w}{C_w^3} \right] - n(1 - P(w))^{n-1} \right)$$

which we know to be $O(n^{1-\varepsilon})$. This completes the proof. ∎

8.2. Size of suffix tree

We now extend our analysis to other parameters of suffix trees. Our methodology applies without major modifications to the evaluation of the average size of a suffix tree. We define the size of the tree as the number of internal nodes.

However, we should point out that our methodology works for the *average* size of a suffix, and we do not yet know how to extend it to the variance and limiting distribution; these are still open problems. Regarding the variance of a suffix tree, one can derive a generating function that counts the occurrences of two distinct words but, so far, attempts to make it suitable for an asymptotic expansion of the variance have not been successful. It is conjectured that the error term between a suffix tree and the corresponding independent trie becomes larger than the order of the variance (which is $O(n)$ for the tries) when the alphabet size is small.

We denote by $s_n = \mathbf{E}[S_n]$ the *average* size S_n of a suffix tree built from n suffixes. It is easy to verify that

$$s_n = \sum_{w \in \mathcal{A}^*} P(O_{n+|w|-1}(w) \geq 2), \tag{8.24}$$

since any two occurrences of a word w within the first $n + |w| - 1$ symbols of X_1^n create an internal node. We denote by $s(z)$ the generating function $\sum_{n=1}^{\infty} s_n z^n$. The following is easy to derive.

Theorem 8.2.1. *The generating function $S(z)$ for the average size of a suffix tree is*

$$s(z) = - \sum_{w \in \mathcal{A}^*} z P(w) \left(\frac{1}{D_w^2(z)} - \frac{1}{(1-z)D_w(z)} \right). \tag{8.25}$$

Proof. The proof is actually quite easy using our results from Section 2.3. First note that

$$s(z) = \sum_{w \in \mathcal{A}^*} \sum_{n=0}^{\infty} \left(1 - P(O_{n+|w|-1} = 0) - P(O_{n+|w|-1} = 1) \right) z^n.$$

From Theorem 2.3.2 we can see that

$$\sum_{n=0}^{\infty} P(O_{n+|w|-1} = 0) z^n = \frac{z^{1-|w|} S_w(z)}{D_w(z)},$$

$$\sum_{n=0}^{\infty} P(O_{n+|w|-1} = 1) z^n = \frac{z P(w)}{D_w^2(z)}.$$

This leads to (8.24).   ∎

The size of tries built from independent strings was discussed in Section 7.2.9. In particular, in Theorem 7.2.9 we gave the average size for tries. Here, we re-derive the generating function for the average size s_n of a trie in a way that is more suitable for our analysis. Noting that

$$s_n = \sum_{w \in \mathcal{A}^*} \left[1 - (1 - P(w))^n - nP(w)(1 - P(w))^{n-1} \right],$$

we obtain

$$s^T(z) = - \sum_{w \in \mathcal{A}^*} zP(w) \left(\frac{1}{(1 - z + P(w))^2} - \frac{1}{(1 - z)(1 - z + P(w))} \right). \quad (8.26)$$

In this section, using Theorem 7.2.9 we will prove the following main result.

Theorem 8.2.2. *There exists $\varepsilon > 0$ such that the following expansion holds:*

$$s_n - s_n^T = O(n^{1-\varepsilon})$$

for large n. Furthermore,

$$s_n = \frac{n}{h} \left(1 + \Phi_0(\log n) \right) + O(n^{1-\varepsilon})$$

where $\Phi_0(\log n)$ is a periodic function with small amplitude if the $\log p_a$, $a \in \mathcal{A}$ are rationally related; otherwise $\Phi_0(\log n)$ converges to zero.

Proof. The proof proceeds as the proof for the depth in a suffix tree. We split $s^T(z) - s(z)$ into two parts, as follows:

$$s^T(z) - s(z) = \sum_{w \in \mathcal{A}^*} zP(w) \left(\frac{1}{D_w^2(z)} - \frac{1}{(1 - z + P(w))^2} \right)$$

$$- \sum_{w \in \mathcal{A}^*} \frac{zP(w)}{1 - z} \left(\frac{1}{D_w(z)} - \frac{1}{1 - z + P(w)z} \right).$$

Using the same approach as in Section 8.1, we set

$$s_n^T - s_n = f_n(1) - d_n, \quad (8.27)$$

where $f_n(1) = \sum_{w \in \mathcal{A}^*} f_n(w, 1)$ was studied earlier, and

$$d_n = \sum_{w \in \mathcal{A}^*} d_n(w)$$

with

$$d_n(w) = P(O_n(w) > 0) - 1 + (1 - P(w))^n$$

$$= \frac{1}{2i\pi} \oint \frac{P(w)z}{1 - z} \frac{dz}{z^{n+1}} \left(\frac{1}{D_w(z)} - \frac{1}{1 - z + P(w)z} \right).$$

We have

$$d_n(w) = \left(\frac{A_w^{-n} P(w)}{(1 - A_w)C_w} - (1 - P(w))^n \right) + J_n(w, \rho) \qquad (8.28)$$

with

$$J_n(w, \rho) = \frac{1}{2i\pi} \oint_{|z|=\rho} \frac{P(w)z}{1 - z} \frac{dz}{z^{n+1}} \left(\frac{1}{D_w(z)} - \frac{1}{1 - z + P(w)z} \right).$$

We already know that it is $O(n^{1-\varepsilon})$.

The term d_n in (8.27) is more intricate since in its present form it is not even clear that the sum of the d_n converges.

We first analyze the sum $\sum_{w \in \mathcal{A}^*} J_n(w)$ which is easier. We notice that when $w \in \mathcal{A}^k - \mathcal{B}_k$ the function $P(w)(1/D_w(z) - (1 - z + P(w))^{-1})$ is $O(P(w)\delta_2^k)$ when $|z| = \rho$. Thus

$$\sum_{w \in \mathcal{A}^k - \mathcal{B}_k} J_n(w) = O(\delta_2^k).$$

Furthermore

$$\sum_{w \in \mathcal{B}_k} P(w)(1/D_w(z) - (1 - z + P(w))^{-1}) = O(\delta_1^k).$$

Therefore the sum of the integrals that make up the $J_n(w, \rho)$ is finite and $O(\rho^{-n})$.

To handle the factors involving the A_w we need to extend the expansion of the root A_w, writing

$$A_w = 1 + \frac{P(w)}{S_w(1)} + P^2(w) \left(\frac{|w|}{S_w^2(1)} - \frac{S_w'(1)}{S_w^3(1)} \right) + O(P^3(w)). \qquad (8.29)$$

Therefore

$$\frac{P(w)A_w^{-n}}{(1 - A_w)C_w} - (1 - P(w))^n = n(1 - P(w))^n O\left(P(w)S_w'(1) + P^2(w) \right).$$

The series $\sum_{w \in \mathcal{A}^*} P^2(w)$ converges. Let us study the series $\sum_{w \in \mathcal{A}^*} P(w)S_w'(1)$. Since $S_w'(1) \le |w|(S_w(1) - 1)$, the convergence of this series holds as long as we can prove that

$$\sum_{w \in \mathcal{A}^*} P(w)(S_w(1) - 1) < \infty.$$

Let $k = |w|$ and first assume that $w \in \mathcal{B}_k$. We know that $S_w - 1 = O(\delta_1^k)$ and thus we have for the corresponding partial series,

$$\sum_{w \in \mathcal{B}_{|w|}} P(w)(S_w(1) - 1) = O\left(\sum_{k \ge 0} \delta_1^k \right).$$

Let us assume now that $w \notin \mathcal{B}_k$; since $S_w(1) = O(1)$ and $\sum_{w \notin \mathcal{B}_k} P(w) = O(\delta_2^k)$, we have this partial series

$$\sum_{w \notin \mathcal{B}_{|w|}} P(w)(S_w(1) - 1) = O\left(\sum_{k \geq 0} \delta_2^k\right).$$

Now, to prove that $d_n = O(n^{1-\varepsilon})$ we split up the sum $d_n = \sum_{w \in \mathcal{A}^*} d_w(n)$, where

$$d_w(x) = \frac{A_w P(w)}{(1 - A_w) C_w} - (1 - P(w))^x. \qquad (8.30)$$

As before, we apply a Mellin transform (see Table 7.1). The Mellin transform of $d_w(x)$ exists in the strip $(0, \infty)$ but we cannot extend it further since $d_w(0) \neq 0$. However, it can be analytically extended for $\Re(s) < 0$ as long as we avoid the poles of $\Gamma(s)$ on the nonpositive integers. Since we want to extract an order $x^{1-\varepsilon}$ for $\sum_{w \in \mathcal{A}^*} d_w(x)$ we must use the same trick as in Section 8.1; namely we define

$$\bar{d}_w(x) = d_w(x) - d_w(0)e^{-x},$$

for which the Mellin transform exists for $\Re(s) \in (-1, \infty)$. We now notice that $\sum_{w \in \mathcal{A}^*} \bar{d}_w(n) - d_n$ tends to zero exponentially fast. The Mellin transform of $\bar{d}_w(x)$, namely $J_w(s)\Gamma(s)$, satisfies

$$J_w(s) = \frac{((\log A_w)^{-s} - 1)P(w)}{(1 - A_w) C_w} + 1 - (-\log(1 - P(w)))^{-s}.$$

We split $J_w(s)$ as follows:

$$j_1(s) = \sum_{w \in \mathcal{B}_{|w|}} J_w(s), \quad j_2(s) = \sum_{w \notin \mathcal{B}_{|w|}} J_w(s).$$

Since $J_w(s) = P(w)^{-s}O(|s|P(w))$, we immediately find that

$$j_2(s) = \sum_{k \geq 0} O(\delta_2^k)$$

for $\Re(s) < 0$, and therefore it has no singularity for $\Re(s) \in (-1, 0)$.

Regarding $j_1(s)$, we consider $w \in \mathcal{B}_k$ and refer to (8.29) for A_w. Since $S_w(1) = O(\delta_1^k)$ and $S'_w(1) = O(k\delta_1^k)$, we find that

$$J_w(s) = O(|s|k\delta_1^k)P(w)^{1-s}$$

and therefore $j_2(s) = \sum_{w \in \mathcal{B}_{|w|}} J_w(s)$ converges as long as

$$\left(\sum_{a \in \mathcal{A}} p_a^{1-\Re(s)} \right) \delta_1 < 1.$$

Thus for $\Re(s) < -1 + c$ with the same value of $c > 0$ as in the proof of Theorem 8.1.2. Therefore, $J_w(s)$ is defined for $\Re(s) \in (-1, -1+c)$, and hence $d_n = O(n^{1-c})$. This concludes the proof of Theorem 8.2.2.   ■

As a consequence of our proof, we can deduce the following corollary regarding the probability $P(O_n(w) \geq 1)$. We will use it in Chapter 10.

Corollary 8.2.3. *Let k be an integer and let $w \in \mathcal{A}^k$. For all $\varepsilon > 0$ and $w \in \mathcal{B}_k$, we have*

$$P(O_n(w) \geq 1) = 1 - (1 - P(w))^n + O(n^{1-\varepsilon} P(w)^{1-\varepsilon} \delta_1^k) + d_w(0)e^{-n}, \quad (8.31)$$

where $d_w(x)$ was defined in (8.30). Furthermore, for $w \notin \mathcal{B}_k$,

$$P(O_n(w) \geq 1) = nP(w)(1 - P(w))^{n-1} + O(n^{1-\varepsilon} P(w)^{1-\varepsilon}) + d_w(0)e^{-n}, \quad (8.32)$$

where $\sum_{w \in \mathcal{A}^*} |d_w(0)| < \infty$.

8.3. Lempel–Ziv'77

We study here the *number* of longest matches using the Lempel–Ziv'77 scheme. Recall that in LZ'77 we find the longest prefix of, say, X_{n+1}^∞, that has a copy in X_1^n; this was discussed in Chapter 6. More precisely, let w be the longest prefix of X_{n+1}^∞ that is also a prefix of X_i^∞ for some i with $1 \leq i \leq n$, that is, $X_i^{i+|w|-1} = X_{n+1}^{n+|w|}$ for $i \leq n$. The number of such i is denoted M_n, the *multiplicity matching parameter*. More formally,

$$M_n = \#\{1 \leq i \leq n \mid X_i^\infty \text{ has } w \text{ as a prefix}\}. \quad (8.33)$$

In other words, M_n is the number of suffixes from among the first n suffixes which *agree maximally* with the $(n+1)$th suffix X_{n+1}^∞, where we measure the degree of agreement between two suffixes by the length of their longest shared prefix. We shall see that the number M_n coincides with the multiplicity parameter (of the associated suffix tree) defined in Chapter 7.

As in Chapter 6, the longest match in LZ'77 (the phrase length) can be found by building the associated suffix tree. We note that in the framework of a suffix tree, M_n is precisely the number of suffixes in the subtree rooted at the node at

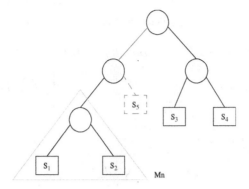

Figure 8.3. This suffix tree has multiple matching parameter $M_4 = 2$ after the insertion of suffix S_5.

which the $(n + 1)$th suffix X_{n+1}^∞ is inserted, that is, the size of such a subtree. This is illustrated in Figure 8.3.

Our goal is to understand the probabilistic behavior of the variable M_n. We will derive the asymptotic distribution $P(M_n = j)$ for large n. We can accomplish this by finding the probability generating function $\mathbf{E}[u^{M_n}]$ and extracting its asymptotic behavior for large n. We will follow the methodology established in Section 8.1.

The main result is presented for a general finite alphabet $\mathcal{A}$ with $p_a > 0$ and $q_a = 1 - p_a$ for any $a \in \mathcal{A}$. Recall also from Definition 7.2.6 that the $\log p_a$, $a \in \mathcal{A}$, are *rationally related* if there exists a real L such that $\log p_a = n_a L$ for an integer n_a (i.e., $\log p_a / \log p_b = n_a/n_b$ is rational for any pair $a, b \in \mathcal{A}$). Otherwise, we say that the $\log p_a$ are *irrationally related*. We also define $p = \max_{a \in \mathcal{A}}\{p_a\}$ and $q = \max_{a \in \mathcal{A}}\{q_a\}$. Our main result is presented next.

Theorem 8.3.1. *For $|u| \leq \min\{p^{-1/2}, q^{-1}\}$ the sequence $\mathbf{E}[u^{M_n}]$ has the following asymptotic form:*

$$\mathbf{E}[u^{M_n}] = -\frac{\sum_{a \in \mathcal{A}} p_a \log(1 - q_a u)}{h} - \frac{1}{h}\delta(\log n, u) + o(1), \qquad (8.34)$$

where $\delta(\log n, u)$ converges to zero as $n \to \infty$ when the $\log p_a$, $a \in \mathcal{A}$, are irrationally related, while when they are rationally related the $o(1)$ estimate can be improved to $O(n^{-\varepsilon})$ for some $\varepsilon > 0$, and the function $\delta(t, u)$ has the form

$$\delta(t, u) = \sum_{k \neq 0} e^{2k\pi it/L}\Gamma(s_k) \sum_{a \in \mathcal{A}} p_a(1 - q_a u)^{-s_k} - p_a^{-s_k+1},$$

where $s_k = 2\pi i k/L$ with L defined for the rational case as the common real factor of the $\log p_a$.
It follows immediately that in the rationally related case,

$$P(M_n = j) = \frac{1}{h}\sum_{a\in\mathcal{A}}\frac{q_a^j p_a}{j} - \frac{1}{h}\sum_{k\neq 0}\frac{e^{2k\pi i \log n/L}\Gamma(s_k)(s_j)^{\bar{j}}\sum_{a\in\mathcal{A}}q_a^j p_a}{j!} + O(n^{-\varepsilon}),$$

(8.35)

while for the irrational case

$$P(M_n = j) = \sum_{a\in\mathcal{A}}\frac{q_a^j p_a}{jh} + o(1),$$

(8.36)

for large n.

The rest of this section is devoted to the proof of Theorem 8.3.1. However, to simplify our presentation we describe the proof only for the binary case, with $p_a = p$ and $q_a = q < p$, leaving the general proof as Exercise 8.9. Our strategy for analyzing M_n is the same as that for the depth of a suffix tree, that is, we compare M_n with the distribution of the multiplicity parameter M_n^T defined for tries built from n *independent* strings. We actually analyzed this in Section 7.3.3 under the name M_n. Now we will relabel it as M_n^T to distinguish it from the multiplicity parameter of a suffix tree.

The road map of the proof follows the method of Section 8.1 with slight variations. After deriving the bivariate generating functions for M_n and for M_n^T, denoted as $M(z,u)$ and $M^T(z,u)$, respectively, we compute

$$Q(z,u) = M(z,u) - M^T(z,u).$$

We then use Cauchy's theorem to prove that $Q_n(u) := [z^n]Q(z,u) \to 0$ uniformly for $u \le p^{-1/2}$ as $n \to \infty$. Another use of Cauchy's theorem proves that

$$P(M_n = k) - P(M_n^T = k) = [u^k z^n]Q(z,u) = O(n^{-\varepsilon}b^{-k})$$

(8.37)

for some $\varepsilon > 0$ and $b > 1$.

parameter M_n is asymptotically the same in suffix trees as in tries built over independent strings. Therefore M_n also follows the logarithmic series distribution plus fluctuations, claimed for M_n^T in Theorem 7.3.6.

Thus our main goal of this section is to prove the following result.

Theorem 8.3.2. *There exists $\varepsilon > 0$ such that, for $|u| < 1+\delta$ and some $\delta > 0$,*

$$|M_n(u) - M_n^T(u)| = O(n^{-\varepsilon}).$$

(8.38)

As a consequence, there exists $b > 1$ such that

$$P(M_n = k) - P(M_n^T = k) = O(n^{-\varepsilon} b^{-k}) \tag{8.39}$$

for large n.

This together with Theorem 7.3.6 suffices to establish our main result, Theorem 8.3.1.

We now start the proof of Theorem 8.3.2 by rederiving a simple formula for the bivariate generating function $M^T(z, u)$ of the multiplicity parameter in an independent trie over a binary alphabet $\mathcal{A} = \{\alpha, \beta\}$. We let w denote the *longest prefix* common to the $(n+1)$th string and at least one of the other n strings. We write $\beta \in \mathcal{A}$ to denote the $(|w| + 1)$th character of the $(n + 1)$th string. When $M_n^T = k$ we conclude that exactly k strings have $w\alpha$ as a prefix with $\alpha \neq \beta$ and the other $n - k$ strings do not have w as a prefix at all. Thus the generating function for M_n^T is exactly

$$M^T(z, u) = \sum_{n=1}^{\infty} \sum_{k=1}^{\infty} P(M_n^T = k) u^k z^n$$

$$= \sum_{n=1}^{\infty} \sum_{k=1}^{\infty} \sum_{\substack{w \in \mathcal{A}^* \\ \alpha \in \mathcal{A}}} P(w\beta) \binom{n}{k} (P(w\alpha))^k (1 - P(w))^{n-k} u^k z^n.$$

After simplifying, it follows immediately that

$$M^T(z, u) = \sum_{\substack{w \in \mathcal{A}^* \\ \alpha \in \mathcal{A}}} \frac{u P(\beta) P(w)}{1 - z(1 - P(w))} \frac{z P(w) P(\alpha)}{1 - z(1 + u P(w) P(\alpha) - P(w))}. \tag{8.40}$$

The same line of reasoning can be applied to derive the generating function $M(z, u)$ for M_n in the associated suffix tree; however, the situation is more complicated because the occurrences of w can overlap. Consider a suffix tree built over the first $n + 1$ *suffixes* $X^{(1)}, \ldots, X^{(n+1)}$ of a string X (i.e., $X^{(i)} = X_i X_{i+1} X_{i+2} \ldots$). We let w denote the *longest prefix* common to both $X^{(n+1)}$ and at least one $X^{(i)}$ for some $1 \leq i \leq n$. As before, we write β to denote the $(|w| + 1)$th character of $X^{(n+1)}$. When $M_n = k$, we conclude that exactly k suffixes $X^{(i)}$ have $w\alpha$ as a prefix and the other $n - k$ strings $X^{(i)}$ do not have w as a prefix at all. Thus, we are interested in finding strings with exactly k occurrences of $w\alpha$ and ending on the right with an occurrence of $w\beta$ and with no other occurrences of w. This set of strings constitutes the words of a language. In Chapter 2 we studied such languages and their generating functions. We therefore follow the methodology developed in Chapter 2. In particular, the language just described (i.e., k occurrences of $w\alpha$ ending on the right with $w\beta$) can be written as

$$\mathcal{R}_w \alpha (\mathcal{T}_w^{(\alpha)} \alpha)^{k-1} \mathcal{T}_w^{(\alpha)} \beta, \tag{8.41}$$

where

$$\mathcal{R}_w = \{v \in \mathcal{A}^* | v \text{ contains exactly one occurrence of } w, \text{ at the right hand end}\}$$
$$\mathcal{T}_w^{(\alpha)} = \{v \in \mathcal{A}^* \mid w\alpha v \text{ contains exactly two occurrences of } w,$$
$$\text{located at the left and right hand ends}\}.$$

In order to understand (8.41) the reader is referred back to Theorem 2.2.3. It follows from (8.41) that

$$M(z, u) = \sum_{k=1}^{\infty} \sum_{\substack{w \in \mathcal{A}^* \\ \alpha \in \mathcal{A}}} \sum_{s \in \mathcal{R}_w} P(s\alpha) z^{|s|+1} u \left(\sum_{t \in \mathcal{T}_w^{(\alpha)}} P(t\alpha) z^{|t|+1} u \right)^{k-1}$$
$$\times \sum_{v \in \mathcal{T}_w^{(\alpha)}} P(v\beta) z^{|v|+1-|w|-1}.$$

After simplifying the geometric sum, this yields

$$M(z, u) = \sum_{\substack{w \in \mathcal{A}^* \\ \alpha \in \mathcal{A}}} u P(\beta) \frac{R_w(z)}{z^{|w|}} \frac{P(\alpha) z T_w^{(\alpha)}(z)}{1 - P(\alpha) z u T_w^{(\alpha)}(z)} \tag{8.42}$$

where

$$R_w(z) = \sum_{v \in \mathcal{R}_w} P(v) z^{|v|}, \quad T_w^{(\alpha)}(z) = \sum_{v \in \mathcal{T}_w^{(\alpha)}} P(v) z^{|v|}$$

are generating functions for the languages $\mathcal{R}_w$ and $\mathcal{T}_w^{(\alpha)}$, respectively. From Lemma 2.3.1 we known that $R_w(z) = z^{|w|} P(w)/D_w(z)$, where

$$D_w(z) = (1 - z) S_w(z) + z^m P(w)$$

and $S_w(z)$ denotes the autocorrelation polynomial for w. It follows that

$$M(z, u) = \sum_{\substack{w \in \mathcal{A}^* \\ \alpha \in \mathcal{A}}} \frac{u P(\beta) P(w)}{D_w(z)} \frac{P(\alpha) z T_w^{(\alpha)}(z)}{1 - P(\alpha) z u T_w^{(\alpha)}(z)}. \tag{8.43}$$

In order to derive an explicit form of $M(z, u)$, we still need to find $T_w^{(\alpha)}(z)$. As in Chapter 2, we introduce the language

$$\mathcal{M}_w = \{v \mid wv \text{ contains exactly two occurrences of } w,$$
$$\text{located at the left and right hand ends}\},$$

then we observe that $\alpha \mathcal{T}_w^{(\alpha)}$ is exactly the subset of words of $\mathcal{M}_w$ that begin with α. We use $\mathcal{H}_w^{(\alpha)}$ to denote this subset, i.e.,

$$\mathcal{H}_w^{(\alpha)} = \mathcal{M}_w \cap (\alpha \mathcal{A}^*),$$

and thus

$$\alpha \mathcal{T}_w^{(\alpha)} = \mathcal{H}_w^{(\alpha)}.$$

So (8.43) simplifies to

$$M(z, u) = \sum_{\substack{w \in \mathcal{A}^* \\ \alpha \in \mathcal{A}}} \frac{u P(\beta) P(w)}{D_w(z)} \frac{H_w^{(\alpha)}(z)}{1 - u H_w^{(\alpha)}(z)}. \tag{8.44}$$

In order to compute the generating function $H_w^{(\alpha)}(z)$ for $\mathcal{H}_w^{(\alpha)}$ we write

$$\mathcal{M}_w = \mathcal{H}_w^{(\alpha)} + \mathcal{H}_w^{(\beta)},$$

where $\mathcal{H}_w^{(\beta)}$ is the subset of words from $\mathcal{M}_w$ that start with β (i.e., $\mathcal{H}_w^{(\beta)} = \mathcal{M}_w \cap (\beta \mathcal{A}^*)$). (Note that every word of $\mathcal{M}_w$ begins with either α or β, because the empty word $\varepsilon \notin \mathcal{M}_w$.) The following useful lemma is the last necessary ingredient to obtain an explicit formula for $M(z, u)$ from (8.44).

Lemma 8.3.3. *Let $\mathcal{H}_w^{(\alpha)}$ denote the subset of words from $\mathcal{M}_w$ that start with α. Then*

$$H_w^{(\alpha)}(z) = \frac{D_{w\alpha}(z) - (1 - z)}{D_w(z)}.$$

Proof. In Chapter 2 we introduced the language

$$\mathcal{U}_w = \{v \mid wv \text{ contains exactly one occurrence of } w,$$
$$\text{located at the left hand end}\}$$

while here we need a new language, namely

$$\mathcal{U}_w^{(\alpha)} = \{v \mid v \text{ starts with } \alpha, \text{ and } wv \text{ has exactly one occurrence of } w\alpha$$
$$\text{and no occurrences of } w\beta\}.$$

We note that the set of words with no occurrences of $w\beta$ can be described as

$$\mathcal{A}^* \setminus \mathcal{R}_{w\beta}(\mathcal{M}_{w\beta})^* \mathcal{U}_{w\beta}$$

with generating function

$$\frac{1}{1 - z} - \frac{R_{w\beta}(z) U_{w\beta}(z)}{1 - M_{w\beta}(z)}. \tag{8.45}$$

Now we will describe the set of words with no occurrences of $w\beta$ in a different way. The set of words with no occurrences of $w\beta$ and at least one occurrence of $w\alpha$ is exactly $\mathcal{R}_w(\mathcal{H}_w^{(\alpha)})^*\mathcal{U}_w^{(\alpha)}$, with generating function

$$\frac{R_w(z)U_w^{(\alpha)}(z)}{1 - H_w^{(\alpha)}(z)}.$$

On the one hand, the set of words with no occurrences of $w\beta$ and no occurrences of $w\alpha$ is exactly

$$\mathcal{R}_w + (\mathcal{A}^* \setminus \mathcal{R}_w(\mathcal{M}_w)^*\mathcal{U}),$$

since the set of such words that end in w is exactly $\mathcal{R}_w$; on the other hand, the set of such words that do not end in w is exactly $\mathcal{A}^* \setminus \mathcal{R}_w(\mathcal{M}_w)^*\mathcal{U}$. So the set of words with no occurrences of $w\alpha$ and no occurrences of $w\beta$ has the generating function

$$\frac{R_w(z)U_w^{(\alpha)}(z)}{1 - H_w^{(\alpha)}(z)} + R_w(z) + \frac{1}{1 - z} - \frac{R_w(z)U_w(z)}{1 - M_w(z)}. \tag{8.46}$$

Combining (8.45) and (8.46), it follows that

$$\frac{1}{1 - z} - \frac{R_{w\beta}(z)U_{w\beta}(z)}{1 - M_{w\beta}(z)} = \frac{R_w(z)U_w^{(\alpha)}(z)}{1 - H_w^{(\alpha)}(z)} + R_w(z) + \frac{1}{1 - z} - \frac{R_w(z)U_w(z)}{1 - M_w(z)}. \tag{8.47}$$

Now we can find the generating function for $\mathcal{U}_w^{(\alpha)}$. For each word $v \in \mathcal{U}_w^{(\alpha)}$, wv has exactly either one or two occurrences of w. The subset of $\mathcal{U}_w^{(\alpha)}$ of the first type is exactly $\mathcal{V}_w^{(\alpha)} := \mathcal{U}_w \cap (\alpha\mathcal{A}^*)$, i.e., the subset of words from $\mathcal{U}_w$ that start with α. The subset of $\mathcal{U}_w^{(\alpha)}$ of the second type is exactly $\mathcal{H}_w^{(\alpha)}$. We observe that

$$\mathcal{V}_w^{(\alpha)} \cdot \mathcal{A} = (\mathcal{H}_w^{(\alpha)} + \mathcal{V}_w^{(\alpha)}) \setminus \{\alpha\} \tag{8.48}$$

(see Exercise 8.10). Hence, its generating function becomes

$$V_w^{(\alpha)}(z) = \frac{H_w^{(\alpha)}(z) - P(\alpha)z}{z - 1}.$$

Since $\mathcal{U}_w^{(\alpha)} = \mathcal{V}_w^{(\alpha)} + \mathcal{H}_w^{(\alpha)}$, it follows that

$$U_w^{(\alpha)}(z) = \frac{H_w^{(\alpha)}(z) - P(\alpha)z}{z - 1} + H_w^{(\alpha)}(z) = \frac{zH_w^{(\alpha)}(z) - P(\alpha)z}{z - 1}.$$

From equation (8.47), we see that

$$\frac{1}{1-z} - \frac{R_{w\beta}(z)U_{w\beta}(z)}{1-M_{w\beta}(z)} = \frac{R_w(z)(zH_w^{(\alpha)}(z) - P(\alpha)z)}{(1-H_w^{(\alpha)}(z))(z-1)}$$
$$+R_w(z) + \frac{1}{1-z} - \frac{R_w(z)U_w(z)}{1-M_w(z)}.$$

Simplifying, and using Lemma 2.3.1 from Chapter 2,

$$U_w(z) = \frac{1-M_w(z)}{1-z}, \quad U_{w\beta}(z) = \frac{1-M_{w\beta}(z)}{1-z},$$

it follows that

$$\frac{R_{w\beta}(z)}{R_w(z)} = \frac{zP(\beta)}{1-H_w^{(\alpha)}(z)}.$$

Solving for $H_w^{(\alpha)}(z)$ and then using $R_w(z) = z^m P(w)/D_w(z)$ and

$$R_{w\beta}(z) = \frac{z^{m+1}P(w)P(\beta)}{D_{w\beta}(z)},$$

it follows that

$$H_w^{(\alpha)}(z) = \frac{D_w(z) - D_{w\beta}(z)}{D_w(z)}. \tag{8.49}$$

Note that

$$D_w(z) - D_{w\beta}(z) = (1-z)S_w(z) + z^m P(w) - (1-z)S_{w\beta}(z) - z^{m+1}P(w)P(\beta)$$
$$= (1-z)(S_{w\alpha}(z) - 1) + z^{m+1}P(w)P(\alpha)$$
$$= D_{w\alpha}(z) - (1-z).$$

Thus, (8.49) completes the proof of the lemma. ∎

In summary, we have just proved the form for $M(z,u)$ given in the following theorem.

Theorem 8.3.4. *Let* $M(z,u) := \sum_{n=1}^{\infty} \sum_{k=1}^{\infty} P(M_n = k)u^k z^n$ *denote the bivariate generating function for* M_n. *Then*

$$M(z,u) = \sum_{\substack{w \in \mathcal{A}^* \\ \alpha \in \mathcal{A}}} \frac{uP(\beta)P(w)}{D_w(z)} \frac{D_{w\alpha}(z) - (1-z)}{D_w(z) - u(D_{w\alpha}(z) - (1-z))} \tag{8.50}$$

for $|u| < 1$ *and* $|z| < 1$. *Here* $D_w(z) = (1-z)S_w(z) + z^m P(w)$ *with* $m = |w|$, *and* $S_w(z)$ *denotes the autocorrelation polynomial for* w.

We now start to make a comparison of $M(z, u)$ and $M^T(z, u)$. Before we do this we need some preliminary results, as in Section 8.1. First, we deal briefly with the autocorrelation polynomial. In Lemma 8.1.6 we proved that, with high probability, w has very few large nontrivial overlaps with itself. Therefore, with high probability, all nontrivial overlaps of w with itself are small. In the next two lemmas we summarize our knowledge about $S_w(z)$ and $S_{w\alpha}(z)$. As before, we use $\rho > 1$ such that $\rho\sqrt{p} < 1$ (and thus $\rho p < 1$ also). Finally, $\delta = \sqrt{p}$. Throughout this section we write $m = |w|$ for the length of w.

Lemma 8.3.5. *If $\theta = (1 - p\rho)^{-1} + 1$ and $\alpha \in \mathcal{A}$ then*

$$\sum_{w \in \mathcal{A}^k} [\![\max\{|S_w(\rho) - 1|, |S_{w\alpha}(\rho) - 1|\} \leq (\rho\delta)^k \theta]\!] P(w) \geq 1 - \delta^k \theta, \qquad (8.51)$$

with the same notation as in Lemma 8.1.6.

Lemma 8.3.6. *Define $c = 1 - \rho\sqrt{p} > 0$. Then there exists an integer $K \geq 1$ such that, for $|w| \geq K$ and $|z| \leq \rho$ and $|u| \leq \delta^{-1}$,*

$$|S_w(z) - uS_{w\alpha}(z) + u| \geq c.$$

Proof. The proof needs to be broken down into several cases. The only condition for K is

$$(1 + \delta^{-1})\frac{(p\rho)^{K/2}}{1 - p\rho} \leq c/2.$$

The analysis is not difficult; the reader is asked to provide details in Exercise 8.11.   ∎

These two lemmas allow us to bound from below the denominator of $M(z, u)$, which we need in order to analytically continue the latter. We establish this bound in the next two lemmas.

Lemma 8.3.7. *If $0 < r < 1$ then there exists $C > 0$ and an integer K_1 (both depending on r) such that*

$$|D_w(z) - u(D_{w\alpha}(z) - (1 - z))| \geq C \qquad (8.52)$$

for $|w| \geq K_1$ and $|z| \leq r$ (where, as before, $|u| \leq \delta^{-1}$).

Proof. Consider K and c as defined in Lemma 8.3.6; this tells us that, for all $|w| \geq K$, we have

$$|S_w(z) - uS_{w\alpha}(z) + u| \geq c \qquad (8.53)$$

for $|z| \leq \rho$. So, for $m =: |w| \geq K$, we have

$$|D_w(z) - u(D_{w\alpha}(z) - (1-z))| \geq (1-r)c - r^m p^m (1 - \delta^{-1} rp).$$

Note that $r^m p^m (1 - \delta^{-1} rp) \to 0$ as $m \to \infty$. Therefore, replacing K by a larger number K_1 if necessary, we can assume without loss of generality that $r^m p^m (1 - \delta^{-1} rp) \leq (1-r)c/2$. So, we define $C = (1-r)c/2$, and the result follows immediately. ∎

Lemma 8.3.8. *If $0 < r < 1$, then there exists $C > 0$ (depending on r) such that*

$$|D_w(z) - u(D_{w\alpha}(z) - (1-z))| \geq C \tag{8.54}$$

for $|z| \leq r$ (and, as before, $|u| \leq \delta^{-1}$).

Proof. Consider K_1 as defined in Lemma 8.3.7. Let C_0 denote the quantity C from Lemma 8.3.7. There are only finitely many values of w with $|w| < K_1$, say $w_1, \ldots, w_i$. For each such w_j, with $1 \leq j \leq i$, we note that $D_{w_j}(z) - u(D_{w_j\alpha}(z) - (1-z)) \neq 0$ for $|z| \leq r$ and $|u| \leq \delta^{-1}$, so that there exists $C_j > 0$ such that $|D_{w_j}(z) - u(D_{w_j\alpha}(z) - (1-z))| \geq C_j$ for all $|z| \leq r$ and $|u| \leq \delta^{-1}$. Finally, we define $C = \min\{C_0, C_1, \ldots, C_i\}$. ∎

Now we are in a position to prove that $M(z, u)$ can be analytically continued for u values beyond the unit disk.

Theorem 8.3.9. *The generating function $M(z, u)$ can be analytically continued for $|u| \leq \delta^{-1}$ and $|z| < 1$ with $\delta < 1$.*

Proof. Consider $|z| \leq r < 1$. We proved in Lemma 8.3.8 that there exists $C > 0$ depending on r such that, for all $|u| \leq \delta^{-1}$, we have

$$\frac{1}{|D_w(z) - u(D_{w\alpha}(z) - (1-z))|} \leq \frac{1}{C}.$$

Setting $u = 0$, we also have $|D_w(z)| \geq C$. Thus

$$|M(z, u)| \leq \frac{P(\beta)\delta^{-1}}{C^2} \sum_{\alpha \in \mathcal{A}} \sum_{w \in \mathcal{A}^*} P(w)|D_{w\alpha}(z) - (1-z)|.$$

Now we use Lemma 8.3.5. Consider w and α with

$$\max\{|S_w(\rho) - 1|, |S_{w\alpha}(\rho) - 1|\} \leq (\rho\delta)^m \theta$$

where, we recall, $m = |w|$. It follows immediately that

$$|D_{wa}(z) - (1 - z)| = |(1 - z)(S_{wa}(z) - 1) + z^{m+1}P(w)P(\alpha)|$$
$$\leq (1 + r)(\rho\delta)^m\theta + r^{m+1}p^m p = O(s^m),$$

where $s = \max\{\rho\delta, rp\}$. Now consider the other values of w and α. We have

$$|D_{wa}(z) - (1 - z)| = |(1 - z)(S_{wa}(z) - 1) + z^{m+1}P(w)P(\alpha)|$$
$$\leq \frac{(1 + r)p\rho}{1 - p\rho} + r^{m+1}p^m p \leq \frac{(1 + r)p\rho}{1 - p\rho} + 1,$$

so we define $C_1 = (1 + r)p\rho/(1 - p\rho + 1)$ to be a value which depends only on r (recall that r is fixed here). Thus

$$|M(z, u)| \leq \frac{P(\beta)\delta^{-1}}{C^2} \sum_{\alpha \in \mathcal{A}} \sum_{m \geq 0} \sum_{w \in \mathcal{A}^m} |P(w)(D_{wa}(z) - (1 - z))|$$

$$\leq \frac{P(\beta)\delta^{-1}}{C^2} \sum_{\alpha \in \mathcal{A}} \sum_{m \geq 0} |(1 - \delta^m\theta)O(s^m) + \delta^m\theta C_1|$$

$$\leq \frac{P(\beta)\delta^{-1}}{C^2} \sum_{\alpha \in \mathcal{A}} \sum_{m \geq 0} O(s^m) = O(1),$$

and this completes the proof of the theorem.   ■

In the final stage of our discussion we compare the generating functions $M(z, u)$ and $M^T(z, u)$, as we did in previous sections when analyzing the depth and size of a suffix tree. Define

$$Q(z, u) = M(z, u) - M^T(z, u). \tag{8.55}$$

Using the notation from (8.40) and (8.50), if we write

$$M_{w,\alpha}^T(z, u) = \frac{uP(\beta)P(w)}{1 - z(1 - P(w))} \frac{zP(w)P(\alpha)}{1 - z(1 + uP(w)P(\alpha) - P(w))},$$
$$M_{w,\alpha}(z, u) = \frac{uP(\beta)P(w)}{D_w(z)} \frac{D_{wa}(z) - (1 - z)}{D_w(z) - u(D_{wa}(z) - (1 - z))}, \tag{8.56}$$

then

$$Q(z, u) = \sum_{\substack{w \in \mathcal{A}^* \\ \alpha \in \mathcal{A}}} (M_{w,\alpha}(z, u) - M_{w,\alpha}^T(z, u)). \tag{8.57}$$

We also define $Q_n(u) = [z^n]Q(z, u)$. We denote the contribution to $Q_n(u)$ from a specific w and α as $Q_n^{(w,\alpha)}(u) = [z^n](M_{w,\alpha}(z, u) - M_{w,\alpha}^T(z, u))$. Then we observe that

$$Q_n^{(w,\alpha)}(u) = \frac{1}{2\pi i} \oint (M_{w,\alpha}(z, u) - M_{w,\alpha}^T(z, u)) \frac{dz}{z^{n+1}}, \tag{8.58}$$

where the path of integration is a circle about the origin with counterclockwise orientation. We define

$$I_{w,\alpha}(\rho, u) = \frac{1}{2\pi i} \int_{|z|=\rho} (M_{w,\alpha}(z, u) - M_{w,\alpha}^T(z, u)) \frac{dz}{z^{n+1}}. \qquad (8.59)$$

To analyze this integral, we apply a singularity analysis. For this we need to determine (for $|u| \le \delta^{-1}$) the zeros of $D_w(z) - u(D_{w\alpha}(z) - (1 - z))$ and in particular the zeros of $D_w(z)$, extending Lemma 8.1.8. The following lemma is easy to establish and the reader is asked to prove it in Exercise 8.12.

Lemma 8.3.10. *There exists an integer $K_2 \ge 1$ such that, for u fixed (with $|u| \le \delta^{-1}$) and $|w| \ge K_2$, there is exactly one root of $D_w(z) - u(D_{w\alpha}(z) - (1-z))$ in the closed disk $\{z \mid |z| \le \rho\}$.*

When $u = 0$, this lemma implies (for $|w| \ge K_2$) that $D_w(z)$ has exactly one root in the disk $\{z \mid |z| \le \rho\}$. Let A_w denote this root, and let $B_w = D_w'(A_w)$. Also, let $C_w(u)$ denote the root of $D_w(z) - u(D_{w\alpha}(z) - (1 - z))$ in the closed disk $\{z \mid |z| \le \rho\}$. Finally, we write

$$E_w(u) := \left(\frac{d}{dz} (D_w(z) - u(D_{w\alpha}(z) - (1 - z))) \right) \Bigg|_{z=C_w}$$

$$= D_w'(C_w) - u(D_{w\alpha}'(C_w) + 1).$$

Now we can analyze the integral in (8.59). By Cauchy's theorem, we observe that the contribution to $Q_n(u)$ from a specific w and α is exactly, after expanding the integral to a larger contour of radius ρ:

$$Q_n^{(w,\alpha)}(u) = I_{w,\alpha}(\rho, u) - \text{Res}_{z=A_w} \frac{M_{w,\alpha}(z, u)}{z^{n+1}} - \text{Res}_{z=C_w(u)} \frac{M_{w,\alpha}(z, u)}{z^{n+1}}$$

$$+ \text{Res}_{z=1/(1-P(w))} \frac{M_{w,\alpha}^T(z, u)}{z^{n+1}}$$

$$+ \text{Res}_{z=1/(1+uP(w)P(\alpha)-P(w))} \frac{M_{w,\alpha}^T(z, u)}{z^{n+1}}, \qquad (8.60)$$

where we write $\text{Res}_{z_0} f(z) := \text{Res}[f(z); z = z_0]$. To simplify this expression, note that

$$\text{Res}_{z=A_w} \frac{M_{w,\alpha}(z, u)}{z^{n+1}} = -\frac{P(\beta)P(w)}{B_w} \frac{1}{A_w^{n+1}},$$

$$\text{Res}_{z=C_w(u)} \frac{M_{w,\alpha}(z, u)}{z^{n+1}} = \frac{P(\beta)P(w)}{E_w(u)} \frac{1}{C_w(u)^{n+1}}, \qquad (8.61)$$

and

$$\mathrm{Res}_{z=1/(1-P(w))} \frac{M_{w,\alpha}^T(z,u)}{z^{n+1}} = P(\beta)P(w)(1-P(w))^n,$$

$$\mathrm{Res}_{z=1/(1+uP(w)P(\alpha)-P(w))} \frac{M_{w,\alpha}^T(z,u)}{z^{n+1}} = -P(\beta)P(w)(1+uP(w)$$
$$\times P(\alpha) - P(w))^n.$$

It follows from (8.60) that

$$Q_n^{(w,\alpha)}(u) = I_{w,\alpha}(\rho,u) + \frac{P(\beta)P(w)}{B_w}\frac{1}{A_w^{n+1}} - \frac{P(\beta)P(w)}{E_w(u)}\frac{1}{C_w(u)^{n+1}} \qquad (8.62)$$
$$+ P(\beta)P(w)(1-P(w))^n - P(\beta)P(w)(1+uP(w)P(\alpha)-P(w))^n.$$

We next determine the contribution of the $z = A_w$ terms of $M(z,u)$ and the $z = 1/(1-P(w))$ terms of $M^T(z,u)$ to the difference $Q_n(u) = [z^n](M(z,u) - M^T(z,u))$.

Lemma 8.3.11. *The $z = A_w$ terms and the $z = 1/(1-P(w))$ terms (for $|w| \geq K_2$) altogether have only an $O(n^{-\varepsilon})$ contribution to $Q_n(u)$, i.e.,*

$$\sum_{\substack{|w| \geq K_2 \\ \alpha \in \mathcal{A}}} \left(-\mathrm{Res}_{z=A_w} \frac{M_{w,\alpha}(z,u)}{z^{n+1}} + \mathrm{Res}_{z=1/(1-P(w))} \frac{M_{w,\alpha}^T(z,u)}{z^{n+1}} \right) = O(n^{-\varepsilon}),$$

for some $\varepsilon > 0$.

Proof. We define

$$f_w(x) = \frac{1}{A_w^{x+1}B_w} + (1-P(w))^x$$

for x real. So by (8.61) it suffices to prove that

$$\sum_{\substack{|w| \geq K_2 \\ \alpha \in \mathcal{A}}} P(\beta)P(w)f_w(x) = O(x^{-\varepsilon}). \qquad (8.63)$$

Now we proceed as in Section 8.1. Note that the left-hand side of (8.63) is absolutely convergent for all x. Also $\bar{f}_w(x) = f_w(x) - f_w(0)e^{-x}$ is exponentially decreasing when $x \to +\infty$ and is $O(x)$ when $x \to 0$ (notice that we utilize the $f_w(0)e^{-x}$ term in order to make sure that $\bar{f}_w(x) = O(x)$ when $x \to 0$; this provides a fundamental strip for the Mellin transform as in Section 8.1. From Table 7.1 we conclude that the Mellin transform

$$\bar{f}_w^*(s) = \int_0^\infty \bar{f}_w(x)x^{s-1}\,dx$$

is well defined for $\Re(s) > -1$, and that

$$\bar{f}_w^*(s) = \Gamma(s)\left(\frac{(\log A_w)^{-s} - 1}{A_w B_w} + (-\log(1 - P(w)))^{-s} - 1\right).$$

Recall now from (8.13) and (8.14) that

$$A_w = 1 + \frac{1}{S_w(1)}P(w) + O(P(w)^2),$$

$$B_w = -S_w(1) + \left(-\frac{2S_w'(1)}{S_w(1)} + m\right)P(w) + O(P(w)^2).$$

Hence we conclude that

$$(\log A_w)^{-s} = \left(\frac{P(w)}{S_w(1)}\right)^{-s}(1 + O(P(w))),$$

$$(-\log(1 - P(w)))^{-s} = P(w)^{-s}(1 + O(P(w)))$$

and

$$\frac{1}{A_w B_w} = -\frac{1}{S_w(1)} + O(|w|P(w)).$$

Therefore,

$$\bar{f}_w^*(s) = \Gamma(s)\left[\left(-\frac{1}{S_w(1)} + O(|w|P(w))\right)\left(\left(\frac{P(w)}{S_w(1)}\right)^{-s}(1 + O(P(w))) - 1\right)\right.$$

$$\left. + P(w)^{-s}(1 + O(P(w))) - 1\right]$$

$$= \Gamma(s)\left(P(w)^{-s}\left(-S_w(1)^{s-1} + 1 + O(|w|P(w))\right)\right.$$

$$\left. + \frac{1}{S_w(1)} - 1 + O(|w|P(w))\right).$$

We now define $g^*(s) = \sum_{\substack{|w| \geq K_2 \\ \alpha \in \mathcal{A}}} P(\beta)P(w)\bar{f}_w^*(s)$ and compute

$$g^*(s) = \sum_{\alpha \in \mathcal{A}} P(\beta) \sum_{|w| \geq K_2} P(w)\bar{f}_w^*(s)$$

$$= \sum_{\alpha \in \mathcal{A}} P(\beta)\Gamma(s) \sum_{m=K_2}^{\infty}\left(\sup\{q^{-\Re(s)}, 1\}\delta\right)^m O(1),$$

where the last equality is true because $1 \geq p^{-\Re(s)} \geq q^{-\Re(s)}$ when $\Re(s)$ is negative and $q^{-\Re(s)} \geq p^{-\Re(s)} \geq 1$ when $\Re(s)$ is positive. We always have $\delta < 1$ and $p > q$. Also, there exists $c > 0$ such that $q^{-c}\delta < 1$. Therefore, $g^*(s)$ is analytic in $\Re(s) \in (-1, c)$. Working in this strip, we choose ε with $0 < \varepsilon < c$. Then we have

$$\sum_{\substack{|w| \geq K_2 \\ \alpha \in \mathcal{A}}} P(\beta)P(w)f_w(x) = \frac{1}{2\pi i} \int_{\varepsilon-i\infty}^{\varepsilon+i\infty} g^*(s)x^{-s}\, ds + \sum_{\substack{|w| \geq K_2 \\ \alpha \in \mathcal{A}}} P(\beta)P(w)f_w(0)e^{-x}.$$

Majorizing under the integral, we see that the first term is $O(x^{-\varepsilon})$ since $g^*(s)$ is analytic in the strip $\Re(s) \in (-1, c)$ (and $-1 < \varepsilon < c$). The second term is $O(e^{-x})$. This completes the proof of the lemma. ∎

Now we bound the contribution to $Q_n(u)$ from the $C_w(u)$ terms of $M(z, u)$ and the $z = 1/(1 + uP(w)P(\alpha) - P(w))$ terms of $M^T(z, u)$.

Lemma 8.3.12. *The $C_w(u)$ terms and the $1/(1 + uP(w)P(\alpha) - P(w))$ terms (for $|w| \geq K_2$) altogether have only an $O(n^{-\varepsilon})$ contribution to $Q_n(u)$, for some $\varepsilon > 0$. More precisely,*

$$\sum_{\substack{|w| \geq K_2 \\ \alpha \in \mathcal{A}}} \left(-\mathrm{Res}_{z=C_w(u)}\frac{M_{w,\alpha}(z,u)}{z^{n+1}} + \mathrm{Res}_{z=1/(1+uP(w)P(\alpha)-P(w))}\frac{M^T_{w,\alpha}(z,u)}{z^{n+1}} \right)$$

$$= O(n^{-\varepsilon}).$$

Proof. The proof technique is the same as that for Lemma 8.3.11 above. ∎

Finally, we show that the $I_{w,\alpha}(\rho, u)$ terms in (8.62) have an $O(n^{-\varepsilon})$ contribution to $Q_n(u)$.

Lemma 8.3.13. *The $I_{w,\alpha}(\rho, u)$ terms (for $|w| \geq K_2$) altogether have only an $O(n^{-\varepsilon})$ contribution to $Q_n(u)$, for some $\varepsilon > 0$. More precisely,*

$$\sum_{\substack{|w| \geq K_2 \\ \alpha \in \mathcal{A}}} I_{w,\alpha}(\rho, u) = O(\rho^{-n}),$$

where $\rho > 1$.

Proof. Here we only sketch the proof. Recall that

$$I_{w,\alpha}(\rho, u) = \frac{1}{2\pi i} \int_{|z|=\rho} uP(\beta)P(w) \left(\frac{1}{D_w(z)} \frac{D_{w\alpha}(z) - (1-z)}{D_w(z) - u(D_{w\alpha}(z) - (1-z))} \right.$$
$$\left. - \frac{1}{1 - z(1 - P(w))} \frac{zP(w)P(\alpha)}{1 - z(1 + uP(w)P(\alpha) - P(w))} \right) \frac{dz}{z^{n+1}}.$$

In Lemma 8.3.10, K_2 was selected to be sufficiently large that

$$(\rho p)^m (1 - \delta^{-1}\rho p) \leq (\rho - 1)c/2.$$

Thus, by setting $C_1 = (\rho - 1)c/2$, we have

$$\frac{1}{|D_w(z) - u(D_{wa}(z) - (1 - z))|} \leq \frac{1}{C_1}$$

and

$$\frac{1}{|D_w(z)|} \leq \frac{1}{C_1}.$$

Also

$$1/|1 - z(1 - P(w))| \leq 1/c_2,$$
$$1/|1 - z(1 + uP(w)P(\alpha) - P(w))| \leq 1/c_2.$$

So, we obtain

$$|I_{w,\alpha}(\rho, u)| = O(\rho^{-n})P(w)(S_{w\alpha}(\rho) - 1) + O(\rho^{-n})P(w)O((p\rho)^m).$$

Thus, by Lemma 8.3.5,

$$\sum_{\alpha \in \mathcal{A}} \sum_{|w|=m} |I_{w,\alpha}(\rho, u)| = O(\rho^{-n})O((\rho\delta)^m).$$

We conclude that

$$\sum_{\substack{|w| \geq K_2 \\ \alpha \in \mathcal{A}}} |I_{w,\alpha}(\rho, u)| = O(\rho^{-n}),$$

and the lemma follows.   ∎

Finally, we consider the contribution to $Q_n(u)$ from small words w. Basically, we prove that for small $|w| \leq K_2$ the contribution to $Q_n(u)$ from those words w is very small.

Lemma 8.3.14. *The terms* $\sum_{\substack{|w| < K_2 \\ \alpha \in \mathcal{A}}} (M_{w,\alpha}(z, u) - M_{w,\alpha}^T(z, u))$ *altogether have only* $O(n^{-\varepsilon})$ *contribution to* $Q_n(u)$.

Proof. Let D_n denote the depth of the $(n + 1)$th insertion in a suffix tree. Similarly, let D_n^T denote the depth of the $(n + 1)$th insertion in a trie built over $n + 1$ independent strings. Therefore,

$$[z^n] \sum_{\substack{|w| < K_2 \\ \alpha \in \mathcal{A}}} (M_{w,\alpha}(z, u) - M_{w,\alpha}^T(z, u))$$

$$= \sum_{i < K_2} \sum_{k=1}^{n} \left(P(M_n = k \text{ and } D_n = i) - P(M_n^T = k \text{ and } D_n^T = i) \right) u^k.$$

Noting that $P(M_n = k$ and $D_n = i) \leq P(D_n = i)$ and that $P(M_n^T = k$ and $D_n^T = i) \leq P(D_n^T = i)$, it follows that

$$[z^n] \sum_{\substack{|w| < K_2 \\ \alpha \in \mathcal{A}}} |M_{w,\alpha}(z, u) - M_{w,\alpha}^T(z, u)| \leq \sum_{i < K_2} \sum_{k=1}^{n} \left(P(D_n = i) + P(D_n^T = i) \right) |u|^k.$$

(8.64)

In Section 7.3.1 we prove that the *typical* depth D_n^T in a trie built over n independent strings is asymptotically normal with mean $h^{-1} \log n$ and variance $\Theta(\log n)$. In Theorem 8.1.3 of this chapter we extended this result to suffix trees. Therefore, we conclude that

$$[z^n] \sum_{\substack{|w| < K_2 \\ \alpha \in \mathcal{A}}} |M_{w,\alpha}(z, u) - M_{w,\alpha}^T(z, u)| = O(n^{-\varepsilon}),$$

since K_2 is a constant. This completes the proof of the lemma. ∎

All contributions to (8.62) have now been analyzed. We are finally ready to summarize our results. Combining the last four lemmas, we see that $Q_n(u) = O(n^{-\varepsilon})$ uniformly for $|u| \leq \delta^{-1}$, where $\delta^{-1} > 1$. For ease of notation, we define $b = \delta^{-1}$. Finally, one more application of Cauchy's theorem yields

$$P(M_n = k) - P(M_n^T = k) = [u^k z^n]Q(z, u) = [u^k]Q_n(u) = \frac{1}{2\pi i} \int_{|u|=b} \frac{Q_n(u)}{u^{k+1}} \, du,$$

and $Q_n(u) = O(n^{-\varepsilon})$ implies

$$|P(M_n = k) - P(M_n^T = k)| \leq \frac{1}{|2\pi i|} 2\pi b \frac{O(n^{-\varepsilon})}{b^{k+1}} = O(n^{-\varepsilon} b^{-k}).$$

Theorem 8.3.2 holds.

In summary, it follows that M_n and M_n^T have asymptotically the same distribution. Theorem 7.3.6 gives the asymptotic distribution of M_n^T. As a result, Theorem 8.3.2 follows immediately, and we conclude that M_n has the logarithmic series distribution, i.e., for a binary alphabet,

$$P(M_n = j) = \frac{p^j q + q^j p}{jh}$$

(plus some small fluctuations if $\ln p / \ln q$ is rational). Theorem 8.3.1 is finally proved.

8.4. Exercises

8.1   Extend Theorem 8.1.2 for Markov sources.

8.2   Prove (8.12) and extend it to Markov sources (see Apostolico and Sz-
       pankowski (1992)).

8.3   Consider a *compact* suffix tree in which all unary nodes (i.e., nodes with
       one child) are skipped as in a PATRICIA trie. Prove that also in this
       case the depth and the average size resemble the depth and average size
       of PATRICIA tries built from independent strings.

8.4   Consider a Markov source that generates a sequence X of length n over
       a finite alphabet $\mathcal{A}$. This sequence enters a binary symmetric channel
       that alters each symbol with probability ε. The output sequence Y
       represents a sequence generated by a *hidden Markov process*. Analyze
       the depth of a suffix tree built over Y, and compare it with a suffix tree
       built from X.

8.5   Let X and Y be two sequences independently generated by a memoryless
       source. Build two suffix trees from X and Y. Estimate the average
       number of common nodes in these two suffix trees. What would be
       the difference if X and Y were generated by two different memoryless
       sources?

8.6   Derive the probability distribution (8.21) of the typical depth in a finite
       suffix tree, that is, prove that

$$P(D_n^{FS} \geq k) = \frac{1}{n} \sum_{w \in \mathcal{A}^k} (n + 1 - |w|)^+ P(w) - N'_{n,w}(0)$$

       where $a^+ = \max\{0, a\}$.

8.7   Prove that $g_n(u)$ as defined in (8.22) is $O(n^{1-\varepsilon})$.

8.8   Establish the estimate (8.23).

8.9   Prove Theorem 8.3.1 for a general alphabet. Attempt to find the limiting
       distribution of the multiplicity parameter M_n for Markovian sources.

8.10   Prove (8.48).

8.11   Prove Lemma 8.3.5 (see Ward (2005) for a detailed proof.)

8.12   Prove Lemma 8.3.10.

8.13   Establish the asymptotic moments of the multiplicity parameter M_n of
       a suffix tree.

8.14   Consider the number of longest phrases of the LZ'77 algorithm for such
       Markov sources. In other words, consider the multiplicity parameter M_n
       for Markov sources. Prove that

$$\mathbf{E}[M_n] \sim \frac{1}{h},$$

where h is the entropy rate of the underlying Markov source. Then find the asymptotic distribution of M_n.

Bibliographical notes

Suffix trees are discussed in a myriad papers and books. We mention here Crochemore and Rytter (1994) and Gusfield (1997) (see also Apostolico (1985)). A probabilistic analysis of suffix trees can be found in Apostolico and Szpankowski (1992), Blumer, Ehrenfeucht, and Haussler (1989), Fayolle (2003), Devroye, Szpankowski, and Rais (1992), Marsan and Sagot (2000), Szpankowski (1993a), and Szpankowski (1993b). Suffix trees are often used for algorithms on words: see Bieganski, Riedl, Carlis, and Retzel (1994), Farach (1997), Giegerich, Kurtz, and Stoye (1999), Kärkkäinen and Sanders (2003), and Sagot (1998).

Sections 8.1 and 8.2 are based on Jacquet and Szpankowski (1994). In particular, Theorems 8.1.2 and 8.2.2 were proved there. However, our presentation follows that discussed in Chapter 7 of Lothaire (2005). An extension to Markov sources was proposed in Fayolle and Ward (2005).

Section 8.3 was based on Ward (2005) and Lonardi et al. (2007). The extension to a finite alphabet is due to Gaither and Ward (2013). It may be observed that suffix trees appear in analyses of data compression schemes, especially Lempel–Ziv'77; see for example Wyner and Ziv (1989), Wyner (1997), Yang and Kieffer (1998), Ziv and Lempel (1978) and Ziv and Merhav (1993).

CHAPTER 9

Lempel–Ziv'78 Compression Algorithm

The Lempel–Ziv'78 (LZ'78) algorithm is a *dictionary-based* scheme that partitions a sequence into phrases or blocks of variable size such that a new phrase is the shortest substring not seen in the past as a phrase. Every such phrase is encoded by the index of its prefix appended by a symbol; thus the LZ'78 code contains the pairs (`pointer`, `symbol`). The LZ'78 algorithm and its pseudo-code were discussed in Chapter 6. In Section 9.1 we provide some additional details and introduce some measures of performance, such as the number of phrases and the redundancy, which we will study in this chapter.

As observed in Chapter 6, a next phrase in the LZ'78 scheme can be easily found by building the associated parsing tree, which in this case is a digital search tree. For example, the string 11001010001000100 of length 17 is parsed as (1)(10)(0)(101)(00)(01)(000)(100), and this process is shown in Figure 9.1 using the digital search tree structure. The root contains the empty phrase; to emphasize it we draw it as a square. All other phrases of the Lempel–Ziv parsing algorithm are stored in internal nodes (represented as circles). When a new phrase is created, the search starts at the root and proceeds down the tree as directed by the input symbols in exactly the same manner as in digital tree construction. The search is completed when a branch is made from an existing tree node to a new node that has not been visited before. Then the edge and the new node are added to the tree. The corresponding phrase is just a concatenation of the symbols leading from the root to this node, which also stores the phrase.

We should observe the differences between the digital search trees discussed in Chapter 6 and that described above. For the Lempel–Ziv scheme we consider a word of *fixed length*, say n, while in Chapters 6 and 7 we dealt with a fixed number of strings, say m, resulting in a digital tree consisting of exactly m nodes. Looking at Figure 9.1, we conclude that the number of nodes in the associated digital tree is exactly equal to the number of phrases generated by the Lempel–Ziv algorithm.

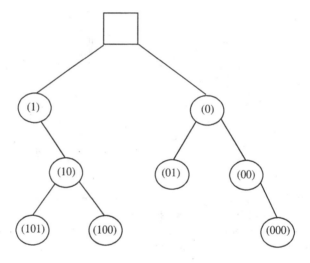

Figure 9.1. A digital tree representation of the Lempel–Ziv parsing of the string 11001010001000100 into phrases (1)(10)(0)(101) $\cdots$.

9.1. Description of the algorithm

For the reader's convenience we will succinctly describe the LZ'78 algorithm again. Let a text w be generated over an alphabet $\mathcal{A}$, and let $\mathcal{T}(w)$ be the associated digital search tree constructed by the algorithm, as illustrated in Figure 9.1. Each node in $\mathcal{T}(w)$ corresponds to a phrase in the parsing algorithm. Let $L(w)$ be the (total) path length in $\mathcal{T}(w)$, that is, the sum of all paths from the root to all nodes (i.e., the sum of the phrases, which is also the text length). We have $L(w) = |w|$ if all phrases are full. If we know the order of node creation in the tree $\mathcal{T}(w)$ then we can reconstruct the original text w; otherwise we construct a string of the same universal type, as discussed in Seroussi (2006b) (see also Knessl and Szpankowski (2005)).

The compression code $C(w)$ is a description of $\mathcal{T}(w)$, node by node in order of creation; each node is identified by a pointer to its parent node in the tree and the symbol that labels the edge linking it to the parent node. The encoding pseudo-code is presented below.

procedure ENCODING(w)
  $\mathcal{T} \leftarrow$ TREE(0)
  $C \leftarrow$ **nil**$k \leftarrow 1$
  while $w \neq$ **nil**
  do $\begin{cases} x \leftarrow \text{READ}(w) \\ \mathcal{T}' \leftarrow \mathcal{T} \\ \textbf{while } \mathcal{T}'.x \neq \textbf{nil} \& w \neq \textbf{nil} \\ \quad \textbf{do } \begin{cases} \mathcal{T}' \leftarrow \mathcal{T}'.x \\ x \leftarrow \text{READ}(w) \end{cases} \\ \textbf{if } \mathcal{T}'.x = \textbf{nil} \\ \quad \textbf{then } \mathcal{T}'.x \leftarrow \text{TREE}(k) \\ \quad \textbf{else } \mathcal{T}'.\$ \leftarrow \text{TREE}(k) \\ k \leftarrow k+1 \end{cases}$
  return $(\mathcal{T})$

The decoding pseudo-code is presented next. Notice how simple it is to implement. The above procedure returns the array wt of phrases from which the text w can be fully reconstructed. Notice that the code is self-consistent and does not need *a priori* knowledge of the text length, since the length is a simple function of the node sequence.

procedure DECODING(C)
  $k \leftarrow 0$
  $wt[k] \leftarrow$ **nil**
  $k \leftarrow k + 1$
  EXTRACT(C, k)
  while $(a \neq$ **nil**$)$
       $\Bigg\{$
  do
      $parent \leftarrow$ NUMBER$(a[1])$
      if $(a[2] = \$)$
        then $wt[k] \leftarrow wt[parent]$
        else $wt[k] \leftarrow wt[parent].a[2]$
      $k \leftarrow k + 1$
      EXTRACT(C, k)
  return (wt)

Example 9.1.1. As an example, consider the string *ababbbabbaaaba* over the alphabet $\mathcal{A} = \{a, b\}$, which is parsed and coded as follows:

Phrase No.	1	2	3	4	5	6	7
Sequence:	(a)	(b)	(ab)	(bb)	(abb)	(aa)	(aba)
Code:	0a	0b	1b	2b	3b	1a	3a

Observe that we need $\lceil \log_2 7 \rceil$ bits to code a phrase and two bits to code a symbol, so in total for seven phrases we need 28 bits.

Now, we are in a position to discuss the performance of the LZ'78 compression scheme. Its performance depends on the number of phrases, but the ultimate goal is to minimize the compression code, and we discuss this next. The pointer to the kth node requires at most $\lceil \log_2 k \rceil$ bits, and the next symbol costs $\lceil \log_2 |\mathcal{A}| \rceil$ bits. We will simply assume that the total pointer cost is $\lceil \log_2(k) \rceil + \lceil \log_2 |\mathcal{A}| \rceil$ bits. Figure 9.2 shows the phrase sequence of the first 100 phrases of a random binary text with $p_a = 0.9$. It spans 973 characters.

In summary, the compressed code length is

$$|C(w)| = \sum_{k=1}^{M(w)} \lceil \log_2(k) \rceil + \lceil \log_2(|\mathcal{A}|) \rceil, \tag{9.1}$$

where $M(w)$ is the number of full phrases needed to parse w (we shall neglect the boundary effect of the last, usually not full, phrase). Clearly, $M(w)$ is also

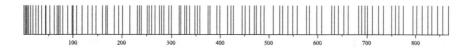

Figure 9.2. The phrase sequence of the first 100 phrases of a binary random text with $p_a = 0.9$.

the number of nodes in the associated tree $\mathcal{T}(w)$. We conclude from (9.1) that

$$|C(w)| = \xi_2(M(w)),$$

where we define

$$\xi_Q(x) = x\lceil\log_Q(|\mathcal{A}|)\rceil + \sum_{0 < k \leq x} \lceil\log_Q(k)\rceil \tag{9.2}$$

for any integer Q and real x. Notice that $\xi_Q(M(w))$ is the code length in a Q-ary alphabet. Actually, a different implementation may add $O(M(w))$ to the code length without changing our asymptotic findings. To simplify, we shall assume throughout that

$$|C(w)| = M(w)\left(\log(M(w)) + \log(|\mathcal{A}|)\right). \tag{9.3}$$

Using a natural logarithm simply means that we are measuring the quantities of information in nat units. In Figure 9.3 we present simulation results for the code length vs. the number of phrases. It confirms (9.3). Thus our goal is to understand the behavior of the number of phrases $M(w)$ when w is generated by a memoryless source.

9.2. Number of phrases and redundancy of LZ'78

Let n be a nonnegative integer. We denote by M_n the number of phrases $M(w)$ and by C_n the code length $C(w)$ when the original text w is of fixed length n. We shall assume throughout that the text is generated by a memoryless source over a finite alphabet $\mathcal{A}$ such that the entropy rate is $h = -\sum_{a \in \mathcal{A}} p_a \log p_a > 0$, where p_a is the probability of symbol $a \in \mathcal{A}$. We respectively define the *compression rate*

$$\rho_n = \frac{C_n}{n}$$

and the *redundancy*

$$r_n = \rho_n - h.$$

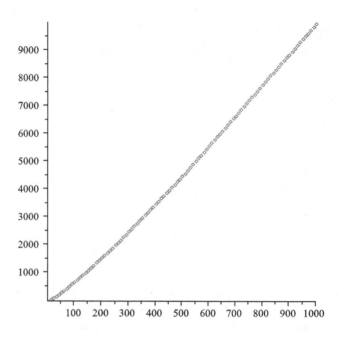

Figure 9.3. Code length as a function of the number m of phrases.

In Chapter 7 we defined $h_2 = \sum_{a \in \mathcal{A}} p_a (\log p_a)^2$ and

$$\eta = -\sum_{k \geq 2} \frac{\sum_{a \in \mathcal{A}} p_a^k \log p_a}{1 - \sum_{a \in \mathcal{A}} p_a^k}. \tag{9.4}$$

Finally, we introduce three functions over integer m:

$$\beta(m) = \frac{h_2}{2h} + \gamma - 1 - \eta + \Delta_1(\log m), \tag{9.5}$$

$$+ \frac{1}{m} \left(\log m + \frac{h_2}{2h} + \gamma - \eta - \sum_{a \in \mathcal{A}} \log p_a - \frac{1}{2} \right),$$

$$v(m) = \frac{m}{h} \left(\frac{h_2 - h^2}{h^2} \log m + c_2 + \Delta_2(\log m) \right), \tag{9.6}$$

$$\ell(m) = \frac{m}{h} \left(\log m + \beta(m) \right), \tag{9.7}$$

where $\gamma = 2.718 \ldots$ is the Euler constant, c_2 is another constant, and $\Delta_1(x)$ and

$\Delta_2(x)$ are periodic functions when the $\log p_a$ for $a \in \mathcal{A}$ are *rationally related*; otherwise $\Delta_1(x)$ and $\Delta_2(x)$ converge to zero as $x \to \infty$. For detailed information about these functions the reader is referred to Theorem 7.2.10 and Remark 7.2.12 of Chapter 7.

The main goal of this chapter is to characterize the probabilistic behavior of the number of phrases M_n. We start with the following result, where we establish the mean, the variance, and the central limit theorem for M_n. The proof is delayed until Section 9.4.

Theorem 9.2.1. *Consider the LZ'78 algorithm over a sequence of length n generated by a memoryless source. The number of phrases M_n has mean $\mathbf{E}[M_n]$ and variance $\mathrm{Var}[M_n]$ satisfying*

$$\mathbf{E}[M_n] = \ell^{-1}(n) + o(n^{1/2}/\log n) \tag{9.8}$$

$$= \frac{nh}{\log \ell^{-1}(n) + \beta(\ell^{-1}(n))} + o(n^{1/2}/\log n)$$

$$\sim \frac{nh}{\log n},$$

$$\mathrm{Var}[M_n] \sim \frac{v(\ell^{-1}(n))}{(\ell'(\ell^{-1}(n)))^2} \sim \frac{(h_2 - h^2)n}{\log^2 n}, \tag{9.9}$$

where $\ell(m)$ and $v(m)$ are defined in (9.7) and (9.6), respectively. Furthermore, the normalized number of phrases converges in distribution and moments to the the standard normal distribution $N(0,1)$. More precisely, for any given real x

$$\lim_{n \to \infty} P(M_n < \mathbf{E}[M_n] + x\sqrt{\mathrm{Var}[M_n]}) = \Phi(x) \tag{9.10}$$

where

$$\Phi(x) = \frac{1}{\sqrt{2\pi}} \int_{-\infty}^{x} e^{-t^2/2} dt.$$

In addition, for all nonnegative k,

$$\lim_{n \to \infty} \mathbf{E}\left[\left(\frac{M_n - \mathbf{E}[M_n]}{\sqrt{\mathrm{Var}[M_n]}}\right)^k\right] = \mu_k \tag{9.11}$$

where

$$\mu_k = \begin{cases} 0 & k \ odd \\ \frac{k!}{2^{k/2}(k/2)!} & k \ even \end{cases} \tag{9.12}$$

are the moments of $N(0,1)$.

We next consider the large and moderate deviation results for M_n, which we will prove in Section 9.4.

Theorem 9.2.2. *Consider the LZ'78 algorithm over a sequence of length n generated by a memoryless source.*

(i) [*Large deviations*]. *For all $1/2 < \delta < 1$ there exist $\varepsilon > 0$, $B > 0$, and $\beta > 0$ such that, for all $y > 0$,*

$$P(|M_n - \mathbf{E}[M_n]| > yn^\delta) \leq A \exp\left(-\beta n^\varepsilon \frac{y}{(1 + n^{-\varepsilon}y)^\delta}\right)$$

for some $A > 0$.

(ii) [*Moderate deviation*]. *There exists $B > 0$ such that*

$$P(|M_n - \mathbf{E}[M_n]| \geq x\sqrt{\mathrm{Var}[M_n]}) \leq Be^{-\frac{x^2}{2}}$$

for all nonnegative real $x < An^\delta$ with $\delta < 1/6$.

Using these large deviation results, we conclude that the average compression rate converges to the entropy rate. Furthermore, our large deviation results allow us also to estimate the average redundancy

$$\mathbf{E}[r_n] = \frac{\mathbf{E}[C_n]}{n} - h,$$

and its limiting distribution when $n \to \infty$. We formulate these results precisely in the next theorem.

Theorem 9.2.3. *The average compression rate converges to the entropy rate, that is,*

$$\lim_{n\to\infty} \frac{\mathbf{E}[C_n]}{n} = h. \tag{9.13}$$

More precisely, for all $1/2 < \delta < 1$,

$$\mathbf{E}[C_n] = \ell^{-1}(n)(\log \ell^{-1}(n) + \log |\mathcal{A}|) + O(n^\delta \log n)$$
$$= \mathbf{E}[M_n](\log \mathbf{E}[M_n] + \log |\mathcal{A}|) + o(n^{1/2+\varepsilon})$$

and

$$\mathrm{Var}[C_n] \sim \mathrm{Var}[M_n](\log \mathbf{E}[M_n] + \log |\mathcal{A}| + 1)^2$$
$$\sim (h_2 - h^2)n.$$

Furthermore,

$$\frac{C_n - \mathbf{E}[C_n]}{\sqrt{\mathrm{Var}[C_n]}} \overset{d}{\to} N(0,1)$$

and also in moments, where $N(0,1)$ represents the standard normal distribution.

Proof. Let $\mu_n = \mathbf{E}[M_n]$ and $\sigma_n = \sqrt{\mathrm{Var}(M_n)}$. Also define

$$g(y) = y(\log|\mathcal{A}| + \log y).$$

Notice that $C_n = g(M_n)$. Clearly, for any fixed $x > 0$

$$P(M_n \geq \mu_n + x\sigma_n) = P(g(M_n) \geq g(\mu_n + x\sigma_n)). \qquad (9.14)$$

Using a Taylor expansion we have

$$g(\mu_n + x\sigma_n) = g(\mu_n) + x\sigma_n g'(\mu_n) + O\left(\frac{(x\sigma_n)^2}{\mu_n}\right), \qquad (9.15)$$

where

$$g'(y) = 1 + \log|\mathcal{A}| + \log y.$$

Given Theorem 9.2.1 we conclude that

$$\lim_{n\to\infty} P(M_n \geq \mu_n + x\sigma_n) = \Phi(x),$$

and then by (9.14)–(9.15) we find that

$$P(C_n \geq g(\mu_n + x\sigma_n)) = P\left(M_n \geq \mu_n + x\sigma_n g'(\mu_n)\left(1 + O\left(\frac{x\sigma_n}{\mu_n g'(\mu_n)}\right)\right)\right),$$

which converges to $\Phi(x)$ since

$$\Phi\left(x + O\left(\frac{x^2\sigma_n}{\mu_n g'(\mu_n)}\right)\right) = \Phi(x) + O(n^{-1/2+\varepsilon}).$$

In other words,

$$\lim_{n\to\infty} P\left(C_n \leq \mu_n(\log\mu_n + \log|\mathcal{A}|) + x\sigma_n(\log\mu_n + \log|\mathcal{A}| + 1)\right) = \Phi(x).$$

Via a similar analysis we find that

$$\lim_{n\to\infty} P\left(C_n \leq \mu_n(\log\mu_n + \log|\mathcal{A}|) - x\sigma_n(\log\mu_n + \log|\mathcal{A}| + 1)\right) = \Phi(x).$$

Thus, the random variable

$$\frac{C_n - g(\mu_n)}{\sigma_n g'(\mu_n)}$$

tends to the normal distribution in probability.

In order to conclude the convergence in moments, we use the moderate deviation result. Observe that by Theorem 9.2.4, to be proved next, the normalized random variable satisfies

$$P\left(\left|\frac{C_n - g(\mu_n)}{\sigma_n g'(\mu_n)}\right| \geq x\right) \leq Be^{-x^2/2}$$

for $x = O(n^\delta)$, when $\delta < 1/6$. Thus

$$\frac{C_n - g(\mu_n)}{\sigma_n g'(\mu_n)}$$

has bounded moments. Indeed, we have for $x = n^\varepsilon$, for $\varepsilon < 1/6$,

$$P\left(\left|\frac{C_n - g(\mu_n)}{\sigma_n g'(\mu_n)}\right| \geq n^\varepsilon\right) \leq Be^{-n^{2\varepsilon}/2}.$$

Since $\sqrt{2n} \leq M_n \leq n$, we conclude that

$$g(\sqrt{n}) \leq g(M_n) \leq g(n) = O(n \log n).$$

Therefore, for all integer k,

$$\mathbf{E}\left[\left|\frac{C_n - g(\mu_n)}{\sigma_n g'(\mu_n)}\right|^k\right] = 2k \int_0^\infty x^{k-1} P\left(\left|\frac{C_n - g(\mu_n)}{\sigma_n g'(\mu_n)}\right| \geq x\right) dx$$

$$\leq 2k \int_0^{n^\varepsilon} x^{k-1} e^{-Bx^2/2} dx + O(n^k \log^k n) e^{-n^{2\varepsilon}/2} = O(1).$$

In summary, the random variable

$$\frac{C_n - g(\mu_n)}{\sigma_n g'(\mu_n)} = \frac{C_n - \mu_n(\log \mu_n + \log|\mathcal{A}|)}{\sigma_n(\log \mu_n + \log|\mathcal{A}| + 1)}$$

has bounded moments. Therefore, by virtue of the dominated convergence and the convergence to the normal distribution

$$\lim_{n \to \infty} \mathbf{E}\left[\frac{C_n - g(\mu_n)}{\sigma_n g'(\mu_n)}\right] = 0$$

$$\lim_{n \to \infty} \mathbf{E}\left[\frac{C_n - g(\mu_n)}{\sigma_n g'(\mu_n)}\right]^2 = 1.$$

In other words, for some $\varepsilon > 0$

$$\mathbf{E}[C_n] = g(\mu_n) + o(n^{-1/2+\varepsilon}) \tag{9.16}$$

$$\mathrm{Var}[C_n] \sim \mathrm{Var}[M_n](\log \mu_n + \log |\mathcal{A}| + 1)^2 \tag{9.17}$$

which proves our variance estimate. ∎

In order to establish the limiting distribution for the redundancy we also need the corresponding large deviation results for the code length C_n.

Theorem 9.2.4. *Consider the LZ'78 algorithm over a memoryless source.*

(i) [Large deviations] *For all $1/2 < \delta < 1$ there exist $\varepsilon > 0$, $B > 0$, and $\beta > 0$ such that, for all $y > 0$,*

$$P(|C_n - \mathbf{E}[C_n]| > yn^\delta \log(n/\log n)) \leq A\exp\left(-\beta n^\varepsilon \frac{y}{(1 + n^{-\varepsilon}y)^\delta}\right) \tag{9.18}$$

for some $A > 0$.
(ii) [Moderate deviation] *There exists $B > 0$ such that for n*

$$P(|C_n - \mathbf{E}[C_n]| \geq x\sqrt{\mathrm{Var}[C_n]}) \leq Be^{-\frac{x^2}{2}} \tag{9.19}$$

for all nonnegative real $x < An^\delta$ with $\delta < 1/6$.

Proof. We start with the moderate deviation result. From Theorem 9.2.2 we know that for $x \leq An^{1/6}$ and some $A, B > 0$ we have

$$P(M_n \geq \mu_n + x\sigma_n) \leq Be^{-x^2/2}.$$

As before we write $g(x) = x(\log |\mathcal{A}| + \log x)$ and note that $g(M_n) = C_n$. We also have

$$P(g(M_n) \geq g(\mu_n + x\sigma_n)) \leq Be^{-x^2/2}.$$

Since

$$g(\mu_n + x\sigma_n) = g(\mu_n) + g'(\mu_n)\sigma_n x\left(1 + O\left(\frac{x\sigma_n}{\mu_n g'(\mu_n)}\right)\right)$$

we arrive at

$$P\left(g(M_n) \geq g(\mu_n) + x\sigma_n g'(\mu_n)\left(1 + O\left(\frac{x\sigma_n}{g'(\mu_n)\mu_n}\right)\right)\right) \leq Be^{-x^2/2}.$$

However, for $x = O(n^{1/6})$

$$x\frac{\sigma_n}{g'(\mu_n)\mu_n} \leq An^{1/6}\frac{\sigma_n}{g'(\mu_n)\mu_n} = O(n^{-1/3}) \to 0,$$

hence

$$P\left(g(M_n) \geq g(\mu_n) + x\sigma_n g'(\mu_n)\right) = P(g(M_n) \geq g(\mu_n) + \sigma_n x(1 + O(n^{-1/3})))$$
$$\leq B e^{-x^2/2(1+O(n^{-1/3}))}$$
$$\leq B' e^{-x^2/2}$$

for some $B' > 0$. Therefore, from (9.16) and (9.17) we conclude that

$$P(C_n > \mathbf{E}[C_n] + x\sqrt{\mathrm{Var}[C_n]}) \leq B'' e^{-x^2/2}$$

and similarly

$$P(C_n < \mathbf{E}[C_n] - x\sqrt{\mathrm{Var}[C_n]}) \leq B'' e^{-x^2/2}$$

for some $B'' > B'$, where B'' absorbs the asymptotics of (9.16) and (9.17).

We now turn our attention to the large deviation result. Since $M_n \leq n$, we observe that if $\mu_n \leq z \leq n$ then

$$g(z) \leq g(\mu_n) + (z - \mu_n)g'(n).$$

Thus, for y such that $\mu_n + yn^\delta \leq n$,

$$g(M_n) \geq g(\mu_n) + yn^\delta g'(n) \Rightarrow g(M_n) \geq g(\mu_n + yn^\delta) \Rightarrow M_n \geq \mu_n + yn^\delta.$$

Thus by Theorem 9.2.2(i) we obtain on the one hand

$$P(g(M_n) \geq g(\mu_n) + yn^\delta g'(n)) \leq A \exp\left(-\beta n^\varepsilon \frac{y}{(1 + n^{-\varepsilon}y)^\delta}\right);$$

The result also holds for $\mu_n + yn^\delta > n$ since $P(M_n > n) = 0$. On the other hand, for $\sqrt{2n} \leq v \leq \mu_n$ we have $g(v) \geq g(\mu_n) + (v - \mu_n)g'(\mu_n)$. Thus

$$g(M_n) \leq g(\mu_n) - yn^\delta g'(\mu_n) \Rightarrow g(M_n) \leq g(\mu_n - yn^\delta) \Rightarrow M_n \geq \mu_n - yn^\delta.$$

Again by Theorem 9.2.2(i),

$$P(g(M_n) \geq g(\mu_n) - yn^\delta g'(\mu_n)) \leq A \exp\left(-\beta n^\varepsilon \frac{y}{(1 + n^{-\varepsilon}y)^\delta}\right).$$

Since $g'(\mu_n)$ and $g'(n)$ are both $O(\log n)$, the order n^δ is not changed in the large deviation result.   ∎

The next finding is a direct consequence of Theorems 9.2.3 and 9.2.4.

Corollary 9.2.5. *The redundancy rate r_n satisfies, for all $1/2 < \delta < 1$,*

$$\mathbf{E}[r_n] = \frac{\mathbf{E}[C_n]}{n} - h$$

$$= h\frac{\log(|\mathcal{A}|) - \beta(\ell^{-1}(n))}{\log \ell^{-1}(n) + \beta(\ell^{-1}(n))} + O(n^{\delta-1}\log n)$$

$$\sim h\frac{\log(|\mathcal{A}|) - \beta\left(hn/\log n\right)}{\log n}, \tag{9.20}$$

and

$$\mathrm{Var}[r_n] \sim \frac{h_2 - h^2}{n}.$$

Furthermore,

$$\frac{r_n - \mathbf{E}[r_n]}{\sqrt{\mathrm{Var}[r_n]}} \xrightarrow{d} N(0,1)$$

and the convergence also holds in moments.

Proof. We will deal here only with $\mathbf{E}[r_n]$ since the rest is a direct consequence of previous findings. We observe that the above Corollary follows from a trivial derivation:

$$\mathbf{E}[r_n] + O(n^{\delta-1}) = \frac{\ell^{-1}(n)(\log(\ell^{-1}(n)) + \log|\mathcal{A}|) - nh}{n}$$

$$= \frac{\ell^{-1}(n)\log|\mathcal{A}| + \ell^{-1}(n)\log\ell^{-1}(n) - h\ell(\ell^{-1}(n))}{n}$$

$$= \frac{\ell^{-1}(n)}{n}\left(\log|\mathcal{A}| - \beta(\ell^{-1}(n))\right),$$

where we have used the fact that $\ell(\ell^{-1}(n)) = n$, by the definition of the inverse function and that

$$h\ell(\ell^{-1}(n)) = \ell^{-1}\log\ell^{-1}(n) + \beta(\ell^{-1}(n))$$

by the definition of $\ell(n)$. ∎

In Figure 9.4 we show experimental histograms of r_n for different values of n. We see that when n increases the mean of r_n decreases, in theory as $1/\log n$. However, the variance decreases much faster, as $1/n$.

9.3. From Lempel–Ziv to digital search tree

In this section we make a connection between the Lempel–Ziv algorithm and digital search trees, using a renewal theory argument. In particular, we prove

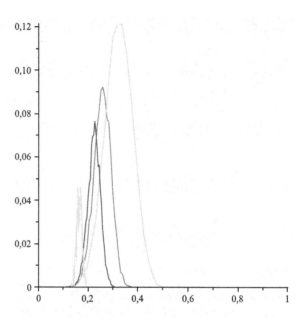

Figure 9.4. Simulation of the redundancy distribution for (right to left) $n = 400$, $n = 1000$, $n = 2000$, and $n = 10000$, with $p_a = 0.9$.

here more precise results for moments and distributions (i.e., the CLT and the large deviations) for the path length in a digital search tree. We may, therefore, view this section as a continuation of our discussion from Chapter 7, in particular Sections 7.2.3 and 7.3.2. We shall use the analytic tools developed in Chapter 7 such as the Mellin transform and analytic depoissonization. However, we need a major strengthening of these tools in order to establish our findings regarding the Lempel–Ziv'78. In particular, we shall develop a more powerful analytic depoissonization.

We recall that our main goal is to derive an estimate on the probability distribution of the number of phrases M_n in the LZ'78 algorithm. We assume that our original text is a prefix of length n of an infinite sequence X generated by a memoryless source over the alphabet $\mathcal{A}$. We build a digital search tree (DST) by parsing the infinite sequence X up to the mth phrase; see Figure 9.1 for an illustration. Here we use m for the number of strings inserted into the associated DST since n is reserved for the string length to be parsed by the LZ'78 algorithm.

Let L_m be the total path length in the associated DST after the insertion of m (independent) strings. The quantity M_n is exactly the number of strings that need to be inserted to increase the path length of the associated DST to n. This observation leads to the following identity valid for all integers n and m:

$$P(M_n > m) = P(L_m < n). \tag{9.21}$$

This is called the *renewal equation*. It allows us to study the number of phrases M_n through the path length L_m of the associated digital search tree built over m fixed independent strings.

We now use generating functions to find a functional equation for the distribution of L_m, from which we can estimate the moments of L_m and its limiting distribution. Let $L_m(u) = \mathbf{E}[u^{L_m}]$ be the moment generating function of L_m. In the following, $\mathbf{k}$ is a tuple $(k_1, \ldots, k_{|\mathcal{A}|})$ where k_a for $a \in \mathcal{A}$ stands for the number of strings that start with symbol a. Since the strings inserted into the DST are independent, we conclude that

$$L_{m+1}(u) = u^m \sum_{\mathbf{k}} \binom{m}{\mathbf{k}} \prod_{a \in \mathcal{A}} p_a^{k_a} L_{k_a}(u), \tag{9.22}$$

where

$$\binom{m}{\mathbf{k}} = \frac{m!}{\prod_{a \in \mathcal{A}} k_a!}.$$

Next, we introduce the exponential generating function

$$L(z, u) = \sum_m \frac{z^m}{m!} L_m(u),$$

leading to the following partial functional-differential equation

$$\frac{\partial}{\partial z} L(z, u) = \prod_{a \in \mathcal{A}} L(p_a u z, u). \tag{9.23}$$

It is clear from the construction that $L(z, 1) = e^z$, since $L_m(1) = 1$ for all integers m. Furthermore, by a Taylor expansion around the mean, we have, for all integers m and for t complex (sufficiently small that $\log L_m(e^t)$ exists),

$$\log(L_m(e^t)) = t\mathbf{E}[L_m] + \frac{t^2}{2} \mathrm{Var}[L_m] + O(t^3). \tag{9.24}$$

Notice that the term $O(t^3)$ is not uniform in m. In passing, we remark that $\mathbf{E}[L_m] = L'_m(1)$ and $\mathrm{Var}[L_m] = L''_m(1) + L'_m(1) - (L'_m(1))^2$. The mean $\mathbf{E}[L_m]$ can be found from Theorem 7.2.10 of Chapter 7. Here we use a Mellin transform and analytic depoissonization to estimate the variance and the limiting distribution.

9.3.1. Moments

We first deal with the moments of the path length in a DST built from m independent strings generated by a memoryless source. We use the Mellin transform and depoissonization to prove the next result. This result can be viewed as an extension of Theorem 7.2.10 of Chapter 7.

Theorem 9.3.1. *Consider a digital search tree built over m independent strings. Then*

$$\mathbf{E}[L_m] = \ell(m) + O(1), \tag{9.25}$$

$$\mathrm{Var}[L_m] = v(m) + o(m), \tag{9.26}$$

where $\ell(m)$ and $v(m)$ are defined in (9.7) and (9.6), respectively.

Proof. Our approach here is different from that in Sections 7.2.3 and 7.3.2. In what follows, we use poissonization to find functional equations for the poissonized mean $\widetilde{X}(z)$ and poissonized variance $\widetilde{V}(z)$, which are defined as follows:

$$\widetilde{X}(z) = \frac{\partial}{\partial u} L(z, 1) e^{-z},$$

$$\widetilde{V}(z) = \frac{\partial^2}{\partial u^2} L(z, 1) e^{-z} + \widetilde{X}(z) - (\widetilde{X}(z))^2.$$

Note that, via straightforward algebra,

$$\mathbf{E}[L_m] = \frac{\partial}{\partial u} L_m(1) = m! [z^m] \widetilde{X}(z) e^z,$$

$$\mathrm{Var}[L_m] = \frac{\partial^2}{\partial u^2} L_m(u) + \frac{\partial}{\partial u} P L_m(1) - (\frac{\partial}{\partial u} L_m(1))^2$$
$$= m! [z^m] (\widetilde{V}(z) + (\widetilde{X}(z))^2) e^z - (\mathbf{E}[L_m])^2.$$

We shall recover the original mean and variance through the depoissonization Theorem 7.2.15 from Chapter 7. In fact, from Theorem 7.2.15 we conclude that, for all $\delta > 0$,

$$\mathbf{E}[L_m] = \widetilde{X}(m) + O(m^\delta), \tag{9.27}$$

$$\mathrm{Var}[L_m] = \widetilde{V}(m) - m(X'(m))^2 + O(m^\delta), \tag{9.28}$$

provided that $\widetilde{X}(z) = O(|z|^{1+\delta})$ and $\widetilde{V}(z) = O(|z|^{1+\delta})$, which we will prove in Lemma 9.4.3 of Section 9.4.3. In passing, we should point out that in Theorem 7.2.10 of Chapter 7 we gave the expected depth, which leads to the expected value $\mathbf{E}[L_m]$. We now recompute $\mathbf{E}[L_m]$ through $X(m)$ and then deal with the variance $\text{Var}[L_m]$ through $V(m)$.

From (9.23), after some algebra we find that $\widetilde{X}(z)$ satisfies the functional equation

$$\widetilde{X}(z) + \widetilde{X}'(z) = z + \sum_{a \in \mathcal{A}} \widetilde{X}(p_a z). \tag{9.29}$$

We apply a Mellin transform, as discussed in Table 7.1 of Chapter 7. Define

$$X^*(s) = \int_0^\infty X(z) z^{s-1} dz$$

as the Mellin transform of $\widetilde{X}(z)$. Using Table 7.1, we conclude that the Mellin transform of $\widetilde{X}'(z)$ is $-(s-1)X^*(s-1)$. Therefore, we introduce another function $\gamma(s)$ defined by

$$X^*(s) = \Gamma(s)\gamma^*(s). \tag{9.30}$$

Then, from (9.29) we obtain the following functional equation for $\gamma^*(s)$:

$$\gamma^*(s) - \gamma^*(s) = \gamma^*(s) \sum_{a \in \mathcal{A}} p_a^{-s} \tag{9.31}$$

for $\Re(s) \in (-2, -1)$. Writing

$$h(s) = 1 - \sum_{a \in \mathcal{A}} p_a^{-s}$$

and

$$Q(s) = \prod_{k=0}^\infty h(s-k)$$

we find by iterating (9.31) and using (9.30)

$$X^*(s) = \frac{Q(-2)}{Q(s)} \Gamma(s). \tag{9.32}$$

Using the inverse Mellin transform and the residue theorem we obtain

$$\widetilde{X}(z) = \frac{z}{h} \log z + \frac{z}{h}\left(\gamma - 1 + \frac{h_2}{2h} - \alpha - \Delta_1(\log z)\right) + O(1), \tag{9.33}$$

where $\Delta_1(\log z)$ is a periodic function defined in Theorem 7.2.10 of Chapter 7. Then by (9.27) we can prove our claim regarding $\mathbf{E}[L_m]$.

The analysis of $\widetilde{V}(z)$ is more delicate but follows a similar pattern. It is more convenient to use $W(z) = \widetilde{V}(z) - \widetilde{X}(z)$, which satisfies

$$W(z) + W'(z) - \sum_{a \in \mathcal{A}} W(p_a z) = (\widetilde{X}'(z))^2 + 2 \sum_{a \in \mathcal{A}} p_a z \widetilde{X}'(p_a z). \qquad (9.34)$$

This equation has no closed-form solution owing to the $(X'(z))^2$ term. We set $W(z) = W_1(z) + W_2(z)$, where

$$W_1(z) + W_1'(z) - \sum_{a \in \mathcal{A}} W_1(p_a z) = 2 \sum_{a \in \mathcal{A}} p_a z X'(p_a z), \qquad (9.35)$$

$$W_2(z) + W_2'(z) - \sum_{a \in \mathcal{A}} W_2(p_a z) = (X'(z))^2. \qquad (9.36)$$

It is proved below that $W_2(z) = O(z)$ when $z \to \infty$, so for now we concentrate on $W_1(z)$. The Mellin transform $W_1^*(s)$ of $W_1(z)$ satisfies

$$h(s) W_1^*(s) - (s-1) W_1^*(s-1) = -2(h(s) - 1) s X^*(s).$$

If we set $W_1^*(s) = \omega_1(s) X^*(s)$ then $\omega_1(s)$ satisfies the following functional equation:

$$\omega_1(s) - \omega_1(s-1) = -2s \left(\frac{1}{h(s)} - 1 \right)$$

which we can solve to find that

$$\omega_1(s) = -2 \sum_{k \geq 0} (s-k) \left(\frac{1}{h(s-k)} - 1 \right).$$

Thus

$$W_1^*(s) = -2 X^*(s) \sum_{k \geq 0} (s-k) \left(\frac{1}{h(s-k)} - 1 \right). \qquad (9.37)$$

The sum on the right-hand side converges since $1 - h(s-k)$ tends exponentially to 0 when $k \to \infty$. After some tedious residue analysis, one finds that

$$W_1(z) = \frac{z \log^2 z}{h^2} + \frac{2z \log z}{h^3} \left(\gamma h + h_2 - \frac{h^2}{2} - \eta h - h \Delta_2(\log z) \right) + O(z), \quad (9.38)$$

where η was defined in (7.35) of Chapter 7 for the binary case and in (9.4) for the general case. The function $\Delta_2(x)$ is identically equal to zero when the numbers $\{\log p_a\}_{a \in \mathcal{A}}$ are irrationally related. For $\{\log p_a\}_{a \in \mathcal{A}}$ rationally related $\Delta_2(x)$ is a periodic function with small amplitude. To complete our estimation of the variance, we use the depoissonization result (7.63) of Theorem 7.2.15 to recover (9.26).

Now we return to $W_2(z)$, which satisfies (9.36). The case of $W_2(z)$ is more difficult to deal with since the Mellin transform of $(X'(z))^2$ involves convolutions. Therefore we will rely on an indirect method to estimate $W_2(z)$. To this end we write

$$W_2(z)e^z = \int_0^z \left((\widetilde{X}'(x))^2 + \sum_{a \in \mathcal{A}} W_2(p_a x) \right) e^x dx. \tag{9.39}$$

Let $\rho = \max_{a \in \mathcal{A}}\{p_a\}$. If $z \leq \rho^{-k-1}$ for some integer k then for all $a \in \mathcal{A}$ we have $p_a z \leq \rho^{-k}$. We denote

$$A_k = \max_{z \leq \rho^{-k}} \left\{ \frac{W_2(z)}{z} \right\}.$$

We will prove in Lemma 9.4.3 below that $X(z) = O(z^{1+\delta})$ for any $\delta > 0$, hence (e.g., by the Ricati theorem) we conclude that $X'(z) = O(z^\delta)$ or more precisely that $|X'(z)| \leq B|z|^\delta$ for some $B > 0$. By equation (9.39) we get, for $\rho^{-k} \leq z \leq \rho^{-k-1}$,

$$|W_2(z)e^z| \leq B^2|z|^{2\delta}e^z + \sum_{a \in \mathcal{A}} A_k p_a |z| e^z = B^2|z|^{2\delta}e^z + A_k|z|e^z$$

since $p_a z \leq \rho^{-k}$ for all $a \in \mathcal{A}$. Therefore we have

$$A_{k+1} \leq B^2 \rho^{(1-2\delta)k} + A_k.$$

Taking $2\delta < 1$ we finally arrive at

$$\limsup_k A_k \leq \frac{B^2}{1 - \rho^{1-2\delta}} + A_0 < \infty,$$

and therefore $W_2(z) = O(z)$. This completes the proof. ∎

9.3.2. Distributional analysis

We will now show that the limiting distribution of the path length is normal for $m \to \infty$. In order to accomplish this, we need an important technical result, which will be proved in Section 9.4.3.

Theorem 9.3.2. *For all $\delta > 0$ and for all $\delta' < \delta$ there exists $\varepsilon > 0$ such that $\log L_m(e^{tm^{-\delta}})$ exists for $|t| \leq \varepsilon$ and*

$$\log L_m(e^{tm^{-\delta}}) = O(m), \tag{9.40}$$

$$\log L_m(e^{tm^{-\delta}}) = \frac{t}{m^\delta}\mathbf{E}[L_m] + \frac{t^2}{2m^{2\delta}}\mathrm{Var}[L_m] + t^3 O(m^{1-3\delta'}) \tag{9.41}$$

for large m.

Given that Theorem 9.3.2 is granted, we present next and prove the central limit theorem for the path length in a DST.

Theorem 9.3.3. *Consider a digital search tree built over m sequences generated by a memoryless source. Then*

$$\frac{L_m - \mathbf{E}[L_m]}{\sqrt{\mathrm{Var}[L_m]}} \to N(0,1)$$

in probability and in moments. More precisely, for any given real number x:

$$\lim_{m\to\infty} P(L_m < \mathbf{E}[L_m] + x\sqrt{\mathrm{Var}[L_m]}) = \Phi(x), \tag{9.42}$$

and, for all nonnegative integers k and $\varepsilon > 0$,

$$\mathbf{E}\left(\left(\frac{L_m - \mathbf{E}[L_m]}{\sqrt{\mathrm{Var}[L_m]}}\right)^k\right) = \mu_k + O(m^{-1/2+\varepsilon}) \tag{9.43}$$

where the μ_k are centralized moments of the normal distribution given by (9.12).

Proof. We apply Levy's continuity theorem, or equivalently Goncharov's result, asserting that

$$\frac{L_m - \mathbf{E}[L_m]}{\sqrt{\mathrm{Var}[L_m]}}$$

tends to the standard normal distribution for complex τ,

$$L_m\left(\exp\left(\frac{\tau}{\sqrt{\mathrm{Var}(L_m)}}\right)\right) e^{-\tau E[L_m]/\sqrt{\mathrm{Var}[L_m]}} \to e^{\tau^2/2}. \tag{9.44}$$

To prove the above we apply several times our main technical result, Theorem 9.3.2, with

$$t = \frac{\tau m^\delta}{\sqrt{\mathrm{Var} L_m}} = O(m^{-1/2-\varepsilon+\delta}) \to 0,$$

where $\delta < 1/2$ and $\varepsilon > 0$. Thus by Theorem 9.3.2 we find that

$$\log L_m\left(\exp\left(\frac{\tau}{\sqrt{\mathrm{Var}(L_m)}}\right)\right) = \frac{\tau E[L_m]}{\sqrt{\mathrm{Var} L_m}} + \frac{\tau^2}{2} + O(m^{-1/2+\varepsilon'}) \tag{9.45}$$

for some $\varepsilon' > 0$. By (9.44) the normality result follows.

To establish the convergence in moments we use (9.45). Observing that the kth centralized moment of L_m is the kth coefficient at $t = 0$ of

$$\exp\left(\frac{\tau}{\sqrt{\text{Var}(L_m)}}\right) \exp\left(-\tau \mathbf{E}[L_m]/\sqrt{\text{Var}[L_m]}\right)$$

we apply the Cauchy formula on a circle of radius R encircling the origin. Thus

$$\mathbf{E}\left[\left(\frac{L_m - \mathbf{E}[L_m]}{\sqrt{\text{Var}[L_m]}}\right)^k\right] = \frac{1}{2i\pi} \oint \frac{d\tau}{\tau^{k+1}} L_m \left(\exp\left(\frac{\tau}{\sqrt{\text{Var}(L_m)}}\right)\right)$$

$$\times e^{-\tau \mathbf{E}[L_m]/\sqrt{\text{Var}[L_m]}}$$

$$= \frac{1}{2i\pi} \oint \frac{d\tau}{\tau^{k+1}} \exp\left(\frac{\tau^2}{2}\right) (1 + O(m^{-\frac{1}{2}+\varepsilon'})$$

$$= \mu_k + O\left(R^{-k} \exp(R^2/2) m^{-\frac{1}{2}+\varepsilon'}\right).$$

This completes the proof.   ∎

In order to compare our theoretical results with experiment, in Figure 9.5 we display the histograms of L_{200} for a binary alphabet with $p_a = 0.8$ and L_{800} for $p_a = 0.9$. As can be seen for $m = 800$ we have a reasonably good approximation.

9.3.3. Large deviation results

We now study the large deviations for L_m and prove the following result.

Theorem 9.3.4. *Consider a digital search tree built over m sequences generated by a memoryless source.*

(i) [Large deviations].   *Let $\frac{1}{2} < \delta < 1$. Then there exist $\varepsilon > 0$, $B > 0$, and $\beta > 0$ such that, for all $x \geq 0$,*

$$P(|L_m - \mathbf{E}[L_m]| > xm^\delta) \leq B\exp(-\beta m^\varepsilon x). \tag{9.46}$$

(ii) [Moderate deviations].   *There exists $B > 0$ such that*

$$P(|L_m - \mathbf{E}[L_m]| \geq x\sqrt{\text{Var}[L_m]}) \leq Be^{-\frac{x^2}{2}} \tag{9.47}$$

for nonnegative real $x < Am^\delta$ with $\delta < 1/6$ and $A > 0$.

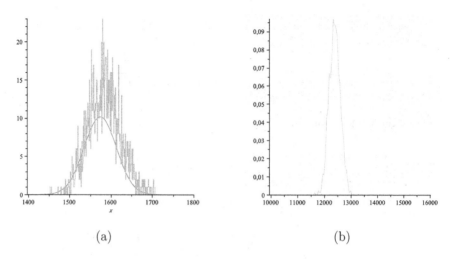

Figure 9.5. Simulation of the histograms of (a) L_{200} for $p_a = 0.8$ and (b) L_{800} for $p_a = 0.9$. In (a) we also show, for comparison, the theoretical limiting distribution for $p_a = 0.8$.

Proof. We apply the Chernov bound. Let $t > 0$ be a nonnegative real number. We have the identity

$$P\left(L_m > \mathbf{E}[L_m] + xm^\delta\right) = P\left(e^{tL_m} > e^{(\mathbf{E}[L_m]+xm^\delta)t}\right).$$

Using Markov's inequality we find that

$$P(e^{tL_m} > e^{(\mathbf{E}[L_m]+xm^\delta)t}) \leq \frac{\mathbf{E}[e^{tL_m}]}{e^{(\mathbf{E}[L_m]+xm^\delta)t}}$$

$$= L_m(e^t)\exp(-t\mathbf{E}[L_m] - xm^\delta t).$$

Here we have taken

$$\delta' = \frac{\delta + 1/2}{2} > \frac{1}{2}, \quad \varepsilon = \delta' - \frac{1}{2} > 0,$$

since $\delta > 1/2$. We now apply Theorem 9.3.2, setting $t = t'm^{-\delta'}$, to obtain

$$\log L_m(e^t) = tE[L_m] + O(t^2\text{Var}[L_m]).$$

By Theorem 9.3.1 we conclude that

$$\log L_m(e^t) - t\mathbf{E}[L_m] = O(m^{-\varepsilon}). \tag{9.48}$$

We complete the lower bound by setting $tm^\delta = t'm^\varepsilon$ with $\beta = t'$.

To obtain an upper bound we follow the same route, but considering $-t$ instead of t and using

$$P\left(L_m < \mathbf{E}[L_m] - xm^\delta\right) = P\left(e^{-tL_m} > e^{-(\mathbf{E}[L_m] - xm^\delta)t}\right)$$

$$\leq L_m(e^{-t})\exp(t\mathbf{E}[L_m] - xm^\delta t).$$

To prove part (ii) we apply again Theorem 9.3.2 with

$$t = \frac{xm^{\delta'}}{\sqrt{\mathrm{Var}[L_m]}}, \tag{9.49}$$

where $\delta < \delta' < 1/6$. Then by Theorem 9.3.2 (with δ and δ' formally interchanged)

$$\log L_m\left(\exp(\frac{x}{\sqrt{\mathrm{Var}(L_m)}})\right) = \mathbf{E}[L_m]\frac{x}{\sqrt{\mathrm{Var}[L_m]}} + \frac{x^2}{2\mathrm{Var}[L_m]}\mathrm{Var}[L_m]$$

$$+ \frac{x^3 m^{3\delta'}}{(\mathrm{Var}[L_m])^{\frac{3}{2}}}O(m^{1-3\delta}).$$

Observe that the error term for $x = O(m^\delta)$ is

$$O(m^{-\frac{1}{2}+3\delta'}(\log m)^{-3/2}) = o(1)$$

since $\delta' < 1/6$, and this leads to

$$\log L_m\left(\exp\left(\frac{x}{\sqrt{\mathrm{Var}(L_m)}}\right)\right) - \mathbf{E}[L_m]\frac{x}{\sqrt{\mathrm{Var}[L_m]}} = \frac{x^2}{2} + o(1). \tag{9.50}$$

Therefore, by the Markov inequality, for all $t > 0$ we have

$$P(L_m > \mathbf{E}[L_m] + x\sqrt{\mathrm{Var}[L_m]}) \leq \exp(\log L_m(e^t) - t\mathbf{E}[L_m] - xt\sqrt{\mathrm{Var}[L_m]}).$$

Using (9.50) we find that

$$P(L_m > \mathbf{E}[L_m] + x\sqrt{\mathrm{Var}[L_m]}) \leq \exp\left(\frac{x^2}{2} + o(1) - x^2\right) \sim \exp\left(-\frac{x^2}{2}\right),$$

where we have set $t = x/\sqrt{\mathrm{Var}[L_m]}$ in the last line. This completes the proof of the lower bound, while for the upper bound we follow the same argument but with t replaced by $-t$. ∎

9.4. Proofs of Theorems 9.2.1 and 9.2.2

In this section we prove our main results, namely Theorems 9.2.1 and 9.2.2 given
that Theorem 9.3.2 is granted.

9.4.1. Large deviations: proof of Theorem 9.2.2

We start with Theorem 9.2.2(i). By (9.21) we have

$$P(M_n > \ell^{-1}(n) + yn^\delta) = P(M_n > \lfloor \ell^{-1}(n) + yn^\delta \rfloor)$$
$$= P\left(L_{\lfloor \ell^{-1}(n)+yn^\delta \rfloor} < n\right).$$

Observe that $\mathbf{E}[L_m] = \ell(m) + O(1)$, and hence

$$\mathbf{E}[L_{\lfloor \ell^{-1}(n)+yn^\delta \rfloor}] = \ell(\ell^{-1}(n) + yn^\delta) + O(1). \tag{9.51}$$

Since the function $\ell(\cdot)$ is convex and $\ell(0) = 0$ we have, for all real numbers $a > 0$
and $b > 0$

$$\ell(a + b) \geq \ell(a) + \frac{\ell(a)}{a}b, \tag{9.52}$$

$$\ell(a - b) \leq \ell(a) - \frac{\ell(a)}{a}b. \tag{9.53}$$

Applying inequality (9.52) to $a = \ell^{-1}(n)$ and $b = yn^\delta$ we arrive at

$$n - \mathbf{E}[L_{\lfloor \ell^{-1}(n)+yn^\delta \rfloor}] \leq -y\frac{n}{\ell^{-1}(n)}n^\delta + O(1). \tag{9.54}$$

Thus

$$P(L_{\lfloor \ell^{-1}(n)+yn^\delta \rfloor} < n) \leq P(L_m - \mathbf{E}[L_m] < -xm^\delta + O(1))$$

with

$$m = \lfloor \ell^{-1}(n) + yn^\delta \rfloor, \qquad x = \frac{n}{\ell^{-1}(n)}\frac{n^\delta}{m^\delta}y. \tag{9.55}$$

We now apply several times Theorem 9.3.4 concerning the path length L_m. That
is, for all $x > 0$ and for all m, there exist $\varepsilon > 0$ and A such that

$$P(L_m - \mathbf{E}[L_m] < xm^\delta) < Ae^{-\beta xm^\varepsilon}. \tag{9.56}$$

In other words,

$$P(L_m - \mathbf{E}[L_m] < xm^\delta + O(1)) \leq Ae^{-\beta xm^\varepsilon + O(m^{\varepsilon-\delta})} \leq A'e^{-\beta xm^\varepsilon}$$

for some $A' > A$. We find that

$$P(M_n > \ell^{-1}(n) + yn^\delta) \le A' \exp(-\beta x m^\varepsilon). \tag{9.57}$$

We know that $\ell^{-1}(n) = \Omega(n/\log n)$. Thus, with x defined as in (9.55), we have

$$x = O((\log n)^{1+\delta}) \frac{y}{(1 + yn^{\delta-1} \log n)^\delta} \le \beta' \frac{n^{\varepsilon_1} y}{(1 + yn^{-\varepsilon_2})^\delta}$$

for some $\beta' > 0$. Setting $\varepsilon_1 < \varepsilon$ and $\varepsilon_2 < \varepsilon$ for some $\varepsilon > 0$, we establish the upper bound.

In a similar fashion, we have

$$P(M_n < \ell^{-1}(n) - yn^\delta) = P(L_{\lfloor \ell^{-1}(n) - yn^\delta \rfloor} > n) \tag{9.58}$$

and

$$\mathbf{E}[L_{\lfloor \ell^{-1}(n) - yn^\delta \rfloor}] = \ell(\ell^{-1}(n) - yn^\delta) + O(1). \tag{9.59}$$

Using inequality (9.53) we obtain

$$n - \mathbf{E}[L_{\lfloor \ell^{-1}(n) - yn^\delta \rfloor}] \ge y \frac{n}{\ell^{-1}(n)} n^\delta + O(1). \tag{9.60}$$

In conclusion,

$$P(L_{\lfloor \ell^{-1}(n) - yn^\delta \rfloor} > n) \le P(L_m - \mathbf{E}[L_m] > x m^\delta + O(1))$$

with

$$m = \lfloor \ell^{-1}(n) - yn^\delta \rfloor, \qquad x = \frac{n}{\ell^{-1}(n)} \frac{n^\delta}{m^\delta} y.$$

Observe that this case is easier since now $m < \ell^{-1}(n)$ and we do not need the correcting term $(1 + yn^\varepsilon)^{-\delta}$.

Now we turn our attention to the moderate deviation results expressed in Theorem 9.2.2(ii) (with $\delta < 1/6$). The proof is essentially the same, except that we now consider

$$y \frac{s_n}{\ell'(\ell^{-1}(n))} \quad \text{with} \quad s_n = \sqrt{v(\ell^{-1}(n))}$$

instead of yn^δ, and we assume $y = O(n^{\delta'})$ for some $\delta' < 1/6$. Thus

$$y \frac{s_n}{\ell'(\ell^{-1}(n))} = O(n^{1/2+\varepsilon}) = o(n)$$

for some $\varepsilon > 0$. By Theorem 9.2.1 we know that

$$\mathbf{E}[M_n] = \ell^{-1}(n) + o(s_n/\ell'(\ell^{-1}(n)));$$

thus, for $y > 0$,

$$P\left(M_n > \ell^{-1}(n) + y\frac{s_n}{\ell'(\ell^{-1}(n))}\right) = P(L_m < n), \qquad (9.61)$$

with

$$m = \lfloor \ell^{-1}(n) + y\frac{s_n}{\ell'(\ell^{-1}(n))} \rfloor.$$

We use the estimate

$$\ell(a + b) = \ell(a) + \ell'(a)b + o(1)$$

when $b = o(a)$ and $a \to \infty$. Thus

$$\ell\left(\ell^{-1}(n) + y\frac{s_n}{\ell'(\ell^{-1}(n))}\right) = n + ys_n + o(1). \qquad (9.62)$$

Since $\sqrt{v(m)} = s_n + O(1)$ we have

$$n = \mathbf{E}[L_m] - y\sqrt{v(m)} + O(1).$$

By Theorem 9.3.4 we know that

$$P(L_m < \mathbf{E}[L_m] - y\sqrt{v(m)} + O(1)) \le A\exp(-y^2/2),$$

where the $O(1)$ term is given by

$$\exp\left(O\left(\frac{y^2}{v(m)}\right)\right) = \exp(o(1)),$$

which is absorbed into A since $\delta < 1/6$. The proof for $y < 0$ follows a similar path.

9.4.2. Central limit theorem: Proof of Theorem 9.2.1

We first show that, for all $1/2 < \delta < 1$

$$\mathbf{E}[M_n] = \ell^{-1}(n) + O(n^\delta).$$

Indeed, for any random variable X, we have

$$|\mathbf{E}[X]| \le \mathbf{E}[|X|] = \int_0^\infty P(|X| > y)dy;$$

we now set $X = M_n - \ell^{-1}(n)$ to find from Theorem 9.2.2(i)

$$|\mathbf{E}[M_n] - \ell^{-1}(n)| \leq n^\delta + n^\delta \int_1^\infty P(|M_n - \ell^{-1}(n)| > yn^\delta)dy = O(n^\delta).$$

By the renewal equation (9.21), for a given y we have

$$P\left(M_n > \ell^{-1}(n) + y\frac{s_n}{\ell'(\ell^{-1}(n))}\right) = P(L_{\lfloor \ell^{-1}(n)+y\frac{s_n}{\ell'(\ell^{-1}(n))}\rfloor} < n).$$

As before, let

$$m = \left\lfloor \ell^{-1}(n) + y\frac{s_n}{\ell'(\ell^{-1}(n))}\right\rfloor.$$

We know that

$$n - \mathbf{E}[L_m] = -ys_n + O(1)$$

and

$$s_n = \sqrt{v(\ell^{-1}(n))} = \sqrt{\text{Var}[L_m]}(1 + o(1)).$$

Therefore

$$P\left(M_n > \ell^{-1}(n) + y\frac{s_n}{\ell'(\ell^{-1}(n))}\right) = P\left(L_m < \mathbf{E}[L_m] + y\sqrt{\text{Var}[L_m]}(1 + o(1))\right).$$

Hence

$$P\left(L_m < \mathbf{E}[L_m] + y(1 + o(1))\sqrt{\text{Var}[L_m]}\right) \geq P\left(M_n > \ell^{-1} + y\frac{s_n}{\ell'(\ell^{-1}(n))}\right),$$

since for all y' we have

$$\lim_{m\to\infty} P\left(L_m < \mathbf{E}[L_m] + y'\sqrt{\text{Var}[L_m]}\right) = \Phi(y'),$$

where, we recall, Φ is the distribution of $N(0,1)$. Therefore, by the continuity of $\Phi(x)$,

$$\lim_{m\to\infty} P\left(L_m < \mathbf{E}[L_m] + y(1 \pm o(1))\sqrt{\text{Var}[L_m]}\right) = \Phi(y).$$

Thus

$$\lim_{m\to\infty} P\left(M_n > \ell^{-1}(n) + y\frac{s_n}{\ell'(\ell^{-1}(n))}\right) = 1 - \Phi(y),$$

and, using the same method, we can also establish the matching lower bound

$$\lim_{m\to\infty} P\left(M_n < \ell^{-1}(n) - y\frac{s_n}{\ell'(\ell^{-1}(n))}\right) = \Phi(y).$$

This proves two things: first, that

$$(M_n - \ell^{-1}(n))\frac{\ell'(\ell^{-1}(n))}{s_n}$$

tends to the normal distribution in probability; second, since by the moderate deviation result the normalized random variable

$$(M_n - \ell^{-1}(n))\frac{\ell'(\ell^{-1}(n))}{s_n}$$

has bounded moments. Then by virtue of dominated convergence and convergence to the normal distribution we have

$$\lim_{n\to\infty} \mathbf{E}\left[(M_n - \ell^{-1}(n))\frac{\ell'(\ell^{-1}n))}{s_n}\right] = 0,$$

$$\lim_{n\to\infty} \mathbf{E}\left[\left((M_n - \ell^{-1}(n))\frac{\ell'(\ell(^{-1}n))}{s_n}\right]^2\right) = 1.$$

In other words,

$$\mathbf{E}[M_n] = \ell^{-1}(n) + o(n^{1/2}\log n),$$

$$\mathrm{Var}[M_n] \sim \frac{v(\ell^{-1}(n))}{(\ell'(\ell^{-1}(n)))^2},$$

which prove (9.8) and (9.9). This completes the proof of our main result in Theorem 9.2.1.

9.4.3. Some technical results

The main goal of this subsection is to prove Theorem 9.3.2. We accomplish this through several technical results.

First, we will work with the Poisson model, that is, the exponential generating function $L(z, u)$ satisfying (9.23) (or its Poisson version $L(z, u)e^{-z}$), from which we can extract information about the probability generating function $L_m(u)$ for large z and u in the vicinity of $u = 1$. Throughout we will use analytic depoissonization, as discussed in Chapter 7. However, here we need an extension of the results presented in Table 7.2 to diagonal exponential depoissonization, reviewed below.

Recall the Poisson mean $\widetilde{X}(z)$ and the Poisson variance $\widetilde{V}(z)$, defined in Section 9.3.1 by

$$X(z) = \frac{\partial}{\partial u}L(z, 1), \qquad \widetilde{X}(z) = X(z)e^{-z},$$

$$\widetilde{V}(z) = e^{-z}\frac{\partial^2}{\partial u^2}L(z, 1) + \widetilde{X}(z) - (\widetilde{X}(z))^2.$$

For a given z and for any t, we then have

$$\log L(z, e^t) = z + \widetilde{X}(z)t + \widetilde{V}(z)\frac{t^2}{2} + O(t^3). \tag{9.63}$$

We first obtain some estimates on the Poisson mean $\widetilde{X}(z)$ and the Poisson variance $\widetilde{V}(z)$ (see Lemma 9.4.3 below), by applying Theorem 9.4.2 proved in Section 9.4.4. Then we derive some estimates on the derivative of $\log L(z, e^t)$ (see Lemma 9.4.4). Finally, we use the depoissonization tool given in Theorem 9.4.1 to prove Theorem 9.3.2.

The main tool of this section is analytic depoissonization. To this end we will use the *diagonal exponential depoissonization* established in Jacquet and Szpankowski (1998). Let θ be a nonnegative number smaller than $\pi/2$, and let $\mathcal{S}(\theta)$ be a complex cone around the positive real axis defined by $\mathcal{S}(\theta) = \{z : |\arg(z)| \leq \theta\}$. We will use the following theorem (see Theorem 8 in Jacquet and Szpankowski (1995)), known as the diagonal exponential depoissonization tool.

Theorem 9.4.1 (Jacquet and Szpankowski, 1998). *Let u_k be a sequence of complex numbers, and $\theta \in]0, \frac{\pi}{2}[$. For all $\varepsilon > 0$ there exist $c > 1$, $\alpha < 1$, $A > 0$, and $B > 0$ such that*

$$z \in \mathcal{S}(\theta) \text{ and } |z| \in [\frac{m}{c}, cm] \Rightarrow |\log(L(z, u_m)| \leq B|z|,$$
$$z \notin \mathcal{S}(\theta), \quad |z| = m \Rightarrow |L(z, u_m)| \leq Ae^{\alpha m}.$$

Then

$$L_m(u_m) = L(m, u_m)(1+o(m^{-1/2+\varepsilon})) \exp\left(-m - \frac{m}{2}\left(\frac{\partial}{\partial z}\log(L(m, u_m)) - 1\right)^2\right) \tag{9.64}$$

for $m \to \infty$.

In Theorems 9.4.7 and 9.4.11 we prove the following main technical result needed to establish Theorem 9.3.2.

Theorem 9.4.2. *Let $\delta \in]0, 1[$. There exist numbers $\theta \in]0, \frac{\pi}{2}[$, $\alpha < 1$, $A > 0$, $B > 0$, and $\varepsilon > 0$ such that for all complex t such that $|t| \leq \varepsilon$:*

$$z \in \mathcal{S}(\theta) \Rightarrow |\log(L(z, e^{t|z|^{-\delta}}))| \leq B|z| \tag{9.65}$$
$$z \notin \mathcal{S}(\theta) \Rightarrow |L(z, e^{t|z|^{-\delta}})| \leq Ae^{\alpha|z|}. \tag{9.66}$$

Granted Theorem 9.4.2, we now proceed to estimate the Poisson mean and variance that will be used to prove Theorem 9.4.5 (the main technical result of this subsection), in which we state an estimate on $\log L_m(e^t)$.

We start with some bounds on the Poisson mean, variance, and $\log L(z, e^t)$.

Lemma 9.4.3. *Let δ be an arbitrary nonnegative number. There exists $\varepsilon > 0$ such that for $|t| \leq \varepsilon$ and $z \in \mathcal{S}(\theta)$ the following estimates hold:*

$$\widetilde{X}(z) = O(|z|^{1+\delta}),$$
$$\widetilde{V}(z) = O(|z|^{1+2\delta}),$$
$$\log L(z, e^{t|z|^{-\delta}}) = z + \widetilde{X}(z)\frac{t}{|z|^\delta} + \widetilde{V}(z)\frac{t^2}{2|z|^{2\delta}} + O(t^3|z|^{1+3\delta}).$$

Proof. We first notice that $\log L(z, 1) = z$. We recall that $\widetilde{X}(z)$ and $\widetilde{V}(z)$ are respectively the first and the second derivative of $L(z, e^t)$ with respect to t at $t = 0$. By Cauchy's formula we have

$$\widetilde{X}(z) = \frac{1}{2i\pi} \oint \log L(z, e^t)\frac{dt}{t^2}, \tag{9.67}$$

$$\widetilde{V}(z) = \frac{2}{2i\pi} \oint \log L(z, e^t)\frac{dt}{t^3}, \tag{9.68}$$

where the integrals are along the circle of center 0 and radius $\varepsilon|z|^{-\delta}$. On this integral contour the estimate $|\log L(z, e^t)| \leq B|z|$ holds, and therefore we have

$$|\widetilde{X}(z)| \leq \frac{B}{\varepsilon}|z|^{1+\delta}, \tag{9.69}$$

$$|\widetilde{V}(z)| \leq \frac{2B}{\varepsilon^2}|z|^{1+2\delta}, \tag{9.70}$$

which proves the first two assertions. For the third, we need to assess the remainder

$$R(z, t) = \log L(z, e^t) - z - \widetilde{X}(z)t - \widetilde{V}(z)\frac{t^2}{2}.$$

We again use the Cauchy formula, obtaining

$$R(z, t) = \frac{2t^3}{2i\pi} \oint \log L(z, e^{t'})\frac{dt'}{(t')^3(t' - t)}. \tag{9.71}$$

The above follows on noting that

$$R(z,t) = \frac{1}{2i\pi} \oint \log L(z, e^{t'}) \frac{dt'}{(t'-t)},$$

$$R(z,0) = \frac{1}{2i\pi} \oint \log L(z, e^{t}) \frac{dt}{t},$$

$$R'(z,0) = \frac{1}{2i\pi} \oint \log L(z, e^{t}) \frac{dt}{t^2},$$

$$R''(z,0) = \frac{1}{2i\pi} \oint \log L(z, e^{t}) \frac{dt}{t^3}.$$

We integrate $R(z,t)$ around the circle of center 0 and radius $\varepsilon|z|^{-\delta}$. If we restrict t in such a way that $|t| \leq \frac{\varepsilon}{2}|z|^{-\delta}$ then $|t - t'| \geq \frac{\varepsilon}{2}|z|^{-\delta}$, and

$$|R(z,t)| \leq \frac{8B}{\varepsilon^3}|t|^3|z|^{1+3\delta},$$

which completes the proof. ∎

Now let

$$D(z,t) := \frac{\partial}{\partial z} \log L(z, e^{t})$$

which is needed in (9.64) to apply the diagonal depoissonization. Our second technical lemma provides estimates on $D(z,t)$.

Lemma 9.4.4. *Let $\delta > 0$. There exist $\varepsilon > 0$ and $B' > 0$ such that, for all t for which $|t| < \varepsilon$, we have*

$$|D(m, tm^{-\delta})| \leq B',$$

$$D(m, tm^{-\delta}) = 1 + \widetilde{X}'(m)\frac{t}{m^\delta} + O(t^2 m^{2\delta}),$$

$$\widetilde{X}'(m) = O(m^\delta)$$

for $m \to \infty$.

Proof. The key point here is to show that $D(m, tm^{-\delta}) = O(1)$. In order to establish this, we again use the Cauchy formula:

$$D(m, tm^{-\delta}) = \frac{1}{2i\pi} \oint \log L(z, e^{tm^{-\delta}}) \frac{dz}{(z-m)^2}, \tag{9.72}$$

where the integration contour encircles m with radius $O(m)$ and lies on the cone $\mathcal{S}(\theta)$. Let $|t| \leq \varepsilon$ such that (9.66) holds, namely $|\log L(z, e^{tm^{-\delta}})| \leq B|z|$ since

$m = O(|z|)$. To this end the contour is chosen to be a circle of center m and radius $m\sin(\theta)$. Noticing that $|z| < m(1 + \sin(\theta))$ we finally arrive at

$$|D(m, tm^{-\delta})| \leq B\frac{1 + \sin(\theta)}{\sin(\theta)} \, . \tag{9.73}$$

From here the proof takes a similar path to that in the proof of the previous lemma. Noting that $D(m, 0) = 1$, we have

$$\widetilde{X}'(m) = \frac{\partial}{\partial t} D(m, 0) = \frac{1}{2i\pi} \oint D(m, t')\frac{dt'}{(t')^2}$$

$$D(m, tm^{-\delta}) = 1 + \widetilde{X}'(m)tm^{-\delta} + + \frac{tm^{-\delta}}{2i\pi} \oint D(m, t')\frac{dt'}{(t')^2(t' - tm^{-\delta})},$$

where the integral contour is now a circle of center $tm^{-\delta}$ and radius $\varepsilon m^{-\delta}$.   ∎

These two lemmas allow us to establish the following intermediate result.

Theorem 9.4.5.   *There exists a number $A > 0$ such that for all arbitrarily small $\delta' < \delta$, and for all complex t such that $|t| \leq A$, we have*

$$\log L_m(e^{tm^{-\delta}}) = \widetilde{X}(m)\frac{t}{m^\delta} + \left(\widetilde{V}(m) - m(\widetilde{X}'(m))^2\right)\frac{t^2}{2m^{2\delta}} + O(t^3 m^{1-3\delta+6\delta'})$$

for $m \to \infty$.

Proof. We need to apply (9.64) of Theorem 9.4.1. Let $\delta' < \delta$ be arbitrarily small. We require Lemma 9.4.3 with t' and δ' $t' = tm^{\delta'-\delta}$; the condition $|t'| \leq \varepsilon$ is then easily checked. From

$$\log L(m, e^{t'm^{-\delta'}}) = m + \widetilde{X}(m)\frac{t'}{m^{\delta'}} + \widetilde{V}(m)\frac{t'^2}{2m^{2\delta'}} + O(t'^3 m^{1+3\delta'})$$

we find that

$$\log L(m, e^{tm^{-\delta}}) = m + \widetilde{X}(m)\frac{t}{m^\delta} + \widetilde{V}(m)\frac{t^2}{2m^{2\delta}} + O(t^3 m^{1-3\delta+6\delta'}).$$

In order to apply (9.64) we need to estimate

$$\left(\frac{\partial}{\partial z}\log(L(m, u_m)) - 1\right)^2 = (D(m, u_m) - 1)^2,$$

where $u_m = e^{tm^{-\delta}}$. Applying Lemma 9.4.4 with $t' = tm^{\delta'-\delta}$ we find that

$$D(m, e^{tm^{-\delta}}) = 1 + \widetilde{X}'(m)\frac{t}{m^\delta} + O(t^2 m^{-2\delta+4\delta'}). \tag{9.74}$$

Then using $X'(m) = O(m^{\delta'})$ we arrive at

$$\left(D(m, e^{tm^{-\delta}}) - 1\right)^2 = (\widetilde{X}'(m))^2 \frac{t^2}{m^{2\delta}} + O(t^3 m^{-3\delta+5\delta'}).$$

Putting everything together and using (9.64) of Theorem 9.4.1, we finally achieve the expected estimate on $\log L_m(e^{tm^{-\delta}})$. ∎

The next result allows us to connect the Poissonized mean and variance with the original mean and variance; it follows directly from Theorem 9.4.5. In fact, we have already established the original mean and variance in Theorem 7.2.15.

Corollary 9.4.6. *For any $\delta' > 0$*

$$\mathbf{E}[L_m] = \widetilde{X}(m) + o(1) = O(m^{1+\delta'}),$$
$$\mathrm{Var}[L_m] = \widetilde{V}(m) - m(X'(m))^2 + o(1) = O(m^{1+2\delta'})$$

as $m \to \infty$.

We are finally in a position to prove Theorem 9.3.2 granted Theorem 9.4.2, which we establish in the next subsection. From Theorem 9.4.1 and Lemma 9.4.4, for any $\delta' > 0$, we obtain the estimate

$$\log L_m(e^{tm^{-\delta'}}) = O(m)$$

which proves (9.40) of Theorem 9.3.2. To prove (9.41) we need to estimate the remainder

$$R_m(t) = \log L_m(e^t) - \mathbf{E}[L_m]t - \mathrm{Var}[L_m]\frac{t^2}{2}.$$

By the Cauchy formula, as in the proof of Lemma 9.4.3 we have

$$R_m(t) = \frac{2t^3}{2i\pi} \oint \log L_m(e^{t'}) \frac{dt'}{(t')^3(t'-t)}, \tag{9.75}$$

where the integral is around a circle of center 0 and radius $\varepsilon|z|^{-\delta}$. If we again restrict t in such a way that $|t| \leq \frac{\varepsilon}{2}|z|^{-\delta}$ then $|t - t'| \geq \frac{\varepsilon}{2}|z|^{-\delta}$. As in the proof of Lemma 9.4.3, we find that

$$R_m(t) = t^3 O\left(\frac{m^{1+3\delta'}}{\varepsilon^3}\right).$$

Therefore, for $\delta > \delta'$ we finally arrive at

$$R_m(tm^{-\delta}) = t^3 O\left(m^{1-3(\delta-\delta')}\right) = t^3 O\left(m^{1-3(\delta'')}\right) \tag{9.76}$$

for some $\delta'' > 0$. This completes the proof of Theorem 9.3.2.

9.4.4.   Proof of Theorem 9.4.2

To complete our analysis we need to prove Theorem 9.4.2; we will establish (9.65) and (9.66) respectively in Theorems 9.4.7 and 9.4.11 below.

We apply the *increasing domains* technique introduced in Section 7.2.5. Recall that this technique allows us to establish a property over an area of the complex plane (e.g., a cone) by mathematical induction. Indeed, let R be a real number. We denote by $\mathcal{S}_0(\theta)$ the subset of the linear cone $\mathcal{S}(\theta) = \{z : \,|\arg(z)| \le \theta\}$ consisting of the complex numbers of modulus smaller than or equal to R. By extension, let k be an integer and denote by $\mathcal{S}_k(\theta)$ the subset of $\mathcal{S}(\theta)$ that consists of complex numbers of modulus smaller than or equal to $R\rho^k$, where

$$\rho = \min_{u \in \mathcal{U}(1), a \in \mathcal{A}} \left\{ \frac{1}{p_a|u|} \right\} > 1 \tag{9.77}$$

for a neighborhood $\mathcal{U}(1)$ of $u = 1$. By construction, if $z \in \mathcal{S}_k(\theta)$ for $k > 0$ and $u \in \mathcal{U}(1)$ then all $p_a uz$ for $a \in \mathcal{A}$ belong to $\mathcal{S}_{k-1}(\theta)$. Thus a property (e.g., recurrence (9.23)) that holds for $\mathcal{S}_{k-1}(\theta)$ can be extended to a larger subset of the cone, namely $\mathcal{S}_k(\theta)$, as in standard mathematical induction.

Our goal is to present a polynomial estimate $\log L(z, u)$ (i.e., $\log L(z, u) = O(z)$) for large z in a cone containing the real positive axis. The main problem is that of the existence of the logarithm of $L(z, u)$, in particular for complex values of z and u. Technically, we can prove the existence and growth of $\log L(z, u)$ only for complex u with a small imaginary part as z increases. For this we fix an arbitrary nonnegative real number $\delta < 1$ and complex t and z such that

$$u(z, t) = e^{t|z|^{-\delta}}. \tag{9.78}$$

The key to our analysis is the following theorem, which proves equation (9.65) of Theorem 9.4.2.

Theorem 9.4.7. *There exists a complex neighborhood $\mathcal{U}(0)$ of $t = 0$ and $B > 0$ such that for all $t \in \mathcal{U}(0)$ and for all $z \in \mathcal{S}(\theta)$ the function $\log L(z, u(z, t))$ exists and*

$$\log L(z, u(z, t)) \le B|z|. \tag{9.79}$$

We will prove the theorem in several steps. The "road map" for the proof is as follows. We first introduce a function $f(z, u)$, which we call the *kernel* function; it is defined by

$$f(z, u) = \frac{L(z, u)}{\frac{\partial}{\partial z} L(z, u)} = \frac{L(z, u)}{\prod_{a \in \mathcal{A}} L(p_a uz, u)}. \tag{9.80}$$

Notice that, formally,

$$\frac{1}{f(z,u)} = \frac{\partial}{\partial z} \log L(z,u).$$

Indeed, if we can show that the kernel function is well defined and is never zero in a convex set containing the real positive line then we will have proved that $\log L(z,u)$ exists, since

$$\log L(z,u) = \int_0^z \frac{dx}{f(x,u)}. \tag{9.81}$$

Furthermore, if we can prove that the estimate $f(x,u) = \Omega(1)$ holds then

$$\log L(z,u) = \int_0^z \frac{dx}{f(x,u)} = O(z) \tag{9.82}$$

as needed to establish (9.65) of Theorem 9.4.2.

Understanding the kernel function is therefore the key to our analysis. In passing we observe that this function satisfies the following differential equation:

$$\frac{\partial}{\partial z} f(z,u) = 1 - f(z,u) \sum_{a \in \mathcal{A}} \frac{p_a u}{f(p_a u z, u)}. \tag{9.83}$$

We proceed now with the proof of Theorem 9.4.7. We start with a trivial lemma, whose proof is left to the reader as an exercise.

Lemma 9.4.8. *For (x,ε) a real positive tuple, let a function $h(x,\varepsilon)$ be defined on an open set containing all tuples $(x,0)$ with $x \geq 0$. Assume that the function $h(x,\varepsilon)$ is real positive and continuously differentiable. If*

$$\forall x \geq 0: \ \frac{\partial}{\partial x} h(x,0) < 1$$

then for all compact sets $\mathcal{K}_x$ there exists a compact neighborhood of $\mathcal{U}(0)$ of 0: $(x_0, t) \in \mathcal{K}_x \times \mathcal{U}(0)$ such that the sequence

$$x_{k+1} = h(x_k, \varepsilon) \tag{9.84}$$

defined for k integer converges to a bounded fixed point when $k \to \infty$.

Let us define the function $a(z,u)$ as follows:

$$\frac{1}{f(z,u)} = 1 + a(z,u).$$

In the next two lemmas we prove that $a(z,u) = O(1)$ for u as in (9.78), and this, by (9.82), will prove (9.65).

Lemma 9.4.9. *Let δ' be a real number such that $\delta' < \delta < 1$. For all number $\hat{a} > 0$ there exists a real number $\varepsilon > 0$ such that for all real t and $|t| < \varepsilon$ we have*

$$|a(z, u(z, t))| \le \hat{a}\frac{|t|}{|z|^{\delta'}} \tag{9.85}$$

for all $z \in \mathcal{S}(\theta)$.

Proof. We apply the increasing domain technique with

$$\rho = \min_{u \in \mathcal{U}(1), a \in \mathcal{A}} \left\{\frac{1}{p_a |u|}\right\} > 1$$

for a compact neighborhood $\mathcal{U}(1)$ of $u = 1$, which is assumed to be small enough so that ρ is greater than 1. To proceed, we make $u(z, t)$ independent of z in the subset $\mathcal{S}_k(\theta)$ of the kth increasing domain, by introducing $u_k(t) = e^{t\nu^k}$ for $\nu = \rho^{-\delta}$, and fix

$$\mu = \rho^{-\delta'} > \nu$$

for $\delta' < \delta$. In the following we will write $f_k(z) = f(z, u_k(t))$ and $u_k = u_k(t)$, omitting the variable t. Recall that the kernel function satisfies the differential equation:

$$f_k'(z) = 1 - f_k(z) \sum_{a \in \mathcal{A}} \frac{p_a u_k}{f(p_a u_k z, u_k)}. \tag{9.86}$$

Let $a_k(z, t) = a(z, u_k(t))$. Since $L(z, 1) = e^z$ for all z, $f(z, 1) = 1$. Since $\frac{\partial}{\partial u} f(z, u)$ is well defined and continuous, we can restrict the neighborhood $\mathcal{U}(1)$ in such a way that $f(z, u)$ is non zero and therefore $a(z, u)$ is well defined for $z \in \mathcal{S}_0(\theta) = \{z \in \mathcal{S}(\theta) : |z| < R\}$ and $u \in \mathcal{U}(1)$. Let a_0 be a nonnegative number such that

$$\forall u \in \mathcal{U}(1) , \quad \forall z \in \mathcal{S}_0(\theta) : \quad |a_0(z, t)| \le a_0|t|. \tag{9.87}$$

Now we fix ε such that $a_0\varepsilon < 1$. We want to prove that there exists a number $\varepsilon > 0$ such that there is an increasing sequence of nonnegative numbers a_k such that

$$|a_k(z, t)| \le a_k|t|\mu^k \tag{9.88}$$

for all $z \in \mathcal{S}_k(\theta)$ and all t for which $|t| \le \varepsilon$, with $\limsup_{k\to\infty} a_k < \infty$.

We now apply the increasing domain approach. Let $z \in \mathcal{S}_k(\theta)$. We set

$$g_k(z) = \sum_{a \in \mathcal{A}} \frac{p_a u_k}{f(p_a u_k z, u_k)}. \tag{9.89}$$

Thus (9.86) can be rewritten as $f'_k(z) = 1 - g_k(z)f_k(z)$, and the differential equation can be solved to give

$$f_k(z) = 1 + \int_0^z (1 - g_k(x)) \exp(G_k(x) - G_k(z)) dx , \qquad (9.90)$$

where $G_k(z)$ is a primitive of the function $g_k(z)$.

We now will give some bounds on $g_k(z)$ for $z \in S_k(\theta)$ and $|t| < \varepsilon$. For all $a \in \mathcal{A}$ we assume that $p_a u_k z \in S_{k-1}(\theta)$. We have $u_k(t) = u_{k-1}(\nu t)$ and we can use the recursion (9.90) since $|\nu t| < \varepsilon$. In particular we have

$$g_k(z) = \sum_{a \in \mathcal{A}} p_a u_k(1 + a_{k-1}(p_a u_k z, \nu t)) = 1 + b_k(z, t) \qquad (9.91)$$

with

$$b_k(z, t) = \sum_{a \in \mathcal{A}} p_a(u_k - 1 + u_k a_{k-1}(p_a u_k z, \nu t)). \qquad (9.92)$$

Since both $|a_{k-1}(p u_k, \nu t)|$ and $|a_{k-1}(q u_k, \nu t)|$ are smaller than $a_{k-1} \nu \mu^{k-1} |t|$, and since $|u_k - 1| \le \beta \nu^k |t|$ for some β close to 1, we have $|b(z, t)| \le b_k |t|$ with

$$b_k = (a_{k-1} \nu \mu^{k-1} + \beta \nu^k)(1 + \beta \nu^k \varepsilon). \qquad (9.93)$$

Thus, substituting into (9.90) we find that

$$|f_k(z) - 1| \le \int_0^z |b_k(x, t)| \exp(\Re(G_k(x) - G_k(z))) dx$$

$$\le \int_0^1 b_k |t| |z| \exp(\Re(G_k(zy) - G_k(z))) dy$$

$$\le \frac{b_k |t|}{\cos(\theta) - b_k |t|}.$$

Clearly,

$$\Re(G_k(yz) - G_k(z)) = -\Re(z)(1 - y) + \int_y^1 \Re(z b_k(zx, t)) dx$$

$$\le -\cos(\theta)|z| + b_k|z|,$$

hence

$$\left| \frac{1}{f_k(z)} - 1 \right| \le \frac{\frac{b_k |t|}{\cos(\theta) - b_k |t|}}{1 - \frac{b_k |t|}{\cos(\theta) - b_k |t|}} = \frac{b_k |t|}{\cos(\theta) - 2b_k |t|} . \qquad (9.94)$$

Therefore,

$$a_k \le \left(a_{k-1}\frac{\nu}{\mu} + \beta\frac{\nu^k}{\mu^k} \right)(1 + \beta\nu^k\varepsilon)\frac{1}{\cos(\theta) - b_k\varepsilon} \ . \tag{9.95}$$

Now let $h(a_k, \varepsilon)$ be the right-hand side of (9.95). Notice that

$$\frac{\partial}{\partial a_k}h(a_k, 0) = \frac{\nu}{\mu\cos(\theta)} < 1$$

for small enough θ. Thus we are in within the remit of Lemma 9.4.8. Moreover, $h(x, \varepsilon)$ is increasing. Since in Lemma 9.4.8 we can make ε as small as necessary, $\limsup_{k\to\infty} a_k < \infty$ and (9.88) is proved, and so is the lemma. ∎

We can extend this lemma to a complex neighborhood of $t = 0$ ($u = 1$).

Lemma 9.4.10. *For all numbers $\alpha > 0$ there exist $\varepsilon > 0$, $\theta \in]0, \pi/2[$ such that, for complex t with $|t| < \varepsilon$,*

$$|a(z, u(z, t))| \le \alpha\frac{|t|}{|z|^{\delta'}} \tag{9.96}$$

for all $z \in \mathcal{S}$.

Proof. The proof is essentially the same as that of the previous lemma except that we have to extend the cone $\mathcal{S}(\theta)$ to a larger set $\mathcal{S}'(\theta)$ defined by $\{z: |\arg(z)| \le \theta + \phi|z|^{\delta-1}\}$ such that if $z \in \mathcal{S}'(\theta)$ then, for all $a \in \mathcal{A}$, $p_a u(z, t)z$ also belongs to $\mathcal{S}'(\theta)$ (with a small rotation of angle $\Im(\frac{t}{|z|^\delta})$ in the case where two points outside $\mathcal{S}(\theta)$ may not satisfy the induction hypothesis). ∎

We can now establish (9.66) of Theorem 9.4.2.

Theorem 9.4.11. *Let $\theta \in]0, \pi/2[$. There exist numbers $A > 0$, $\alpha < 1$, and $\varepsilon > 0$ such that, for all complex t with $|t| \le \varepsilon$,*

$$z \notin \mathcal{S}(\theta) \Rightarrow |L(z, u(z, t))| \le Ae^{\alpha|z|} \ . \tag{9.97}$$

Proof. We proceed as for the previous proof. First we prove the statement for t real (near $t = 0$) and then consider complex t. We take a neighborhood $\mathcal{U}(1)$ of $u = 1$ (or $t = 0$) and define ρ as in (9.77). We define $\bar{\mathcal{C}}(\theta)$ as the complement of $\mathcal{S}(\theta)$ in the complex plane. We also introduce

$$\lambda = \min_{u\in\mathcal{U}(1), a\in\mathcal{A}}\{p_a|u|\}. \tag{9.98}$$

We set $R > 0$ and define $\bar{C}_0(\theta)$ and $\bar{C}_k(\theta)$ for integer $k > 0$ as subsets of $\bar{C}(\theta)$:

$$\bar{C}_0(\theta) = \{z \in \bar{C}(\theta), |z| \le \lambda R\},$$
$$\bar{C}_k(\theta) = \{z \in \bar{C}(\theta), \lambda R < |z| \le \rho^k R\}.$$

With these definitions, if $u \in \mathcal{U}(1)$ when z is in $\bar{C}_k(\theta) - \bar{C}_{k-1}(\theta)$ then both puz and quz are in $\bar{C}_{k-1}(\theta)$. This determines the increasing domains in this case.

Since $L(z, 1) = e^z$, if $\alpha > \cos(\theta)$ then $|L(z, 1)| \le e^{\alpha|z|}$. There exist $A_0 > 0$ and ε such that for all t with $|t| \le \varepsilon$ and for all $z \in \bar{C}_0(\theta)$: $|L(z, e^t)| \le A_0 e^{\alpha|z|}$. We also tune ε so that $\alpha \prod_k u_k(\varepsilon) < 1$.

We proceed with the same analysis for $z \in \bar{C}_1(\theta)$. However, since $|L(z, 1)|$ is strictly smaller than $e^{\alpha|z|}$ for all $z \in \bar{C}_1(\theta)$, we can find $A_1 < 1$ and $\varepsilon > 0$ such that for all t with $|t| \le \varepsilon$ and for all $z \in \bar{C}_1(\theta)$ we have $|L(z, e^t)| \le A_1 e^{\alpha|z|}$. In fact, since

$$\min_{z \in \bar{C}_1(\theta)} \left\{ \frac{|e^z|}{e^{\alpha|z|}} \right\} \to 0$$

when $R \to \infty$ we can make A_1 as small as we want.

We now define $\alpha_k = \alpha \prod_{i=0}^{i=k} u_k(\varepsilon)$. We will prove by induction that there exists an increasing sequence $A_k < 1$ such that, for t with $|t| \le \varepsilon$,

$$z \in \bar{C}_k(\theta) \Rightarrow |L(z, u_k(t))| \le A_k e^{\alpha_k|z|}. \tag{9.99}$$

Our plan is to prove this property by induction. Assume that is true for all integers smaller than or equal to $k - 1$; we will then prove that it is true for k. Assume that $z \in \bar{C}_k(\theta) - \bar{C}_{k-1}(\theta)$. We use the differential equation

$$L(z, u_k) = L(z/\rho, u_k) + \int_{z/\rho}^{z} \prod_{a \in \mathcal{A}} L(p_a u_k x, u_k) dx.$$

Clearly,

$$|L(z, u_k)| \le |L(z/\rho, u_k)| + |z| \int_{1/\rho}^{1} \prod_{a \in \mathcal{A}} |L(p_a u_k z y, u_k)| dy.$$

Using the induction hypothesis,

$$|L(z/\rho, u_k)| \le A_{k-1} e^{\alpha_{k-1}|z|/\rho},$$

and so for all $a \in \mathcal{A}$,

$$|L(p_a u_k y z, u_k)| \le A_{k-1} e^{\alpha_{k-1} p_a |u_k||z|y} \le A_{k-1} e^{\alpha_k p|z|y}$$

(we have $\alpha_{k-1}|u| \le \alpha_{k-1}e^{\varepsilon} = \alpha_k$). Thus

$$|L(z, u_k)| \le A_{k-1}e^{\alpha_{k-1}|z|/\rho} + \frac{A_{k-1}^2}{\alpha_k}\left(e^{\alpha_k|z|} - e^{\alpha_k|z|/\rho}\right).$$

This gives an estimate

$$A_k \le \frac{A_{k-1}^2}{\alpha_k} + A_{k-1}e^{-\rho^{k-2}(\rho-1)\alpha_k R}.$$

Evidently, the term in $e^{-\rho^{k-2}(\rho-1)\alpha_k R}$ can be made as small as we want by increasing R. If we choose A_1 such that

$$\frac{A_1}{\alpha_1} + e^{-\rho^{k-2}(\rho-1)\alpha_k R} < 1$$

for all k then we get $A_k \le A_{k-1}$ and the theorem is proven for t real. Figure 9.6 displays the function $\log L(z, u_k(t))/z$ for $t = 0.1$ and $t = -0.1$ for $u_k(t) = e^{t\nu^k}$ with $\nu = \rho^{-0.5} \approx 1.34524$ and $k = 1, \dots, 6$. This confirms graphically our assertion.

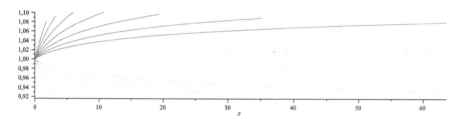

Figure 9.6. The function $(\log L(z, u_k))/z$ when $p_a = p_b = 0.5$ and $u_k = e^{t\nu^k}$ for $t = 0.1$ and $t = -0.1$ for $k = 1, \dots, 6$.

Now, we need to expand our proof to the case where t is complex and $|t| \le \varepsilon$. To this end we use a trick similar to that in the proof of Lemma 9.4.10. We expand $\bar{C}(\theta)$ as

$$\bar{C}'(\theta) = \{z : \arg(z)| \ge \theta + \phi R^{\delta-1} - \phi|z|^{\delta-1}\},$$

for $|z| > R\rho$, in order to ensure that $p_a u_k z$ stays in $\bar{C}'(\theta)$ for all $a \in \mathcal{A}$ when

$$z \in \bar{C}'_k(\theta) - \bar{C}'_{k-1}(\theta)$$

(absorbing, if needed, a tiny rotation that the factor u_k implies when t is complex). Of course, one must choose ϕ such that $\theta + \phi R^{\delta-1} < \pi/2$ and tune ε. Figure 9.7 displays the function $\log P(z, u_k(t))/z$ for $t = 0.1i$ and $k = 6$ with the usual convention for complex function display. Again it confirms our statement.

■

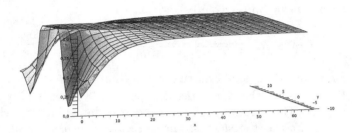

Figure 9.7. The function $\log L(x+iy, u_k(t)))/(x+iy)$ when $p_a = p_b = 0.5$ and $u_k = e^{t\nu^k}$ for $t = 0.1.i$ and $k = 6$.

9.5. Exercises

9.1   Prove Lemma 9.4.8.

9.2   Analyze the phrase length D_n in the LZ'78 algorithm; that is, compute the mean and the variance, as well as proving the CLT and large deviation results for D_n.

9.3   Consider a digital search tree built over an unbiased binary memoryless source, that is, one with $p_a = p_b = 0.5$. Prove that the variance of the path length grows linearly in this case, that is, $\mathrm{Var}[L_m]\Theta(m)$ and compute precisely the term in front of m (see Kirschenhofer et al. 1994).

9.4   Study the problem of Gilbert and Kadota (1992), namely: How many parsings of total length n can one construct from m words? For example, for $m = 2$ we have four parsings of length 3, namely $(0)(00)$, $(0)(01)$, $(1)(10)$ and $(1)(11)$, and two parsings of length 2, namely $(0)(1)$ and $(1)(0)$. Let $F_m(n)$ be the number of parsings built from m words of total length n, and let $F_m(x) = \sum_{n=0}^{\infty} F_m(n)x^n$ be its generating function.

Note that

$$F_{m+1}(x) = x^m \sum_{k=0}^{m} \binom{m}{k} F_k(x) F_{m-k}(x).$$

Observe that

$$F_m(n) = 2^n P(L_m^{sym} = n)$$

where L_m^{sym} is the path length in a symmetric digital tree. In particular, for $n = m \log_2 m + O(\sqrt{m})$ show that

$$F_m(n) \sim \frac{2^n}{\sqrt{2\pi(C + \delta(\log_2 n))m}} \exp\left(-\frac{(n - m \log_2 m)^2}{2(C + \delta(\log_2 n))m}\right)$$

for a constant C and a fluctuating function $\delta(x)$.

9.5   First consider the generalized Lempel–Ziv'78 scheme. Fix an integer $b \geq 1$. The algorithm parses a sequence into phrases such that the next phrase is the *shortest* phrase seen in the past by *at most* $b - 1$ phrases ($b = 1$ corresponds to the original Lempel–Ziv algorithm). For example, consider the sequence *ababbababababaaaaaaaaaac* over the alphabet $\mathcal{A} = \{a, b, c\}$. For $b = 2$ it is parsed as follows:

$$(a)(b)(a)(b)(ba)(ba)(baa)(aa)(aa)(aaa)(c)$$

with seven *distinct* phrases and eleven phrases altogether. Analyze this algorithm, its compression rate, its redundancy and the number of phrases (see Louchard, Szpankowski, and Tang (1999)).

9.6   In Theorem 9.3.3 we established the central limit theorem for the path length L_m in a digital search tree. Using the Berry–Esseen inequality establish the rate of convergence to the CLT.

9.7   In Theorem 9.2.1 we establish the central limit theorem for the number of phrases M_n in the LZ'78 algorithm. Using the Berry–Esseen inequality establish the rate of convergence to the CLT.

9.8   The multiplicity parameter for tries is defined in Section 7.2.4 and for suffix trees in Section 8.3. Consider the LZ'78 scheme and the associated digital search tree and define the corresponding parameter. This parameter coincides with the number of previous phrases that are equal to the new inserted phrase (without the last symbol). Analyze this parameter.

9.9   Consider two strings X^n and Y^m. Parse the string X^n using the Lempel–Ziv'78 algorithm. Then consider parsing the other string, Y^m, with respect to X^n by the LZ'78 algorithm. Analyze the phrase length and the number of phrases of Y^m (see Ziv and Merhav (1993)).

9.10   Extend the main results of this chapter to Markov sources (see Jacquet et al. (2001)).

Bibliographical notes

In this chapter we studied the limiting distribution, the large deviations, the moments of the number of phrases, and the redundancy of the Lempel–Ziv'78 compression scheme when the text is generated by a memoryless source. Among other things we proved that the number of phrases satisfies the central limit law and that the (normalized) redundancy rate of the LZ'78 code obeys the CLT. We accomplished this by studying the path length in a digital search tree with a fixed number of strings, as discussed in depth in Chapter 7.

The Lempel–Ziv algorithm was introduced in Ziv and Lempel (1978). It has been analyzed in several papers, e.g., Aldous and Shields (1988), Louchard and Szpankowski (1995), Louchard et al. (1999), Jacquet et al. (2001), Merhav (1991), Plotnik, Weinberger, and Ziv (1992), Savari (1997), Wyner (1997) and Ziv and Merhav (1993). In particular, the limiting distribution for the number of phrases in LZ'78 was studied in Aldous and Shields (1988) and Jacquet and Szpankowski (1995). In Aldous and Shields (1988) only an unbiased (symmetric) memoryless source was analyzed ($p_a = 0.5$). Aldous and Shields (1988) wrote: "It is natural to conjecture that asymptotic normality holds for a larger class of processes .... But in view of the difficulty of even the simplest case (i.e., the fair coin-tossing case we treat here) we are not optimistic about finding a general result. We believe the difficulty of our normality result is intrinsic ... ." The general memoryless case was solved in Jacquet and Szpankowski (1995) using analytic tools of a similar nature to those in this chapter. A simplified and generalized analysis was presented in Jacquet and Szpankowski (2011, 2014). However, the proof of the CLT in our 1995 paper was quite complicated: it involves a generalized analytic depoissonization over convex cones in the complex plane. It should be pointed out that, since this 1995 paper, no simpler proof, in fact, no new proof of the CLT has been presented except for that by Neininger and Rüschendorf (2004); however, that was only for *unbiased* memoryless sources (as in Aldous and Shields (1988)). The proof of Neininger and Rüschendorf (2004) applies the so-called *contraction method*.

The redundancy of the Lempel–Ziv'78 remained an open problem for some time. It was conjectured in Plotnik et al. (1992) that the average redundancy decays as $O(\log \log n / \log n)$. It was finally settled in Louchard and Szpankowski (1997) and Savari (1997). The variance and the limiting distribution of the redundancy were presented for the first time in Jacquet and Szpankowski (2011, 2014).

Finally, universal types based on LZ'78 are discussed in Seroussi (2006b); see also Knessl and Szpankowski (2005) and Seroussi (2006a).

CHAPTER 10

String Complexity

In this chapter we analyze a set of distinct substrings (factors, words) of a sequence X. We denote this set as $I(X)$. Our goal is to estimate the cardinality of $I(X)$, known as the *string complexity*. More interestingly, we shall also study the cardinality of $I(X) \cap I(Y)$ when X and Y are two sequences. This is called the *joint string complexity*.

The string complexity captures the richness of the language used in a sequence. For example, sequences with low complexity contain a large number of repeated substrings and they eventually become periodic (e.g., the tandem repeats in a DNA sequence). On the one hand, in order to identify unusually low- or high-complexity strings one needs to determine how far their complexities are from the average or maximum string complexity. On the other hand, the joint string complexity is a very efficient way of evaluating the degree of similarity of two sequences. For example, the genome sequences of two dogs will contain more common words than the genome sequences of a dog and a cat; the set of common words of one author's text is larger than the set of common words between two texts from two different authors. Similarly, two texts written in the same language have more words in common than texts written in very different languages. Also, the joint complexity is larger when languages are quite close (e.g., French and Italian), and smaller when languages are rather different (e.g., English and Polish). In fact this can be verified experimentally as will be discussed in the last section of this chapter (see Figure 10.2).

Here we will analyze the average (joint) string complexity under the assumption that the underlying sequences are generated by memoryless sources. We should point out that the technique proposed in this chapter can be extended to Markov sources, as recently proposed in Jacquet and Szpankowski (2012) and in Jacquet et al. (2013).

We first present the average string complexity of a single string of length n and prove that it equals $n^2/2 - O(n \log n)$. Then, we will show that the average joint string complexity is $\Theta(n)$ when two strings are generated by the same source model and $\Theta(n^\kappa)$, for some $\kappa < 1$, when the strings are generated by two different independent sources. When proving these results we use techniques discussed in Chapters 7 and 8 as the string complexity is related to some parameters of the associated suffix tree. Furthermore, we need an extension of the methodology used so far to include the two-dimensional Mellin transform and depoissonization.

10.1. Introduction to string complexity

In this section, we formally introduce string complexity as well as the joint string complexity. We also present some simple properties that will be used throughout this chapter.

10.1.1. String self-complexity

We first consider the string complexity of a single string, which we also call the self-complexity. Throughout we denote by X the string (text) whose complexity we plan to study. Define by $I(X)$ the set of *distinct* substrings of X. For example, if $X = aabaa$, then $I(X) = \{\varepsilon, a, b, aa, ab, ba, aab, aba, baa, aaba, abaa, aabaa\}$; if $X = abbba$, then $I(X) = \{\varepsilon, a, b, ab, bb, ba, abb, bbb, bba, abbb, bbba, abbba\}$. The string complexity is the cardinality of $I(X)$.

In this chapter we study the *average* string complexity. Clearly,

$$\mathbf{E}[|I(X)|] = \sum_{X \in \mathcal{A}^n} P(X)|I(X)|,$$

where $|I(X)|$ denotes the cardinality of $I(X)$. Let $|X|_w$ denote the number of times that the word w occurs in X; it is nothing other than our familiar frequency count $O_X(w)$ analyzed in depth in Chapter 2. It is now easy to observe that

$$|I(X)| = \sum_{w \in \mathcal{A}^*} \min\{1, |X|_w\},$$

since we count only *distinct* occurrences of w in X. Furthermore, since between any two positions in X there is one and only one substring, we also have

$$\sum_{w \in \mathcal{A}^*} |X|_w = \frac{(|X| + 1)|X|}{2}.$$

This we can rewrite in a more convenient form as

$$|I(X)| = \frac{(|X| + 1)|X|}{2} - \sum_{w \in \mathcal{A}^*} \max\{0, |X|_w - 1\}.$$

Now let $|X| = n$, and denote the average string complexity by

$$C_n := \mathbf{E}[|I(X)| \mid |X| = n].$$

Then, in terms of our regular notation $O_n(w) = |X|_w$ from Chapter 2, we finally arrive at

$$C_n = \frac{(n + 1)n}{2} - \sum_{w \in \mathcal{A}^*} \sum_{k \geq 2} (k - 1)P(O_n(w) = k). \tag{10.1}$$

10.1.2. Joint string complexity

Let X and Y be two sequences, not necessarily of the same length. We define $J(X, Y)$ as the set of common factors between X and Y, that is, $J(X, Y) =$

$I(X) \cap I(Y)$. For example, if $X = aabaa$ and $Y = abbba$, then $J(X, Y) = \{\varepsilon, a, b, ab, ba\}$. We call $|J(X, Y)|$ the *joint* complexity of sequences X and Y.

Our goal is to estimate the average joint complexity $J_{n,m} = \mathbf{E}[|J(X, Y)|]$ of two random sequences X and Y of lengths n and m, respectively, generated by two (possibly different) independent sources. We denote these sources as source 1 and source 2. We have

$$|J(X, Y)| = \sum_{w \in \mathcal{A}^*} \min\{1, |X|_w\} \cdot \min\{1, |Y|_w\}.$$

Therefore, for $|X| = n$ and $|Y| = m$

$$J_{n,m} = \mathbf{E}[|J(X, Y)|] - 1 = \sum_{w \in \mathcal{A}^* - \{\varepsilon\}} P(O_n^1(w) \geq 1) P(O_m^2(w) \geq 1)$$

where $O_n^i(w)$ is the number of w-occurrences in a string of length n generated by source i. We have removed the empty word to ease the presentation.

10.2.   Analysis of string self-complexity

Now we briefly discuss the average string self-complexity when the underlying string is generated by a memoryless source.

Theorem 10.2.1. *Assume that the string X of length n is generated by a memoryless source over a finite alphabet $\mathcal{A}$. Then the average string complexity C_n is*

$$C_n = \frac{(n+1)n}{2} - \frac{n}{h}(\log n - 1 + Q_0(\log n) + o(1))$$

where h is as usual the entropy rate per symbol of the text source while $Q_0(x)$ is a periodic function of small amplitude, with zero mean when the $\log p_a$, $a \in \mathcal{A}$, are rationally related, and zero otherwise.

Proof. From (10.1) we conclude that

$$C_n = \frac{(n+1)n}{2} + s_n^{FS} - n(D_n^{FS})'(1) \tag{10.2}$$

where s_n^{FS} is the average size of a *finite suffix tree* and $D_n^{FS}(u) = \mathbf{E}[u^{D_n^{FS}}]$ is the probability generating function for the depth of insertion in the finite suffix tree as described in Section 8.1.2. Furthermore, by Theorem 8.1.13 we know that there exists $\varepsilon > 0$ such that $s_n^{FS} = s_n^T + O(n^{1-\varepsilon})$ and $D_n^{FS}(u) = D_n^T(u) + O(n^{-\varepsilon})$, where s_n^T and $D_n^T(u)$ are the respective quantities for the independent tries. As in Chapter 7 we denote by, respectively, $\mathbf{E}[S_n] = s_n^T$ and $\mathbf{E}[L_n] = n(D_n^{FS})'(1)$ the average size and the external path length in the associated (independent) trie. In Theorem 7.2.9 and Theorem 7.2.7 we show that

$$\mathbf{E}[S_n] = \frac{1}{h}(n + \Psi(\log n)) + o(n),$$

$$\mathbf{E}[L_n] = \frac{n \log n}{h} + n\Psi_2(\log n) + o(n),$$

where $\Psi(\log n)$ and $\Psi_2(\log n)$ are periodic functions when the $\log p_a$, $a \in \mathcal{A}$ are rationally related. This completes the proof. ∎

For a more detailed analysis of the average string complexity for an unbiased memoryless source the reader is referred to Janson, Lonardi, and Szpankowski (2004) and Exercise 10.4.

10.3. Analysis of the joint complexity

We now concentrate on the average case analysis of the joint string complexity. In this section we present some preliminary results. In particular, in Theorem 10.3.1 we establish – as we did in Chapter 8 for suffix trees – that we can analyze the joint string complexity through independent strings. Then we extend the depoissonization technique discussed in Chapter 7 to the two-dimensional case needed for our current analysis. We finish this section by establishing some recurrences on the average joint string complexity.

10.3.1. Independent joint complexity

We first define the independent joint complexity. Consider n independent strings. We denote by $\Omega_n^i(w)$ the number of strings for which w is a prefix when the n strings are generated by a source i, for $i \in \{1, 2\}$. In this case we define

$$C_{n,m} = \sum_{w \in \mathcal{A}^* - \{\varepsilon\}} P(\Omega_n^1(w) \geq 1)P(\Omega_m^2(w) \geq 1) \tag{10.3}$$

and call it the average independent string complexity. In Chapter 7 we noticed that

$$P(\Omega_n^i(w) \geq 1) = 1 - (1 - P_i(w))^n,$$
$$P(\Omega_n^i(w) \geq 2) = 1 - (1 - P_i(w))^n - nP_i(w)(1 - P^i(w))^{n-1}.$$

Our main key result established below shows that the joint string complexity $J_{n,n}$ is well approximated by $C_{n,n}$.

10.3.2. Key property

In the first part of this book, we studied the number of word w occurrences, denoted as $O_n(w)$, in a random text of length n. We now compare it with $\Omega_n(w)$. Using Corollary 8.1.12 we can easily prove (see Exercise 10.6) the following important relationships.

Theorem 10.3.1. *Let k be an integer and let $w \in \mathcal{A}^k$. Define*

$$p = \max_{a \in \mathcal{A}}\{P(a)\} \ . \tag{10.4}$$

Then for all $\varepsilon > 0$ and $w \in \mathcal{B}_k$ we have

$$P(O_n(w) \geq 1) - P(\Omega_n(w) \geq 1) = O(n^{-\varepsilon} P(w)^{1-\varepsilon} p^{k/2}) \tag{10.5}$$

$$P(O_n(w) \geq 2) - P(\Omega_n(w) \geq 2) = O(n^{-\varepsilon} P(w)^{1-\varepsilon} p^{k/2}), \tag{10.6}$$

where, as we recall from Chapter 8, $\mathcal{B}_k$ is the set of words w of length k such that $\max P(w) - \{k\} \leq k/2$ and $\sum_{w \in \mathcal{A}^k - \mathcal{B}_k} P(w) = O(p^{k/2})$. Furthermore, when $w \notin \mathcal{B}_k$,

$$P(O_n(w) \geq 1) - P(\Omega_n(w) \geq 1) = O(n^{-\varepsilon} P(w)^{1-\varepsilon}) \tag{10.7}$$

$$P(O_n(w) \geq 2) - P(\Omega_n(w) \geq 2) = O(n^{-\varepsilon} P(w)^{1-\varepsilon}) \tag{10.8}$$

for large n.

We now assume that both sources are memoryless and write $P_i(a)$ for the probability of occurrence of symbol $a \in \mathcal{A}$ generated by source i. Our main key result is presented next.

Theorem 10.3.2. *There exists $\varepsilon > 0$ such that*

$$J_{n,m} - C_{n,m} = O(\min\{n, m\}^{-\varepsilon}) \tag{10.9}$$

for large n.

Proof. For $w \in \mathcal{A}^*$ and n integer, let

$$\Delta_n^i(w) = P(O_n^i(w) \geq 1) - P(\Omega_n^i(w) \geq 1). \tag{10.10}$$

We have

$$|J_{n,m} - C_{n,m}| \leq \sum_{w \in \mathcal{A}^*} \left(|\Delta_n^1(w)| + |\Delta_m^2(w)| + |\Delta_n^1(w)\Delta_m^2(w)| \right) .$$

Let us consider the sum of the $|\Delta_n^1(w)|$. We set $\sum_{w \in \mathcal{A}^*} |\Delta_n^1(w)| = \delta_1 + \delta_2$ with $\delta_1(n) = \sum_{w \in \mathcal{B}_{|w|}} |\Delta_n^1(w)|$ and $\delta_2(n) = \sum_{w \in \mathcal{A}^* - \mathcal{B}_{|w|}} |\Delta_n^1(w)|$. Using Theorem 10.3.1 we know that, for all $\varepsilon > 0$,

$$\delta_1(n) = O\left(\sum_{w \in \mathcal{A}^*} n^{-\varepsilon} P(w)^{1-\varepsilon} p^{|w|/2} \right) = O\left(\sum_k n^{-\varepsilon} q^{-k\varepsilon} p^{k/2} \right),$$

$$\delta_2(n) = O\left(\sum_{w \in \mathcal{A}^* - \mathcal{B}_{|w|}} n^{-\varepsilon} P(w)^{1-\varepsilon} \right) = O\left(\sum_k n^{-\varepsilon} q^{-k\varepsilon} p^{k/2} \right),$$

for $p = \max_{a \in \mathcal{A}} \{P(a)\}$ and $q = \min_{a \in \mathcal{A}} \{P(a)\}$. We conclude that $\delta_1(n)$ and $\delta_2(n)$ are both of order $n^{-\varepsilon}$ as long as $q^{-\varepsilon} p^{1/2} < 1$.

We can prove similarly that $\sum_{w \in \mathcal{A}^*} |\Delta_m^2(w)| = O(m^{-\varepsilon})$ when the same condition is applied to the second source model. The evaluation of the sum $\sum_{w \in \mathcal{A}^*} |\Delta_n^1(w)\Delta_m^2(w)|$ is left as Exercise 10.7.   ∎

10.3.3.   Recurrence and generating functions

From now on we will exclusively concentrate on $C_{n,m}$ (see (10.3)) for memoryless sources. We start with a recurrence for the independent joint string complexity.

Lemma 10.3.3.   *For $n, m \geq 1$ we have the recurrence*

$$C_{n,m} = 1 + \sum_{a \in \mathcal{A}} \sum_{k, \ell \geq 0} \binom{n}{k} P_1(a)^k (1 - P_1(a))^{n-k} \binom{m}{\ell} P_2(a)^\ell (1 - P_2(a))^{m-\ell} C_{k,\ell},$$

$$\tag{10.11}$$

with $C_{0,m} = C_{n,0} = 0$.

Proof. Let us assume that $n, m > 0$. Partitioning $\mathcal{A}^*$ as $\{\varepsilon\} + \sum_{a \in \mathcal{A}} a\mathcal{A}^*$ and using (10.3) we arrive at

$$C_{n,m} = 1 + \sum_{a \in \mathcal{A}} \sum_{w \in \mathcal{A}^*} (1 - (1 - P_1(aw))^n)(1 - (1 - P_2(aw))^m). \tag{10.12}$$

Factoring $P_i(aw)$ as $P_i(a)P_i(w)$ and expanding, we obtain

$$1 - (1 - P_1(a)P_1(w))^n = \sum_k \binom{n}{k} P_1(a)^k (1 - P_1(a))^{n-k} \left(1 - (1 - P_1(w))^k\right),$$

$$1 - (1 - P_2(a)P_2(w))^m = \sum_\ell \binom{m}{\ell} P_2(a)^\ell (1 - P_2(a))^{m-\ell} \left(1 - (1 - P_2(w))^\ell\right).$$

We now establish (10.11) using (10.3) with n, m replaced by k, ℓ.   ∎

In passing, we observe that

$$C_{1,1} = \frac{1}{1 - \sum_{a \in \mathcal{A}} P_1(a)P_2(a)}.$$

As already seen in previous chapters, recurrences like the above are easier to solve in the poissonized version. However, this time we need a two-dimensional poissonized generating function, defined by

$$C(z_1, z_2) = \sum_{n,m \geq 0} C_{n,m} \frac{z_1^n z_2^m}{n!m!} e^{-z_1 - z_2}.$$

Then (10.11) becomes

$$C(z_1, z_2) = (1 - e^{-z_1})(1 - e^{-z_2}) + \sum_{a \in \mathcal{A}} C\left(P_1(a)z_1, P_2(a)z_2\right). \tag{10.13}$$

Clearly,

$$n!m!C_{n,m} = [z_1^n][z_2^m]C(z_1, z_2)e^{z_1 + z_2}$$

which is a two-dimensional (double) depoissonization operation. As mentioned earlier, we presented one-dimensional depoissonization in Table 7.2. However, in our present case we have two variables, z_1 and z_2, and we need a generalized depoissonization that will allow us to claim that $C_{n,n} = C(n, n) + O(1)$. This is discussed in the next subsection.

10.3.4.   Double depoissonization

Let $a_{n,m}$ be a two-dimensional (double) sequence of complex numbers. We define the double Poisson transform $f(z_1, z_2)$ of $a_{n,m}$ as

$$f(z_1, z_2) = \sum_{n,m \geq 0} a_{n,m} \frac{z_1^n z_1^m}{n! \, m!} e^{-z_1 - z_2}.$$

It is relatively straightforward to obtain an extension of the one-dimensional depoissonization result presented in Table 7.2 to the two-dimensional case.

Lemma 10.3.4. *Let $\mathcal{S}_\theta$ be a cone of angle θ around the real axis. Assume that there exist $B > 0$, $D > 0$, $\alpha < 1$ and β such that for $|z_1|, |z_2| \to \infty$:*

(i) *if $z_1, z_2 \in \mathcal{S}_\theta$ then $|f(z_1, z_2)| = B(|z_1|^\beta + |z_2|^\beta)$;*

(ii) *if $z_1, z_2 \notin \mathcal{S}_\theta$ then $|f(z_1, z_2)e^{z_1 + z_2}| = De^{\alpha|z_1| + \alpha|z_2|}$;*

(iii) *if $z_i \in \mathcal{S}_\theta$ and $z_j \notin \mathcal{S}_\theta$ for $\{i, j\} = \{1, 2\}$ and $|f(z_1, z_2)e^{z_j}| < D|z_i|^\beta e^{\alpha|z_j|}$.*

Then

$$a_{n,m} = f(n, m) + O\left(\frac{n^\beta}{m} + \frac{m^\beta}{n}\right)$$

for large m and n.

Proof. Let

$$f_n(z_2) = \sum_m a_{n,m} \frac{z_2^m}{m!} e^{-z_2}.$$

We notice that $f(z_1, z_2)$ is the Poisson transform of the sequence $f_n(z_2)$ with respect to the variable z_1.

First depoissonization. For $z_2 \in \mathcal{S}_\theta$ we have the following estimates

$$\text{for } z_1 \in \mathcal{S}_\theta, \quad |f(z_1, z_2)| < B(|z_1|^\beta + |z_2|^\beta)$$
$$\text{for } z_1 \notin \mathcal{S}_\theta, \quad |f(z_1, z_2)e^{z_1}| < D|z_2|^\beta e^{\alpha|z_1|}.$$

Therefore, for $z_2 \in \mathcal{S}_\theta$ we have, for all integers $k > 0$,

$$f_n(z_2) = f(n, z_2) + O\left(n^{\beta-1} + \frac{|z_2|^\beta}{n}\right) + O(|z_2|^\beta n^{\beta-k}).$$

Similarly, when $z_2 \notin \mathcal{S}_\theta$ we have

$$\text{for } z_1 \in \mathcal{S}_\theta, \quad |f(z_1, z_2)e^{z_2}| < D|z_1|^\beta e^{\alpha|z_2|}$$
$$\text{for } z_1 \notin \mathcal{S}_\theta, \quad |f(z_1, z_2)e^{z_1+z_2}| < De^{\alpha|z_1|+\alpha|z_2|}.$$

Thus for all integer k and $\forall z_2 \notin \mathcal{S}_{th}$

$$f_n(z_2)e^{z_2} = f(n, z_2)e^{z_2} + O(n^{\beta-1}e^{\alpha|z_2|}) + O(n^{\beta-k}e^{\alpha|z_2|}).$$

Second depoissonization. The two results for $f_n(z_2)$, respectively for $z_2 \in \mathcal{S}_\theta$ and $z_2 \notin \mathcal{S}_\theta$, allow us to depoissonize $f_n(z_2)$. Then

- for $z_2 \in \mathcal{S}_\theta$, $f_n(z_2) = O(n^\beta + |z_2|^\beta)$;

- for $z_2 \notin \mathcal{S}_\theta$, $f_n(z_2)e^{z_2} = O(n^\beta e^{\alpha|z_2|})$.

The "big oh" terms are uniform. Therefore, for all $k > \beta$,

$$a_{n,m} = f_n(m) + O\left(\frac{n^\beta}{m} + \frac{m^\beta}{n}\right) + O\left(n^\beta m^{\beta-k}\right).$$

Since

$$f_n(m) = f(n, m) + O\left(n^{\beta-1} + \frac{m^\beta}{n}\right),$$

setting $k > \beta + 1$ we prove the desired estimate.   ■

We will now prove that $C(z_1, z_2)$ satisfies the conditions of Lemma 10.3.4, to conclude that

$$C_{n,m} = C(n, m) + O\left(\frac{n}{m} + \frac{m}{n}\right).$$

Lemma 10.3.5.   *The generating function $C(z_1, z_2)$ satisfies the condition of Corollary 10.3.4 with $\beta = 1$.*

Proof. We will prove that the generating function $C(z_1, z_2)$ satisfying the functional equation (10.13) fulfills the conditions of Lemma 10.3.4 with $\beta = 1$. More specifically, we will prove that when z_1 and z_2 belong to a cone $\mathcal{S}_\theta$ with angle $\theta < \pi/2$ around the positive real axis, $C(z_1, z_2) = O(|z_1| + |z_2|)$.

We now use the increasing domain technique discussed in Section 7.2.5. Let $\rho = \max_{a \in \mathcal{A}, i \in \{1,2\}} \{P_i(a)\}$. We denote by $\mathcal{S}_k$ the fraction of the cone containing points such that $|z| < \rho^{-k}$. Notice that $\mathcal{S}_k \in \mathcal{S}_{k+1}$ for all integer k. We also notice that $C(z_1, z_2) = O(|z_1| + |z_2|)$ when $z_1, z_2 \to 0$; therefore we can define

$$B_k = \max_{(z_1,z_2) \in \mathcal{S}_k \times \mathcal{S}_k} \left\{ \frac{|C(z_1, z_2)|}{|z_1| + |z_2|} \right\} < \infty.$$

We know that $C(z_1, z_2)$ satisfies the functional equation (10.13). If $(z_1, z_2) \in \mathcal{S}_{k+1} \times \mathcal{S}_{k+1} - \mathcal{S}_k \times \mathcal{S}_k$ then, for all $a \in \mathcal{A}$ $(P_1(a)z_1, P_2(a)z_2)$ are in $\mathcal{S}_k \times \mathcal{S}_k$ and therefore we have

$$|C(z_1, z_2)| \leq B_k \left(\sum_{a \in \mathcal{A}} P_1(a)|z_1| + P_2(a)|z_2| \right) + 1 = B_k(|z_1| + |z_2|) + 1,$$

since $|1 - e^{-z_i}| < 1$ for $i = 1, 2$. Thus we can derive the recurrence for all $k \geq 1$:

$$B_{k+1} \leq B_k + \max_{(z_1,z_2) \in \mathcal{S}_{k+1} \times \mathcal{S}_{k+1} - \mathcal{S}_k \times \mathcal{S}_k} \left\{ \frac{1}{|z_1| + |z_2|} \right\} = B_k + \rho^k.$$

We need to note carefully that

$$\min_{(z_1,z_2) \in \mathcal{S}_{k+1} \times \mathcal{S}_{k+1} - \mathcal{S}_k \times \mathcal{S}_k} \{|z_1| + |z_2|\} = \rho^{-k},$$

since only one of z_1 and z_2 can have modulus greater than ρ^{-k}. It turns out that $\lim_{k \to \infty} B_k < \infty$ and therefore condition (i) of Lemma 10.3.4 holds.

Now we will prove condition (iii) of Lemma 10.3.4. To this end we define $\mathcal{G}$ as the complementary cone of $\mathcal{S}_\theta$ and $\mathcal{G}_k$ as the portion consisting of points of modulus smaller than ρ^{-k}. We will use $\cos\theta < \alpha < 1$; therefore $\forall z \in \mathcal{G}$: $|e^z| < e^{\alpha|z|}$. We define D_k as follows:

$$D_k = \max_{(z_1, z_2) \in \mathcal{G}_k \times \mathcal{G}_k} \left\{ \frac{|C(z_1, z_2)\exp(z_1 + z_2)|}{\exp(\alpha|z_1| + \alpha|z_2|)} \right\}.$$

Defining $G(z_1, z_2) = C(z_1, z_2)e^{z_1 + z_2}$, we have the equation

$$G(z_1, z_2) = \sum_{a \in \mathcal{A}} G(P_1(a)z_1, P_2(a)z_2)\exp((1 - P_1(a))z_1 + (1 - P_2(a))z_2)$$
$$+ (e^{z_1} - 1)(e^{z_2} - 1).$$

We notice that if $(z_1, z_2) \in \mathcal{G}_{k+1} \times \mathcal{G}_{k+1} - \mathcal{G}_k \times \mathcal{G}_k$, then all $(P_1(a)z_1, P_2(a)z_2)$ are in $\mathcal{G}_k \times \mathcal{G}_k$ and therefore we have

$$|G(z_1, z_2)| \leq D_k \left(\sum_{a \in \mathcal{A}} \exp\left((P_1(a)\alpha + (1 - P_1(a))\cos\theta)|z_1| \right.\right.$$
$$\left.\left. + (P_2(a)\alpha + (1 - P_2(a))\cos\theta)|z_2| \right) \right)$$
$$+ (e^{\cos\theta|z_1|} + 1)(e^{\cos\theta|z_2|} + 1).$$

Now we notice that $\forall a \in \mathcal{A}$ and $\forall i \in \{1, 2\}$:

$$P_i(a)\alpha + (1 - P_i(a))\cos\theta - \alpha \leq -(1 - \rho)(\alpha - \cos\theta);$$

therefore

$$\frac{|G(z_1, z_2)|}{\exp(\alpha(|z_1| + |z_2|))} \leq D_k|\mathcal{A}|\exp(-(1 - \rho)(\alpha - \cos\theta)(|z_1| + |z_2|))$$
$$+ 4\exp(-(\alpha - \cos\theta)(|z_1| + |z_2|)) .$$

Since $(z_1, z_2) \in \mathcal{G}_{k+1} \times \mathcal{G}_{k+1} - \mathcal{G}_k \times \mathcal{G}_k$ implies $|z_1| + |z_2| \geq \rho^{-k}$, it follows that

$$D_{k+1} \leq \max\{D_k, |\mathcal{A}|D_k \exp\left(-(1 - \rho)(\alpha - \cos\theta)\rho^{-k}\right)$$
$$+ 4\exp\left(-(\alpha - \cos\theta)\rho^{-k}\right)\}.$$

We clearly have $\lim_{k \to \infty} D_k < \infty$ and condition (iii) holds. We leave the proof of condition (ii) as Exercise 10.8. ∎

10.4.   Average joint complexity for identical sources

We assume here that the two sources are probabilistically identical, that is, $\forall a \in \mathcal{A}$ we have $P_1(a) = P_2(a) = p_a$. In this case, we define $c(z) = C(z, z)$ which satisfies

$$c(z) = (1 - e^{-z})^2 + \sum_{a \in \mathcal{A}} c(p_a z). \tag{10.14}$$

To this end, in order to extract the asymptotics of the generating function we will use the Mellin transform given in Table 7.1.

Theorem 10.4.1.   (i) *For a biased memoryless source, the joint complexity is asymptotically*

$$C_{n,n} = n\frac{2 \log 2}{h} + Q(\log n)n + o(n),$$

where $Q(x)$ is a small periodic function (with amplitude smaller than 10^{-6}) which is nonzero only when the $\log p_a$, $a \in \mathcal{A}$, are rationally related.
(ii) *For a binary unbiased memoryless source, if $\forall a \in \mathcal{A}$ we have $p_a = 1/2$ then it holds that*

$$C_{n,n} = 2n - 1 + (-1)^n, \qquad n \geq 2$$

with $C_{1,1} = 2$.

Proof. We first consider $p_a = 1/2$ (the binary symmetric case) for which

$$c(z) = 2z - 1 + e^{-2z}.$$

This can be directly verified by substituting it into (10.14). Then an easy calculation leads to $C_{n,n} = 2n + O(1)$ or more precisely $C_{n,n} = 2n - 1 + (-1)^n$, for $n \geq 2$.

  We now consider the general case. Since $c(z)$ is $O(z^2)$ when $z \to 0$ and is $O(z)$ when $z \to \infty$, taking z as a positive real number, the Mellin transform $C^*(s)$ of $c(z)$ is defined for $\Re(s) \in (-2, -1)$ and satisfies

$$c^*(s) = \frac{(2^{-s} - 2)\Gamma(s)}{1 - \sum_{a \in \mathcal{A}} p_a^{-s}}, \tag{10.15}$$

where $\Gamma(s)$, as always, is the Euler gamma function. We use the inverse Mellin transform

$$c(z) = \frac{1}{2i\pi} \int_{d-i\infty}^{d+i\infty} c^*(s) z^{-s} ds$$

for $d \in (-2, -1)$ in the definition domain of $c^*(s)$. The reader is referred to Chapter 7 for a more in-depth discussion of the Mellin transform.

The next step is to use the Cauchy residue theorem. The poles of the integrand of (10.15) are:
(i) the double pole at $s = -1$ with residue $-2z \log 2/h$;
(ii) $s_k = -1 + 2\pi i k/L$ for integer $k \neq 0$ when the $\log p_a$, $a \in \mathcal{A}$, are rationally related (L was introduced in Definition 7.2.6), with residues

$$z^{-s_k} \frac{2^{-s_k} - 2}{h'(s_k)} \Gamma(s_k).$$

Therefore

$$c(z) = \frac{2z \log 2}{h} - \sum_{k \neq 0} z^{-s_k} \frac{2^{-s_k} - 2}{h'(s_k)} \Gamma(s_k) + O(1)$$

with

$$Q(z) = \sum_{k \neq 0} z^{-s_k} \frac{2^{-s_k} - 2}{h'(s_k)} \Gamma(s_k).$$

By Lemma 7.2.4 the behavior of the fluctuating function $Q(z)$ depends on the rationality of the $\log p_a$ ratios. This completes the proof. ∎

10.5. Average joint complexity for nonidentical sources

We now handle the much more complicated case of nonidentical sources. We will again use the functional equation (10.13) but now we need double depoissonization, double Mellin transform, and the saddle point method. In fact, we will establish our main result only for the special case when one source is symmetric.

10.5.1. The kernel and its properties

As in the case of identical sources, the asymptotic behavior of the joint complexity depends crucially on the location of the roots of the denominator of the corresponding (double) Mellin transform (see (10.23) below). This set of roots is much more complex than in the previous case, so we dedicate this subsection to understanding its properties.

Let us define

$$H(s_1, s_2) = 1 - \sum_{a \in \mathcal{A}} (P_1(a))^{-s_1} (P_2(a))^{-s_2}.$$

The *kernel* of $H(s_1, s_2)$ is the set $\mathcal{K}$ of tuples (s_1, s_2) such that $H(s_1, s_2) = 0$. For example, $(-1, 0)$ and $(0, -1)$ belong to $\mathcal{K}$. With this definition set

$$\kappa = \min_{(s_1, s_2) \in \mathcal{K} \cap \mathbb{R}^2} \{(-s_1 - s_2)\}.$$

We will prove that $C_{n,n}$ is of order $n^\kappa/\sqrt{\log n}$.

Let (c_1, c_2) be the unique *real* pair in $\mathcal{K}\cap\mathbb{R}^2$ such that $c_1+c_2 = -\kappa$. We denote by $\partial\mathcal{K}$ the subset of $\mathcal{K}$ consisting of the tuples (s_1, s_2) such that $\Re(s_1+s_2) = -\kappa$ and let $\partial\mathcal{K}^* = \partial\mathcal{K} - \{(c_1, c_2)\}$. Although the set $\mathcal{K}$ is continuous, the subset $\partial\mathcal{K}$ is an enumerable set. A careful analysis will show that there is a positive minimum distance that separates any pair of elements in $\partial\mathcal{K}$.

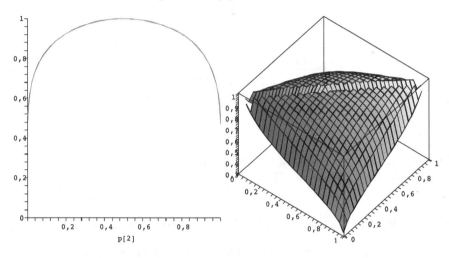

Figure 10.1. The quantity κ versus p_2 for $p_1 = q_1 = 1/2$ (left) and versus (p_1, p_2) (right).

Example 10.5.1. Consider now a binary alphabet $\mathcal{A} = \{a, b\}$, and let $P_i(a) = p_i$ and $P_i(b) = q_i$ for $i \in \{1, 2\}$. Then in Exercise 10.9 the reader is asked to prove that

$$\kappa = \frac{\log\frac{q_2}{q_1}\log\log\frac{q_2}{q_1} + \log\frac{p_1}{p_2}\log\log\frac{p_1}{p_2} - \log\frac{q_2 p_1}{q_1 p_2}\log\log\frac{q_2 p_1}{q_1 p_2}}{\log p_1 \log q_2 - \log p_2 \log q_1}. \tag{10.16}$$

Figure 10.1 displays κ as a function of p_1, p_2. Observe that, for $p_1 = q_1 = 1/2$ κ does not reach zero when p_2 or q_2 is close to zero. ∎

Now we will dwell on some important properties of the set $\partial\mathcal{K}$. We prove the following property.

Lemma 10.5.2. *The set $\partial \mathcal{K}$ consists of pairs $(c_1 + it_1, c_2 + it_2)$ with $(t_1, t_2) \in \mathbb{R}^2$ satisfying $\forall a \in \mathcal{A}$,*

$$(P_1(a))^{it_1} (P_2(a))^{it_2} = 1. \tag{10.17}$$

Proof. Indeed, assume that $(s_1, s_2) \in \partial \mathcal{K}$: hence

$$\sum_{a \in \mathcal{A}} P_1^{-s_1}(a) P_2^{-s_2}(a) = 1.$$

Consequently,

$$\sum_{a \in \mathcal{A}} \left| P_1^{-s_1}(a) P_2^{-s_2}(a) \right| \geq 1$$

or, equivalently,

$$\sum_{a \in \mathcal{A}} P_1^{-\Re(s_1)}(a) P_2^{-\Re(s_2)}(a) \geq 1.$$

Actually, the last inequality is an equality; that is,

$$\sum_{a \in \mathcal{A}} (P_1(a))^{-\Re(s_1)} (P_2(a))^{-\Re(s_2)} = 1.$$

Indeed, assume the contrary, i.e., that

$$\sum_{a \in \mathcal{A}} (P_1(a))^{-\Re(s_1)} (P_2(a))^{-\Re(s_2)} > 1;$$

then by continuity there exists $c_2' < \Re(s_2)$ such that

$$\sum_{a \in \mathcal{A}} (P_1(a))^{-\Re(s_1)} (P_2(a))^{-c_2'} = 1.$$

Thus $(\Re(s_1), c_2') \in \mathcal{K}$. But $\Re(s_1) + c_2' < \Re(s_1) + \Re(s_2) = \kappa$, which contradicts the definition of κ. Therefore, $\sum_{a \in \mathcal{A}} P_1^{-\Re(s_1)}(a) P_2^{-\Re(s_2)}(a) = 1$ implies that $(\Re(s_1), \Re(s_2)) = (c_1, c_2)$. Furthermore, since

$$(P_1(a))^{s_1} (P_2(a))^{s_2} = (P_1(a))^{i\Im(s_1)} (P_2(a))^{i\Im(s_2)} (P_1(a))^{c_1} (P_2(a))^{c_2},$$

each factor $(P_1(a))^{i\Im(s_1)}$ and $(P_2(a))^{i\Im(s_2)}$ must be equal to 1 because this is the only way in which the identity $\sum_{a \in \mathcal{A}} P_1^{-s_1}(a) P_2^{-s_2}(a) = 1$ can be obtained. This completes the proof. ∎

Example 10.5.3. We will illustrate Lemma 10.5.2 for the binary case. Then $(c_1 + it_1, c_2 + it_2) \in \mathcal{K}$ must satisfy (10.17), which further means there exist pairs $(k, \ell) \in \mathbb{Z}$ such that

$$it_1 \log p_1 + it_2 \log p_2 = 2ik\pi,$$
$$it_1 \log q_1 + it_2 \log q_2 = 2i\ell\pi.$$

Therefore,

$$t_1 = \frac{2\pi}{D}(k \log q_2 - \ell \log p_2), \quad t_1 = \frac{2\pi}{D}(-k \log q_1 + \ell \log p_1)$$

with $D = \log p_1 \log q_2 - \log p_2 \log q_1$. ∎

10.5.2. Main results

To present succinctly our main results for nonidentical sources, we need a generalization of the rationally related set of numbers that we introduced in Definition 7.2.6. This will lead us to the notion of *commensurability*.

Let $\mathbf{x} = (x_1, \ldots, x_k)$ be a vector of k real numbers. We say that it is *commensurable* if there exists a real number $\nu \neq 0$ such that $\nu\mathbf{x} \in \mathbb{Z}^k$. We realize that in this case commensurability is equivalent to the numbers $x_1, \ldots, x_k$ being rationally related (in Definition 7.2.6 we used L rather than ν). However, in order to handle the joint complexity we need an extension of the idea of rational relationship to two vectors; then the concept commensurability is more appropriate. Consider two vectors $\mathbf{x}$ and $\mathbf{y}$. We say that they are *mutually commensurable* if there exists a pair of nonzero real numbers, (ν_1, ν_2), such that $\nu_1\mathbf{x} + \nu_2\mathbf{y} \in \mathbb{Z}^k$. The pair (ν_1, ν_2) is called the *integer conjugate* of $(\mathbf{x}, \mathbf{y})$. Furthermore, a pair of vectors is called *mutually fully commensurable* when the set of integer conjugates is of dimension 2 (i.e., the integer conjugates are linearly independent). In this case the set of integer conjugates forms a lattice $\{k\mathbf{a} + \ell\mathbf{b}), (k, \ell) \in \mathbb{Z}^2\}$, where $\mathbf{a}$ and $\mathbf{b}$ are two independent vectors. Finally, if two vectors are mutually commensurable but not fully commensurable, then the integer conjugates form a set of the form $\{k\mathbf{a}, k \in \mathbb{Z}\}$. If $\mathbf{x}$ and $\mathbf{y}$ are not commensurable, then we call them *incommensurable*. We should point out that in our case we shall view the vectors $\mathbf{x}$ and $\mathbf{y}$ as $(\log P_1(a_1), \ldots, \log P_1(a_k)) =: (\log P_1(a))_{a \in \mathcal{A}}$ and $(\log P_2(a_1), \ldots, \log P_2(a_k)) =: (\log P_2(a))_{a \in \mathcal{A}}$, respectively.

We now formulate our main result; however, as mentioned earlier, in the next subsection we prove it only for the special case when one source is unbiased (i.e., symmetric). We need some additional notation. Let $f(s_1, s_2)$ be a C^2 function;

then we define

$$\Delta f(s_1, s_2) = \frac{\partial^2}{\partial s_1^2} f(s_1, s_2) + \frac{\partial^2}{\partial s_2^2} f(s_1, s_2),$$

$$\nabla f(s_1, s_2) = \frac{1}{2} \left(\frac{\partial}{\partial s_1} f(s_1, s_2) + \frac{\partial}{\partial s_2} f(s_1, s_2) \right).$$

We claim that in general the average joint string complexity $C_{n,n}$ (see Theorem 10.4.1) behaves asymptotically as follows

$$C_{n,n} = \frac{n^\kappa}{\sqrt{\log n}} \left(\frac{\Gamma(c_1)\Gamma(c_2)}{\sqrt{\pi \Delta H(c_1, c_2)\nabla H(c_1, c_2)}} + Q(\log n) + o(1) \right), \qquad (10.18)$$

where

$$Q(x) = \sum_{(s_1, s_2) \in \partial \mathcal{K}^*} \frac{\Gamma(s_1)\Gamma(s_2)}{\sqrt{\pi \Delta H(s_1, s_2)\nabla H(s_1, s_2)}} \exp(-i\Im(s_1 + s_2)x).$$

The behavior of $Q(x)$ depends on whether $(\log P_1(a))_{a \in \mathcal{A}}$ and $(\log P_2(a))_{a \in \mathcal{A}}$ are commensurable, which in turn depends on the structure of the set $\partial \mathcal{K}^*$. The properties of $Q(x)$ are discussed in Lemma 10.5.4 below.

In particular, we shall see that $Q(x)$ may exhibit periodic or doubly periodic behavior. Recall that a function f is periodic if there exists $T \neq 0$ such that, for all x, $f(x+T) = f(x)$; a two-variable function $f(x, y)$ is doubly periodic if there exist T_1 and T_2 such that, for all x and y, we have $f(x+T_1, y+T_2) = f(x, y)$. In our case we need to modify this definition slightly, since $Q(x) = F(x, x)$ where $F(x, y)$ is defined formally in (10.19) below.

Lemma 10.5.4. *If $(\log P_1(a))_{a \in \mathcal{A}}$ and $(\log P_2(a))_{a \in \mathcal{A}}$ are not mutually commensurable then*

$$\forall x : \ Q(x) = 0.$$

Otherwise $Q(x)$ is doubly periodic unless $(\log P_1(a))_{a \in \mathcal{A}}$ and $(\log P_2(a))_{a \in \mathcal{A}}$ are not fully mutually commensurable; then the function $Q(x)$ is simply periodic.

Proof. Clearly, the set of integer conjugates (t_1, t_2) of $((2\pi)^{-1} \log P_i(a))_{a \in \mathcal{A}}$ mapped into $(c_1 + it_1, c_2 + it_2)$ corresponds to $\partial \mathcal{K}$. We will consider the commensurable and incommensurable case separately.

If the vectors $(\log P_1(a))_{a \in \mathcal{A}}$ and $(\log P_2(a))_{a \in \mathcal{A}}$ are *not commensurable* then there is no (t_1, t_2) such that, $\forall a \in \mathcal{A}$,

$$\frac{t_1}{2\pi} \log P_1(a) + \frac{t_2}{2\pi} \log P_2(a) \in \mathbb{Z}.$$

But this is not sufficient for us to infer that $\partial \mathcal{K}^* = \emptyset$. To conclude the latter we must prove that the existence of (t_1, t_2) such that $t_1 \log P_1(a) + t_2 \log P_2(a) = 0$, $\forall a \in \mathcal{A}$, implies $(t_1, t_2) = (0, 0)$. Since the vectors $(P_1(a))_{a \in \mathcal{A}}$ and $(P_2(a))_{a \in \mathcal{A}}$ both sum to 1 and are different, there is necessarily at least one symbol $a \in \mathcal{A}$ such that $P_1(a) > P_2(a)$. This implies that $t_1/t_2 < 1$. There is necessarily another symbol $b \in \mathcal{A}$ such that $P_1(b) > P_2(b)$ implies that $t_1/t_2 > 1$. Thus, there is no $(t_1, t_2) \neq (0, 0)$ such that, $\forall a \in \mathcal{A}$, $t_1 \log P_1(a) + t_2 \log P_2(a) = 0$; consequently $\partial \mathcal{K}^* = \emptyset$.

Now we assume that $(\log P_1(a))_{a \in \mathcal{A}}$ and $(\log P_2(a))_{a \in \mathcal{A}}$ are *commensurable*. In this case, the elements of $\partial \mathcal{K}$ form a lattice of the form $(s_1^{k,\ell}, s_2^{k,\ell}) := (c_1 + i(ka_1 + \ell b_1), c_2 + i(ka_2 + \ell b_2))$ with $(k, \ell) \in \mathbb{Z}^2$. Consequently

$$Q(x) = \sum_{(k,\ell) \in \mathbb{Z}^2 - \{(0,0)\}} \gamma_{k,\ell} \exp\left(-ix\left((a_1 + a_2)k + (b_1 + b_2)\ell\right)\right),$$

where

$$\gamma_{k,\ell} = \frac{\Gamma(s_1^{k,\ell})\Gamma(s_2^{k,\ell})}{\sqrt{\pi \Delta H(s_1^{k,\ell}, s_2^{k,\ell}) \nabla H(s_1^{k,\ell}, s_2^{k,\ell})}}.$$

If we set $Q(x) = F(x, x)$ then we can write

$$F(x, y) = \sum_{(k,\ell) \neq (0,0)} \gamma_{k,\ell} \exp\left(-(a_1 + a_2)ikx - (b_1 + b_2)i\ell y\right), \qquad (10.19)$$

which is doubly periodic of period $(2\pi/(a_1 + a_2), 2\pi/(b_1 + b_2))$. When the commensurability is not full, we have $\partial \mathcal{K} = \{(c_1 + ika_1, c_2 + ika_2), k \in \mathbb{Z}\}$ and $Q(x)$ is periodic of period $2\pi/(a_1 + a_2)$.   ■

The binary case is special since, surprisingly, there is no incommensurability at all.

Corollary 10.5.5. *In the binary case, for which $|\mathcal{A}| = 2$, $Q(x)$ is always doubly periodic. When $\log p_1, \log q_1, \log p_2, \log q_2$ are commensurable, $Q(x)$ is simply periodic.*

Proof. The elements of $\mathcal{K}$ corresponding to the pairs $(c_1 + it_1, c_2 + it_2)$ satisfy the conditions discussed in Example 10.5.3 above. Consequently, the elements of $\mathcal{K}$ form a lattice and therefore $Q(x)$ is doubly periodic.   ■

10.5.3. Proof of (10.18) for one symmetric source

Here we will not prove (10.18) in the general case. We investigate in detail only the case when one probability distribution is uniform over the alphabet, i.e., when $\forall a \in \mathcal{A}$ we have $P_1(a) = 1/|\mathcal{A}|$ (an unbiased or symmetric source). To simplify the notation we write $p_a = P_2(a)$. We also write $r(s) = \sum_{a \in \mathcal{A}} p_a^{-s}$.

Theorem 10.5.6. *Let the first source be uniform with $P_1(a) = 1/|\mathcal{A}|$, while the second is a general memoryless source with $p_a = P_2(a)$.*
(i) *If the $\log p_a$, $a \in \mathcal{A}$, are rationally related and ν is the smallest nonnegative real such that, $\forall a \in \mathcal{A}$, $\nu^{-1} \log p_a \in \mathbb{Z}$ then*

$$
C_{n,n} = \frac{n^\kappa}{\sqrt{\log n}} \left(\frac{\Gamma(c_1)\Gamma(c_2)}{\sqrt{\pi \Delta H(c_1, c_2) \nabla H(c_1, c_2)}} + Q(\log n) + O(1/\log n) \right),
$$
$$
(10.20)
$$

where

$$
Q(x) = \sum_{(s_1, s_2) \in \partial \mathcal{K}^*} \frac{\Gamma(s_1)\Gamma(s_2)}{\sqrt{\pi \Delta H(s_1, s_2) \nabla H(s_1, s_2)}} \exp(-i\Im(s_1 + s_2)x)
$$

with

$$
\mathcal{K}^* = \left\{ c_1 + \frac{2ik\pi}{\log |\mathcal{A}|} + 2i\pi\ell \left(\frac{1}{\log \nu} + \frac{1}{\log |\mathcal{A}|} \right), c_2 + \frac{2i\ell}{\log \nu} \right), (k, \ell) \in \mathbb{Z}^2 \setminus \{(0,0)\} \right\}.
$$

(ii) *If the $\log p_a$, $a \in \mathcal{A}$, are not commensurable, then*

$$
C_{n,n} = \frac{n^\kappa}{\sqrt{\log n}} \left(\frac{\Gamma(c_1)\Gamma(c_2)}{\sqrt{\pi \Delta H(c_1, c_2) \nabla H(c_1, c_2)}} + Q(\log n) + o(1) \right), \qquad (10.21)
$$

with

$$
\mathcal{K}^* = \left\{ \left(c_1 + \frac{2ik\pi}{\log |\mathcal{A}|}, c_2 \right), k \in \mathbb{Z}^* \right\}.
$$

Remark 10.5.7. Notice that the error term $O(1/\log n)$ for the rational case is smaller than the error term $o(1)$ in (10.18). ∎

In the rest of this section we provide a proof of Theorem 10.5.6. The heart of it relies on showing that $C(z_1, z_2) = O(z^\kappa)$ for $z_1 = z_2 = z$ and in giving an explicit expression of the factor in front of z^κ. We accomplish this by using a double Mellin transform, which we discuss next.

The two-dimensional (double) Mellin transform $C^*(s_1, s_2)$ of the function $C(z_1, z_2)$ is defined as follows

$$C^*(s_1, s_2) = \int_0^\infty \int_0^\infty C(z_1, z_2) z_1^{s_1-1} z_2^{s_2-1} dz_1 dz_2.$$

However, it is easy to see that it does not exist: the convergence strip is empty. Indeed, let $\{i, j\} = \{1, 2\}$; for fixed z_j we have $C(z_1, z_2) = O(z_i)$ when $z_i \to 0$ and $z_i \to \infty$, $i \in \{1, 2\}$. More precisely, we have $C(z_1, z_2) = O(z_1 z_2)$ when z_1, z_2 when both tend to zero. To circumvent this difficulty, we define

$$\tilde{C}(z_1, z_2) = C(z_1, z_2) - D(z_1, z_2),$$

where

$$D(z_1, z_2) = z_1 e^{-z_1} D_1(z_2) + z_2 e^{-z_2} D_2(z_1) - C_{1,1} z_1 z_2 e^{-z_1 - z_2}$$

with

$$D_1(z) = \frac{\partial}{\partial z_1} C(0, z), \quad D_2(z) = \frac{\partial}{\partial z_2} C(z, 0).$$

We now show that the Mellin transform of $\tilde{C}(z_1, z_2)$ exists in $-2 < \Re(s_i) < -1$. Indeed, notice that the $\tilde{C}(z_1, z_2)$ expansion contains no terms in z_1, z_2 or $z_1 z_2$. Thus $\tilde{C}(z_1, z_2) = O(z_i^2)$ when $z_i \to 0$, and so the double Mellin transform

$$\tilde{C}^*(s_1, s_2) = \int_0^\infty \int_0^\infty \tilde{C}(z_1, z_2) z_1^{s_1-1} z_2^{s_2-1} dz_1 dz_2$$

of $\tilde{C}(z_1, z_2)$ exists in the strip $-2 < \Re(s_i) < -1$.

To find $\tilde{C}^*(s_1, s_2)$ we need first to estimate $D_i(z)$, $i \in \{1, 2\}$, for large z_i. We shall prove, using the standard (one-dimensional) Mellin transform, that

$$D_i(z) = \frac{z \log z}{h_{ij}} + O(z) \tag{10.22}$$

where $h_{ij} = -p_i \log p_j - q_i \log q_j$ for $z \to +\infty$. Indeed, to find its strip of convergence, observe that by (10.13) we have

$$C(z_1, z_2) = C_{1,1} z_1 z_2 + z_1^2 g_1(z_1, z_2) + z_2^2 g_2(z_1, z_2)$$

with analytic $g_i(z_1, z_2)$ and such that

$$D_1(z) = z^2 \frac{\partial}{\partial z_1} g_2(0, z_2).$$

Thus $D_1(z) = O(z^2)$ when $z \to 0$. Similarly, $D_2(z)$. Furthermore, we have

$$\frac{\partial}{\partial z_1} C(0, z_2) = \frac{1}{2i\pi} \oint C(z_1, z_2) \frac{dz_1}{z_1^2}$$

where the integral over z_1 is around any contour encircling zero, using the fact that uniformly in $z_2 \in \mathbb{C}$ we have

$$C(z_1, z_2) = O(|z_2| e^{\alpha |z_1|})$$

and

$$\frac{\partial}{\partial z_1} C(0, z_2) = O(|z_2|)$$

for $z_2 \to +\infty$. Therefore, $D_1(z) = O(z)$ when $z \to +\infty$ and also $D_2(z) = O(z)$ by symmetry. Thus the Mellin transform $D_i^*(s)$ of $D_i(z)$ exists in the complex vertical strip $\Re(s) \in (-2, -1)$, and is given by

$$D_i^*(s) = -\frac{\Gamma(s)}{1 - \sum_{a \in \mathcal{A}} P_i(a)(P_j(a))^{-s}},$$

since, by (10.13),

$$\frac{\partial}{\partial z_i} C(z_1, z_2) = e^{-z_i}(1 - e^{-z_j}) + \sum_{a \in \mathcal{A}} P_i(a) \frac{\partial}{\partial z_i} C(P_1(a)z_1, P_2(a)z_2);$$

thus

$$D_i(z) = (1 - e^{-z}) + \sum_{a \in \mathcal{A}} P_i(a) D_i(P_j(a)z)$$

and this implies (10.22).

Now, knowing $D_i(z)$ we can move on to compute the Mellin transform of $\tilde{C}(z_1, z_2)$. Let us return for now to the general case of two nonidentical sources. Observe first that on modifying the basic functional equation (10.13) we obtain

$$\tilde{C}(z_1, z_2) = (1 - e^{-z_1})(1 - e^{-z_2}) - D(z_1, z_2)$$
$$+ \sum_{a \in \mathcal{A}} \tilde{C}(P_1(a)z_1, P_2(a)z_2) + D(P_1(a)z_1, P_2(a)z_2) .$$

The double Mellin transform is then

$$\tilde{C}^*(s_1, s_2) = \Gamma(s_1)\Gamma(s_2) \left(\frac{1}{H(s_1, s_2)} + \frac{s_1}{H(-1, s_2)} + \frac{s_2}{H(s_1, -1)} + \frac{s_1 s_2}{H(-1, -1)} \right).$$
$$(10.23)$$

In passing we observe that

$$C_{1,1} = \frac{1}{H(-1,-1)}.$$

To recover $\tilde{C}(z,z)$ we apply the inverse Mellin transform

$$\tilde{C}(z,z) = \frac{1}{(2i\pi)^2} \int_{\Re(s_1)=c_1} \int_{\Re(s_2)=c_2} C^*(s_1, s_2) z^{-s_1-s_2} ds_1 ds_2. \qquad (10.24)$$

We move the integration domain of s_1 to $\Re(s_1) = \rho_1$ and the integration domain of s_2 to $\Re(s_2) = \rho_2$, for $\rho_1, \rho_2 = -1 + \varepsilon$ with $\varepsilon > 0$ such that $H(s_1, s_2)$ stays far away from 0. The only poles encountered are at $s_1 = -1$ and $s_2 = -1$ but they are canceled by the additional terms.

Therefore, (10.24) remains valid for $\Re(s_1) = \rho_1$ and $\Re(s_2) = \rho_2$ for some $\rho_1, \rho_2 > -1$. On the new integration domain we need to focus only on the term

$$\int \int \frac{\Gamma(s_1)\Gamma(s_2)}{H(s_1, s_2)} z^{-s_1-s_2},$$

since the other leading terms contribute $o(z^{-M})$ for any $M > 0$ (these terms have no singularities on the right-hand side of the double integration domain). Indeed the term

$$\frac{s_1 \Gamma(s_1)\Gamma(s_2)}{H(-1, s_2)}$$

has no singularity for $\Re(s_1) > -1$, and the term

$$\frac{s_2 \Gamma(s_1)\Gamma(s_2)}{H(s_1, -1)}$$

has no singularity for $\Re(s_2) > -1$. The term

$$\frac{s_1 s_2 \Gamma(s_1)\Gamma(s_2)}{H(-1, -1)}$$

has no singularity at all. In fact the above terms are exponentially negligible since the contribution of $D(z_1, z_2)$ is exponentially small when (z_1, z_2) tend to $+\infty$. In view of this, for general nonidentical sources we arrive at

$$C(z,z) = \left(\frac{1}{2i\pi}\right)^2 \int_{\Re(s_1)=\rho_1} \int_{\Re(s_2)=\rho_2} \frac{\Gamma(s_1)\Gamma(s_2)}{H(s_1, s_2)} z^{-s_1-s_2} ds_1 ds_2 + o(z^{-M}),$$
$$(10.25)$$

for arbitrary $M > 0$.

We now look at the simplified case where one source is uniform, so that $\forall a \in \mathcal{A}$, $P_1(a) = 1/|\mathcal{A}|$. Recall that in this case we write $P_2(a) = p_a$ and $H(s_1, s_2) = 1 - (|\mathcal{A}|)^{s_1} r(s_2)$, where $r(s) = \sum_{a \in \mathcal{A}} p_a^{-s}$. Furthermore,

$$\left(-\frac{\log(r(s)) + 2ik\pi}{\log(|\mathcal{A}|)}, s \right) \in \mathcal{K}$$

for s complex and $k \in \mathbb{Z}$. It is also easy to compute κ in this case. Indeed,

$$\kappa = \min_{s \in \mathbb{R}} \{ \log_{|\mathcal{A}|}(r(s)) - s \},$$

$$c_2 = \min \arg_{s \in \mathbb{R}} \{ \log_{|\mathcal{A}|}(r(s)) - s \}.$$

We will need the following technical lemma.

Lemma 10.5.8. *Let* $L(s) = \log_{|\mathcal{A}|}(r(s))$. *Then,* $\forall s \in \mathbb{C}$, *we have* $\Re(L(s)) \leq L(\Re(s))$.

Proof. The following holds:

$$\Re(L(s)) = \log_{|\mathcal{A}|}(|r(s)|) \leq \log_{|\mathcal{A}|} \left(\sum_{a \in \mathcal{A}} |p_a^{-s}| \right).$$

Thus $\log_{|\mathcal{A}|}(\sum_{a \in \mathcal{A}} |p_a^{-s}|) = L(\Re(s))$. ∎

Now we prove a lemma which is a special case of Theorem 10.5.6. Later we will show that the additional condition in that lemma can be removed.

Lemma 10.5.9. *Assume that* $r(s)$ *has no root for* $\Re(s) \leq c_2$. *Let* $-\alpha_2$ *be the second derivative of* $\log(r(s)) - s$ *at its local minimum* c_2 *on the real axis. The average number of common words* $C_{n,n}$ *between two sequences of the same length* n *for nonidentical sources satisfies*

$$C_{n,n} = \left(\frac{1}{\sqrt{2\pi\alpha_2 \log n}} \Gamma(c_1)\Gamma(c_2) + Q(\log n) + o(1) \right) n^\kappa,$$

where $Q(\log n)$ *is a periodic function of order* 10^{-6} *when the* $\log p_a$, $a \in \mathcal{A}$, *are rationally related.*

Remark 10.5.10. The condition $\Re(s) \leq c_2 \Rightarrow r(s) \neq 0$ will be removed in the final proof of Theorem 10.5.6 presented in the next subsection. Notice that this condition is fulfilled when the alphabet is binary. Indeed, $r(s) = 0$ is equivalent to $(p_a/p_b)^s = -1$; thus $(p_a/p_b)^{\Re(s)} = 1$, which can occur only when $\Re(s) = 0$. ∎

Proof. We move the integration line of s_1 in (10.25) towards the positive real axis direction and meet one pole at $s_1 = 0$ (residue 1). The poles of the function $(1 - |\mathcal{A}|^{s_1}(r(s_2)))^{-1}$ are at

$$s_1 = -\log_{|\mathcal{A}|}(r(s_2)) + \frac{2ik\pi}{\log(|\mathcal{A}|)},$$

for k integer with residues $-1/\log(|\mathcal{A}|)$. Therefore we have

$$\tilde{C}(z,z) = -\frac{1}{2i\pi}\int \frac{\Gamma(s_2)}{h(s_2)}z^{-s_2}ds_2 + \sum_k \frac{1}{2i\pi\log(|\mathcal{A}|)}\int \Gamma\left(-L(s_2) + \frac{2ik\pi}{\log(|\mathcal{A}|)}\right)$$
$$\times\Gamma(s_2)z^{L(s_2)-s_2-2ik\pi/\log(|\mathcal{A}|)}ds_2 + O(z^{-M}),$$

where, as before, $h(s) = \sum_{a\in\mathcal{A}} p_a^{-s}\log p_a$ and $L(s) = \log_{|\mathcal{A}|}(r(s))$ with $M > 0$ arbitrary (but fixed to ensure the uniformity of $O(\cdot)$). It turns out that the function $(h(s))^{-1}$ and the function

$$\sum_k \frac{\Gamma\left(-L(s) + 2ik\pi/\log(|\mathcal{A}|)\right)}{\log(|\mathcal{A}|)}z^{L(s)-2ik\pi/\log(|\mathcal{A}|)}$$

have the same poles and their residues cancel out. Indeed the roots of $\log(r(s)) - 2ik\pi$ are exactly the roots s_k of $h(s)$ and the residue of $\Gamma\left(L(s) - 2ik\pi/\log(|\mathcal{A}|)\right)$ is the same as the residue of $(h(s))^{-1}$.

There is no other potential singularity except the root of $r(s)$. Since by hypothesis there is no root such that $\Re(s) \leq c_2$, the integration path can be moved towards a position c_2 that contributes $z^{L(c_2)-c_2} = z^\kappa$. We can ignore the term in $z^{-s}/h(s)$ since it is $o(z^\kappa)$, because $L(s) > 0$ and thus $L(s) - s > -s$ for s between -1 and 0. Therefore we have

$$C(z,z) = \frac{1}{2i\pi\log(|\mathcal{A}|)}\int_{\Re(s)=c_2} \sum_k \Gamma\left(-L(s) + \frac{2ik\pi}{\log(|\mathcal{A}|)}\right)$$
$$\times\Gamma(s)z^{L(s)-s-2ik\pi/\log(|\mathcal{A}|)}ds + O(z^{\kappa-\varepsilon}).$$

We notice that $L(s) - s$ is a saddle point at $s = c_2$, i.e., it attains a local minimum on the real axis and a local maximum on the imaginary axis at $s = c_2$. This is a natural consequence of the fact that the first and second derivative of $L(s) - s$ at the point $s = c_2$ are respectively zero and nonpositive. Let $-\alpha_2$ be the second derivative of $L(s) - s$ at $s = c_2$.

Now we will handle the rational and irrational cases separately.

Rational or Commensurable Case. In the case where $L(c_2 + it)$ is a periodic function of t of period $2\pi/\log \nu$, the function $L(c_2 + it) - c_2 - it$ is therefore periodic in t if we omit a linear term. Therefore it has a sequence of saddle points at $c_2 + it_\ell$ with $t_\ell = 2i\ell\pi/\log\nu$ for all $\ell \in \mathbb{Z}$. These saddle points are the maxima of $\Re(L(c_2 + it))$ and each has the same second derivative α_2. In fact it turns out that $\exp((L(c_2 + it) - c_2 - it)$ is periodic in t. Around each saddle point we have uniformly

$$L(c_2 + it) - c_2 - it = \kappa - \frac{\alpha_2}{2}(t - t_\ell)^2 + O((t - t_\ell)^3).$$

This property is valid for some $A > 0$ and for t real as long as $|t - t_\ell| < A$ for some $\ell \in \mathbb{Z}$. Assuming that $2A < |\log\nu|$, we define intervals $[t_\ell - A, t_\ell + A]$ such that

$$I = \mathbb{R} - \cup_{\ell\in\mathbb{Z}}[t_\ell - A, t_\ell + A].$$

Outside these intervals, namely if t is such that for all $\ell \in \mathbb{Z}$, $|t - t_\ell| > A$, we have $\Re(L(c_2 + it) - c_2) < \kappa - \varepsilon$ uniformly for some $\varepsilon > 0$. We set

$$\frac{1}{2i\pi}\int_{\Re(s)=c_2} \Gamma(L(s))\Gamma(s)z^{L(s)-s}ds = \sum_{\ell\in\mathbb{Z}} \frac{1}{2\pi}\int_{t_\ell-A}^{t_\ell+A}$$
$$\times \Gamma(-L(c_2 + it))\,\Gamma(c_2 + it)z^{L(c_2+it)-c_2-it}dt$$
$$+ \frac{1}{2\pi}\int_{t\in I}\Gamma(-L(c_2 + it))$$
$$\times \Gamma(c_2 + it)z^{L(c_2+it)-c_2-it}dt.$$

As a consequence we find that

$$\int_{t_\ell-A}^{t_\ell+A}\Gamma(-L(c_2 + it))\,\Gamma(c_2 + it)z^{L(c_2+it)-c_2-it}dt$$

can be estimated as follows:

$$\frac{1}{\sqrt{\log z}}\int_{-A\sqrt{\log z}}^{A\sqrt{\log z}}\Gamma\left(L\left(c_2 + it_\ell + \frac{it}{\sqrt{\log z}}\right)\right)\Gamma\left(c_2 + it_\ell + \frac{it}{\sqrt{\log z}}\right)$$
$$\times z^{\kappa - it_\ell}e^{-\alpha_2/2t^2}\left(1 + O\left(\frac{t^3}{\sqrt{\log z}}\right)\right)dt.$$

This expression becomes

$$\frac{z^\kappa}{\sqrt{2\pi\alpha_2\log z}}\Gamma\left(c_1 - it_\ell(1 + \log_{|\mathcal{A}|}\nu)\right)\Gamma(c_2 + it_\ell)\left(1 + O\left(\frac{1}{\sqrt{\log z}}\right)\right)$$

with $c_1 = -c_2 - \kappa$. In fact, a more careful analysis shows that the order-3 term disappears, and thus we have an $O(1/\log z)$ term instead of an $O(1/\sqrt{\log z})$ term. Finally, observe that each term such as

$$\int_{-\infty}^{+\infty} \Gamma\left(-L(c_2 + it) + \frac{2ik\pi}{\log|\mathcal{A}|}\right)\Gamma(c_2 + it)z^{L(c_2+it)-c_2-it}dt$$

can be treated similarly.

The sum of these terms with their respective factors $z^{-2ik\pi/\log|\mathcal{A}|}$ is asymptotically equivalent to

$$\frac{z^\kappa}{\sqrt{2\pi\alpha_2 \log z}}\Gamma(c_1)\Gamma(c_2)$$

and ultimately contributes

$$\sum_\ell \frac{z^\kappa}{\sqrt{2\pi\alpha_2 \log z}}\Gamma\left(c_1 - it_\ell(1 + \log_{|\mathcal{A}|}\nu)\right)\Gamma(c_2 + it_\ell)\left(1 + O\left(\frac{1}{\log z}\right)\right).$$

This becomes the double periodic function with error term $\log z$.

Irrationals/Incommensurable Case. Here the function $L(c_2 + it)$ is not periodic. However, there still may be a sequence of local maxima of $\Re(L(c_2 + it))$, and we need to deal with this.

Lemma 10.5.11. *For $c_2 < 0$, let $\{t_k\}$ be a sequence of local maxima of $\Re(L(c_2 + it_k))$ such that*

$$\lim_{k\to\infty} \Re(L(c_2 + it_k)) = L(c_2).$$

Then the sequence of the second derivatives of $\Re(L(c_2 + it))$ at $t = t_k$ tends to the second derivative of $-L(s)$ at $s = c_2$. Also, there exist $A > 0$ and $\alpha_3 > 0$ such that

$$\limsup_{k\to\infty} \max_{t\in[t_k-A,t_k+A]} \left\{\frac{\Re(L(c_2 + t)) - \Re(L(c_2 + it_k))}{(t - t_k)^2}\right\} \le -\frac{\alpha_3}{2}.$$

Proof. We have

$$\log(r(c_2 + it)) = -it \log p_b + \log\left(\sum_{a\in\mathcal{A}} p_a^{-c_2}\left(\frac{p_a}{p_b}\right)^{-it_k}\right)$$

and

$$\Re(\log(r(c_2 + it)) = \log\left|\sum_{a\in\mathcal{A}} p_a^{-c_2}\left(\frac{p_a}{p_b}\right)^{it_k}\right|.$$

We know that if $\Re(L(c_2 + it_k))$ tends to $L(c_2)$ then $\forall a \in \mathcal{A}$, $(p_a/p_b)^{-it_k} \to 1$. The second derivative of $L(c_2 + it)$ with respect to t is equal to

$$\frac{\sum_{a \in \mathcal{A}} (\log p_a)^2 (p_a/p_b)^{-c_2-it_k}}{\sum_{a \in \mathcal{A}} (p_a/p_b)^{-c_2-it_k}} - \left(\frac{\sum_{a \in \mathcal{A}} (\log p_a)(p_a/p_b)^{-c_2-it_k}}{\sum_{a \in \mathcal{A}} (p_a/p_b)^{-c_2-it_k}} \right)^2 ;$$

hence the first part of the lemma is proved.

For the second part, we note that the derivative of any given order of $\Re(L(c_2 + it)$ is uniformly bounded as t varies from $-\infty$ to $+\infty$. Therefore, for all $\varepsilon > 0$, there exists A such that for all $t \in [t_k - A, t_k + A]$ the derivative at t is within ε of the derivative at t_k. Now let $L^{(2)}(t)$ be the second derivative of $\Re(L(c_2 + it))$. We find that $\forall t \in [t_k, t_k + A]$, since the first derivative of $\Re(L(c_2 + it))$ is zero, we have

$$\Re(L(c_2 + it)) = \Re(L(c_2 + it_k)) + \int_{t_k}^{t} (t - t_k) L^{(2)}(t) dt$$

$$\leq (L^{(2)}(t_k) + \varepsilon) \frac{(t - t_k)^2}{2}$$

as required. ∎

Corollary 10.5.12. *There exists $A > 0$ such that, in the sequence of local maxima, the separation of adjacent maxima tends to an interval larger than A.*

For the irrational and incommensurable case, for all $t \in \mathbb{R}^*$ we know that $\Re(L(c_2 + it)) < -c_1$. We use the fact that, for all s, $\sum_k |\Gamma(s + 2ik\pi/\log|\mathcal{A}|)|$ converges to a continuous function $g(s)$. Therefore, the contribution of the external terms is smaller in modulus than

$$\int_{t \notin (-A,A)} g(L(s))|\Gamma(c_2 + it)z^{L(c_2+it)-c_2-it}|dt.$$

Since $L(c_2 + it)$ is bounded as t varies from $-\infty$ to $+\infty$, $g(L(s))$ is uniformly bounded. The function $|\Gamma(c_2 + it)|$ is absolutely integrable; therefore

$$|z^{L(c_2+it)-c_2-it-\kappa}| \to 0, \quad z \to +\infty$$

implies that

$$\sum_k \int_{t \notin (-A,A)} \Gamma\left(-L(c_2 + it) + \frac{2ik\pi}{\log|\mathcal{A}|} \right)$$

$$\times \Gamma(c_2 + it)z^{L(c_2+it)-c_2-it-2ik\pi/\log|\mathcal{A}|}dt = o(z^\kappa).$$

We still need to show that the error term is $o(z^\kappa/\sqrt{\log z})$. To this end we must prove that, for a sequence of local maxima of $\Re(L(c_2 + it))$, with t real, tending to κ, the function $\Re(L(c_2 + it))$ is locally bounded on such maxima by a Gaussian function. In fact this is established by Lemma 10.5.11. We know that there exist $\alpha_3 > 0$ and $A > 0$ such that, for all $t \in [t_k - A, t_k + A]$,

$$\Re(L(c_2 + it) \leq \Re(L(c_2 + it_k)) - \frac{\alpha_3}{2}(t - t_k)^2$$

and that there exists $\varepsilon > 0$ such that, for t not in such an interval, $\Re(L(c_2+it)) < \Re(L(c_2)) - \varepsilon$. Therefore

$$\int_{t\notin(-A,A)} g(L(c_2 + it))|\Gamma(c_2 + it)|z^{\Re(L(c_2+it))-c_2} dt$$

$$< O(z^{\kappa-\varepsilon}) + \sum_k \int_{t_k - A}^{t_k + A} g(L(c_2 + it))|\Gamma(c_2 + it)|z^{\Re(L(c_2+it))-c_2} dt.$$

By an easy change of variable, i.e., setting $t = t_k + \sqrt{\log z}\theta$, any term on the right-hand side can be written as

$$\frac{1}{\sqrt{\log z}} \int_{-A\sqrt{\log z}}^{A\sqrt{\log z}} g(L(c_2 + it))|\Gamma(c_2 + it)|z^{\Re(L(c_2+it_k))-c_2} e^{-\alpha_3\theta^2/2} d\theta.$$

Notice that the right-hand side is a uniformly dominated sum even when multiplied by $\sqrt{\log z}$. This follows from the fact that $z^{\Re(L(c_2+it_k))-c_2} < z^\kappa$ and that the sum of

$$\max_{t\in[t_k-A,t_k+A]} \{|\Gamma(c_2 + it)|\}$$

is uniformly dominated. Since $z^{\Re(L(c_2+it_k))-c_2} = o(z^\kappa)$, we conclude that the resulting sum is $o(z^\kappa/\sqrt{\log z})$.   ∎

10.5.4. Finishing the proof of Theorem 10.5.6

To complete the proof of Theorem 10.5.6 we must remove from Lemma 10.5.9 the condition that for all s such that $\Re(s) < c_2$ there are no roots of $r(s)$. Assume in the following that in fact there are such roots. Let θ be such that $r(\theta) = 0$ with $\Re(\theta) \leq c_2$. On such points the function $L(s)$ is no longer analytic but multi-valued, that is, it can have ambiguous values. Indeed, the domain of the definition of $L(s)$ in a complex neighborhood of θ must exclude a half line starting from θ, i.e., a horizontal line towards the right. Below and above the line, $L(s)$ has well-defined values by continuity but crossing the line adds a term

$2i\pi/\log|\mathcal{A}|$ to $L(s)$, creating a discontinuity. We call this line the *interdiction line* of θ. Therefore, it is impossible to move the line of integration in

$$\int_{\Re(s)=\rho_2} \Gamma(-L(s))\Gamma(s)z^{L(s)-s}ds$$

without distorting it in order to avoid the interdiction line of θ. Fortunately, when we sum all the contributions

$$\Gamma(s)\Gamma\left(-L(s)+\frac{2ik\pi}{\log|\mathcal{A}|}\right)z^{L(s)-s+2ik\pi/\log|\mathcal{A}|}$$

for $k \in \mathbb{Z}$, the sum converges because

$$\sum_k \left|\Gamma\left(-L(s)+\frac{2ik\pi}{\log|\mathcal{A}|}\right)\right|$$

is absolutely convergent. It turns out that the discontinuity terms due to the interdiction line cancel out. Indeed, crossing the interdiction line is equivalent to incrementing the integer k; therefore

$$\sum_k \Gamma(s)\Gamma\left(-L(s)+\frac{2ik\pi}{\log|\mathcal{A}|}\right)z^{L(s)-s+2ik\pi/\log|\mathcal{A}|}$$

has no discontinuity on this line. In other words, the function

$$\sum_k \Gamma(s)\Gamma\left(-L(s)+\frac{2ik\pi}{\log|\mathcal{A}|}\right)z^{L(s)-s+2ik\pi/\log|\mathcal{A}|}$$

converges and is analytic around θ.

There is still a problem, because θ is a singularity. If $s \to \theta$ we obtain $\Re(L(s)) \to -\infty$ and therefore $|\Gamma(-L(s))z^{L(s)}| \to \infty$. Therefore, moving the integration line of

$$\sum_k \Gamma(s)\Gamma\left(-L(s)+\frac{2ik\pi}{\log|\mathcal{A}|}\right)z^{L(s)-s+\frac{2ik\pi}{\log|\mathcal{A}|}}$$

generates an isolated integration contour around θ. But since $\Re(L(s)) \to -\infty$ when $s \to \theta$ we can make the contour close enough to θ that the exponent $z^{L(s)-s}$ is $o(z^{-M})$ for any arbitrary $M > 0$. In conclusion, we can ignore the $O(z^{-M})$ term.

To conclude our discussion we must also take into account the fact that the roots of $r(s)$ form an enumerable set $\{\theta_\ell\}_{\ell \in \mathbb{N}}$. We must estimate whether the sum of the contributions of the isolated loops is $o(z^{-M})$. A simple analysis shows the existence of a minimum in the discrepancy between the roots, so that $|\Im(\theta_\ell)| \geq A'\ell$ for some $A' > 0$ and hence the sum of the $|\Gamma(\theta_\ell)|$ converges. Furthermore, the sum of the integrals of $\Gamma(-L(s))\Gamma(s)z^{L(s)-s}$ around the isolated roots θ_ℓ is dominated by the sum of the $|\Gamma(\theta_\ell)|$.   ∎

Remark 10.5.13. Finally, let us look at the general formula (10.18), which we are not going to prove here. In the general setting, $\{-L_k(s_2)\}_{k\in\mathbb{N}}$ is the set of roots of $H(s_1, s_2)$. This set of roots corresponds to multivalued functions $L_k(s)$ having continuous branches. In other words, the $(-L_k(s), s)$ are analytic descriptions of $\mathcal{K}$. For θ such that $(\infty, \theta) \in \mathcal{K}$ we have the infinite branch of $\mathcal{K}$ corresponding to the singularities of the $L_k(s)$ branch. As discussed above, we need to consider

$$C(z, z) = \sum_{k\in\mathbb{N}} \int_{\Re(s)=c_2} \Gamma(-L_k(s))\Gamma(s)z^{L_k(s)-s}ds + O(z^{-M}).$$

We expect that the same sort of analysis based on the sequence of saddle points, applies for the general case.   ∎

10.6.   Joint complexity via suffix trees

Enumerating the common words in sequences is not an easy task as we have seen in the previous sections. An alternative (and almost equivalent) method is to enumerate common words that appear at least twice. This turns out to be equivalent to counting the number of common nodes in the corresponding associated suffix trees. We now discuss this method.

The suffix tree S_X of a word X describes the set of subwords of X that have at least two copies in X, possibly on overlapping positions. In other words,

$$S_X = \{w : O_X(w) \geq 2\},$$

where $O_X(w)$ is the number of times that w appears in X. Clearly, $S_X \subset A_X$. We sometimes will call S_X the string semi-complexity. We know that

$$|A_X| \approx \frac{(|X|+1)|X|}{2}$$

leads to a quadratic complexity, while $|S_X| = O(|X|)$. In fact, there exist algorithms that build S_X in linear time in $|X|$ (see Chapter 6).

10.6.1. Joint complexity of two suffix trees for nonidentical sources

Our aim is to evaluate the cardinality of $S_X \cap S_Y$ when X and Y are two sequences generated from two distinct random sources. The cardinality of this set may be called the joint string semi-complexity. Let R_n be the average of $|S_X \cap S_Y|$ when X and Y are both of length n and the two strings are generated by two nonidentical memoryless sources. We have

$$R_n := \mathbf{E}[|S_X \cap S_Y|] = \sum_{w \in \mathcal{A}^*} P(O_n^1(w) \geq 2) P(O_n^2(w) \geq 2). \qquad (10.26)$$

As in Theorem 10.3.1 we can establish a key property, that R_n is well approximated by the average number of common nodes in two independent tries built over two sets of n independent strings. We call the latter $T_{n,n}$ and, as is easy to see,

$$T_{n,m} = \sum_{w \in \mathcal{A}^*} (1 - (1 - P_1(w))^n - n p_1(w)(1 - P_1(w))^{n-1})$$
$$\times (1 - (1 - P_2(w))^m - m p_2(w)(1 - P_2(w))^{m-1})$$

where $P_i(w)$ is the word probability in source model i. Throughout we will now assume that $R_n = T_{n,n} + O(n^{-\varepsilon})$ and study only $T_{n,n}$.

Let us start with a recurrence for $T_{n,m}$. Observe that $T_{0,m} = T_{n,0} = T_{1,n} = T_{m,1} = 0$ and, for $n, m \geq 1$, we have

$$T_{n,m} = 1 + \sum_{a \in \mathcal{A}} \sum_{k,\ell} \binom{n}{k} P_1(a)^k (1 - P_1(a))^{n-k} \binom{m}{\ell} P_2(a)^\ell (1 - P_2(a))^{m-\ell} T_{k,\ell}.$$
$$(10.27)$$

Then, using the double poissonized generating function

$$T(z_1, z_2) = \sum_{n,m} T_{n,m} \frac{z_1^n z_2^m}{n! m!} e^{-z_1 - z_2}$$

yields

$$T(z_1, z_2) = \sum_{a \in \mathcal{A}} T(P_1(a)z_1, P_2(a)z_2) + (1 - (1 + z_1)e^{-z_1})(1 - (1 + z_2)e^{-z_2}).$$
$$(10.28)$$

In fact, using the same approach as in the proof of Lemma 10.3.5, we conclude that $T(z_1, z_2)$ satisfies the conditions of the depoissonization Lemma 10.3.4. We formulate the result in the following lemma.

Lemma 10.6.1. *The function $T(z_1, z_2)$ satisfies the conditions of Lemma 10.3.4 with $\beta = 1$.*

We have $T_{n,n} = T(n,n) + O(1)$ via double depoissonization. To estimate $T(n,n)$ we use a double Mellin transform $T^*(s_1, s_2)$ defined for $-2 < \Re(s_1) < -1$ and $-2 < \Re(s_2) < -1$ which becomes

$$T^*(s_1, s_2) = \frac{\Gamma(s_1 + 1)\Gamma(s_2 + 1)}{H(s_1, s_2)}$$

as is easy to see from (10.28). Using the same techniques as in the previous section we can prove the theorem below which mimics Theorem 10.5.6. In fact, in Exercise 10.10 we ask the reader to provide the details of the proof.

Theorem 10.6.2. *Consider the joint string semi complexity when one string is generated by a general memoryless source with $p_a = P_2(a)$ while the second source is unbiased, that is, $P_1(a) = 1/|\mathcal{A}|$.*
(i) If the $\log p_a$, $a \in \mathcal{A}$, are rationally related, i.e., commensurable, with ν the smallest nonnegative real number such that, $\forall a \in \mathcal{A}$, $1/\nu \log p_a \in \mathbb{Z}$ then

$$T_{n,n} = \frac{n^\kappa}{\sqrt{\log n}} \left(\frac{\Gamma(1 + c_1)\Gamma(1 + c_2)}{\sqrt{\pi \Delta H(c_1, c_2)\nabla H(c_1, c_2)}} + R(\log n) + O\left(1/\log n\right) \right),$$
(10.29)

where

$$R(x) = \sum_{(s_1, s_2) \in \partial \mathcal{K}^*} \frac{\Gamma(1 + s_1)\Gamma(1 + s_2)}{\sqrt{\pi \Delta H(s_1, s_2)\nabla H(s_1, s_2)}} \exp(-i\Im(s_1 + s_2)x)$$

with

$$\mathcal{K}^* = \left\{ (c_1 + \frac{2ik\pi}{\log |\mathcal{A}|} + 2i\pi\ell \left(\frac{1}{\log \nu} + \frac{1}{\log |\mathcal{A}|} \right), c_2 + \frac{2i\ell}{\log \nu} \right), (k, \ell) \in \mathbb{Z}^2 \setminus (0, 0) \right\}.$$

(ii) If the $\log p_a$, $a \in \mathcal{A}$ are irrational, i.e., incommensurable, then

$$T_{n,n} = \frac{n^\kappa}{\sqrt{\log n}} \left(\frac{\Gamma(1 + c_1)\Gamma(1 + c_2)}{\sqrt{\pi \Delta H(c_1, c_2)\nabla H(c_1, c_2)}} + R(\log n) + o(1) \right)$$
(10.30)

with

$$\mathcal{K}^* = \left\{ (c_1 + \frac{2ik\pi}{\log |\mathcal{A}|}, c_2), \ k \in \mathbb{Z}^* \right\}.$$

In fact, we believe the above finding holds true for the generally case when both of the sources are generally memoryless. In this case, we expect

$$T_{n,n} = \frac{n^\kappa}{\sqrt{\log n}} \left(\frac{\Gamma(1 + c_1)\Gamma(1 + c_2)}{\sqrt{\pi \Delta H(c_1, c_2)\nabla H(c_1, c_2)}} + R(\log n) + o(1) \right).$$
(10.31)

However, details of the proof are quite tricky and so we will skip them.

10.6.2. Joint complexity of two suffix trees for identical sources

Let $t(z) = T(z, z)$. When, $\forall a \in \mathcal{A}$, $P_1(a) = P_2(a) = p_a$ we have

$$t(z) = (1 - (1 + z)e^{-z})^2 + \sum_{a \in \mathcal{A}} t(p_a z).$$

The Mellin transform $T^*(s)$ of $t(z)$, as is easy to see, satisfies

$$T^*(s) = \frac{(1 + s)(2^{-s}s/4 - 2 + 2^{-s})\Gamma(s)}{h(s)}, \qquad (10.32)$$

from which, by following the same footsteps as in previous sections, we conclude that (see Exercise 10.11)

$$T_n = [z^n]t(z) = \frac{1}{2}\frac{n}{h} + nQ_5(\log n) + o(n) \qquad (10.33)$$

where Q_5 is periodic when the members of the set $\{\log p_a\}_{a \in \mathcal{A}}$ are rationally related, i.e., commensurable, and zero otherwise.

10.7. Conclusion and applications

In this chapter, we studied the joint string complexity and proved that the joint complexity of two strings generated by the same source grows as $O(n)$ while for strings generated by different sources it grows as $O(n^\kappa/\sqrt{\log n})$ for some $\kappa < 1$. In fact these findings can be extended to Markov sources, as proved in Jacquet and Szpankowski (2012) and Jacquet et al. (2013). In view of these facts, we can apply the joint string complexity to discriminate between identical and nonidentical sources. We introduce a discriminant function as

$$d(X, Y) = 1 - \frac{1}{\log n} \log J(X, Y)$$

for two sequences X and Y of length n. This discriminant allows us to determine whether X and Y are generated by the same memoryless or Markov source by verifying whether $d(X, Y) = O(1/\log n) \to 0$ or $d(X, Y) = 1 - \kappa + O(\log \log n/\log n) > 0$, respectively. In Figure 10.2 we compare the joint string complexities of a simulated English text and the same-length texts simulated in French and in Polish. We compare these experimental results with our theoretical results (extended to Markov sources). In the simulation we used a Markov model of order 3. It is easy to see that even for texts of lengths smaller than 1,000, one can discriminate between these languages. In fact, computations show that for English and French we have $\kappa = 0.18$ while for English and Polish we

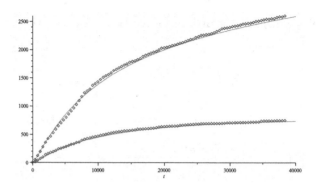

Figure 10.2. Joint string complexity of simulated texts (we used third-order Markov analysis) for English and French (upper set of points), and English and Polish (lower set of points) languages, in each case versus the average theoretical results (solid lines).

have $\kappa = 0.01$. Furthermore, as indicated in Jacquet et al. (2013), the joint string complexity can be used for automated Twitter classification. In closing, we observe that our algorithm based on the joint complexity was one of the top finishers in the SNOW 2014 Challenge of Tweets Detection.

10.8. Exercises

10.1   Consider an unbiased memoryless source over alphabet $\mathcal{A}$ of cardinality $|\mathcal{A}|$. We denote by $C_n(|\mathcal{A}|)$ the string complexity. Prove the following results for the average and variance of the string complexity, for small values of n:

$$\mathbf{E}\left[C_2(|\mathcal{A}|)\right] = 3 - (1/|\mathcal{A}|),$$
$$\mathbf{E}\left[C_3(|\mathcal{A}|)\right] = 6 - (3/|\mathcal{A}|),$$
$$\mathbf{E}\left[C_4(|\mathcal{A}|)\right] = 10 - (6/|\mathcal{A}|) + (1/|\mathcal{A}|^2) - (1/|\mathcal{A}|^3),$$
$$\mathbf{E}\left[C_5(|\mathcal{A}|)\right] = 15 - (10/|\mathcal{A}|) + (4/|\mathcal{A}|^2) - (6/|\mathcal{A}|^3) + (2/|\mathcal{A}|^4)$$

and

$$\mathrm{Var}\left[C_2(|\mathcal{A}|)\right] = (|\mathcal{A}| - 1)/|\mathcal{A}|^2,$$
$$\mathrm{Var}\left[C_3(|\mathcal{A}|)\right] = 3(|\mathcal{A}| - 1)/|\mathcal{A}|^2,$$
$$\mathrm{Var}\left[C_4(|\mathcal{A}|)\right] = (|\mathcal{A}| - 1)(6|\mathcal{A}|^4 - 5|\mathcal{A}|^3 + 12|\mathcal{A}|^2 - |\mathcal{A}| + 1)/|\mathcal{A}|^6,$$

$$\text{Var}\,[C_5(|\mathcal{A}|)] = 2(|\mathcal{A}| - 1)(5|\mathcal{A}|^6 - 10|\mathcal{A}|^5 + 33|\mathcal{A}|^4 - 28|\mathcal{A}|^3$$
$$+16|\mathcal{A}|^2 - 10|\mathcal{A}| + 2)/|\mathcal{A}|^8$$

(see Janson et al. (2004)).

10.2   Consider a strongly, that is, exponentially, mixing stationary source. Prove that

$$\mathbf{E}[C_n] = \binom{n+1}{2} - O(n \log n)$$

using Szpankowski (1993b) result on the height of a suffix tree.

10.3   Define C_n^ℓ as the the *ℓ-subword complexity* or *ℓ-spectrum* of a string, which is the number of distinct ℓ-length subwords of the underlying string. Prove for an unbiased memoryless source that

$$\mathbf{E}[C_n^\ell] = k^\ell(1 - e^{-nk^{-\ell}}) + O(\ell) + O(n\ell k^{-\ell})$$

(see Janson et al. (2004) or Gheorghiciuc and Ward (2007)).

10.4   Consider again an unbiased memoryless source over a finite alphabet $\mathcal{A}$. Prove the Janson et al. (2004) result

$$\mathbf{E}[C_n] = \binom{n+1}{2} - n \log_{|\mathcal{A}|} n + \left(\frac{1}{2} + \frac{1-\gamma}{\ln |\mathcal{A}|} + \phi_{|\mathcal{A}|}(\log_{|\mathcal{A}|} n) \right) n$$
$$+ O(\sqrt{n \log n})$$

where $\gamma \approx 0.577$ is the Euler constant and

$$\phi_{|\mathcal{A}|}(x) = -\frac{1}{\log |\mathcal{A}|} \sum_{j \neq 0} \Gamma\left(-1 - \frac{2\pi i j}{\ln |\mathcal{A}|} \right) e^{2\pi i j x}$$

is a continuous function with period 1. Observe that $|\phi_{|\mathcal{A}|}(x)|$ is very small for small $|\mathcal{A}|$: $|\phi_2(x)| < 2 \times 10^{-7}$, $|\phi_3(x)| < 5 \times 10^{-5}$, and $|\phi_4(x)| < 3 \times 10^{-4}$.

10.5   Extend Theorem 10.2.1 for an ℓ-subword complexity C_n^ℓ as defined in Exercise 10.3 above (see Gheorghiciuc and Ward (2007)).

10.6   Provide the details of the proof of Theorem 10.3.1.

10.7   Using the notation from the proof of Theorem 10.3.2, prove that

$$\sum_{w \in \mathcal{A}^*} |\Delta_n^1(w)||\Delta_m^2(w)| = O(\min\{n, m\}^{-\varepsilon})$$

where n and m are integers representing the lengths of respective strings.

10.8 Complete the proof of Lemma 10.3.5 by showing that condition (ii) of Lemma 10.3.4 holds for the joint string complexity $C(z_1, z_2)$ defined in (10.13).

10.9 Prove (10.16) for a binary alphabet.

10.10 Provide the details of the proof of Theorem 10.6.2.

10.11 Considering identical memoryless sources, prove that the average number of common nodes of the two associated suffix trees can be expressed by (10.33).

Bibliographical notes

String complexity is discussed in many books and articles, mostly from the worst-case point of view: see Li and Vitanyi (1993), Niederreiter (1999), Shallit (1993), and Wang and Shallit (1998). In this chapter we focused on the average-case complexity. It was first studied in Janson et al. (2004) for random strings generated by an unbiased memoryless source. It was then extended by Jacquet (2007) to two unbiased memoryless sources. The joint string complexity from the average-case point of view was first studied by Jacquet (2007), and then extended to Markov sources by Jacquet and Szpankowski (2012). The experimental results presented in the last section of this chapter were taken from Jacquet et al. (2013). We would like to point out that the classification of sources was also investigated by Ziv (1988).

Bibliography

Abramowitz, M. and Stegun, I. (1964). *Handbook of Mathematical Functions*. Dover, New York.

Adebiyi, E. F., Jiang, T., and Kaufmann, M. (2001). An efficient algorithm for finding short approximate non-tandem repeats, In *Intelligent Systems for Molecular Biology (ISMB)*, pp. 5–12.

Aldous, D. and Shields, P. (1988). A diffusion limit for a class of random-growing binary trees, *Probab. Th. Rel. Fields*, *79*, 509–542.

Alon, N. and Spencer, J. (1992). *The Probabilistic Method*. John Wiley and Sons.

Apostolico, A. (1985). The myriad virtues of suffix trees, In Apostolico, A. and Galil, Z. (Eds.), *Combinatorial Algorithms on Words*, Vol. 12 of *NATO Advanced Science Institutes, Series F*, pp. 85–96. Springer-Verlag.

Apostolico, A. and Szpankowski, W. (1992). Self-alignments in words and their applications, *J. Algorithms*, *13*, 446–467.

Arratia, R., Goldstein, L., and Gordon, L. (1990). Poisson approximation and the Chen-Stein method, *Statist. Sci.*, *5*, 403–434.

Arratia, R. and Waterman, M. (1994). A phase transition for the score in matching random sequences allowing deletions, *Ann. Appl. Probab.*, *4*, 200–225.

Arratia, R. and Waterman, M. S. (1989). The Erdös-Rényi strong law for pattern matching with a given proportion of mismatches, *Ann. Probab.*, *17*, 1152–1169.

Banderier, C., Bodini, O., Ponty, Y., and Bouzid, H. (2012). On the diversity of pattern distributions in rational language, In *ANALCO*, pp. 107–116.

Bassino, F., Clement, J., Fayolle, J., and Nicodeme, P. (2007). Counting occurrences for a finite set of words: an inclusion-exclusion approach, In *Conference on Analysis of Algorithms*, pp. 29–44.

Bassino, F., Clement, J., and Nicodeme, P. (2012). Counting occurrences for a finite set of words: an inclusion-exclusion approach, *ACM Trans. Algorithms*, *8*(3), Article No. 31.

Bender, E. (1973). Central and local limit theorems applied to asymptotic enumeration, *J. Combin. Th. A*, *15*, 91–111.

Bender, E. and Kochman, F. (1993). The distribution of subword counts is usually normal, *European J. Combin.*, *14*, 265–275.

Bieganski, P., Riedl, J., Carlis, J. V., and Retzel, E. (1994). Generalized suffix trees for biological sequence data: applications and implementations, In *27th Hawaii Int. Conf. on Systems Science*, pp. 35–44. IEEE Computer Society Press.

Billingsley, P. (1961). Statistical methods in Markov chains, *Ann. Math. Statist.*, *2*, 12–40.

Billingsley, P. (1968). *Convergence of Probability Measures*. John Wiley and Sons.

Blumer, A., Blumer, J., Ehrenfeucht, A., Haussler, D., Chen, M. T., and Seiferas, J. (1985). The smallest automaton recognizing the subwords of a text, *Theoret. Comput. Sci.*, *40*(1), 31–55.

Blumer, A., Ehrenfeucht, A., and Haussler, D. (1989). Average size of suffix trees and DAWGS, *Discr. Appl. Math.*, *24*, 37–45.

Bourdon, J. and Vallée, B. (2002). Generalized pattern matching statistics, In *Mathematics and Computer Science II (Versailles, 2002)*, Trends. Math., pp. 249–265. Birkhäuser.

Bradley, R. (1986). Basic properties of strong mixing conditions, In Eberlein, E. and Taqqu, M. (Eds.), *Dependence in Probability and Statistics*, pp. 165–192.

Breen, S., Waterman, M. S., and Zhang, N. (1985). Renewal theory for several patterns, *J. Appl. Probab.*, *22*, 228–234.

Briandais, R. de la (1959). File searching using variable length keys, In *Proceedings of the AFIPS Spring Joint Computer Conference*, pp. 295–298.

Bucklew, J. A. (1990). *Large Deviation Techniques in Decision, Simulation, and Estimation*. John Wiley and Sons.

Burrows, M. and Wheeler, D. J. (1994). A block sorting data compression algorithm, Tech. rep., Digital System Research Center.

Choi, Y., Knessl, C., and Szpankowski, W. (2012). On a Recurrence Arising in Graph Compression, *Electronic J. Combinatorics*, *15*(3), P15.

Choi, Y. and Szpankowski, W. (2011). Pattern Matching in Constrained Sequences, *ACM Trans. Algorithms*, *7*(2), 25:1–25:19.

Chryssaphinou, O. and Papastavridis, S. (1988a). A limit theorem for the number of non-overlapping occurrences of a pattern in a sequence of independent trials, *J. Appl. Probab.*, *25*, 428–431.

Chryssaphinou, O. and Papastavridis, S. (1988b). A limit theorem on the number of overlapping appearances of a pattern in a sequence of independent trials, *Probab. Theory Related Fields*, *79*, 129–143.

Chryssaphinou, O., Papastavridis, S., and Vaggelatou, E. (2001). Poisson approximation for the non-overlapping appearances of several words in Markov chains, *Combin. Probab. Comput.*, *10*, 293–308.

Clément, J., Flajolet, P., and Vallée, B. (2001). Dynamical sources in information theory: a general analysis of trie structures, *Algorithmica*, *29*, 307–369.

Cobbs, A. L. (1995). Fast identification of approximately matching substrings, In Galil, Z. and Ukkonen, E. (Eds.), *Combinatorial Pattern Matching*, Vol. 937 of *Lect. Notes Comp. Sci.*, pp. 41–54. Springer-Verlag.

Coffman, E. and Eve, J. (1970). File structures using hashing functions, *Commun. ACM*, *13*(7), 427–432.

Cowan, R. (1991). Expected frequencies of DNA patterns using Whittle's formula, *J. Appl. Probab.*, *28*, 886–892.

Crochemore, M., Mignosi, F., Restivo, A., and Salemi, S. (2000). Data compression using antidictionaries, *Proceedings of the IEEE*, *88*(11), 1756–1768. Special issue *Lossless data compression* edited by J. Storer.

Crochemore, M. and Rytter, W. (1994). *Text Algorithms*. The Clarendon Press Oxford University Press.

Dembo, A. and Kontoyiannis, I. (2002). Source coding, large deviations, and approximate pattern matching, *IEEE Trans. Information Theory*, *48*(6), 1590–1615.

Dembo, A. and Zeitouni, O. (1993). *Large Deviation Techniques and Applications*. Jones and Bartlett.

Denise, A. and Régnier, M. (2004). Rare events and conditional events on random strings, *Discrete Math. Theor. Comput. Sci.*, *6*, 191–214.

Denise, A., Régnier, M., and Vandenbogaert, M. (2001). Assessing the statistical significance of overrepresented oligonucleotides, In Gascuel, O. and Moret, B. M. E. (Eds.), *Algorithms in Bioinformatics (WABI 2001)*, Vol. 2149 of *Lect. Notes Comp. Sci.*, pp. 85–97. Springer-Verlag.

Devroye, L. (1982). A note on the average depth of tries, *Computing*, *28*, 367–371.

Devroye, L. (1984). A probabilistic analysis of the height of tries and of the complexity of triesort, *Acta Informatica*, *21*, 229–237.

Devroye, L. (1992). A study of trie-like structures under the density model, *Ann. Appl. Probab.*, *2*, 402–434.

Devroye, L. (1999). Universal limit laws for depths in random trees, *SIAM Journal on Computing*, *28*, 409–432.

Devroye, L. (2002). Laws of large numbers and tail inequalities for random tries and PATRICIA trees, *Journal of Computational and Applied Mathematics*, *142*, 27–37.

Devroye, L., Lugosi, G., Park, G., and Szpankowski, W. (2009). Multiple Choice Tries, *Rand Structures & Algorithms*, *34*, 337–367.

Devroye, L., Szpankowski, W., and Rais, B. (1992). A note of the height of suffix trees, *SIAM J. Comput.*, *21*, 48–53.

Drmota, M. (2009). *Random Trees*. Springer, Wien-New York.

Drmota, M., Reznik, Y., and Szpankowski, W. (2010). Tunstall Code, Khodak Variations, and Random Walks, *IEEE Trans. Information Theory*, *56*, 2928–2937.

Drmota, M. and Szpankowski, W. (2009). (Un)Expected Behavior of Digital Search Tree Profile, In *ACM-SIAM Symposium on Discrete Algorithms*, pp. 130–138.

Durrett, R. (1991). *Probability: Theory and Examples*. Wadsworth, Belmont.

Farach, M. (1997). Optimal suffix tree construction with large alphabets, In *38th Foundations of Computer Science (FOCS)*, pp. 137–143, Miami Beach, FL.

Fayolle, J. (2003). Parameters des arbes suffixes dans le cas de sources simples, Tech. rep., INRIA.

Fayolle, J. and Ward, M. (2005). Analysis of the average depth in a suffix tree under a Markov model, In *2005 International Conference on Analysis of Algorithms*, pp. 95–104.

Feller, W. (1970). *An Introduction to Probability Theory and its Applications*, Vol. I. John Wiley and Sons.

Feller, W. (1971). *An Introduction to Probability Theory and its Applications*, Vol. II. John Wiley and Sons. Second edition.

Flajolet, P. (1983). On the performance evaluation of extendible hashing and trie searching, *Acta Informatica*, *20*, 345–369.

Flajolet, P., Guivarc'h, Y., Szpankowski, W., and Vallée, B. (2001). Hidden pattern statistics, In Oreijas, F., Spirakis, P., and Leeuwen, J. van (Eds.), *Automata, Languages and Programming (ICALP 2001)*, Vol. 2076 of *Lect. Notes Comp. Sci.*, pp. 152–165. Springer-Verlag.

Flajolet, P. and Sedgewick, R. (2009). *Analytic Combinatorics*. Cambridge University Press.

Flajolet, P. and Steyaert, J.-M. (1982). A branching process arising in dynamic hashing, trie searching and polynomial factorization, *Lecture Notes in Computer Science*, *140*, 239–251.

Flajolet, P., Szpankowski, W., and Vallée, B. (2006). Hidden word statistics, *J. ACM*, *53*(1), 147–183.

Fredkin, E. (1960). Trie memory, *Communications of the ACM*, *3*, 490–499.

Fudos, I., Pitoura, E., and Szpankowski, W. (1996). On Pattern Occurrences in a Random Text, *Information Processing Letters*, *57*, 307–312.

Gaither, J. and Ward, M. (2013). The Asymptotic Distribution of the Multiplicity Matching Parameter in Tries and Suffix Trees, Tech. rep., Purdue University.

Gantmacher, F. R. (1959). *The Theory of Matrices,* Vols 1, 2. Chelsea. Translated from the Russian original.

Gentleman, J. (1994). The distribution of the frequency of subsequences in alphabetic sequences, as exemplified by deoxyribonucleic acid, *Appl. Statist.,* *43*, 404–414.

Gentleman, J. and Mullin, R. (1989). The distribution of the frequency of occurrence of nucleotide subsequences, based on their overlap capability, *Biometrics, 45,* 35–52.

Geske, M. X., Godbole, A. P., Schaffner, A. A., Skolnick, A. M., and Wallstrom, G. L. (1995). Compound Poisson approximations for word patterns under Markovian hypotheses, *J. Appl. Probab., 32,* 877–892.

Gheorghiciuc, I. and Ward, M. D. (2007). On correlation polynomials and subword complexity, *Discrete Mathematics and Theoretical Computer Science, AH,* 1–18.

Giegerich, R., Kurtz, S., and Stoye, J. (1999). Efficient implementation of lazy suffix trees, In *3rd Workshop on Algorithmic Engineering (WAE99),* Vol. 1668 of *Lect. Notes Comp. Sci.,* pp. 30–42. Springer-Verlag.

Gilbert, E. and Kadota, T. (1992). The Lempel-Ziv Algorithm and Message Complexity, *IEEE Trans. Information Theory, 38,* 1839–1842.

Godbole, A. P. (1991). Poisson approximations for runs and patterns of rare events, *Adv. in Appl. Probab., 23,* 851–865.

Godbole, A. P. and Schaffner, A. A. (1993). Improved Poisson approximations for word patterns, *Adv. in Appl. Probab., 25,* 334–347.

Goulden, I. P. and Jackson, D. M. (1983). *Combinatorial Enumeration.* John Wiley and Sons.

Guibas, L. and Odlyzko, A. (1981a). Periods in strings, *J. Combin. Th. A, 30,* 19–43.

Guibas, L. and Odlyzko, A. (1981b). String overlaps, pattern matching, and nontransitive games, *J. Combin. Th. A, 30,* 183–208.

Gusfield, D. (1997). *Algorithms on Strings, Trees, and Sequences.* Cambridge University Press.

Gwadera, R., Atallah, M., and Szpankowski, W. (2003). Reliable detection of episodes in event sequences, In *3rd IEEE Conf. on Data Mining*, pp. 67–74. IEEE Computer Soc.

Henrici, P. (1997). *Applied and Computational Complex Analysis.* John Wiley.

Hwang, H.-K. (1994). Théorèmes limites pour les structures combinatoires et les fonctions arithmétiques,. Thèse de Doctorat, Ecole Polytechnique.

Hwang, H.-K. (1996). Large deviations for combinatorial distributions I: Central limit theorems, *Ann. in Appl. Probab.*, *6*, 297–319.

Jacquet, P. (2007). Common words between two random strings, In *IEEE Intl. Symposium on Information Theory*, pp. 1495–1499.

Jacquet, P., Milioris, D., and Szpankowski, W. (2013). Classification of Markov Sources Through Joint String Complexity: Theory and Experiments, In *IEEE Intl. Symposium on Information Theory*, pp. 2289–2293.

Jacquet, P. and Régnier, M. (1986). Trie partitioning process: limiting distributions, In *CAAP '86 (Nice, 1986)*, Vol. 214 of *Lect. Notes Comp. Sci.*, pp. 196–210. Springer-Verlag.

Jacquet, P. and Regnier, M. (1998). Normal limiting distribution of the size of tries, In *Proceedings of Performance'87*, pp. 209–223.

Jacquet, P. and Szpankowski, W. (1991). Analysis of digital tries with Markovian dependency, *IEEE Trans. Inform. Theory*, *37*, 1470–1475.

Jacquet, P. and Szpankowski, W. (1994). Autocorrelation on words and its applications: analysis of suffix trees by string-ruler approach, *J. Combin. Th. A*, *66*, 237–269.

Jacquet, P. and Szpankowski, W. (1995). Asymptotic behavior of the Lempel-Ziv parsing scheme and digital search trees, *Theoret. Comput. Sci.*, *144*, 161–197.

Jacquet, P. and Szpankowski, W. (1998). Analytical de-Poissonization and its applications, *Theoret. Comput. Sci.*, *201*, 1–62.

Jacquet, P. and Szpankowski, W. (2011). Limiting Distribution of Lempel Ziv'78 Redundancy, In *IEEE Intl. Symposium on Information Theory*, pp. 1424–1428.

Jacquet, P. and Szpankowski, W. (2012). Joint String Complexity for Markov Sources, In *23rd International Meeting on Probabilistic, Combinatorial and Asymptotic Methods for the Analysis of Algorithms*, pp. 1–12.

Jacquet, P. and Szpankowski, W. (2014). On the Limiting Distribution of Lempel Ziv'78 Redundancy for Memoryless Sources, *IEEE Trans. Information Theory*, *60*, 1–14.

Jacquet, P., Szpankowski, W., and Apostol, I. (2002). A universal predictor based on pattern matching, *IEEE Trans. Inform. Theory*, *48*, 1462–1472.

Jacquet, P., Szpankowski, W., and Tang, J. (2001). Average profile of the Lempel-Ziv parsing scheme for a Markovian source, *Algorithmica*, *31*, 318–360.

Janson, S. (2004). Large deviations for sums of partially dependent random variables, *Random Structures & Algorithms*, *24*, 234–248.

Janson, S., Lonardi, S., and Szpankowski, W. (2004). On the Average Sequence Complexity, *Theoretical Computer Science*, *326*, 213–227.

Jolivet, R., Rauch, A., Luscher, H. R., and Gerstner, W. (2006). Predicting spike timing of neocortical pyramidal neurons by simple threshold models, *J. Computational Neuroscience*, *21*, 35–49.

Kärkkäinen, J. and Sanders, P. (2003). Simple linear work suffix array constructio, In Baeten, J. C. M., Lenstra, J. K., Parrow, J., and Woeginger, G. J. (Eds.), *30th Automata, Languages and Programming (ICALP '03)*, Vol. 2719 of *Lect. Notes Comp. Sci.*, pp. 943–955. Springer-Verlag.

Karlin, S. and Ost, F. (1987). Counts of long aligned word matches among random letter sequences, *Adv. in Appl. Probab.*, *19*, 293–351.

Karlin, S. and Taylor, H. (1975). *A First Course in Stochastic Processes* (Second edition). Academic Press.

Kato, T. (1980). *Perturbation Theory for Linear Operators*. Springer-Verlag.

Khodak, G. (1969). Connection Between Redundancy and Average Delay of Fixed-Length Coding, In *All-Union Conference on Problems of Theoretical Cybernetics*.

Kirschenhofer, P. and Prodinger, H. (1988). Further results on digital search trees, *Theoretical Computer Science*, *58*, 143–154.

Kirschenhofer, P. and Prodinger, H. (1991). On some applications of formulae of Ramanujan in the analysis of algorithms, *Mathematika*, *38*, 14–33.

Kirschenhofer, P., Prodinger, H., and Szpankowski, W. (1989a). On the Balance Property of PATRICIA Tries: External Path Length Viewpoint, *Theoretical Computer Science*, *68*, 1–17.

Kirschenhofer, P., Prodinger, H., and Szpankowski, W. (1989b). On the variance of the external path in a symmetric digital trie, *Discrete Applied Mathematics*, *25*, 129–143.

Kirschenhofer, P., Prodinger, H., and Szpankowski, W. (1994). Digital Search Trees Again Revisited: The Internal Path Length Perspective, *SIAM J. Computing*, *23*, 598–616.

Kleffe, J. and Borodovsky, M. (1992). First and second moment of counts of words in random texts generated by Markov chains, *Comput. Appl. Biosci.*, *8*, 433–441.

Knessl, C. and Szpankowski, W. (2004). On the number of full levels in tries, *Random Structures and Algorithms*, *25*, 247–276.

Knessl, C. and Szpankowski, W. (2005). Enumeration of Binary Trees and Universal Types, *Discrete Mathematics and Theoretical Computer Science*, *7*, 313–400.

Knessl, C. and Szpankowski, W. (2009). On the Average Profile of Symmetric Digital Search Trees, *Analytic Combinatorics*, *4*.

Knuth, D. E. (1998). *The Art of Computer Programming. Sorting and Searching* (Second edition)., Vol. 3. Addison-Wesley.

Kolesnik, V. D. and Krachkovsky, V. Y. (1991). Generating functions and lower bounds on rates for limited error-correcting codes, *IEEE Trans. Information Theory*, *37*(3), 778–788.

Kucherov, G. and Rusinowitch, M. (1997). Matching a set of strings with variable length don't cares, *Theoret. Comput. Sci.*, *178*, 129–154.

Landau, G. and Schmidt, J. (1993). An algorithm for approximate tandem repeats, In Apostolico, A., Crochemore, M., Galil, Z., and Manber, U. (Eds.), *4th Combinatorial Pattern Matching (Padova)*, Vol. 684 of *Lect. Notes Comp. Sci.*, pp. 120–133. Springer-Verlag.

Li, M. and Vitanyi, P. (1993). *Introduction to Kolmogorov Complexity and its Applications*. Springer Verlag.

Li, S.-Y. (1980). A martingale approach to the study of occurrence of sequence patterns in repeated experiments, *Ann. Probab.*, *8*, 1171–1176.

Lonardi, S., Szpankowski, W., and Ward, M. (2007). Error Resilient LZ'77 Data Compression: Algorithms, Analysis, and Experiments, *IEEE Trans. Information Theory*, *53*, 1799–1813.

Lothaire, M. (2005). *Applied Combinatorics on Words*, Vol. 105 of *Encyclopedia of Mathematics and its Applications*. Cambridge University Press.

Louchard, G. (1994). Trie size in a dynamic list structure, *Random Structures and Algorithms*, *5*, 665–702.

Louchard, G. and Szpankowski, W. (1995). Average profile and Limiting distribution for a phrase size in the Lempel-Ziv parsing algorithm, *IEEE Trans. Information Theory*, *41*, 478–488.

Louchard, G. and Szpankowski, W. (1997). On the Average Redundancy Rate of the Lempel-Ziv Code, *IEEE Trans. Information Theory*, *43*, 2–8.

Louchard, G., Szpankowski, W., and Tang, J. (1999). Average Profile of Generalized Digital Search Trees and the Generalized Lempel-Ziv Algorithm, *SIAM J. Computing*, *28*, 935–954.

Luczak, T. and Szpankowski, W. (1997). A suboptimal lossy data compression based on approximate pattern matching, *IEEE Trans. Inform. Theory*, *43*, 1439–1451.

Magner, A., Knessl, C., and Szpankowski, W. (2014). Expected External Profile of PATRICIA Tries, In *Analytic Algorithmics and Combinatorics (ANALCO)*.

Mahmoud, H. (1992). *Evolution of Random Search Trees*. John Wiley and Sons.

Marcus, B., Roth, R., and Siegel, P. (1988). Constrained Systems and Coding for Recording Channels in Handbook of Coding Theory,. chap. 20. Elsevier Science.

Marsan, L. and Sagot, M.-F. (2000). Extracting structured motifs using a suffix tree. Algorithms and application to consensus identification, In *4th Research in Computational Molecular Biology (RECOMB)*, pp. 210–219. ACM Press.

McCreight, E. M. (1976). A space-economical suffix tree construction algorithm, *J. Assoc. Comput. Mach.*, *23*(2), 262–272.

Merhav, N. (1991). Universal Coding with Minimum Probability of Codeword Length Overflow, *IEEE Trans. Information Theory*, *37*, 556–563.

Moision, B. E., Orlitsky, A., and Siegel, P. H. (2001). On codes that avoid specified differences, *IEEE Trans. Information Theory*, *47*(1), 433–442.

Naor, M. and Wieder, U. (2003). Novel architectures for P2P applications: The continuous-discrete approach, In *Proc. 15th ACM Symposium on Parallelism in Algorithms and Architectures (SPAA)*, pp. 50–59.

Neininger, R. and Rüschendorf, L. (2004). A general limit theorem for recursive algorithms and combinatorial structures, *Ann. Appl. Probab.*, *14*, 378–418.

Nicodème, P., Salvy, B., and Flajolet, P. (1999). Motif Statistics, In *European Symposium on Algorithms, Lecture Notes in Computer Science*, pp. No. 1643, 194–211.

Nicodème, P., Salvy, B., and Flajolet, P. (2002). Motif statistics, *Theoret. Comput. Sci.*, *287*(2), 593–617. Algorithms (Prague, 1999).

Niederreiter, H. (1999). Some computable complexity measures for binary sequences, In *Sequences and Their Applications*, pp. 67–78. Springer Verlag.

Olver, F. W. J. (1974). *Asymptotics and Special Functions*. Academic Press.

Paninski, L. (2003). Estimation of Entropy and Mutual Information, *Neural Comp.*, *15*(6), 1191–1253.

Park, G. (2006). *Profile of Tries*. Ph.d. thesis, Purdue University.

Park, G., Hwang, H., Nicodeme, P., and Szpankowski, W. (2009). Profile in Tries, *SIAM J. Computing*, *38*, 1821–1880.

Pittel, B. (1985). Asymptotic growth of a class of random trees, *Ann. Probab.*, *18*, 414–427.

Pittel, B. (1986). Paths in a random digital tree: limiting distributions, *Adv. Appl. Probab.*, *18*, 139–155.

Plotnik, E., Weinberger, M., and Ziv, J. (1992). Upper Bounds on the Probability of Sequences Emitted by Finite-State Sources and on the Redundancy of the Lempel-Ziv Algorithm, *IEEE Trans. Information Theory*, *38*, 66–72.

Prum, B., Rodolphe, F., and Turckheim, É. (1995). Finding words with unexpected frequencies in deoxyribonucleic acid sequences, *J. Roy. Statist. Soc. Ser. B*, *57*, 205–220.

Rabiner, L. (1989). A tutorial on hidden Markov models, *Proceedings of the IEEE*, *77*(2), 257–286.

Rachev, S. T. and Ruschendorf, L. (1995). Probability metrics and recursive algorithms, *Adv. Appl. Probab.*, *27*, 770–799.

Régnier, M. (2000). A unified approach to word occurrence probabilities, *Discr. Appl. Math.*, *104*, 259–280.

Régnier, M. and Jacquet, P. (1989). New results on the size of tries, *IEEE Trans. Information Theory*, *35*, 203–205.

Régnier, M. and Szpankowski, W. (1998a). On pattern frequency occurrences in a Markovian sequence, *Algorithmica*, *22*, 631–649.

Régnier, M. and Szpankowski, W. (1998b). On the approximate pattern occurrences in a text, In *Compression and Complexity of Sequences*, pp. 253–264. IEEE Computer Society Press.

Reinert, G. and Schbath, S. (1998). Compound Poisson and Poisson process approximations for occurrences of multiple words in Markov chains, *J. Comput. Biol.*, *5*, 223–253.

Reinert, G., Schbath, S., and Waterman, M. (2000). Probabilistic and statistical properties of words: an overview, *J. Comput. Biol.*, *7*, 1–46.

Robin, S. (2002). A compound Poisson model for word occurrences in DNA sequences, *J. Roy. Statist. Soc. Ser. C*, *51*, 437–451.

Robin, S. and Daudin, J.-J. (1999). Exact distribution of word occurrences in a random sequence of letters, *J. Appl. Probab.*, *36*, 179–193.

Robin, S. and Daudin, J.-J. (2001). Exact distribution of the distances between any occurrences of a set of words, *Ann. Inst. Statist. Math.*, *36*(4), 895–905.

Sagot, M.-F. (1998). Spelling approximate repeated or common motifs using a suffix tree, In Lucchesi, C. and Moura, A. (Eds.), *LATIN'98: Theoretical Informatics: Third Latin American Symposium*, Vol. 1380 of *Lect. Notes Comp. Sci.*, pp. 111–127. Springer-Verlag.

Salvy, B., Sedgewick, B., Soria, M., Szpankowski, W., and Vallee, B. (2011). Philippe Flajolet, the Father of Analytic Combinatorics, *ACM Transactions on Algorithms*, *7*.

Savari, S. (1997). Redundancy of the Lempel-Ziv Incremental Parsing Rule, *IEEE Trans. Information Theory*, *43*, 9–21.

Savari, S. and Gallager, R. (1997). Generalized Tunstall codes for sources with memory, *IEEE Trans. Information Theory*, *43*, 658–668.

Schachinger, W. (1995). On the variance of a class of inductive valuations of data structures for digital search, *Theoretical Computer Science*, *144*, 251–275.

Schachinger, W. (2000). Limiting distributions for the costs of partial match retrievals in multidimensional tries, *Random Structures & Algorithms*, *17*, 428–459.

Schachinger, W. (2001). Asymptotic normality of recursive algorithms via martingale difference arrays, *Discrete Mathematics and Theoretical Computer Science*, *4*, 363–397.

Schachinger, W. (2004). Concentration of size and path length of tries, *Combinatorics, Probability and Computing*, *13*, 763–793.

Schbath, S. (1995). *Étude asymptotique du nombre d'occurrences d'un mot dans une chaîne de Markov et application à la recherche de mots de fréquence exceptionnelle dans les séquences d'ADN*. Ph.D. thesis, Université René Descartes, Paris V.

Sedgewick, R. (1983). *Algorithms*. Addison-Wesley.

Sedgewick, R. and Flajolet, P. (1995). *An Introduction to the Analysis of Algorithms*. Addison-Wesley.

Seroussi, G. (2006a). On the Number of t-Ary Trees with a Given Path Length, *Algorithmica*, *46*, 557–565.

Seroussi, G. (2006b). On Universal Types, *IEEE Trans. Information Theory*, *52*, 171–189.

Shallit, J. (1993). On the maximum number of distinct factors in a binary string, *Graphs and Combinatorics*, *9*, 197–200.

Shields, P. C. (1969). *The Ergodic Theory of Discrete Sample Paths*. Amer. Math. Soc.

Stefanov, V. (2003). The intersite distances between pattern occurrences in strings generated by general discrete- and continuous-time models: an algorithmic approach, *J. Appl. Probab.*, *40*.

Szpankowski, W. (1987). Average complexity of additive properties for multiway tries: a unified approach, *Lecture Notes in Computer Science*, *249*, 13–25.

Szpankowski, W. (1988a). The Evaluation of an Alternating Sum with Applications to the Analysis of Some Data Structures, *Information Processing Letters*, *28*, 13–19.

Szpankowski, W. (1988b). Some results on V-ary asymmetric tries, *Journal of Algorithms*, *9*, 224–244.

Szpankowski, W. (1991). On the height of digital trees and related problems, *Algorithmica*, *6*, 256–277.

Szpankowski, W. (1993a). Asymptotic properties of data compression and suffix trees, *IEEE Trans. Inform. Theory*, *39*, 1647–1659.

Szpankowski, W. (1993b). A generalized suffix tree and its (un)expected asymptotic behaviors, *SIAM J. Comput.*, *22*, 1176–1198.

Szpankowski, W. (2001). *Average Case Analysis of Algorithms on Sequences*. John Wiley and Sons.

Temme, N. (1996). *Special Functions*. John Wiley & Sons, New York.

Titchmarsh, E. C. and Heath-Brown, D. (1988). *The Theory of the Riemann Zeta-Functions*. Oxford University Press.

Tunstall, B. (1967). *Synthesis of Noiseless Compression Codes*. Ph.d. thesis, Georgia Inst. Tech.

Ukkonen, E. (1995). On-line construction of suffix trees, *Algorithmica*, *14*(3), 249–260.

Vallée, B. (2001). Dynamical sources in information theory: fundamental intervals and word prefixes, *Algorithmica*, *29*, 262–306.

Vitter, J. and Krishnan, P. (1996). Optimal Prefetching via Data Compression, *Journal of the ACM*, *43*, 771–793.

Wang, M. and Shallit, J. (1998). On minimal words with given subword complexity, *Electronic Journal of Combinatorics*, *5*.

Ward, M. (2005). *Analysis of the Multiplicity Matching Parameter in Suffix Trees*. Ph.d. thesis, Purdue University.

Ward, M. and Szpankowski, W. (2005). Analysis of the Multiplicity Matching Parameter in Suffix Trees, *2005 Conference on Analysis of Algorithms - DMTCS Proc.*, pp. 307–322.

Waterman, M. (1995a). *Introduction to Computational Biology.* Chapman & Hall.

Waterman, M. S. (1995b). *Introduction to Computational Biology. Maps, Sequences and Genomes.* Chapman and Hall.

Weiner, P. (1973). Linear pattern matching algorithm, In *14th IEEE Symposium on Switching and Automata Theory (SWAT)*, pp. 1–11.

Wu, S. and Manber, U. (1995). Fast text searching allowing errors, *Comm. Assoc. Comput. Mach.*, *35*, 983–991.

Wyner, A. and Ziv, J. (1989). Some asymptotic properties of the entropy of a stationary ergodic data source with applications to data compression, *IEEE Trans. Inform. Theory*, *35*, 1250–1258.

Wyner, A. J. (1997). The redundancy and distribution of the phrase lengths of the fixed-database Lempel-Ziv algorithm, *IEEE Trans. Inform. Theory*, *43*, 1439–1465.

Yang, E. and Kieffer, J. (1998). On the performance of data compression algorithms based upon string matching, *IEEE Trans. Inform. Theory*, *44*, 47–65.

Zehavi, E. and Wolf, J. K. (1988). On runlength codes, *IEEE Trans. Information Theory*, *34*(1), 45–54.

Ziv, J. (1988). On classification with empirically observed statistics and universal data compression, *IEEE Trans. Information Theory*, *34*, 278–286.

Ziv, J. and Lempel, A. (1977). A universal algorithm for sequential data compression, *IEEE Trans. Inform. Theory*, *IT-23*, 337–343.

Ziv, J. and Lempel, A. (1978). Compression of individual sequences via variable-rate coding, *IEEE Trans. Inform. Theory*, *24*, 530–536.

Ziv, J. and Merhav, N. (1993). A measure of relative entropy between individual sequences with application to universal classification, *IEEE Trans. Inform. Theory*, *39*, 1270–1279.

Index